Sophie Yablon
Ms. Peck
SS5 Blue 1
Locker #425

Dear

Mrs. Mudbrick

I would

I would

like to welcome

dear

you and you

Mrs. Mudb—

out.. you are

Sophie

Dear

To

Sophi Ya

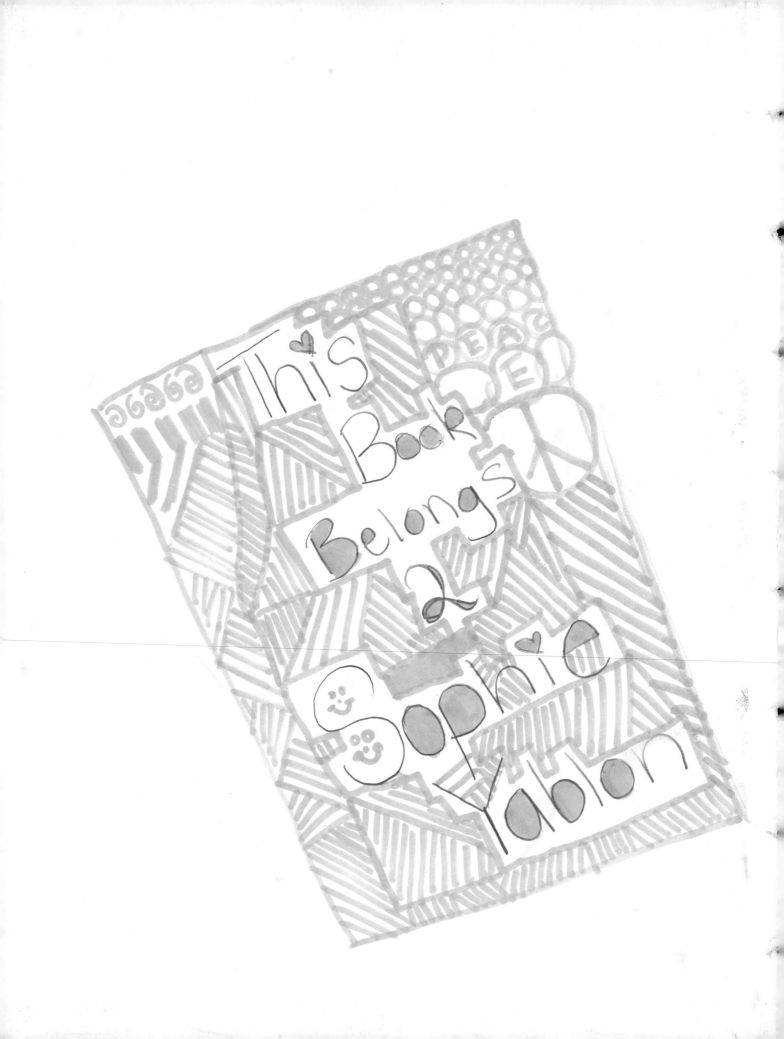

HOUGHTON MIFFLIN SOCIAL STUDIES

A Message of Ancient Days

*H*istory truly bears witness
to the passage of time,
sheds light upon the truth,
breathes life into the power
of memory, provides instruction
for daily life, and carries
a message of ancient days.

Cicero

Beverly J. Armento
Jacqueline M. Córdova
J. Jorge Klor de Alva
Gary B. Nash
Franklin Ng
Christopher L. Salter
Louis E. Wilson
Karen K. Wixson

A Message of Ancient Days

HOUGHTON MIFFLIN   BOSTON • MORRIS PLAINS, NJ

California • Colorado • Georgia • Illinois • New Jersey • Texas

Consultants

Sandra Alfonsi
Academic Advisory Board
Hadassah
Queens, New York

Alison S. Brooks
Department of
Anthropology
The George Washington
University
Washington, D.C.

Ross Dunn
Department of History
San Diego State
University
San Diego, California

Benjamin Elman
Department of History
University of California,
Los Angeles
Los Angeles, California

Erich Gruen
Department of Classics
and History
University of California,
Berkeley
Berkeley, California

Charles Haynes
Senior Scholar for
Religious Freedom
Freedom Forum First
Amendment Center
Arlington, Virginia

Lidwien Kapteijns
Department of History
Wellesley College
Wellesley, Massachusetts

Michelle Maskiell
Department of History
Montana State University
Bozeman, Montana

Jacob Meskin
Department of Religion
Princeton University
Princeton, New Jersey

Skirball Institute
Rabbi Alfred Wolf
Founding Director
Los Angeles, California

Elliot N. Dorff
Rector
University of Judaism
Los Angeles, California

Robert Ellwood
School of Religion
University of Southern
California
Los Angeles, California

B. Srinivasa Murthy
Department of Religious
Studies (retired)
California State
University, Long Beach
Long Beach, California

Ven. Dr. Havanpola
Ratanasara
Buddhist Sangha Council
of Southern California
Los Angeles, California

Rev. Thomas P. Rausch,
S.J.
Rector, Jesuit Community
Loyola Marymount
University
Los Angeles, California

Teacher Reviewers

David E. Beer (Grade 5)
Weisser Park Elementary
Fort Wayne, Indiana

Jan Coleman (Grades 6–7)
Thornton Junior High
Fremont, California

Barbara J. Fech (Grade 6)
Martha Ruggles School
Chicago, Illinois

Deborah M. Finkel
(Grade 4)
Los Angeles Unified
School District,
Region G
South Pasadena,
California

Jim Fletcher (Grades 5, 8)
La Loma Junior High
Modesto, California

Susan M. Gilliam
(Grade 1)
Roscoe Elementary
Los Angeles, California

Lorraine Hood (Grade 2)
Fresno Unified School
District
Fresno, California

Jean Jamgochian
(Grade 5)
Haycock Gifted and
Talented Center
Fairfax County, Virginia

Susan Kirk-Davalt
(Grade 5)
Crowfoot Elementary
Lebanon, Oregon

Carol Siefkin (K)
Garfield Elementary
Sacramento, California

Norman N. Tanaka
(Grade 3)
Martin Luther King Jr.
Elementary
Sacramento, California

John Tyler (Grades 5, 8)
Groton School
Groton, Massachusetts

Acknowledgments

Grateful acknowledgment is made
for the use of the material listed below.
The material in the Minipedia is
reprinted from *The World Book* *Encyclopedia* with the expressed permission of the publisher. © 1999
by World Book, Inc.

—Continued on page 541.

From Your Authors

*T*hrough the tall cedar trees of the Forbidden Forest appeared the terrifying giant Huwawa. The towering creature had a head like a lion's and the teeth of a fierce dragon. His fiery breath struck fear into the hearts of all his enemies.

So begins one of the stories in Gilgamesh, a long poem first written down more than 4,000 years ago. In the poem, Gilgamesh appears as a superhero with magical powers. But the real Gilgamesh was the king of an ancient city in present-day Iraq. In Chapter 6 of this book, you will read more about both the legendary Gilgamesh and the amazing Sumerian civilization in which the real Gilgamesh lived.

Most of the people you will meet in this book lived long ago in places that may seem very far away from your home. But they all had feelings just like yours and faced many of the same challenges you will face in your life. And whether they were great leaders or ordinary people, their actions helped shape the world you live in now.

As you read about these people, places, and events, we hope you will ask many questions. Some questions may be about history: "What caused these people to make the decisions they did?" or "How do we know about these events?" Other questions may be about geography: "What are the land and weather like in that place?" or "Why did people choose to settle there?" Still other questions may be about economics: "How did people meet their needs for food and shelter?" or "How did people work out ways for using scarce resources?"

Most of all, we hope you catch the excitement of thinking, questioning, and discovering answers about your world—now and in the 21st century.

Beverly J. Armento
Professor of Social Studies
Education
Department of Middle/
Secondary Education and
Instructional Technology
Georgia State University

Jacqueline M.K. Córdova
Professor of Spanish
and TESOL
Department of Foreign
Languages and Literatures
California State University,
Fullerton

J. Jorge Klor de Alva
President
University of Phoenix

Gary B. Nash
Professor of History
University of California,
Los Angeles

Franklin Ng
Professor of Anthropology
California State University,
Fresno

Christopher L. Salter
Professor and Chair
Department of Geography
University of Missouri

Louis E. Wilson
Associate Professor and Chair
Department of
African American Studies
Smith College

Karen K. Wixson
Professor of Education
University of Michigan

Contents

Understanding Skills

Each "Understanding Skills" feature gives you the opportunity to learn and practice a skill related to the topic you are studying.

Understanding Concepts

Each "Understanding Concepts" feature gives you more information about a concept that is important to the lesson you are reading.

Making Decisions

Much of history is made of people's decisions. These pages take you step-by-step through fascinating problems from history and today. What will you decide?

Exploring

The story of the past is hidden all around you in the world of the present. "Exploring" pages tell you the secrets of how to find it.

Literature

Throughout history people have expressed their deepest feelings and beliefs through literature. Reading these stories, legends, poems, and shorter passages that appear in the lessons will help you experience what life was like for people of other times and places.

Primary Sources

Reading the exact words of the people who made and lived history is the best way to get a sense of how they saw themselves and the times in which they lived. You will find more than 50 primary sources throughout this book, including the following:

A Closer Look

Take a closer look at objects and pictures spread out on these special pages. With the clues you see, you'll become a historical detective.

Charts, Diagrams, and Timelines

These visual presentations of information help give you a clearer picture of the people, places, and events you are studying.

A Moment in Time

A person in the past is frozen at an exciting moment. Get to know these people by reading about where they are, what they're wearing, and the objects around them.

Maps

The events of history have been shaped by the places in which they occurred. Each map in this book tells its own story about these events and places.

Maps

Starting Out

What makes this textbook so much more interesting than others you've used? In this book, the people of the past speak directly to you, through their actual words and the objects they used. You'll walk inside their houses and look inside their cooking pots. You'll follow them as they go to school, build cities, fight wars, work out settlements for peace.

When and where? The timeline at the beginning of each lesson and the lesson title tell you the time and place.

From unit to chapter to lesson—each step lets you see history in closer detail. The maps and photos show you where events happened. The art introduces you to the people.

Right from the beginning the lesson opener pulls you into the sights, the sounds, the smells of what life was like at that time, in that place.

Like a road sign, the question that always appears here tells you what to think about while you read the lesson.

Look for these key terms. They are listed here so that you can watch for them. The first time they appear in the lesson they are shown in heavy black print and defined. Key terms are also defined in the Glossary.

Letters, diaries, books—short passages from these primary sources let people from the past speak to you. When you see a tan background, a red initial letter, and a gray bar, you know that the quotation is a primary source.

B.C. A.D.
100   50   250
27   235

LESSON 3

Daily Life in Ancient Rome

THINKING FOCUS

How was daily life different for rich and poor Romans?

Key Terms

• rhetoric
• ritual

Before it is light I wake up, and, sitting on the edge of my bed, I put on my shoes and leg-wraps because it is cold. . . . Taking off my nightshirt I put on my tunic and belt; I put oil on my hair, comb it, wrap a scarf around my neck and put on my white cloak. Followed by my school attendant and my nurse I go to say good morning to daddy and mummy and I kiss them both. I find my writing things and exercise book and give them to a slave. I set off to school followed by my school attendant. . . .

I go into the schoolroom and say "Good morning master." He kisses me and returns my greeting. The slave gives me my wax tablets, my writing things and ruler. . . . When I finish learning my lesson I ask the master to let me go home to lunch. . . . Reaching home I change, take some white bread, olives, cheese, dried figs, and nuts and drink some cold water. After lunch I go back to school where the master is beginning to read. He says, "Let's begin work."

At the end of the afternoon I'm off to the Baths with some towels with my slave. I run up to meet the people going to the Baths and we all say to each other "Have a good bathe and a good supper."

A Roman schoolboy, quoted by F. R. Cowell,
Everyday Life in Ancient Rome

A boy from a wealthy Roman family wrote the above description of a typical day in about A.D. 300.

Accounts like this are one source of information about daily life in ancient Rome.

Rich and Poor

The boy who wrote this account belonged to an elite family in Rome. Only the rich could send their children to school and have slaves wait on them. His home may have looked like the Roman house shown in A Closer Look on page

442. What parts of the house were open to let in light, air, and rain? Where would you spend the most time if you lived in this house?

A rich family in one of these homes might own 500 slaves. Some very wealthy Roman families

440

Chapter 14

Take a closer look, in this case at a Roman house. Look at the couches in the dining room, the pictures on the floors.

A CLOSER LOOK

A Roman House

Imagine living in a home that was also your parents' work place. Relatives, friends, servants, and clients would always be coming and going. There might be a vegetable garden and a couple of stores under your roof, too.

Would you walk on your artwork? The Romans did. Romans decorated their floors with mosaics like this one.

If you put out this dog-shaped oil lamp, your bedroom would be totally dark—even during the day! That's because bedrooms rarely had windows.

The father of the family sits here, where he can see all the action.

Back yard

Garden

Kitchen

Statue of great-grandfather

Stores

Door, open all day

Reading room

Bedroom

Like a living room today, the *atrium* was the place where Roman families entertained their guests. But the Roman living room had a hole in its roof. Rainwater poured into a pool where it was stored for drinking and washing.

Can you eat lying down? Romans held dinner parties in a room called the *triclinium*, which means "three-couch place." The room had three couches, and dinner guests ate while lying on their sides.

Only the rich could afford glass pitchers and bowls like these.

442

Chapter 14

Family Life in the Empire

By the time Rome had become the center of an empire, family life was changing. In the days of the Republic, the father was the undisputed head of the family. He could even sell his children as slaves. He could arrange marriages for his daughters when they were only 12 to 15 years old. He would do this for the political and economic benefits it would bring to the family. The young bride and groom had little to say about it.

By the A.D. 100s, however, family discipline had become less harsh, and the father's power had been reduced. A father no longer had the right to sell his children or to force marriages. In addition, women had more freedom. Unlike women in other ancient cultures such as Greece, Roman women were independent under the law. They could have their own property and slaves.

Families that could afford the cost of private education sent their children and even household slaves to school beginning at about age seven. These children studied basic reading, writing, and arithmetic. The schools were small, and one teacher was responsible for all subjects. Teachers followed the rule of the Greek playwright Menander: "A man who has not been flogged [beaten] is not trained."

Girls usually did not have any formal education after age 15. Usually at 15, the sons of wealthy parents continued their education by taking classes in Latin and Greek literature and **rhetoric**—the art of effective writing and speaking. Students needed to learn rhetoric in order to enter law or politics. Romans believed that skill in rhetoric was the mark of a gentleman.

The Roman schools rarely had classes in science, engineering, or complex mathematics. The few professional people—engineers, doctors, or lawyers, for example—learned through apprenticeships, not through formal education. ■

◄ *Some people in Pompeii were eating their midday meal when Vesuvius erupted. (See How Do We Know? on page 444.) Several foods, preserved intact under the ashes, can be seen today in the Pompeii Museum, including this loaf of bread.*

◄ *This young Roman student looks thoughtful. Is she thinking about the day's lesson?*

■ *What were family life and schooling like for young people growing up in the Roman Empire?*

Benefits of Life in Rome

The city of Rome was a crowded, busy, thriving place—the center for the best and worst of the Mediterranean world. Disease, crime, and fires raged there. But life in Rome also had its benefits. The emperors made a point of trying to keep the city people happy.

443

The Roman Empire

---

emperor might command a personal slave population of 20,000. Household slaves did just about every job imaginable. They cooked, served meals, cleaned, and took care of the children. Each slave might have only one job—folding the master's clothes or fixing the mistress's hair, for example.

In contrast, the vast majority of those who lived in the city had tiny apartments in five-story apartment buildings called *insulae* (IHN suh ly). In some cases, an entire family would crowd into a single room.

For every wealthy home in Rome, there were 26 blocks of *insulae*. Most *insulae* were dark

The Roman writer Juvenal described the poorer neighborhoods of Rome in the A.D. 100s:

*M*ost of the city [is] propped up with planks to stop it collapsing. Your landlord stands in front of cracks that have been there for years and says, "Sleep well!" although he knows that the house itself may not last the night. I wish I lived where there were no fires, no midnight panics.

In these crowded conditions, fires and crime were serious problems. Lack of sanitation also contributed to the spread of disease. The problem was so severe that about one-fourth of the babies born in Rome did not live through their first year. Half of all Roman children did not live to be 10 years old. ■

In the mosaic, he may be answering the age-old question, "What did you learn in school today?"

◄ *This make-up box and the hairpin shown with it once belonged to a wealthy Roman woman.*

■ *How did the housing of the rich Roman compare with the housing of the poor?*

441

The Roman Empire

Every age has its great storytellers.
Each chapter includes short examples of fine writing from or about the period. The literature is always printed on a tan background with a blue initial letter and a multicolored bar.

Frozen at a moment in time, this Roman engineer transports you back to the past. You learn all about him, through his equipment, his clothes, the place he's working.

A MOMENT IN TIME

A Roman Engineer

8:43 A.M., August 20, 109 B.C.
On what will be the Via Aemilia seven outside Pisa

Crossbars

Cap

Class

Robe

Measuring Cord

Metal Point

471

Continuing On

As you get to know the people of the past, you'll want ways of understanding and remembering them better. This book gives you some tools to use in learning about people and places and remembering what you've learned.

Giving you the inside story is the purpose of two special paragraphs. How Do We Know? tells you where information about the past comes from. Its companion, Across Time & Space, connects what you're reading to things that happened centuries ago or continents away. (See page 417 for an example.)

The titles outline the lesson. The red titles tell you the main topics discussed in the lesson on "Daily Life in Ancient Rome." The blue titles tell you the subtopics.

A picture is worth a thousand words. But just a few words in a caption can help you understand a picture, a photograph, a map, or in this case, an illustration of a Roman circus.

(textbook spread reproduced as an illustration)

Public Services

The government gave free wheat to male citizens on a regular basis. This gift of food was important to the poor people of Rome, who often went hungry. On special occasions, the emperor also gave money to the citizens of Rome. The wheat and money came from taxes that farmers and other people in the provinces paid.

Another benefit of living in Rome was the plentiful water supply. The system of aqueducts carried 200 million gallons of water to Rome daily. With so much water available, the city built public baths where residents, rich and poor, could bathe and swim for a small fee. These baths became important gathering places.

Entertainment

The emperors spent enormous sums of money to entertain the people. In fact, 159 days each year

had been declared holidays by the A.D. 50s. Later emperors found it necessary to limit the number of holidays each year. Still, nearly one-third of the days of each year remained holidays throughout the A.D. 100s.

On these holidays the emperors provided elaborate circuses and games to keep the people content. The Circus Maximus was a gigantic Roman arena that could hold nearly 200,000 spectators. There, spectacular daredevil chariot races took place. "All Rome today is in the circus," wrote Juvenal. "Such sights are for the young, whom it befits to shout and make bold wagers with a smart damsel by their side."

Chariot racing was also popular at the Colosseum, but so were some of the more bloody sports. Wild beasts were hunted and killed by the hundreds. Gladiators fought each other to the death. During

the years A.D. 106 to 114, 23,000 gladiators fought to entertain the citizens. The Romans were so fond of bloody events that during the intermissions, Roman officials executed condemned criminals for the entertainment of the audience.

However, the benefits of life in Rome such as free food and spectacular entertainment did not appeal to all Romans. Some claimed that the citizens took too much interest in those things and not enough interest in their government. Even members of the elite class, who benefited the most, saw problems. The Roman historian

Tacitus said that the empire made slaves of free men. The Roman writer Juvenal also complained that the public "longs for just two things—bread and circuses." ■

▲ Circuses were a major form of entertainment in the Roman Empire. This "Mosaic of the Circus Games" was found in Roman Gaul. It dates from about A.D. 175.

■ How did the emperors provide "bread and circuses" for the people of Rome?

▼ The Roman public baths were complex structures. (1) A furnace heated (2) a tank of water. (3) Pipes carried the hot water to the pools. The Romans began their bath in a hot-water pool, continued it in (4) a warm-water pool, and ended it in (5) a cool-water pool.

Religious Practices

Many Romans believed that they had been able to build their empire and find peace because they had kept their gods happy. Like many other ancient peoples, the Romans had gods for every act and event in their lives.

The Many Gods of the Romans

The great gods of the Roman state were Jupiter, Juno, and Minerva. Jupiter was the supreme god. He controlled the thunder and lightning and was the special guardian of Rome. Juno was his wife. She was the queen of the gods and the protector of women. Minerva was the goddess of wisdom and guardian of craftworkers. The Romans joined together on specific days to worship these gods. In this way they showed their unity and their loyalty to the state.

At home, the Romans worshiped household gods, such as Vesta, Lares (LAIR eez), and Penates (puh NAY teez). Vesta guarded the fireside, where people

cooked and kept warm. Lares guarded the land, and Penates watched over the stored food. Family members made daily offerings to these gods and asked for protection in exchange.

Many of these Roman gods had been borrowed from the Greeks at an earlier time. For example, Jupiter was the Greek god Zeus, and Juno was the Greek goddess Hera. Diana, the Roman goddess of the hunt, was the Greek goddess Artemis. Mars, the Roman god of war, was the Greek god Ares.

In A.D. 126, the Romans erected a magnificent temple called the Pantheon (PAN thee uhn) to honor all the Roman gods and goddesses. They built it in the shape of a drum, with a dome rising 14 stories above the ground. They covered the dome with gleaming brass so that people could see it

▼ Found in the ruins of Pompeii, this household shrine contains small statues that include one of Lares, the guardian of houses.

444
Chapter 14

Cutaway diagrams show you what's under the roof—in this case, the famous Roman baths. Other illustrations, charts, and graphs tell you how things work and how one bit of information relates to another.

You're in charge of your reading. See the red square at the end of the text? Now find the red square over in the margin. If you can answer the question there, then you probably understood what you just read. If you can't, perhaps you'd better go back and read that part of the lesson again.

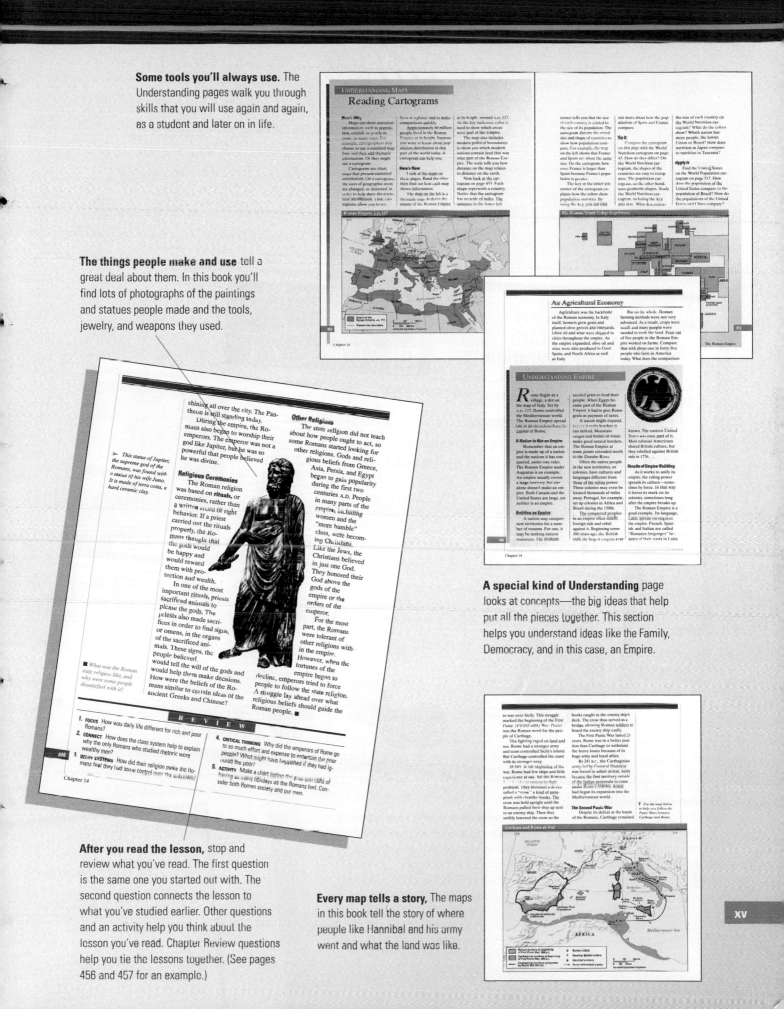

Some tools you'll always use. The Understanding pages walk you through skills that you will use again and again, as a student and later on in life.

The things people make and use tell a great deal about them. In this book you'll find lots of photographs of the paintings and statues people made and the tools, jewelry, and weapons they used.

A special kind of Understanding page looks at concepts—the big ideas that help put all the pieces together. This section helps you understand ideas like the Family, Democracy, and in this case, an Empire.

After you read the lesson, stop and review what you've read. The first question is the same one you started out with. The second question connects the lesson to what you've studied earlier. Other questions and an activity help you think about the lesson you've read. Chapter Review questions help you tie the lessons together. (See pages 456 and 457 for an example.)

Every map tells a story, The maps in this book tell the story of where people like Hannibal and his army went and what the land was like.

Also Featuring

Some special pages show up only once in every unit, not in every lesson in the book. These features continue the story by letting you explore an idea or activity, or read a story about another time and place. The Time/Space Databank in the back of the book brings together resources you will use again and again.

School isn't the only place where you can learn social studies. This feature gives you a chance to explore history and geography outside the classroom—at home or in your own neighborhood.

EXPLORING

Greek Architecture in Your Community

◄ This scale model of Buckingham Palace is entirely made up of interlocking plastic bricks. What elements of Greek architecture can you identify?

You don't have to travel to Greece to see what the...

▲ *The three classical types of Greek capitals are Doric (top), Ionic (middle), and Corinthian (bottom).*

Chapter 12

MAKING DECISIONS

Public Policy: Spend Less? Raise Taxes?

Uncontrolled prices are widespread in the sales taking place in the markets and in the daily life of the cities. . . we have decided that maximum prices of articles for sale must be established. . . Thus, when the pressure of high prices appears anywhere . . . [greed] will be checked by the limits. . . of the law.

Emperor Diocletian, Edict on Prices, A.D. 301

When . . . he brought about enormously high prices, he attempted to legislate the prices of [goods]. Then much blood was spilled. . . nothing appeared on the market because of fear, and prices soared much higher. In the end, after many people had lost their lives, it became absolutely necessary to repeal the law.

Lactantius, Christian writer living in Rome, A.D. 245-325

▼ *Diocletian and his co-emperor Maximian ruled the empire together.*

Background

When Diocletian became emperor of Rome in A.D. 284, he faced an empire in crisis. Enemies along the empire's borders were constantly waging war against Rome. The once-powerful Roman army was no longer strong enough to fight off their attacks. Warfare left the cities and countryside in ruins.

In addition, the empire had grown so large that the government in Rome wasn't able to rule it efficiently. Lawsuits in distant provinces were often left unsettled

because there were no government officials to hear them.

Closer to home, arguments and civil wars broke out each time an emperor died or retired: Who would follow him to the throne? Prices were also rising rapidly, making it harder for people to survive.

Finally, the treasury—the money used to pay for the government and army—was running out. The empire was falling apart. What could Diocletian do to save it?

Chapter 15

Diocletian began by making a number of decisions. First he reorganized the government. He appointed a co-emperor and two junior emperors. Each of these men ruled a portion of the empire. In this way a local problem could be quickly brought to the attention of one of the rulers. This same system would help ensure a peaceful transfer of power at the end of an emperor's reign.

The four regions of the empire were further divided into more than a hundred provinces—double the number that had existed before. Each province was run by a governor and hundreds of government officials.

To safeguard the borders, Diocletian increased the size of the army. In addition to the troops stationed along the empire's frontiers, he created specially trained troops stationed in cities nearby. These troops stood ready to move quickly to any point along the border in case of enemy attack.

To fight rising prices, Diocletian issued his Edict on Prices, setting the top price to be charged or paid for any item. He also introduced a new system of coins.

What should be done about attacks on the empire?

Decision Increase size of army

Outcomes
- More soldiers
- Borders defended
- Cities, countryside safe
- Empire strong, unified
- Fewer workers
- More money spent on army
- Increased taxes
- Unhappy taxpayers

▲ *What were the goals behind Diocletian's decision to increase the size of the army? Did the outcome of that decision support his goals?*

The Cost of Decisions

What did Diocletian hope to achieve with these changes? He wanted to bring peace and make the empire secure. He also wanted to make government more effective and efficient and to keep the economy stable.

Though many Romans agreed that these were worthy goals, some of the decisions Diocletian

made based on these goals were not so popular. All of these changes cost money, and that meant higher taxes. Now there were four royal courts to pay for, not just one. There were nearly three times the number of government workers as before, and all of these workers had to be paid. As the army increased in size, more money had to be spent on soldiers' salaries, training, and supplies.

Christianity and the Fall of Rome

What would you do? The Making Decisions pages show you an important decision from the past. Then you practice the steps that will help you to make a good choice.

Stories have always been important parts of people's lives. Each unit in the book has at least one story about the time and place you're studying. In this case, it's a retelling of a Roman tale. Roman schoolboys and girls probably read this story, too.

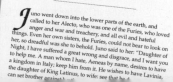

LITERATURE

The War over Latium

Alfred J. Church

The Roman poet Virgil wrote the Aeneid (ih NEE uhd), an epic poem about the beginnings of Rome. Here is a retelling of parts of the Aeneid.

Aeneas (ih NEE uhs)

treachery betrayal

After Troy was destroyed by the Greeks, the hero Aeneas and the other Trojan survivors left to find a new home in Italy. In this story from The Aeneid for Boys and Girls, the goddess Juno, who hates Aeneas, is determined to keep the Trojans from settling in the Latium Plain. She decides to seek help from the underworld.

Juno went down into the lower parts of the earth, and called to her Alecto, who was one of the Furies, who loved anger and war and treachery, and all evil and hateful things. Even her own sisters, the Furies, could not bear to look on her, so dreadful was she to behold. Juno said to her: "Daughter of Night, I have suffered a great wrong and disgrace, and I want you to help me. A man whom I hate, Aeneas by name, desires to have a kingdom in Italy; keep him from it. He wishes to have Lavinia, the daughter of King Latinus, to wife: see that he d can set brother against

Mapping Our Planet

A map is a representation of all or part of the earth's surface. Look at the pictures and map on this page. The picture on the right shows our planet in space. You can hardly see any details of the land. The picture below shows a smaller area of the earth. You can see the islands of Japan. You can also see North and South Korea and other parts of the East Asia coast. Now look at the map of the same area. Notice how carefully the mapmaker has drawn the shapes and sizes of the coastal lands and islands. The map is like a diagram of the area in the picture.

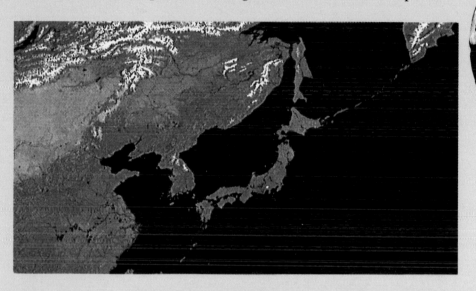

◄ You can see that Japan is really many islands and that North and South Korea are on a peninsula. In both pictures, computers have added color to make the images clearer.

Korea and Japan: Political

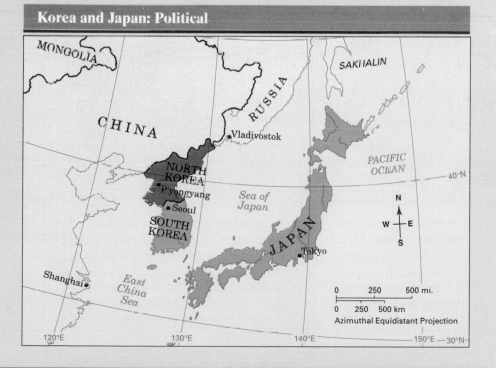

MONGOLIA

CHINA

RUSSIA

SAKHALIN

Vladivostok

NORTH KOREA

P'yongyang

Seoul

SOUTH KOREA

Sea of Japan

PACIFIC OCEAN

40°N

JAPAN

Tokyo

Shanghai

East China Sea

N
W E
S

0   250   500 mi.

0   250   500 km

Azimuthal Equidistant Projection

120°E   130°E   140°E   150°E — 30°N

◄ Look at the coastline of Japan on the map and in the photo above it. Check to see how accurately the mapmaker drew this coastline.

Understanding a Map

Take a quick look at the maps in this handbook. You will see maps of different sizes showing different places. Some maps show the surface of the entire world, but most show a smaller area. You get different information from different kinds of maps.

Even though maps look different, they share many of the same features. Every part of a map tells you something important. Knowing how to read the parts of a map will help you understand the information on a map. Look at the different features on this map of Australia.

The **compass rose** points out directions. The tips of this compass rose point to north **(N)**, south **(S)**, east **(E)**, and west **(W)**, as well as to in-between, or intermediate, directions.

Latitude and **longitude** are imaginary lines that form a grid over the earth. A **grid** is a pattern of lines that cross one another. You can use the grid to locate places on the map.

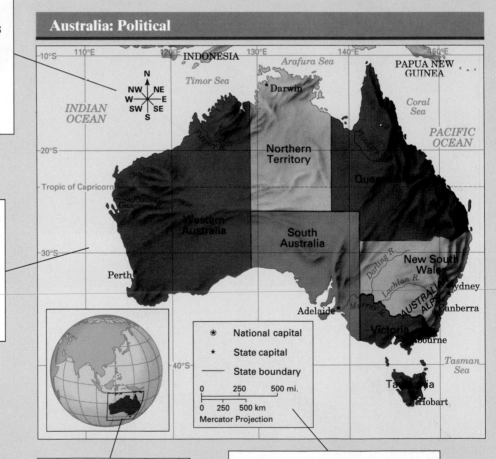

Australia: Political

An **inset** is a small map related to a larger one. The inset gives different information than is shown on the larger map. This map's **locator inset** helps you find Australia on the earth.

The **legend** explains what the map's symbols mean. Sometimes the legend includes a **scale** line that tells you how much smaller the map is than the real area it represents. This legend also tells you the kind of **projection** used on this map to show the earth's curved surface on flat paper.

Using the Legend, Inset, and Grid

Imagine that you are visiting Mexico City with your family. You want to see the beautiful flowers of the city's famous Botanical Gardens. You have heard about the castle in Chapultepec *(chuh POOL tuh pehk)* Park and want to see that, too. This map of Mexico City can help you find these and many other interesting sights around the city.

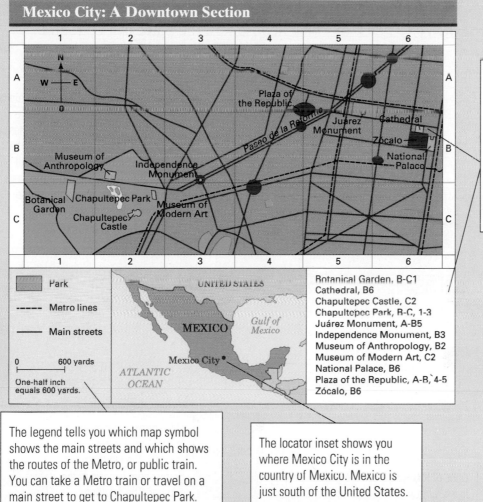

Mexico City: A Downtown Section

The grid helps you find places on the map. To find Mexico City's cathedral, look up the cathedral in the map's index and read the letter and number next to it, *B6*. The letter and number name the square on the map's grid where you can find the cathedral.

Botanical Garden, B-C1
Cathedral, B6
Chapultepec Castle, C2
Chapultepec Park, B-C, 1-3
Juárez Monument, A-B5
Independence Monument, B3
Museum of Anthropology, B2
Museum of Modern Art, C2
National Palace, B6
Plaza of the Republic, A-B, 4-5
Zócalo, B6

The legend tells you which map symbol shows the main streets and which shows the routes of the Metro, or public train. You can take a Metro train or travel on a main street to get to Chapultepec Park.

The locator inset shows you where Mexico City is in the country of Mexico. Mexico is just south of the United States.

MAP SKILLS

1. REVIEW What monument stands on the Paseo de la Reforma? In which grid square on the map do you find the monument?

2. REVIEW Look at the map on page 39 of your book. What does the main map show? What does the inset map on that page show?

3. THINK ABOUT IT Why would a grid and index be necessary on the map of a big city?

4. TRY IT Make a simple map of your town or city. Include places that would be of interest to a tourist. Make sure you add a legend, locator inset, and grid. Have you added a compass rose?

Understanding Globes and Hemispheres

Both maps and globes show the location of land and water on the earth. However, a globe does something a flat map can't do. A globe shows that the earth is shaped like a ball, or sphere. Geographers use certain imaginary lines of latitude and longitude on the globe to divide the earth into halves, or hemispheres. When you want to locate a place on a globe, it helps to know in which hemisphere the place can be found.

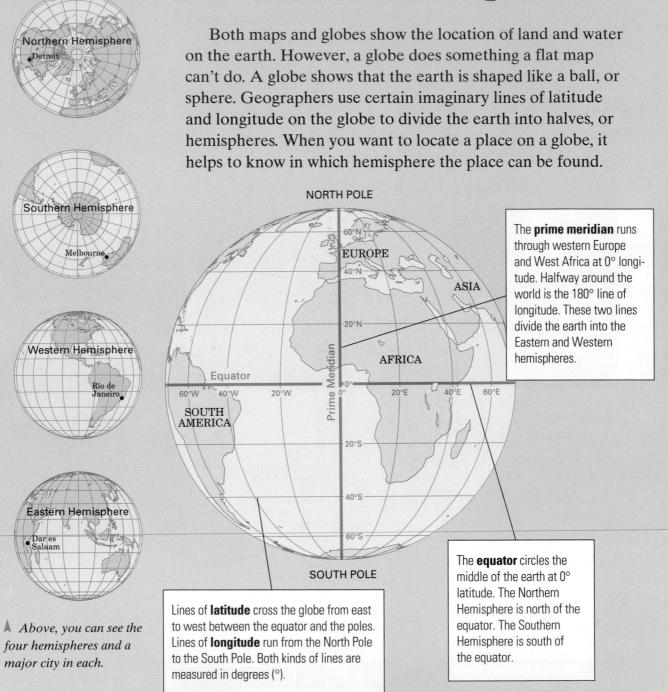

Northern Hemisphere
Detroit

Southern Hemisphere
Melbourne

Western Hemisphere
Rio de Janeiro

Eastern Hemisphere
Dar es Salaam

▲ *Above, you can see the four hemispheres and a major city in each.*

NORTH POLE

60°N

EUROPE

40°N

ASIA

20°N

AFRICA

Prime Meridian

Equator

60°W   40°W   20°W   0°   20°E   40°E   60°E

SOUTH AMERICA

20°S

40°S

60°S

SOUTH POLE

The **prime meridian** runs through western Europe and West Africa at 0° longitude. Halfway around the world is the 180° line of longitude. These two lines divide the earth into the Eastern and Western hemispheres.

The **equator** circles the middle of the earth at 0° latitude. The Northern Hemisphere is north of the equator. The Southern Hemisphere is south of the equator.

Lines of **latitude** cross the globe from east to west between the equator and the poles. Lines of **longitude** run from the North Pole to the South Pole. Both kinds of lines are measured in degrees (°).

GLOBE SKILLS

1. **REVIEW** Why is it helpful to know the four hemispheres of the earth?

2. **THINK ABOUT IT** One continent lies in four hemispheres. What continent is it and how is this possible?

3. **TRY IT** Find three countries on a globe. Give the name of each country to a classmate. Have each classmate find the country on the globe and tell you the two hemispheres in which it lies.

Using Latitude and Longitude on Maps

Suppose someone asks you the location of the small country of Singapore. You might say it is in Southeast Asia. If you need to tell exactly where Singapore is, you can give its latitude and longitude. Singapore is located at about 1° north latitude and 103° east longitude. That means Singapore lies one degree north of the equator and 103 degrees east of the prime meridian.

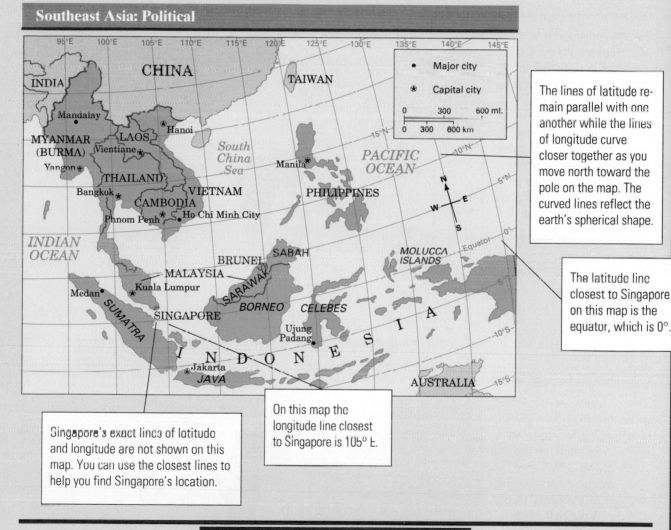

Southeast Asia: Political

The lines of latitude remain parallel with one another while the lines of longitude curve closer together as you move north toward the pole on the map. The curved lines reflect the earth's spherical shape.

The latitude line closest to Singapore on this map is the equator, which is 0°.

Singapore's exact lines of latitude and longitude are not shown on this map. You can use the closest lines to help you find Singapore's location.

On this map the longitude line closest to Singapore is 105° E.

MAP SKILLS

1. **REVIEW** Use latitude and longitude to tell the location of Ujung Padang on the island of Celebes in Indonesia.

2. **THINK ABOUT IT** How could you use latitude and longitude to tell the location of an entire nation, such as Vietnam in Southeast Asia?

3. **TRY IT** Use a globe or atlas to find the lines of latitude and longitude closest to your city or town.

4. **TRY IT** Look at the map of Eurasia on pages 508–509. List European and Asian cities located near 45° N latitude and cities near 45° E longitude.

Understanding Projections

Picture yourself peeling an orange. Once you finish, try to flatten out the peel. What happens? Most likely, the peel breaks apart. Because the peel is shaped like a sphere, or ball, you change its shape when you try to flatten it. Mapmakers face a similar problem when they show the sphere-shaped earth on a flat map. Each map uses a certain projection, or way of changing the size or shape of oceans and continents on the earth's surface. Compare the shape and size of the continent of Africa on four projections.

Flemish-born mapmaker Gerardus Mercator made this projection in 1569. Near the poles, the land areas look larger than the same areas on a globe. For example, Greenland appears much larger on the Mercator projection than it does on a globe. The globe shows Greenland more accurately. Notice how much smaller Africa looks than North America.

Mercator Projection

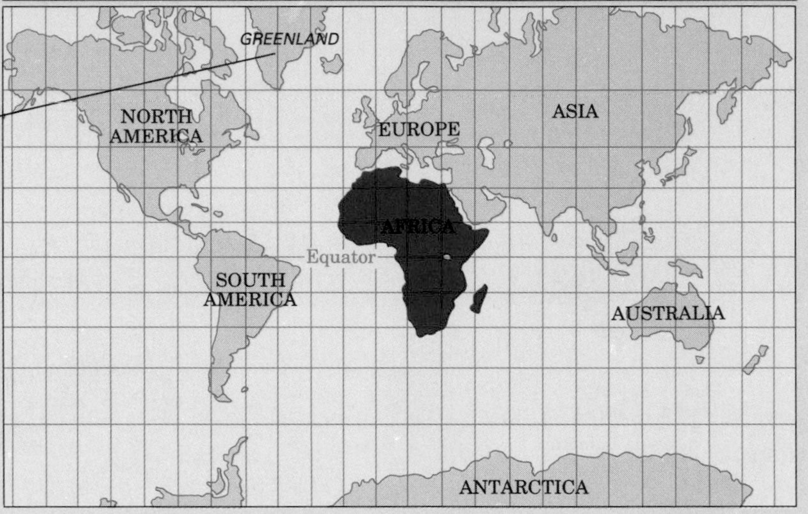

German mapmaker Arno Peters made this projection in 1974. The relative size of the continents on the projection and on a globe look about the same. The Peters projection, however, changes the continents' shapes. Compare Africa on the Peters projection with Africa on the Mercator projection.

Peters Projection

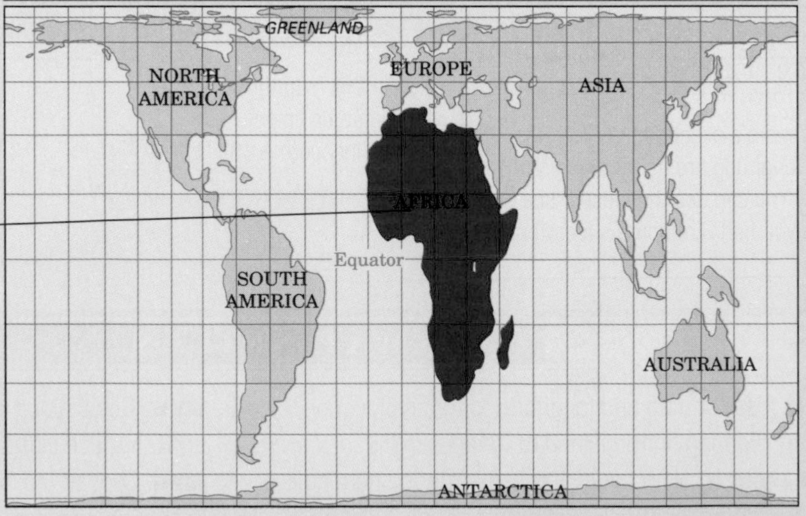

Goode Projection

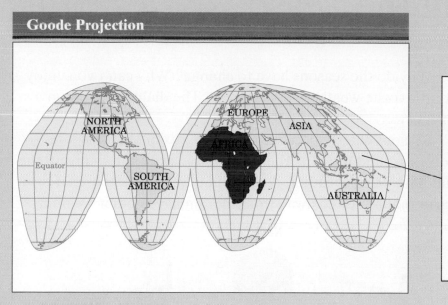

In 1923 American map-maker Paul Goode created a projection showing the continent sizes and shapes as they appear on a globe. Because this projection divides the earth into segments, or pieces, near the poles, the distances between places cannot be easily measured.

Robinson Projection

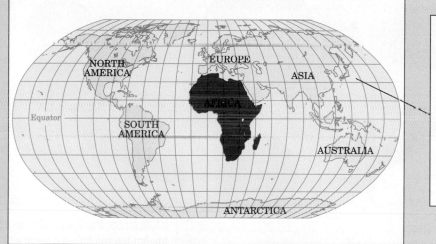

Another American map-maker, Arthur Robinson, made this projection in 1963. The sizes, shapes, and distances of land and water areas on this projection are closest to the ones on a globe. Most of the world maps in this book use the Robinson projection.

MAP SKILLS

1. **REVIEW** Which projections show Africa closest to the way it looks on a globe?

2. **THINK ABOUT IT** Look at Africa on the Mercator projection and the Goode projection. Why do you think Africa looks alike on the two projections when Greenland and other areas at the top of the projections are so different? Use a globe to help you answer the question.

3. **TRY IT** Find the land areas of Greenland, Antarctica, and Africa on a globe and trace them. Compare each tracing to the same area on a flat world map. They will not be exactly the same because your globe and map are different sizes. Notice differences in the shapes of the land areas. Which shapes show the most change? Why did the changes occur?

Observing the Seasons

Why do the seasons have to change? Why can't you enjoy your favorite weather all year long? The diagram below gives the answer.

Seasons change because the earth tilts or slants as it revolves around the sun. The parts of the earth tilted toward the sun have warm weather. At the same time, those parts of the earth that are tilted away from the sun have cooler weather.

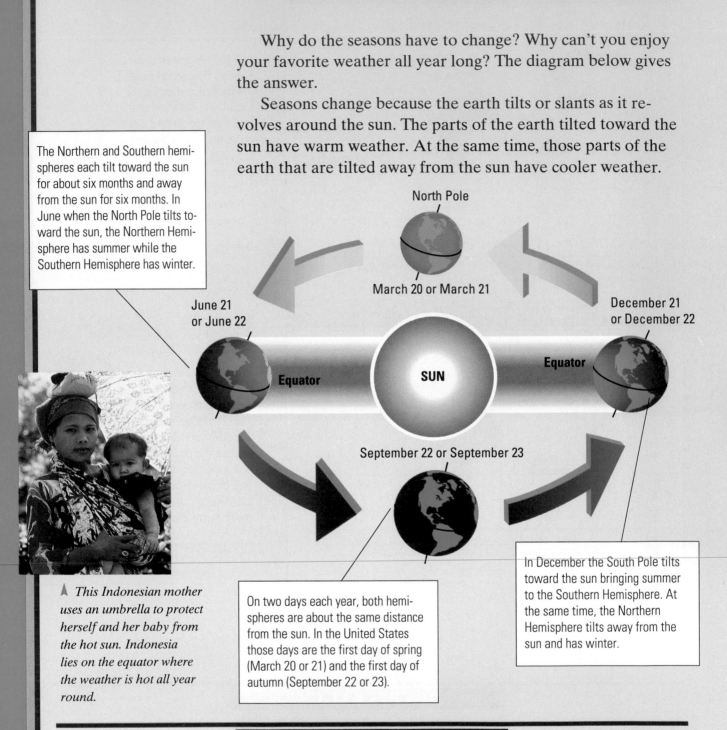

The Northern and Southern hemispheres each tilt toward the sun for about six months and away from the sun for six months. In June when the North Pole tilts toward the sun, the Northern Hemisphere has summer while the Southern Hemisphere has winter.

North Pole

March 20 or March 21

June 21 or June 22

December 21 or December 22

Equator

SUN

Equator

September 22 or September 23

On two days each year, both hemispheres are about the same distance from the sun. In the United States those days are the first day of spring (March 20 or 21) and the first day of autumn (September 22 or 23).

In December the South Pole tilts toward the sun bringing summer to the Southern Hemisphere. At the same time, the Northern Hemisphere tilts away from the sun and has winter.

▲ *This Indonesian mother uses an umbrella to protect herself and her baby from the hot sun. Indonesia lies on the equator where the weather is hot all year round.*

GLOBE SKILLS

1. **REVIEW** When does summer begin in Australia? Why?
2. **THINK ABOUT IT** What season is it right now in the nation of Chile in South America? How do you know?
3. **TRY IT** Place a ball on a table. Hold a smaller ball and move it around the larger ball. Draw two dots on the smaller ball, one for the North Pole and the other for the South Pole. Watch how its position changes in relation to your "sun." Use the balls to explain to a classmate why winter in the Northern Hemisphere begins in December.

Reading Different Kinds of Maps

Maps do more than show the shape of the land. Study the maps on the following pages and think about what you learn.

A Physical Map with a Profile

A physical map shows the elevation of land, or its height compared to sea level. Sometimes a physical map includes a diagram called a profile. The profile below shows a side view of the mountains, hills, and flat lands you would see in the area marked by the red line on the map.

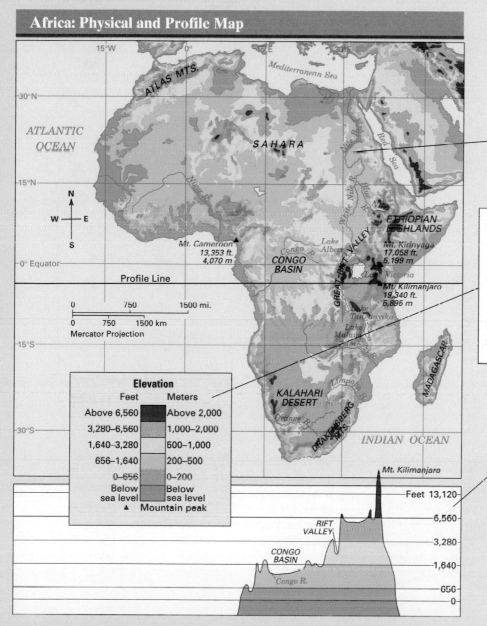

Africa: Physical and Profile Map

On the map, the color of an area shows the land's elevation.

The legend tells you what elevation each color represents. An elevation of "0" means that the land is at sea level. The number "6,560" means that the land rises 6,560 feet higher than sea level.

This map's profile shows how the land falls and rises across the Congo Basin, the Great Rift Valley, and Mt. Kilimanjaro. The Profile Line on the map shows where this profile, or side view, cuts across Africa. Notice that Mt. Kilimanjaro is the highest point on the profile and the map.

Elevation

Feet	Meters
Above 6,560	Above 2,000
3,280–6,560	1,000–2,000
1,640–3,280	500–1,000
656–1,640	200–500
0–656	0–200
Below sea level	Below sea level
▲ Mountain peak	

A Time Zone Map

When you want to call a friend in another part of the country, think about the time zone where your friend lives. When it is 12:00 noon in Los Angeles, California, the time is 10:00 A.M. in Honolulu, Hawaii, and 3:00 P.M. in Miami, Florida.

Before official time zones existed, people had difficulty planning travel and doing business far from their homes. Each area set its own time. In order to end the confusion, government leaders agreed in 1884 to divide the earth into 24 time zones.

When you go west across the International Date Line at 180° longitude, the date immediately changes to one day later. It is Monday noon west of the International Date Line at the same time that it is Sunday noon east of the Line.

▼ *This diagram shows why the earth has 24 time zones. The earth rotates, or spins like a top. It takes 24 hours for the earth to make a complete rotation. At all times, half of the earth is getting daytime sunlight while the other half has nighttime darkness.*

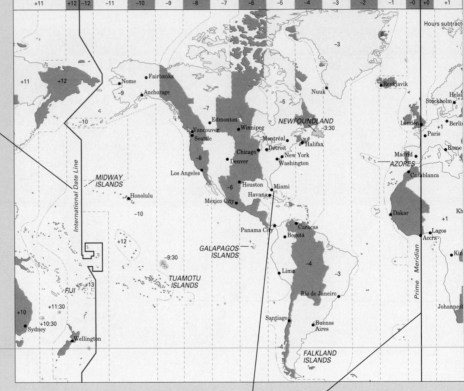

Time Zones of the Western Hemisphere

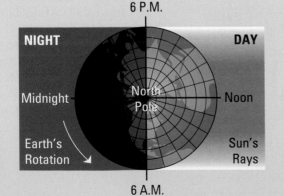

The zone that contains the prime meridian is the starting point of the time zone map. West of the prime meridian, the time gets earlier. Miami is in the "-5" time zone that is five hours earlier than the prime meridian time zone.

A Historical Map

Historical maps tell about the history of a group of people or a part of the world. These maps give information about countries that existed in the past. Some of these maps show how the boundaries of an area have changed over time. The historical map below gives information about the land controlled by Rome from 338 B.C. to 133 B.C. The map shows three stages in the expansion of the lands controlled by Rome.

Roman armies conquered most of this peninsula by 270 B.C. This land, gained during the second stage of Roman expansion, appears in orange on the map.

Roman Expansion, 338 B.C.–133 B.C.

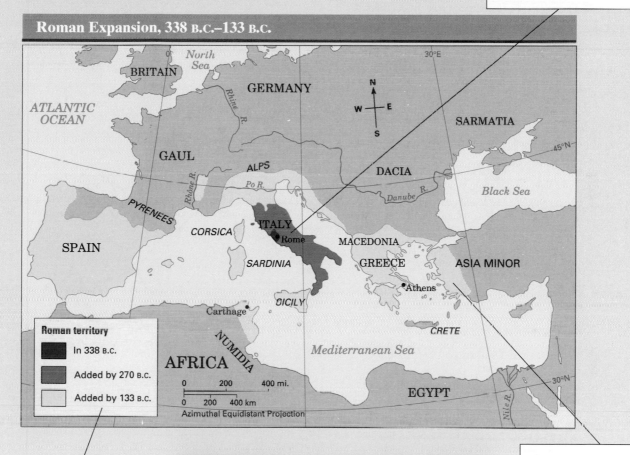

Roman territory

- In 338 B.C.
- Added by 270 B.C.
- Added by 133 B.C.

The legend explains the meaning of each color used on the map. Areas of the same color represent the land gained during one time period. In 338 B.C., the land controlled by Rome included only the city and the area around it

The land under Roman control more than doubled during the third stage of expansion, between 270 B.C. and 133 B.C. Land added during this stage has the color yellow.

◄ *Roman engineers built aqueducts to carry water between towns. This one near Nîmes, France, was built in the first century A.D.*

A Route Map

A route map shows the movement of people or goods across an area. Some route maps show the paths explorers used. Other route maps show the roads to take on a family trip. This route map shows the path Alexander's army followed.

Alexander the Great set out from Macedonia in southeastern Europe to conquer the mighty Persian Empire. Follow the heavy line on this route map to see where Alexander and his troops traveled.

Alexander's route starts at Pella in Macedonia. Alexander and his troops left Pella in 334 B.C.

The map area colored yellow shows Alexander's empire at its height—around 323 B.C.

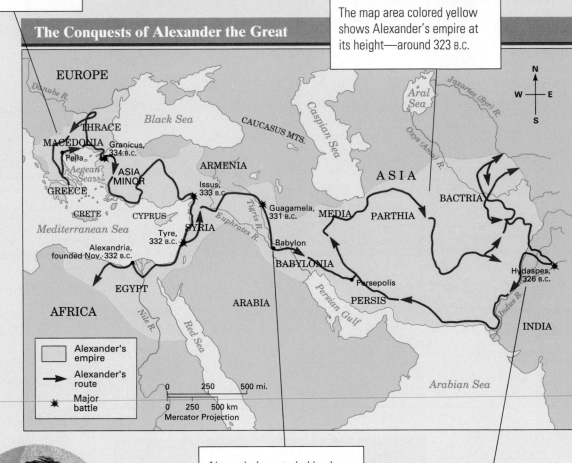

The Conquests of Alexander the Great

Alexander's route led back to Babylon, the capital of his empire. Alexander died there in 323 B.C. after a sudden illness. He did not leave an heir to his empire. These lands were divided up among Alexander's generals, who established kingdoms of their own.

Alexander reached northwest India in 326 B.C. and defeated the army of the Indian prince Porus. Alexander planned to continue across India, but his troops rebelled. Instead, he sailed down the Indus River, then led his troops west. Notice how the arrows point south, then west.

▲ *Alexander the Great lived only 33 years (356–323 B.C.) but changed the world of his time.*

Comparing Maps

These two maps show different facts about the country of Argentina. The land regions map shows the main physical areas in Argentina. The population density map shows the number of people in different areas of Argentina. You can compare the maps to figure out why people in Argentina live where they do.

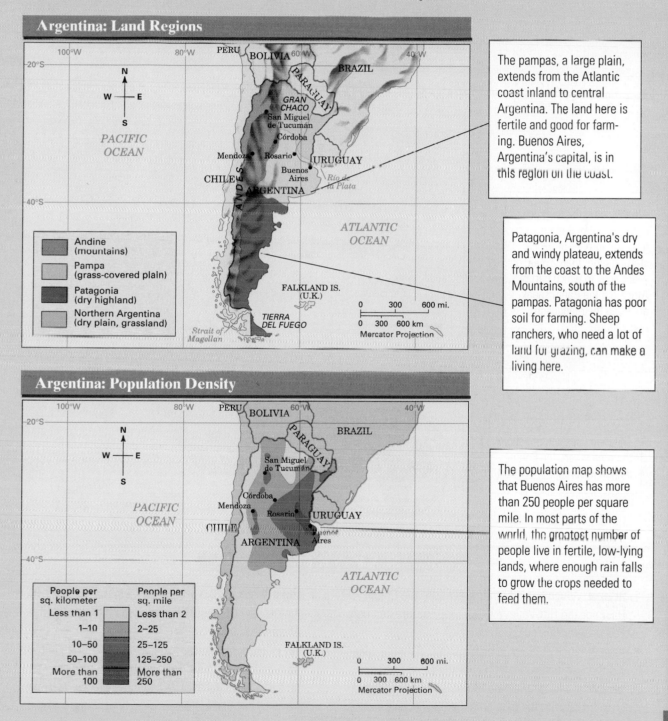

Argentina: Land Regions

Legend:
- Andine (mountains)
- Pampa (grass-covered plain)
- Patagonia (dry highland)
- Northern Argentina (dry plain, grassland)

0 300 600 mi.
0 300 600 km
Mercator Projection

The pampas, a large plain, extends from the Atlantic coast inland to central Argentina. The land here is fertile and good for farming. Buenos Aires, Argentina's capital, is in this region on the coast.

Patagonia, Argentina's dry and windy plateau, extends from the coast to the Andes Mountains, south of the pampas. Patagonia has poor soil for farming. Sheep ranchers, who need a lot of land for grazing, can make a living here.

Argentina: Population Density

People per sq. kilometer	People per sq. mile
Less than 1	Less than 2
1–10	2–25
10–50	25–125
50–100	125–250
More than 100	More than 250

0 300 600 mi.
0 300 600 km
Mercator Projection

The population map shows that Buenos Aires has more than 250 people per square mile. In most parts of the world, the greatest number of people live in fertile, low-lying lands, where enough rain falls to grow the crops needed to feed them.

A Cultural Map

A people's culture includes everything that is a part of their way of life. Cultural maps can show how all or part of one group's culture spread and influenced other people. This map shows what happened as a result of the migration of Bantu-speaking peoples in Africa.

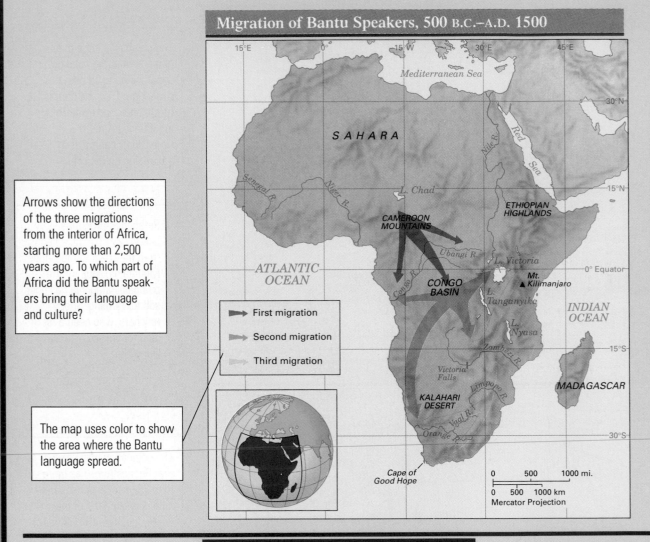

Migration of Bantu Speakers, 500 B.C.–A.D. 1500

Arrows show the directions of the three migrations from the interior of Africa, starting more than 2,500 years ago. To which part of Africa did the Bantu speakers bring their language and culture?

First migration
Second migration
Third migration

The map uses color to show the area where the Bantu language spread.

0   500   1000 mi.
0   500   1000 km
Mercator Projection

MAP SKILLS

1. REVIEW Which has a higher elevation, the Congo Basin or the Rift Valley? What map feature can help you answer this question quickly?

2. REVIEW Look at the map on page 200. By what year did the Egyptians gain land near the Dead Sea?

3. REVIEW Compare the map of China's climate regions on page 28 with the map on page 33 showing economic use. What kind of climate do most of the rice farming regions of China have?

4. THINK ABOUT IT How would the route map of Alexander the Great's conquests help you write a report about Alexander?

5. TRY IT Think of three to five places in the United States you would like to visit. Then imagine your family going on a two-week vacation to see these places. You might travel by car, plane, train, or even boat. Trace a map of the United States. On it, draw a route map of your imaginary vacation.

Using Geographic References

What countries border El Salvador? What does a volcano look like? Where is Haiti? The different parts of the Time/Space Databank on pages 488–532 of this book will help you answer many geography questions.

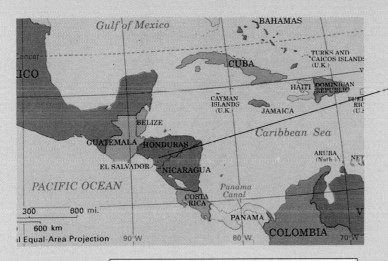

The Atlas on pages 502–517 has maps of the world and continents. This segment from the Atlas shows the northwest corner of South America, Central America, and major islands in the Caribbean Sea. You can see that El Salvador is bordered by two countries, Guatemala and Honduras.

The Glossary of Geographic Terms on pages 518–519 shows some of the earth's natural features. This entry for volcano tells you what a volcano is and shows a picture of what one looks like.

This entry from page 520 of the Gazetteer tells you where the city of Alexandria, Egypt, is. It tells the city's latitude and longitude and on what page you can find Alexandria on a map.

A

Aegean Sea (in southern Europe)	39°N	25°E	**329**
Aegospotami (ancient town of Thrace)	40°N	26°E	**370**
Ain Mallaha (ancient settlement near Jordan R.)	32°N	35°E	**121**
Alexandria (city in Egypt founded by Alexander the Great)	31°N	30°E	**451**

volcano
an opening in the earth, usually raised, through which lava and gasses from the earth's interior escape

---

MAP SKILLS

1. **REVIEW** Which part of the Time/Space Databank will have a map of the world's vegetation regions? Look at the vegetation map there and find out which continent is mostly desert.

2. **REVIEW** What is the exact location of Cairo, Egypt? On which pages of your Atlas will you find a map of Egypt?

3. **THINK ABOUT IT** What is the difference between a canyon and a cliff? Which part of the Time/Space Databank helped you answer this question?

4. **TRY IT** Suppose you are the new editor of the Time/Space Databank. You decide to add more information to the Glossary of Geographic Terms. Pick two geographic features, write their definitions, and draw pictures of them.

Unit 1

The World Past and Present

Like a snapshot in a family album, this sculpture records a moment in time. The happy husband and wife lived 2,500 years ago in what is now Italy. They are shown seated together at a grand banquet. What could their lives have been like? Certainly, they lived in a world that was different from ours. Yet the people of the past shared many of our feelings and needs. Their experiences helped shape our world.

6500 B.C.

Terra cotta sarcophagus from an Etruscan tomb at Cerveteri, Italy, c. 600 B.C. Louvre, Paris

Chapter 1
Peoples of Our World

A child gently sways back and forth in a swing. Other children shout and laugh as they toss a ball. Still others scamper to launch kites in the afternoon breeze. These are familiar scenes of daily life. The time could be the present, but it also could be thousands of years ago. In ancient Greece, children swung in swings. In Rome they played catch. The Chinese flew kites. In many ways, the lives of the people of the past were not so different from our own.

Just as we play board games today, the ancient Egyptians used this game board and these "throwing sticks" about 1400 B.C.

In some parts of the world, people have been writing down their thoughts and feelings for more than 5,000 years. This message was written on the walls of a cave in southern China about 1100 B.C.

This might have been a toy or a religious object. It was made about 700 B.C. by the Etruscans, a people who lived in what is now Italy.

Today

LESSON 1

Links with the Past

THINKING
FOCUS

What do we have in common with the people of the past?

Key Term

• history

The Romans called him "the Scourge of God." Attila the Hun and his men swept across Europe 1,500 years ago and conquered the cities of the once-proud Roman Empire. The Romans, who thought these invaders were uncivilized, called them barbarians. Yet one Roman had a different view of the leader of the Huns. After one dinner with Attila and his captains, the Roman historian Priscus wrote the following:

➤ *What impression of Attila the Hun does this portrait give you?*

A lavish meal, served on silver trenchers [platters], was prepared for us and the other barbarians, but Attila just had some meat on a wooden platter. . . . Gold or silver cups were presented to the other diners, but his own goblet was made of wood. His clothes, too, were simple, and no trouble was taken except to have them clean. The sword that hung by his side, the clasps of his barbarian shoes and the bridle of his horse were all free from gold, precious stones or other valuable decorations. . . .

As twilight came on torches were lit, and two barbarians entered before Attila to sing some songs they had composed, telling of his victories and valor in war. . . . After the songs a Scythian entered, a crazy fellow who told a lot of strange and completely false stories, not a word of truth in them, which made everyone laugh . . . all that is except Attila. He remained impassive, without any change of expression, and neither by word or gesture did he seem to share in the merriment except that when his youngest son, Ernas, came in and stood by him, he drew the boy towards him and looked at him with gentle eyes.

Priscus, *History*, c. A.D. 448

The People of the Past

People of ancient times may seem like distant mysteries to us. Yet descriptions like Priscus's account of his dinner with Attila help us see them more clearly. We can begin to understand what kind of people they were.

Think about the portrait of Attila that Priscus presents. For example, Priscus notes that Attila eats from a wooden tray and drinks from a wooden goblet, or cup. Attila was the leader of the Huns. Why didn't he eat off the silver platters like the rest of his guests?

He and his men took great treasures from the cities they conquered. Why did Attila dress so plainly? Think about the way that he looked at his son. Can't you almost see the tender expression on his face?

The Romans saw Attila as a fierce warrior, but as this portrait shows, he was more than that. He was also a man with a unique personality and a family, just like people today.

◄ *The Egyptians painted portraits of the dead on the wrappings of mummies, like this portrait of a child from about A.D. 100.*

Lives of the Past

Studying the past allows you to "see" the faces of the famous and the nameless people who lived thousands of years before you. It helps you understand what their lives were like.

In Boston's Museum of Fine Arts, for example, you can see the 1,800-year-old mummy of a young Egyptian girl. Her portrait was painted where the wrappings cover her face.

The portrait shows that her hair is bobbed short in the style of the Roman emperor's court (Egypt was ruled by Rome during her lifetime). Her large, round eyes, dark brown, look out at you. Her lips are colored gold with something like lipstick.

The same sun you play under once warmed her skin. The same earth spun her through space. The light you see from a nearby star was just leaving the star when she laughed in the night.

Surely children like this Egyptian girl lived in a world that was much different from ours. Yet in many ways it was the same. Think about how people treat their pets today. Now look at A Moment in Time on the next page.

▼ *A young girl in ancient Egypt might have used a bronze and gold make-up kit like this one.*

A Nubian Princess

9:11 A.M., May 10, 1341 B.C.
In a house in Nubia, an ancient African
kingdom south of Egypt

Makeup
Her mother helped her grind the colors and put them on in the cool air of early morning. Our princess wants to look as grown-up and royal as she feels.

Hand
The princess is directing her servants. They are loading her boat with ivory, rare African wood, and other gifts for the king of Egypt. She'll be leaving for Egypt in a few minutes.

Earrings
She has never worn such long earrings, but her older sister told her that Egyptian teen-agers wear even longer ones. The king is a teen-ager, too. She wonders what he looks like.

Jewel Box
Carved from white stone, this is the gift that she will hand to the king of Egypt. Her parents asked her to pick the best jewelry from local crafts-people. She did, but not before she hid her favorite ring in her room.

Gown
Late last night servants finally got the folds of her new linen dress to fall perfectly. The wooden ma-chine that presses the folds broke last week and wasn't repaired until yesterday.

Cat
Her shy pet, named Miu, has been rushing around the house with her all morning. All the princess's friends have cats, too.

Sandals
She's wearing leather sandals for this special occasion. Her everyday sandals are made from the same plant used to make paper.

Connections to the Past

Evidence from the past shows that ancient people used many of the same kinds of objects we use today. In Egyptian tombs from 5,000 years ago, "chew sticks," a primitive form of toothbrushes, have been found. Dolls with arms and legs that move have been discovered in Greek and Roman tombs from about 2,200 years ago. And in Babylonia about 5,000 years ago, boys and girls were spinning tops.

Ancient people enjoyed some of the same snacks we do. Four thousand years ago people first started eating ice cream in China. Two thousand years ago Romans were munching on cookies.

Ancient people also shared our concerns about appearance. About 6,000 years ago, women were using eye make-up and arranging their hair with combs. Men in ancient Egypt wore wigs.

As you can see, the people of the past were like us in many ways. As we study the past, we learn about ourselves as well. ■

How Do We Know?

HISTORY *The objects dug up at ruins of ancient settlements are an important source of information about life in the past. By studying these objects, we can begin to understand the lifestyles and values of ancient people.*

◄ *"Chew sticks" served as toothbrushes in Egypt 5,000 years ago.*

■ *What are two examples of objects used by ancient people that are still used today?*

Daily Life in the Past

Daily life in the past was not so different from daily life today. Take, for example, the ordinary sounds of a city.

You can probably appreciate why the man who wrote the following description was annoyed by the noise of his neighborhood.

My lodgings are right over a public bath-house, and you can imagine what that means! It's enough to make a man hate his own ears. First there are the strenuous types exercising, swinging lead weights about in their hands, and grunting and groaning whenever they find it hard—or want people to think they do. Their other favorite trick is holding their breath and then letting it out with sharp gasps and whistles. . . .

Next you get a ball-player yelling out his score—could anything be worse?

Doesn't that sound like a description of the sights and sounds of a modern fitness center? Can't you almost see the weightlifters and hear the shout of the ball-player? But this account was actually written nearly 2,000 years ago. A Roman writer named Seneca, who lived from 4 B.C. to A.D. 65, was describing life near one of the bath-houses that were popular gathering spots for the citizens of Rome.

Family Life

Do you think family relationships in the past were different than today? Listen to this exchange between a father and his son.

"Where did you go?"
"I did not go anywhere."
"If you did not go anywhere, why do you idle about? Go to school.
. . . Don't stand about in the public square or wander on the boulevard."

That account is from a student's essay. It was written in the 600s B.C. in Sumer, part of what is now the Middle East.

The people of ancient times faced many of the same social problems as well. Consider the account on page 9 in which a gambler tells of his ruined life.

UNDERSTANDING FAMILY

"Where did you go?" The question a father in Sumer asked his son 2,500 years ago is still asked in families today. Families are one of the basic institutions of human societies.

What is a family? How do families differ? What roles do families play in society?

What is a Family?

In many societies, members of a family are related people, but in some societies the term applies to unrelated people brought together by common bonds.

Sometimes, families live together in one household. In other cases, family members may be living in scattered places. No matter where they live, members of a family are tied together by many interests or concerns.

How Do Families Differ?

Families vary from one part of the world to another, but they generally fall into three categories: nuclear, extended, and alternative. The nuclear family consists of a father, a mother, and their children. Many families in the United States are nuclear families.

The extended family consists of the nuclear family plus the families of the children when they grow up and marry. Extended families are commonly found in some regions of India and Indonesia.

Alternative families consist of individuals who live together for economic, political, social, or religious reasons. Members of alternative families may or may not be related. Workers who live together in Israel on a farm called a kibbutz form this type of family.

What Is a Family's Role?

In most societies the family is responsible for raising the children. It also passes on values, beliefs, and customs from one generation to the next.

The family plays a major role in teaching the types of behavior that are accepted in a society. Children learn what is expected of them in their society by watching their parents and other members of their family. In addition, parents teach children basic attitudes and values of their society. Whether the time is today or 600 B.C., a parent is carrying out a family role by asking a child, "Where did you go?"

**Aristotle, 384–322 B.C.,
ancient Greece:**
"We should behave to our
friends as we would wish
our friends to behave to us."

| 500 | 400 | 300 | 200 | 100 | B.C. | A.D. | 100 |

**Confucius, 551–479 B.C.,
ancient China:**
"What you do not want
done to yourself, do not
do to others."

**Jesus, c. 4 B.C.–A.D. 29,
ancient Israel:**
"So whatever you wish
that men would do to
you, do so to them."

*B*ecause of one throw of the
dice I have driven away a devoted wife. My wife's mother hates
me, and my wife pushes me away;
the man in trouble finds no one
with sympathy. They all say, "I
find a gambler as useless as an old
horse that someone wants to sell."

The sad story told above is
more than 3,000 years old. It is
part of the Vedas, a collection of
sacred poems from what is now the
country of India.

The Story of the Past

The study of the past is called
history. When we set out to study
history, we are able to draw the
people and events of ancient times
closer to us.

We can see how our lives are
similar to theirs and also how they
are different. We can see how people of the distant past had to face
some of the very same problems we
face today. And we can appreciate
the connections that bind together
people of all time periods and all
areas of the world. ■

▲ *Notice how people
from different time peri-
ods and different parts of
the world have expressed
similar ideas.*

■ *What are two examples
of written sources that tell
us about daily life in ancient times?*

R E V I E W

1. **FOCUS** What do we have in common with the people
of the past?
2. **CONNECT** What are some ways American history has
been affected by the experiences of people of ancient
times?
3. **SOCIAL SYSTEMS** What are two concerns people faced
in the past that we still face today?
4. **CRITICAL THINKING** You have read about how people

today are similar to the people of the past. In what
ways are we different?

5. **WRITING ACTIVITY** Imagine that you could have a conversation with a 12-year-old child who lived 2,000
years ago. What kinds of common experiences do you
think you could talk about? Write the dialogue of your
conversation.

9

Making Hypotheses

Here's Why

Some maps provide geographical information about the modern world. Others provide geographical information about the past, such as the sea routes used by Greek traders or the extent of empires in ancient Africa. These are called historical thematic maps because they show specific historical information.

Historical thematic maps can help you see links between events that happened in different places and at different times. Using your observations, you can form a

hypothesis. The hypothesis, or explanation based on available facts, may be about what has occurred or is likely to occur.

As you have read, the present is connected to the past. For example, many Europeans today speak Romance languages, such as French, Italian, Portuguese, Romanian, and Spanish. Romance languages come from Latin, which was the language spoken by early Romans. By studying historical thematic maps, you may be able to form a hypothesis about the spread of languages.

Here's How

Look at the map that shows where Romance languages are spoken in Europe today. Next study the map that shows the roads linking the Roman Empire. Compare the two maps.

Notice how well developed the roads are that connect Rome to the territories that are now Spain and Portugal. From these maps, you can form a hypothesis that Rome had a strong influence on these territories. Through this network of roads, the Roman army was able to move soldiers and supplies.

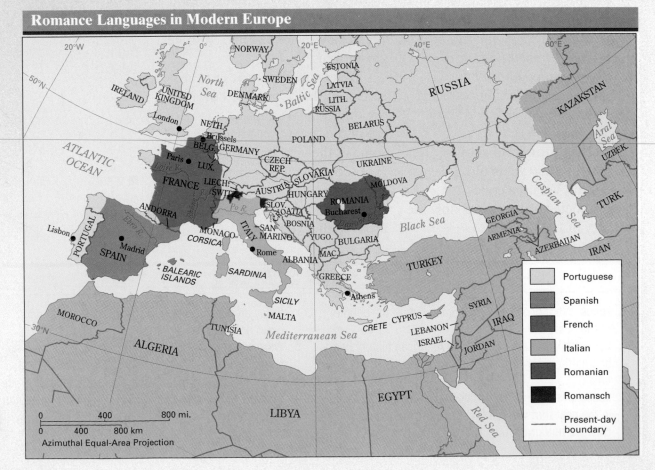

Romance Languages in Modern Europe

Legend:
- Portuguese
- Spanish
- French
- Italian
- Romanian
- Romansch
- Present-day boundary

0   400   800 mi.
0   400   800 km
Azimuthal Equal-Area Projection

Roman traders used the roads to transport goods.

Roman soldiers and traders probably spread the Latin language throughout these territories as they traveled the roads. The fact that two Romance languages, Spanish and Portuguese, are still spoken there seems to support this hypothesis.

Where else is the road system well developed? In the second map, you can see that a complex system of roads links France to Rome.

Now look at Germany. The Romans built fewer roads into Germany. From the lack of roads, you might hypothesize that the Romans had less influence here. Look at the map of Romance languages. Does it support your hypothesis? Is German a Romance language?

After studying these two maps, you can form a hypothesis. The Romance languages spread through Europe by means of the road and trade network that was part of the Roman Empire.

Try It

Find the map of major languages of the world on page 515 in the Atlas. Where is English spoken? Why do you think English is spoken in both the United States and Australia? Why do you think Portuguese is spoken in Brazil?

Apply It

Look at the map of World Religions on page 515 of the Atlas. Which religion has spread the least? The most? Knowing what you do about how cultures, languages, and ideas spread, what hypothesis can you form about these two religions?

Look again at the map. Try to find other patterns of information on the map. What hypothesis can you form from these patterns?

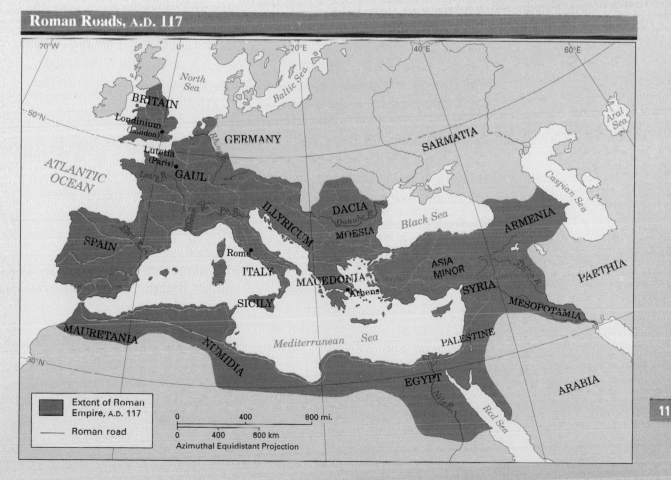

Roman Roads, A.D. 117

Extent of Roman Empire, A.D. 117

Roman road

0   400   800 mi.

0   400   800 km

Azimuthal Equidistant Projection

LESSON 2

Building on the Past

How have we learned from the past?

Key Terms

- myth
- culture

> *I*carus, beating his wings in joy, felt the thrill of the cool wind on his face and the clear air above and below him. He flew higher and higher into the blue sky until he reached the clouds. His father called out in alarm. He tried to follow, but he was heavier and his wings would not carry him. Up and up Icarus soared, through the soft moist clouds and out again toward the glorious sun. He was bewitched by a sense of freedom; he beat his wings frantically so that they would carry him higher and higher to heaven itself.
>
> Greek myth, "The Flight of Icarus," retold by Sally Benson

Did you ever wish you could fly? The idea of flight has intrigued people throughout the ages. Three thousand years ago the ancient Greeks told the story of a boy named Icarus who wanted to fly. Icarus flew toward the sun on wings made of feathers and wax. But he flew too close to the sun, and the wax melted. He fell from the sky to his death.

The story of Icarus is not true. It is a **myth,** a story told by people to explain their past. Nevertheless, it shows that people long ago were also fascinated with flight.

People have been experimenting with flying machines since the days of the ancient Greeks. In the 300s B.C., a Greek named Archytas *(ahr KY tuhs)* built a "wooden pigeon" that moved through the air. Around the same time, the Chinese discovered how to make kites. Today, we have learned to make machines that let us fly. But like Icarus, we still try to fly higher, now reaching toward the stars.

Learning from the Past

The dream of flight is one of the many ideas we share with the people who came before us. In fact, we owe much to the inventions and accomplishments of people of the past.

Many things we take for granted today were made possible by the achievements of the people who came before us. Take, for example, something as simple as a bicycle. The bicycle as we know it dates back only to about 1790, when a Frenchman invented a two-wheeled wooden scooter. On the next page, A Closer Look shows some of the inventions that had to come first. ■

■ *In what way do modern inventions depend on the past?*

Bicycle Technology

When you ride a bicycle, you are pedaling a machine that took thousands of years to create. Each part of a bicycle has a long history.

How do you make a faster wheel?
That's what people in Mesopotamia were wondering about 2,000 B.C. They came up with the idea of spokes to lighten the heavy, solid wheels on their chariots (below). With spokes the chariots rolled faster.

Life didn't have much bounce before rubber was discovered in Mexico 2,000 years ago. The statue below shows an ancient Mexican athlete playing a sport that used a rubber ball. Spanish explorers brought rubber back to Europe. In 1888, an Englishman made the first inflatable rubber tires.

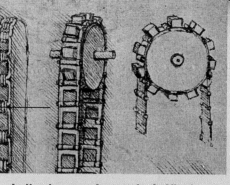

Italian inventor Leonardo da Vinci drew this chain drive around A.D. 1500. In 1770, a European inventor used a chain drive in silk-making machinery. From that idea the chain drive was adapted for use in bicycles in 1869.

13

Learning from Other Cultures

As the example of the bicycle shows, we have built on inventions from many different periods of time and from many different cultures. A **culture** consists of the behaviors, beliefs, customs, and attitudes of a group of people. It is reflected in the artwork, the literature, the language, the inventions, and traditions of the people. It is affected by the geography and climate where people live.

We have benefited from the accomplishments of human cultures reaching back millions of years. Throughout this book you will learn about the many contributions of these ancient cultures. You will also recognize how the decisions and actions of people in the past affect our lives today.

The Earliest Cultures

The first human cultures began developing about two million years ago. One of the first accomplishments of these cultures was learning to make and use crude stone tools. With simple tools such as sharp-edged rocks, people could hunt animals for food. They also learned to work together to go after large animals. These groups of people then developed rules of behavior for members to obey.

A second important accomplishment of early cultures was learning to farm. About 9000 B.C., people in some parts of the world began to settle down in one place for long periods and produce their own food. Once farmers could produce enough crops to feed other people, some people had time to develop other skills, such as pottery making or weaving.

Another important development was the rise of cities in some

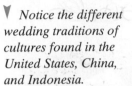

▼ *Notice the different wedding traditions of cultures found in the United States, China, and Indonesia.*

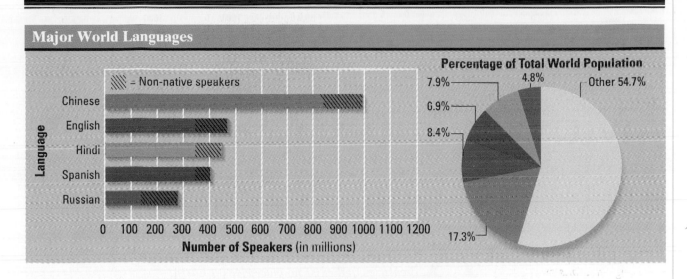

Major World Languages

= Non-native speakers

Language (vertical axis):
- Chinese
- English
- Hindi
- Spanish
- Russian

Number of Speakers (in millions) — axis: 0 100 200 300 400 500 600 700 800 900 1000 1100 1200

Percentage of Total World Population

- 7.9%
- 6.9%
- 8.4%
- 4.8%
- Other 54.7%
- 17.3%

parts of the world beginning about 3500 B.C. As larger groups of people gathered together in cities, more opportunities for specialized workers, such as builders, bakers, and artists were created. In addition, city life resulted in the need for more extensive systems of government. And bringing people together also meant a greater exchange of ideas.

Changes in Cultures

What causes cultures to change? New ideas and inventions often lead people to develop new ways of doing things. For example, the invention of writing systems allowed people to record their thoughts and discoveries and to communicate them to other people.

Changes in the environment also cause cultures to change. Over time, the climate in an area can change. Also, natural disasters such as floods and earthquakes can alter the landscape. People must then move or learn to adjust to new living conditions.

Another major source of change is contact with other cultures. When people from different cultures meet, they are exposed to the ways of life of each culture.

Cultures change from within as well. Factors such as population growth and conflicts between groups within a culture can bring about new ways of doing things.

The Cultures of Today

Today we live in a world of many cultures—a multicultural world. We have learned from cultures of all parts of the world, and we continue to interact with other cultures. We are linked to the cultures of the past, just as cultures of the future will be linked to us. ■

▲ *Languages often vary from one culture to another. Turn to the map of world languages on page 515 of the Atlas to see where these languages are spoken.*

Across Time & Space

When cultures come in contact, they learn from each other. For example, Native Americans taught European settlers how to grow corn and sweet potatoes. The settlers passed the information back to Europe. Now these foods are cultivated all around the world.

■ *What is a culture?*

R E V I E W

1. **FOCUS** How have we learned from the past?
2. **CONNECT** What do cultures of today have in common with cultures of the past?
3. **SOCIAL SYSTEMS** How are cultures different from each other?
4. **CRITICAL THINKING** What will the cultures of the future be able to learn from the cultures of today?
5. **ACTIVITY** Select an everyday object and investigate how it is connected to the past. Make a list showing at least three inventions that are linked to the object you selected.

15

LESSON 3

Moving into the Future

THINKING FOCUS

How will our decisions affect the lives of people in the future?

Key Terms

- rain forest
- deforestation

Antisiranana, Madagascar—The rain forest that crowns Amber Mountain still echoes like a cathedral with the strange cries of creatures that exist no place else on Earth.

As they have for centuries, sorcerers from the local Antakarena tribe climb into the hills to bathe beneath sacred waterfalls, strictly observing taboos aimed at pleasing the spirits of ancestors buried there. . . .

The mountain is besieged, however, by others driven by hunger or greed to plant crops in the forest, burn off areas for grazing, cut firewood or drag away massive rosewood logs to sell as lumber.

"Enchanting Forest," by Tom Masland, *Chicago Tribune*, May 31, 1989

What will become of the rain forests of Madagascar, an island nation off the coast of East Africa? **Rain forests** are lush green regions, brimming with plant and animal life, that receive more than 140 inches of rain a year. Today the rain forests throughout the world are in danger.

Issues such as the fate of rain forests have faced people throughout the ages. And just as the decisions of the past have affected our lives, the decisions made today will affect people for ages to come.

➤ *Rain forests, like the one at the right, are sometimes cleared using a method called slash and burn, shown above.*

An Age-Old Problem

As long as people have settled in groups, they have cut down or cleared away forests. This process is called **deforestation.** People cut down trees for lumber. They use the land for grazing animals, growing crops, or building settlements.

Nevertheless, the loss of forest land has caused problems throughout time. For example, 2,300 years ago an important Greek teacher named Plato complained about the deforestation of his homeland.

> *There are mountains in Attica which now can keep nothing but bees, but which were clothed not so long ago with fine trees, producing timber suitable for roofing the largest buildings.*
>
> Plato, *Critias*, c. 360 B.C.

Plato said that without the forest cover, rain just flowed over the mountains to the sea. The water supply from mountain streams that the Greeks once depended upon dried up.

In ancient Rome, deforestation caused flooding. A Roman scholar, Pliny the Elder, wrote 2,000 years ago that, "Indeed devastating torrents unite when the wood that used to hold the rivers and absorb them has been cut away from hills."

Much of the United States was once covered with forests. But as the European settlers moved westward, they cleared vast areas to

This drawing, called Plan of an American New Cleared Farm, shows how European settlers cut down the forests of America.

Find the areas where rain forests are expected to remain in the year 2000.

Destruction of Tropical Rain Forests

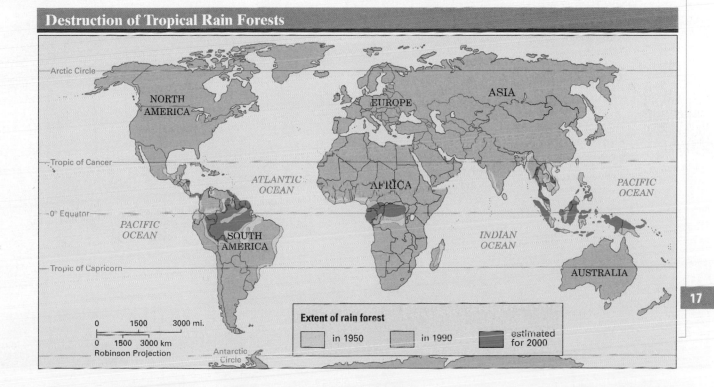

Arctic Circle

NORTH AMERICA

EUROPE

ASIA

Tropic of Cancer

ATLANTIC OCEAN

AFRICA

PACIFIC OCEAN

PACIFIC OCEAN

0° Equator

PACIFIC OCEAN

SOUTH AMERICA

INDIAN OCEAN

Tropic of Capricorn

AUSTRALIA

Antarctic Circle

| 0 | 1500 | 3000 mi. |
| 0 | 1500 | 3000 km |

Robinson Projection

Extent of rain forest

in 1950   in 1990   estimated for 2000

build towns, graze animals, and grow crops. Logging operations continue to reduce the size of American forests.

Today, deforestation is a global problem. Look at the map on page

17. How has the area covered by rain forests changed from 1950 to 1990? The United Nations predicts that at the present rate, one-fifth of the remaining rain forests will be cleared by the year 2000. ∎

■ What is deforestation?

▼ What are the effects of deforestation?

A Current Problem

In Madagascar, an island about the size of Texas 300 miles off the coast of East Africa, 80 per cent of the rain forests have been destroyed already.

As has happened in the past, Madagascar faces strong pressures to clear the land of the rain forests. Cutting down the trees for lumber and other wood products helps Madagascar's economy. Clearing the land for farming helps Madagascar feed its people.

Nevertheless, the destruction of the rain forests causes serious problems. The chart below shows the effects of deforestation. How does it affect the world's atmosphere? How does it contribute to flooding?

If the rain forests of Madagascar disappear, so will their unique plant and animal species. Almost all the world's lemurs live in Madagascar. These large-eyed, furry mammals make their home in the forest. Scientists

Rare plant and animal species that rely on the unique habitats found in rain forests become extinct.

The slash and burn method pollutes the air and may contribute to the "greenhouse effect," the gradual warming of the earth's atmosphere.

The livelihoods of native people, such as those who extract material from rubber trees for making rubber, are destroyed.

When logging operations clear vast areas, topsoil is washed away, so nothing will grow.

When the roots of trees and plants that soak up water are removed, flooding can result.

estimate that 86 per cent of the plants, 95 per cent of the reptiles, and 65 per cent of the birds in Madagascar's rain forests exist nowhere else. Destruction of the rain forests would also ruin the homelands of native cultures.

The rivers that run from these lush forests will also dry up. Without this water, the farmers in Madagascar will suffer. Finally, the long-term effects of deforestation on the earth's atmosphere could cause problems far beyond the borders of Madagascar. ■

Tropical Rain Forest Timber

Usage
- Pulp 16%
- Construction and furniture 51%
- Fuelwood 33%

Consumers
- United States 6%
- Other 8%
- Producing regions 60%
- Japan 15%
- Europe 11%

▲ *How much of the timber from rain forests does the United States use?*

■ *Why does Madagascar face pressure to clear its rain forests?*

Looking for Answers

What can the past tell us about the problems of today? By studying the past, we can see how previous cultures dealt with similar problems. We can understand the effects of their actions, and we can make judgments about how our actions might affect the future.

Examining the Past

In the case of deforestation, people have recognized its effects for centuries. Yet in the past, people did not choose to conserve the forests. They made other choices. Those choices affected their lives and the lives of the generations that followed.

Today, we can examine the choices made in the past as we make new choices. What choices will we make about deforestation?

Learning from the Past

Deforestation is a global problem. Dealing with it will take an international effort. In our multicultural world, we must understand the history of other cultures in order to solve problems together. By studying the past, we can see the roots of the present and we can better understand our world neighbors.

Learning about the past gives us a framework for making decisions about the issues that we face today. It also helps us understand how our actions will affect the people of tomorrow. ■

■ *How can learning about the past help us understand the problems of today?*

R E V I E W

1. **FOCUS** How will our decisions affect the lives of people in the future?
2. **CONNECT** Why might people from different cultures have differing views on the problem of deforestation?
3. **CITIZENSHIP** What are two ways that learning about the past helps us make decisions today?
4. **CRITICAL THINKING** You have read that Plato and Pliny warned of the effects of deforestation more than 2,000 years ago. Why did people continue to destroy rain forests?
5. **WRITING ACTIVITY** Imagine someone said to you, "Why should I care about the rain forests of Madagascar?" How would you answer that person? Write an essay that gives your response.

Rain Forests: Preserve Them? Use Them?

We simply cannot replace this invaluable resource once it is gone. The rain forests . . . once lost, can never be regained. Every second of every day, we are losing a tropical forest the size of a football field.

Hon. John E. Porter
U.S. Representative, Illinois

How can Brazil be expected to control its economic development, [Brazil's President José Sarney] asks, when it is staggering under a $111 billion foreign debt load? By what right does the U.S. . . . lecture poor countries like Brazil on their responsibilities to mankind?

Time,
September 18, 1989

Background

From the air, Brazil's great forests look like a giant green cushion. Once the earth nourished many such rain forests. Now only a few remain. The loss of these rain forests affects the entire world.

How? Like all plants, the huge trees of the forest take in carbon dioxide from the air. They use this gas to make their food. The enormous forests, therefore, help balance the carbon dioxide and oxygen in the earth's atmosphere. When trees are cut down, we reduce the amount of carbon dioxide taken from the air. At the same time, we are burning more gasoline and other fossil fuels, releasing more carbon dioxide

into the air. Some scientists predict that this build-up of carbon dioxide in the atmosphere will cause the world's climate to grow warmer and warmer. We cannot foresee all the results of this global warming. One possibility, though, is that fertile farmland could someday become barren desert.

A close look at the rain forests reveals bare patches, some as big as the state of Connecticut. Other effects of deforestation are more difficult to see. When trees go, so do animals, plants, insects, and birds. Species as unique as the frogs shown here may become extinct if this trend continues. Such extinctions could have far-reaching effects. For example, many of our medicines come from plants. What if a plant growing in a rain forest today contains a cure for a form of cancer? What if the plant becomes extinct as the forest shrinks?

Roots of the Problem

If you look only at the effects of this loss of rain forests, the solution may seem clear: Put a stop to it. To see how complicated the problem really is you have to study the causes—the reasons for clearing the rain forests.

Brazil has a large and rapidly growing population. Providing jobs and housing requires space. Some forests are cleared to build homes, factories, roads, and bridges.

Like most countries, Brazil wants to keep a balance of trade. This means that Brazil tries to sell to other nations as much as it buys from them. Brazil imports steel and other products. It exports beef and lumber. Forests are cleared to provide grazing land for cattle. Lumber, of course, comes from the forests.

In addition, Brazilian miners bring nearly 70 tons of gold a year out of the rain forests. Some areas are cleared to give the miners room to work.

Brazilians want to raise their standard of living. If the rain forests can be useful, why should they not benefit the nation in which they grow?

Decision Point

1. After reading about the problem of the rain forests, what questions do you have?
2. Where would you look for more information about global warming? About Brazil's economy?
3. Are there ways to both preserve and use the rain forests? How can you find out?
4. Choose one topic related to the rain forest problem. What more do you need to know about it? Find the information in newspapers and magazines.
5. Discuss the new information you and your classmates found. Based on this very limited information, what ideas and alternatives can you suggest?

Chapter Review

Reviewing Key Terms

culture (p. 14)   myth (p. 12)
deforestation (p. 17)   rain forest (p.16)
history (p. 9)

A. Imagine you are playing a game in which your partner tries to guess the key term you are thinking of. For each of the four key terms below, think of a phrase you could give to your partner as a clue. Write each phrase on your own paper. An example has been done for you.
1. rain forest: huge numbers of different plants and animals
2. deforestation
3. culture
4. history

B. Be sure you understand the meanings of the five key terms. Then answer each question by writing one or more sentences.
1. Was the reading by Priscus an example of history or of myth? Explain why you think so.
2. What is one way in which culture and history are related?
3. In the selection entitled "Enchanting Forest," what do we learn about the Antakarena culture?
4. What do we learn about Madagascar's rain forest in that selection?
5. What examples from history of deforestation are given in the chapter?

Exploring Concepts

A. On your own paper, copy and complete the outline below. Then use it to write a summary of the chapter. For each main idea, write a short paragraph.

  I. The present is like the past.
    A.
      1. Playing with toys
      2. Eating snacks
      3.
    B. Problems of daily life
 II. The present builds on the past.
    A.
    B. Accomplishments of early cultures
      1.
      2.
III. The present affects the future.
    A. An old and new problem
    B. Ways of solving the problem
      1.
      2.

B. Answer each question with information from the chapter.
1. What are three ways in which the lives of people from the past were similar to our lives today? List specific examples.
2. How do the examples of the flight of Icarus, the wooden pigeon, and the invention of the bicycle show how people build on the past?
3. What messages from the past can help us understand the problem of deforestation today? How do these messages help us to understand the problem?
4. How is cultural development seen in the daily lives of the people of a culture?
5. What accomplishments led to people's jobs being specialized? What were some important results of building cities?
6. Why might a very important part of the Antakarena culture disappear if all of the rain forests of Madagascar are destroyed?

Reviewing Skills

1. Compare the Africa rainfall map on this page and the world vegetation map on page 516 in the Atlas. What hypothesis might you make about the relationship between vegetation and rainfall amount?
2. What observations based on these maps support your hypothesis?
3. Looking only at the rainfall map, if your hypothesis is accurate, in what part of Madagascar would you expect to find rain forests?
4. Now look at the vegetation map. What part of Madagascar is covered by rain forests? Compare this information with your answer to question 3.
5. Suppose you wanted to write a report on why deforestation has occurred throughout history to the present. The only information you have to begin with is two maps: a map showing world deforestation, and a world land-use map. How would you begin?

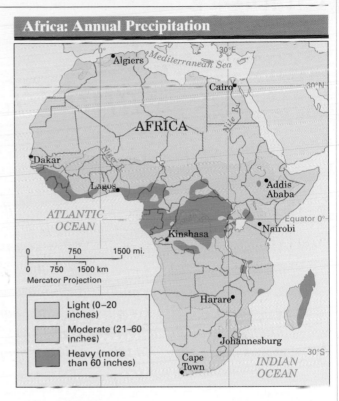

Africa: Annual Precipitation

Light (0–20 inches)

Moderate (21–60 inches)

Heavy (more than 60 inches)

0   750   1500 mi.

0   750   1500 km

Mercator Projection

Using Critical Thinking

1. In the chapter, you got a glimpse of the attitudes of Sumerian children and parents toward each other around 600 B.C. What might historians of the future learn about your culture from things that you have written? Write a short paragraph describing how your attitudes are reflected in the clothes you wear as well as in things you say and do.

2. A people's culture is partly reflected in its inventions. The personal computer was invented in the United States in the 1970s. Suppose you are a historian in the future. What would you say the use of the personal computer represented about our culture? Make a list of behaviors, beliefs, and attitudes you think are reflected in the use of the personal computer.

Preparing for Citizenship

1. **WRITING ACTIVITY** Describe the setting and main character for the beginning of a story about an Antakarena child. Learn as much as you can about Madagascar's rain forests and the people who live there. Find out about the culture and the plant and animal life of Madagascar. Use that information in your description.

2. **COLLABORATIVE LEARNING** The people of the past were in many ways very much like the people of the present. Team up with three other people. Each person in the group should research a well-known person of the distant past. As a group, decide who of the four historical figures interests you most. Choose one important event in that person's life. Work together to create a short scene about that event. Set the scene in modern times without changing the historical figure's attitudes, beliefs, or behavior.

Chapter 2

People and Places

Today astronauts explore new frontiers, just as ancient sea captains once did. Modern builders change the face of the earth with their skyscrapers and freeways, just as early people changed the land with their fields and villages. Settlers still seek gentle landscapes and mild climates, while they avoid rugged mountain ranges and harsh climates. Throughout time, the world has shaped the way people live. And the actions of people have reshaped the world.

3000 B.C.

The people of ancient Egypt used the waters of the Nile River to make the desert bloom. This model of farmers plowing a field was made in about 2000 B.C.

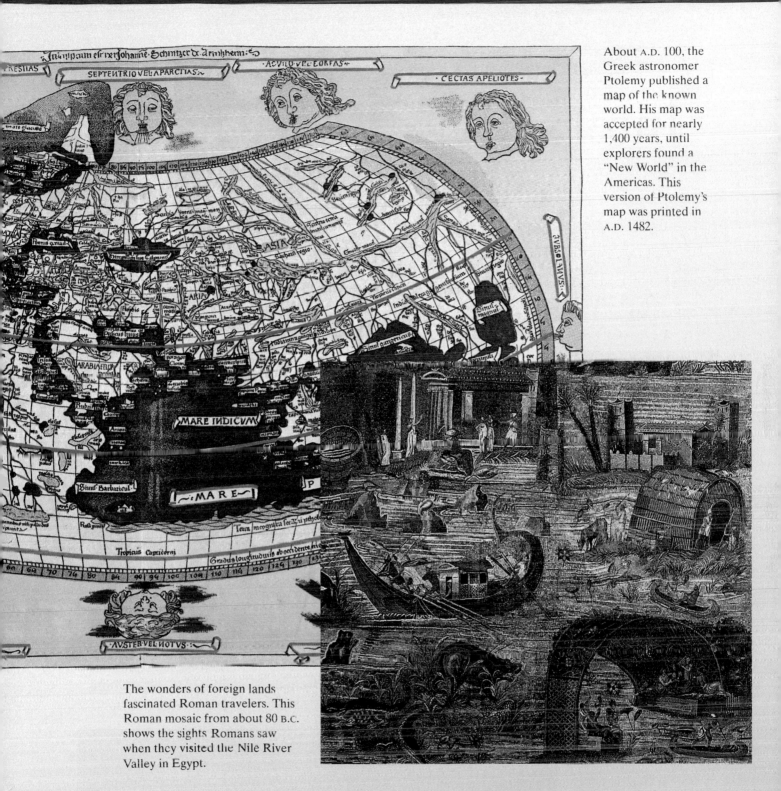

About A.D. 100, the Greek astronomer Ptolemy published a map of the known world. His map was accepted for nearly 1,400 years, until explorers found a "New World" in the Americas. This version of Ptolemy's map was printed in A.D. 1482.

The wonders of foreign lands fascinated Roman travelers. This Roman mosaic from about 80 B.C. shows the sights Romans saw when they visited the Nile River Valley in Egypt.

Today

Interacting with the World

THINKING FOCUS

How do climate and topography affect human life?

Key Terms

- topography
- climate
- diffusion
- region

➤ *In some parts of China, farmers have conquered the mountains by carving out terraces for their crops.*

The day had turned very hot. It was now in the nineties. I saw eighteen sheep crowded into a little blot of shade under a frail hawthorn tree. Children cooled themselves by kicking water in a ditch. Farmers with lamp shade hats planted crops by pushing one sprout at a time into the ground, in a process that had a greater affinity to needlepoint than to farming, as though they were stitching a design into the furrows. And though there were black peaks and mountain ranges on both sides of the train, the land fell away, and it was as if we were approaching the ocean—the land dipped and had the smooth, stony look of the seashore. It was the hottest part of the day, but even so the land was full of people. Hours later, in an immense and stony desert I saw a man in a faded blue suit, bumping over the stones on his bike.

Then there were sand dunes near the track—big soft slopes and bright piles; but the snowy peaks in the distance still remained. I had not realized that there was anything so strange as this on this planet.

Paul Theroux, *Riding the Iron Rooster*

In 1988, Paul Theroux, an American writer, wrote about his travels across China by train. As he traveled, Theroux observed many people and places. He noticed how certain kinds of places affected people and their ways of life.

Theroux boarded the train in Lanzhou *(lahn joh)* at about midnight the night before his account above. The next evening, from

the window of the dining car, he could see the town of Jiayuguan (*jyuh yoo kwahn*). It lay "glowing in the sand" of the Gobi, an immense desert. Trace his journey on the map of China below.

Living in the World

Like Paul Theroux, geographers study the relationships between people and their world. They study the factors that influence where people settle and how they live. Among these are topography and climate.

Topography refers to the surface, or physical, features of an area. These include mountains and valleys, rivers and lakes, sandy shores and grassy plains. Examine the map of China below.

China is a land of topographic extremes. Mount Everest, the highest peak in the world, soars 29,028 feet above sea level. That's more than five miles high! The Turfan Depression, a fertile area in the middle of a desert, lies 505 feet below sea level. Vast dry plains stretch across parts of western China. Limestone hills in the southeast shoot almost straight up, 100 to 600 feet from the ground. Two rivers rise in the highlands of

▼ *Why do you think fewer people live in the Plateau of Tibet than in eastern China?*

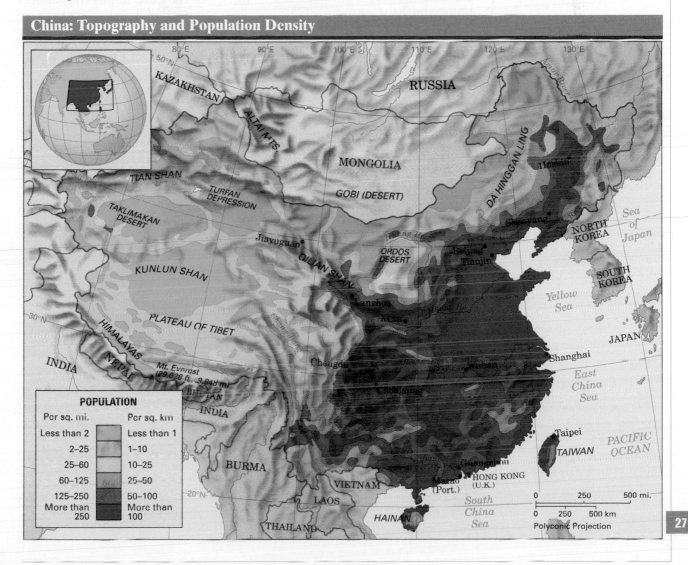

China: Topography and Population Density

People and Places

western China. They are the Chang Jiang *(chahng jyahng)* and the Huang He *(hwahng hay)*. They water the hilly, fertile fields to the east. In the words of Paul Theroux, China is "more like a whole world than a mere country."

The climates of China are as varied as its topography. **Climate** is the general pattern of weather in an area over time. The most important elements of climate are precipitation and temperature. Precipitation is water or ice that falls to the earth, such as rain, snow, or sleet.

The Tibetan Highlands of southwest China are dry and cold. They get less than 20 inches of rain annually, and July temperatures average less than 45° F. But parts of southeast China along the coast are rainy and hot. Some areas get more than 80 inches of rainfall a year, with January temperatures averaging more than 60° F.

Where People Live

Look at the map on page 27. Note that China's 1.24 billion people are spread unevenly over the country's 3.7 million square miles. Which areas are most densely populated? Many people live in the southeast and along the east coast. Fewer live in the north and west.

To understand settlement patterns, first examine China's topography. How does the topography of the southeast differ from that of the north and west? Some parts of eastern China and the coast are hilly, but they are not as mountainous as the north and west. Also, southeastern China has plenty of rivers for water and transportation. For example, trace the Chang Jiang River and its tributaries.

➤ *Compare this map to the map on page 27. In what climate region of China do most people live?*

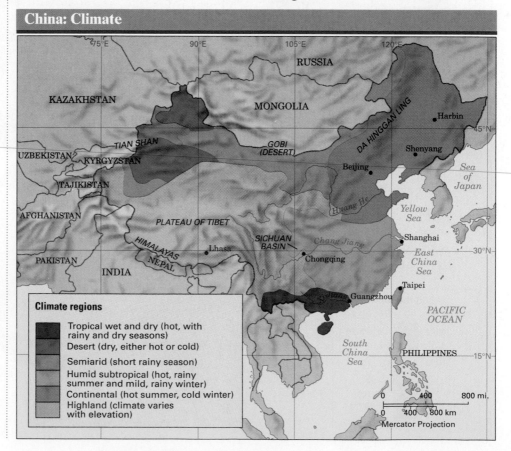

China: Climate

Climate regions

- Tropical wet and dry (hot, with rainy and dry seasons)
- Desert (dry, either hot or cold)
- Semiarid (short rainy season)
- Humid subtropical (hot, rainy summer and mild, rainy winter)
- Continental (hot summer, cold winter)
- Highland (climate varies with elevation)

The north and west, however, lack sources of water and are covered by vast areas of desert instead of fertile fields. What is the population density of the desert area known as the Gobi?

China's climate also affects settlement patterns. Look at the map on page 28. The climate along China's coast is mild—warmer in the winter and cooler in the summer than the climate farther inland. The coast also receives a great deal of rain. Most people in China are farmers. Think about what farmers need—fertile land, water, and a long growing season. Can you see why most of the people in China live in the eastern part of the country?

Throughout the world, people's choices of where they live are influenced by topography and climate. The first human settlements, farms, and cities developed in places where the climate and topography made farming possible.

For the most part, people are still drawn to places where the land is level and climates are warm or mild with plenty of rain. Study the world physical map on pages 504 and 505 and the world climate map on page 516 of the Time/Space Databank. Besides eastern China, other areas with this favorable mix of nature include western Europe, northern India, and much of the eastern United States, as well as its West Coast. You won't be surprised to learn that these areas are some of the most heavily populated in the world.

How People Live

Not all places in the world have mild temperatures, rivers suited for transportation, and level land. Find the Sichuan *(SEE shwahn)* Basin on the map on page 28. It is cut off from the rest of China by high mountains. The climate is good for farming, but the topography is not. The area is far too hilly. Even so, the Sichuan Basin is an important farming area. People have dug into the sides of the hills to create level strips of land, or terraces, that they can farm. These people have modified their environment to suit their needs as farmers.

Now find the Plateau of Tibet on the map. Here both the climate and the topography of the plateau make farming difficult. The temperatures are very cold, and little rain falls. Most of the plateau is a rocky wasteland. But in some areas, people can live by herding the yak, a tough animal capable of surviving the cold.

These herders depend upon the yak for their survival. They live in tents made of yak hair. They use yak hides to make their shoes. The yak also provides the Tibetans with milk, meat, and transportation. ■

▲ *Amid the highest mountains and plateaus in the world, these Tibetans are yak herders. The yak, a sort of hairy buffalo, provides the Tibetans with nearly everything they need, from milk to rope.*

■ *Where do humans tend to settle and why?*

Moving Through the World

Faced with an environment that makes farming difficult, the people of the Sichuan Basin came up with an answer— they decided to modify their environment. The people of Tibet chose another answer. They adapted to their environment by developing other means of getting food—herding yaks. But sometimes people are unable to modify or adapt. In these cases, people may choose to move to a different environment.

Kinds of Movement

People move to other areas for a variety of reasons. One type of movement is only temporary. You, for example, travel to and from school every day. Many adults are daily commuters, going to and from their work. This type of movement happens over and over in a cycle. Thus, it's called cyclic movement.

A second type of movement is periodic. It's when you move to a new place and stay for a period of time. For example, you might spend summer vacations at camp. But, eventually, you return home.

Periodic movement is a part of life for the Mongols and Kozakhs of northern China. These people herd sheep and goats. They move often, whenever their herds have eaten all the grass in a place. They move periodically, never staying permanently in one place.

A third type of movement is called migration. When people migrate, they leave their homeland to live permanently in another place. Archaeologists believe that people first migrated to the Americas from Asia between 20,000 and 40,000 years ago, across the Bering Strait.

One Effect of Movement

Whenever people move from place to place, they discover new ideas, values, languages, and inventions. Sometimes they adopt elements of a new culture, such as a religion or a custom, and change them if necessary to fit their own needs. **Diffusion** is the spread of the ideas, values, and inventions of one culture into another culture.

The spread of the yo-yo is one possible example of diffusion. You probably played with a yo-yo at one time. But did you know that the yo-yo has a worldwide reputation? At the left is a map that

This world map is centered on the North Pole. Compare it to the world political map on pages 502 and 503 in the Atlas. What differences do you notice?

The Yo-yo Around the World

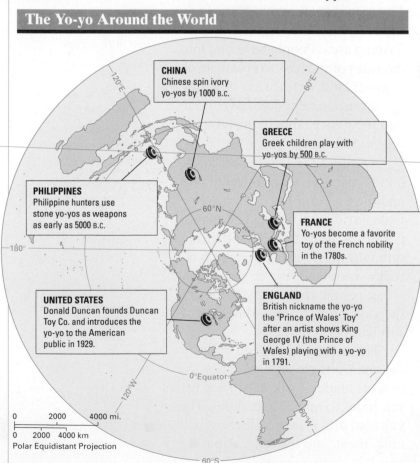

CHINA
Chinese spin ivory yo-yos by 1000 B.C.

GREECE
Greek children play with yo-yos by 500 B.C.

PHILIPPINES
Philippine hunters use stone yo-yos as weapons as early as 5000 B.C.

FRANCE
Yo-yos become a favorite toy of the French nobility in the 1780s.

UNITED STATES
Donald Duncan founds Duncan Toy Co. and introduces the yo-yo to the American public in 1929.

ENGLAND
British nickname the yo-yo the "Prince of Wales' Toy" after an artist shows King George IV (the Prince of Wales) playing with a yo-yo in 1791.

0   2000   4000 mi.
0   2000   4000 km
Polar Equidistant Projection

shows the cultures where the yo-yo has appeared over the years. As the yo-yo moved from culture to culture, it changed. In prehistoric times, Philippine hunters used stone yo-yos as weapons. Later, the Chinese used ivory yo-yos as toys. Many centuries later, the yo-yo became a fad among the French nobility, who called the yo-yo *l'emigrette* or "the migrant." Inspired by the Philippine yo-yo, American inventor Donald Duncan began producing yo-yos in the 1920s. Duncan introduced the first plastic yo-yo in 1957. In its diffusion, the yo-yo has changed from a weapon to a toy and from stone to plastic.

The story of the alphabet is another case of diffusion. About 4,000 years ago, the Phoenicians *(fih NIHSH uhns),* who lived in what is now Lebanon, developed an alphabet. When Phoenician merchants traded with the Greeks, the alphabet traveled to many Greek-speaking areas. Through exploration, trade, and war, the Greeks carried the alphabet even farther, eventually to the Italian peninsula. There, the Romans dropped several letters and gave the rest of the letters Latin names. When Roman soldiers marched into Britain, their alphabet went with them. Over time, this alphabet was transported to the New World. The alphabet in use today by English-speaking peoples is known as the Roman alphabet. You can learn more about it and other common alphabets on pages 488 and 489 in the Minipedia.

All cultures owe much to other cultures. For example, people played a game similar to modern football 5,000 years ago in Egypt. What examples of cultural diffusion can you see in your daily life—in your music, food, and clothes? ∎

▲ *The word* yo-yo *means "to return" in Tagalog, a Philippine language.*

■ *Why do large groups of people sometimes move from their homeland?*

▼ *These farmers live in one of China's farming regions. They're harvesting grain.*

Looking at the World

Geographers study the world and how people relate to it. They need to find ways of making sense of all the information they gather.

One way to better understand it all is to think about the world in terms of regions. Areas having similar characteristics that differ from surrounding areas are called **regions.** Geographers divide the world into various kinds of regions—language regions, topographic regions, religious regions, and even sports regions. For example, geographers divide China into several climate regions.

As Paul Theroux traveled through China, he crossed several boundaries. He crossed one boundary as he entered China. He crossed others as he passed from one climate region to another. A boundary is a dividing line between regions, countries, or other areas of the world.

Two Kinds of Boundaries

Boundaries may be natural or artificial. Natural boundaries are geographical features of the earth such as mountains or rivers. For example, the Amur River runs along the eastern part of the border between Russia and China. This powerful river serves as an unmistakable boundary between the two countries.

Artificial boundaries are those created by humans. While natural boundaries like a river are easily recognized, artificial boundaries are not always so easy to find in the real world. Some kinds of artificial boundaries, such as the borders between countries, are indicated only by signs. The border between Canada and the United States is marked by signs across major highways that pass between the two countries. In less-traveled areas, however, the U.S.-Canada border is unnoticeable. It even passes through some people's back yards.

The Effect of Boundaries

The main purpose of boundaries is to show the extent of a state, country, or region. If there were no boundary between Canada and the United States, how would each government know who could vote?

Another purpose of boundaries is to prevent passage. Chinese rulers ordered the building of the Great Wall of China between the 400s B.C. and A.D. 1600. They hoped that the 1,500 mile wall and the guards who stood on top of it would keep the Mongols from invading China.

Boundaries serve a purpose but they can also cause problems. People don't always agree on artificial boundaries. In 1846, the United States and Mexico went to war, partly over a dispute about their border.

But even natural boundaries can lead to disagreements. Mexico and the United States finally agreed that the Rio Grande would represent part of the boundary between the two countries. Since that agreement, however, the Rio Grande has constantly shifted its course, forcing the two countries to adjust the border often.

So boundaries can be walls, preventing the movement of people and ideas. Or they can be doorways. Since boundaries mark the places where two countries or regions meet, they provide an opportunity for contact between people and the spread of ideas.

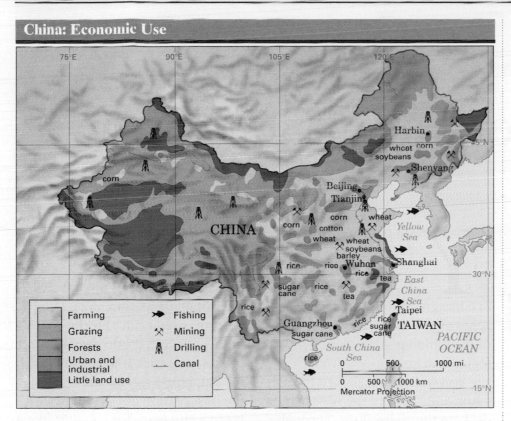

China: Economic Use

75°E 90°E 105°E 120°E

Harbin
wheat corn
soybeans
Shenyang
45°N

CHINA

corn

Beijing
Tianjin
corn wheat
corn
cotton
wheat wheat
soybeans
barley
Yellow
Sea

rice rice Wuhan Shanghai
rice
tea East
China
Sea
30°N

sugar
cane rice tea
Taipei
rice TAIWAN
Guangzhou rice sugar
sugar cane cane PACIFIC
OCEAN

South China
rice Sea
0 500 1000 mi.

0 500 1000 km
Mercator Projection

15°N

Farming   **Fishing**
Grazing   **Mining**
Forests   **Drilling**
Urban and industrial   **Canal**
Little land use

Geographers also divide China into regions according to the ways people use the land to make a living. The map on this page shows China's economic use regions. Where are China's forest regions? Where are China's industrial regions?

Compare the climate map with the economic use map, focusing on the continental climate region in northeastern China. This region has hot summers and cold winters. According to the economic use map, how is the land in this region used? What connection do you notice between the area's climate and economic use of the land?

Now, for contrast, examine the northern and western regions. In these areas climate and terrain make life rugged. What do the people do for a living?

Geographers use regions to help them understand the ways in which people interact with the world. But there is also another way that geographers learn about the world. They create and study maps. ■

◄ *How do the people of Guangzhou use the land?*

■ *Why do people divide the world into regions?*

R E V I E W

1. **FOCUS** How do climate and topography affect human life?

2. **CONNECT** What examples of diffusion can you find in Chapter 1?

3. **ECONOMICS** Examine the world maps in the Time/Space Databank. How do climate and topography affect the use of land in some countries? Consider Greece, Saudi Arabia, and Brazil as examples.

4. **CRITICAL THINKING** Climate and topography clearly affect human life. But how do humans affect the climate and topography of the areas where they live? How do these effects in turn end up affecting human life?

5. **ACTIVITY** Draw a map of your city, town, or neighborhood. Then divide it into regions. Explain what distinguishes each region.

LESSON 2

Understanding a Map

What do you need to know in order to use a map?

Key Terms

- scale
- cartographer
- legend
- inset

▼ *A map at this angle is often called a bird's-eye view.*

You're standing at the foot of one of the world's tallest buildings—the Sears Tower in Chicago, Illinois. Your neck aches as you strain to see the top of the building—110 stories—1,454 feet above you.

You walk inside, board the elevator, and zoom to the observation deck on the 103rd floor. Through floor-to-ceiling windows, you look at the city, which spreads out in all directions below you.

Looking east, you see Lake Michigan dotted with boats. Looking west, you see the University of Illinois and a tangle of streets and freeways. Elsewhere are high-rise buildings, factories, schools, parks, churches, parking lots, and train tracks. Bright blue swimming pools gleam from a few apartment rooftops.

From 103 stories up, the city looks flat—something like a map. Of course, you can't lift the edges of the city, fold it into a small packet, and stick it into your pocket. However, the view from the observation deck is quite similar to a city map, for a map is like a picture of a place taken from above. In fact, mapmakers often use aerial photos—photos taken from the air—to help them make accurate maps.

Look closely at the photograph and the map below. Both show portions of the city of Chicago. What are the differences between the photo and the map?

Sears Tower

34

The Extent of a Map

How does the view from the observation deck differ from a map of the city? One obvious difference is size.

Scale

A map is a flat representation of the earth's surface. But a map is usually much smaller than the area it represents. A map must be drawn to scale in order to accurately represent the area shown. **Scale** is the relationship between distance on a map and actual distance on the earth.

Examine the illustration on this page. Look at the bottom layer. It shows a portion of a city. Find the museum in the city. Now look at the layer above. It shows only the museum and the sidewalks around it. The third layer shows the layout of the museum's rooms. Finally, the top layer shows one room in the museum.

Each drawing is the same size. But each one shows a different area. The bottom layer shows the largest area—a part of the city. The top layer shows the smallest area—a room in the museum.

Each layer is drawn to a different scale. Compare the scale bars beside each layer. The bottom layer is drawn to the smallest scale. A half inch on this layer represents 60 feet in the real world. That half inch covers the distance from the street corner to the sidewalk leading to the museum entrance. The top layer is drawn to the largest scale. According to the scale bar, a half inch on this layer represents five feet in the real world. This half inch takes you only a short distance, from the cat display to the mummy. The top layer is drawn closer to actual size than the bottom layer. In general, a large-scale map shows a small area, and a small-scale map shows a large area.

In A Closer Look on pages 36 and 37, you'll find several maps of the same area, some even drawn at the same scale. But each map looks different because each was created for a different purpose.

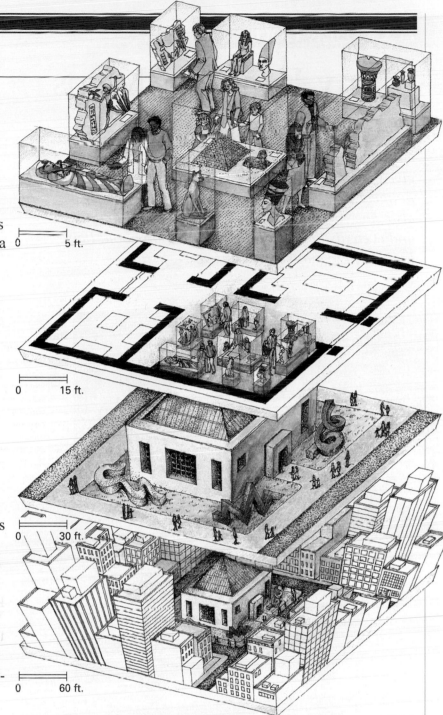

0 5 ft.

0 15 ft.

0 30 ft.

0 60 ft.

▲ *Use the scale in the top layer. How many feet long is the mummy case on the left side of the room?*

People and Places

Many Kinds of Maps

If you have a question about a place, there's probably a map that will answer it. The most common maps give the location of cities, roads, lakes, rivers, and political boundaries. But more specialized maps can also give you information on temperature, rainfall, and even history. If you have a question about Italy, look at these maps for an answer.

Compass

Italy political map

National park (N.P.)

International boundary
Regional boundary
Expressway
Other road
Railroad
National capital
Regional capital
Other city or town

WORLD BOOK map

Holy Roman Empire

Italy c. A.D. 1500 is the subject of the historical map above. The map reveals how the area was split into many small, independent states at that time.

*Maps pp. 36–37 from The World Book Encyclopedia.
© 1998 World Book, Inc. By permission of the publisher.*

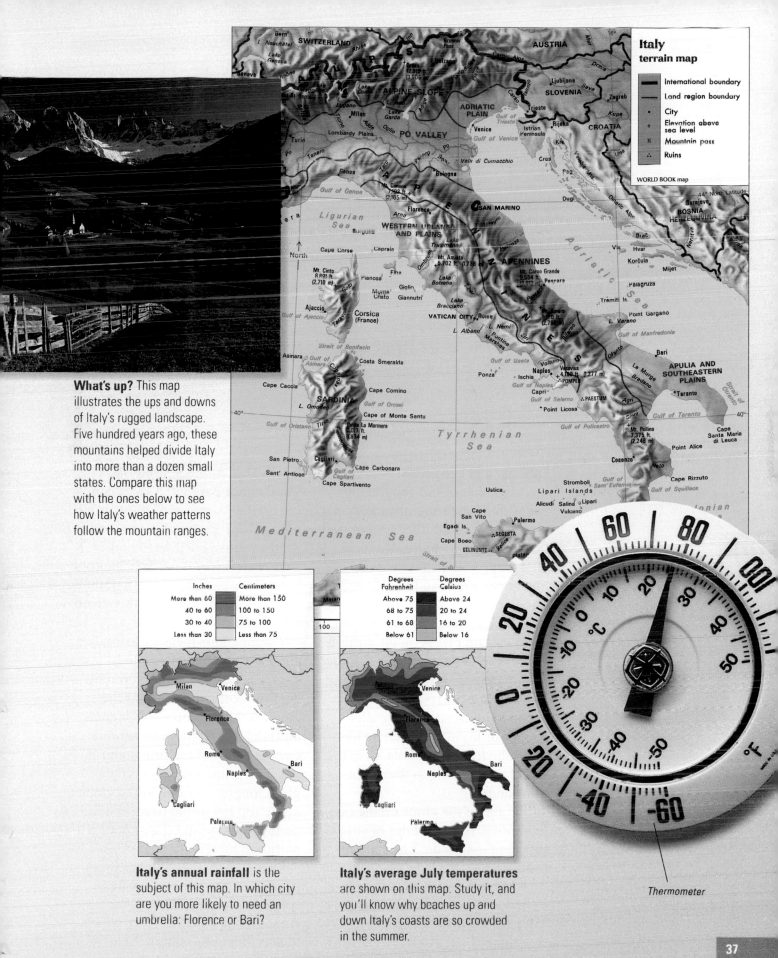

Italy terrain map

▬	International boundary
─	Land region boundary
•	City
+	Elevation above sea level
)(	Mountain pass
∴	Ruins

WORLD BOOK map

What's up? This map illustrates the ups and downs of Italy's rugged landscape. Five hundred years ago, these mountains helped divide Italy into more than a dozen small states. Compare this map with the ones below to see how Italy's weather patterns follow the mountain ranges.

Inches	Centimeters
More than 60	More than 150
40 to 60	100 to 150
30 to 40	75 to 100
Less than 30	Less than 75

Degrees Fahrenheit	Degrees Celsius
Above 75	Above 24
68 to 75	20 to 24
61 to 68	16 to 20
Below 61	Below 16

Italy's annual rainfall is the subject of this map. In which city are you more likely to need an umbrella: Florence or Bari?

Italy's average July temperatures are shown on this map. Study it, and you'll know why beaches up and down Italy's coasts are so crowded in the summer.

Thermometer

37

People and Places

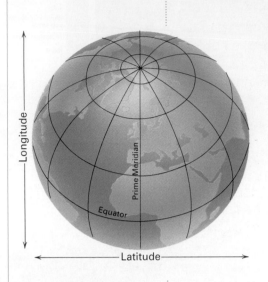

Northern Hemisphere

Southern Hemisphere

Eastern Hemisphere

Western Hemisphere

▲ *Find the equator and the prime meridian on the globe above. Which of the four hemispheres at the right looks most familiar to you? Why?*

Latitude and Longitude

Mapmakers and geographers use scale to measure distances on a map. They use another system—an imaginary grid—to locate places on a map. This grid is made up of intersecting lines of latitude and longitude.

The idea of using a grid to pinpoint certain places on the earth is not new. In 300 B.C., in what is now Turkey, a mapmaker named Hipparchus *(hih PAHR kuhs)* drew a grid of equally spaced, parallel lines over his maps. Then he identified the locations of places in the world by referring to their locations on the grid.

Examine the globe on the far left above. It shows lines of latitude and longitude. Lines of latitude, or parallels, run east and west around the globe. All lines of latitude are parallel to the equator. They never meet.

Lines of longitude, or meridians, run north and south from the North Pole to the South Pole. They're not parallel. As you can see on the globe, lines of longitude are farthest apart at the equator. As they move northward and southward away from the equator, these lines become closer together until finally they meet at the North and South poles.

Mapmakers measure latitude and longitude in units called degrees. Latitude is measured in degrees north and south of the equator. The equator is 0 degrees latitude. Longitude is measured east and west of the prime meridian. The prime meridian is 0 degrees longitude. Look at the globe at the top left of the page. Where do the equator and the prime meridian meet?

The four smaller globes on this page show the earth's four hemispheres. The word *hemisphere* comes from a Greek word, which means "half of a sphere." The equator divides the earth into two equal halves—the northern and southern hemispheres. The prime meridian and the longitude line opposite it at 180 degrees divide the earth into the eastern and western hemispheres.

The small globes show you that North and South America are found in the western hemisphere. Can you name three continents in the eastern hemisphere?

If you wanted to visit Asia, would you start out for the northern or southern hemisphere? In which of the four hemispheres is Africa found? ■

■ *What do you need to know about a place in order to locate it on a map?*

The Content of a Map

In order to read a map, you need to know more than just how to use scale and lines of latitude and longitude. **Cartographers,** or mapmakers, also use symbols to communicate information. To read a map, you need to know how to decode these symbols.

Understanding Symbols

Take a look at the map on this page. This map shows the Iberian Peninsula, which includes modern-day Spain and Portugal. In ancient times, the Romans ruled this area. Now examine the legend in the lower left corner. A **legend** explains the symbols used on a map.

Can you find the tiny symbol of an aqueduct, a structure built to transport water? These symbols show where the ancient Romans built aqueducts centuries ago. The famous aqueduct at Segovia still stands in Spain today. Can you find it near the center of the peninsula? How many other aqueducts can you find on this map?

The Romans also built roads to help them move troops and supplies quickly from town to town. A red line on the map stands for their roads on the peninsula.

The orange area on the map represents a senatorial province. Roman senators were expected to oversee this area. The yellow areas were provinces under the control of the Roman emperor. What are the names of the imperial provinces? In which province is Carthago Nova located?

Using Insets

The map shows you where the Romans built aqueducts and roads and how they organized their rule

The Romans named the temples at Carthago Nova after gods or heroes. Hercules was a hero of superhuman strength, and Mercury was the god of commerce and travel. What does this information tell you about the ancient Romans of Carthago Nova?

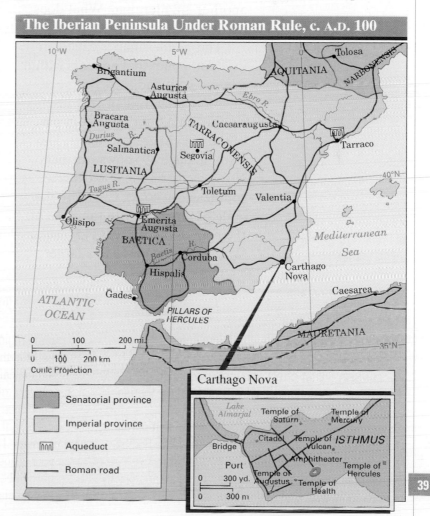

The Iberian Peninsula Under Roman Rule, c. A.D. 100

The Romans used many arches to build this aqueduct at Segovia, Spain. The water flowed through a channel along the top.

over the Iberian Peninsula. But the map offers even more information. In the bottom right corner there is another, smaller map. What does this map tell you?

The smaller map is called an **inset,** or a map that appears within a larger map and shows some of the same area. Usually the inset shows a small but important part of the area in greater detail. The inset on page 39 shows Carthago Nova, a city on the peninsula's southeastern coast. Compare the scale of the inset with the scale of the map of the Iberian Peninsula. Which map is drawn to a larger

■ *What is the purpose of an inset map?*

scale? What distance does one-fourth of an inch represent on the inset? What distance does it equal on the larger map? Using the scale on the inset, how far is it from the bridge to the amphitheater?

Lines of latitude and longitude, legends, symbols, insets, and scale make up the basic language of most maps. Once you understand this language, you're ready to begin putting maps to work.

Maps can be valuable tools whether you're learning about an ancient culture or simply trying to find an unfamiliar street in your own hometown. ■

R E V I E W

1. **FOCUS** What do you need to know in order to use a map?

2. **CONNECT** What effect of human movement discussed in Lesson 1 is illustrated by the map of the Iberian Peninsula?

3. **GEOGRAPHY** Based on what you know about patterns of human settlement, why do you think the Romans settled in Carthago Nova?

4. **CRITICAL THINKING** Imagine two maps that are exactly the same size. One of the maps is a map of world cli-

mate regions. The other map is a map of national parks in the United States. Which map is made at a larger scale?

5. **CRITICAL THINKING** What hemisphere would you expect to be shown at the center of most world maps made in the United States? Why?

6. **ACTIVITY** Draw a map of the neighborhood around your school. Include a legend with the map. Don't forget symbols for stop lights, crosswalks, stores, and any special buildings.

Locating Places

Here's Why

Suppose someone asked you the location of a city. You could go to the map and help the person find the city. Or you could provide the person with the latitude and longitude of the city. How would you figure out the latitude and longitude of Chongqing, China?

Here's How

As you know, latitude and longitude are used to tell the exact location of places on the earth. Look at the map on this page. Notice that the grid on this map has latitude and longitude lines every 10 degrees. Chongqing is just below the 30 degree line of latitude, so it is about 29°N. Now look at the lines of longitude. Chongqing is between 100°E and 110°E. To get a more exact location, imagine a line of longitude at 105°E, halfway between 100°E and 110°E. Chongqing is about halfway between 105°E and 110°E, at about 107°E. The location of Chongqing, China, is 29°N, 107°E. Note that latitude is always given first, then longitude.

Try It

Look at the map again. Identify the cities that are found at these locations:

1. 25°N, 67°E
2. 36°N, 140°E
3. 44°N, 88°E

Give the latitude and longitude for these cities:

4. Colombo, Sri Lanka
5. Manila, Philippines
6. Harbin, China

Apply It

Turn to the Eurasia map on pages 508-509 in the Atlas. Write the latitude and longitude of five cities or islands. Then play the "Where am I?" game with a partner. For example, one person says, "I am visiting a place at 29°N, 50°E. Where am I?" The other person then uses the map to find the answer.

Southern Asia

★ Capital city
• Other city
— National boundary

600   1000 mi.
0   500 1000 km
Two-Point Equidistant Projection

41

L E S S O N   3

Putting Maps to Work

What decisions must cartographers make?

Key Terms

- thematic map
- projection

A cholera epidemic! In the 1820s, these words were enough to strike fear into the bravest heart. Cholera *(KAHL ur uh)* was usually fatal, killing its victims in less than seven days.

The epidemic spread quickly from India to Russia and then through central Europe, reaching Scotland by 1832. In 1849, severe outbreaks hit Paris and London. Today, doctors know how to treat and prevent cholera. But in the early 1800s, no one knew much about the disease.

John Snow, a doctor in the London neighborhood of Soho, grew discouraged. By 1854, cholera had claimed the lives of 500 people in Soho, and there was no sign that

things would improve. Dr. Snow tried everything he knew, but none of his cholera patients recovered.

But Dr. Snow had an idea. He'd had some training in geography, and he decided to use his training to track down the source of the disease. One night he listed the addresses of all the cholera victims in Soho. Then he took a street map and marked each victim's address with a dot.

Before you read on and learn what happened, look at Dr. Snow's map on this page. Do you see any pattern in the dots? Dr. Snow did. The map revealed that almost all of the cholera victims lived near a public well, known as the Broad Street Pump. The map supported what Dr. Snow suspected—the epidemic was somehow related to the city's water supply.

Dr. Snow contacted city officials. Workers quickly removed the handle from the Broad Street Pump, forcing people to go elsewhere for water. Almost immediately, the number of new cholera cases dropped to zero.

Today, few people contract cholera where there are working sewage systems. Even fewer die from it where there is medical care. In the 1850s, Dr. Snow's map provided a needed clue to the source of this disease—bad water.

➤ *How many cholera deaths were recorded near the Oxford Street water pumps? The Piccadilly pump?*

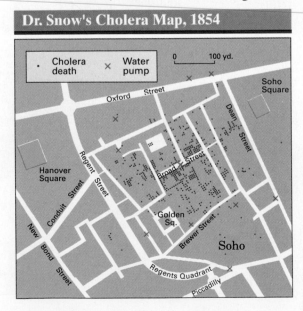

Dr. Snow's Cholera Map, 1854

- Cholera death   × Water pump

0   100 yd.

Oxford Street
Soho Square
Dean Street
Hanover Square
Regent Street
Conduit Street
Broad Street
New Bond Street
Golden Sq.
Brewer Street
Soho
Regents Quadrant
Piccadilly

Maps for Different Purposes

Dr. Snow's purpose was to find a link between the addresses of cholera victims and the location of Soho water supplies. For his base map, he chose a general map of Soho, showing people's houses. By marking victims' addresses and the water pumps, he created a thematic map. A **thematic map** shows information on a special theme or subject.

Like Snow, all mapmakers choose base maps and thematic information to fit their needs. Both maps on this page are thematic, but each has a different purpose.

The map at the right shows the London subway system. What's the purpose of this map? Who would use it? Shoppers, tourists, and workers might use it to find their way around the city. In this map, cartographers limited their thematic information to subway stops and routes.

The second map shows statistical information. It uses numbers and translates them into colors on the map. The map below shows the percentage of women working for pay in each country. How do the colors show different percentages? Compare the map below with the map of China on page 27. The map of China gives you statistical information, too. How does its use of numbers differ from the

The London subway is known as the Under-ground or the Tube. How would you use a map like this?

What percent of women work for pay in India and Mexico?

Women in the Work Force

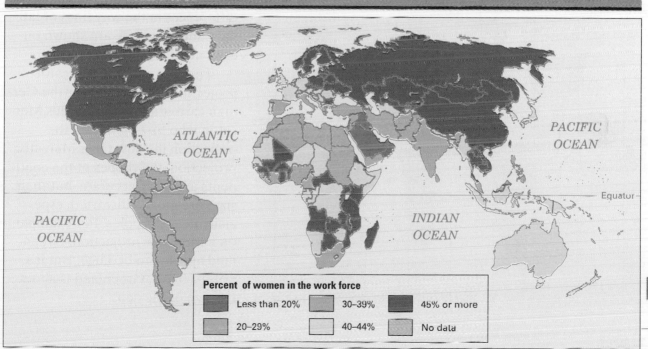

Percent of women in the work force

Less than 20%	30–39%	45% or more
20–29%	40–44%	No data

ATLANTIC OCEAN

PACIFIC OCEAN

PACIFIC OCEAN

INDIAN OCEAN

Equator

■ *On what do cartographers base their decisions when choosing types of maps?*

▼ *Compare the size of Greenland, which is highlighted in red, on the four projections.*

map of women in the work force? Does it use percentages? As you can see from comparing both maps, there are different ways to measure numbers of people.

Who might want to use a map of women in the work force? Organizations who are helping women start businesses could find it helpful. ■

The Shape of the Earth

Whether a map shows working women or subway routes, it's a means of giving information about the earth. But as cartographers try to make accurate maps, they face one serious problem: the shape of the earth. The earth is a sphere, and a map is flat. It's impossible for cartographers to accurately show the earth's curved surface on the flat surface of a map.

Imagine trying to flatten a basketball. No matter how you do it, some parts will tear, and other parts will stretch. Mapmakers face the same kind of problem when they try to map the earth.

Over time, however, cartographers have developed different map **projections,** or ways of transferring the curved surface of the earth onto a flat map. All projections are compromises, though, because they all distort distance, direction, size, or shape.

Each world map on this page and the facing page is based on a different projection. Notice how the shapes and sizes of continents vary from map to map. Also notice differences in the way lines of latitude and longitude are shown on each map.

The first map is a Mercator projection. It is named for the German cartographer Gerhardus Mercator, who first published the projection in 1569. On a Mercator projection, the shapes of the continents are fairly accurate, but their sizes are greatly distorted, especially near the poles. For example, on a Mercator projection, Greenland appears to be huge. But it's not. Actually, Greenland is about the size of Mexico.

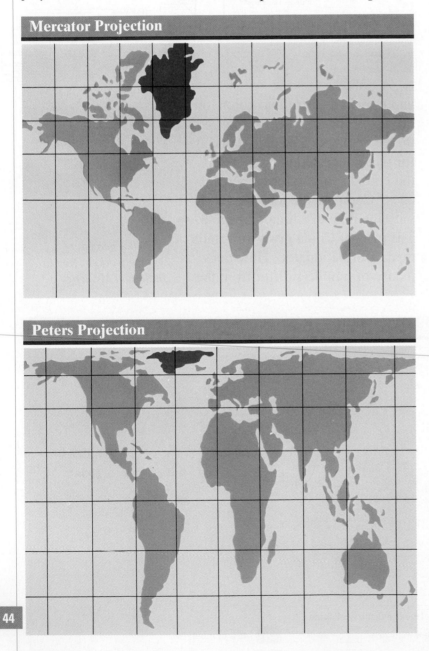

Mercator Projection

Peters Projection

The second map on page 44 is the Peters projection, created by the West German cartographer Arno Peters. On this projection, the sizes of the continents are accurate as compared with each other, but the shapes of the continents are distorted. For example, compare the size and shape of Africa on the Peters projection with its size and shape on the Mercator projection.

The third map, at the right, is Goode's interrupted homolosine *(hoh MAHL uh syn)* projection. In 1923, Paul Goode, a cartographer at the University of Chicago, combined parts of two other projections to create this one. Goode's map shows little distortion of size or shape. In order to achieve this type of accuracy, though, areas of the world are split into sections, making it more difficult to figure out distances.

The fourth map is the Robinson projection. It was created by the American cartographer Arthur Robinson. On this projection the sizes and shapes of continents and the distances between places are fairly accurate. The Robinson projection is a good compromise. This type of projection is used as a base

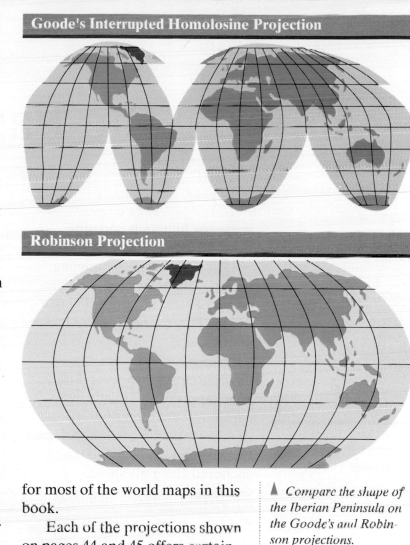

Goode's Interrupted Homolosine Projection

Robinson Projection

for most of the world maps in this book.

Each of the projections shown on pages 44 and 45 offers certain advantages and disadvantages. Which projection would be your choice if you wanted to show accurate distances? Accurate sizes? Accurate shapes? ■

▲ *Compare the shape of the Iberian Peninsula on the Goode's and Robinson projections.*

■ *What are some of the problems with map projections?*

R E V I E W

1. **FOCUS** What decisions must cartographers make?
2. **CONNECT** Suppose Dr. Snow had chosen a map of the entire city of London for his base map. What problems might this decision have created?
3. **GEOGRAPHY** Examine the map showing the diffusion of the yo-yo on page 30. This map is a polar projection of the world. It is centered on the North Pole. What are its advantages and disadvantages?
4. **CRITICAL THINKING** Dr. Snow used his map to save possibly hundreds of lives. Think of another instance when a map might be life-saving.
5. **CRITICAL THINKING** Because it's a sphere, the earth has no top or bottom. Yet, most maps show north at the top. Turn a flat world map upside down. How might this new view change the way you think about other parts of the world?
6. **ACTIVITY** Create a chart of the four projections presented in this lesson. In column one, list the projections. In the next two columns, list the advantages and disadvantages of each type of projection. In the last column, give an example of how each projection might be used.

45

L E S S O N   4

Mapping the Past

Key Term

• monsoon

Thousands of people crowded the port of Carthage, a booming Phoenician city on the northern coast of Africa. On that day in 480 B.C., the port was busier than usual.

Hungry babies screamed in their parents' arms, several traders argued noisily, and family members embraced tearfully. Others simply watched while sailors tested the oars and sails of the 60 ships anchored along the shore.

Silently, Commander Hanno studied the scene. He and hundreds of Carthaginians would soon set out on an official mission to settle on the west coast of Africa. The new settlements would help protect Phoenician ships that traveled to islands off Africa's west coast—today's Canary and Madeira islands. These islands were the source of a valuable purple dye that was important to Phoenician trade. Hanno was eager to set sail for those far-off lands.

➤ *Estimate how far Hanno sailed from Carthage to Gytta. Now, figure the distance by using the scale.*

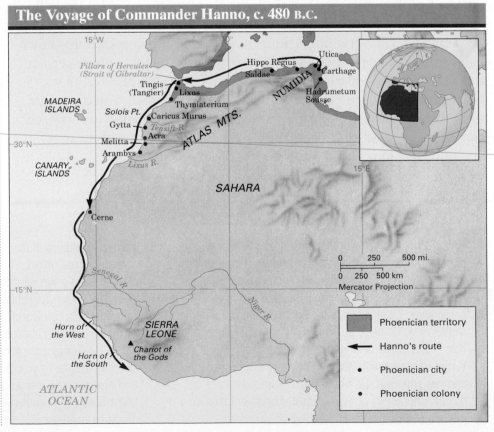

The Voyage of Commander Hanno, c. 480 B.C.

Over time, Hanno's fleet settled several Phoenician colonies on Africa's west coast. With that mission completed, he and his crew sailed on. Hanno and his crew explored the coast as far south as present-day Sierra Leone and possibly even farther. Look at the map on page 46. Trace the route of Hanno and his crew.

Exploring the World

Centuries ago, missions like Commander Hanno's provided most of the information about the world. As people began to travel farther and farther from their homelands, their geographic knowledge grew. Why did people begin to reach out beyond their borders? One reason was the desire to trade.

The Drive to Trade

Before Hanno's time, Phoenicia was just a narrow strip of land between the Mediterranean Sea and the Lebanon Mountains. It was slightly more than 100 miles long and only 16 miles wide in places.

The Phoenicians weren't able to grow enough food to feed their population. But they discovered other ways to meet their needs. They were expert traders who made use of the resources in their environment. Tall trees blanketed the surrounding mountains. They cut these down for lumber. From the sea, they gathered a special type of shellfish. They crushed the shells to make a purple dye. They used the dye to color their finely woven cloth, which was highly prized in the ancient world.

The Phoenicians traded their lumber and purple-dyed cloth for food and other necessities. As their trade increased, the Phoenicians expanded their territory by building ports in southern Spain and northern Africa. One of these ports was Carthage, founded about 750 B.C.

Trade with India

In those days, trading and exploring went hand-in-hand. Traders were always looking for new markets and faster routes. In their search they brought back knowledge of distant lands and people.

About 2,000 years ago, Mediterranean traders dreamed of far-off India and its treasures. India offered rare spices, gems, perfumes, sugar, woods, gold, brass, and iron to any traders brave enough to risk the difficult trip.

The journey from the shores of the Mediterranean to Indian markets was a rough one. On land, traders faced muddy roads, burning deserts, mountain ranges, and bandits. Sea travel was also risky. After crossing the Red Sea or the Persian Gulf, sailors faced the dangers of the Arabian Sea. Powerful seasonal winds called monsoons swept across these waters. The **monsoon** is a wind system that has an effect on the climate in southern Asia. These powerful winds blow from the southwest from April to October, bringing heavy rains much of

▲ *This is one type of shellfish the Phoenicians crushed to make their purple dye. The Greeks named the Phoenicians after the purple-dyed goods they traded. The Greek word* phoinix *means "red-purple."*

➤ *Using the scale, find the round-trip mileage from Rome to Patala, India. Take the route that goes to Alexandria, through the Red Sea, then follows the coast.*

How Do We Know?

HISTORY *We know about ancient trade partly from written records. The oldest remaining record of a voyage refers to an Egyptian trading mission. According to the record, around 3200 B.C., Egyptian traders sailed "forty ships of one hundred cubits with cedar wood from Byblos (BIHB luhs)," one of Phoenicia's cities.*

■ *What areas of the world did Mediterranean peoples learn about?*

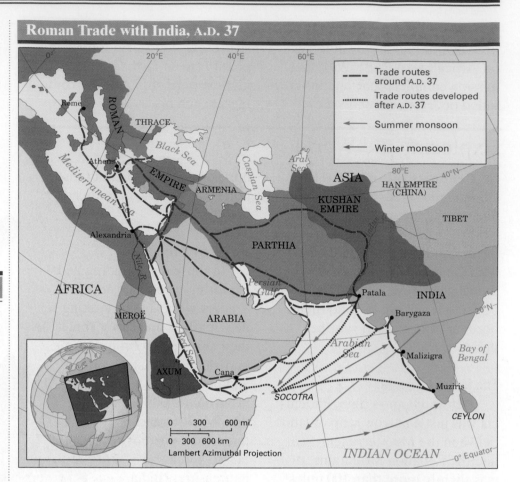

Roman Trade with India, A.D. 37

the time. From November to March, the winds are dry and blow from the northeast.

Ancient ships hugged the coast so they could seek shelter from the fierce winds. Those who braved the open seas for a direct route to India were often shipwrecked.

Around A.D. 37, a Greek named Hippalus used his knowledge of geography and monsoons to sail from the Red Sea directly across the Arabian Sea to India. He used the monsoons to work in his favor. On the way to India, his ship was pushed by the monsoon blowing from the southwest. On the return voyage, it was helped by the monsoon blowing from the northeast. Use the scale on the map above to compare Hippalus's trade route with the older sea routes. How much shorter was Hippalus's route? ■

Learning About the World

Early explorers and traders knew the importance of keeping careful records of their journeys so that more accurate maps might be made. In some cases, they took along historians and geographers to help them keep track of their travels.

Some early maps were based on records made during the conquests of Alexander the Great, one of history's most famous military leaders. Alexander ruled Macedonia, a kingdom that lay to the north of Greece. He had maps made as his huge army battled to victory from Egypt to India between 334 and 326 B.C. On his marches, Alexander took geographers, a historian, and astronomers—scientists who study stars and planets. He also took *bematistae* (*buh MAH tees ty*) or "steppers," who measured distance by the steps they took. This army of soldiers and scholars covered 20,000 miles, fighting and conquering, but also recording and mapping.

Written Records

As people traveled and learned about the world, they recorded their knowledge in writing, as well as on maps. For example, Chinese scholars spent about 800 years, between 1122 and 256 B.C., putting together a guide to China's geography called *Shanhai jing*.

Ancient historians also noted geographic information when recording events. Herodotus, for example, was a Greek historian and geographer. In the 400s B.C., he included geographic descriptions in his history of the world. Gaius Fannius Strabo was a Roman historian. In A.D. 18, he wrote a 17-volume work called *Geography,* in which he described every place known to the Greeks and Romans. Claudius Ptolemy, a Greek geographer and astronomer, published his *Guide to Geography* in A.D. 100. In his work he included the latitudes and longitudes of 8,000 places, 26 maps of parts of the world, and one map of the entire known world.

Ancient Maps

People have been making maps for thousands of years. One of the oldest existing maps is a clay map found in northern Iraq. It dates to around 2300 B.C. and shows rivers, hills, and settlements with measurements of farm plots.

Ancient mapmakers were able to make fairly accurate maps of areas they knew well. When dealing with unknown lands, however, they often left unexplored areas blank or filled them in with their imaginations. An ancient "world map" made of clay was also found in Iraq, in an area that was once known as Mesopotamia. In this map, shown below, the world was pictured through the eyes of the Assyrians, who ruled Mesopotamia between about 722 and 626 B.C. They saw the world as round and flat. Can you find the Euphrates River that flowed through the middle of their world?

Advances in Cartography

Information from explorers and traders helped early cartographers improve their maps. Technological developments also led to more accurate mapmaking.

About 2,000 years ago, the Chinese discovered a way to find direction with a piece of magnetized iron ore called a lodestone. They placed the lodestone on wood or reeds, then floated it in water. The lodestone always swung around to point toward the north. The Chinese had created a simple compass.

▼ *Can you locate the sea that encircles the earth in this ancient map of the "world"?*

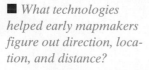

> *The earliest astrolabes probably date back to the 200s B.C. in Greece. Sailors used astrolabes like the one shown here to help them navigate.*

■ *What technologies helped early mapmakers figure out direction, location, and distance?*

Ancient people also learned how to use the planets and stars to help them determine location and distance on the earth. Two early scientific instruments that helped them were the astrolabe *(AS truh layb)* and the gnomon *(NOH mahn)*.

An astrolabe is a disk with marks around its edge like a ruler. Scholars and sailors used the astrolabe to sight the positions of the sun and stars and to figure out their height in the sky. This information aided them in determining latitude.

A gnomon is the blade that stands upright in the center of a sundial. When the sun shines, the gnomon casts a shadow, pointing to the hour. Early scholars learned they could use gnomons to find the height of the sun at different times during the day. They then used this information to help them figure out the distance between two points. Around 240 B.C., the Greek mathematician Eratosthenes *(ehr uh TAHS thuh neez)* used a gnomon to help him figure out the earth's circumference.

Through the centuries, technological advances have continued to help cartographers improve their maps. In the A.D. 1400s, for example, improvements in navigational equipment allowed European sailors to explore much of the world. Their explorations provided valuable information for mapmakers.

Today's cartographers rely on space-age technology. Like the ancient sailing ships, satellites now circle the earth, sending back information and adding to our knowledge of the world. Aerial photography, using infrared film, allows mapmakers to record information not visible to the eye. Computers and radar also make the mapmaker's job easier. ■

R E V I E W

1. **FOCUS** How did people begin to learn about the world?

2. **CONNECT** In Chapter 1 you learned how the present is built on the past. Give three examples of ways in which present geographical knowledge is built on past developments.

3. **ECONOMICS** Why were the Phoenicians willing to make the effort to settle the west coast of Africa?

4. **CRITICAL THINKING** What might historians learn about the Assyrians from their map of the ancient world on page 49?

5. **CRITICAL THINKING** What advantages do aerial and satellite cameras offer mapmakers?

6. **WRITING ACTIVITY** Imagine that you traveled with Commander Hanno from Carthage to Africa or with Hippalus from the Mediterranean shores to India. Write a page about one of your experiences in diary form.

Locating Cities on a Map

Here's Why

You know that maps can help you understand history. Suppose you wanted to find the location of Carales, a Phoenician port city. You could look in a historical atlas.

Here's How

An atlas is a book of maps and geographical facts. Historical atlases contain maps that show geographical information about the past. For example, a historical world atlas might have maps showing China in A.D. 200, trade routes of the Roman Empire, or the kingdoms of ancient Egypt. Usually an atlas has an index in the back of the book that lists place names and the pages on which you can find them.

Look at the sample index page below. Find "Carales." Notice the letter-number combination "B1" following the entry "Carales." Next to B1 is the listing for a page number. If this was a real atlas, you would turn to page 51. Instead, just look at the map below. The grid location B1 can help you find Carales on the map.

First find the letter "B" along the right side of the map. Next find the number "1" at the top. With your finger, trace a line across from the B, meeting another line coming from the 1. Carales is located in the square formed by the grid lines.

Grid lines sometimes appear only along the sides of the map with the reference letters and numbers. In such cases it is up to you to follow the imaginary lines across the map as if they were actually present.

Try It

Look again at the sample index below. Find Cyrene. What are the grid references for Cyrene? Find Cyrene on the map. Where is Cyrene located in relationship to the grid lines? What are the grid references for Crete? Find Crete on the map.

Apply It

Find the location of the earliest cities in your state. What cities already existed at the time your state joined the union? Give the grid location for these cities.

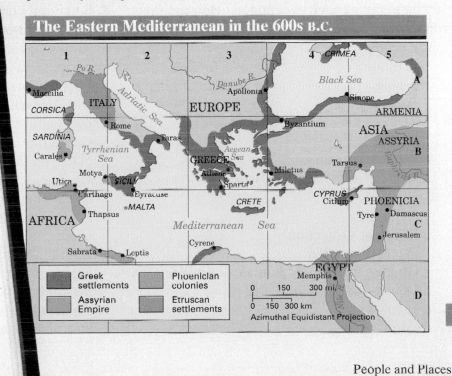

The Eastern Mediterranean in the 600s B.C.

Chapter Review

Reviewing Key Terms

cartographer (p. 39) projection (p. 44)
climate (p. 28) region (p. 31)
diffusion (p. 30) scale (p. 35)
inset (p. 40) thematic map (p. 43)
legend (p. 39) topography (p. 27)
monsoon (p. 47)

A. Which key term can be defined by using one of these word groups? Include the words in a sentence that defines the term.
1. smaller, details
2. powerful, seasonal
3. adopt, culture
4. purpose, represent
5. shape, round, flat
6. mountains, valleys, rivers, lakes

B. Some of the following statements are true and some are false. Write *True* or *False* for each statement. Then rewrite the false statements to make them true.
1. Diffusion occurs when people change their land to make farming easier.
2. The climate region of northeastern China is heavily populated.
3. All maps have the same scale so people can see the distance between two cities.
4. Ancient cartographers had difficulty making maps of areas that were far away from their homelands.
5. The legend on a map explains how the world is divided into hemispheres.

Exploring Concepts

A. Each of the six groups of words below have something in common. They are also different in important ways. For each group, answer the following questions on your own paper. What do these things have in common? How are they different?
1. farming
   herding
   fishing
2. cyclic
   periodic
   migratory
3. natural boundary
   artificial boundary
4. latitude
   longitude
5. Mercator projection
   Peters projection
   Goode's interrupted homolosine projection
   Robinson projection
6. gnomon
   astrolabe

B. Support each statement with facts and details from the chapter.
1. Geographers divide the world into various kinds of regions.
2. Sometimes large groups of people move from their homeland to another place.
3. Most of China's people live in the eastern part.
4. People sometimes change an invention from one culture to fit the needs of their own culture.
5. Cartographers still use map grids to locate places on the world.
6. Dr. Snow's map showed the reason for the cholera epidemic.
7. Mediterranean traders traveling to India needed to know topography and climate.
8. Both the Mercator projection and the Peters projection distort the appearance of the continents.
9. Ancient historians included geographic information in their records.

52

Reviewing Skills

1. Look at the latitude and longitude lines on the map of the Iberian peninsula on this page. What is located at 36° N, 5° W?
2. Using the map, give the latitude and longitude of these cities:
   a. Toledo, Spain
   b. Cartagena, Spain
   c. Segovia, Spain
   d. Tarragona, Spain
3. Use the map on page 51. Find Damascus, Leptis, and Athens. Give the grid references for each as they would appear in their atlas index entries.
4. Study the world nutrition map on page 43. What general information about hunger can you learn from the map?
5. What terms does a navigator use to give the exact location of the ship?

Iberian Peninsula

Using Critical Thinking

1. How do topography and climate influence the kinds of sports played in a particular region? Give examples to explain your answer.
2. Imagine you could choose another country to live in for one year. Before you make your final choice, what things would you be interested in finding out? What kinds of maps would you need to consult?
3. Some animals, such as the yak in Tibet, help people to survive in the environment. Would people in the desert and arctic climates have difficulty surviving without the help of animals? Name specific animals and tell how they are useful. Which animals make life in your climate region easier? How would your life be different without those animals?

Preparing for Citizenship

1. **WRITING ACTIVITY** Cut out a weather map from a recent newspaper. Study the content of the map, including the symbols. Write a brief weather report based on information on the map. Compare your report with others in the class.
2. **GROUP ACTIVITY** Meet with a small group of classmates to discuss what you have learned about cyclic movement. Make a chart listing the cyclic activities of five people. Use examples based on people in your neighborhood. For instance, your postal carrier travels the same route every working day.
3. **COLLABORATIVE LEARNING** Working in groups of four, create a map of your school. Each person in the group should be in charge of one of the following four tasks:
   a. drawing a general map of the school building and school grounds
   b. making a legend for the map
   c. figuring out the scale of the map
   d. creating an inset of a particular school area (gym, lunchroom, library)
   Exchange maps with another group. Measure the distance between where you are now and the area shown in the inset.

Chapter 3

Learning About the Past

A fleck of gold flashes in the dust. Could it be the clue that leads researchers to the tomb of an ancient king? A farmer stumbles upon a broken piece of pottery. Could this be evidence of a city that disappeared thousands of years ago? Children exploring a cave find strange writing on the walls. Could these words unlock the secrets of a lost civilization? Learning about the past is a search for clues to hidden worlds.

In 1822, a French scholar figured out how to read the strange writing of the ancient Egyptians. Historians could then finally understand Egyptian records, like this list of Egyptian kings from about 1270 B.C.

Fascinated by tales of the ancient Greeks, German businessman Heinrich Schliemann dug beneath the ruins of Mycenae, an ancient Greek city. In 1876, he unearthed treasures like this gold lion's head from about 1570 B.C.

6500 B.C.

Chinese peasants digging a well in 1974 accidentally discovered an underground army. These life-size pottery warriors once guarded the tomb of Chinese Emperor Qin Shihuangdi, who died in 210 B.C.

Modern archaeologists continue to examine ancient objects in order to piece together the story of the past.

Today

LESSON 1

Understanding History

> My mother now began to beg, urge, and command me to escape as best I could. . . . I replied that I would not be saved without her. Taking her by the hand, I hurried her along. . . . And now came the ashes, but at first sparsely. I turned around. Behind us, an ominous thick smoke, spreading over the earth like a flood, followed us. . . . To be heard were only the shrill cries of women, the wailing of children, the shouting of men. Some were calling to their parents, others to their children, others to their wives—knowing one another only by voice.
>
> Pliny the Younger, from letters written to the historian Tacitus

THINKING FOCUS

How do historians learn about the past?

Key Terms

- prehistory
- fossil
- artifact
- oral tradition
- primary source
- secondary source

➤ *During the eruption, many people were buried in volcanic ash. The bodies later decayed, but the impressions left were preserved in the hardened ash. Archaeologists then filled the impressions with plaster to make casts of the victims, like the one shown here.*

Pliny the Younger wrote this about the eruption of the volcano Mount Vesuvius in A.D. 79, when he was just 18 years old. His letters give valuable information about the disaster that destroyed the Roman cities of Pompeii and Herculaneum. However, written records like these aren't the only sources of information about the eruption. Volcanic lava and ash sealed Pompeii and Herculaneum exactly as they were almost 2,000 years ago, so the cities are like time capsules. Archaeologists (ahr kee AHL uh jihsts) have uncovered many clues that tell how the people of Pompeii and Herculaneum lived.

For example, one wall painting in Pompeii shows the games that were being held in the local sports arena. Campaign slogans on other walls within the city show that, at the time of the volcano's eruption, Pompeii was getting ready for elections. Other evidence shows that, like us, the Romans kept watchdogs. Colored tiles on a floor uncovered at Pompeii spell out the message *cave canem*. This means, "Beware of the dog."

Archaeologists even have an idea of what ancient Romans ate. Sealed in the ash were loaves of bread, eggs, nuts, and lentils.

Historical Evidence

Pliny's letter and the wall paintings at Pompeii are examples of the two kinds of sources historians use to study the past: written sources and nonwritten sources. To learn about the past, historians must seek out as many different sources as they possibly can, both written and nonwritten, and then try to find out what they mean.

Kinds of Sources

To most people, written sources mean books. But to historians, written sources might also be letters, diaries, speeches, popular songs, poems, business records, or campaign slogans. They could be the marks on ancient tombs or old calendars and maps—anything with writing on it.

Anything written down can give historians clues about the people and events of the past. However, written sources only go back to about 3000 B.C. That's

when writing developed in Mesopotamia, an ancient country in what is now the Middle East. History before the development of writing is called **prehistory.** To learn about prehistoric times, historians must rely completely on nonwritten sources.

Nonwritten sources include **fossils**—the remains or imprints of once-living plants or animals. Dinosaur fossils, for example, can tell about the kinds of dinosaurs that lived in a certain time and place.

Other nonwritten sources are **artifacts,** or objects made by humans. Ancient jewelry, tools, coins, and toys teach about the customs and beliefs of people of the past.

Still other nonwritten sources are tombs, monuments, and even entire cities. The streets and buildings of Pompeii, preserved beneath the ashes, give a picture of life as it was in A.D. 79.

Another important nonwritten source is a culture's **oral tradition,**

◄ *This ancient carving of Egyptian scribes is a nonwritten source. The carving shows that the Egyptians wrote with penlike instruments.*

▲ *The pages above from a French songbook of 1470 are a valuable written source. They show how music was written down at the time.*

◄ *Will today's compact discs like the one at left be a nonwritten source for historians of the future?*

57

Learning About the Past

the legends, myths, and beliefs passed on by word of mouth from generation to generation. Over time, many myths and legends have been written down. For example, the legend of King Odysseus was part of the ancient Greek oral tradition. It was finally written down by the Greek poet Homer between 800 and 700 B.C., and it is Homer's version that is known today.

The Historian's Job

Historians do not just collect facts. They also must examine the information they collect and then decide how to interpret it. Doing this carefully often can take a long time. For example, in the 400s B.C., a Greek historian named Thucydides *(thoo SID ih deez)* spent 27 years studying the war between the Greek city-states of Athens and Sparta. Here is how Thucydides

UNDERSTANDING ORAL TRADITION

Legends describe ancient events, such as how people first learned to make iron tools and spears. According to the oral tradition of the Yoruba people in Nigeria, they learned to make iron from Ogun, one of their orishas, or gods. The legends, stories, ideas, customs, and beliefs that a culture passes on by word of mouth make up its oral tradition.

Word of Mouth

An oral tradition may change from generation to generation as the interests, opinions, fears, and needs of each generation change.

How useful is oral tradition to historians if accounts told by word of mouth change and become inaccurate? Historians can't be sure that an oral tradition portrays events from long ago accurately. However, oral traditions do tell about the kinds of things that were important to people of the times.

A Source of Information

Ancient cultures that existed before the development of writing depended on oral tradition to communicate their ideas and record events. Through oral traditions the elders taught the younger members of the society about their culture. This is why historians are interested in oral traditions.

India and China are two places where ancient oral traditions are still remembered and passed on. But in many places oral traditions have been forgotten. Historians can only learn about the oral traditions of most ancient cultures if someone has recorded them in writing.

The oral tradition still exists in modern societies, side by side with written records. In most African societies, especially West African, the storyteller is an important member of society who records family histories and recites them on special occasions.

Historians must be careful when interpreting oral tradition. Nevertheless, oral tradition can be a useful source for information about people of the past.

described the difficult job of the historian:

> H e must not be misled by the exaggerated fancies of the poets, or by the tales of chroniclers who seek to please the ear rather than speak the truth. . . . At such a distance of time he must make up his mind to be satisfied with conclusions resting upon the clearest evidence which can be had. . . . Of the events of the war I have not ventured to speak from any chance information, nor according to any notion of my own; I have described nothing but what I either saw myself, or learned from others of whom I made the most careful and particular enquiry. The task was a laborious one, because eye-witnesses of the same occurrences gave different accounts of them, as they remembered or were interested in the actions of one side or the other.
>
> Thucydides, 400s B.C.

The Interpretation of Sources

As Thucydides says, sources are open to interpretation. Has one of your teachers ever asked you to tell your side of the story after a disagreement with another student? Did your version differ from your friend's?

Now consider two written records of a war—one from the winner's point of view; one from the loser's. How might the two be different?

Historians must keep in mind that everyone has his or her own point of view. Whether or not the author of a source is a man or a woman, rich or poor, or young or old will affect the way he or she sees and describes an event.

Nonwritten sources are, of course, also open to interpretation. Suppose, for example, that archaeologists uncover the remains of an ancient walled structure. Some historians might think it is a fort. Others, however, might argue it is a cattle corral. ∎

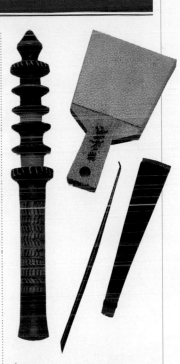

▲ Can you identify the modern-day artifacts shown above? Imagine the difficulty interpreting ancient artifacts.

■ What kinds of sources do historians use to learn about the past?

The Evaluation of Sources

Historians ask questions about a source to determine how accurate and useful it is. A historian studying Pliny's account of the eruption would start by asking these questions:

Who was the writer? Pliny was a well-educated young man from a wealthy family. He had studied science under his uncle. As a result, his description of the process of the eruption is very valuable to historians. They want to know how the writer's background might affect his or her account.

What kind of source is it? Pliny's account was one of many letters he wrote about life in the Roman Empire. His letters have given historians valuable information about the life and politics of the Roman Empire.

Different kinds of sources offer different kinds of information. Letters or diaries, for example, may tell a great deal about people's daily lives. Political speeches, on the other hand, might help explain a government's policies.

When was the source produced? Pliny wrote his description of the eruption shortly after it happened. Sources produced during the same time period as the events

Across Time & Space

In the early 1800s, the British artist Sir William Gell visited and sketched the houses of Pompeii as they might have looked before the eruption of Vesuvius. His drawings helped make Pompeii popular. In fact, people began building new houses in the Pompeiian style.

Compare the photo above with the painting on the next page. Both depict eruptions of Mt. Vesuvius. What can you learn from each?

■ Why do historians ask questions about their sources?

are secondary sources. They are likely to be more accurate because they were recorded when the event was fresh in people's minds.

Where was the source produced? Pliny's account was an eyewitness account. Therefore, it is more valuable to historians than one written by someone who merely heard about the disaster. Even if a source was produced during the time period of the event, historians want to know if the author was actually at the event.

Why was the source produced? Pliny wrote about the eruption in letters to the Roman historian Tacitus. Most of Pliny's letters were a mix of historical information and literature. Writing such letters was a fashionable thing for wealthy young Roman men to do.

Writers have many different reasons for writing. One writer may just want to describe an event. Another might want to prove a point, impress someone, or make someone else look bad. Understanding why a source was produced helps historians judge the accuracy of the information that is presented. ■

they describe are called **primary sources.** Materials that were created later by people who studied the original sources are called **secondary sources.** The photo at the top of this page shows the eruption of Mt. Vesuvius in 1944. Because the photo records an event at the time of the event, it is a primary source. The painting of Mt. Vesuvius on the next page shows the eruption of A.D. 79. However, the painting wasn't made until 1785, so it's a secondary source.

Primary sources are generally more valuable to historians than

The Puzzle of History

History has been called a conversation between the present and the past. People of the past communicate with people of today through the writing, artifacts, and structures they leave behind.

Each generation has historians who gather and evaluate sources of information about the past. However, the way these historians interpret the sources they find varies from generation to generation.

After all, every generation sees the world differently. And because each generation and each individual looks at things from a new point of view, history is always open to different interpretations.

History also has been compared to a jigsaw puzzle. Some pieces of the puzzle have been lost forever. Pieces once considered lost have now been found. The available pieces can be fitted together in many ways. Each generation of historians tries to put together the available pieces of the puzzle and to interpret the picture that emerges. In doing so, they hope to understand not only what happened in the past, but how it happened, and why it happened. ■

▲ *In 1785, artist Angelica Kauffmann painted the A.D. 79 eruption of Mt. Vesuvius. Pliny the Younger studies with his mother at Misenum as they learn of the eruption.*

■ *Why do historians study the past?*

1. **FOCUS** What methods and sources do historians use to learn about the past?
2. **CONNECT** Is the map on page 39 a primary source or a secondary source? Why?
3. **HISTORY** Why do historians ask questions about their sources?
4. **CRITICAL THINKING** In ancient Rome fewer women than men left behind written sources. How might this have affected historians' knowledge of the history of Rome?
5. **WRITING ACTIVITY** Look around your home. What written and nonwritten sources do you see? Make a list of the sources. Then, using one or two of the sources on your list, try to write a history of your family. Follow Thucydides' advice as you write and evaluate your sources carefully.

Evaluating Information

Here's Why

People learn about the past in many ways. Written records, fossils, artifacts, and oral traditions are all keys to understanding the past. By gathering and evaluating these sources, historians form their ideas about past events.

As you study the past, you also need to evaluate historical evidence. To do this, you must be able to tell the difference between facts, reasoned judgments, and opinions.

Look at the picture below of the gigantic stone statues found on Easter Island. This island is located in the eastern Pacific Ocean, 2,300 miles west of Chile.

The Polynesian name for Easter Island is Rapa Nui *(rap uh NOO ee)*. Its Chilean name is Isla de Pascua *(EEZ lah thay PAHS kwah)*.

The statues, called moai *(MOH eye),* were made hundreds of years ago. Suppose you read an account of how these statues were made. How would you know whether or not to believe the account?

Here's How

To decide whether information is accurate, look for facts, reasoned judgments, and opinions. An interpretation that depends on facts and reasoned judgments is likely to be correct. An explanation that offers only opinions has little value.

Read "The Easter Island Story" on

EASTER
•ISLAND

this page. It contains facts, reasoned judgments, and opinions.

A fact is a statement that can be proven. There are many forms of proof. The findings of archaeologists can be proof, or proof can come from written sources or direct observation.

Find the statement highlighted in blue in "The Easter Island Story." This statement is a fact because there is proof that it is true. Photographs and other records show the statues and stone picks that archaeologists found at the volcano.

A reasoned judgment is a statement that is based on fact but has not been proven. Key words like *probably*, *perhaps*, and *possibly* can help you to identify reasoned judgments.

The statement highlighted in purple is a reasoned judgment. It explains how the statues may have been lifted onto their platforms. Can you find the facts that support this idea? They directly follow the reasoned judgment. People on Easter Island tested this idea in the 1950s. Using two logs as levers, they lifted a 25-ton statue. Yet it has not been proven that the statues' makers used logs as levers. It only has been shown that this is possible.

An opinion is a statement of personal preference, feelings, or ideas. Words such as *think* and *feel* often indicate that a statement is an opinion. The statement highlighted in green is an opinion. It tells you how the writer feels about the statues.

Try It

Look again at "The Easter Island Story." Find a fact, a reasoned judgment, and an opinion. Be sure to choose examples that have not been discussed already.

Apply It

Listen to a newscast or read a newspaper or magazine article. Record one fact, one reasoned judgment, and one opinion. Point out any key words that helped you identify the types of statements.

The Easter Island Story

I think the moai of Easter Island are exciting artifacts. They are certain to interest people in the future.

Islanders used stone picks to carve the moai from the rock of the extinct volcano Rano Raruku. Both inside and outside of the crater, archaeologists have found many unfinished statues and thousands of stone picks. All of the moai are made of a yellow-gray stone called tuff. The tuff comes from the crater walls of Rano Raruku.

The islanders probably dragged the statues from the volcano to the places where they stand now. In the 1950s, people from Easter Island tested this idea. They found that it took 180 people to pull a medium-sized statue!

The people who built the statues probably used log levers to lift the statues onto their platforms. Trees grow on the island today. And by studying pollen deposits, scientists have learned that there were trees on the island in the past. Also, people in other times and places have used logs for the same purpose.

Learning About the Past

LESSON 2

Examining Sources

How do archaeologists investigate ancient cultures?

Key Terms

- archaeology
- excavation
- radiocarbon dating

➤ *Tollund man was found in a Danish peat bog like the one shown here. After scientists determined what Tollund Man ate for his last meal, they prepared a similar meal of seeds and grain. The resulting mixture tasted quite bitter.*

The dead man lay on his side in a swampy area called a peat bog. His face was so calm that he appeared to have died in his sleep. But it was clear that he hadn't; a rope was wound tightly around his neck.

Two Danish workers discovered the man's body in 1950. They had come to Tollund Bog to cut peat, a form of rotted plant material that is used for fuel. The peat cutters wondered if they should call the police. As it turned out, the body in the bog was hardly a case for the Danish police. Instead, it was a lucky find for archaeologists. **Archaeology** is the recovery and study of artifacts, ruins, bones, and fossils remaining from the past.

In Denmark, archaeologists soon learned that Tollund Man hadn't been hanged and buried that day, that year, or even this century. The airtight peat bog had perfectly preserved Tollund Man's body for thousands of years. Using a technique called radiocarbon dating, archaeologists found out

that the man had died around 210 B.C. Using other scientific techniques, they even found out what Tollund Man ate for his last meal: cereal, made with seeds of plants that grew in Denmark more than 2,000 years ago. No one can say for sure why Tollund Man died. But evidence indicates he may have been killed in a religious ritual.

Unlocking the Archaeological Record

Airtight peat bogs like the one at Tollund have preserved many other things, too. Archaeologists have found many things in the bogs such as parts of ancient horse-drawn carriages, plows, canoes, and weapons.

The artifacts, ruins, bones, and fossils that archaeologists discover and study make up the archaeological record. By studying the archaeological record, archaeologists can learn many things about people of the past: how they lived, what they ate, what diseases they had, and even how they died.

The Formation of the Record

Imagine a village where no one has lived for thousands of years. Over the centuries the wind and rain have swept through its streets, destroying many of its buildings. Eventually, all that is left of the village are the ruins of the buildings and a few artifacts. As more time passes, soil covers the site. Trees and brush grow over the remains. The archaeological record of the village becomes sealed in layers within the earth.

Centuries later, however, signs of the village may be brought back to the earth's surface. This uncovering occurs in many ways. Erosion, the gradual wearing away of soil, might reveal the remains of the ruined buildings. Animals rooting in the ground might dig up artifacts. New settlers clearing the land for farming might uncover more evidence.

Archaeologists then are able to examine the surface of the site and can begin to put together the archaeological record. In most cases,

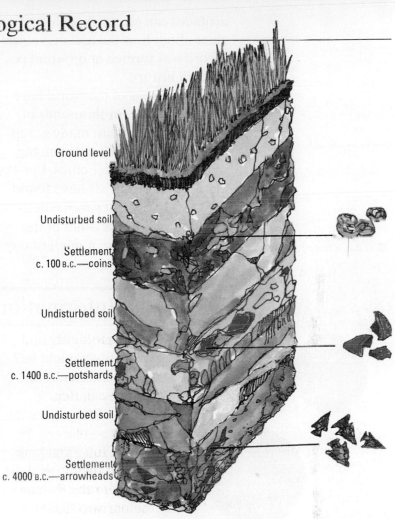

Ground level

Undisturbed soil

Settlement
c. 100 B.C.—coins

Undisturbed soil

Settlement
c. 1400 B.C.—potshards

Undisturbed soil

Settlement
c. 4000 B.C.—arrowheads

however, evidence remains buried in layers in the earth, and archaeologists must use excavation to examine the site. **Excavation** is the process of digging up the remains of the past.

The Excavation of a Site

Once archaeologists have located a site, they carefully remove the earth, layer by layer. They divide the surface of the site into squares with grids. As they dig, they carefully record the exact location of every object they find.

The study of the remains that are found in various layers of soil and rock is called stratigraphy *(struh TIHG ruh fee)*. Studying the layers themselves, as well as the

▲ *Modern archaeologists place grids horizontally over a site and even vertically as they excavate. This helps them record the location of artifacts in the layers.*

artifacts, can give archaeologists clues about how the archaeological record was formed at different periods in history.

Some areas of the world have been inhabited for thousands of years. In these areas, many groups of people have built cities on top of the ruins of earlier cities. For example, archaeologists have found evidence of at least seven cities built on top of each other at the site of ancient Troy in modern-day Turkey.

■ *What is the archaeological record?*

In general, archaeologists believe that the deepest layers are the oldest. However, this may not always be true. Over time, new cultures disturb the layers by digging up soil and artifacts from deeper layers. Shifts in the earth's crust, such as earthquakes, can also disturb the layers. Therefore, things of different ages may be buried together. In such cases, archaeologists must use other techniques to date the layers and the objects found in them. ■

Dating the Information

How can archaeologists find out how old an artifact might be? They use two methods, cultural dating and scientific dating.

Cultural Dating

Suppose you are taking part in an archaeological dig in Italy, where the Roman Empire flourished 2,000 years ago. As you carefully sift through one layer of soil, you find a small object. When you clean it off, you discover that it is a metal coin. It's decorated with the portrait of a man, but it does not have a date on it. How would you go about finding out how old it is?

A little research about the Roman Empire from written sources will tell you about the history of Roman coins. Coins were decorated with the face of the emperor who was in power when the coin was made. Some research into Roman art will lead you to sculptures and portraits of Roman emperors. You might find out that the emperor

Compare United States currency with these Roman coins. What would a historian of the future learn about you from your pocket change?

pictured on the coin you uncovered is Augustus. You then learn that he ruled from 31 B.C. to A.D. 14. Now you know that the coin you found was made between 31 B.C. and A.D. 14.

This process of gathering information is an example of cultural dating. Archaeologists are using cultural dating when they compare objects they find with information they already have. To find the date of the Roman coin, for example, you compared it with information you could get about Roman coins and emperors.

Absolute and Relative Dating

Archaeologists use two types of cultural dating: absolute dating and relative dating. With absolute dating, archaeologists decide the age in years of an object. Finding the date of the Roman coin is an example of absolute dating.

However, archaeologists cannot always find out exactly how old an object is. Sometimes, they can only find out whether it is older or newer than other objects. This is called relative dating.

Using Pottery to Date Archaeological Finds

The bird on the shard below is similar to those found on the bowl. So the shard probably dates to the same period as the bowl, from 1450 to 1100 B.C.

The shard and amphora, or wine jug, have similar patterns scratched on their surfaces. So the shard probably dates to the same period as the amphora, from 3000 to 2000 B.C.

The portion of the animal shown on the shard is similar to the animals on the vase. Also, both shard and vase have a shiny finish. The shard probably dates to the same period as the vase, the 1200s B.C.

◄ *Archaeologists rarely find complete pots. More often, they find shards, or broken pieces of pottery like the one below. To establish the date of the shard, they compare it to similar pots that have already been dated. The chart at left shows three examples of potshard dating.*

Pottery is an important tool in relative dating. Pottery was very common in early cultures and so it is often found in excavations. Because pottery styles changed a great deal over time, archaeologists can identify different pottery styles. They can determine which styles were developed first and which came later. Using this information, archaeologists can then decide the relative age of other objects found at the same site as the pottery.

Scientific Dating

Some ancient objects can be dated more accurately by analyzing them in a laboratory. This kind of analysis is called scientific dating. The oldest form of scientific dating is dendrochronology *(dehn droh kruh NAHL uh jee)*, or tree-ring counting. It has been used since the 1700s.

Dendrochronology is based on the fact that a tree grows a new ring every year. So, you can figure out the age of a tree by counting the number of rings in its trunk. In addition, changes in the climate, including temperature and rainfall, affect a ring's thickness, so trees in one area have a specific pattern of rings.

Archaeologists compare tree-ring patterns from many trees and piece together a master pattern

▼ *Which method would you use to date each of the following objects—a fossil trilobite, a prehistoric sea animal; a bone from a prehistoric human; and a wooden sculpture from ancient Peru?*

Determining the Age of Archaeological Finds

Method	Age Range	Process
Written records	Up to about 5,000 years ago	Use written records of known age to date artifacts found along with them.
Tree-ring dating	Up to about 8,000 years ago	Match the pattern in a wooden object to a master tree-ring pattern; count the rings.
Radiocarbon dating	From about 1,000 to 60,000 years ago	Measure the amount of radioactive carbon remaining in the object (used to date the remains of plants and animals).
Potassium-argon dating	More than 500,000 years ago	Compare the amounts of potassium and argon present in volcanic rock (used to date bones and tools found in the rock).

that covers a period of many hundreds of years. Then the archaeologists match the pattern of the rings with the pattern in ancient wooden objects to find out how old the objects are.

Radiocarbon Dating

Archaeologists have developed many other scientific dating techniques. The most significant is **radiocarbon dating.** In this method, the radioactive carbon within an archaeological discovery is measured to determine the age of the object. Radiocarbon dating can only be used to date the remains of once-living things, such as wood or bones.

Here's how radiocarbon dating works. Every living thing absorbs carbon from the atmosphere. A small amount of the carbon is radioactive. When a plant or animal dies, it stops absorbing carbon. The radioactive carbon absorbed when it was alive begins to decay at a known rate.

Archaeologists have figured out methods of

measuring the amount of radioactive carbon left in things like bones and wood. Using this information, they can figure out when a plant or animal died. They can even figure out how long ago the tree used to make an artifact lived.

Radiocarbon dating has helped solve many mysteries. For example, in 1950 archaeologists used this method to figure out the age of Tollund Man. But radiocarbon dating is not perfect. It does not work on objects less than 1,000 years old or more than 60,000 years old. In addition, the accuracy of radiocarbon dating can be affected by pollution. Even the smoke from a cigarette can affect the accuracy of a sample.

In spite of these problems, radiocarbon dating has had a great impact on archaeology. For one thing, it has forced archaeologists to rethink some of their ideas about the past. For example, archaeologists used to believe that the great pyramids in Egypt were the oldest stone monuments in the world. However, radiocarbon dating of objects within the tombs has proved that giant stone tombs found in western Europe were built hundreds of years before the pyramids. ■

■ *What are two methods of dating artifacts?*

Chapter 3

Interpreting the Evidence

▲ *This cave painting from Lascaux, France, is 17,000 years old.*

Techniques such as radiocarbon dating have given archaeologists valuable information about the past. Nevertheless, people can interpret the archaeological record in many ways. Archaeologists must interpret the evidence they collect just as historians do.

People tend to interpret past events in light of their own experiences. For example, imagine you are on an archaeological dig and you come upon a row of stones. You might assume the stones are part of a wall, because you are familiar with stone walls. However, the people of an ancient culture might have brought these stones together for other reasons. Perhaps they were trying to create an altar to their god or to keep track of lunar eclipses.

Reconsidering the Past

As different archaeologists examine the archaeological record, they come to different conclusions about its meaning. For example, archaeologists disagree about the meaning of objects depicted in ancient cave art. These paintings were made by humans more than

◄ *At left is a detail from the cave painting above. Some think the object shown is a spear; others identify it as a stalk of wheat. What do you think?*

69

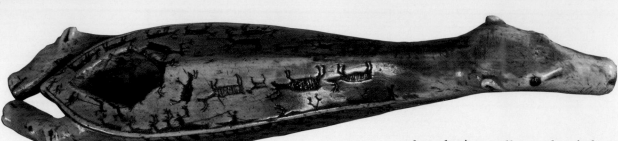

Examine the object above. It is made of bone and engraved with caribou designs. What do you think it is? Archaeologists have identified it as an arrow straightener, a tool used by prehistoric hunters.

How Do We Know?

HISTORY *Archaeologists conduct experiments to help them interpret the archaeological record. For example, they sometimes construct replicas of ancient buildings to observe how they decay. They even study garbage to find out what kinds of things people throw away.*

■ *Why do archaeologists reach different conclusions about the past?*

10,000 years ago. Some archaeologists believe the objects are weapons such as arrows, spears, and harpoons. If they are, it would indicate that early humans were hunters and warriors.

In recent years, however, some people have begun to challenge that interpretation. A scholar named Alexander Marshack, for example, used a microscope to examine these works of art closely. Marshack decided that the objects depicted in these early paintings might be plants, tree branches, and leaves instead of weapons. He believes the artwork may celebrate nature, not hunting. Perhaps our early ancestors were not as warlike as archaeologists have long believed.

Interpreting the Past

Archaeologists must use all the evidence they can gather to interpret the archaeological record. The case of Tollund Man shows how archaeologists pull together information from many sources. Through radiocarbon dating, they were able to find out that the man in the peat bog died in about 210 B.C. But how and why did he die?

To find out, archaeologists had to do more research. From written records, they learned that the ancient Nordic people sometimes sacrificed people to their gods by hanging them. The archaeologists even learned that the food Tollund Man ate for his last meal might have been a part of the ritual of the sacrifice. Although archaeologists still cannot be sure, they think that Tollund Man was hanged, not as a punishment but as an offering to the gods.

Perhaps future generations of archaeologists will find additional information about Tollund Man. Future generations also might interpret the information that is already available differently. For archaeologists as well as for historians, interpreting the evidence is a never-ending process. ■

R E V I E W

1. **FOCUS** How do archaeologists investigate ancient cultures?

2. **CONNECT** How are grids used by cartographers similar to those used by archaeologists?

3. **ARCHAEOLOGY** Imagine you are an archaeologist working at a dig. You find a piece of wood used in building an ancient house. What are two techniques you might use to find out how old it is, and how would you apply them?

4. **CRITICAL THINKING** Imagine that 1,000 years from now a team of archaeologists discovers the remains of your home. What conclusions might they draw about life in the 20th century from the artifacts they find in your room?

5. **ACTIVITY** Pick four modern artifacts, for example, a coin, a tool, a wooden object, and a piece of pottery. Examine each artifact and then list the method you would use to determine its date.

LESSON 3

Examining Archaeology

At first I could see nothing, the hot air escaping from the chamber causing the candle flame to flicker, but presently, as my eyes grew accustomed to the light, details of the room emerged slowly from the mist, strange animals, statues and gold—everywhere the glint of gold. For the moment—an eternity it must have been to the others standing by—I was struck dumb with amazement, and when Lord Carnarvon, unable to stand the suspense any longer, inquired anxiously, "Can you see anything?" it was all I could do to get out the words, "Yes, wonderful things."

Howard Carter, *Tomb of Tut-Ankh-Amen*

THINKING FOCUS

What can archaeologists learn from an archaeological dig?

Key Terms

- sarcophagus
- kitchen midden

After five seasons of failure, archaeologist Howard Carter and his wealthy employer, Lord Carnarvon, finally were successful on November 26, 1922. They had found the tomb of the young. Egyptian pharaoh Tutankhamen *(tut ahngk AH muhn).*

The pharaoh's tomb had been sealed since the time shortly after his burial in 1352 B.C. It was crowded full of beautiful carvings and many objects made of gold and precious stones. As a matter of fact, Tutankhamen's tomb contained everything a wealthy king would need for his afterlife. In the most splendid of the tomb's four rooms lay Tutankhamen's mummy. It was buried in a solid gold **sarcophagus** *(sar KAHF uh guhs),* or coffin.

A Classic Excavation

Tutankhamen is not remembered for his political leadership or his military ability. The boy-king died before he was 20, after ruling for only nine years. But his tomb was an important find for archaeologists. Ancient tomb robbers had taken the treasures from the other tombs in Egypt's Valley of the Kings. Robbers had apparently even broken into one room of Tutankhamen's tomb, but for some reason, had left much of it alone. Until Howard Carter discovered it in 1922, Tutankhamen's tomb remained well hidden underneath the ancient foundations of workers' huts.

The excavation of Tutankhamen's tomb is an example of what is called classic archaeology. Carter and his employer were searching for spectacular artifacts from a past culture.

71

Tutankhamen's Treasure

What did Howard Carter see when he looked inside the tomb? He saw four small rooms piled to the ceiling with gold jewelry, life-sized statues, furniture, games, chariots, and more.

Made of gold and colored glass, this necklace represents a vulture goddess. It was one of 143 objects tucked into the cloth wrapped around Tutankhamen's body. Some were the king's favorite possessions. Others had a religious value.

Fit to cool a king on a hot day, this fan once had 30 ostrich feathers. The feathers were destroyed by insects over the centuries. The fan's golden surface still shows Tutankhamen hunting the ostriches whose feathers were used to make it.

The head and shoulders of the king's body were covered by this gold mask. Pictures of the king appear in many places in the tomb. This mask may be the best indication of what he looked like.

> *L*ast week, Lord Carnarvon and Mr. Howard Carter revealed what has been described as promising "the most sensational Egyptological discovery of the century"—the finding of the complete funeral paraphernalia of King Tutankhamen . . . and other objects of priceless value and the utmost importance. . . . After covering up the site, [Carter] telegraphed to Lord Carnarvon to come out from England. On his arrival, the search was continued. It revealed, as we have said, an unrivalled store of treasures!
>
> *The Illustrated London News*, December 9, 1922

In the newspaper above article from *The Illustrated London News,* note the excitement that followed the discovery of the incredible artifacts in the Egyptian pharaoh's tomb. ■

■ *What was Howard Carter's goal in excavating the Egyptian tomb?*

The New Archaeology

For centuries, the hope of finding beautiful objects lured wealthy people like Lord Carnarvon to archaeological adventures in foreign lands. The great value of the treasures uncovered in the digs paid for the expensive excavations. Beginning in the 1700s, people tried to find rare objects for their private art collections. By the late 1800s, nations had joined in the race to excavate ancient treasures for display in their museums.

New Goals

Since the beginning of this century, however, archaeology has changed its focus. Most archaeologists no longer look only for beautiful objects and the treasures of dead kings. Today, most archaeologists search instead to understand the lives of all people, rich and poor.

To do so, archaeologists must look in different places and use different methods than they did less than 100 years ago. Instead of seeking art objects and throwing out "rubbish," archaeologists now try to study all the things early people left behind. As a matter of fact, archaeologists today do study ancient people's rubbish. This rubbish, known as **kitchen midden,** often contains artifacts, bones, and other evidence of early human settlements. Archaeologists study kitchen midden to learn important information about diet, daily activity, and contact with other cultures.

Modern archaeologists also work closely with other specialists. Geologists study soil and minerals to give archaeologists clues about the condition of the earth at different periods in time. Botanists *(BAHT n ihsts)* and zoologists *(zoh AHL uh jihsts)* provide information about the plants and animals that lived at different times. Chemists and physicists use the scientific dating techniques that tell archaeologists the age of ancient artifacts.

A Modern Dig

The archaeological dig conducted at Koster, a site in western Illinois, shows how modern archaeologists go about their work.

A Modern Excavation

For years, farmers in the Illinois River Valley found stone tools and potshards in their fields. Archaeologists could tell ancient people must have lived here. With the help of students and other volunteers, they began excavating Theodore Koster's cornfield in Kampsville, Illinois.

Can you tell this isn't just gravel? As early North Americans made tools, pieces of stone like this flaked off. Archaeologists can often tell from their shape what kind of tool the flakes were chipped from.

These spear heads were made around 9500 B.C. They have shallow grooves on each side. The grooves made it easier to attach the spear heads to the spears.

The dig at Koster is featured above. Between 1970 and 1979, archaeologists uncovered evidence of 15 settlements built on the site, dating back to 6500 B.C. Studying the evidence has allowed archaeologists to reconstruct the ways of life of the early inhabitants of North America.

At the Koster site, archaeologists and students gathered and studied pollen, snail shells, and fish scales. It doesn't sound nearly as exciting as finding a gold-covered mummy in Tutankhamen's tomb. However, the Koster dig provided valuable information about how people adapted to and changed their surroundings.

The Koster dig shows just how much archaeology has changed over time. No longer is archaeology merely a search for beautiful and valuable buried treasures. It is a search for knowledge about the past. ■

■ *How has archaeology changed during the past century?*

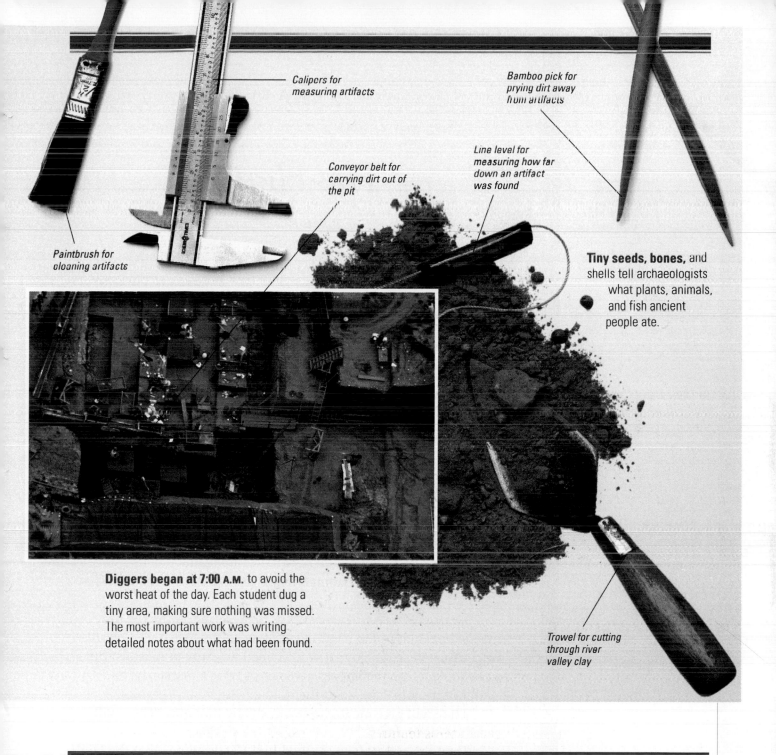

Calipers for measuring artifacts

Bamboo pick for prying dirt away from artifacts

Conveyor belt for carrying dirt out of the pit

Line level for measuring how far down an artifact was found

Paintbrush for cleaning artifacts

Tiny seeds, bones, and shells tell archaeologists what plants, animals, and fish ancient people ate.

Diggers began at 7:00 A.M. to avoid the worst heat of the day. Each student dug a tiny area, making sure nothing was missed. The most important work was writing detailed notes about what had been found.

Trowel for cutting through river valley clay

REVIEW

1. **FOCUS** What can archaeologists learn from an archaeological dig?

2. **CONNECT** Imagine you are a historian studying the artifacts found in Tutankhamen's tomb. What can you learn from these sources about daily life in ancient Egypt? What kinds of things cannot be learned from these sources?

3. **ECONOMICS** How have archaeologists like Howard Carter been able to get money to finance their many excavations?

4. **CRITICAL THINKING** Why are everyday objects as valuable as rare treasures to modern archaeologists?

5. **ACTIVITY** Observation skills are particularly important to archaeologists. Practice your observation skills by closely studying a location, such as your backyard, a garage, or a park. Look for artifacts on and even below the surface of the site, if possible. Record where you find each artifact. What conclusions can you make about the artifacts you find and the people who left them?

The Henge

Edward Rutherfurd

Stonehenge is a huge stone temple built between 1800 and 1400 B.C. in England. The circle of large stones is still a mystery today—archaeologists aren't certain why or even how it was built. This story from the novel Sarum *suggests some answers.*

In Lesson 4 of Chapter 3, you will read about Stonehenge.

Nooma was excited that the priests had chosen him to build the new henge: not only was this a great honour that made him stick out his chest with pride, but it was also a challenge to his craftsmanship; and he hurried towards the sacred grounds with eager anticipation.

But when he heard the priests' instructions, and when finally he comprehended the enormous scale of their plan, and the short time in which the work was to be completed, his solemn eyes grew larger. Despite the chill autumn day, he felt small beads of perspiration breaking out on his broad forehead.

"Such huge stones? Completed in ten years?" It was a wail of dismay.

The priests took no notice of his protests, and now the little mason began to tremble with fear. How could such a vast temple be completed so quickly? It would need an army of masons! But as he looked into the impassive faces of Dluc's priests, he had no doubt of his fate if he failed them.

"They will give me to the sun god," he thought. "They will sacrifice me at dawn."

When the priests next showed him the drawings that the High Priest had made and he bent his head to study them, his large oval face fell even further.

"Nothing like this has ever been done before," he muttered as he stared at the great arches. And jabbing his finger at one of the drawings he protested: "How am I to do that?"

For Dluc's designs made clear that each of the massive lintels of the ring of sarsens was to be slightly curved so that together they would form a perfect circle. How could such huge stones be transformed—thirty of them—into identical blocks each shaped with such precision?

"You must find a way," they told him.

lintel the horizontal stone that rests on top of two upright stones
sarsen an upright stone that supports the lintel

Nooma shook his head slowly. "I shall certainly be led to the altar stone," he thought sadly.

But there was nothing he could do. The priests could not be refused. Somehow, he must devise a way to build this huge new henge.

"I should need fifty masons to work under me," he said finally. "And as for labourers . . ." He tried to calculate the size of the army of men that would be needed to haul such enormous stones. For each sarsen would weigh up to thirty-five tons— the largest half as much again—and would have to be moved nearly twenty miles across the rolling high ground. "Why," he exclaimed, "it would take five hundred men at least, and teams of oxen too."

But the priests were unmoved by these astounding demands.

"You shall have all the men you need, and oxen," he was informed.

Nooma thought. The practical problems of organising such a force, of feeding and housing them would occupy much time. He could not do this and supervise the stone-working alone. "I shall need help to organise the men," he said.

"Choose whom you wish."

The little fellow considered.

"I should like Tark the riverman," he said.

It was a good choice. No one on the five rivers was cleverer than Tark, the best known and most highly regarded of all the riverfolk. The riverfolk at Sarum were an extensive tribe, somewhat apart from the farmers, and mostly descended in one way or another from the crafty fishermen and hunters who had first inhabited the place millennia before. It was not uncommon to see mean, hard little faces and long toes which bore a remarkable resemblance to those of Tep the hunter, along the riverbanks of any of the five rivers, as these people went about their business as trappers, fishermen and traders. Water rats they were often called by the Sarum people.

Tark was of this tribe, but a nobler specimen than most. Though he, too, had the long toes of the water rat, he was a tall, good-looking man with strong, rugged features, long black hair which he swept back, and a black beard which he kept meticulously trimmed and singed. His eyes, black as jet, could be hard when he was driving a bargain, but could also become gentle and luminous, especially when he sang, which he did in a fine, tuneful bass; and it was partly for this reason that he was well known from the trading post to the port to be popular with the women. Tark was an expert trader, with six boats and men of his own working under him. He was everywhere, even crossing the sea sometimes in search of slaves or special items that he knew would please Krona or the priests. Above all, he was wily in his dealing

wily sly

with the priests, always making himself useful to them, while at the same time seeing to it that each transaction was to his benefit. He liked the little mason, whom he found slightly absurd, admired his craftsmanship and had formed a kind of friendship with him, often letting him have small items from his river-trading which the mason would never have been clever enough to bargain for himself.

Nooma was sure that he would know how to organise the provisioning and quartering of his men, and he was right.

"You have a month to prepare," the priests told the mason. "At the next moon, work must begin."

In the days that followed, Nooma found that his needs were more than supplied. The priests moved from house to house, picking young men whenever they were needed. Before the work was done, over a third of the adult male population would be engaged on the task at any one time. Under Tark's direction, grain stores were built near the site from which the sarsens would be brought, and the work of felling trees, which would be used as rollers over which the huge stones could be moved, was begun.

By the end of the month, despite the huge size of the task before him, Nooma felt the first dawning of a new confidence. Encouraged by Tark, who was delighted by such an opportunity to make himself useful to the priests, he began to go about his great work with a new optimism and before the end of the month confided to the trader: "Perhaps, after all, it can be done."

While the preparations were in hand, he also set his mind to the technical problems presented by the stones themselves: how were they to be handled, and above all, how were such cumbersome objects to be fitted together in so precise a design?

It was in this that Nooma showed a practical genius which amply justified the choice that the priests had made in putting the work under his hands.

For when he came to report to the priests at the end of the month, the little mason was brimming with suppressed excitement.

As he outlined his plans, jabbing the air with his stubby little fingers, he announced:

"We must cut the stones into their final shape before we move them."

The priests were surprised. It had been assumed that the rough-hewn rocks would be brought to the henge before they were shaped. But Nooma shook his head.

"First," he explained, "it is foolish to move the sarsens before they are almost shaped, because they will be heavier. And second, if we cut and dress the stones at the henge, the mess will be enormous: thousands of stone chippings to carry away."

"Then you mean to shape every stone of the temple a day's

quartering assigning lodgings to people

78

journey away, carry the finished stones to the sacred ground and assemble them there?" one of the priests asked in astonishment.

He nodded calmly. "Why not?"

Next he produced his own drawings.

To produce the identically curved lintels he proposed to make a wooden block, along which each stone could be cut, and in order to fix them in place he had devised an ingenious solution.

"See," he explained, "at the top of each upright we can make two tenons—these bumps—and on the underside of each lintel two matching sockets for the tenons to fit into."

He pointed them out to the priests.

"They will be fitted into each other just as we do blocks of wood," he explained. "And then," he continued, "I can make tongue and groove joints at the end of the lintels so that each one slots into the next."

"They will be solid," the priest who had spoken before remarked.

"Solid!" the quiet little fellow suddenly burst out. "Why each stone will be married to the next like husband to wife. The temple will be indestructible!" He was flushed with excitement.

It was from that moment that the priests knew the new temple of Stonehenge would be a masterpiece; and that night, when they gave Dluc an account of the mason's plans, the High Priest was pleased.

Further Reading

Canyons Beyond the Sky. Lawrence Kettleman. An archaeological dig forms the backdrop for this story of time travel between modern and ancient cultures.

Country of Broken Stone. Nancy Bond. The excavation of a Roman fort provides a link to the past when hostile acts by some people opposed to the dig unleash supernatural forces.

The Faraway Lurs. Harry Behn. The love and friendship of a Bronze Age boy and girl is opposed by their families and tribes. This author based the story on an actual archaeological discovery.

Pyramid. David Macauley. How were the pyramids built? David Macauley's book offers a step-by-step illustrated description of the building of a pyramid.

LESSON 4

Interpreting Sources

Key Term

• megalith

▲ *This Roman amphora dates from about 700 B.C. The owner's name is shown on its surface.*

During the Roman Empire, nearly 2,000 years ago, people eagerly flocked to Roman ports to watch foreign ships empty their cargo. Nearly every day new items arrived from many lands abroad: fierce lions from central Africa, bolts of fine silk from China, and majestic horses from Spain. From India came the pepper and spices Romans needed for cooking, along with diamonds and pearls for the wealthy to wear. Pliny the Younger, author of the account of the eruption of Mount Vesuvius, wrote that the wealthy women of Rome even wore pearls on their shoes.

But a special treat for Romans was to watch a ship unload its cargo of fantastic beasts from India. Bengal tigers, elephants, apes, and peacocks would emerge from the holds of the ship. The noisy crowd would suddenly hush, gasping in amazement at the fantastic sight.

To obtain these luxuries, the Roman traders sailed to distant ports. The ships were loaded down with Roman goods such as gold, glass, silver coins, and amphorae *(AM fuh ree)*—pottery containers filled with wine and olive oil.

Evidence of Cultural Contact

How do people today know about the ancient Roman markets and the goods traded there? In addition to the written records, such as Pliny's account, archaeologists have found Roman goods far beyond the empire's borders. For example, they have discovered amphorae in India, along with coins dating from before A.D. 100. These finds indicate that India and Rome once enjoyed a thriving trade.

The map on page 81 shows some of what archaeologists and historians have learned about the contacts between ancient cultures.

Notice the routes linking China and Rome. Archaeologists know about Chinese-Roman trade from many sources including accounts by Pliny who wrote, "Our imports from China and Arabia cost a hundred million sesterces per annum," the equivalent of 25 million silver Roman coins per year.

Acquainted Cultures

Trade was one of several forms of contact between the cultures of the ancient world: China, Egypt, India, Mesopotamia, Greece, and Rome. Individuals traveled to foreign lands, even in ancient times.

Chapter 3

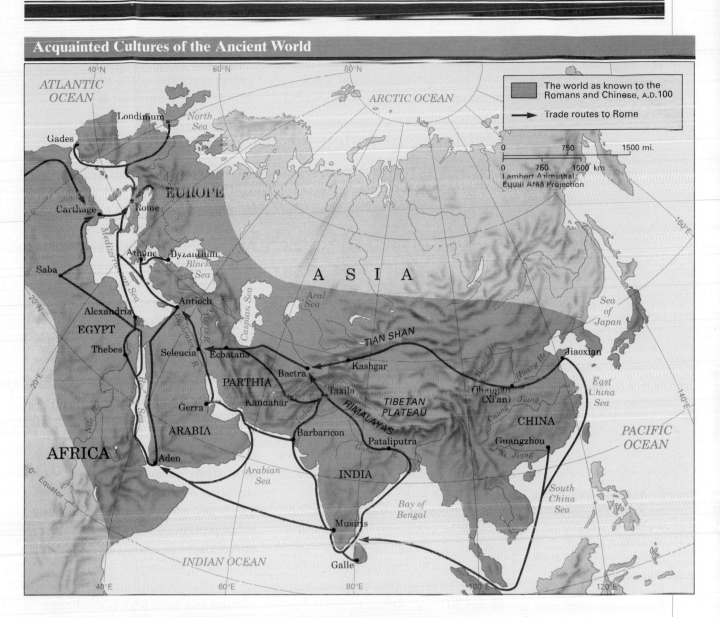

Sometimes these travelers left behind evidence of their visits, such as the Romans who scratched their names on stone monuments in Greece and Egypt. Sometimes travelers and explorers left written accounts of their travels. For example, the Chinese monk Faxian (FAH shee EHN) traveled to India to study in the early A.D. 400s. He later wrote about his travels.

Different cultures came into contact not only through trade and travel, but also through war and migration. Clues about the different contacts between cultures are found in the archaeological record.

Archaeologists sometimes find signs that at a particular time, new types of food, pottery, or weavings appeared in a certain location. This might show that new people migrated to the area during the time period, bringing with them new ideas.

Cultural Diffusion

Whenever different cultures come in contact, they exchange goods and ideas. This process is what is known as cultural diffusion, and it is one way that ideas have spread from one area of the world to another.

▲ Use the scale on the map to find the shortest route from China to Rome.

Some historians believe developments in writing, art, architecture, and agriculture from a few areas spread throughout the world through cultural diffusion. Others argue that groups of people developed similar ideas independently of one another. ■

Evidence of Independent Invention

The archaeological record shows that some cultures borrowed ideas and technology from other people they were in contact with. Yet the record also shows that, in some cases, different groups created similar technologies without coming into contact with each other. Instead, these peoples each came up with their similar ideas independently.

The Mystery of Stonehenge

A great example of independent development is found in the south of what is now Britain. More than 4,000 years ago, the people of this area built Stonehenge. It is a monument of huge stones, or **megaliths,** arranged in a circular pattern, as shown below.

Originally, this monument included 81 megaliths, each weighing about 50 tons. Archaeologists have determined that the stones were carted to their present location from a rock quarry 25 miles away. Scholars figure it must have taken 1,100 people seven weeks to move just one of the stones, using twisted hide ropes and wooden rollers. At that rate, it would have taken at least 10 years to get all 81 upright stones into place.

Imagine how hard it would be to stand one of these megaliths upright without the aid of modern machinery. Try to imagine hoisting the seven-ton horizontal stones found on top of each pair of upright stones. Builders began constructing Stonehenge around 2800 B.C. Later generations changed the arrangement of the huge stones and added new ones over a period of about 1,700 years.

Archaeologists and historians are still not sure why Stonehenge

▼ *To help them estimate the age of the megaliths, archaeologists used radiocarbon dating on charcoal found in underground pits at Stonehenge. The charcoal dates from around 1848 B.C.*

was built. The position of these megaliths could mean that the monument was built to help track the movements of the stars and planets. Whatever its purpose, Stonehenge has sparked debate among those who have studied it.

Reinterpreting the Past

In the 1920s, many archaeologists and historians argued that the people who built Stonehenge could not have figured out by themselves how to build such a monument. They insisted that the builders of Stonehenge must have learned how from people of another culture. Most archaeologists believed that the pyramids of Egypt, which were built beginning in the 2600s B.C., were the oldest stone monuments in the world. The archaeologists argued that ideas about building large monuments were spread from Egypt by cultural diffusion to areas such as Britain.

However, the development of radiocarbon dating proved them wrong. In the 1960s, radiocarbon dating of the artifacts found inside the pyramids showed that stone monuments like Stonehenge were built in western Europe hundreds of years before the pyramids. The builders of Stonehenge figured out how to do it on their own—not by cultural diffusion.

Most archaeologists now believe that people in different parts of the world struggled with similar problems and had similar needs. People searched for ways to feed themselves, to adapt to or change their environment, to record information, and to get along with their neighbors. In some cases, cultures adapted each other's ideas to meet their needs. In other cases, they independently came up with similar ideas on their own.

As archaeologists and historians debate the different ways in which ideas have spread throughout the world, they examine their sources again and again. They also reinterpret the information. As a result of this continuing study, the present-day view of the past is always changing. ■

▲ *Before 2800 B.C., the Egyptians made paper, similar to that shown at right, from the papyrus plant. In A.D. 105, a Chinese clerk independently invented rag paper, much like the paper shown at left. It was made from mulberry bark, old rags, and fishnet.*

■ *Why do archaeologists accept the idea of independent invention?*

R E V I E W

1. **FOCUS** How have new historical sources and methods changed some interpretations of the past?
2. **CONNECT** What written source discussed on page 48 provides evidence of Phoenician trade?
3. **ARCHAEOLOGY** Why did radiocarbon dating force archaeologists to reconsider their assumptions about how ideas spread into the ancient world?
4. **CRITICAL THINKING** How do groups of people today come into contact? What evidence of that contact might historians and archaeologists of the future find?
5. **ACTIVITY** What evidence is there of your presence in different places? Make a list of the evidence that exists of your presence at school, at a friend's home, or in a different town.

Learning About the Past

Chapter Review

Reviewing Key Terms

archaeology (p. 64)
artifact (p. 57)
excavation (p. 65)
fossil (p. 57)
kitchen midden (p. 73)
megalith (p. 82)

oral tradition (p. 57)
prehistory (p. 57)
primary source (p. 60)
radiocarbon dating (p. 68)
sarcophagus (p. 71)
secondary source (p. 60)

A. The following phrases could be headlines for newspaper articles. Pretend that you are a reporter. Write a paragraph for each headline. Use the key term in each headline at least once.
1. Artifacts from Pompeii Uncovered
2. Archaeologists Study Illinois Rubbish from 6500 B.C.

3. Lord Carnarvon Reveals 1352 B.C. Sarcophagus of King Tutankhamen
4. Archaeologists Debate the Mystery of Stonehenge Megaliths

B. The two words in each pair are related in some way. Write a sentence or two explaining how the words are related.
1. radiocarbon dating, fossil
2. primary source, secondary source
3. kitchen midden, excavation
4. oral tradition, prehistory
5. artifact, archaeology

Exploring Concepts

A. Copy and complete the following outline to show the main ideas in the chapter.

I. Understanding history
   A. Historical evidence
      1. Nonwritten sources
      2.
   B. Evaluation of sources
      1. Primary sources
      2.
II. Examining sources
   A. Unlocking the archaeological record
      1.
      2. Study of the remains
   B. Dating the information
      1.
      2.
III. Examining archaeology
   A. Classic excavation
   B.
IV. Interpreting sources
   A. Evidence of cultural contact
   B.

B. Support each of the following statements with facts and details from the chapter.
1. Our understanding of history will always be changing.
2. Historians gather information about the past from many sources.
3. Historians should always evaluate the sources of their information.
4. The excavation of a site is an important part of putting together the archaeological record of an area.
5. There are many ways an archaeologist can find out the age of an artifact.
6. The goals of archaeology have changed over the years.
7. Radiocarbon dating changed people's ideas about the relationship between Stonehenge and the Great Pyramids.
8. Similar developments in writing, architecture, agriculture, and art have been found in different parts of the world. However, archaeologists do not always agree on how such similar developments took place in locations so far apart.

Reviewing Skills

1. Some archaeologists think that Tollund Man was hanged as an offering to the gods. Is this statement a fact, an opinion, or a reasoned judgment? Explain your answer.

2. The ancient Romans traded with people from many other parts of the world. How do you know that this statement is a fact? Use examples to support your answer.

3. Archaeologists used evidence from the Koster dig to reconstruct what life was like for the settlement's inhabitants. Are their conclusions facts, opinions, or reasoned judgments? Why?

4. Look at the map on page 81 in your book. This map indicates known trade routes in A.D. 100. Notice the place names. Then compare this map with the map of Eurasia on page 508 of the Atlas. List two city or town names that appear on the map of the ancient world but do not appear on the modern map. Then list two city or town names that appear on both maps.

5. Imagine that you have discovered some artifacts in an Egyptian tomb. First you write an exact description of the artifacts. Then you write all the uses the artifacts probably had. Finally you write your feelings and ideas about the importance of the artifacts. What three types of information are you writing down?

Using Critical Thinking

1. Historians often study popular songs of the past. Select a song from the 1940s, the 1950s, or the 1960s. What does the song tell you about Americans of that time period? Now select a modern song. What feelings or thoughts are being expressed? What does this song reveal about your generation?

2. "Those who cannot remember the past are condemned to repeat it." A great thinker made this statement about the past and its connection to the future. Think of a past mistake that you have repeated. How should you have learned a lesson? What problems in our society do we seem "condemned to repeat"?

3. We are creating written sources for archaeologists thousands of years from now. Which of these will be written sources: soup can labels, clay models, paintings, homework papers? Think of three more written sources.

Preparing for Citizenship

1. **INTERVIEWING** A family's stories could be the beginning of an oral tradition. Interview an older family member to find out what his or her life was like at the age of 11 or 12. Prepare your questions before the interview. Some topics could be school, hobbies, games, friends, chores, or music. Write down or tape any stories from the interview. Think about your life. Has life changed? What have you learned about another time?

2. **GROUP ACTIVITY** Historians examine a variety of sources and evidence before forming an opinion. In small groups, select a major historical event to research. What sources could be used to find out what really happened? Have each member of the group bring in information about the event. Discuss your findings.

3. **COLLABORATIVE LEARNING** Archaeologists use many sources to study Mt. Vesuvius and Pompeii. With three classmates, give a presentation which compares information on a modern disaster with that on Pompeii. Two people can research Pompeii and two research the modern disaster. Together, decide how to present your comparison of ancient and modern sources.

Unit 2

The Earliest People

These people are preparing a feast fit for a king. The farmers are carrying grain. The herders are bringing livestock. This mosaic was made 4,500 years ago in Ur, a city in what is now Iraq. Our earliest ancestors lived by hunting and gathering whatever food they could find. After they learned to farm, small settlements, towns, and then cities such as Ur began to grow.

3,000,000 B.C.

The Standard of Ur. Sumerian mosaic,
c. 2500 B.C. British Museum, London

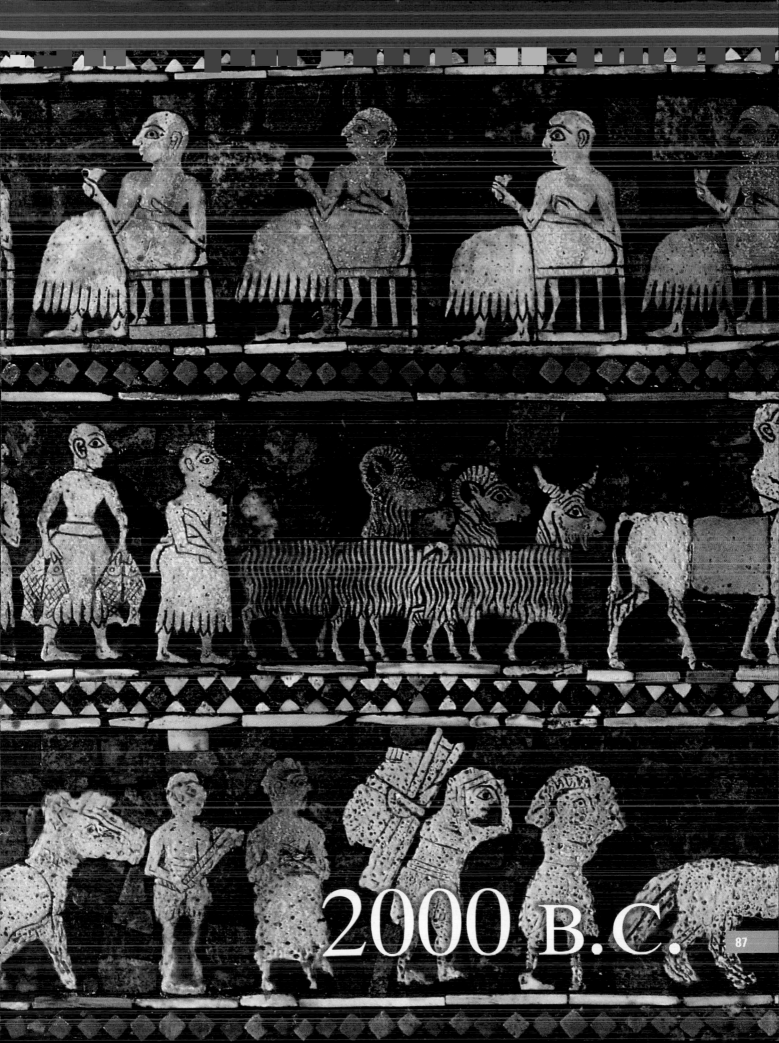

2000 B.C.

Chapter 4

The Depths of Time

*Pieces of bone, chipped stones, and the
ashes of ancient campfires—these are the
clues that have helped archaeologists
uncover the story of our earliest ancestors.
This story goes back to a time when simple
discoveries, such as toolmaking or fire
building, represented great achievements.*

3,000,000 B.C. Ancient ancestors of humans gather wild
plants on the plains of what is
now East Africa (above).

3,500,000	3,000,000	2,500,000	2,000,000

2,500,000 B.C. Early humans make
the first stone tools. People use
them to scavenge meat and gather
foods more easily.

3,000,000 B.C.

Our early ancestors were artists, too. The ivory horse (right) from Europe was carved between 18,000 and 11,000 years ago. The cave painting (above) in France was done around 30,000 years ago.

500,000 B.C. By this date, early human ancestors learn how to control fire.

1,500,000	1,000,000	500,000	B.C.	A.D.

10,000 B.C.

LESSON 1

Uncovering Clues to Our Past

THINKING FOCUS

What have scientists learned about our earliest ancestors?

Key Term

• glacier

> *O*n the morning of November 30, 1974, I awoke, as I usually do on a field expedition, at daybreak. I was in Ethiopia, camped on the edge of a small muddy river, the Awash, at a place called Hadar. . . .
>
> As a paleoanthropologist—one who studies the fossils of human ancestors—I am superstitious. Many of us are, because the work we do depends a great deal on luck. The fossils we study are extremely rare, and quite a few distinguished paleoanthropologists have gone a lifetime without finding a single one. I am one of the more fortunate. This was only my third year in the field at Hadar, and I had already found several. I know I am lucky, and I don't try to hide it. . . . When I got up that morning I felt it was one of those days when you should press your luck. One of those days when something terrific might happen.
>
> Donald Johanson and Maitland Eddy,
> *Lucy: The Beginnings of Humankind*, 1981

Something terrific did happen to Don Johanson, the archaeologist who wrote the above description. On that day, he and fellow scientist Tom Gray discovered the bones of an exceptionally complete skeleton of an early human ancestor. Johanson and his team named their skeleton Lucy.

Lucy is over 3 million years old and one of the oldest skeletons yet found. Her brain must have been quite small, about the size of a softball. Nevertheless, she walked on two feet just as modern humans do. By studying Lucy, archaeologists have learned a lot about our earliest ancestors.

➤ *Don Johanson, shown here on a dig in Africa, made one of the most important discoveries in archaeology when he and his team found Lucy.*

90

Clues from Archaeology

Archaeologists learn about ancient human cultures by studying the artifacts that those cultures left behind. Using this and other methods, archaeologists and historians have put together a good picture of the last few thousand years of human history. But the farther back in time we go, the more incomplete is the evidence available to archaeologists. To learn about our earliest ancestors, archaeologists rely on their analysis of fossil bones, tools, and other artifacts.

Fossil Finds

Archaeologists rarely find complete fossil skeletons. Instead, they usually find bone fragments so small that few people would even notice them. They fit these bone fragments together like the pieces of a puzzle. All of the pieces together might form the back of a skull, a jawbone with a few teeth, or part of a leg bone and kneecap.

To the untrained eye, fossil bones are not much to look at. However, a trained scientist can learn a lot about our ancestors from these bones. Take a look at the Lucy skeleton on the right. By piecing together these bone fragments, Johanson and Gray found that Lucy was only about 3.5 feet tall, shorter than an average five-year-old today.

Scientists also gathered many other bits of information about Lucy by carefully analyzing the bones. From the shape of the pelvic bone, they could tell that she was female. From the size and shape of the leg bones, they determined that she walked upright and was

Lucy, shown below, is one of the most complete early skeletons ever found. Note how scientists have been able to piece the skeleton together even though many of the bones are still missing. Johanson and his team found Lucy near the site shown in the picture at left, at Hadar, Ethiopia, in eastern Africa.

Scientists often provide a date for an important event, such as when a particular species appeared on earth. However, because no written records exist, scientists can only estimate the date. When estimating, they often use the Latin word circa, *meaning "approximately." Circa is often abbreviated c.*

about 25 years old when she died. And finally, the skull bones provided clues about the size of her brain—approximately one-third the size of the brain of modern humans.

Sometimes scientists find other artifacts along with fossil bones. In 1961, Louis and Mary Leakey, a husband-and-wife team working in eastern Africa, found fossil bones in the same layer of earth with simple stone tools. The Leakeys concluded that the fossils were the remains of early humans who had made and used these tools. They gave these early people the name *Homo habilis,* which means "handy human." Scientists use a two-word Latin name, such as *Homo habilis,* to distinguish one species, or type, of organism from another. The first word is the name

of the genus—the large group to which the species belongs. The second word describes a characteristic of the individual species.

In addition to tools, archaeologists sometimes find the crushed bones of animals that were eaten by early human ancestors. They may also find ashes from prehistoric campfires. They combine the evidence they find with fossils and tools to put together a picture of how our ancestors changed over time.

Earliest Ancestors

Lucy belongs to the oldest group of human ancestors, which are also known as australopithecines *(aw stray low PITH uh synz).* Various groups of australopithecines lived between 3.75 million and 1 million years ago.

➤ *Archaeologists make careful records of where they have found fossils, tools, and other artifacts. This information helps them piece together a picture of how our early ancestors may have lived.*

Archaeologists have found australopithecine fossils throughout Africa. The first such fossil found, a child's skull, was discovered at Taung, in South Africa. Raymond Dart, the scientist who made this important discovery in 1924, was the first person to recognize the humanlike features of australopithecines. In the 1950s, Louis Leakey found more australopithecine fossils in the Olduvai *(OL duh vy)* Gorge in eastern Africa.

Although scientists disagree about the exact relationship

between the australopithecines and modern humans, they do agree that *Homo habilis* was an important member of our ancestral group. *Homo habilis* lived from about 2.5 to 1.5 million years ago. These early ancestors had larger brains than the australopithecines. Their long arms, fingers, and toes, made it possible for them to get around in trees as well as on the ground.

Homo habilis was followed by another type of early human, *Homo erectus*. The oldest *Homo erectus* fossils found in Africa are about 1.8 million years old.

Homo erectus had a larger brain than *Homo habilis* and made more complex tools. These early humans are believed to be the first of our ancestors to leave Africa. By about 100,000 years ago, *Homo erectus* had died out.

Homo heidelbergensis was named after a jaw found in Heidelberg, Germany. This ancient human lived between 600,000 and 100,000 years ago. Its brain was about the same size as ours, but it had a much bigger face and teeth.

Neanderthals

In 1856, stone workers found the bones of an ancient people who were more advanced than *Homo heidelbergensis*, but who did not look exactly like modern humans. They had bony ridges above their eyes, broad noses, and big, strong chests. They were Neanderthals, named after the Neander Valley in Germany where they were found.

The Neanderthals lived in Europe and in the Middle East from about 230,000 years ago until they disappeared around 30,000 years ago. Scientists have different theories about why they died out

and whether they are related to modern humans.

Modern Humans

Modern *Homo sapiens* probably began in Africa before 130,000 years ago. *Homo sapiens*, means "wise human." You are a member of the group called *Homo sapiens*. Recently, archaeologists were fascinated by some very old footprints they found in a rock in South Africa. They belonged to a *Homo sapiens* woman who was walking along the seashore about 117,000 years ago.

By at least 60,000 years ago *Homo sapiens* had spread to the Middle East, Asia, and Australia. Modern humans only appeared in Europe about 40,000 years ago. *Homo sapiens* were living in different parts of the world at the same time that the Neanderthals were alive.

The first modern humans in Europe were called Cro-Magnons. Their name comes from the cave in southwestern France where their bones were first found.

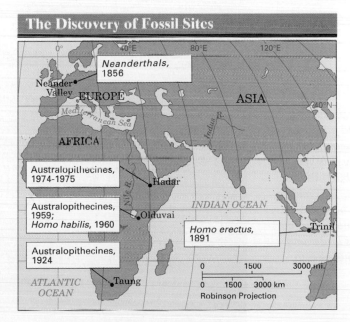

▲ *By fitting together pieces of fossil bone found in La Ferrasie, France, scientists reconstructed this Neanderthal skull.*

▼ *The map below shows where and when fossil remains of early human ancestors were found.*

The Discovery of Fossil Sites

Neanderthals, 1856
Neander Valley
EUROPE
Mediterranean Sea
ASIA
AFRICA
Indus R.
Australopithecines, 1974-1975
Hadar
Nile R.
Australopithecines, 1959;
Homo habilis, 1960
Olduvai
INDIAN OCEAN
Homo erectus, 1891
Trinil
Australopithecines, 1924
ATLANTIC OCEAN
Taung
0   1500   3000 mi.
0   1500   3000 km
Robinson Projection

93

The Depths of Time

Toolmaking began with *Homo habilis* about 2.5 million years ago. This very important development marks the beginning of the Paleolithic *(pay lee oh LIHTH ihk)* Age, or Old Stone Age, which scientists believe ended between 10,000 and 7,000 years ago on most continents.

The discovery of Stone Age tools has given us clues to the Paleolithic culture. You can find other clues to our past by studying geology. ■

The Ice Age

Geologists—scientists who study the earth—have learned that at times in our planet's history, huge sheets of ice and snow called **glaciers** covered large areas of the earth. Today, in the Northern Hemisphere, glaciers cover parts of Alaska, Canada, Scandinavia, and the Soviet Union. However, thousands of years ago, glaciers extended from the North Pole southward into the middle latitudes of North America, Europe, and Asia. Glaciers also covered parts of South America, Africa, New Zealand, and Australia.

From about 2.5 million years ago until about 12,000 years ago, glaciers advanced and retreated

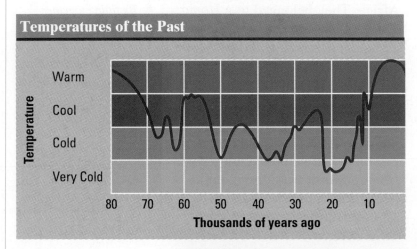

Temperatures of the Past

Temperature: Warm, Cool, Cold, Very Cold

Thousands of years ago: 80 70 60 50 40 30 20 10

▲ *Note the wide variations in temperature shown on the graph above.*

➤ *Glaciers still exist in very cold parts of the world. Glaciers form when snow falls year after year but only partially melts. This melted snow then becomes ice. As more snow falls, the glacier gets larger and heavier, causing it to move.*

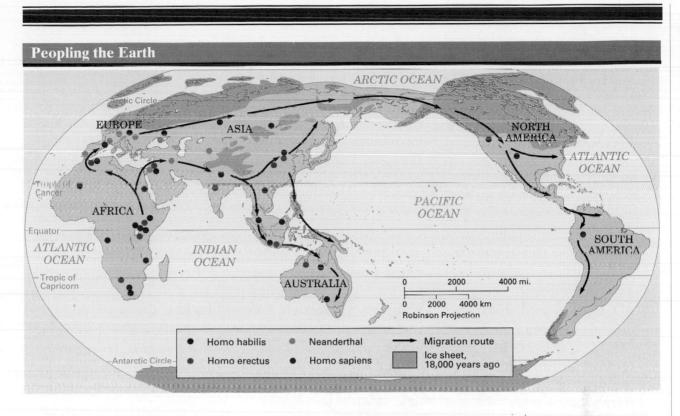

across the surface of the earth. This period was called the Ice Age. However, it included warmer periods as well as periods of intense cold. Each of these periods lasted thousands of years. During cold periods huge glaciers formed. During warmer periods the glaciers melted and retreated.

Adapting to the glacial periods was a challenge for our ancestors. Without a thick coat of fur, they had to find other ways to keep warm. *Homo erectus* learned to make fire. *Homo sapiens* sewed clothing from animal hides.

The glaciers also opened up new worlds for our ancestors. With much of the world's water frozen in these blankets of ice, the level of the oceans dropped dramatically. Land bridges, previously covered by water, emerged. One such land bridge connected Asia with the Americas across what is now the Bering Strait. Land bridges also linked the islands of Southeast Asia with Australia.

Look at the map on this page. Note how these land bridges made it possible for early humans to follow the animals they hunted into new lands. In this way, as the map above shows, our earliest ancestors colonized every continent except Antarctica. ■

▲ *Note how the presence of land bridges allowed early humans to migrate from southern Africa to Europe, Asia, Australia, and the Americas. In 1998, archaeologists found evidence that early humans may have also migrated to the Americas by boat.*

■ *What can geologists tell us about conditions during the Ice Age?*

R E V I E W

1. **FOCUS** What have scientists learned about our earliest ancestors?

2. **CONNECT** What method would archaeologists use to date the remains of Cro-Magnons?

3. **GEOGRAPHY** How did conditions during the Ice Age make it possible for human settlement to spread to new areas?

4. **CRITICAL THINKING** What evidence might scientists have used to discover that *Homo erectus* was able to make fires?

5. **ACTIVITY** Make a poster or a three-dimensional scene showing how people adapted to the cold temperatures of the Ice Age.

95

The Depths of Time

Organizing Fossil Finds

Here's Why

A table is one way to organize information so that it is clear and easy to read. Bus schedules, television listings, and team standings are usually presented in table form. Suppose you want to get a quick overall picture of where evidence of early humans has been found. Making a table can help you organize that information.

Here's How

Look at the table below. Read the title. It tells you what kind of information the table contains. The table shows when and where some of the evidence of early humans has been found.

The information is arranged in rows and columns. Rows run across the table; columns run down the table. Look at the headings at the top of each column—Type, Location, Year, Discoverer. A heading tells what kind of facts is in each column.

Suppose you want to know where evidence of *Australopithecus* has been found. Look in the column headed "Type" to find *Australopithecus*. You will find two entries for *Australopithecus* because evidence of *Australopithecus* has been found in at least two locations. Then move across to the column headed "Location." Now you have the information: evidence of *Australopithecus* sites has been found in Taung, South Africa, and in Hadar, Ethiopia.

Continue across to the "Year" column. The two dates are 1924 and 1974. Where was the evidence of *Australopithecus* found first?

Has all evidence of early humans been found in the same part of the world? By reading down the column headed "Location," you can quickly see that discoveries have been made in many different places.

Try It

Make a table comparing *Homo habilis, Homo erectus,* and *Homo sapiens.* Use the following terms as column headings: Time Period, Physical Development, and Location. Use the information presented in this chapter to help you fill in the table.

Apply It

Make a table showing a week's homework assignments. What title will you use? What will the column headings be? How can you use the table?

Evidence of Early Humans

Type	Location	Year	Discoverer
Australopithecus	Taung, South Africa	1924	Raymond Dart
Australopithecus	Hadar, Ethiopia	1974	Donald Johanson
Homo erectus	Trinil (Java), Indonesia	1891	Eugène Dubois
Homo heidelbergensis	Terra Amata, France	1965	Henry de Lumley
Neanderthal	Neander Valley, Germany	1856	Johann Fuhlroyt and Herman Schaaffhausen
Neanderthal	Shanidar, Iraq	1953	Ralph Solecki
Homo sapiens (Cro-Magnon)	Altamira, Spain	1879	Marcelino de Sautuola
Homo sapiens (Cro-Magnon)	Lascaux Cave, France	1940	Henri Breuil
Homo sapiens	Kwazulu, South Africa	1972	C. Powell and P. Beaumont

LESSON 2

The Development of Culture

Imagine you could be moved back in time about two million years to the plains of eastern Africa. You find yourself settled on the shores of a large, quiet lake. Resting under the shade of a tree, you soak up the unfamiliar landscape.

Hours pass, and you begin to get hungry. At home, you might have gone to the kitchen for a snack. What will you do here on the plains of ancient Africa? You search along the lake shore for food but collect only a few sour berries. How will you survive?

Two naked persons walk down to the lake not far from you. Your only hope of survival is to make friends with them. You put on a friendly smile and walk towards them.

Their first reaction to you is to laugh. Giggling, they point at your clothes and shoes. You point to your open mouth to show them you are hungry. They nod, talk to each other in a strange language, and motion for you to wait.

One person walks off toward a field. The other person picks up two rocks and begins striking one

THINKING FOCUS

Why were toolmaking and language important for the development of human culture?

Key Term

- technology

◄ *The lush lands of eastern Africa were a place where early humans lived.*

against the other, to make a sharp edge. Soon the first person returns with a bone. The people place it on the ground and pound it with the sharpened stone. They invite you to eat the marrow found inside the bone.

During your imaginary visit, you would come to appreciate the skill your friends possess at finding food. You might also be impressed with the way they are able to make simple tools from the materials at hand to meet their needs.

Making Tools

The earliest flint tools were not complicated, but even these simple stone tools took skill and planning. First, the tool-maker had to choose the right kind of stone. The stone had to be hard enough not to crumble or shatter when struck. However it could not be so hard that it couldn't be chipped.

After finding a suitable stone, the toolmaker had to shape it into a tool. This task was usually done by striking that stone with another stone. By hitting the first stone at different angles, early toolmakers could make different kinds of tools. Even the small flakes that flew from the stone were useful. Their edges were almost as sharp as a razor.

Tools made life easier for early humans. Using tools, people could take advantage of a wider range of food sources. They were no longer limited to what they could kill or gather with their bare hands. With the sharp stone flakes, they could butcher larger animals, such as elephants, rhinos, and hippos. With sharpened pieces of antler, they could dig for underground roots.

Early Tools

As far as we know, *Homo habilis* was the first of our early ancestors to make tools. The stone flakes found with *Homo habilis* fossils date back 2.5 million years.

▼ *Early humans used stones from landscapes similar to the one shown below. A variety of tools could be made from stones like the one at the far right.*

They were probably used for cutting meat.

As humans slowly developed and changed, so did their tools. The tools of *Homo erectus* were more sophisticated than the earlier tools. For example, *Homo erectus* made hand axes that could be used in many ways. Hand axes were mainly used for butchering animals, but the patterns of wear show that they were also used for digging roots and cutting wood.

Early toolmaking marked the dawn of technology. **Technology** includes all the tools, methods, and materials that people use to control and improve their lives.

Homo sapiens' Tools

Homo erectus used the same tool for a variety of purposes. In contrast, early *Homo sapiens* made tools that were used for specific purposes. They made spear points for hunting big animals such as the hippopotamus or the wild ox, and thin scrapers for cleaning hides. They made piercing tools to poke holes in the hides so they could lace the hides together to make simple clothing.

Over thousands of years, *Homo sapiens* learned to make more sophisticated tools. They carved fishhooks, needles, and three-pronged fishing spears from pieces of bone or antlers. Before this time, bone tools were very rare. They even made specific tools for creating other tools. Notice the type of tool the person in A Closer Look on the following page is using to make a harpoon point.

▼ *The spear point, shown below, is an example of the careful workmanship of 18,000 years ago.*

UNDERSTANDING TECHNOLOGY

Think back to your imaginary trip at the beginning of this lesson. Your new friends used a simple tool to obtain food from the inside of a bone.

Hand-axe to Jackhammer

Toolmaking by early humans marked the beginning of technology, the knowledge that people use to fashion tools. Technology can be simple, such as modifying a stone into a hand axe. Or it can be complex, such as shaping steel into a jackhammer.

Importance of Technology

Think of a few ways technology has improved the quality of life throughout history. First, technology can make work easier. If you needed wood, would you rather search for a fallen tree or buzz through an upright tree with a saw?

Second, technology helps people produce more goods. Before the printing press was invented, people had to painstakingly copy books by hand. Books were thus extremely rare and expensive.

Finally, technology can improve people's lives. For instance, personal computers with special features help people who cannot see or hear.

As our technology has changed, our way of life has changed. The earliest hand axe was merely the beginning. Just as early technology allowed humans to hunt and cook in new ways, so too, modern technology has helped us to live and work in different ways.

Toolmaking in Africa

Early African toolmakers used their intelligence and creativity to develop better tools for daily living. For example, in eastern Africa, archaeologists have found different kinds of harpoon points made only with stone and bone. As you read, notice what other materials were used to improve the lives of the early African people.

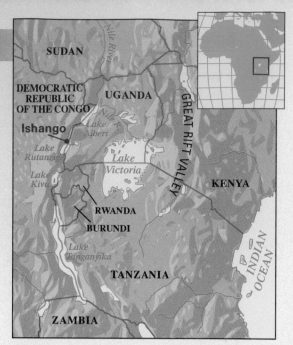

These 20,000 year-old harpoon points are shown at actual size. They were used to spear a type of fish called tilapia. The person throwing the harpoon pulled in the fish by a cord attached to one end of the point.

Ishango, where the harpoon points were found, is located on the shores of Lake Rutanzige, in what is presently the Democratic Republic of the Congo. The people of Ishango also may have made boats or rafts to go out on the lake to fish.

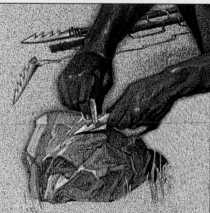

To make harpoon points, the toolmaker ground a piece of an antelope bone into a point. Next, the toolmaker cut into the side with a sharp quartz stone to make triangular teeth. Then, the toolmaker put notches at the tail end to fasten a cord to the harpoon point.

Ostrich Eggs as Tools and Jewels African toolmakers fashioned broken bits of ostrich shells into flat beads with holes in the center. The beads were strung together and worn as jewelry. Empty ostrich egg shells could have been used by ancient humans to carry water.

Importance of Tools

With more than a hundred kinds of tools, the Cro-Magnons and other modern humans were able to take full advantage of their surroundings. They thrived in all different parts of the world, from the frozen Arctic to the tropical jungles. *Homo sapiens* had a tool kit that fitted their environment. For example, tools in Asia may have been made of bamboo. Archaeologists have not found all the tools used in Asia. Bamboo, though hard, could not survive many thousands of years.

Tools helped *Homo sapiens* make contact with each other. Different families became trading partners as they traded their tools and ornaments.

The ability to make tools was a key factor in the survival of early humans. Another key factor was the ability of early humans to create and use language. ■

■ *How did early humans make and use tools?*

Using Language

People often communicate with one another without using language. For example, when you smile, cry, or shrug your shoulders, you are communicating. Indeed, all animals communicate in one way or another. Humans, however, are the only animals that can communicate through language. When you use language, you can talk about the past or the future. You can discuss real things or imaginary things. You can even invent new words.

When did your early ancestors develop their ability to use language? No one knows for certain. However, scientists have learned that specific parts of the brain are involved in using language. Fossil skulls of *Homo habilis, Homo erectus,* and early *Homo sapiens* show that the parts of the human brain important for language became larger over time. Therefore, scientists conclude that humans have had an increasing ability to create and use language beginning around 2.5 million years ago. This language may have been slower and simpler than ours.

Why was language important to early humans? Language allowed them to share information, to work together, and to pass on their traditions. With language, early humans could discuss the advantages of different kinds of tools or plan hunting strategies. In other words, the ability to use language spurred the development of early human culture. ■

■ *Why was language important to early humans?*

R E V I E W

1. **FOCUS** Why were toolmaking and language important for the development of human culture?

2. **CONNECT** Discuss how tools changed over time, beginning with the tools developed by *Homo habilis* and ending with those used by the *Homo sapiens.* How did this change in tools correspond to a change in brain size?

3. **HISTORY** How did tools help early humans survive?

4. **CULTURE** How is language more complex than other forms of animal communication?

5. **CRITICAL THINKING** How might an increasing ability to use language have affected the early humans' abilities to make tools?

6. **ACTIVITY** Invent a tool that will help you do something more easily. Make a drawing of the tool. Explain how the tool will be used and what it is made of.

101

Attar

Leonard Wibberley

Hunting for food was serious business for early humans. In this selection from Attar of the Ice Valley, *a young boy finds an unexpected hunting partner. His discovery changes how he and his descendants hunt wild animals.*

Attar began to see that the dungo had in fact been hunting with him rather than on his own. There was enough in the dungo's actions to suggest that it had deliberately driven the rua to where Attar had been hiding.

This was so great a wonder for Attar that he could scarcely believe it. Was it possible that there could be a lasting comradeship between a man and a dungo? Was it possible that they could help each other to get food, for the speed of the dungo would be of great aid in running down game? It often happened that a spear wounded an animal and then the man who had thrown the spear had to trail the animal, sometimes for days, before his prey was sufficiently exhausted for him to catch and kill it. But if he, Attar, could wound an animal and then the dungo could bring it down and kill it, the whole art of hunting would be changed.

These ideas came to him unbidden and greatly excited him. If this was so—if this new way of hunting was what the Great Bear had planned to bring about—there was one point that had to be made clear. The point was this: that the man was the master and director of the hunt and the dungo would be the assistant. The dungo must not get the idea that he was master and the man the assistant.

Watching the dungo gorging itself on the rua, Attar knew that he must assert his mastery. "Move," he cried. "That is my kill." And he took the butt end of his spear and brought it down sharply over the dungo's rump. The dungo howled, snarled, and backed away, but only an inch or two.

"Off," cried Attar. "Away. The rua is mine."

The dungo snarled and, made brave by the smell of the blood, crouched to leap at Attar despite its injured leg. Attar brought the shaft of the spear down sharply again on the animal's back. This time it yelped and moved away and, settling down on the snow, glared at Attar from yellow eyes full of anger.

"Farther," said Attar. "Move back more." He feinted as if to clout the dingo again, and without waiting for the blow, it slunk back in the snow.

"Good," said Attar. "Now you can eat. But it is I who feed you. You do not feed me." He took one of the snow rabbits he had killed and threw it at the dungo. The dungo disposed of the rabbit in three tearing gulps.

"That will do you," said Attar. "You will have more of the rua later. I myself have eaten nothing for two days." He was, in fact, so hungry that he trembled. With the edge of his spear, he cut a sliver of neck meat from the rua and ate it. It was delicious and immediately gave him strength. He cut another strip of the tender meat and that tasted just as good.

The dungo came bellying closer to him, its lips curled back a little, baring its teeth. Attar hit it on the nose, firmly but not savagely, with his spear shaft. The dungo moved back, yelping. Then Attar cut him a piece of meat and gave it to him. This time, having disposed of the meat with one gulp, the dungo moved its large tail slowly from side to side. Attar moved to place himself between the rua and the dungo and reached out a hand to pat the dungo on the head. The dungo not only accepted the pat but gave Attar's hand a brief lick.

"You and I, then, will hunt together, dungo," said Attar. "It is a wonder and something that has never been heard of before. But it is plain that by killing Black Ear I have become bound to you. This has been the plan of the Great Bear."

It was not Teth and Gurth who came to help Attar carry the carcass of the rua, but Odo, a young hunter not much older than Attar himself. He was especially skillful in catching birds and small animals and very good-natured. Everybody liked him because he was willing. Also, he could make very fine sounds by blowing through the hollow thighbone of a deer in which he had cut a hole in a special place.

The sounds he made were like the wind in all its differing moods—the morning wind and the night wind, which are quite different from each other, and also the wind of summer and that of winter; or to put it another way, which was the way Attar and his people put it, the wind of the flowers and the wind of the ice. All these varieties of sounds Odo could make on the thighbone of the deer. Although others could produce some sounds from it, none could do it with the accuracy and delicacy of Odo. For this, then, as well as his other qualities, he was very popular in his tribe, and nobody grumbled at him that he captured only small animals and birds when he went hunting.

As he approached Attar, however, he saw the dungo sitting in the snow beyond the rua and he stopped immediately. He surveyed the scene for a moment and then said softly to Attar, his

feint   to fake an attack

carcass   the dead body of an animal

103

eyes on the dungo, "I will move behind him, and when he turns his head to watch me, take him in the chest with your spear."

Attar laughed. "Welcome, Odo," he said. "Meet my new hunting mate. Mikdoo." He made up the name Mikdoo on the spur of the moment, and it was entirely suitable, for it meant Son of the Black One.

"If you run hunting with such as that," said Odo, "you will soon be in the miserable Cave of the Bear." He started to back away, frightened. "He has bitten you, Attar, and made you into a dungo like himself. That has happened before."

"No, Odo," said Attar. "He has not bitten me. See. We are friends." He reached down and touched the dungo's ears. The mane of thicker hair on the dungo's shoulders was bristling because of the presence of Odo, but it still permitted Attar to touch it. "I will tell you all about it," said Attar, and did so, without elaboration.

"You see, then, how it is," he concluded. "This is now my dungo. But let us get the rua up to the cave, where Huru will tell us if such a thing has ever happened before."

"First send the dungo away," said Odo.

"I cannot," said Attar. "His own people will not have him. I have touched him. He has my scent on him. They will tear him to pieces if he approaches them."

"Attar," said Odo. "You also have the scent of the dungo on you. I do not know if the others are going to agree with your pact with the dungo."

Attar shrugged. "We will see what will happen," he said. "This is not something I decided. It is something that was decided for me. Come, let us pick up the rua."

They slung the carcass on their spears and set off for the cave. The going was hard because the strange warm wind that had followed the storm had melted the snow, which was soft in many places where a few hours before it had been firm. Also, the weight of the rua made them sink even in the firmer places. They had not gone far before they were both sweating.

They sweated not only from the weight of the deer but from the warmth of the wind, which had started fitfully and was now blowing gently but evenly down from the ice cliffs. On the top of the cliffs themselves, three thousand feet above the floor of the valley, the air was colder than ever. But this mass of cold air, being heavy, tumbled down the cliff face and, in so doing, warmed up, so that the wind on the valley floor was like the south wind of summer. It first softened the snow and then melted it.

The two young hunters were two hours getting the rua back to the cave, and in that time a river of melted snow formed and was flowing over the still frozen surface of the true river down the center of the valley. High up on the cliffs, the terrible pendants

pendant something hanging from something else

of ice still draped the valley sides. Lower down, the black face of rocks began to show through the shroud of snow and ice.

A matting of drab brown grass and undergrowth appeared here and there, and from first one side of the valley and then the other came a rumbling growl, angry and deep. Masses of snow thundered downward to the valley in horrifying avalanches. It was, in fact, dangerous to be traveling along the valley, and Odo and Attar moved as fast as they could to get to the safety of the cave before they were cut off or trapped by a moving mass of snow.

All the while Mikdoo, the dungo, followed along, snarling at the avalanches, limping from his wound, and thoroughly uncomfortable because of the wetness of his coat, now drenched with melted snow. Mikdoo did not follow close. He kept some distance away and several times stopped as if debating whether to follow farther. But follow he did. Once, however, he stopped on a small knoll in the bottom of the valley and turned to where his home lay. Lifting his snout, he gave a long, mournful howl, either of pleading to be allowed to return or of farewell. Whatever the message, it was not answered, and Mikdoo started once again to follow Attar.

A decision had been made. Mikdoo would hunt with men in the future. He would lose his old freedom but gain security. For him and his descendants, there was no way back.

knoll a small rounded hill or mound

Further Reading

The Ice Is Coming. Patricia Wrightson. This fantasy takes place in present-day Australia, but the hero, an aborigine boy, must adopt the lifestyle of his prehistoric ancestors to prevent a second Ice Age.

Light in the Mountain. Margaret J. Anderson. Surviving in a harsh and cold climate is a challenge for the early Maori people of New Zealand.

Prehistory. Keith Branigan. Using evidence from early archaeological sites, the author recreates the food, technology, society, and religion of prehistoric peoples.

The Way Home. Joan Phipson. Three children, lost in the Australian Outback after an accident, travel between the present and the prehistoric time of early Aborigines while finding their way home.

						B.C.	A.D.
3,500,000	3,000,000	2,500,000	2,000,000	1,500,000	1,000,000		

750,000   12,000

LESSON 3

Hunters and Gatherers

**THINKING
FOCUS**

*How did human culture
develop from the time of
Homo heidelbergensis to
the time of the Cro-
Magnons?*

Key Terms

- hunter-gatherer
- band

▼ *Fire played an impor-
tant role in the lives of
Homo heidelbergensis,
allowing them to live in
cold climates, hunt large
animals, and cook plant
foods.*

A group of people sit in a circle around a large campfire. The leaping flames light up their faces, which shine with warmth and pleasure. A master storyteller has captured their attention with a fascinating tale. He is reciting a legend about a magic hunter who can transform himself into the animals he hunts. The storyteller's voice falls softly as he comes to the end of the story. The people sitting around the campfire are still and peaceful. The only other sounds are the crackle of the fire and the howl of a lone wolf baying in the distance.

The scene described in the paragraph above could have taken place at a present-day outing in northern Michigan. Or it could just as easily have taken place at a campsite along the shores of the Mediterranean Sea 400,000 years ago. Since prehistoric times, people have enjoyed gathering together around the light and the warmth of campfires. However, for early humans, fire was much more than a source of comfort—it was essential for survival.

Early Fire Users

For hundreds of thousands of years during the glacial periods of the Ice Age, the climate in most of the Northern Hemisphere was much colder than it is today. Southern Europe, which now has a warm climate, was as cold as northern Alaska is today. To survive in this harsh world, people had to learn how to use fire. *Homo erectus* was the first to control fire. There is evidence that groups of *Homo heidelbergensis* who lived in the colder parts of Europe knew the advantages of building fires, too.

Hunting and Gathering

Fire was important for many reasons. It provided warmth and scared off animals. Early people also used fire to cook plant foods to make them easier to digest.

By studying these fire pits and other remains, archaeologists have learned a lot about how *Homo heidelbergensis* lived. Like all other Paleolithic peoples, these early humans were **hunter-gatherers**. That is, they hunted wild animals and gathered wild plants.

Homo heidelbergensis lived in **bands**—small, loosely organized groups of perhaps 20 to 30 individuals. During the year, they moved over a wide area, searching for ripe plants and following migrating animals. Evidence from sites in Spain indicates that groups of *Homo heidelbergensis* worked together to drive large animals, such as elephants, rhinos, and wild oxen, into traps. Coordinating such group hunting must have required some type of social organization and probably some type of language.

Women as Gatherers

The women in hunter-gatherer groups probably had children to care for much of their lives. For that reason, it is likely that women would not be running after buffalo, but instead might be gathering shellfish or food plants. Women could also skin animals, prepare food, and make clothes and baskets, while caring for children.

Let's visit a site called Terra Amata on the Mediterranean coast of southern France. Here *Homo heidelbergensis* set up a camp every spring for several years in a row.

Terra Amata

Early humans camped on this spot, where the modern city of Nice, France, now stands. The first thing archaeologists found at Terra Amata was the foundation of a hut large enough to sleep about 20 people. The hut was most likely built of sturdy branches, with stones around the base of the hut for support.

At the center of the hut, archaeologists found the remains of a fire pit. Small stones on one side of the fire pit shielded the fire from the wind. The people of Terra Amata might have slept on animal hides near the pit, huddled close to the fire for warmth. Near the fire pit was a flat stone. The people of Terra Amata probably used this hard surface for shaping their tools. Stone flakes were scattered all around the area. These flakes flew off rocks as people chipped them into tools.

A second flat stone in another corner of the hut probably served as a cutting board for meat. The surface of this stone had many small scratches, and animal bones were strewn all around. From

▼ *Oval huts built at Terra Amata by visiting hunters probably looked something like this.*

Work space

Work space

Work space

Hearth

Residents of Terra Amata ate a number of different kinds of foods, including almonds, plants, and oysters.

■ *Based on evidence from Terra Amata, describe how* Homo heidelbergensis *lived.*

these bones archaeologists learned what kinds of meat the people of Terra Amata ate. Deer was the most common meat, but they also ate many other types of animals, including elephants, oysters, and turtles.

By studying the layers of sand, archaeologists learned that Terra Amata was occupied for only a few days or a week at a time. If people had stayed there longer, the sand would have been more packed down. The layers also show that people came back and rebuilt their huts at Terra Amata year after year.

Because the area around Terra Amata was rich in resources, it was a good place to live. The land teemed with animals for hunting. People gathered dandelion leaves, wild wheat, almonds, figs, berries and quail eggs. They could spear salmon in the rivers and harvest seafood from the Mediterranean Sea. Fresh water bubbled up from a nearby spring. It's no wonder that *Homo heidelbergensis* returned to Terra Amata again and again.

If you visit Terra Amata today, you might be shocked. All you would see are modern buildings, several stories high, surrounded by busy streets. So, how do we know what Terra Amata looked like? Archaeologists studied Terra Amata before the apartment buildings went up.

Human life changed very little during the 500,000 years that *Homo heidelbergensis* roamed the earth. Sometime thereafter, the Neanderthals appeared. Although the Neanderthal people still lived as hunter-gatherers, their culture became more complex, The community became more important to them. ■

The Neanderthals: Community Builders

In the summer of 1856, workers blasted open a cave in the cliffs bordering the Neander Valley in Germany. The cave was a quarry, rich in limestone. It was also rich in fossils. However, the workers weren't interested in old bones. They saved a few bones to show the quarry owner but chopped up most of the fossils as they dug out the limestone.

The quarry owner showed the bones to a local schoolteacher, who eventually showed them to an anatomist. (An anatomist studies the structure of humans.) This fossil was named Neanderthal, after the valley where it was found. Neanderthal fossils were found later as far east as Israel and Iraq.

Early Studies

False conclusions based upon the Neanderthal fossil have led to many misconceptions. Archaeologists who first studied the Neanderthal fossil concluded that these were brutish people with little intelligence and bad posture. However, these archaeologists made some mistakes. Careful study of Neanderthal skulls has shown that, on average, the Neanderthal brain was at least as large as that of modern humans. They had the intelligence they needed to adapt to the cold, harsh environment of central Europe.

Reexamination of other bones has shown that, in general, Neanderthal posture was just as good as that of modern humans. However, some Neanderthals suffered from the disease called arthritis. The first archaeologists who studied the Neanderthal fossils failed to recognize the signs of this disease. That is why they incorrectly described all Neanderthals as stoop-shouldered people with bowed legs.

Community Spirit

The camps Neanderthals built were generally larger than those *Homo heidelbergensis* built. This indicates that Neanderthals probably lived in larger groups—perhaps 20 to 50 people—and stayed in one place longer.

The Neanderthals probably had a strong sense of community and took care of one another. The evidence for this is in the Neanderthals' bones. As you have read, fossils of aged Neanderthals show that some were crippled with arthritis. These people would not have survived unless other people helped them and gave them food.

Other examples of this community spirit are even more dramatic.

At Shanidar cave in present-day Iraq, archaeologists found the skeleton of a man with an injury that paralyzed the right side of his body. This handicapped man was probably one of the oldest people in his community when he died at age 40. Members of his community must have taken care of him. Perhaps he was valued for his wisdom, knowledge, or sense of humor, even though he could not have hunted or gathered food.

Shanidar cave also provides information about other aspects of Neanderthal culture, including burials. These Neanderthal burials are the earliest evidence we have of funeral ceremonies held to mourn the passing away of loved ones. For instance, at Shanidar, a man was buried on a bed of wildflowers gathered from nearby fields.

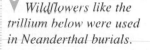

▼ *Wildflowers like the trillium below were used in Neanderthal burials.*

◄ *These remains of a Neanderthal youth may be 50,000 years old. They were found in Kebara cave in modern Israel.*

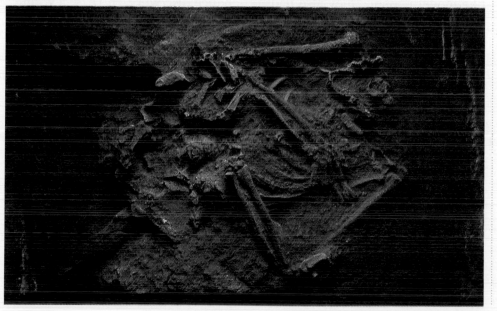

The Depths of Time

At a grave in France, a teenage boy was found buried in a pit. He was lying on his right side with his head on his forearm and a pillow of flints. A stone axe and the bones of wild cattle were near his hand. The bones may be all that remain of an offering of meat placed in the pit at the time of burial. The axe and the meat suggest the Neanderthals had some belief in a life after death in which the boy would need the food and the trusted tool.

The burial sites at Shanidar show that some similarities exist between certain burial customs of the Neanderthals and the customs of some modern peoples. These similarities indicate that both early and modern humans probably have many of the same feelings about death. But however much we share with the Neanderthals, we have even more in common with our direct ancestors, the *Homo sapiens*. ■

Cro-Magnons: Modern Humans

▼ *Cro-Magnons used spear throwers, like the one pictured here, to enable them to throw spears faster and further. A hunter would put the dull end of the spear in the hook on top of the spear thrower. Holding the thrower over his head, he would then snap his arm forward. Such a thrower would greatly improve his ability to hunt animals.*

About 30,000 years ago, the Neanderthals died out. Cro-Magnons and other *Homo sapiens*, however, survived. The Cro-Magnons looked much like people today. In fact, if Cro-Magnons could come back to life dressed in modern clothes, you might not be able to pick them out from a crowd.

Cro-Magnon Life

Cro-Magnons not only looked like modern people, they also had a lifestyle similar to that of modern hunter-gatherers. They used some of the same tools: nets for fishing, spear throwers for launching spears, and probably even bows and arrows. These tools were much more advanced than those of the Neanderthals. With these, the Cro-Magnons became better hunters.

Cave Paintings

The clearest sign of the Cro-Magnons' advanced culture, however, was their art. They carved designs in their tools. They whittled small sculptures

of female figures out of bone, ivory, and antlers. Women wove string skirts. The Cro-Magnon painted graceful pictures of animals on cave walls. These cave paintings are so beautiful and look so much like modern paintings, that when the famous artist Pablo Picasso saw them for the first time he exclaimed, "We [modern artists] have invented nothing!"

As with many other important archaeological finds, the first cave paintings came to the attention of the modern world through a chance discovery. In 1879, a young Spanish girl and her father, Marcelino de Sautuola, were exploring a cave in northern Spain where Sautuola had found some stone tools. Sautuola had to crawl on his hands and knees to squeeze through some of the cave's narrow side chambers.

However, his daughter, Maria, was only five years old and short enough to walk through these tight passages. Maria wandered into one chamber, looked up, and saw a herd of life-sized bison painted on the ceiling. She called to her father to come see the lifelike paintings.

Sautuola was amazed by the ancient paintings. He showed them to an archaeologist, who was also very impressed. However, many other archaeologists did not believe that the cave paintings were real. One even accused Sautuola of paying an artist to paint the animals in the cave. Disgraced and disillusioned, Sautuola had the cave closed up and spoke no more about the paintings.

However, over the next 30 years, archaeologists discovered a number of caves in France with paintings similar to those found in Sautuola's cave. Research showed that these paintings, as well as those discovered by Sautuola, were authentic ancient art, painted between 12,000 and 35,000 years ago.

Some of the most stunning paintings were discovered in 1940 in a French cave called Lascaux. Four boys were playing in a forest when their dog disappeared down a hole. One of the boys lowered himself carefully down the hole to

The French government closed the Lascaux caves in 1963 because the visitors' breath was destroying the Paleolithic masterpieces. In 1983, the French opened a copy of the cave, called Lascaux II. In this artificial cave, artists copied the paintings using the same techniques the Cro-Magnon artists used.

◄ *Cro-Magnon artists covered the ceiling of the entrance to the Lascaux caves, shown at left, with vivid paintings of animals. The drawing below shows the entrance to the cave.*

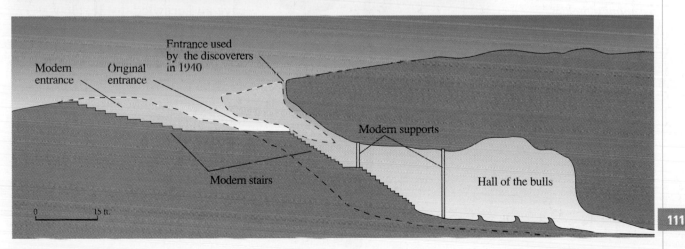

Modern entrance

Original entrance

Entrance used by the discoverers in 1940

Modern supports

Modern stairs

Hall of the bulls

0   15 ft.

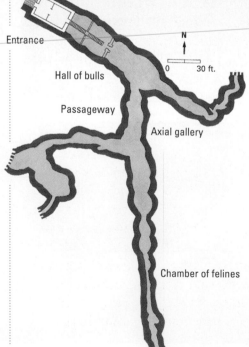

The paintings in the hall of the bulls, shown above, vividly illustrate the animals hunted by Cro-Magnons. Note how the artists have used color to highlight the details of the animals' bodies.

The overhead diagram of the Lascaux caves, shown at right, illustrates how large the caves are.

Entrance

Hall of bulls

Passageway

N

0   30 ft.

Axial gallery

Chamber of felines

fetch the dog. When the boy returned, he was shaking. He thought he'd seen ghosts of wild animals. The next day the boys told their schoolmaster what they had found. The schoolmaster returned to the cave and crawled inside. He was astonished by what he saw. Huge, lifelike images of horses, deer, and bison covered the damp walls.

Examine these cave paintings. To see them as the Cro-Magnons did, you must imagine walking through the long, twisting passages of a dark cave. The air smells dank and moisture drips down the walls. A torch casts looming shadows in front of you, and the air is thick with smoke. You enter a large

chamber, your footsteps echoing as you walk to the center of the room. Animated by the flickering light, bulls and deer seem to leap across the walls.

Perhaps these paintings played a part in hunting rituals of the Cro-Magnons. Modern hunting peoples sometimes draw pictures of animals and stab them as a way of bringing luck in the real hunt. The Cro-Magnons were probably trying to gain greater control of their unpredictable world by painting wild animals on cave walls. Magic rituals involving these paintings may have been an important part of Cro-Magnon life, because survival hinged on a successful hunt.

In time, as early people learned to tame animals and plant crops, their world became more predictable. They no longer had to rely on the magic of the paintings.

We will never know exactly what the cave paintings meant to the Cro-Magnons. Nevertheless, we can appreciate the artistic skill of the people who made these paintings. The paintings show us that the Cro-Magnons had a strong feeling for beauty and a sense of wonder like our own. Use the chart on page 114 to compare the achievements of Cro-Magnons to those of the other early humans you have learned about in this chapter. ■

■ *Why do we call the Cro-Magnons modern humans?*

Achievements of Early Humans

	Homo habilis, 2,500,000–1,500,000 years ago	Homo erectus, 1,800,000–200,000 years ago	Neanderthal 230,000–30,000 years ago	Homo sapiens 130,000 years ago–present
Tools	Crude stone tools, 2,500,000 years ago	Hand-axe, 1,500,000 years ago	Side scraper, 100,000 years ago	Bone harpoon with barbs, 12,000 years ago
Fire	No evidence	Controlled fire by 400,000 years ago	Used fire to keep warm	Fired clay, 27,000 years ago
Burial Rites	No evidence	No evidence	Planned burial, 50,000 years ago	Bead blanket at burial, 23,000 years ago
Art	No evidence	No evidence	Used colors to decorate themselves	Bison sculpture, 14,000 years ago

R E V I E W

1. **FOCUS** How did human culture develop from the time of *Homo heidelbergensis* to the time of Cro-Magnons?

2. **CONNECT** How has our picture of the Neanderthals changed with more careful study of early human remains?

3. **HISTORY** Which early humans first used fire, and why was fire such an important discovery?

4. **CULTURE** What evidence do we have of Cro-Magnons' advanced culture?

5. **CRITICAL THINKING** What are some stereotypes of "cavemen"? Based on what you have learned in this chapter, do you think these stereotypes are true? Explain your answer.

6. **WRITING ACTIVITY** Write a short story about a day at Terra Amata, Neander, Shanidar, or Lascaux. Set it in prehistoric times. Give your story a main character. Include a description of several events. Explain how your main character feels about the things that happen in his or her life.

Recognizing Patterns

Here's Why

Writers organize material in different patterns according to their purpose. To explain how to do something, writers may organize material in steps. To show how events relate to one another, they may use a cause-and-effect pattern. To make differences and similarities clear, a compare/contrast pattern is often used.

You will more easily understand the material you read if you can recognize the organizational pattern used.

You can then use the same pattern as you take notes.

Here's How

The paragraphs below describe two methods that archaeologists use to date fossils and artifacts. The paragraphs are organized in a compare/contrast pattern.

Several clues tell you that these paragraphs follow a compare/contrast pattern. The first sentence tells you that you will be reading about two things—radiocarbon dating and potassium-

argon dating. The second sentence provides a clue to the organizational pattern: the phrase *but how they are used differs* tells you that you will be reading about differences in the two methods.

Now read the remaining paragraphs. Each paragraph describes one of the dating methods. Look at the notebook page below. The notes show how you can use the compare/contrast pattern to organize these ideas in your notebook.

Try It

Copy the sample notes from the notebook onto a sheet of paper. Then add information to each column about the time limit of each dating method.

Apply It

Find an example of this same organizational pattern in another textbook. Take notes that show the compare/contrast pattern.

Radiocarbon and potassium-argon dating are two methods used by scientists to determine the age of fossils and artifacts. Both methods determine age based on the decay of radioactive elements, but how they are used differs.

Radiocarbon dating measures the breakdown of an organic material, carbon-14. Thus it is used to establish the age of once-living things—wood, bones, and shells. Using radiocarbon dating, scientists can determine the age of objects up to 60,000 years old.

Unlike radiocarbon dating, potassium-argon dating is used to determine the age of inorganic material, usually volcanic rocks. Fossil remains found in the rock are then dated according to the age of the rock. This method is not accurate for objects less than 500,000 years old. However, it can be used to determine the age of objects up to 10 million years old.

	Radiocarbon Dating	Potassium-Argon Dating
Purpose:	To determine age	To determine age
Method:	measures breakdown of carbon-14	Dates fossils by age of rock
Time limit:		

Chapter Review

Reviewing Key Terms

band (p. 107) hunter-gatherer (p. 106)
glacier (p. 94) technology (p. 99)

A. Suppose you are an early human who has traveled forward in time to the present. You can speak English now. While talking to a person from the twentieth century, you want to explain what the following three words mean. On your own paper, write one or two sentences to describe each key term.

1. glacier
2. band
3. hunter-gatherer

B. Some of the following statements are true. The rest are false. Write *True* or *False* for each statement. Then rewrite the false statements to make them true.

1. Because the earth used to be warmer, glaciers covered nearly 30 percent of the earth's surface, more than today.
2. Trying to cut wood with a rock instead of a hand axe showed progress.
3. *Homo heidelbergensis* may have organized themselves in bands to hunt better.
4. Hunter-gatherers would enjoy sitting around and listening to stories.

Exploring Concepts

A. The diagram below should show three groups of early humans belonging to genus *Homo*. The names of two are filled in. Copy the diagram, and fill in the name of the third group. Then add to the diagram three traits, inventions, or other features of each group.

B. Support each statement with facts and details from the chapter.

1. If you look at fossil bones from early human ancestors, you will find clues about what they looked like and what their habits were.
2. You could easily tell apart the skulls of australopithecines, *Homo sapiens,* and Neanderthals.
3. People have made and used tools from *Homo habilis* through *Homo sapiens,* but the tools and their uses have changed very much.
4. Glaciers made it possible for our ancestors to cross areas that are now under water.
5. Choosing the right stone was important to the early toolmakers.
6. Language is related to the development of culture.
7. *Homo erectus* was the first early human to leave Africa.
8. There were many differences between Neanderthals and *Homo sapiens.*

Reviewing Skills

1. On a separate sheet of paper, copy the table Early Toolmakers. Then fill in the appropriate facts under each heading.
2. After completing the table, answer the following questions: Which tool was used for several different purposes? Which tools were made for specific purposes?
3. Review the section Modern Humans on pages 93 and 94. Then do the following:
   a. Tell what organizational pattern the author uses.
   b. Use that organizational pattern to take notes on the section.
4. Suppose you are preparing a bulletin board display that shows how much of the earth was covered by glaciers 20,000 years ago and how much is covered by glaciers today. Trace a map of the earth to make two copies and color in the appropriate areas. In what kind of book will you find the map?

Early Toolmakers		
Type	Tools Used	Purpose
Homo habilis		
Homo erectus		
Homo sapiens		

Using Critical Thinking

1. To our ancestors, fire was more than a source of heat; it was essential for survival. Do we need fire to survive today, or have other energy sources replaced fire for our everyday needs? Explain your answer. Give specific examples of other methods or materials necessary for survival today.
2. Ancient hunter-gatherers lived very well in some areas, such as Terra Amata. There were plenty of fish, animals for hunting, leaves and berries, and fresh drinking water. How would they live in your area if all the modern conveniences and inventions were not there?
3. Scientists know that Cro-Magnons lived in huts lined with animal furs. Scientists also believe that they may have lived in caves sometimes. What evidence is reported in this chapter that supports scientists' ideas about Cro-Magnons?

Preparing for Citizenship

1. **WRITING ACTIVITY** Imagine you are going back in time to observe a group of early humans. Choose the time period and one of these early human groups to observe: *Homo erectus,* Neanderthal, or Cro-Magnon. Now hide behind a rock, listen, and watch the early humans go about their daily lives. What kinds of tasks are they doing? Are the tasks helping to make their lives easier, more comfortable, or somehow better? How similar are their tasks to the jobs that we perform today? How are they different from jobs we perform today? Write down your observations and share them with the class.

2. **COLLABORATIVE LEARNING** Plan and create a display called "Tools of Yesterday and Today." Show early tools and the modern tools that grew out of them. Divide the class into groups of four. Then have each group choose two early tools and two modern tools to draw or make from clay. Choose early tools made from stone, shell, animal part, or wood. Then form two pairs within your group. The first pair will read about and make the early tools; the second pair will read about and make the modern tools. For each tool, write what it was made of, how it was used, who used it, and when it was used.

Chapter 5

Development of Societies

A handful of seeds and a few captured animals helped start a quiet revolution. Instead of just harvesting wild grains and moving on, hunter-gatherers learned to save some seeds. Now they could plant crops in one place year after year. Instead of just hunting wild animals, they learned to tame them. Groups of hunter-gatherers settled down, becoming farmers and herders. Once they could control their food supply, they began to build villages and then cities.

c. 8500 B.C. Groups of hunter-gatherers settle along the Tigris River in what is now the Middle East and begin farming.

12,500	10,000	7500

11,000 B.C.

c. 8000–7000 B.C. Settlers in Egypt and the Middle East begin planting crops including barley, shown above.

People learned to raise cattle and sheep to provide food and clothing. This sculpture, from about 2600 B.C., shows a milking scene. Today, shepherds like the man in Syria (below) still tend flocks of sheep.

Farmers used stone tools to tend their crops. This hoe found in Egypt dates to between 7000 and 4000 B.C.

c. 3500 B.C. The first cities, such as Ur in present-day Iraq, begin to develop.

5000	2500	B.C.	A.D.

c. 6000 B.C. Improved farming methods lead to larger settlements. One of the largest towns in the Middle East is Çatal Hüyük, with a population of about 5,000.

2000 B.C.

LESSON 1

Learning to Farm

How did people's lifestyle change as they began to domesticate plants and animals?

Key Terms

- surplus
- environment
- domesticate
- agriculture

Imagine yourself standing on a hill overlooking a broad, rich valley. Several gazelles are grazing on tall grasses. A fish breaks the surface of a peaceful lake. Birds are nesting in the dense reeds along the shore. In the air is the spicy smell of evergreen shrubs. You reach down and pick a handful of ripe berries, popping them into your mouth one by one, enjoying their tart flavor.

For you, a hunter-gatherer living in 10,000 B.C., this valley is a wonderful spot. A spring provides fresh, cold water. Wildlife and plants to eat are everywhere. You and your family have camped here since spring when you gathered armful after armful of grain. Food is plentiful in this valley. Perhaps you should stay here all year.

The preceding description is based on the region around Ain Mallaha *(YN MAHL ah hah)*, an archaeological site in the Jordan River Valley. Of course, we can only guess at the thoughts of ancient hunter-gatherers. But the evidence from Ain Mallaha and other sites shows that between about 11,000 and 8,000 B.C., some people in this region began to settle down.

Find Ain Mallaha on the map on page 121. It is located in a green-colored area that's shaped like a crescent. Because this strip of land had particularly good soil, it was given the name Fertile Crescent.

Living in Settled Communities

The trend toward settling down and living in one location also occurred in other places around the globe. But it happened at different times in different places. This change didn't happen overnight with people suddenly switching their lifestyle from wandering to staying put. It all came about gradually. In this chapter you'll learn about sites in the Middle East, one of the first areas where the hunter-gatherers started to settle in villages.

Hunter-gatherers searched for areas where they could hunt game, harvest wild grains, gather berries and nuts, and find tasty plants and roots. Surrounded by plenty of food, they were tempted to stay for months at a time. As they became more attached to one place, they built longer-lasting homes.

The structures at Ain Mallaha give clues to the changing lifestyle of the hunter-gatherers. The picture on the next page shows the remains of one structure. This home was a circular pit, dug well below ground level. Stones covered the dirt walls. The walls that extended above ground and the roof were made of reeds.

Artifacts found in this home show some of the activities that took place inside. Notice the fire pit in the center of the floor where meat and grain were roasted. Look near the fire pit for the mortar, a round object hollowed out in the center. Grain was placed in the mortar and pounded with a blunt tool called a pestle. Both mortar and pestle were made of stone.

Storage bins were kept along the wall. These bins were used for storing the **surplus**, or extra, grain. Surplus grain was important. It was needed for times when food wasn't as plentiful.

Both the mortars and storage bins provided good reasons for the hunter-gatherers to stay permanently in one place. The mortars were much too heavy to carry around. People also didn't want to wander far because intruders might steal their precious surplus from the storage bins. You'll see how these ancient people stored and processed their grain when you read A Closer Look on pages 122 and 123. ∎

Early Settlements in the Middle East, 11,000–8000 B.C.

The Fertile Crescent of ancient times extended through parts of today's Middle East. See the Time/Space Databank to learn what modern countries make up this particular area.

∎ *What conditions allowed some hunter-gatherers to start settling down?*

◀ *Ruins of a hunter-gatherer dwelling at Ain Mallaha in present-day Israel. Nearby are a burial pit and a spring.*

Development of Societies

Taming Animals and Sowing Seeds

How Do We Know?

HISTORY *We learn about food gathering in ancient times from experiments today. Scientist Jack Harlan harvested wild grain in Turkey with a crude sickle like those used by hunter-gatherers 10,000 years ago. He gathered six pounds of wild wheat per hour.*

As the hunter-gatherers began to settle down, they learned more about their **environment**—all the living and nonliving things that made up their surroundings. They observed wild grains in different stages of growth. They noticed the conditions that allowed these grains to thrive. At harvest time, they didn't gather up all the grain. They left some of the plants so their seeds or kernels could drop to the ground and sprout next season, starting a new crop.

Hunter-gatherers also learned more about the habits of the animals they hunted: gazelle, wild sheep, and wild goats. Scientists believe that they might have protected these herds by driving away wolves and other enemies. Then the animals could breed and the herds would grow. In this way, people were learning to have an influence over the plants and animals in their environment.

As people gained greater knowledge, they did even more.

A CLOSER LOOK

Early Food Storage

What can happen to grain that isn't stored properly? It can get smelly and moldy enough to make you sick. As people developed safe ways to harvest, store, and process grain, their inventions helped sprout civilization.

You can't just eat wheat. Wheat and barley have to be changed into a form people can eat. Early farmers learned to cut the grain, separate the usable part from the chaff, and then grind the grain into flour for baking.

Prehistoric people set sharp flint stones in wooden handles and used them to cut grain. If they didn't work fast, wild birds would eat all the grain.

The hunter-gatherers searched the countryside, taking seeds from wild grain and other edible plants. Then they sowed these seeds and grew their own plants closer to home. They learned to save enough seeds so they could re-plant the same plants the next season. They also captured wild cattle, sheep, goats, and pigs and tamed them. Slowly, people learned how to control both the growth and the behavior of plants and animals. They **domesticated** plants and animals, making them more useful to humans.

The first evidence of domesticated plants—wheat, barley, and lentils—comes from archaeological sites in the Middle East dated around 8000 to 7000 B.C. Hunter-gatherers probably noticed that some plants were more productive than others. By collecting and sowing the seeds of these plants, they could increase their harvest. Today's varieties of domesticated barley produce more than six times as many seeds as wild barley.

Sheep, goats, and dogs were among the first domesticated animals. Sheep were domesticated

Was this the first kitchen pantry? Early villagers stored their extra grain in underground storage pits lined with rock, grass, and sometimes clay. The pits kept the grain dry and safe from rats.

Stored wheat

Grass lining

Stone lining

Heavy, breakable pots were impractical for nomads to carry around. But when people began to settle in one place, they needed a good way to store their food. In time, pottery became beautiful as well as useful.

Neolithic quern used to grind grain into flour for bread

Development of Societies

Wild sheep

Domesticated sheep

▲ *How many differences can you see between the domesticated sheep on the right and the wild one on the left?*

about 8500 B.C. Archaeologists know this because they can tell the difference between the bones of domesticated sheep and those of wild sheep. Over hundreds of years, animals living in a domesticated environment undergo physical changes. They tend to become smaller than wild animals of a related species. Their muzzles become shorter. Horns may disappear entirely or change their shape. Archaeologists can make out these differences in animal bones unearthed at sites.

■ *How are domesticated plants and animals more useful to humans than wild ones?*

Domestication causes another important change. When animals and plants are domesticated, they rely on humans for survival. For

example, a wild dog knows how to find its own shelter, hunt its own food, and flee or fight when faced with an enemy. But once a dog is domesticated, its survival skills fade because the dog now looks to humans for its home, supper, and safety.

Examine the chart below to help you understand that plants and animals were domesticated at different times in different places. Which animal was the first to be domesticated? Which people first domesticated rice? Which plants were domesticated in the Middle East? Which plants were domesticated first in America, and when did this happen? ■

➤ *By excavating the remains of animals and plants, archaeologists learned the approximate dates of domestication shown on the chart.*

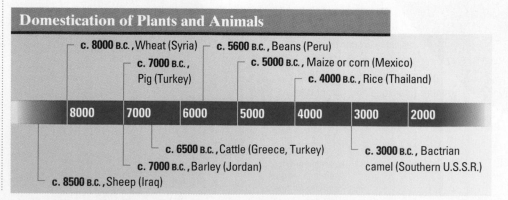

Domestication of Plants and Animals

c. 8000 B.C., Wheat (Syria)	c. 5600 B.C., Beans (Peru)
c. 7000 B.C., Pig (Turkey)	c. 5000 B.C., Maize or corn (Mexico)
	c. 4000 B.C., Rice (Thailand)

8000	7000	6000	5000	4000	3000	2000

c. 6500 B.C., Cattle (Greece, Turkey)

c. 3000 B.C., Bactrian camel (Southern U.S.S.R.)

c. 7000 B.C., Barley (Jordan)

c. 8500 B.C., Sheep (Iraq)

Chapter 5

Farming as a Way of Life

Plant and animal domestication made possible the beginning of **agriculture**, or farming. Agriculture is the growing of plants and the raising of animals to supply food for humans. Evidence shows that by 11,000 to 8000 B.C. people in parts of the Middle East had learned to farm.

The Advantages of Agriculture

Women may have done some of the earliest farming, because women may have been plant gatherers before. The shift to farming and herding was a slow process, taking many hundreds of years. Even after agriculture had taken hold, many people continued to hunt, and many hunter-gatherers never adopted an agricultural lifestyle.

Agriculture offered some important advantages. Farmers and herders could raise much more food than hunter-gatherers could collect. They could support more people on small plots of land. And when the land was fairly fertile, they could move into regions where wild food and game were scarce. Perhaps most important of all, a farmer could grow more food than he needed to feed the family. The surplus could be traded or stored for winter months.

Certainly, farmers and herders faced problems, such as insects, bad weather, and plant and animal diseases. When such disasters struck, a farmer's food supply could be wiped out in a matter of days. Farmers had altered plants so that they could not survive without attention. Farmers and plants were now dependent on each other.

Different Occupations

With the arrival of agriculture, not everyone was needed all day in the fields to raise food for the group. So, some people explored other activities. Gradually, they moved into other occupations, becoming tool makers, builders, fishers, craftspersons, priests, and leaders. The farming was eventually left to the farmers. Over time, agriculture had brought about a division of daily labors.

Farming also affected wild animals and open lands. Wild animals were often forced out of areas when farmers needed land for grazing domesticated flocks. Farmers also planted crops in areas once blanketed with wild plants and trees. Thus, through agriculture, people were changing their environment and their lifestyle in lasting ways.

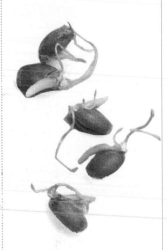

▲ *Ancient farmers learned to save some wheat kernels for future planting.*

◄ *Some farmers in the Middle East still use the traditional farming methods of their ancestors.*

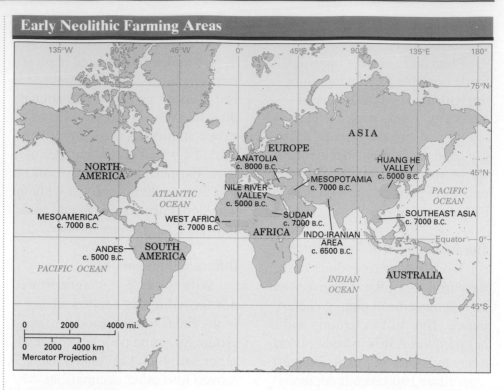

➤ *The map shows areas where Neolithic people actually farmed. These cultures had advanced beyond the simple domestication of plants and animals to agriculture.*

■ *What were the pros and cons of agriculture in ancient times?*

A Major Change

Remember that humans had been on the earth for an extremely long time before they began to grow crops and herd animals. In all those thousands of years, they had lived by hunting and gathering. The beginning of agriculture was a new chapter in the human story.

Agriculture began during the Neolithic Era. *Neos* in Greek means "new" and *lithos* means "stone." The Neolithic Era, so named because people used new, more efficient stone tools, stretched from about 8000 to 5000 B.C. in the Middle East. In other parts of the world, the era covered different time periods. On the map above, locate the various areas showing Neolithic farming.

The Neolithic people also took steps in another new direction. They began to live in villages. They learned to make pottery for storing food and water. They mastered weaving, so that now they had cloth as well as animal hides for coverings. Basket weaving was another new skill. Toward the end of the Neolithic Era, villagers started to work with metal—first copper, then bronze.

In the next lessons, you'll discover how these advances were hints of things to come. These were the establishment of towns and the building of cities. ■

R E V I E W

1. **FOCUS** How did people's lifestyle change as they began to domesticate plants and animals?
2. **CONNECT** Compare food gathering in Terra Amata with early farming.
3. **GEOGRAPHY** Use the map on page 121 to name six modern countries that had early settlements.

4. **CRITICAL THINKING** Why do dogs and cats often live only a short time when abandoned in cities or woods by their owners?
5. **ACTIVITY** By using pantomime, show how the hunter-gatherers and early farmers and herders obtained their food.

LESSON 2

Living in an Early Farming Town

If someone were to give you the object in the picture below, what would you do with it? Before you read on, take out a piece of paper and jot down as many ideas as you can. The bowllike part of the object is made of solid stone and is very heavy. It might make a good doorstop. It has a dent in the center, so maybe you could use it for a salad bowl or candy dish. What ideas did you come up with?

It might be difficult to think of practical ways to use this object today. However, it was very useful about 8,000 years ago in the Neolithic Era when it was made. Take a closer look. The edges of the stone are bumpy, but other areas seem smooth. What do you think caused this?

Now look at the rounded object inside the stone. Archaeologists found this small object just as you see it, resting in the hollow of the large one. If you guessed that these two objects were used together, you're right. Maybe you also noticed that they're very similar to the mortar and pestle

found in the excavated ruins at Ain Mallaha. If so, you're right again.

The bowllike object is a mortar and the smaller object is a pestle. The pestle is used to grind food against the mortar. An ancient farmer would use this mortar and pestle, or quern *(kwurn)*, to grind grain into flour.

People ground so much grain that they wore the stone smooth in certain places. In this smoothing process, tiny pieces of grit chipped off the stone, mixing with the grain. Archaeological evidence shows that as people ate this gritty mixture over a long period of time, it gradually wore down their teeth. Querns similar to the one pictured below were used in many early settlements around the world where Neolithic farmers grew grains.

THINKING
FOCUS

What would life be like in a Neolithic farming town?

Key Terms

- shrine
- self-sufficient

▼ *Querns varied in size but, generally, were as big as large bowls.*

Development of Societies

A Large Neolithic Town

Let's look at what life may have been like in one of those Neolithic towns. You've been transported back in time about 8,000 years. You're standing on the flat roof of a mud-brick building. Far off are the large twin cones of a volcano. You can see fields of wheat stretching out before you, making a golden carpet over the dry earth. A river winds lazily across the plain. A woman climbs out from a hole in the roof. With her broad smile she warmly welcomes you to her hometown, Çatal Hüyük *(chah TUHL hoo YUHK)*.

Turn to the map on page 121. You will see that Çatal Hüyük was located on a plain in present-day Turkey. Around 6000 B.C., the town covered about 32 acres. That's roughly the size of 24 football fields put together. The town had about 1,000 houses, and the population numbered between 5,000 and 6,000. By today's standards, Çatal Hüyük wasn't large. But so far, it's the biggest Neolithic town discovered by archaeologists in the Middle East.

When dwellings in Çatal Hüyük collapsed from age or fire or other reasons, people simply built new homes on top of the old ones. That is the reason why these archaeological ruins are layered like a cake. The diagram below shows ruins with the most ancient remains on the bottom and the most recent on the top. These remains tell us much about the lifestyle, farming, and beliefs of the people of ancient Çatal Hüyük.

Daily Life

Didn't you find it odd that your time travel took you to a Çatal Hüyük rooftop? Why didn't you land on a street corner or, at least, on someone's doorstep? That was not possible in Çatal Hüyük. This town had no streets, lanes, or alleys, and the doors of buildings opened onto roofs. To get from place to place, people walked across their neighbors' roofs. Notice, in the diagram on page 129, that the roofs were at different levels. You can see the ladders that allowed people to get from one level to the next. Ladders also led from the doors, at roof level, down into the houses. All that ladder climbing must have caused some nasty tumbles. It's no wonder that archaeologists have found many broken bones at the Çatal Hüyük site.

The houses of Çatal Hüyük were all about the same size. Most had two rooms—a small room for

Across Time & Space

Most people in the United States today buy their flour at the supermarket. However, some people in the southwestern United States and in Mexico still grind grain by hand. Their tools, called the metate *and the* mano, *are made of stone and are similar to those used by the ancient Middle Eastern farmers.*

▼ *In a cutaway view, each layer of ruins represents a different time period when Çatal Hüyük was occupied. Only about three percent of the ruins have been excavated.*

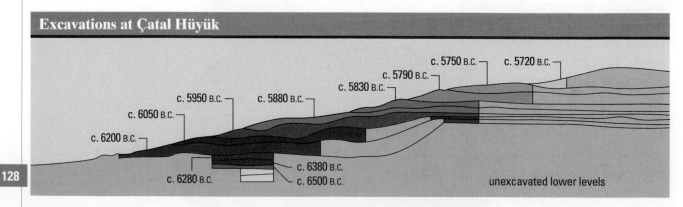

Excavations at Çatal Hüyük

c. 6200 B.C.
c. 6050 B.C.
c. 5950 B.C.
c. 5880 B.C.
c. 5830 B.C.
c. 5790 B.C.
c. 5750 B.C.
c. 5720 B.C.
c. 6280 B.C.
c. 6380 B.C.
c. 6500 B.C.
unexcavated lower levels

storing food and a large room with a kitchen area and living quarters. By examining the storerooms, archaeologists have learned that wheat was Çatal Hüyük's main crop. Other evidence also shows that people raised cattle and

hunted deer, bear, and wolves. For variety, they grew peas and gathered crab apples, juniper berries, and nuts such as acorns and almonds.

The kitchen area in each house featured both a hearth and a clay oven. Smoke escaped through the same hole in the roof that people used to climb in and out of the house. Basically, the furniture was built-in. Platforms that extended from the walls served as tables or benches during the day and as beds at night.

Burial Practices

In some homes, simple graves were found under the platforms. Archaeologists think that people buried their relatives there. No one is sure why. Possibly, dead relatives were still considered part of the family so they were kept within the household.

Evidence suggests that a number of the buildings were **shrines,** or sacred places where people worship. Çatal Hüyük's shrines, however, may have been used for other activities, too. The shrines were no larger than the houses, but they were special inside. Bull horns decorated the benches, and plaster

▲ *The drawing of Çatal Hüyük's mud dwellings shows how the different roof levels allowed sunlight to enter the rooms.*

This Çatal Hüyük ceremonial dagger has a blade of flint. The handle is shaped like a coiled snake.

sculptures of leopards, rams, and bulls adorned the walls.

The Çatal Hüyük people also painted in color on their shrines' white plastered walls. Subjects for the pictures ranged from colorful patterns to wild beasts to a village with volcanoes in the background. Archaeologists think that the paintings were connected with special events. These shrines with their paintings and sculptures may have attracted people from other areas of the plain. If so, Çatal Hüyük probably became the region's religious center.

A Farming Economy

Fertile soil and a river helped to make Çatal Hüyük a large town. With good crops supplying plenty of food, people decided to stay in the town. As the population increased, the town grew. But sometimes groups of people left the town to start settlements nearby. They carried the Çatal Hüyük way of life with them.

The Çatal Hüyük people lived in their mud-brick homes and left town to tend their fields. Since the region was dry, farmers probably waited until the river flooded in late spring. After flood waters went down, they planted seeds in the moist earth.

The townspeople produced ample grain and cattle. They also had salt, reeds, a limited amount of wood, and plenty of mud for shaping bricks. These basic items made them **self-sufficient,** meaning they weren't dependent upon others for their survival.

Çatal Hüyük Crafts

Since not everyone in Çatal Hüyük had to farm full time, the townspeople set up small industries. Archaeologists discovered the Neolithic talent for crafts.

The Çatal Hüyük craftspeople made tools by both grinding and chipping stone. From bone, they crafted needles, beads, hairpins, and fish hooks. They also wove woolen cloth, made baskets, and fashioned leather into pouches. From wood, they made bowls and boxes with lids. ■

■ *What kind of lifestyle did people have in Çatal Hüyük, and how do we know?*

➤ *Shrines like this were mixed in among the houses at Çatal Hüyük. Find the sculpture of the bull head, a religious image that occurred often at Çatal Hüyük.*

Chapter 5

◀ *In some areas of Iraq today, women still carry on the ancient tradition of making sun-dried bricks. Iraq also has large cities with modern buildings.*

Trade in the Neolithic World

Çatal Hüyük was the hub of trade on the plain. Its people were excellent at crafts, making items that neighboring settlements wanted.

This town also had an item valued throughout the Neolithic Middle East—a black volcanic glass called obsidian. This shiny, dark glass is formed when hot lava from a volcano cools quickly. Obsidian is valued because it can be chipped to make fine, sharp-edged tools. Even today surgeons use obsidian blades for delicate operations.

The Çatal Hüyük people journeyed more than 120 miles to get obsidian at volcanic lava flows. Archaeologists believe they transported it on the backs of their domesticated cattle. At other times, Çatal Hüyük traders got their obsidian from neighboring towns. Then, they turned around and traded it to distant towns. Sometimes, they crafted the obsidian first, making arrowheads, tools, and mirrors.

Obsidian from Çatal Hüyük's area was unearthed about 620 miles away at the archaeological site of Jericho. Trade items from afar that were excavated at Çatal Hüyük include turquoise and copper from the Sinai Peninsula, also more than 600 miles away.

Çatal Hüyük was only one of a number of Neolithic towns in the Middle East that engaged in trade. One example was Umm Dabaghiyah *(OOM dah bah GEE ah)*, a small settlement that archaeologists

◀ *Learning to make clay pots like this one was a giant step forward for the Neolithic people.*

131

Development of Societies

believe existed at the same time as Çatal Hüyük.

In about 6000 B.C., Umm Dabaghiyah was a village located on the dry northern plain between the Tigris *(TY gruhs)* and Euphrates *(yu FRAYT eez)* rivers. Find the site on the map on page 121. This town was tiny compared with Çatal Hüyük. It had fewer than ten houses.

But Umm Dabaghiyah had other buildings. These were long, narrow structures with rows of cell-like rooms. The walls were unplastered; the floors were dirt, and the roofs had trap doors. These rooms lacked the hearths, platforms, and tools needed for daily living.

What was the purpose of these cell-like rooms? In some rooms were large numbers of the same item. For example, one room held thousands of clay balls—ammunition for slingshots. This shows that

UNDERSTANDING SURPLUS

When you have a surplus, you have an extra supply of something. It can be a surplus of just about anything imaginable—shoes or ships, timber, coal, or even baseball cards.

Through the ages, a surplus of food has kept people alive during lean years. It has also allowed them to change their lifestyles. For example, once the hunter-gatherers had a surplus of grain and wild game, they didn't have to roam to hunt food. If they chose, they could then become settlers instead of wanderers.

Over and Above

The English word *surplus* comes from the Latin words *super*, meaning "over," and *plus*, meaning "more." Although ancient Romans coined this term, the idea of surplus goes much farther back. The first successful mammoth hunters, for example, certainly enjoyed a surplus of meat.

Surplus and Trade

Think about surplus and how it affects us today. If oranges grow well in my state but not in yours, I'll have a surplus of oranges. You'll have the opposite of a surplus, which is a scarcity. However, if your state grows a surplus of apples and my state grows none, the answer seems easy. We can trade apples for oranges.

As a matter of fact, trade turned out to be the answer for people in early societies as well. In Çatal Hüyük, people traded their own surplus of obsidian for items they lacked, and soon trade became a vital part of their lifestyle.

Note, however, that each one involved in a trade must have something the other wants. One nation may have a surplus of something, such as coconuts, but unless another nation has a coconut scarcity, trade won't solve the problem.

Surplus and Scarcity

In our day, too, the balance of surplus and scarcity has an effect on trade. The Middle Eastern countries, with their surplus oil, have become among the richest in the world. In recent years, the United States and many other countries throughout the world have had a scarcity of oil. How do you think our country's scarcity of oil might affect its trade with Middle Eastern countries?

hunting was important to these people. In fact, because of the number and types of animal bones found there, archaeologists concluded that this town was a hunting and trading outpost. These rooms must have been used for storage.

The people who lived in Umm Dabaghiyah hunted a wild, donkeylike animal called an onager *(AHN uh juhr)*. They skinned the onager and then traded the hides. During a 1974 dig, archaeologists discovered how this animal was hunted when they found a detailed wall painting. Hunters stampeded the onagers into an enclosed area built from stakes and nets.

The people of Umm Dabaghiyah did little farming because crops didn't grow well in their dry

area. Thus, they weren't self sufficient. However, they had a surplus of onager hides. This surplus allowed them to trade for necessities and luxuries they couldn't produce. By focusing on trade, this small town pioneered a new way of life. ■

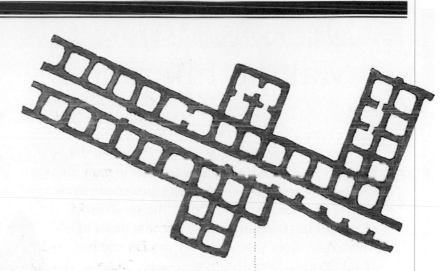

▲ *An archaeologist at Umm Dabaghiyah sketched this floor plan of the storerooms.*

■ *What was the surplus item produced at Umm Dabaghiyah and how did the people make use of it?*

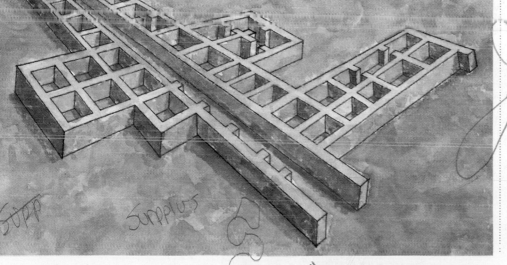

◄ *This artist's drawing, based on the floor plan above, shows how the storerooms at Umm Dabaghiyah might have looked. Entrance was through a trap door in the roof.*

R E V I E W

1. **FOCUS** What was life like in a Neolithic farming town?

2. **CONNECT** In the area of industry, how did the Çatal Hüyük people differ from hunter-gatherers? What caused this difference?

3. **CULTURE** What is obsidian, and how is it formed?

What did the Çatal Hüyük people do with it?

4. **CRITICAL THINKING** Why do you think the Çatal Hüyük houses had only rooftop entries?

5. **ACTIVITY** Make a poster showing something about daily life in Çatal Hüyük or Umm Dabaghiyah.

Making Inferences

Here's Why

You know that when you read stories, not every detail is always explained. Sometimes you must look for clues and think about your own experiences to understand information the author did not state directly. This is called making inferences.

You can use the clues shown on a map and what you already know to make inferences. For example, suppose you wanted to know how obsidian was transported through Anatolia. If a map did not show the trade route, could you use the clues along with what you already know to figure it out? Could you make an inference?

Here's How

Look at the light green area on the map below. Note the symbols for the sources of obsidian and for sites where obsidian objects, like those shown here, have been found. These are places where obsidian was used and traded. The locations of symbols are clues that will help you guess, or infer, how obsidian was transported.

Because the sources of obsidian are in the Taurus Mountains, you can infer that the trade route would begin there. You can also see that the route would go overland from the mountains to Çatal Hüyük. You already know that water routes were used. So you can infer that once the obsidian reached the Mediterranean Sea, it was probably loaded on boats and shipped to towns on or near the coast. By using clues and what you already knew, you were able to infer how obsidian was transported.

Try It

Look at the pink area on the map. Where was the source of this region's obsidian? How do you think the obsidian was transported from place to place? Base your answers on map clues and what you already know.

Apply It

Draw a map that shows the location of your school and home. Include streets and landmarks. Show your map to someone who lives in another area. Help that person infer the route you walk or ride to school each day. Give clues about landmarks you pass.

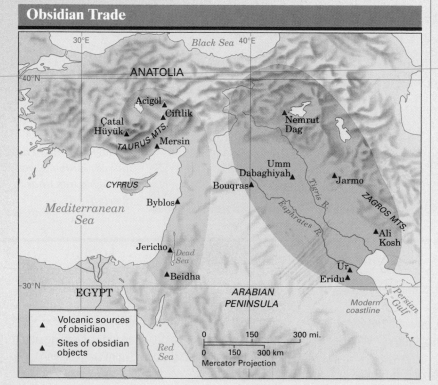

Obsidian Trade

Legend:
▲ Volcanic sources of obsidian
▲ Sites of obsidian objects

0 — 150 — 300 mi.
0 — 150 — 300 km
Mercator Projection

LESSON 3

Starting Cities

In 1927, Sir Leonard Woolley dug into a cemetery at the ancient city of Ur, in what is now Iraq. The first shovelfuls of the British archaeologist yielded only dirt. However, over the next two years, Woolley dug up treasures beyond his wildest hopes. Buried in that cemetery were the kings and queens of the ancient city of Ur.

One of Woolley's priceless finds was the Standard of Ur. A standard is often carried before a king or queen in a procession. Usually, it's a flag. But the Standard of Ur is something quite different. It consists of two separate solid panels, one called War, and the other, Peace. Both panels are detailed mosaics—pictures made by putting together many small pieces of stones, shells, gems, or tiles.

The panels, each measuring 22 inches, were carried on a pole. Look at the War panel below. Woolley wrote this about it in his book, *Ur of The Chaldees:*

In the second row, at the back, comes the phalanx of the royal army, heavy-armed infantry in close order with copper helmets exactly like those found by us in the king's grave, and long cloaks of some stiff material which I take to be felt, just such cloaks as are worn by the shepherds of Anatolia [part of Turkey] to-day, holding axes in their hands; in front of them are the light-armed infantry without cloaks, wielding axes or short spears.

The king stands out because of his greater height and central location. His figure dominates the top

THINKING
FOCUS

What are the characteristics of a city?

Key Terms

- irrigation
- famine
- civilization

◄ *In a royal grave at the city of Ur, this War panel was found lying next to a man thought to be the king's standard-bearer.*

135

Development of Societies

These figures from the Peace panel show a harpist and a singer entertaining the king. The entire Peace panel appears on pages 86 and 87.

row. Facing him stand prisoners of war, their hands bound behind their backs.

"The Standard is a remarkable work of art, but it has yet greater value as an historical document," said Woolley. He explained further that these panels make up the earliest known detailed picture of the army that fought throughout the Middle East.

Earlier in this chapter, a quern taught you about an important task carried out by Neolithic farm families. What does the Standard of Ur tell you about a warrior's duties in one of the world's first cities?

A City on the Plain

The city of Ur was located on the dry plain of the Tigris and Euphrates rivers. Find Ur on the map on page 121.

This city didn't just spring up on the plain. Ur and other cities in that river area arose because of advances in agriculture and changes in society. Here's how it happened at the city of Ur.

The Sun-baked Land

Many farmers in the ancient world could count on rain to water their crops until harvest time. But this natural method didn't work in the land between the Tigris and Euphrates rivers. There, rain was scarce.

For most of the year, the land between the rivers is scorched by the sun. The clay soil bakes to a surface so hard you'd need a jackhammer to drill through it. When the rain finally arrives, it rolls right off. How could anyone farm such land? The people of Ur did it with irrigation. When people use **irrigation,** they bring needed water

The land around the Tigris and Euphrates rivers is still a sun-baked plain.

to their fields through canals, ditches, or pipes.

An Irrigation System

People who settled by the Tigris and Euphrates rivers dug canals and tunnels from the riverbeds to their fields. Their irrigation system made the dry, dusty plains bloom. In Chapter 6, you'll learn more about the workings of this irrigation system used by Ur and other cities on the plain.

Irrigation farming worked well because the times of watering and also the amounts of water could be controlled. Farmers produced surplus food, preventing famine and starvation. **Famine** is a terrible shortage of food that can cause starvation. Fields yielded bountiful harvests of barley, wheat, and vegetables. Date palms and grapevines also grew well on this land.

As you learned in Lesson 1, a food surplus enabled people to leave farming and take on specialized jobs, such as building or toolmaking. Where irrigation farming was practiced, the population grew rapidly. The boom in population around the Tigris and Euphrates rivers led to the growth of cities such as Ur. ■

This treasure from a royal tomb at Ur is called Ram-in-a-Thicket. When the statue was found, it was crushed and twisted. Only earth held the gems, shells, and gold in place.

■ *How did irrigation make it possible for a city to grow in the land around the Tigris and Euphrates?*

Features of a City

Ur, like every ancient or modern city, had a large number of people living close together. But it was more than just population that made Ur a city.

Leadership and Planning

One characteristic or special feature of a city is that there is some kind of leadership or government. We know from written records that Ur had a "big man" that led people into battle. Success in battle could have pushed the man who had trained and led the army in the fighting to the top and made him king. The king was rewarded by owning the best land.

The king had control over many people's lives. Farmers worked the king's land. Soldiers fought in his army. Servants lived in his palace. Even so, the king did not have total power. His decisions had to be set before a group of counselors and warriors for their approval. A set of codes, or laws, governed the king as well as the common people.

There were many projects in Ur that required the labor and talent of lots of people. Planning, or organization of workers, is another characteristic of a city. If you had been living in Ur you might have been part of the group that harvested the wheat crop. You could have built walls or repaired the colorful tiles in the temple. Shearing the wool of sheep needed organized workers, too. The priests and kings of Ur were rich and strong and could use their influence and power to make people work for them.

Let's look at the evidence of organization that archaeologists have found. The region around the city of Ur was crisscrossed by a complicated network of irrigation canals. In Ur hundreds of people had to work together to build and to maintain the canals. A complex

➤ *If you walked up this stairway, you'd find yourself on the first platform of the Ziggurat of Ur. The ruins are in good condition.*

▼ *This drawing shows you what the Ziggurat of Ur looked like in ancient times. A one-room shrine to the moon god crowns its top.*

Across Time & Space

When we use the words city, town, *and* village *today, we are usually saying something about population. A city has more people than a town, and a village has fewer. A sub-urb may be small or large. It may be a town, a village, or a city. What makes a suburb?*

job like that could not have been done without good organization and strong, clear leadership.

Large public buildings also show how well Ur was organized. The structure in the above drawing is a ziggurat *(ZIHG uh raht)*, a type of temple tower with a one-room shrine at the top. The people who lived on this level land in effect had built themselves a mountain where they could worship their god. The ziggurat had many storerooms in addition to the temple. It also contained a large number of workrooms.

Constructing something as huge and grand as this ziggurat took a great deal of planning and organization. This meant that a large number of people had to work together to get the job done.

Specialized Workers

Another characteristic of a city is that people are employed in all sorts of different jobs. Since irrigation gave Ur abundant crops, not everyone was needed to till the soil. People began to develop skills other than farming. These skills led them into a variety of jobs.

Sir Leonard Woolley excavated a tablet listing several of Ur's special workers. The chisel worker made sculptures; the gem cutter cut and polished gems, and the fuller stomped on woven wool to make it soft. The metalworker crafted everything from weapons to mirrors. Although Ur imported its wood from afar, the carpenter kept busy making boats and chariots. To the leatherworker went the job of making soldiers' tunics.

Ur also had judges and doctors and musicians who played harps, lyres, and drums. When different people in a society do different jobs, the arrangement is called specialization of labor.

Richer and Poorer

Cities usually have different social groups, too. That is, some people are richer and more powerful than others.

Ur had three levels of society. At the top were the most powerful—government officials, priests, and soldiers. The society's second level was made up of merchants, teachers, laborers, farmers, and craftspeople. At the bottom of the social scale were the slaves, who often had been captured during battle.

Burials at Ur give insight into people's social standing. As you have seen, kings and queens had tombs filled with treasures. Other wealthy people were buried with cups of stone or metal, even gold. But the graves of common people held only a few simple items such as cups, axes, and fish hooks. Generally, the plainer the pottery in a grave, the poorer the person.

Trade Near and Far

Long-distance trade is another sign of a city. For Ur, this trade was a lifeline to survival. Ur was located on a treeless, sun-baked plain, hundreds of miles from many valuable resources. The people of Ur traded grain and woven cloth for the items they needed. They traded for timber, for the stone used in making tools, and for the gems in their jewelry. They also traded for the gold, silver, tin, lead, copper, and bronze needed by their metalworkers.

As the population of Ur grew larger, trade expanded as never before. The priests kept records of goods that flowed in and out of the city. How did they do this? Ur had a unique system of writing. Fortunately, some records have survived to let us know that Ur was a key trading center.

Seagoing boats navigated along the Mediterranean coasts. Some also ventured to India. Crowding the river waterways were round basketlike boats made of reeds and covered with hides. ■

■ *What archaeological evidence tells us that Ur was a city?*

▼ *This bearded bull of gold decorates the sounding box of a lyre (a musical instrument) from a royal tomb. Lyres were frequently found in royal graves.*

An Early Civilization

Cities like Ur often signal the rise of a **civilization.** Just what is a civilization? It's a complex society that usually has these five characteristics, or features:

1. Stable food supply
2. Specialization of labor
3. A system of government
4. Social levels
5. A highly developed culture that includes art, architecture, religion, music, and law. Frequently, civilizations also have a system of writing.

Would hunter-gatherer groups make up a civilization? No, they wouldn't because these people didn't always have a stable food supply, and they didn't develop much specialization of labor. They often had leaders but not organized government. Some had art, religion, and music, but not architecture. Although hunter-gatherers had a culture, they were not considered a civilization.

Ur, however, and other cities in the Fertile Crescent did have all the needed characteristics that make a civilization. In fact, these

➤ *This woman's fancy headdress of gold was unearthed in the Fertile Crescent.*

▼ *The chart shows how early farming with its surplus food often led to the rise of cities.*

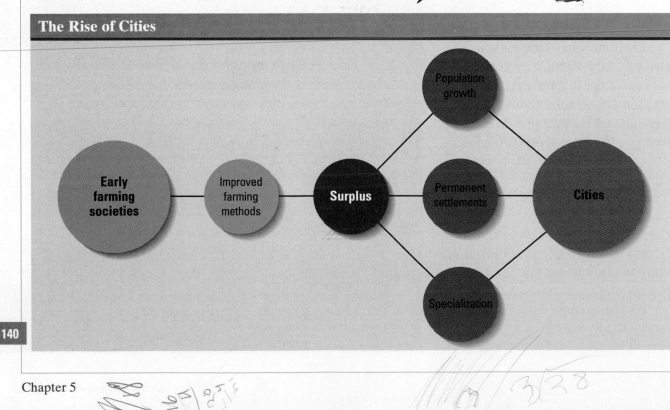

The Rise of Cities

Early farming societies → Improved farming methods → Surplus → Population growth

Surplus → Permanent settlements

Surplus → Specialization

Population growth → Cities

Permanent settlements → Cities

Specialization → Cities

140

cities around the Tigris and Euphrates rivers formed one of the world's earliest civilizations.

You'll find that cities often speed up the growth of a civilization, but not always. For example, ancient Egyptian civilization reached an advanced level before cities were even built there. You'll read about this Egyptian civilization in Chapter 7.

Cities and civilizations often share the same features. So it's not surprising that both words come from the same Latin word, *civitas*, meaning "city."

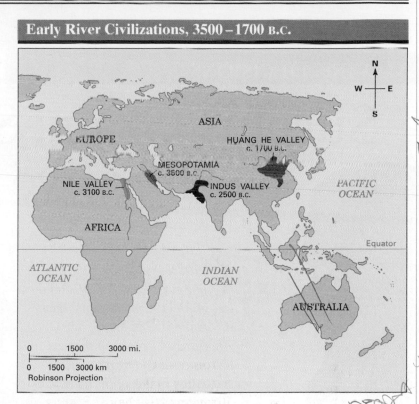

Early River Civilizations, 3500–1700 B.C.

0   1500   3000 mi.

0   1500   3000 km
Robinson Projection

The Fertile Crescent and the Nile Valley were only two of the world's first civilizations. On the map above, find where other early civilizations began. Rivers often played a major role in their growth, as they did in the Fertile Crescent and Egypt.

More than 7,000 years have passed since hunter-gatherers began to settle down in villages of the Middle East. The very gradual change in their lives shows that it takes century upon century to mold a civilization. ■

▲ *On the map, notice the time periods associated with each of the early civilizations.*

◄ *These vessels of gold found in tombs indicate the advanced artistry of the Ur civilization.*

■ *What are five features of a civilization?*

R E V I E W

1. **FOCUS** What are characteristics of a city?
2. **CONNECT** Hunter-gatherer groups were not civilizations. Give at least three elements that they lacked.
3. **GEOGRAPHY** How did the Euphrates River help Ur's development?
4. **ECONOMICS** Why was trade vital to the city of Ur?
5. **CRITICAL THINKING** An archaeologist unearthed a midden containing broken pottery, a dog bone, dried wheat, and a golden hairpin. What do these tell about the ancient people who once lived in that area?
6. **ACTIVITY** Make a picture chart showing the various elements of a city.

Surplus Grain: Store? Sell? Give It Away?

I n 1988—perhaps for the first time ever—the U.S. produced less grain (196 metric tons) than it consumed (206 metric tons)... . Another bad harvest in the next few years could trigger massive starvation in any of the more than 100 nations that buy U.S. grain.

The Worldwatch Institute

W orld food production is growing faster than population . . . if the food supply can be increased at the current pace (or even a slower one), there will be enough food for a stable world population of 10 billion in 100 years.

Pierre R. Crosson and Norman J Rosenberg, *Scientific American*

Background

Surpluses have always been important to human communities. In prehistoric times, they allowed people to survive hard winters or blazing summers when food was scarce. With surpluses, large groups of people could live together, because there was enough food for everyone. Surpluses also made it possible for people to specialize, since not everyone had to spend the day hunting or gathering food. Finally, surpluses led to trade. When one group had extra meat or grain on hand, they would try to exchange it for something else they needed—tools, seeds, or animal skins.

From the beginning of civilization, people have had to decide what to do with surpluses. The United States is frequently faced with this decision today. This is a fertile and wealthy nation, and it often produces more than enough food for its own people. In the 1960s, new and more productive kinds of plants were introduced, along with new, more efficient farm machinery. With chemical fertilizers and insecticides, these advances made the land produce even more grain and added to our surpluses. Look at the graph on

Total Grain Surplus, United States, 1974–1986

page 142. What should we do with the grain we have left each year? We have three alternatives: to keep our surplus grain, to sell it, or to give it away.

Considering Alternatives

Maybe we'd be wise to keep our surpluses. In 1988, a drought made the U.S. harvest 10 percent smaller than it was in 1985. In 1970, a fungus cut the corn crop 15 percent. These natural events are unpredictable. We have to protect ourselves and be sure there is enough food. Why give away or sell our own insurance against hunger?

But with good weather, future harvests in the United States may bring us huge surpluses. Scientists are developing new varieties of plants and animals. Some experts predict that by the year 2000, annual U.S. corn production could reach almost 10 million bushels.

Then why not sell our surpluses? After all, we buy a great deal from other countries. The goods we buy are harvested or manufactured by workers in those countries, so they help to provide jobs. To assure work for our own people, we need to sell as much as possible to other nations. American farmers have had difficult years. Keeping our surpluses does not help them, but selling our surpluses does. It increases the demand for grain and keeps grain prices up.

We could give away our surplus grain to countries whose people are starving. In spite of advances in technology, starvation remains a fact of life in many parts of the world.

Decision Point

1. What alternatives do we have in how we use our surplus grain?
2. What are the advantages of each alternative?
3. What disadvantages can you identify for each alternative?
4. Grain can also be used as feed for animals and in the production of certain fuels. Where would you look for more information about these uses?
5. What are some advantages and disadvantages of these other uses?

What should we do with our surplus grain?

Store	Sell	Give Away
• Advantages	• Advantages	• Advantages
• Disadvantages	• Disadvantages	• Disadvantages

Development of Societies

Chapter Review

Reviewing Key Terms

agriculture (p. 125)
civilization (p. 140)
domesticate (p. 123)
environment (p. 122)
famine (p. 137)

irrigation (p. 136)
self-sufficient (p. 130)
shrine (p. 129)
surplus (p. 121)

A. Some of the following statements are true. The rest are false. Write *True* or *False* for each statement. Then rewrite the false statements to make them true.

1. When hunter-gatherers learned to control their environment, their lifestyle changed.
2. Agriculture could not have developed without the domestication of plants.
3. Famine would make people self-sufficient.

4. Surplus food helped the growth of trade.
5. The shrines of Çatal Hüyük, with their paintings and sculptures, were much like our art museums today.
6. Ur is considered a civilization because it learned to domesticate plants and animals.

B. If you were a farmer living 5,000 years ago, why would the following be important to you? Write an explanation of how each of these things would influence your farm life.

1. domesticated plants and animals
2. irrigation
3. surplus
4. environment

Exploring Concepts

A. Ain Mallaha, Çatal Hüyük, Umm Dabaghiyah, and Ur were all very different types of communities. Copy the following chart on your paper. Then compare the size, occupation, and types of dwellings that these four historic areas had. Complete all the sections in your chart.

Location and Date	Size	Lifestyle	Dwellings
Ain Mallaha			Round pits, dirt walls, reed roofs
Çatal Hüyük 6,000 B.C.			
Umm Dabaghiyah		Hunters and traders	
Ur 3,000–2,000 B.C.	City		

B. You could draw the following conclusions from studying the ancient Middle East. Using facts and details from the chapter, give proof that these conclusions are correct.

1. Some hunter-gatherers began to settle down between 11,000 and 8000 B.C.
2. Early farmers domesticated plants and animals.
3. Neolithic farmers learned to make flour.
4. The people of Çatal Hüyük traded with distant communities.
5. Umm Dabaghiyah was a much different community than Çatal Hüyük and Ur.
6. The city of Ur was organized; it also had leadership.
7. The residents of Çatal Hüyük and Ur were self-sufficient, but the residents of Umm Dabaghiyah were not.
8. The early communities of Ain Mallaha, Çatal Hüyük, and Ur were formed because of their geography and environment.
9. Archaeologists' work is important.

Reviewing Skills

1. The map on this page shows areas in the Middle East that receive at least 12 inches of rain each year. This is the minimum amount needed for growing wheat without irrigation. Suppose you were an archaeologist. Would you expect to find traces of ancient irrigation ditches at Eridu or Ali Kosh? Explain your answers.

2. Make a table that will show that Ur was a civilization. Across your paper write these column headings: Food Supply, Specialization, Government, Social Levels, and Cultural Development. Down the left-hand side of your paper, write Evidence of Ur's civilization. Use information on pages 135–139 to give examples of how Ur shows the characteristics of a civilized society.

3. The people of Ain Mallaha, Çatal Hüyük, Umm Dabaghiyah, and Ur all invented tools that helped them in their work. How could you show the tools used by these communities on a map?

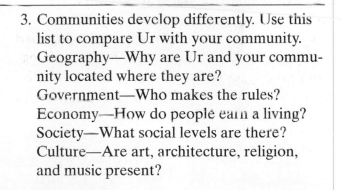

Middle East: Annual Rainfall

Annual Rainfall
☐ Less than 12 inches
☐ 12 inches or more

0   150   300 mi.
0 150 300 km
Mercator Projection

Using Critical Thinking

1. From earliest times, people have changed their environments. How have people changed their environment today? Discuss both good and bad changes.

2. Ancient peoples valued obsidian, copper, gazelle skins, and onager hides. Societies that had these resources developed a flourishing trade. Which resources do we prize in modern life? Why?

3. Communities develop differently. Use this list to compare Ur with your community. Geography—Why are Ur and your community located where they are? Government—Who makes the rules? Economy—How do people earn a living? Society—What social levels are there? Culture—Are art, architecture, religion, and music present?

Preparing for Citizenship

1. **ARTS ACTIVITY** The drawings and symbols on the Standard of Ur tell us about the people of Ur and their beliefs. How would you design a standard for the United States? What symbols and words would tell about us and our beliefs? For ideas, look at the flag, coins, songs, the presidential seal, and monuments. When you show your standard, explain why you chose your design.

2. **COLLABORATIVE LEARNING** Ur was a successful city. It had planning and leadership. As a class, decide what problems need solving in your community. For each problem—such as litter or dangerous crosswalks—form a small group to decide what can be done about it. Each group should choose a leader and then plan tasks for its members. Present the group's plan to the class.

145

Unit 3

Early Middle Eastern Civilizations

A nobleman and his wife, pleading for eternal life, make lavish offerings to a god. This beautifully painted scene, found in an Egyptian tomb, shows the richness of the Egyptian civilization 3,500 years ago. The people of ancient Egypt and Mesopotamia tamed the bleak land of the Middle East by controlling its rivers. Then they built two of the world's first great civilizations.

5300 B.C.

From The Book of the Dead of Kha, painted on papyrus, 1400 B.C. Torino, Museo Egizio

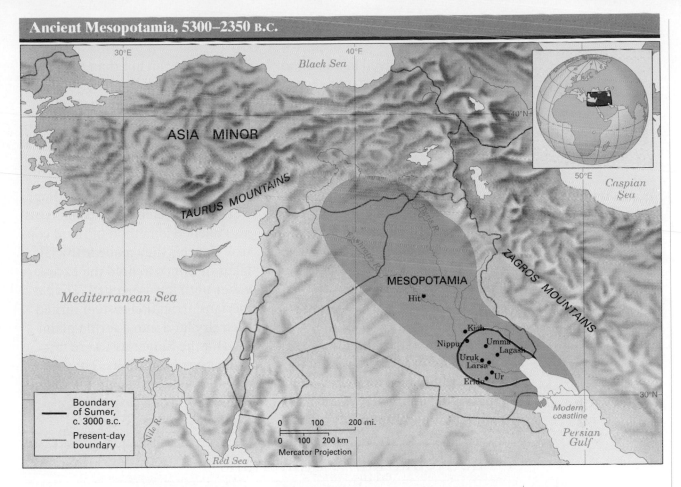

Boundary
of Sumer,
c. 3000 B.C.

Present-day
boundary

0   100   200 mi.

0   100   200 km
Mercator Projection

the Euphrates River to the Persian Gulf, then up the Tigris River and back to Hit. The area you have circled is a **plain**—a broad area of flat, open land, that is lower than the plateau. On the plain lay the region called Sumer *(SOO mur)*, making up much of the southern half of Mesopotamia.

Sumer spread over more than 10,000 square miles, an area about the size of Maryland. It was in Sumer that the world's first cities, including Ur and Kish, arose.

Scholars believe that the course of both rivers has changed a great deal in the last 5,000 years. The city of Kish was probably built just west of the ancient course of the Euphrates River.

Sumer was the homeland of the young canal worker we met earlier. Imagine him working on the irrigation canals in the 110-degree heat and the scorching, dusty wind. Historians believe that it was struggles with their harsh environment that caused the Sumerians,

▲ Use the map to locate Mesopotamia in relation to modern nations. Then describe the geography of northern and southern Mesopotamia.

◄ This modern Iraqi boat strongly resembles boats used 4,500 years ago in Mesopotamia.

151

Mesopotamia

the people who lived in Sumer, to develop many important new ways of life.

The Mesopotamian plain had a number of disadvantages—very hot summers, little rain, few resources, and parched, dry land. Heavy spring floods created spongy marshes and often killed young crops, and fall floods could destroy the harvest. Yet the Sumerians saw possibilities. The flooding, for example, spread rich soil, perfect for growing wheat and barley.

The ingenious Sumerians found a way to bring the land to life. They created an irrigation system with dams, gates, and canals. The Tigris and Euphrates rivers were slightly higher than the plain. The farmers dug canals from the rivers to the fields. Then, at the proper times in the growing cycle, they opened the gates and allowed gravity to pull the precious water down to the fields.

Because the times of flooding were unpredictable, the Sumerians also needed a method of flood control. For this they made artificial lakes or ponds to hold the excess water until it was needed. The Sumerians' irrigation system turned their dry land into a fertile plain.

But the Sumerians were not just successful farmers. They were also the builders of a great civilization. Let's take a closer look at what they achieved. ■

■ *Give evidence to support this statement: Irrigation was essential to the development of civilization in Mesopotamia.*

▼ *Delicately carved stone cylinder seals like the one below illustrate the artistry of the Sumerians. The design on the seal impression at the right was made by rolling the seal in wet clay. The result was a raised picture that could be used to show ownership or record an agreement.*

The Remarkable Sumerians

The Sumerians were a creative and energetic people. In their land, archaeologists have discovered traces of farming villages and irrigation systems from as early as 5000 B.C. They have also found evidence of great cities and a complex civilization that developed around 3500 B.C.

The Sumerian City-State

By 3000 B.C., 12 great Sumerian cities dotted the Mesopotamian plain. On the map on page 151, find Ur, Kish, and Lagash. Many thousands of Sumerians lived in these and other cities at this time. It is estimated that Lagash, for example, had as many as 20,000 people.

These centers of population were not just cities; they were city-states. Each **city-state** was made up of a city and the surrounding villages and farmland that it controlled. The farmers produced the food. City dwellers did other kinds of work. Some were brick makers,

canal builders, butchers, potters, and so forth. These workers exchanged their goods and services for food.

Mesopotamia is a region, not a country or nation. No central power controlled all the city-states, and there were no boundary lines. Each city-state was independent.

Priests ruled the early city-states, an indication of the primary role that religion played in Sumerian life. In fact, religion and government were combined. The priests ran the irrigation systems. They watched over the canals, planned new ones, gathered work crews, appointed inspectors, and settled arguments. They stored the surplus grain in the temples and distributed it during droughts and other hard times for farmers. In return, they collected taxes in the form of grain, animals, and other farm products. They also prayed and made sacrifices to please the Sumerian gods.

A Typical City-State

Kish, like the other Sumerian city-states, was built of mud brick. Its streets were narrow and winding. Its houses were small, windowless, and closely packed. In the photo above, you can see the ruins

of houses on a typical Sumerian street. Try to imagine how these houses once looked. What do you think it would have been like to live in one?

Most houses were like those described above. But the cities also had larger houses, the homes of the wealthy. Some had two stories and were built around a courtyard, like the one in the drawing below.

Kish also had a number of large public buildings. No doubt the most impressive of these buildings was the temple. And, by about 2700 B.C., Kish also had a huge royal palace.

Finally, like the other Sumerian cities, Kish had a thriving marketplace. Farmers and merchants came to the market with their wares. Traders from far-off lands brought products that were not available in Mesopotamia. Like other Sumerian cities, Kish was a

◄ *The photo shows the ruins of typical Sumerian houses in the ancient town of Larsa.*

▼ *From excavations at Ur, an archaeologist created the drawing below to show what a large Sumerian house, perhaps the home of a wealthy family, might have looked like.*

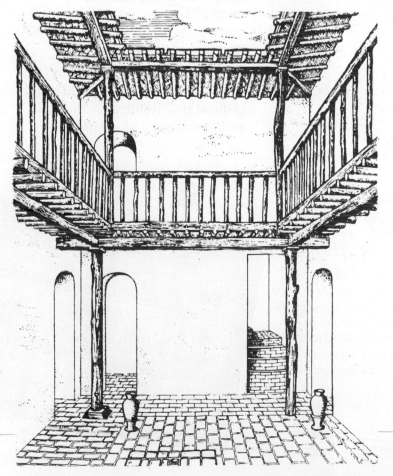

Irrigation allowed farmers to produce a surplus of food. The surplus freed some people to live in cities and work at occupations other than farming.

To run the vast irrigation systems, the Sumerians had to work together. They needed **administrators,** or managers, to organize the building and upkeep of the canals. The first of these administrators were the priests.

To please the gods and to store the surplus, the people built great temples. These building projects required stone, wood, and metal. Sumer lacked these, so the Sumerians traded with merchants from places near and far, including the lands we know today as Iran and India. Farmers exchanged wheat, barley, dates, wool, and dairy products for the tools and other supplies they needed. These included large items, such as lumber for building projects, and smaller items, such as stone hoes and clay pots.

As trade became increasingly important, other workers made goods to exchange at the market. Some created glittering jewelry. Others crafted decorative pottery,

▲ *The first wheel, invented sometime around 3500 B.C. by a Sumerian craftsman, was a solid wooden one, similar in design to this reconstruction. Lighter, spoked wheels came over a thousand years later.*

busy, exciting place, and trade was its lifeblood. This growing long-distance trade was an important part of the civilization that arose in the great cities of the Mesopotamian plain.

Builders of Civilization

Why did the harsh land of Sumer give rise to the world's first civilization? Remember that irrigation was most likely the key.

➤ *This well-preserved game-board, about 4,500 years old, is a fine example of Sumerian craftsmanship. What other information does it give us about the Sumerians?*

musical instruments, and colorful fabrics. Some even invented fascinating board games like the one pictured at the bottom of page 154. A skilled worker who makes such goods by hand is called an **artisan.**

With the growth of trade, the Sumerians needed a way to keep track of business deals. For example, how much grain does this farmer owe for that stone plow? In order to help keep records, the Sumerians used small clay or stone tokens in various shapes. Each shape stood for a different item or product.

People put the tokens into a round or football-shaped clay container called a *bulla.* The bulla was sealed while the clay was still wet. With the bulla sealed in this way, no one could change or remove its contents. However, no one could tell what tokens were inside the bulla, either.

After a time, people began to press marks into the wet clay of the new bulla to stand for the tokens inside. Archaeologists believe that this simple system of keeping records with tokens and bullae may have led to the invention of writing. In the next lesson, you will discover how this great invention may have come about.

Another important achievement of the Sumerians was the development of new kinds of technology to meet their daily needs. To break through the hard clay soils of their farmlands, they invented the plow. To transport the goods they traded, they developed the wheel and the sailboat. The Sumerians traded for metal, and they became skilled at working with various metals. They made strong tools and weapons, mixing copper and tin to make bronze. All these advances were just the beginning of the wondrous civilization that the Sumerians formed in their harsh homeland. ∎

▲ *The bulla and tokens shown here represent an early record-keeping system that may have led to the Sumerians' greatest invention, the world's first writing system.*

■ *What were some important advances that the Sumerians made in government, technology, and communication?*

REVIEW

1. **FOCUS** What was the relationship between the geography of Mesopotamia and the civilization that developed there?

2. **CONNECT** How were the cities of Ur and Kish examples of civilization?

3. **GOVERNMENT** Kish was a city-state. How was it governed? What was its relationship to the other city-states?

4. **CRITICAL THINKING** The Sumerians traded grain, wool, and other products for the stone, metal, and wood they lacked. What can you conclude about surplus in the lands they traded with?

5. **ACTIVITY** Sumerian cylinder seals were something like a person's signature. Draw a seal you could use to mark property and sign agreements. Make its design show something distinctive about you.

LESSON 2

The Contributions of the Sumerians

What were the Sumerian contributions in government, religion, and education?

Key Terms

- epic
- nomad
- polytheism
- pictograph
- cuneiform
- scribe

➤ *A Sumerian sculptor carved this stone relief of Gilgamesh about 2,000 years after the reign of the ancient king. By that time, Gilgamesh had long been a legendary hero in Mesopotamia.*

Through the tall cedar trees of the Forbidden Forest appeared the terrifying giant Huwawa. The towering creature had a head like a lion's and the teeth of a fierce dragon. His fiery breath struck fear into the hearts of all his enemies.

Facing the terrible monster were two men, both handsome, strong, and brave. One man, Gilgamesh, was king of the city of Uruk *(OO ruk).* No one rivaled this great adventurer in strength and courage. Next to Gilgamesh stood Enkidu, his valiant friend and servant.

Gilgamesh approached the fearsome Huwawa. Seven huge trees blocked the king's way, but he ripped them from the ground. The angry monster stared at Gilgamesh with his "eye of death." Huwawa then let out a cry so frightening that even the brave Gilgamesh trembled and felt weak. The time was perfect for the giant to attack.

So begins one of the stories in *Gilgamesh*, which was probably the world's first **epic,** or long poem about a hero. The story goes on to tell how the two friends attacked the giant Huwawa. Later, aided by the sun god Utu, Gilgamesh and Enkidu defeated Huwawa.

The story of Gilgamesh was first written down sometime before 2000 B.C., but it had probably been a part of an oral tradition for hundreds of years before that.

The real Gilgamesh was the king of the Sumerian city of Uruk around 2700 B.C. The epic about him is myth, not history, but it teaches us a great deal about how the Sumerians viewed their kings and their gods.

Gilgamesh may have been the world's first super-hero. The epic introduces him this way:

> *I* will proclaim to the world the deeds of Gilgamesh. This was the man to whom all things were known; this was the king who knew the countries of the world. He was wise, he saw mysteries and knew secret things.
>
> N.K. Sanders, editor
> from, *The Epic of Gilgamesh*

The First Kings

The earliest Sumerian city-states were ruled by priests, not kings, and the largest structure in each city was the temple. By 3000 B.C., the ruling priests had begun to share power with kings. Soon most cities had a magnificent royal palace in addition to the temple. These changes came about because the Sumerians had enemies; their cities were no longer safe.

The Rise of Kingship

Silently, under cover of night, they came. They swarmed through the streets, killing defenseless villagers and running off with precious grain and livestock. Who were these invaders? They were warriors from tribes that lived in the nearby mountains. No doubt they were attracted by the wealth of the thriving city-state.

An attack like this could have happened in any Sumerian city around 2900 B.C. Sometimes the raiders were **nomads,** people who moved with their flocks and herds. As the seasons changed, the nomads looked for water and pasture in new places, and they came into increasing conflict with their settled neighbors in the cities.

The population grew, and so did competition for land and water. Small skirmishes and great battles became common. The city-states even fought each other.

In the face of all these threats, the city-states looked for ways to protect themselves. Some cities built high walls to keep out invaders. But walls were not enough. The Sumerians needed strong military leaders. One by one, each city chose a temporary leader to rule during wars.

Each military leader eventually became a full-time ruler—a king,

In the Middle East, nomads and their flocks and herds still move with the changing seasons. Here a modern shepherd is watering his flock in the Euphrates River.

157

Mesopotamia

who took over many of the priests' duties. He managed irrigation works, stored surplus grain, and became the chief judge.

Kings and Gods

Over the years, the kings and priests took on separate tasks. The kings ruled the city-states, while the priests worked to please the gods. Yet kings remained closely tied to the Sumerian religion. Each city had its own god. The people believed that the city god gave the king his power and that their kings were appointed by the gods. They believed that kingship "came down from heaven." ■

■ *What circumstances in Mesopotamia led to the rise of kings?*

▼ *The Sumerians made these small statues of their gods and of themselves. They are wearing the typical Sumerian clothes, which were made of wool.*

The Sumerian Religion

The religion of Sumer was a kind of **polytheism**—belief in many gods. The Sumerians believed that their gods controlled everything. Without the gods' help, cities could not be safe, and farmers could not grow crops. Drought, disease, floods, and invading armies—all of these evils came and went at the will of the gods. The Sumerians felt helpless against the forces of nature. Only by pleasing the gods, they believed, could they feel confident of good fortune.

The Gods of Sumer

According to Sumerian legends, four all-powerful gods created the world and ruled over it. The father of all the gods was An, who ruled the sky. Later Enlil, the god of the air, replaced An as supreme god. Enki ruled the waters, and Ninhursag was the mother goddess. Other great gods were the moon god, the sun god, and the goddess of love and war.

Below these gods reigned about 3,000 lesser gods. The most important ones ruled the forces of nature. There was a lower god for each everyday object, such as the pickax or the mud brick.

The great Sumerian gods each ruled a city-state. Enki, for example, ruled the city of Eridu, and the moon god, Nanna, ruled Ur. Each city had a high priest, who worked to please all the gods.

Imagine a Sumerian priest explaining about the gods: "Our gods are hard to please. Like humans, they change their minds, get angry, feel love and hate. Sometimes they are happy. Other times they fall into a great sadness. Like us, they need to eat, and sleep. They even look like us.

"Yet they are not like us at all. They reign immortal and all powerful. They behave better than the best of us but can be more evil than the worst villain. At any time, a god's anger may strike as a flood, a disease, or a savage enemy raid.

"But remember," the priest might conclude, "they are the masters, and we are the servants. Our only purpose is to serve the gods."

Service to the Gods

All Sumerians served the gods. Even the mightiest king was a servant of the city's god and of the god Enlil, who gave kings their power. One of the king's most important tasks was to oversee the building and repair of the temples. The priests spent their lives serving the gods. They left food in the temple for the city god, recited prayers, and presented offerings. The Sumerians believed that the work kept away misfortune, such as drought or illness.

Serving the gods was not only the task of kings and priests. All Sumerians sent food and animals to the temple. They prayed, attended religious ceremonies, and tried to live a good life. They believed that in return the gods would protect them and bring them good fortune. Many Sumerians used their artistic skills to serve the gods. Stoneworkers created sculptures for the temple. They made small statues of the gods and of their worshippers. They carved the cylinder seals that were used to show ownership. Metalworkers created beautiful religious art. From gold and silver, they crafted good-luck charms, vases, and small statues of priests, kings, and heroes.

▼ *This small copper chariot pulled by donkey-like animals was found in a Sumerian temple.*

From these works of art, buried for centuries, archaeologists have learned much about life in ancient Sumer. ■

■ *Describe the Sumerians' religion and explain its important role in the lives of the people.*

The People of Sumer

Step for a moment into one of the weaving workshops in Lagash. Over in the corner of the weaving house, four of the younger women are sitting on low stools learning to spin sheep wool into yarn. In the middle of the room, two experienced weavers are squatting on either side of a loom, weaving a thick cloth of bright red. This cloth will be sent on donkey caravans and traded for copper. Some of these women are free business women, others are slaves. They all work for Urukagina, the king of this city-state.

Three social classes lived in Sumerian cities. Some members of all three classes are mentioned in the paragraph you just read. The highest class was made up of the king, government officials, the most important priests, and the wealthiest merchants and landowners. The lowest class was made up of slaves. All other people were part of the free middle class that included farmers, fishermen, and artisans such as the women weavers.

Slavery

Sumer has some of the first records of slavery in the ancient world. Slaves were often prisoners from wars between city-states. Because farming needed large numbers of workers, prisoners were used to farm the land while soldiers were off fighting. This was a change from earlier times when prisoners were often killed.

People who didn't own land sometimes sold themselves as slaves just to eat and have a place to sleep. Parents could legally sell their children into slavery. Though slaves were the property of a master and could be beaten, they did have certain rights. They could be in business and borrow money. If a slave was married to a free person, their children were born free. Slaves could also buy their own freedom. ■

■ *What were the three social classes in Sumerian cities and how did their lives differ?*

▼ *Sumerian scribes used a reed stylus to press the cuneiform letters onto moist clay tablets. Notice the wedge-shaped letters on the tablet. Then use the chart to trace the development of several cuneiform letters.*

The Beginnings of Writing

By inventing writing, the Sumerians were the first people to keep lasting written records of the human past.

Using Picture Writing

The Sumerians' first written symbols were pictures of items that were used in trade, such as a bull or a sack of grain. Such symbols are **pictographs**, or pictures that stand for words or ideas. The Sumerians used a sharpened reed, called a stylus, to draw the pictographs on moistened clay.

Look at the chart on this page. As you can see, a pictograph might stand for an object or a related idea. For example, a picture of a sword might mean "power."

Next, the Sumerians extended the pictures to make them stand for syllables related only by sound, not meaning. For example, the word for "fish" was *ha*. A picture of a fish could stand for the word *fish*,

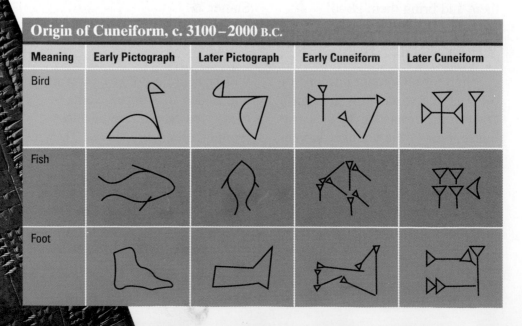

Origin of Cuneiform, c. 3100–2000 B.C.				
Meaning	**Early Pictograph**	**Later Pictograph**	**Early Cuneiform**	**Later Cuneiform**
Bird				
Fish				
Foot				

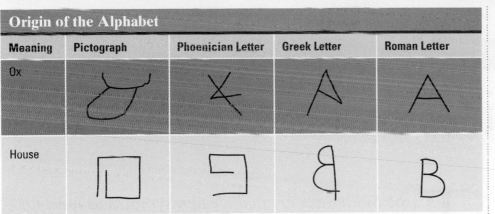

Origin of the Alphabet

Meaning	Pictograph	Phoenician Letter	Greek Letter	Roman Letter
Ox				
House				

◄ The shapes of our letters originated in Sumerian pictographs. The chart shows how we got the Roman alphabet we use today.

or it could stand for the syllable *ha* as a part of any word. Here is an example in English:

🐝 + 🍃 = belief

Now writers could string syllables together to form words and express abstract ideas like "belief."

Simplifying the Pictures

Picture writing changed over time. By 2500 B.C., writers had simplified their symbols and made them wedge shaped. This type of writing is known as **cuneiform** (*KYOO nee uh fawrm*), meaning "wedge shaped." Cuneiform consisted of around 600 symbols, which range from a single wedge to complex patterns of about 30 wedges. Few people could read or write. Even kings could not do so. To read and write messages, people employed scribes—professional writers and record keepers.

Using Symbols for Sounds

The cuneiform system was used in the Middle East for about 2,000 years. Later, around 900 B.C., the Phoenicians (*fih NIHSH uhns*) devised a simpler way to keep records. The Phoenicians lived on the east coast of the Mediterranean Sea. They were seafaring merchants who traded throughout the area. Cuneiform, with its many symbols, was just too complicated to use in their growing trade. They invented a new writing system with only 22 symbols. Each symbol stood for one sound. If you think this system sounds familiar, you're right. The Phoenicians invented the alphabet. ■

How Do We Know?

HISTORY *For many years, historians studying Mesopotamia could not read cuneiform. Then, in 1835, linguists began to decipher a message carved in three languages on a giant rock formation in the Zagros Mountains. By 1857, all three languages had been translated. One was Sumerian. Deciphering cuneiform led to much of our knowledge of the ancient Middle East, including Sumer and the Sumerian people.*

■ *Describe the important steps in the invention of writing, including pictographs, cuneiform, and the alphabet.*

REVIEW

1. **FOCUS** What were the Sumerian contributions in government, religion, and education?
2. **CONNECT** Explain how Sumerian achievements in technology and communication helped to advance long-distance trade.
3. **HISTORY** What were the needs of the Sumerians that led to the establishment of kingships? To the invention of writing?
4. **CRITICAL THINKING** Religion had great importance for the Sumerians. What conditions of their lives might help to explain why?
5. **WRITING ACTIVITY** Examine the picture writing for *belief* on page 160. Try writing other words in the same way—*pantry* and *football*, for example. Combine letters and pictures as necessary—for example, in writing *catalog*.

161

Writing Systems

T he Sumerians created written symbols to meet an everyday need—tracking the goods they traded. You, too, can develop symbols and use them to send secret messages. Like the Sumerians, you'll be limited only by your imagination—and your tools and materials.

Get Ready

Find a clear, flat surface, such as a desk, table, or floor space. Use waxed paper, plastic, or oilcloth to protect the surface. Get a ball of pottery clay the size of an orange. Find a tool—a new, unsharpened pencil, a paper clip, or a popsicle stick.

Find Out

Work the clay to soften it. Then flatten it into a sheet. Using the tool you've chosen, press symbols into the clay. Your symbols can stand for sounds, as our alphabet letters do. They can also stand for ideas, as in cuneiform or hieroglyphics (see the charts on the facing page), or for syllables. For instance, if you decide that / is the syllable *par,* and # is the syllable *tee,* how would you write *party?*

Work out a system of symbols. Use them to "write" each word below on your clay tablet:

flower flour   knee needle paddle
friend ship friendship   am is are
give take jump   true truth truly
I you they

Write a few sentences using these words.

Move Ahead

Find a place in the classroom to display the clay tablets. Can you tell which tool a person used, just by looking at his or her tablet? Do any of the written "languages" look alike? Can your classmates read the sentence you "wrote"?

Look at the examples of cuneiform and hieroglyphic writing on the charts. Which pictographs really look like the objects they represent?

Transfer your new language from clay to paper. Use a pen, pencil, crayon, or marker. Will the writing tool make a difference in the way your "words" look?

Explore Some More

Make a "dictionary" of your new language. A friend can use it to read your messages. Also keep a list of symbols you notice in everyday life such as road signs and flags.

Create a special symbol to stand for your signature. That symbol on a note or drawing will show that it came from you.

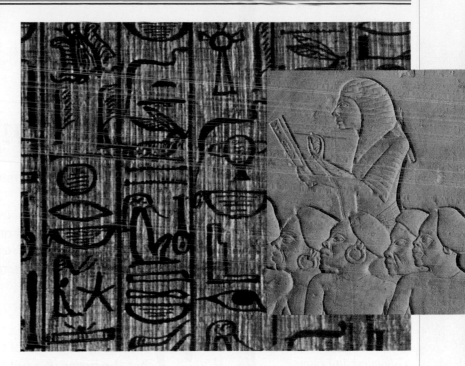

▲ An Egyptian scribe keeps accounts for his master in this sculpture, inset against a detail of hieroglyphics from an Egyptian wall-hanging.

Hieroglyphics Versus Alphabet

	Hieroglyphics	Greek Script
Soldier		στρατιώτης
Eye		ὀφθαλμός
Beetle		χάνθαρος
Swallow		χελιδών

Development of Cuneiform Writing

	Early Pictograph	Later Pictograph	Early Cuneiform	Later Cuneiform
Donkey				
Ox				
Sun				
Grain				
Orchard				

▲ How do hieroglyphic writing and cuneiform differ from an alphabetic system?

163

The Luring of Enkidu

Bernarda Bryson

Many myths have survived about the Mesopotamian King Gilgamesh. This selection from a book called Gilgamesh *tells about the education of Enkidu, the wild man. Enkidu later becomes King Gilgamesh's friend and servant. Here, a shepherd's son describes Enkidu.*

You learned about King Gilgamesh in Lesson 2. This is another myth involving the well-known king.

gazelle a hoofed, horned mammal of Africa and Asia

The hair springs out of his head like a field of grain, and he has the horns of a wild beast!"

"If he stole your catch of game, my son, why didn't you stop him?"

"He is taller and more powerful than Gilgamesh the King. I was numbed with fear!"

"If what you say is true, son, then we must report the matter to the King. But if you have lied, we will be in disgrace forever!"

The shepherd and his son went into the city of Uruk to make their complaint. But there the populace were already spreading rumors about the wild man. Some said, "He is covered with hair from head to foot," and others, "He is taller than a giant and eats grass with the gazelles!"

It was the eldest of the elders who led the hunter and his father before the King. "O Gilgamesh," said the elder, "there is a wild man that terrorizes the countryside. He robs the hunter of his game and disperses the herds of the shepherd. He turns all who see him numb with fear—indeed I've heard that he is taller and more powerful than Gilgamesh the King!"

Gilgamesh, who feared nothing, might have been expected to say, "Then it's I who will go out and subdue him and bring him captive to the city!" Not at all; he sent to the temple of Ishtar for a certain priestess, one called Harim, servant of the goddess.

He said to her, "Harim, I have a certain task for you; it is one that turns the boldest hunters numb with fear!"

"Then I am afraid," said Harim.

The eldest of the elders spoke angrily, "This is not a girl's task, O King; it is a task for a brave man—a hero!"

"Tut tut," said Gilgamesh. "It is a girl's task of smiles and charm. Go, Harim; soften the heart of the wild man and bring him back to the city!"

Harim was led by the hunter to the edge of the forest, and she noted that he began to tremble with fear. "Go back to the hut of your father," she commanded. "If I can tame the wild man, I will lead him into the city alone."

The hunter was shamed by the girl's bravery. "Do not enter the forest, O Harim; I myself will go." But the priestess laughed at him and sent him home.

She went among the dark cedars; she listened to the sounds of birds and of monkeys chattering. She noted the bits of sunlight that filtered through the branches and lit up the flowers, moss, and bracken on the forest floor. "How peaceful a place this is! How could any evil thing lurk here?" Harim found a fresh spring bubbling with cool water. She sat beside it on a stone, untied her sandals, and dipped her feet in the water.

Enkidu came to the place with the small wild horse and the gazelle. As they drew near, the two beasts became nervous, sniffed the air, and fled. But Enkidu stood still; he wondered what new danger was near, what unknown beast might have come to the water.

When he saw the girl sitting there his breath failed and he was overcome. He had not yet seen a human being, and this creature seemed to him the most admirable, the most enchanting being that he had ever seen. He stood quietly in order not to frighten her.

Harim gazed at this giant figure, his soaring horns, and his unkempt looks and would have run away, but she could not move. She opened her mouth to scream and could not make a sound. She was numb with terror. And Enkidu noting this remained quiet; he had made friends with many timid creatures and he knew their ways.

When the priestess saw the gentleness of his manner, her courage returned to her somewhat. She called out shyly, "Hello!"

Enkidu knew no words. He could babble somewhat as the monkeys did. He could bark quite like a fox, or trill like many birds. He had various calls of greeting for his wild friends, but this new animal made sounds that he could not understand.

He neither barked nor roared, but stood perplexed looking at the girl. Again she spoke, and now held out her hands to him in greeting.

Enkidu approached slowly and sat on the earth beside the white feet of Harim. She said all sorts of things to him and he understood nothing. She asked him many questions and he could not reply. But he felt ecstasy in his heart, and great contentment in merely sitting beside her.

How easy was her conquest of Enkidu! Harim smiled, but she now began to feel a new sort of fear. How could she lead this great fellow, so gentle and so innocent, back to the city of Uruk?

Would the people set on him and kill him? Would they jeer at him? Would the King have him put into a cage and carried through the streets on the backs of soldiers? She shuddered.

No, first she must teach him the ways of people, the conformity of life.

"Al-ka ti-ba i-na ga-ag-ga-ri!" said Harim. "Come, rise from the ground!" But the wild man did not understand. Thus, she taught him the word for standing, and then after that, the word for sitting. She taught him the words for walking, running, talking, laughing, eating, and he repeated each one, learning it. She taught him the words for trees and for stones and for water, for earth and for the trailing vines that grew beside the spring, and for the spring itself. She taught him the words for feet and hands and the names of all the fingers and all the myriad words of love.

Thus patiently, Harim taught Enkidu to be like ordinary men. She cut his hair and combed it in the way of people of the city. She made him bathe; she tore her long tunic into two parts, making of one-half a garment for Enkidu, keeping the other half for herself.

Again she spoke to him, and now he understood, "A-na-tal-ka En-ki-du ki-ma ili ta-ba-as-si!"—"I gaze upon you, Enkidu; you are like a god!"

He brought her gifts—all the things that he had come to know and love in the forest and from the open steppes; wild cucumbers and cassia melon, grapes and figs and caper buds from the dry rocks. He brought her blossoms of golden mimosa and fragrant branches of jasmine.

After some time had passed Harim said, "Now I will lead Enkidu out among the people and everyone will admire him!" But still she feared for his life so she took him first to the hut of the shepherd.

At the edge of the forest Enkidu stopped and turned back. He was overcome with regret; how could he leave forever his friends of the woods and wild places? Who would protect them? Who would release them from the traps? How could he leave behind his friend the little wild horse, or the gazelle, the rabbits, the monkeys that had taught him to play games?

But as he approached they leaped away startled. The rabbit hid trembling in the grass and the birds took off with a wild flutter of wings.

Enkidu threw himself to the ground weeping. "O Harim, what have I done? How have I made all my friends into strangers? Why do they run from me?"

"Enkidu is no longer a wild creature. He is no longer a beast of the forest and the open plain. Enkidu is now a man. He will live among men and be eminent among men!"

Enkidu followed regretfully as the priestess led him toward the hut of the shepherd. This man greeted him with awe and

myriad many; innumerable

eminent distinguished; outstanding

166

admiration, but his son fled from the place and hid in the sheep-fold. After some time he returned, running. "Father, a lion has entered the fold! It is devouring the lambs!"

Enkidu went to the sheepfold where again he wrestled with the lion, his friend who no longer knew him. Again he overcame the beast, but he let it go free. He lifted the lambs gently, washing and tending the ones that bled. To his great joy they did not shun him or run away. Neither did the young calves nor the barnyard fowl A dog followed him wagging its tail. A cat smoothed its fur against his legs, and again he was content.

In the hut of the shepherd Enkidu learned to sit on a chair and to wash his hands before eating. He learned how to care for animals, to make plants grow, and to build with mud and brick and reeds. He learned to play on a flute. He ate bread. There he drank the juice of the wild grape. His face shone, he rejoiced; he sang.

Harim smiled. "Now Enkidu has become like a man, we shall go into the city!"

Further Reading

Gilgamesh and Other Babylonian Tales. Jennifer Westwood.

He Who Saw Everything: The Epic of Gilgamesh. Anita Feagles. This book and *Gilgamesh and Other Babylonian Tales* are other versions of the Gilgamesh epic.

In the Land of Ur. Hans Baumann. The author describes archaeological finds in Mesopotamia and tells what they reveal about the ancient civilizations of that area.

The Three Brothers of Ur. Jennifer G. Fyson. Here is an adventure story about three boys in the ancient city of Ur. The story also teaches about the boys' religion and customs.

7000   6000   5000   4000   3000

2350   1000

L E S S O N   3

The First Empires

THINKING FOCUS

How did three great rulers build and maintain empires in Mesopotamia?

Key Terms

- empire
- code

> *This bronze head is believed to be of Sargon of Akkad or his grandson, Naram-Sin, who extended Sargon's empire.*

"Invaders! We're under attack!" The words resounded through Uruk as a fearsome army thundered toward the great city. First came the chariots pulled by hardy, donkeylike animals. In each chariot stood a driver, and behind him a warrior, shooting deadly arrows. Next came the foot-soldiers, rushing forward as a solid block—metal helmets, a wall of metal shields, spears leveled to face their foes.

The attack caught Uruk unprepared. Who were these invaders? Who would dare to rouse the anger of the great Lugal-zaggesi *(LOO guhl zuh GEE see),* king of Uruk and ruler of all Sumer? But Lugal-zaggesi was not in Uruk at the time, and the forces that he had left behind to protect the city could not stop the invaders.

The bold attackers battered down the city's gate. They ravaged the streets and avenues, burning and tearing down buildings. They killed some residents and terrorized the rest, seizing whatever riches they found. When Uruk lay in ruins, they used battering rams and ropes to tear down the city's wall.

A few days later, Lugal-zaggesi returned with his troops. The king saw his ruined city and savagely attacked the invaders. Again, arrows whizzed through the air. Metal clanked against metal as swords and shields met. After many hours, the battle ended. Now a captive, the great Lugal-zaggesi stood before his conquerors.

Who were those fierce warriors, and who was their general, who barked orders in a foreign tongue? He called himself Sargon, meaning "true king." Soon this warrior-king would be known throughout all Mesopotamia.

Sargon of Akkad

Unlike most kings, Sargon did not begin his life in a palace. His parents were probably herders on the north edge of Sumer near the Euphrates River. They spoke a language called Akkadian.

When Sargon left home, he went to Kish and became a servant of its king. Historians believe he later killed the king and usurped his throne. Next, he gathered an army and founded a new capital—the city of Akkad *(AHK ahd),* on the Euphrates River.

Sargon's power grew. He led his strong army to the cities of Uruk, Ur, Lagash, and Umma, conquering each one. Finally, he reached the Persian Gulf. According to legend, he washed his weapons in the waters of the gulf as a sign that he had conquered all of Sumer's city-states.

Later, Sargon conquered northern Mesopotamia and lands as far east as modern Iran and as far west as the Mediterranean coast. His kingdom may have reached to Egypt.

Until Sargon's rule, the city-states were independent, each with its own king. They had walls to protect them from enemies, including other city-states. With each conquest, Sargon tore down the walls, showing that the city was part of his vast kingdom. He created the world's first **empire**—a nation and the city-states and nations it has conquered, under one ruler. Sargon ruled until 2279 B.C., about 55 years. For another 60 years, his sons and grandsons ruled.

As the years passed, problems developed, and the empire grew weaker. One problem was rebellion. The city-states never accepted the rule of a central government. They continued to struggle for independence. A second problem was frequent invasions. Enemies could easily invade the city-states on their flat, open plain. Around 2250 B.C., the Gutians, fierce warriors from the neighboring Zagros Mountains, invaded Akkad and left it in ruins. Sargon's empire had collapsed. ■

How Do We Know?

HISTORY *As you read about the ancient world, do not be surprised if two sources give two different dates for the same event. Sargon of Akkad provides a good example, since historians do not agree about the exact years of his life and reign. To find out why this is true, review Chapter 3, Lesson 1. Remember that historians are constantly finding and interpreting new evidence.*

■ *What important change did Sargon make in the way Mesopotamia was governed?*

◄ *There were no official boundaries for Sargon's empire. The map shows the extent of the great king's influence.*

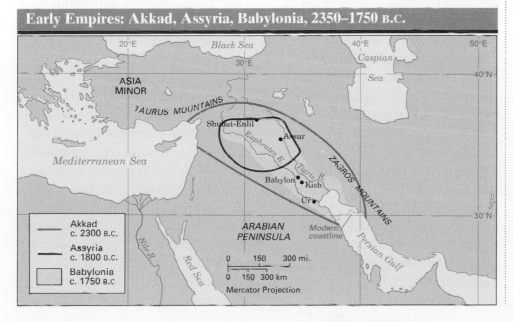

Early Empires: Akkad, Assyria, Babylonia, 2350–1750 B.C.

Akkad c. 2300 B.C.
Assyria c. 1800 B.C.
Babylonia c. 1750 B.C.

Black Sea · Caspian Sea · ASIA MINOR · TAURUS MOUNTAINS · Shubat-Enlil · Assur · Euphrates R. · ZAGROS MOUNTAINS · Mediterranean Sea · Babylon · Kish · Tigris R. · Ur · ARABIAN PENINSULA · Modern coastline · Persian Gulf · Nile R. · Red Sea

0   150   300 mi.
0 150 300 km
Mercator Projection

Mesopotamia

169

Letters between the king of Mari and his sons were written on clay tablets like this one, shown with its clay envelope.

Rival Empires

During the next four centuries, the Sumerians recovered some of their lost power and made great achievements under the kings of Ur. But then power shifted to two new centers. Assyria, centered at the city-state of Assur in the north, and Babylonia, centered at the city-state of Babylon in the south, vied for power. In fact, the struggle between north and south, with power swinging from one to the other, became the pattern for much of Mesopotamia's history.

A Strong Assyrian Ruler

Assyria reached its peak under the ruler Shamshi-Adad *(SHAM shee uh DAD)*, in power from about 1813 to 1781 B.C. Like Sargon, Shamshi-Adad was a great conqueror. He led his army west and conquered what is now Lebanon, with its thick forests and mineral-rich mountains. Next he overthrew the King of Mari on the Euphrates, installing his son as the new king of the city.

Shamshi-Adad held his lands together by trade as well as force. Assyrian merchants exchanged Mesopotamian products such as fine cloth for valuable foreign goods including tin, copper, and silver. Their trade agreements were prepared by scribes like the one in A Moment in Time on page 171.

Shamshi-Adad appointed his two sons to help him rule his vast, rich kingdom. But he and his sons never felt safe. They feared attack by nomads who envied Assyria's riches. Even more, they worried about neighboring kingdoms. One neighbor, Babylonia, especially worried them.

A Wise Babylonian Ruler

A young ruler named Hammurabi *(hah moo RAH bee)* came to power in Babylonia in 1792 B.C., during the last years of Shamshi-Adad's life. The Assyrians were right to fear him. One day, he would take over Assyrian lands and rule all of Mesopotamia.

In the fifth year of his rule, he set out with his strong army to gain control of the neighboring kingdoms. Over the next five years, he conquered lands east to the Zagros Mountains and south to Uruk.

Later, around 1760 B.C., the Assyrians joined some neighboring peoples and attacked Hammurabi's kingdom. The battles were fierce and bloody, but the great king defeated the invaders.

Hammurabi felt strong enough to begin extending his lands. He marched his victorious army north. He defeated other armies and added new lands, including Assyria, to his kingdom. Finally, Hammurabi ruled all of Mesopotamia. His kingdom included 24 great cities. Now Mesopotamia formed one enormous empire. Use the map on page 169 to find out the extent of Hammurabi's Babylonian Empire.

Hammurabi was a capable ruler. He sent governors to all his lands. He also sent out judges, tax collectors, and military commanders. He kept tight control over his far-flung cities and maintained a strong central government. Hammurabi was a wise king and a great military leader. Today, however, we remember him mainly for one of his achievements—the Code of Hammurabi.

A Mesopotamian Scribe

8:33 A.M., December 17, 1794 B.C.
On the bank of the Euphrates River,
in the port of the city of Mari

Seals
Inside a purse under the scribe's robe are two seals. One prints her name. The other prints this important message: "May the gods curse anyone who changes what is here written!"

Hands
Her quick hands wrote as fast as the merchant dictated to her. Now she's making an envelope to protect the document.

Pot
Inside is a day's supply of wet clay and water. Her sister collected the clay at a special place near the Euphrates where it contains less sand.

Envelope
She pats it thin as a piecrust. Next she'll write on the envelope and wrap it around the tablet.

Skirt
A customer who expected to see her father was shocked to find a woman in the dead scribe's place. Since her father had no sons, he taught his elder daughter his trade. It took 11 years.

Stylus
She uses this sharpened reed to press words into the wet clay in the neat "handwriting" her father taught her.

Tablet
It lists the items being shipped—110 pounds of cedar wood, 10 pounds of silver, 60 lengths of cloth, 12 pounds of dyed wool, and 6 tanned cowhides. The tablet ends with a promise: "The boat captain will pay the merchant 100 pounds of silver in two years."

c. 2334–c. 2279 B.C.,
Sargon of Akkad

1813–1781 B.C.,
Shamshi-Adad of Assyria

2000

1500

1792–1750 B.C.,
Hammurabi of Babylonia

▲ *On the timeline, locate the rulers of the three early empires presented in this lesson. In Lesson 4, you will read about the two later rulers.*

The Code of Hammurabi

"I have brought justice to all my subjects." So boasted Hammurabi in words that were carved on an eight-foot slab of black stone. Below the king's words, the remarkable structure listed 282 laws of Babylonia. Most people couldn't read, but the laws were public now. Anyone could find out what they were, so no one could be punished at a ruler's whim.

Hammurabi chose carefully among the laws of his empire. He tried to cover all matters that were important to his people. He made sure that one law did not conflict with any other. Such a complete and organized set of laws is called a **code**. The Code of Hammurabi was not the first or even the best of the early law lists. But we know more about it than about others, since it was preserved on stone.

Some of Hammurabi's laws covered religion, irrigation, and military service. Others dealt with trade, slavery, and the duties of workers such as surgeons. The Code of Hammurabi also gave protection to women and the family. The purpose of all these laws was "to set right the orphan and widow . . . and wronged person."

➤ *The top of the stone slab that is inscribed with Hammurabi's Code is shown in this photo. Hammurabi is standing in front of the god, possibly the Babylonians' chief god Marduk, who is delivering the laws to him.*

Items from The Code of Hammurabi:

If a freeman has destroyed the eye of another freeman, they shall destroy his eye.

If he has destroyed the eye of a commoner or broken the bone of a commoner, he shall pay one mina [one to two pounds] of silver.

If a freeman hired an ox and has destroyed its eye, he shall give one-half its value in silver to the owner of the ox.

744–727 B.C.,
Tiglath-Pileser III of the
New Assyrian Empire

1000   500   B.C. A.D.

605–562 B.C.,
Nebuchadnezzar of the
New Babylonian Empire

Read the laws again. Which one suggests the importance of agriculture in Mesopotamian life? From our perspective today, we may see problems with these laws. Which one seems unfair? How do some laws vary according to a person's position in society?

Hammurabi's Code was an important advance. It helped to establish the kind of life that people should live, a responsible life framed by law and order. Some laws showed concern for the less powerful. For example, there were laws that protected wives from being beaten or neglected by their husbands.

Hammurabi's Code helped the king rule his empire. Yet even with a law code, with governers, and with armies, Hammurabi's kingdom began to crumble after the great king's death in 1750 B.C.

The Next 750 Years

In this chapter you have seen that invasions by people from surrounding deserts and mountains were common throughout the history of Mesopotamia. Around 1600 B.C., the Hittites, a fierce mountain people from the northwest, invaded Mesopotamia and conquered the city of Babylon.

Other invaders included the Kassites from the Zagros Mountains to the northeast. The Kassites gained control of Babylonia and ruled the city for four centuries. They adopted the Babylonian language and culture. In addition, they brought peace and order to the land.

By now, several kingdoms outside of Mesopotamia were becoming increasingly prominent in the Middle East. Some of them made important contributions. For example, it was during this period that the Phoenicians invented the alphabet. The Jews developed their belief in one God. And by the 1200s B.C., in the north, a new Assyrian Empire was emerging that would become more powerful than ever. ■

■ *Support this statement: Although their empires did not survive long after they died, in many ways Shamshi-Adad and Hammurabi were capable rulers.*

R E V I E W

1. **FOCUS** How did three great rulers build and maintain empires in Mesopotamia?
2. **CONNECT** Besides land, what resources and achievements made the city-states desirable to conquerors?
3. **GEOGRAPHY** What features of the geography of Mesopotamia forced the Sumerians to develop trade?
4. **CRITICAL THINKING** Military leaders have often performed actions that serve as signs of power or conquest, such as Sargon's washing his weapons in the Persian Gulf. Why are such actions important?
5. **ACTIVITY** Plan a panel discussion about crime and punishment, focusing on what makes a punishment fair or unfair. In your discussion, refer to Hammurabi's Code and to present-day laws.

Using Telescoping Timelines

Here's Why

Some timelines give a broad view of events over many centuries. Other timelines, called telescoping timelines, give a more detailed view of a shorter period. Like a telephoto lens, a telescoping timeline allows you to "zoom in" on a certain period of time.

Suppose you wanted to use a timeline to present key events from one period in the history of Mesopotamia. A telescoping timeline is an effective way to do this.

Here's How

The 2,000-year timeline at the bottom of the page shows major events in Mesopotamian history. The dates on the thick bar show you that the timeline covers the period from 2400 to 400 B.C.

Now look at the 150-year telescoping timeline above it. This timeline's subject is the rise and decline of Babylonian power. It covers the period from 650 to 500 B.C. The shaded triangle between the timelines helps you see where the telescoping timeline "fits" on the 2,000-year timeline.

On which timeline should an event from the chapter be plotted? That depends on when the event occurred. For example, Hammurabi's reign belongs on the 2,000-year timeline. His reign was over before 650 B.C. However, the burning of Jerusalem in 587 B.C. belongs on the 150-year timeline.

Try It

Copy both of the timelines from the book onto your own paper. Decide on which timeline each of the following events belongs: the end of Nabonidus's rule, in 539 B.C.; Adad-Nirari's defeat of northern Mesopotamia, in 911 B.C.; the Hittite conquest of Babylon, in 1600 B.C. Plot each event in its proper place on the timeline.

Apply It

Make your own timeline and telescoping timeline. Use the events of your own life, from birth until now, as your base timeline. Make a telescoping timeline of one year. Include any special events, such as a family trip, that happened during that year.

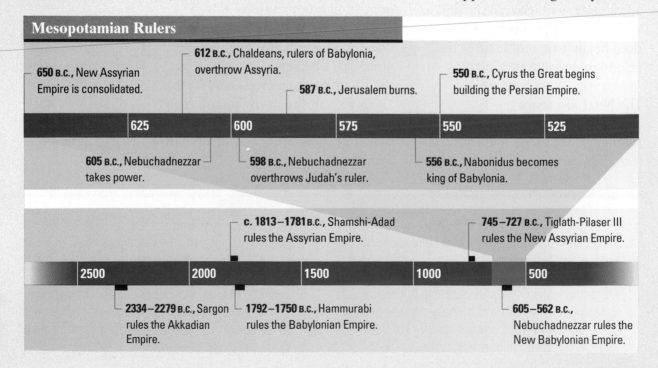

Mesopotamian Rulers

650 B.C., New Assyrian Empire is consolidated.

612 B.C., Chaldeans, rulers of Babylonia, overthrow Assyria.

587 B.C., Jerusalem burns.

550 B.C., Cyrus the Great begins building the Persian Empire.

| 625 | 600 | 575 | 550 | 525 |

605 B.C., Nebuchadnezzar takes power.

598 B.C., Nebuchadnezzar overthrows Judah's ruler.

556 B.C., Nabonidus becomes king of Babylonia.

c. 1813–1781 B.C., Shamshi-Adad rules the Assyrian Empire.

745–727 B.C., Tiglath-Pilaser III rules the New Assyrian Empire.

| 2500 | 2000 | 1500 | 1000 | 500 |

2334–2279 B.C., Sargon rules the Akkadian Empire.

1792–1750 B.C., Hammurabi rules the Babylonian Empire.

605–562 B.C., Nebuchadnezzar rules the New Babylonian Empire.

L E S S O N 4

New Empires

Three hundred feet above the city of Babylon towered the majestic ziggurat—seven stories high. Each story was smaller than the one below it, giving the whole structure a pyramid shape. In the shrine at the top, priests chanted prayers to Marduk, who was their chief god. The Babylonians believed that Marduk was the creator of the world, so they called the ziggurat E-temen-anki, "The House of the Foundation of Heaven and Earth."

Babylon had other marvels besides the grand ziggurat. Not far from the tower were the magnificent "hanging gardens." Sweetly scented plants and trees grew from high terraces, creating a lush, cool resting place, out of the blazing sun.

Beyond the gardens stood the city walls. These walls were so thick that a chariot drawn by four large horses could easily travel along on top of them. The great king of Babylon, Nebuchadnezzar *(neh buh kuhd NEHZ ur),* had rebuilt the towering ziggurat, planted the gardens, and constructed the vast walls.

These glorious building projects tell us something important about the age that we are about to explore. In ancient Mesopotamia, the period after 1000 B.C. is recognized as the age of the great new empires of Assyria and Babylonia. The giant structures built at this time in Babylon and other cities were displays of the fabulous wealth and power of these empires and their rulers.

THINKING
FOCUS

How were the New Assyrian and New Babylonian empires alike, and how were they different?

Key Terms

- exile
- astronomer

◄ *The ziggurat at Babylon was probably as old as the city itself. It had been destroyed and rebuilt more than once before Nebuchadnezzar's reign. This picture shows one artist's idea of what the ziggurat might have looked like.*

175

Mesopotamia

A New Assyrian Empire

In the late 900s B.C., power again swung north to Assyria. But this New Assyrian Empire would reach far beyond Mesopotamia.

A Path of Conquest

How did the Assyrians build such a vast empire, and how did they maintain it? The Assyrians had long been rugged warriors. Their tightly organized and well-equipped army stormed enemy cities like a mighty machine—on foot, in chariots, and on swift horses. Once Assyrian troops battered down a city's gates, they showed no mercy. They murdered, tortured, and enslaved their enemies. Those conquered by the Assyrians hated them forever.

The king of Assyria, Adad-Nirari *(uh DAD nih RAH ree)*, set out to conquer new lands and gather riches around 911 B.C. The king secured the northern part of Mesopotamia for the Assyrians. Everywhere his army went, they looted and plundered, gathering gold, silver, jewels, and other wealth. The rulers who followed Adad-Nirari enlarged his path of conquest, moving west as far as the Mediterranean Sea.

Almost 200 years later, in 745 B.C., King Tiglath-Pileser III *(TIHG lath puh LEE zur)* came to the throne. He succeeded in extending the empire to the south by taking over Assyria's age-old rival, Babylonia.

Tiglath-Pileser III struggled to hold his far-flung empire together as many of the conquered peoples rebelled. Early in his reign, he developed a strategy to end rebellion. He forced many people to move from their homelands to faraway parts of the empire. For example, Assyrian soldiers took 30,000 Syrians on a scorching march across desert, valley, and highland into the Zagros Mountains. By doing this, he hoped to break the spirit of rebellion.

By 650 B.C., the New Assyrian Empire covered lands from the Persian Gulf to Egypt to present-day Turkey. Use the map below to

Compare the extent of the New Assyrian and New Babylonian empires. Then compare them both with the early empires shown in the map on page 169.

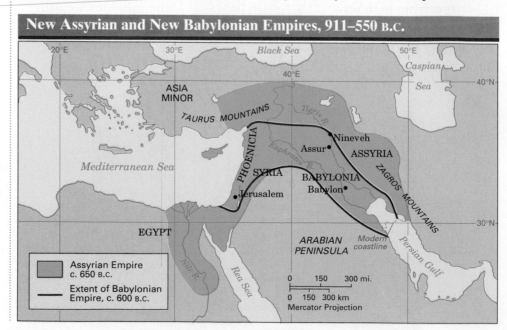

New Assyrian and New Babylonian Empires, 911–550 B.C.

Assyrian Empire c. 650 B.C.

Extent of Babylonian Empire, c. 600 B.C.

0 150 300 mi.

0 150 300 km

Mercator Projection

see the extent of the New Assyrian Empire at its peak.

The Fall of Assyria

The Assyrians did little to win the favor of their subjects. They took much from them —slaves, silver, gold, iron, copper, crops, livestock. They used this wealth to build their own magnificent cities.

Their practice of relocating rebellious peoples made them even more despised, and the rebellions continued. The groups that had been displaced never gave their loyalty to Assyria. Neighboring armies built up their strength to defeat the empire. Finally, the Chaldeans *(kal DEE uhns)*, who then ruled Babylonia, joined the Medes from the Zagros Mountains on the east to overthrow the Assyrians in 612 B.C. Once again, power had swung to the south. ■

■ What policies of the Assyrian rulers helped to cause the eventual downfall of their empire?

A New Babylonian Empire

The Chaldeans of Babylonia ruled from their capital, the city of Babylon. Find this city on the map on page 176. Notice how large the New Babylonian Empire would become at its peak.

Like the Assyrians, the Babylonians were great conquerors. They were also great traders. Archaeologists have found thousands of cuneiform tablets telling of their complex trade networks. The Babylonians traded with Lebanon, Egypt, and Greece. To protect their trade routes, they sent their armies west.

A Babylonian Emperor

Leading the Babylonian armies was the great king Nebuchadnezzar whose grand building projects you have read about. Nebuchadnezzar ruled from 605 to 562 B.C. He captured major cities such as Jerusalem and the Phoenician city of Tyre *(tyr)*. He also drove

177

Mesopotamia

The present-day city of Al Hillah, Iraq, is near the site of ancient Babylon. Little remains of the magnificent city. However, parts of it are now being restored by the Iraqi government, based on the discoveries of archaeologists. The restorations in process include the hanging gardens, the ziggurat, and Nebuchadnezzar's main palace.

the Egyptians out of Syria and Phoenicia and thus was able to secure a rich trade gateway to the Mediterranean Sea.

The Phoenicians, the Philistines, and the Jews lived to the west of Babylonia, near the Mediterranean Sea. These conquered peoples were no better off than they had been under the Assyrians. They bitterly resented paying taxes to the Babylonians. Nebuchadnezzar was forced to work hard to maintain his empire. Every year he led his troops west to put down rebellions.

In 598 B.C., the Jews of the kingdom of Judah, the south part of Israel, refused to pay taxes to

Nebuchadnezzar. The Babylonian king overthrew Judah's ruler and forced 3,000 Jews on a torturous march to Mesopotamia. In 587 B.C., he put down another rebellion by burning the city of Jerusalem and destroying its great temple. This time, he sent thousands of Jews to Babylon as slaves.

The poem on page 179 expresses the sadness of the Jews in **exile**—forced absence from their country. The Babylonians had ordered the Jews to entertain them by playing stringed instruments, called lyres, and singing about their Lord, the God of the Jews. Zion is a Hebrew name for Israel, their homeland.

UNDERSTANDING LIMITS OF AUTHORITY

When Sargon was king of Akkad, he had no authority over other city-states. Nor did other kings have authority over Akkad. Each king ruled within the territorial limits of his city-state.

Real but Invisible

Territorial limits are not, of course, lines drawn on the earth, like the boundary lines drawn on maps. They are real, though, and they are recognized by people and governments everywhere in the world.

War and Negotiation

Countries establish territorial limits either by war or by making agreements. Sargon conquered neighboring city-states and combined them to make a single empire. He destroyed city walls to symbolize the end of the old limits. More recently, the United States and Great Britain signed a treaty in 1846 setting the U.S. border with Canada at 49° north latitude.

Kinds of Territorial Limits

Territorial limits are applied to states, such as California, as well as to countries. What other examples can you think of?

Today, territorial limits often involve more than the boundaries we see on maps

and globes. For example, modern countries now claim air space. Airplanes may not fly over a foreign country without permission. Countries with coastlines claim part of the ocean waters as their own. For the United States, this area extends 3 nautical miles, or 3.6 land miles, from shore.

In 1969, the American flag was planted on the moon. That event focused the world's attention on problems of territorial limits in space. As space exploration continues, the countries of the world will have to work at solving these new problems.

The famous Ishtar Gate was the only structure still partially standing when archaeologists excavated Babylon. The gate, which stood at the city's entrance, was covered with a layer of glazed brickwork. The photo at left shows a detail of a dragon from the reconstruction in Iraq.

By the waters of Babylon,
there we sat down
and wept, when we remembered Zion.
On the willows there we hung
up our lyres.
For there our captors required
of us songs,
And our tormentors, mirth,
saying, "Sing us one of the
songs of Zion!"
How shall we sing the Lord's
song in a foreign land?

Psalms 137:1–4

Babylonian Achievements

Nebuchadnezzar used much of the wealth from his conquests in grand building projects. He built walls and fortifications to protect Babylon and great temples to glorify the gods. He rebuilt the ziggurat. Travelers from Greece listed the "hanging gardens" as one of the seven wonders of the world. To learn more about the seven wonders, turn to the Minipedia in the back of this book.

Scientific studies flourished during Nebuchadnezzar's reign. Many priests became **astronomers,** scientists who observe and record the movements of stars and planets. For centuries, the Babylonians had excelled in astronomy and mathematics. Early astronomers developed calendars based on the phases of the moon. At first their calendars were not synchronized with the movements of the sun. Later, by adding a total of seven months every nineteen years, the astronomers created a more accurate calendar.

Another outstanding scientific achievement was the division of the hour into 60 minutes. Our current use of an hour that is 60 minutes long is a daily reminder of the Babylonians.

A third achievement was the introduction of place value into mathematics. Place value refers to the position of a numeral in relation to other numerals. For example, the numeral 6 has a different value in the numbers 6, 61, and

▲ Many artists have tried to portray the glorious "hanging gardens of Babylon," but no one knows what they really looked like.

611. To find out how important place value is, try to multiply two numbers in Roman numeral form, such as XIV and XVIII.

The Fall of Babylonia

The rulers of Babylonia made the same mistakes as the Assyrians. Like the Assyrians, they worked to maintain their empire but did little to make life better for the people they conquered. Instead, they drained the conquered lands of wealth through taxes and plunder. Like the Assyrians, they made many enemies. Babylonia was ready for a fall.

The story of that fall involves an odd Babylonian king. King Nabonidus *(na buh NY duhs)* ruled Babylon from 556 to 539 B.C.

Historians are baffled by his behavior. Nabonidus bragged of great victories he never won. He left Babylon for years at a time, perhaps to avoid civil war and a famine the city suffered during his reign. He tried to replace Babylon's god Marduk with another god named Sin. For all these reasons, Nabonidus had many enemies.

When a foreign invader came, he was welcomed by the people. The conqueror of Babylonia, Cyrus the Great, came from Persia, a region of mountains and plateaus to the east of Mesopotamia. Around 550 B.C., Cyrus began winning new lands and building an empire. His empire would grow to be the largest the world had known. ■

■ Why were the Babylonians finally unable to maintain their empire?

R E V I E W

1. **FOCUS** How were the New Assyrian and New Babylonian empires alike, and how were they different?

2. **CONNECT** How do the geography and earlier history of Mesopotamia help to explain the importance of trade to both the Assyrians and the Babylonians?

3. **HISTORY** What were the policies of Tiglath-Pileser III and Nebuchadnezzar that led to the downfall of their empires?

4. **CRITICAL THINKING** Both the Assyrians and the Babylonians relocated conquered people, moving them from their homeland. What other way of dealing with conquered people might have helped the Assyrians and Babylonians maintain their empires?

5. **WRITING ACTIVITY** Imagine you've come from a Mesopotamian farm to the great city of Babylon. Write a letter home, describing what you've seen.

Holding a Mesopotamian Fair

Here's Why

Many accomplishments in sports, business, government, and other areas of activity are the result of group efforts. Working as a group to reach common goals is a complex task. It requires cooperation in setting goals, planning actions, and making decisions. For example, suppose your class decided to hold a Mesopotamian World's Fair. Like the students in the photograph, you would begin by organizing your project. How would you proceed?

Here's How

Here are five steps for organizing your World's Fair:

1. Elect a moderator, or leader, to run meetings. This person should keep class meetings focused.
2. Decide, as a class, what to do and how to proceed. The class should develop a list of goals and ways of achieving them.
3. Divide up jobs, form committees, and select committee leaders. Each committee should have a list of specific tasks, and the leader should make sure the group stays on target.
4. Hold individual committee meetings to set goals and assign tasks. Each member should have specific jobs that lead to achieving the committee's goals.
5. Meet again as a class to review plans, report progress, and make recommendations. The class should consider what progress has been made, what problems have come up, and what changes should be made.

Following these steps, you should be able to plan a successful Mesopotamian World's Fair.

Try It

Using the steps described in Here's How, plan a World's Fair at your school. Highlight Mesopotamian achievements in the following areas: public works, tools and inventions, literature, writing, and law.

Apply It

Now you have seen how to effectively organize a group effort. How would you divide the jobs if you were planning a paper-recycling campaign for your school or a Saturday project to clean up your school's grounds?

181

Chapter Review

Reviewing Key Terms

administrator (p. 154)
artisan (p. 155)
astronomer (p. 179)
city-state (p. 152)
code (p. 172)
cuneiform (p. 160)
empire (p. 169)
epic (p. 156)

exile (p. 178)
nomad (p. 157)
pictograph (p. 160)
plain (p. 151)
plateau (p. 150)
polytheism (p. 158)
scribe (p. 161)

A. Compare the key terms in each pair.
1. plateau, plain
2. city-state, empire
3. nomad, exile
4. pictograph, cuneiform

B. The following sentences are false. Explain each key term correctly.
1. <u>Artisans</u> held high positions as <u>administrators</u> in the city-states.
2. <u>Epics</u> tell us about how the Sumerians kept track of business deals.
3. The Sumerians, who believed in <u>polytheism</u>, worshiped only one god.
4. Hammurabi's <u>code</u> of law allowed rulers to freely punish criminals.
5. <u>Astronomers</u> developed the first systems of writing and became <u>scribes</u> for their kings and priests.

Exploring Concepts

A. Copy and complete this outline.

I. The land between two rivers
  A. The Mesopotamian plain
  B. The remarkable Sumerians
    1. The Sumerian city-state
    2.
II. The contributions of the Sumerians
  A. The first kings
  B.
    1. The gods of Sumer
    2. Service to the gods
  C. The beginnings of writing
    1.
    2. Simplifying the pictures
III. The first empires
  A. Sargon of Akkad
  B. Rival empires
    1.
    2. A wise Babylonian ruler
IV. New empires
  A. A new Assyrian empire
  B.

B. The history of Mesopotamia is marked by the rise and fall of many strong leaders. Support each of the following statements with facts and details from the chapter.
1. Sargon changed Mesopotamia's government by creating the world's first empire.
2. Shamshi-Adad was one of the most powerful rulers of the Assyrian Empire.
3. Hammurabi, like Sargon and Shamshi-Adad, was a fierce conqueror, but he also showed concern for his people.
4. Adad-Nirari's greatest interest was gaining wealth and power.
5. The policies of Tiglath-Pileser III were partly responsible for the fall of the New Assyrian Empire.
6. Nebuchadnezzar's reign was both cruel and magnificent.
7. The policies of Nebuchadnezzar resembled those of Tiglath-Pileser III and had similar results.
8. Nabonidus's kingdom was not secure because the people of Babylonia did not like his practices.

Reviewing Skills

1. Look at the timeline on this page. Suppose you wanted to make a telescoping timeline of events during Hammurabi's rule. Would you make a 1,000-year timeline? A 150-year timeline? A 50-year timeline? Why?

2. Find a timeline and a map scale in your book. How are they alike? How are they different?

3. Suppose your class wanted to put on a Reader's Theater presentation of "The Luring of Enkidu" from *Gilgamesh*. Reader's Theater is a dramatic reading of a play or story without acting it out. To prepare for such a presentation, some class members might make posters for publicity. Others might print programs. How would you apply to your group preparation the five main steps for organizing a group project?

4. "I have brought justice to all my subjects," Hammurabi said. Was this a statement of fact or opinion? Use information from the chapter to support your view.

5. Suppose that you have taken many notes on the Babylonians and Sumerians. Now you have to give an oral report comparing the two societies. How could you help listeners to see both the likenesses and differences of Babylonians and Sumerians?

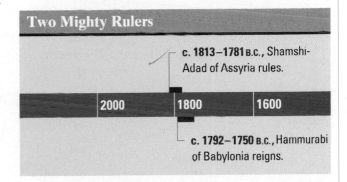

Two Mighty Rulers

c. 1813–1781 B.C., Shamshi-Adad of Assyria rules.

2000   1800   1600

c. 1792–1750 B.C., Hammurabi of Babylonia reigns.

Using Critical Thinking

1. Ancient cultures had clearly defined roles for priests, kings, artisans, and scribes. What were the functions of these groups in Mesopotamian society? How are these groups of people and their roles different in American society today?

2. The first tools of written communication were a stylus and a piece of clay. The stylus, a sharpened reed, was used to draw pictographs on moist clay. Much later, paper replaced the clay tablets. What other tools of written communication have been invented since then?

3. The Sumerians' religion was extremely important to them. Their gods were involved in all aspects of their lives. Review the Sumerians' religious beliefs on pages 158 and 159. Then read in Lesson 3 about the war between King Lugal-zaggesi and Sargon. How do you think a Sumerian priest might have explained the invasion of Uruk to someone?

Preparing for Citizenship

1. **WRITING ACTIVITY** Nebuchadnezzar built the towering ziggurat. He also built the Hanging Gardens, one of the seven wonders of the ancient world. What do these structures tell us about the values and beliefs of Babylonian society? Now choose two structures in American cities, and write an essay on the wonders of the modern world. What do these wonders reveal about the values and beliefs of our society?

2. **COLLABORATIVE LEARNING** The epic of *Gilgamesh* tells the story of a real king who became a legendary hero. Who are our American heroes today? Consider both the past and present. With two classmates, select an American hero. Have each person in your group research one part of your hero's life: childhood, public life, and private life. Together, decide how to present your hero to the class.

Chapter 7

Ancient Egypt

Tombs filled with dazzling treasures tell us of the ancient Egyptians. Their civilization flourished in the valley along the Nile River in North Africa, a region rich in resources and protected from enemies by a vast desert. The valley seemed like heaven on earth to the Egyptians. In fact, life was so good that they hoped it would continue after death, in the afterlife.

4000 B.C. People begin to settle along the Nile. In this tomb painting from a later period, an Egyptian couple happily plow their fields in the afterlife.

4000

3000

4000 B.C.

c. 3100 B.C. According to legend, the king of Upper Egypt conquers Lower Egypt and unites the two lands. This figure wears the crown of Upper Egypt.

Throughout this period, Egyptian kings built massive royal tombs. These pyramids date from the 2600s B.C. The giant figures (below) guard the temple built by King Ramses II about 1250 B.C.

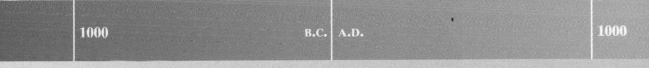

c. 1570–1070 B.C. Egyptian rulers conquer their neighbors and expand trade. This model boat, found in the tomb of King Tutankhamen, resembles the trading ships that sailed the Nile.

1000		B.C.	A.D.		1000

1489 B.C. Queen Hatshepsut takes control. A skillful ruler, she promotes trade and brings peace. Like earlier rulers, she orders a grand temple built so she will be remembered forever.

A.D. 350

LESSON 1

The Gift of the Nile

THINKING
FOCUS

*What did the ancient
Egyptians accomplish be-
cause of the "gifts of the
Nile"?*

Key Terms

- cataract
- delta
- papyrus
- dynasty

Grain was scarce, and fruit was dried up. People robbed their neighbors. Babies were crying, and old men were sad as they sat on the ground with their legs bent and their arms folded.

So begins an ancient legend about the Nile River. The Egyptians depended on the flooding of the Nile to water their fields. Some years there were "high Niles," when crops grew well and people had plenty to eat. Other years there were "low Niles," when the fields became dry, baked by the sun, and few had enough food.

The legend tells of a time of low Niles, when Egypt had seven years of famine. This time fell during the reign of King Zoser in the 2600s B.C. The king watched the crops withering, and he saw his people starving. He turned to his chief advisor, Imhotep, for help. The answer was to learn the name of the god of the Nile so they could pray to him, said Imhotep. Later, he told the king that the Nile slept in two caverns below a temple near Egypt's southern border. The god Khnum *(kuh NOOM)* controlled the floodgates and let the Nile rush toward Egypt.

Later that night, Zoser dreamed that Khnum spoke to him: "I am Khnum. I know the Nile. When it covers the fields, it gives them life. Now the Nile will pour over the land without stopping. Plants will grow, bowing down with fruit. The years of starvation will be over."

When the king awoke, he told the people to honor Khnum by giving him a portion of each year's harvest. The "high Niles" returned, and the years of hunger ended.

➤ *In this scene at
Aswan in south Egypt,
the fertile riverbank contrasts sharply with the
barren desert.*

The Geography of the Nile

Egypt is on the northeastern coast of Africa. Look at the map below, and locate Egypt on the globe in the inset. Now find the Nile River on the large map.

The Nile is Egypt's lifeline. Without it, the land would be mostly desert. It is the longest river in the world, traveling over 4,000 miles from its source in the lakes and marshes of East Africa to its outlet in the Mediterranean Sea.

At six places along the Nile's winding course, stone cliffs and boulders force its waters through narrow channels. The rushing water forms waterfalls and rapids called **cataracts**. The first cataract marked the southern boundary of ancient Egypt. Find it on the map.

From the first cataract, the Nile flows north for about 650 miles. For most of this journey, it flows as a single river. But just south of what is today Cairo (KY roh), it divides into many small channels and streams. This triangle of marshy wetlands is called the delta.

Droughts and Floods

From the air, the ancient Egypt Nile looks like a brown snake wriggling north across a vast desert. Its narrow banks are green with crops and palms. Abruptly they turn into desert—red stone and hot sands. The people who lived there 4,000 years ago called their fertile, dark-soiled valley the Black Land. The desert was the Red Land.

Egypt gets almost no rain. The deserts on the east and west are

parts of the Sahara, the desert that covers much of northern Africa. Desert on two sides, mountains on the south, and the Mediterranean Sea on the north—all of these natural barriers isolated ancient Egypt and thus protected it from invaders.

In this desert land, Egyptians depended on the Nile for water and for life. The amount of water the Nile carried on its journey to

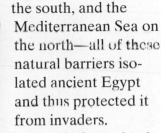

The Egyptians used stone nilometers like this one to measure the yearly flood level of the Nile.

▼ *Some have compared the shape of Egypt with that of a lotus flower. Can you see the flower's blossom and stem?*

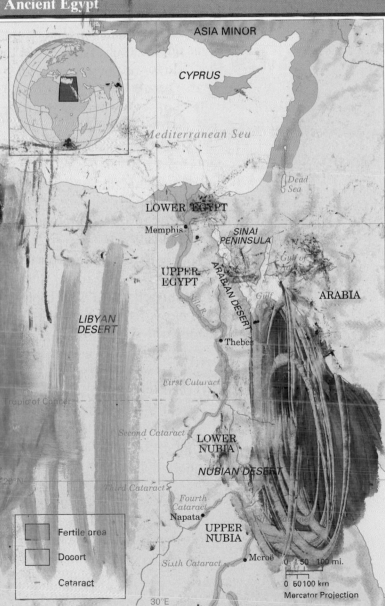

Ancient Egypt

ASIA MINOR

CYPRUS

Mediterranean Sea

Dead Sea

LOWER EGYPT

Memphis

SINAI PENINSULA

Gulf of

UPPER EGYPT

ARABIAN DESERT

Nile R.

ARABIA

LIBYAN DESERT

Thebes

First Cataract

Tropic of Cancer

Second Cataract

LOWER NUBIA

NUBIAN DESERT

Third Cataract

Fourth Cataract

Napata

UPPER NUBIA

Meroë

Sixth Cataract

Fertile area

Desert

- Cataract

0   50   100 mi.

0 60 100 km

Mercator Projection

30°E

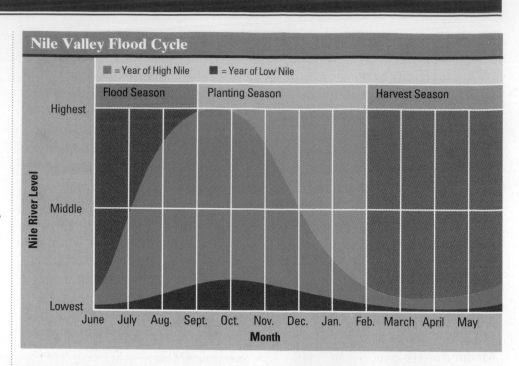

Nile Valley Flood Cycle

■ = Year of High Nile ■ = Year of Low Nile

| Flood Season | Planting Season | Harvest Season |

Nile River Level: Highest, Middle, Lowest

June July Aug. Sept. Oct. Nov. Dec. Jan. Feb. March April May

Month

➤ *Which months made up each of Egypt's three seasons? How did the years of "high Niles" differ from the years of "low Niles"? What might you be doing now if you were a farmer in ancient Egypt?*

➤ *Notice the fine carving and bright coloring in this small wooden statue of a woman who is carrying an offering.*

the Mediterranean varied from season to season. When rains fell in central Africa and snows began to melt in the mountains of east Africa, the water level of the river rose. As the river reached Egypt, it overflowed its banks. Farmers depended on the annual flooding to water their crops.

The floods of Egypt were more predictable than those of Mesopotamia. Farmers each year knew when the Nile would rise, and they planned ahead. The Egyptians measured time by the river, dividing the year into three seasons. Study the chart above. What was the season for planting? What was the season for harvesting? This seasonal cycle of flooding, planting, and harvesting gave a pattern to Egyptian life.

The River's Gifts

About 2,500 years ago, Herodotus *(hih RAHD uh tuhs)*, a Greek visitor to ancient

Egypt, called this land the "gift of the Nile." The Egyptians sang special hymns of praise to the river. The example below was first written down during the period known as the New Kingdom (from about 1570 to 1070 B.C.):

> *H*ail to thee O Nile that issues from the earth and comes to keep Egypt alive! . . . He that waters the meadows which Ra created.
>
> *Hymn to the Nile,* from papyrus documents, 1350-1100 B.C.

To take advantage of the annual flooding of the Nile, the people built irrigation channels to carry water into the fields. They also built dams to hold back the water for use during droughts. What they did may sound familiar to you. In some ways it was the same thing the Sumerians did. But the floods came at predictable times in Egypt, and farming was easier.

Besides water, another gift of the Nile was the thick, black mud

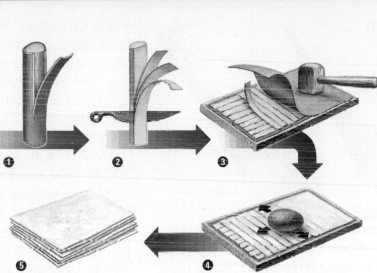

(1) Paper makers cut the stem of the papyrus and removed the inner pith. (2) They cut the pith into strips, (3) put one layer across another, and beat the layers into a single sheet. (4) They polished the sheet with a stone, and (5) finally, they trimmed the edges.

left behind in the flooding. This dark mud enriched the soil and made the farmland extremely productive. As you can see from the map on page 187, the delta had the largest area of rich farmland.

The Nile gave other gifts as well. Fish, ducks, geese, and other edible water birds made their homes in the marshlands of the delta. **Papyrus** *(puh PY ruhs)*, a long, thin reed, grew wild along the riverbanks. The Egyptians harvested papyrus and made baskets, boats, sandals, and a lightweight writing material. Our word *paper* comes from the word *papyrus*.

The Egyptians used the gifts of the Nile wisely. Here in this land of contrasts—fertile riverbanks and barren deserts, floods and droughts, Black Land and Red Land—they managed to build a remarkable civilization. ■

■ *Explain how water, mud, plants, and animals were all "gifts of the Nile" to the Egyptians.*

The Union of Two Lands

Ancient Egypt had two parts, Upper Egypt and Lower Egypt. Upper Egypt, the southern part, stretched for over 500 miles from the first cataract northward to the beginning of the Nile Delta. Lower Egypt, the northern part, was the Nile Delta. It was only 100 miles long but many times wider than Upper Egypt.

Red and White Crowns

By about 3300 B.C., both Upper Egypt and Lower Egypt had kings. The king of Upper Egypt wore a tall, white, pear-shaped crown. The king of Lower Egypt wore a short, boxy, red crown with a tall spike at the back and a curlicue at the front.

Much of our knowledge of prehistoric Egypt is mixed with legend. One famous legend tells about Menes *(MEE neez)*, a king of Upper Egypt. Around 3100 B.C., Menes defeated the king of Lower Egypt, united the two lands, and named himself King of both Upper and Lower Egypt.

The legend goes on to tell how Menes designed a new crown to celebrate his victory. This double crown stood for the union of the two lands. Menes and his family

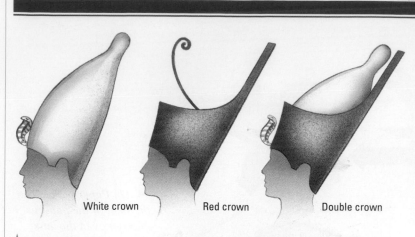

White crown   Red crown   Double crown

▲ *The white crown of the king of Upper Egypt was placed inside the red crown of the king of Lower Egypt, forming the double red and white crown that symbolized the union of the two lands.*

➤ *The slate palette of Narmer is from around 2950 B.C. King Narmer, who is wearing the white crown, is striking a kneeling prisoner.*

■ *What were some important early accomplishments of the Egyptians?*

formed the first Egyptian dynasty. A **dynasty** is a series of rulers from the same family. After Menes died, his son became king, and later his grandson. Throughout its history, 30 different dynasties ruled ancient Egypt.

Menes chose the city of Memphis as his capital. Find Memphis on the map on page 187. How do you think the city's location helped the king keep firm control of both parts of his newly united kingdom?

Historians believe that the "Menes" of this legend may have been a real king, possibly Narmer. They also believe it wasn't that king who first wore the red and white crown, but a later one.

Three Kingdoms

History for ancient Egypt began around 3000 B.C., with the invention of hieroglyphic writing.

Within the history of ancient Egypt, historians have identified three periods when many important events took place.

In the Old Kingdom period, from 2686 to 2181 B.C., the Egyptians built the great pyramids. The Middle Kingdom lasted from 2055 to 1650 B.C. This was when Egypt became stronger, and the Egyptians achieved a great deal in literature, art, and architecture. In the New Kingdom period, from 1570 to 1070 B.C., Egypt became a world power by conquering other nations and building an empire.

People of many cultures mingled in Egypt. It was a crossroad for people from different parts of the ancient world. To the south was Nubia and to the north were countries that bordered the Mediterranean Sea, such as Greece and Rome.

In the 1,000 years before the Old Kingdom began, the Egyptian people accomplished many things. They learned to irrigate their fields. They formed governments. They invented hieroglyphic writing. Finally, the Egyptians created the belief systems and _____ Egyptian life unique. These early achievements formed the basis of ancient Egyptian society. ■

R E V I E W

1. **FOCUS** What did the ancient Egyptians accomplish because of the "gifts of the Nile"?
2. **CONNECT** Compare and contrast the conditions for farmers in Mesopotamia and Egypt.
3. **GEOGRAPHY** Explain how the geography of the Nile marked the southern border of Egypt.
4. **CRITICAL THINKING** The ancient Egyptians valued a

quiet, orderly life. They did not want things to change. How might these preferences help to explain why the story of Menes was important to them?

5. **WRITING ACTIVITY** Imagine you are a travel writer who has just visited ancient Egypt by time machine. Write an article called "Egypt: A Land of Contrasts."

LESSON 2

Life in Ancient Egypt

The photo below might surprise you if you have seen pictures of Egyptian pyramids. This pyramid is different. It is called the Step Pyramid, and the name fits. To find out more about this unusual structure, we will revisit King Zoser.

Sometime in the middle of the 2600s B.C., the king began to plan for his burial. He called on Imhotep, his chief advisor and also a fine architect, to design his tomb. Until then, a royal tomb was a flat-topped, mud-brick structure built over a burial chamber that lay deep under the ground. Imhotep designed a grander, more permanent tomb for the king, and he did not build it of mud brick, but of stone.

No one knows whether Imhotep planned the design in advance or thought of it as the work went along. At any rate, his builders put one flat-topped structure on top of another. They made each level a few feet smaller than the one below it.

When Imhotep's pyramid was finished, a chamber for the king's body lay about 80 feet under the ground. A mile-long, 133-foot-high stone wall surrounded the tomb. The wall had 14 doors, only one of which actually opened.

Architects of later periods built on Imhotep's ideas to design and construct pyramids that were even grander. King Zoser had started an age of pyramid building that would last for more than a thousand years. Pyramid building reached its height during the Old Kingdom period. More than 80 pyramids have survived as reminders of that distant age.

THINKING FOCUS

Describe the religious ideas and the social structure of the ancient Egyptians.

Key Terms

- afterlife
- embalm
- mummy
- hieroglyphics

◄ *Zoser's Step Pyramid, the first large-scale stone structure in the world, was built in the mid-2600s B.C. on a plateau overlooking the ancient city of Memphis.*

191

Ancient Egypt

The Egyptian Religion

> ➤ *The Egyptians considered some animals sacred or as representatives of gods. Cat mummies were used as offerings to the cat goddess Bastet.*

King Zoser's pyramid was undoubtedly more than just a new idea in architecture. It showed the religious beliefs of the Egyptian people. Early Egyptian literature pictured the king climbing up to heaven on a stairway formed by the rays of the sun. People may have thought of that stairway when they looked at the Step Pyramid. The shape of the later pyramids might have seemed like the slope of the sun's rays. In that way, the later pyramids, too, might have pictured a king's passage to heaven.

Preparing for the Afterlife

The Egyptians believed in an **afterlife,** a life that would continue after death. Their belief was so strong and important to the people that great preparation was made for death and burial. Pyramid building was just one part of this preparation.

Another part was the preparation of the body itself. Before an Egyptian's body could be placed in a pyramid or other tomb, it had to be prepared for the afterlife.

The Egyptians believed that without a body, a person's spirit couldn't eat, drink, dance, or enjoy the other pleasures that the afterlife would offer. If the body decayed, the spirit would die too. So the Egyptians developed a process called **embalming,** treating the body to protect it from decay. Embalming changed the body into a **mummy.** To learn more about this process, see A Closer Look on pages 194 and 195.

Once the mummy had been prepared, it was placed in the tomb along with items for use in the afterlife. These items ranged from food and drink to gold and jewelry. They included many objects that were useful in daily life, such as clothes, games, and hand mirrors. Some tombs even held mummies of cats, dogs, horses, and apes or contained small carved statues of servants. Tomb walls were painted with scenes from the everyday life of the dead person. See the example on pages 204 and 205.

Most of these objects and paintings were found in the tombs of royal or wealthy families. Burying pharaohs in huge pyramids was one way to show the difference between the special, godlike pharaoh and the common people. But even many of the less privileged people were buried with some of their favorite possessions.

According to Egyptian belief, the objects and paintings in the tomb would help to ensure that the person would continue to have and enjoy the good things of this life.

After a mummy was placed in its tomb, priests recited prayers or

> ▼ *The sky god Horus, depicted with the head of a hawk, was closely connected with the king. In fact, the Egyptians saw their king as Horus on earth. Here Horus is shown standing in his sun boat. With him is an ibis, a sacred bird of ancient Egypt.*

chanted magic spells. They called on the gods to help the person make the trip from this world to the next. The following words appear on the tomb of an Old Kingdom ruler named Pepi: "Gates of sky, open for Pepi, Gates of heaven, open for Pepi, Pepi comes to you, make him live!"

The Book of the Dead

Hymns, prayers, and magic spells from the tombs are found in the Egyptian *Book of the Dead*. One part describes a trial in which the soul of a dead person argues its case before a jury of the gods. "In life, I fed the hungry," says the soul. "I respected my parents."

The soul also tells what it did not do. "I never stole." The gods then weigh the heart of the dead person against the feather of truth. The Egyptians believed the heart was the center of intelligence and memory. If the soul was too heavy with sin, they believed, it died a second death from which there was no returning. But the soul that passed the test would go on to a happy afterlife. Such a judgment scene is shown in the picture above.

The Gods of the Egyptians

The religion of ancient Egypt, like that of Mesopotamia, was a form of polytheism, belief in a number of gods. Some of these gods were, of course, linked with death and the afterlife. Osiris *(oh SY ruhs)* was chief god of the underworld, or home of the dead. One helper of Osiris was Anubis *(uh NOO buhs)*, who had the body of a human and the head of a jackal. His job was to prepare the bodies of the dead for the afterlife.

Like the Mesopotamians, the Egyptians had great gods that they believed created and ruled the world. One of these was Ra *(rah)*, the sun god, who was later joined with another great god, Amon *(AH muhn)*, to become Amon-Ra.

Some Egyptian gods, like Anubis, had the body of a human and the head of an animal. Hathor *(HAH thawr)*, the goddess of love, had the head of a cow. Horus, the sky god, had the head of a hawk.

Each Egyptian village or city had its own local god. There were also gods of music and dancing, of love and beauty, and of healing and learning. Ordinary Egyptians built small shrines at home and dedicated them to their favorite gods. Especially popular was a dwarf like god named Bes, the god of the family. ■

This picture, painted on papyrus around 1250 B.C., shows the jackal-headed god Anubis weighing the heart of a dead person named Ani against the feather of truth.

◄ *At one time Amon was a minor god, but he became the most powerful of all the Egyptian gods. This small gold statue shows Amon with a curved sword in his right hand and a key, the symbol of life, in his left hand*

■ *What religious beliefs account for the pyramids and mummies of ancient Egypt?*

193

Egyptian Burial

Preparing for the afterlife was like packing for a long trip. Every step in the process, from preparing the body to protecting the tomb against robbers, had to be done just right.

This huge boat was buried near the Great Pyramid of Khufu, a king of the Old Kingdom. Was it used at his funeral, or was it for his use in his afterlife? No one knows for sure. Perhaps it symbolizes the soul's journey after death.

To get the body ready, embalmers removed all the internal organs except the heart and put them inside jars like this. Then they covered the body for about 40 days with natron, a kind of salt, which dried it out.

Magic amulets were tucked into the wrappings next to the body. A scarab over the heart, for instance, would make sure the heart could not speak against its owner during the trial in the afterworld.

Embalmers sealed the dried corpse in a coat of hot, liquid tree sap. Then they washed and oiled the mummy. Finally, they wrapped it in up to 400 yards of linen strips.

194

Once the body was placed in the burial room of the pyramid, the workers needed to seal the tomb. As they left, the workers let huge stones crash into place and block the main passageway. To fool robbers, some Egyptian royal tombs had traps and false stairs that led nowhere.

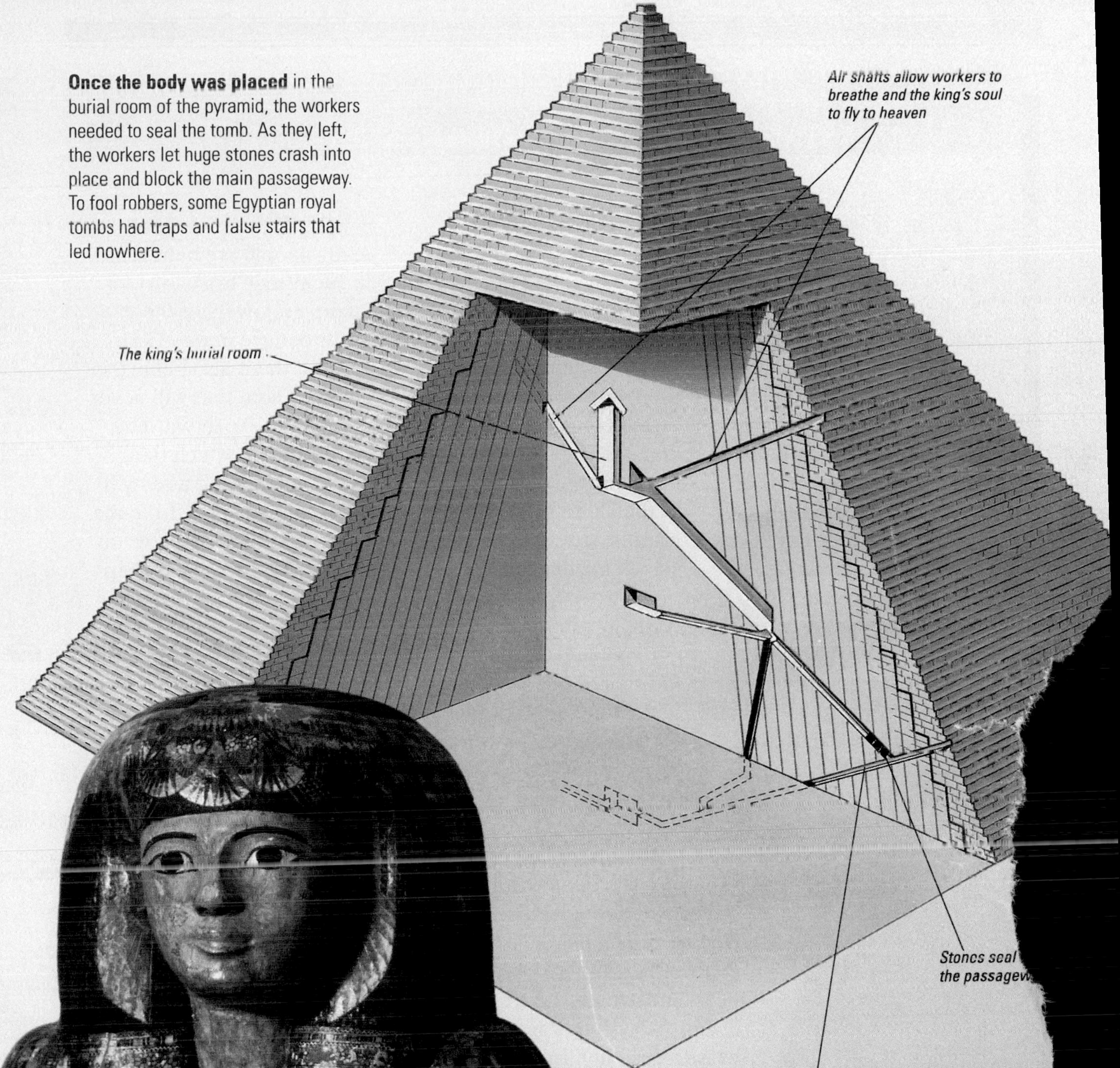

Air shafts allow workers to breathe and the king's soul to fly to heaven

The king's burial room

Stones seal the passageway

Workers' escape corridor

Craftsmen made coffins look like humans and wrote spells and prayers of protection outside and inside. The face of the coffin was often a portrait of the dead person.

Ancient Egypt

*T*o us, the ancient Egyptians sometimes seem more interested in death than life. We marvel at the time, energy, and other resources they put into making pyramids and mummies. Yet we know that their love of life caused them to do these things. They thought an afterlife would be like this one, only better.

In every time and place, people have asked, "Is there life beyond this life?" and if so, "What kind of life is it?" These questions ask about the afterlife—life that continues after death.

A Place of Darkness

The Mesopotamians painted a gloomy picture of the afterlife. For them, the world of the dead was under the earth. One of their stories called it a place "where they see no light and live in darkness." The hero-king Gilgamesh tried but failed to gain a happy afterlife. Eternal life was reserved for the gods.

A Happy Afterlife

People's ideas about an afterlife are tied to their ideas about God or the gods. In our own twentieth-century Western society, many people are believers in Judaism, Christianity, or Islam. Followers of these faiths believe in one God. Most of them also believe in a human soul that will never die. They look forward to an afterlife in which they will live with God and with other human souls. Like the Egyptians, many believe in an afterlife that will be happier and better than this life. However, few cultures have placed more importance on the idea of an afterlife than the ancient Egyptians.

A Writing System

The earliest Egyptian writing, also called **hieroglyphics** *(hy roh GLIH fihks),* used pictures to stand for objects, ideas, and sounds. Like cuneiform, the system was not easy to decipher. In fact, language specialists and archaeologists studied the symbols for years without success.

Then, in 1799, French soldiers near Rosetta, a village in the Nile Delta, unearthed a black stone slab. They found that on it the same passage was written in three ways: in Greek, in Egyptian hieroglyphs, and in a cursive form of Egyptian.

For 20 years, scholars tried in vain to decode the hieroglyphic writing on the Rosetta Stone. Then a brilliant Frenchman named Jean Champollion found the key. Champollion knew that part of the message was the same in all three cases. It praised the pharaoh Ptolemy V for gifts he had given the temples. One day in 1822, Champollion was comparing the hieroglyphs with the Greek words. He identified and compared the proper names *Ptolemy* and *Cleopatra*. He matched the sounds with the hieroglyphs as follows:

▲ *The Rosetta Stone provided the key that unlocked hieroglyphics.*

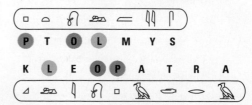

Now Champollion was able to decode the Rosetta Stone. Later, he went on to publish a dictionary of ancient Egyptian.

Fortunately, the Egyptians left us many written texts. Once scholars could decode hieroglyphic writing, they could read laws, songs, tales, jokes, magic spells, and business contracts. From these texts and others, scholars have learned about Egypt's past.

The hieroglyphic system was complex. It was made up of over 700 different signs that a person had to memorize in order to master it. Young people who wanted to be scribes spent years attending special schools. Their school day was long, sometimes lasting from just after sunrise until sunset. Teachers expected their students to pay attention, and punishments could be harsh. One father sent the following words of advice to his son, who was learning to be a scribe: "Learn to write, for this will be of greater advantage to you than all the trades. One day at school is useful to you and the work done there will last forever, like mountains."

Few Egyptian students, studying hard and copying the same lines over and over, would have found these words encouraging. However, those who completed the training would be well rewarded. Only a few people learned to read and write. As experts with special skills, they would have a good job and a respected place in society. ■

■ *Compare and contrast the writing systems of the Egyptians and the Mesopotamians.*

◄ *This Old Kingdom sculpture is called "The Seated Scribe." Students in schools for scribes memorized and copied passages like this: "Do not spend time in daydreaming or you will surely come to a bad end." Is this scribe daydreaming or taking a well-deserved break?*

A Social Pyramid

Scribes and farmers, potters and brick makers—all Egyptians had a place in the social class system of ancient Egypt. A diagram of Egyptian society might look something like a pyramid.

Kings and Priests

At the top of the social pyramid was the king. Remember that the Mesopotamians believed that their kings ruled on behalf of the gods. The Egyptians considered their kings even more powerful. They believed that their kings *were* gods.

The Egyptian king was extremely powerful. He owned all the land and had complete control over all of his people. Every worker, from farmer to artist, served the king, directly or through royal officials. The members of the royal family and the nobility ranked just below the king on the social pyramid.

▲ *This fine painted woodcarving of a plowing scene was found in a Middle Kingdom tomb of around 2000 B.C. Why do you think it was put in the tomb? Where would these farmers have been on the social pyramid?*

■ *What were the occupations of people at the top, middle, and bottom of the Egyptian social pyramid?*

Officials and Scribes

The king relied on government officials, who were also in the upper level of society. He counted on them to assist him in governing the country. Many were tax collectors. Some were responsible for the royal storehouses. When crops were poor, officials distributed grain to the people.

The scribes, another group of officials, held a privileged position. They were Egypt's writers and record keepers. Scribes might work at the king's palace, travel with high officials, or serve as public letter writers or record keepers. They assisted the tax collectors in making careful records of what everyone owed and how they paid their taxes.

Slaves who had been captured in wars may have served the king, too. Some slaves fought as soldiers in the Egyptian army or worked as servants in the homes of Egyptian nobles.

Artisans and Farmers

Below scribes on the social pyramid were the artisans and other skilled workers. These included carpenters, painters, jewelers, brick makers, and stonemasons. Many of these skilled workers provided goods for the king and his family. For example, they might create furniture, make jewelry, weave fine cloth, and paint pictures inside the royal tombs. The king paid them in food, such as bread, beer, and milk.

Farmers formed the large base of the Egyptian social pyramid. Most Egyptians were farmers, and they spent their lives growing and marketing the products they raised on their farms. In this way, they supported all the other levels of Egyptian society.

But the farmers didn't provide food only. During the flood season, they could not work in the fields. They were required to work on royal building projects. These included the irrigation works, the pyramids, and later the temples. The great stone monuments that the farmers helped to build have outlasted both kings and commoners. ■

R E V I E W

1. **FOCUS** Describe the religious ideas and the social structure of the ancient Egyptians.

2. **CONNECT** Compare and contrast the Egyptians' beliefs about their kings and their gods with the beliefs of the Mesopotamians.

3. **ECONOMICS** What was the importance of farming to the economy of ancient Egypt?

4. **CRITICAL THINKING** Give reasons for and against a young Egyptian's decision to become a scribe.

5. **ACTIVITY** Work with a group of three or four classmates, and make a pyramid diagram to illustrate the social structure of ancient Egypt. Draw pictures of people with different occupations and place them on your pyramid.

LESSON 3

The New Kingdom

The sculpture on the right shows a ruler of ancient Egypt wearing a false beard. False beards were not unusual in ancient Egypt. Sometimes, for a special occasion, a king would paste one on his chin as a symbol, or sign, of royal authority. Americans had the same kind of custom when Colonial judges wore long white wigs, also as symbols of authority.

Look again at the sculpture in the picture. What you see is something more unusual than just a false beard. It's a false beard pasted on the face of a woman. The woman is Hatshepsut *(hat SHEHP soot),* a ruler of ancient Egypt. Hatshepsut was the daughter of one king and the wife of another, but she is best remembered as a ruler in her own right.

But it seems that some Egyptian scribes became confused. In telling the story of their woman ruler, they called her "his majesty herself."

THINKING FOCUS

What were the achievements of the Egyptians during the New Kingdom period?

Key Terms

- pharaoh
- obelisk

◄ *Hatshepsut's beard, a sign of her kingship, does not hide the beauty of the pharaoh. In this sculpture from her temple, Hatshepsut is presenting an offering to the god Amon.*

New Kingdom Rulers

The New Kingdom period lasted around 500 years, from about 1570 to 1070 B.C. During that time, Egyptians began to call their kings pharaohs. The term *pharaoh* meant "great house." Earlier, during the Old Kingdom, the term referred to the royal palace. However, the Egyptians later used it to refer to the king himself. The word was used as a sign of respect. Today Hatshepsut, too, is often called an Egyptian pharaoh.

She was the daughter of the pharaoh Thutmose I *(thoot MOH suh).* After his death, his son, Thutmose II, became pharaoh. Hatshepsut, the new king's half-sister, became queen.

But Thutmose II lived only about seven more years. In ancient Egypt, the oldest male in line for the throne usually became the next ruler. Thutmose III, Hatshepsut's nephew, was next in line. But he was about 10 years old, too young

Egyptian Expansion

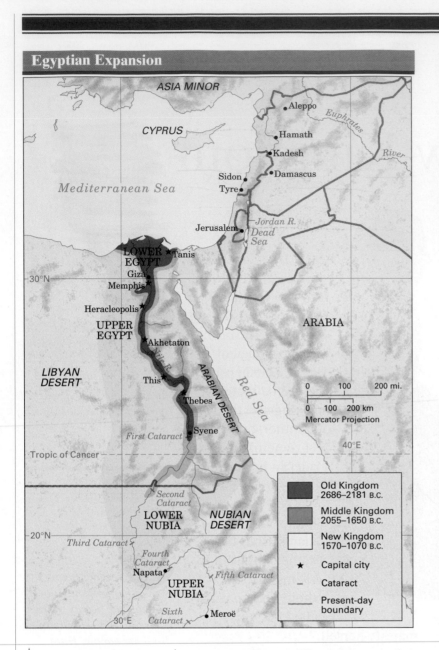

Notice the extent of ancient Egypt during the three periods of its greatness.

Old Kingdom 2686–2181 B.C.	
Middle Kingdom 2055–1650 B.C.	
New Kingdom 1570–1070 B.C.	
★	Capital city
-	Cataract
—	Present-day boundary

to govern Egypt. Hatshepsut took over the government in his place. The Egyptian people probably expected her to rule only until young Thutmose III was old enough to take over his royal duties.

Hatshepsut's Reign

But Hatshepsut had other ideas. This bold queen seized power for herself and became the new pharaoh. She ruled Egypt for about 20 years, and she turned out to be a shrewd and skillful ruler.

Like earlier Egyptian rulers, Hatshepsut wanted to make sure

she would be remembered for all time. She ordered a great temple to be built along the banks of the Nile. She also had two enormous granite pillars called **obelisks** placed at the temple of the sun god Amon-Ra at Karnak. Stonecutters carved words on the four sides of each obelisk. They proclaimed the devotion of Hatshepsut to the sun god and declared her right to rule Egypt.

Note that Hatshepsut built a great temple and erected obelisks, but she did not build a pyramid. By the time of the New Kingdom, pyramids were no longer built. Instead, rulers dug secret tombs deep in the cliffs west of their capital, Thebes. There they were buried in what we call today the Valley of the Kings.

Hatshepsut's Achievements

As a ruler, Hatshepsut concerned herself with improving life at home rather than expanding Egypt's borders and building a great empire. One example is a trade expedition she sent to Punt, a kingdom near present-day Somalia or Djibouti. Its exact location is unknown. Relief pictures on the walls of her temple portray five large sailing ships carrying Egyptian products. The artist also portrayed the people and houses of Punt, providing us with pictures of traditional life in Africa. The expedition returned to Egypt with many items, including gold, ivory, leopard skins, ostrich feathers, incense, rare woods, and monkeys.

Hatshepsut was responsible for a number of public projects. She restored old temples that had been destroyed during foreign invasions

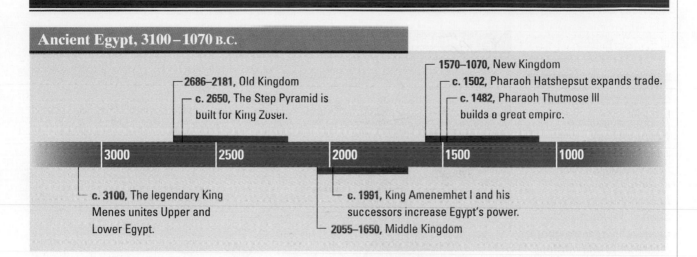

2686–2181, Old Kingdom

c. 2650, The Step Pyramid is built for King Zoser.

1570–1070, New Kingdom

c. 1502, Pharaoh Hatshepsut expands trade.

c. 1482, Pharaoh Thutmose III builds a great empire.

| 3000 | 2500 | 2000 | 1500 | 1000 |

c. 3100, The legendary King Menes unites Upper and Lower Egypt.

c. 1991, King Amenemhet I and his successors increase Egypt's power.

2055–1650, Middle Kingdom

of an earlier era, the time between the Middle and New Kingdoms. She also sent workers to mine the deserts for ores, a practice that those earlier invasions had interrupted. Under Hatshepsut's rule, Egypt enjoyed a time of renewed peace and prosperity.

Later Pharaohs

After Hatshepsut died, her nephew Thutmose III took the power she had denied him. Now at last he had the chance to govern, and he became a successful military leader, one of Egypt's mightiest pharaohs.

In a period of 20 years, Thutmose led 16 military raids into the Middle East, conquering Syria and Palestine. Fear of him, and of the Egyptian army, maintained Egypt's southern border at the fourth cataract of the Nile. Find the fourth cataract on the map on page 200. Notice the extent of Thutmose's empire, stretching from

Nubia to the Euphrates River. Nubia was Egypt's neighbor to the south. Egypt traded and fought with Nubia for its riches, including gold.

Scribes recorded Thutmose's campaigns in detail. In his fifth campaign, for example, a list of items taken from two ships that were seized includes slaves, copper, lead, wheat, and "every good thing." The scribe adds, "Afterwards his majesty proceeded southward to Egypt . . . with joy of heart."

Victories brought great wealth to Egypt. Conquered nations were forced to send yearly gifts to prove their loyalty to Egypt's rulers. Even rulers of unconquered states such as Babylonia and Assyria sent gifts to show their friendship with one of the Mediterranean's most powerful kingdoms.

Later rulers continued to enlarge Egypt's empire abroad and build

▲ *During the Old, Middle, and New Kingdom periods, a number of strong and effective rulers were in power. Later, as you read more about ancient Egypt, you can add other great rulers to this timeline.*

◄ *The obelisk of Hatshepsut, erected in the temple of the god Amon-Ra, was carved from Aswan granite. The shaft is 97 feet tall. Its pyramid-shaped top was once covered with precious metal to reflect the sun's rays.*

201

Ancient Egypt

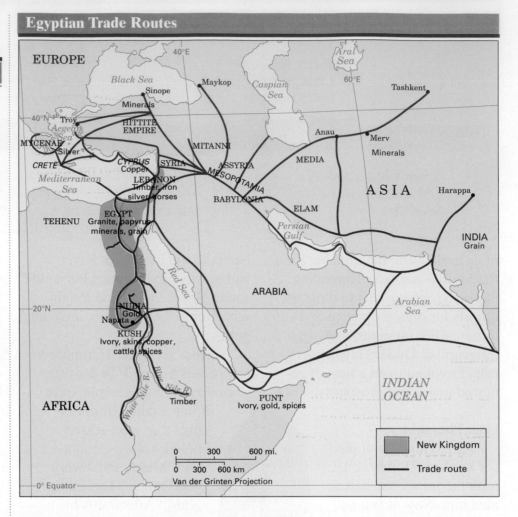

Egyptian Trade Routes

In 1960, planners of Egypt's Aswan High Dam realized that the lake it created would cover the two temples built by Ramses II at Abu Simbel. Saving them required cutting them into huge blocks and hoisting them by machine to higher ground. There they were rebuilt to look as much as possible as they had before.

➤ How far did Egypt's trade routes extend during the New Kingdom? What products did Egypt give and receive in trade with other nations?

■ Compare and contrast the two strong rulers Hatshepsut and Thutmose III.

impressive monuments at home. Ramses II, who ruled in the 1200s B.C., ordered four enormous stone statues of himself placed in front of the temple he had workmen build in his honor. Each statue was 67 feet tall, about the height of a modern four-story building. Ramses' temple can be seen today at Abu Simbel. Read Across Time and Space on this page to find out more about it. ■

Achievements of the Egyptians

The Egyptian rulers of the New Kingdom built great temples that are lasting reminders of their skills as architects, sculptors, and engineers. The Egyptians excelled in other areas as well.

A Better Calendar

Remember that the Babylonians created a lunar calendar, one that was based on the moon. The Egyptians also invented a lunar calendar, but it was based on both the moon and a star. The Egyptians had observed the annual appearance of Sirius, the brightest star in the sky. They noticed that it was invisible for several months, but then it appeared each year just at the time of the flooding. Their calendar was more accurate than the Babylonian one, corresponding almost exactly to the seasons.

Medicine

An unknown Egyptian doctor wrote the world's oldest known scientific document in the first part of the 1500s B.C. Scholars think it may have been a handbook for army surgeons. He described 48 injuries and illnesses, their symptoms, and their treatments. Although no modern doctor would use his cures, his attention to detail and the accuracy of his observations of the human body were remarkable for that time.

In one case the writer described the treatment of "a man having a wound in his head" but not "a perforation [hole], a split, or a smash." He advised doctors to treat this type of injury by wrapping it "with fresh meat the first day and treat afterward with grease, honey, and lint every day until he recovers."

The Arts

Some of the best information we have about the daily lives of the Egyptian people comes from the paintings on the inner walls of their tombs. Remember that these paintings were not meant to be interior decoration but were to provide for the afterlife of the deceased.

Unlike most modern artists, the painters and sculptors of ancient Egypt did not seek to make a name for themselves. Instead, their works were done to serve the king, his officials, the community, and the gods. Nevertheless, the works of these artists reveal great ability and probably represent long years of apprenticeship. For us today, tomb paintings are among the finest achievements of ancient Egypt. ■

■ *What were some important achievements of the Egyptians during the New Kingdom period?*

▼ *These statues of Ramses II are part of the temple to the sun god Ra at Abu Simbel.*

R E V I E W

1. **FOCUS** What were the achievements of the Egyptians during the New Kingdom period?

2. **CONNECT** Which Egyptian ruler was more like Sargon of Akkad in goals and achievements, Hatshepsut or Thutmose III? How?

3. **HISTORY** After the death of an Egyptian ruler, who usually ruled next? How does this custom explain why some texts call Hatshepsut a king?

4. **CRITICAL THINKING** Scholars have concluded that the Egyptians feared change and disorder. Both Hatshepsut and Thutmose III brought changes to Egypt. What changes might have worried the Egyptians?

5. **WRITING ACTIVITY** Imagine that you are Hatshepsut, and your first Egyptian trading ship has just returned from Punt. Write a diary entry describing the event and your feelings about it.

Interpreting Egyptian Art

Here's Why

One way to learn about the daily lives and beliefs of people of the past is to study their art. Suppose you wanted to learn more about what life was like in Thebes, the capital of Egypt at the time of the New Kingdom. Art from that time period is rich in information about daily life. But first you must know how to interpret art from the past.

Here's How

When you look at art from the past, ask yourself these questions:

1. What was its purpose?
2. What is its main subject?
3. What does it tell you about the past?

The illustration on these pages is from a wall painting found in a tomb at Thebes. The tomb, which dates from about 1380 B.C., belonged to Nebamun *(NEHB uh muhn)* and Ipuky *(ee POO kee).* Both were important artists who worked for the king.

Now ask: What was the painting's purpose? Why was the painting created? The chapter tells you that a tomb painting's purpose was to help ensure a happy afterlife for the person buried in the tomb.

Next, what is the main subject of the painting? To answer this question, you need to figure out who is shown in the painting and what each person is doing.

Notice that horizontal lines divide the painting into sections, called registers. Look at the large, seated figure to the left of the registers. In Egyptian paintings, people of high rank are often shown as being larger than others. In this case, the large figure is a supervisor.

Look at the man on the far left of the upper register. He is weighing gold rings against a counterweight shaped like a bull's head.

The four seated men in the upper register are all carving symbols. To the right, two craftsmen are fitting the symbols into a framework. They are building a catafalque *(KAT uh fawlk),* an ornamental structure used in funerals.

Now look at the bottom register. Here you see six artisans at work. To their left, two men show finished objects to the supervisor.

Now do you know what the painting is about? If you guessed that it shows a royal workshop of artisans, you are right. Both Nebamun and

Ipuky were supervisors in the royal workshop. The items being made were for the king's tomb.

Next, consider the third question. What does the painting tell you about the past? Most important, it shows how deeply the Egyptians believed in the afterlife. As you can see, much effort went into the crafting of items for the next life.

The painting also tells you about Egyptian customs. For example, think about how the people in the painting are dressed. Notice that the supervisor wears a large ornamental collar and a thin, full-length garment. The workers dress in simple cloths wrapped at the waist.

Try It

Look closely at the bottom register. Try interpreting the rest of the painting by answering the following questions. What are the six seated men in the bottom register making? What kinds of tools are they using? What does this tell you about ancient Egyptian technology? What are the workers wearing? What does this say about Egypt's climate?

Apply It

Now that you have learned some skills for interpreting wall paintings, try your hand at making a painting of your own. Working alone or in a small group, create a mural that shows some scene from your daily life. For example, you might paint a scene from the lunchroom. Or you could paint a scene of your classroom or a special area such as the library. Be sure to show a number of different activities in detail. Display your murals. Then study and interpret each other's paintings.

Isis and Osiris

Charles Mozley

This 5,000-year-old Egyptian myth tells the story of Isis, who became a goddess but lived as a mortal on earth, and her husband Osiris, who became a god and left earth to rule the underworld. In this excerpt from The First Book of Ancient Egypt, *read how Isis and Osiris win over evil.*

Osiris (oh SY rihs)

In Lesson 3 you read about some of the Egyptian gods. Now read a myth about two of the most popular gods.

Under the rule [of Osiris and Isis] Egypt prospered and all men loved them. All, that is, but a few who were under the influence of the jealous brother of Osiris, Set. Being a goddess, Isis could see the wickedness in Set's heart and she warned her husband against him. But Osiris could not believe that there was evil in his own brother.

One day, Set invited Osiris to his palace on the River Nile. That night there was a huge banquet for the King. There was much feasting and drinking and merrymaking.

Suddenly eight huge Ethiopian slaves marched into the great hall, bearing upon their shoulders a large chest. This they set upon the floor and Set said,

"My brother! See this magnificent chest. It is made of the most precious wood I could find. It is bound with gold and silver bands, and as you see, I have had gems set into the lid. I shall give this chest to one of my guests—and you, dear brother, shall help me decide which one it shall be."

"How can I do that?" Osiris asked.

"Well," said the evil brother. "It will really be simple. The chest shall belong to that one of my guests who best fits into it. He must, however, fit into it exactly. Therefore he must not be too tall or too short, too fat or too thin. And, you, my brother, shall be the judge of all, as befits your rank."

"An unusual game," Osiris commented smiling. "Proceed."

Now the guests at this banquet had been carefully selected for two reasons: one, because they hated the good Osiris and wished to make the evil Set Pharaoh in his place; two, because not one of them could comfortably fit into the chest.

After all had tried and this became evident, Osiris said, "Now what do you suggest, dear brother?"

Set had the answer ready. "Since obviously I am too short for the chest, you are the only one left to try it—but first, let me hold your crown."

"Of course," replied the unsuspecting Osiris, and handing the crown over to his brother, he stepped into the chest and lay down full length. "Why," he exclaimed, "it is a perfect fit! As if it were made for me!"

"And so it was!" shouted the traitor, Set, and with a mighty heave slammed the lid shut upon Osiris.

The Ethiopian slaves were then ordered to lock the clasps and take the chest up on their shoulders. Thus they marched out of the palace, straight to a deep part of the river, and heaved the chest into the rushing water.

So the good Osiris perished, and the chest bearing his body floated down the River Nile. Seeing it pass, the birds ceased their singing, the fish sank to the bottom of the river, and the wind, like a great sigh of sorrow, swept over the land.

Isis, playing in the royal palace with her little son, Horus, lifted up her face and listened to the wind. With a broken-hearted cry she buried her face in her hands. "Set has slain Osiris!" she wailed. "My beloved husband is dead."

She had lived as a mortal woman for so long that in her sorrow she did not remember she was a goddess who knew the secret of life and death. All at once, however, power and knowledge came to her and she leaped to her feet. If she could but find the body of Osiris she might yet bring him back to life! But first she must put her little son, Horus, into a safe place.

Taking the child, she hastened to a distant part of the kingdom and gave him into the care of a dear friend. Then she cast a spell over the area, so none could find the boy and harm him. Having done this, Isis set out on her sad search along the River Nile.

Many people had seen the mysterious chest float down the river, but none knew where it had gone. At long last some children told Isis that they had found the chest, cast up by the waves into a bush near the shore.

"And then," the children cried, "the bush grew into a great tree, all around the chest!"

"Yes, yes!" Isis cried. "Where is this tree? Show it to me!"

"We can't," said a little boy. "The tree was so tall and so straight, our King had it made into a pillar for his palace."

Within that pillar was the body of her beloved husband, Isis knew, and hastened to the palace. But she did not go inside. Instead she sat weeping beside the fountain. Presently the Queen's maidens came out and seeing the sad stranger, spoke kindly to her.

Isis smiled at the maidens. "You are so kind to me, a lonely wanderer," she said, "that I wish to do something for you. I am skilled in beauty arts. Let me braid your hair more becomingly."

raven tresses long,
black and shiny hair

Astarte (a STAHR tee)

pined for missed

And this she did, and as she arranged the maiden's hair, each one seemed to become more beautiful. As Isis worked with the raven tresses of the girls, she breathed upon their hair and it instantly took on a wonderful fragrance.

When the maidens returned to the palace they ran to their Queen, Astarte, and told her of the stranger at the fountain.

"Remarkable," said the Queen, "and the scent which she has given you is exquisite. Bring this woman to me."

And so Isis came into the palace, looking like a humble servant, for all that she was a far greater Queen than Astarte. But though she served the Queen well, she spent every moment possible playing with one of the young princes, who was rather sickly. Whenever Isis was with the child, Astarte noticed that the little prince appeared stronger and rosier, and whenever she left him, he pined for her. Before long, Isis was made chief nurse for the child and the prince thrived under her care.

There were some in the palace who were jealous of the preference shown to the stranger, and they spied upon her. One night, after Isis had put the little prince to bed, these jealous ones peeked through a crack in the door and what they saw sent them racing to Astarte. They related so horrifying a tale, that the mother forgot all her queenly dignity. Picking up her fine linen skirts she ran down the palace halls and burst into the room where Isis had the young prince.

Imagine the mother's feelings when she saw her child lying in a pile of burning sticks and a swallow flying around the flames and twittering mournfully.

With a loud cry Astarte rushed forward and plucked her child from the flames.

In that instant Isis returned to her human form—and to all her queenly dignity. "You have deprived the prince of immortality!"

treacherous not to be
trusted; dangerous

she said. "Another few moments and all would have been accomplished." Then she told the frightened mother who she was, and Astarte fell on her knees and begged forgiveness.

"I forgive you," Isis said sadly. "But you must give me the central pillar from this palace, for it contains the body of my slain husband, Osiris."

"You shall have it," Astarte promised, and commanded slaves to take the pillar down at once. "Why did you not tell me your story in the beginning?" she then asked gently.

Isis shook her head. "After the treacherous murder of my husband, I dared trust no-one," she said.

When the slaves had taken the pillar down, Isis caused it to be split open, and there was the casket. A magic boat of papyrus reeds was built for Isis, and having had the casket put in it, she guided the boat into the marshes of the Nile.

There she opened the casket and gazed at the face of her beloved. At daybreak, she spoke magic words over Osiris, calling his soul back into his body, as she breathed into his nostrils.

Again and again she did this, but, alas, the soul of Osiris had been gone too long from his body. It was of no avail.

In her grief Isis gave a terrible cry. "By the secret name of Ra, let the sun stand in the heavens, for Osiris is indeed dead!"

And lo! the sun stood still, and time stood still, and every thing all over the world stood still.

And then there was a mighty rushing through the air. Suddenly Thoth, the god of wisdom, stood before the grieving Isis. "What has happened here?" he asked, and Isis told him her story.

"And now," she finished, "all my power is as nothing, for I cannot bring my beloved back to life."

Thoth shook his mighty head. "It is not right that you should," he said. "He that has known the mysteries of death cannot walk among mortal men again. But because Osiris was a good man and a great King, and because your love is so strong for him, I will recall his soul into his body and make him live forever—"

Isis' eyes brightened, but Thoth held up his hand. "Osiris shall live forever as a king among the deserving spirits."

Further Reading

Ancient Egyptians. Pierre Miguel. The Egyptians used hieroglyphic writing to tell the story of a person's life. This book uses hieroglyphs to recreate the history of ancient Egypt.

Egyptian Adventures. Olivia Coolidge. These 12 short stories tell about ancient Egyptian superstitions, magic, festivals, and funerals.

Mara, Daughter of the Nile. Eloise Jarvis McGraw. Spies and political intrigue in ancient Egypt are the backdrop for this story about a mistreated slave during the reign of Pharaoh Hatshepsut.

Voyage of Osiris: A Myth of Ancient Egypt. Gerald McDermott. Here is another version of Osiris's story.

Egypt and the Nubian Kingdom of Kush

THINKING FOCUS

Why is Kush called one of the great civilizations of ancient Africa?

Key Terms

- access
- tribute

▼ The Kushites gave their own style to Egyptian ideas, such as pyramids.

E arly in the 1800s, two French explorers came upon the ruins of an ancient city. One of them, Frédéric Caillaud, wrote:

I magine my joy when I saw the tops of a crowd of pyramids . . . tipped by the rays of the sun. I climbed to the summit of the highest of them. . . . Looking around, I saw a second group of pyramids to the west, and, not far from the river, a huge field of ruins . . . indicating the site of an ancient city.

Frédéric Caillaud, *Voyage à Meroé,* 1822

Who were the people that had lived there? Why had they built pyramids?

The ancient city that those early French explorers saw was Meroë (*MAIR uh wee*). The city of Meroë was once the capital of the Nubian kingdom of Kush (*kuhsh*).

Nubia is the geographical region that stretches along the Nile Valley from the first cataract to the fifth cataract. Several kingdoms prospered in Nubia at different times and in different places. Each one had its own works of art, its own borders, and capital city, but they shared common traditions.

Egypt Dominates Kush

Find Kush on the map below. The map shows the boundaries of Kush when its capitals were at Napata and Meroë. Note that it is south of Egypt in what is now known as the Sudan. It was part of the area known as Nubia. Like Egypt, Kush lies on both banks of the Nile River.

As early as the Old Kingdom, Egypt's rulers sent ships south to trade with the Nubians. They brought back gold, and tropical valuables such as ivory, ostrich feathers, and a black wood called ebony. Trading brought wealth to both countries. The Nubians charged Egyptian traders a fee as they passed through Nubia. The traders made a profit, too, because the goods they brought from Nubia were in great demand in Egypt. Egyptian stonecutters carved huge granite blocks from the cliffs in Nubia and floated them on barges back to Egypt. The pharaohs used the granite for their temples, tombs, and obelisks.

Egyptian rulers realized the riches that Nubia offered. During the Middle Kingdom, they had their soldiers build forts and trading posts in Kush. In this way, they protected their trade routes and made sure they had **access** to, or the ability to reach, Nubia's gold and ivory. Egyptian rulers came to depend on Kush for police and soldiers as well.

Since the time of the Middle Kingdom, the Egyptians had considered Kush to be part of their empire. However, Egyptian rulers had to "reconquer" Kush from time to time in order to maintain their control. In the 1400s B.C.,

Thutmose III invaded Kush again. Egypt demanded that Kush pay an annual **tribute**, or gift—ebony, ivory, ostrich feathers, perfumes, oils, and grains. Tribute scenes—pictures of Kushites carrying and presenting their tribute to Egyptian rulers—became popular during the New Kingdom.

▼ *How far north did Kush extend when its capital was Meroë?*

The Nubian Kingdoms of Kush

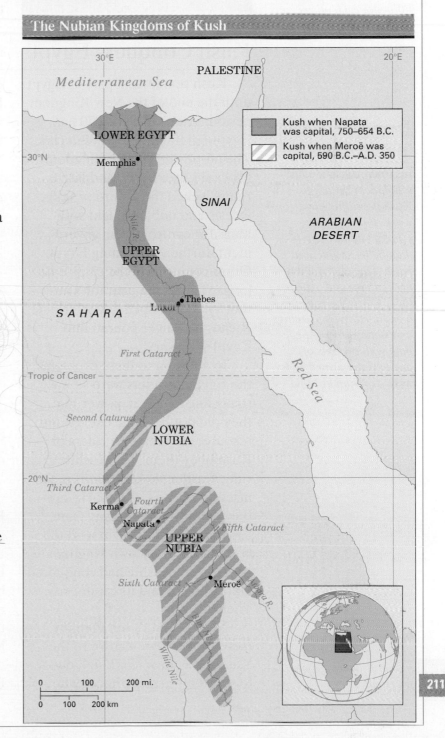

Kush when Napata was capital, 750–654 B.C.

Kush when Meroë was capital, 690 B.C.–A.D. 350

➤ *This painting was found in a c. 1420 B.C. Egyptian tomb. Kushites are carrying tribute to their Egyptian rulers.*

■ *How did Kushite society and Egyptian society influence each other?*

How Do We Know?

HISTORY *Much of what scholars know about Kush is skillful guesswork. For example, scholars think some Indian beliefs influenced Kush. One clue is a three-headed lion god, Apedemak, which the Kushites worshiped. Wall paintings and statues show Apedemak with two sets of arms. Many-armed gods were common in India.*

■ *How did the Kushite leaders become Egyptian pharaohs when Egypt was weak?*

Not surprisingly, Egyptian culture had a strong influence on the Kushites. For example, Egyptian priests built temples in Kush where the Kushites worshiped Egyptian gods. The Kushites also adopted the Egyptian belief in the afterlife. Kushites learned Egyptian crafts. Some learned Egyptian hieroglyphic writing, too. Some Kushite leaders even studied at the Egyptian court. ■

Kush Conquers Egypt

Kush remained a part of Egypt until the end of the New Kingdom period. Then, around 1070 B.C., Egypt fell into a period of decline. The all-powerful New Kingdom pharaohs were dead, and later rulers lacked their military skills. Priests and nobles fought with kings for control of the government, further weakening Egypt. Other countries in the empire no longer feared the pharaoh's authority and stopped paying tribute. Riches no longer poured into Egypt's treasury.

In addition to these problems, the Egyptian rulers were so busy struggling to stay in power that they did not have the energy and resources to make the rulers of Kush obey them. The Kushite ruler Kashta *(KAHSH tuh)* recognized Egypt's weakness. He saw the chance to break away from Egyptian control and extend the boundaries of his own kingdom. By 750 B.C., Kashta had conquered Upper Egypt and its capital city, Thebes.

Next, Kashta's son Piankhy *(pee AHNG kee)*, known to the Kushites as Piye *(PEE ay)*, defeated the warring princes who controlled the Nile Delta. Later, Piankhy put up a granite tablet on which he described the attack on the city of Memphis. It began:

> W hen day broke, at early morning, his majesty reached Memphis. . . . Then his majesty saw that it was strong, and that the wall was raised by a new rampart, and battlements manned with mighty men. There was found no way of attacking it.
>
> . . .
>
> But his majesty was enraged against it like a panther. He said, "I swear, as Ra loves me . . . this shall befall it [the city]. . . . I will take it like a flood of water."
>
> Piankhy, from a granite tablet near Napata, 700s B.C.

The city of Memphis fell to the Kushite army. Piankhy then went on to complete his conquest of Egypt by taking the rest of Lower Egypt. His successor, Shabaka, became the first Kushite pharaoh of Egypt. Shabaka's kingdom extended from the shores of the Mediterranean Sea to the borders of what is today the country of Ethiopia in Africa. ■

Kush's Last Thousand Years

The dynasty that began with Kashta did not last long. Kush controlled Egypt for less than a hundred years. By 671 B.C., Assyria, which was by now the strongest power in the Middle East, attacked Egypt and attempted to overthrow the Kushite ruler King Taharqa *(tuh HAHR kuh)*. Assyrian soldiers, armed with iron weapons, easily defeated the Kushites, whose weapons were made of bronze and stone. King Taharqa's troops fled south. By 654 B.C., Assyrian troops had expelled the Kushites from Egypt.

Kushite kings continued to rule their former kingdom from their capital at Napata *(nuh PAH tuh)*. No longer the rulers of Egypt, they still wore the double crown of the Egyptian pharaoh. Their court ceremonies and religious practices remained Egyptian, and scribes still used the Egyptian language for official documents.

Meroë, a New Capital

In 591 B.C., an Egyptian army defeated Kushite forces. For reasons still unexplained, the kings of Kush soon after moved their capital city from Napata to Meroë, a city about 150 miles south on the banks of the Nile River. Meroë became a great city, the center of Kushite culture.

Meroë was a good choice for the new capital of Kush. The area was rich in the natural resources necessary for iron production—iron ore and a good supply of wood.

Meroë became an important center of iron making. It also became a meeting place for traders from the Middle East, Asia, and parts of Africa. Camel caravans from the south brought leopard skins and ostrich eggs to Meroë's markets. Merchants from Syria and Palestine came to Meroë seeking gold and ivory. In ports on the Red Sea, Kushite merchants exchanged iron tools and spearheads for glass, fine cloth, and other luxury goods from China and India.

Arts and crafts flourished at Meroë. Workers made delicate vases and bowls decorated with sketches of hunters, animals, and flowers. Jewelers cast bracelets and earrings of silver and gold.

Some Egyptian practices continued. As in Egypt, the Kushite kings built great palaces along the Nile. They built temples to

▲ *This small gold sheath with its intricate design illustrates the fine work done by the Nubians.*

▼ *Leopard skins, ostrich feathers, granite, and ivory were some of the products Kush traded with Egypt and other nations.*

Ancient Egypt

honor the gods and pyramids in which royal families were buried.

Nubian Queens

During the time of Meroë, at least five queens governed Nubia. Some of the queens are shown on temples as warriors holding swords. The wealth of their tombs shows the influence and high position these women held.

The Fall of Kush

Over time, Egyptian influence on Kushite life lessened. The Kushites developed their own hieroglyphic writing. Later they worshiped a lion god called Apedemak, their god of war.

Meroë remained an important cultural and trade center for more than 600 years. In A.D. 350, King Ezana, the ruler of a neighboring kingdom called Axum, invaded and conquered Meroë. Ezana left a record of the defeat:

I made war on them. . . . They fled without making a stand, and I pursued them. . . . killing some and capturing others . . . I burnt their towns, both those built of bricks and those built of reeds, and my army carried off their food and copper and iron . . . and destroyed the statues in their temples, their granaries, and cotton trees and cast them into the [Nile].

Ezana, ruler of Axum, A.D. 300

For many centuries after this brutal conquest, Meroë was forgotten. Modern archaeologists have explored the city and other ruins of ancient Kush. They have learned much about them, but much more is still unknown. Meroitic hieroglyphic writing remains a mystery.

Almost everything we know about Kush comes from two sources. One source is the writings of other ancient peoples whose languages have been deciphered. The other source is writings from the time when Egyptian writing was still used in Kush. Someday, when scholars learn to read the Meroitic language, we will learn much more about the kings, queens, and commoners of one of the world's great civilizations. ■

■ *What happened to the Egyptian influence in Kush in the centuries after the Assyrian conquest?*

➤ *This elaborate royal crown made of silver was found in an excavation of ancient Nubia. Archaeologists date the crown in the A.D. 200s or 300s.*

R E V I E W

1. **FOCUS** Why is Kush called one of the great civilizations of ancient Africa?
2. **CONNECT** What was the meaning of the double crown of Egypt? What achievement of King Piankhy made it an appropriate crown for Kushite kings?
3. **HISTORY** What benefits did Egypt receive from Kush, and what benefits did Kush receive from Egypt?

4. **CRITICAL THINKING** Why did Meroë become an important center of culture and trade?
5. **ACTIVITY** Imagine that you live during the time of Kush's greatness. Using information from this lesson, draw or paint a travel poster urging people to visit your country.

Reading a Cross Section

Here's Why

A cross section is a special kind of diagram. It shows how the inside of an object looks, how it is made, what it is made of, or how it works. Cross sections are often used to show how things such as toys and machines are put together.

Cross sections can be especially helpful for understanding how something works. For example, cross sections can help you understand how smelting furnaces, such as those used during the iron age, worked.

Here's How

Look at the diagrams on this page. Get the "big picture" first—read the titles and look over the diagrams to see what they show in general. Then read the labels and refer to the glossary as you study each diagram closely.

Look at the cross section on the left. The labels tell you what each part of the diagram is. For example, the labels explain that the furnace walls were made of clay bricks covered by a layer of mud. The labels also identify hollow clay pipes and bellows. The bellows were used to pump air through the pipes. Find the arrows that indicate the movement of the bellows.

Now look at the contents of the furnace. The labels tell you there are alternating layers of charcoal and iron ore in the upper part of the furnace. What is in the bottom part of the furnace?

Try It

The diagram on the right shows the same furnace after it was fired. Compare this diagram to the one on the left. What is the same in the two diagrams? What is different? What happened to the charcoal? What happened to the iron ore?

Apply It

Find a cross-sectional diagram in your science textbook or another source. Explain the diagram by answering these questions: What does the diagram show? What parts are labeled? Why is the cross section useful?

Glossary

bellows (bĕl´ōz) A pump device used to produce a current of air

bloom (blōōm) Purified iron that is the result of the smelting process

slag (slăg) Impurities and waste from the smelting process

smelting (smĕlt´ĭng) The use of heat to remove pure metal from ore

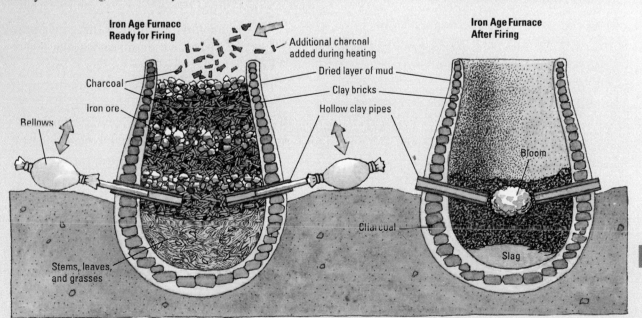

Iron Age Furnace Ready for Firing

Additional charcoal added during heating

Dried layer of mud

Charcoal

Clay bricks

Iron ore

Hollow clay pipes

Bellows

Stems, leaves, and grasses

Iron Age Furnace After Firing

Bloom

Charcoal

Slag

215

Chapter Review

Reviewing Key Terms

access (p. 211)
afterlife (p. 192)
cataract (p. 187)
delta (p. 187)
dynasty (p. 190)
embalm (p. 192)

hieroglyphics (p. 196)
mummy (p. 192)
obelisk (p. 200)
papyrus (p. 189)
pharaoh (p. 199)
tribute (p. 211)

A. The two words in each pair are related in some way. On your own paper, write a sentence explaining how the words are related.

1. cataract, delta
2. papyrus, hieroglyphics
3. pharaoh, tribute
4. dynasty, pharaoh
5. mummy, afterlife
6. hieroglyphics, obelisk

B. Some of the following statements are true. The rest are false. Write *True* or *False* for each statement. Then rewrite the false statements to make them true.

1. A dynasty was made up of several rulers from different families.
2. Cataracts are the plants from which papyrus is made.
3. Hatshepsut placed pillars called obelisks across the river from her temple.
4. The Egyptians built forts in Kush to protect their access to Kush's gold and ivory.
5. Embalming turned the body into a mummy.
6 The part of the Nile called the delta is found in southern Egypt.

Exploring Concepts

A. The following cause-and-effect chart about ancient Egypt lists facts about the Nile, an important discovery, a new ruler, and a power struggle. Copy the chart on your own paper. Then, fill in a sentence to the right of each cause that tells the effect. The first one has been done for you.

Cause	Effect
1. The Nile flooded its banks each year, depositing rich mud in farmers' fields.	Ancient Egypt could grow crops in the desert and feed its people.
2. In 1799, soldiers found a stone with three kinds of ancient writing.	
3. Thutmose III was next in line for the throne, but he was only 10 years old.	
4. The rulers of Egypt could no longer make the rulers of Kush obey.	

B. Support each statement with facts and details from the chapter.

1. Natural borders isolated ancient Egypt and protected it from invaders.
2. The seasons in Egypt were based on the flooding of the Nile.
3. A famous Egyptian legend tells the story of King Menes.
4. Historians have identified three periods in Egypt's history when many important events took place.
5. Imhotep, advisor to King Zoser, brought about an important change in Egypt.
6. The Egyptians left many written texts.
7. As a ruler, Hatshepsut concerned herself with improving life at home rather than building an empire.
8. The Babylonians and the Egyptians each created a lunar calendar.
9. Kush's riches were important to the Egyptians.
10. King Kashta's dynasty did not last long.

Reviewing Skills

1. Look again at the picture of the god Anubis on page 193. You can see that the figure representing Anubis is larger than the figures to his left. Do you think that the difference in the size of these figures is significant? Use what you have learned about interpreting Egyptian paintings to help you explain your answer.

2. Turn to the cross-section diagram on page 422. The ancient Romans built many roads, some of which are still in use today. This diagram shows how the Romans built roads. You can see that rubble forms the road's bottom layer. This means that the rubble was the first layer that workers laid down. What were the next two layers?

What material makes up the road's surface? Look at the diagram again. Notice that the Roman road is higher in the middle than it is near the curbs. Why might the Romans have constructed roads this way?

3. Imagine that your class plans to present a short play about ancient Nubia. Explain how to prepare this project by using the five steps for organizing a class project described on page 181.

4. Imagine that you are an ancient Egyptian sailor measuring the depth of the Nile River at different times of the year. What is the best way to organize the measurements you have recorded?

Using Critical Thinking

1. One way scientists learn about early people is by studying the objects they left behind. Which Egyptian artifacts are the most helpful for learning about ancient Egypt? Why?

2. Having paper allowed the Egyptians to leave many written records. From such records and the objects the people left behind, we learned the information you read in this chapter. Do you think this information gives us a full picture of Egyptian society? If not, tell what you think is missing.

3. The ancient Egyptians accomplished many things. They formed governments, became a world power, and built an empire. They invented a writing system and developed a belief system and customs. The ancient Egyptians also created outstanding literature, art, and architecture. If you had lived in ancient Egypt, which achievement would you have wanted to be a part of? How might a person do something similar today?

4. To become a scribe, a student copied the same lines over and over. What kinds of schoolwork do you think best prepare students for life in our society today?

Preparing for Citizenship

1. **ARTS ACTIVITY** Make a diorama of a pharaoh's burial chamber. The illustrations in A Closer Look on pages 194 and 195 will help you. Include a model of a mummy and objects buried with the pharaoh. Decorate part of the wall with a mural. On the other part, write a message about the afterlife using hieroglyphic symbols from page 488 of the Minipedia. Explain why we display objects from Egyptian tombs in museums today.

2. **COLLABORATIVE LEARNING** Form groups, one for each Egyptian achievement mentioned in Using Critical Thinking (3) on this page. In your group, decide what modern achievement can be compared to the ancient one. Have one group member describe the Egyptian achievement. Have another describe a modern achievement that can be compared to it. Have two students illustrate the achievements. Combine the work of all the groups into a class presentation.

Unit 4

Early Asian Civilizations

Horse-drawn chariots carried the wealthy people of China 1,800 years ago. By then, the civilizations in the Near East had fallen, but Asian civilizations continued to flourish. China, cut off from the rest of the world by mountains and deserts, grew with little outside influence. India accepted people and ideas from many places. Both civilizations developed traditions that live on into the present.

2500 B.C.

Bronze horse and chariot from a tomb at Wuwui, c. A.D. 100

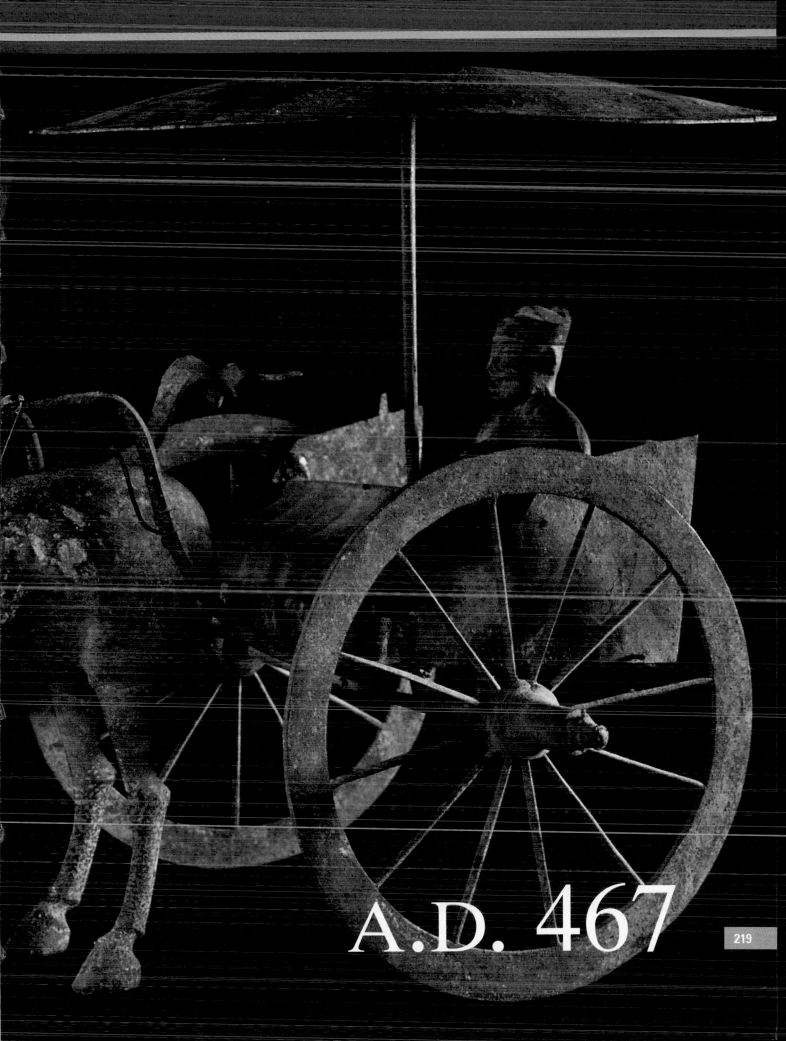

A.D. 467

Chapter 8
Ancient India

Like the brightly colored cotton cloth woven in India for thousands of years, the culture of India has been fashioned from many strands. The earliest Indian civilization arose about 4,500 years ago. Gradually, other ancient peoples moved to India. Over the centuries, the people blended old and new customs and beliefs, just as weavers blend the multicolored threads of their fabrics. The unique mixture of religious and social traditions continues in India today.

More than 4,000 years ago people in the Indus Valley were weaving cotton cloth. Hand looms like this are used today in some parts of India.

c. 2500–1500 B.C. The Indus Valley civilization flourishes along the Indus River. This bead necklace is from the ancient city of Harappa.

| 3000 | 2500 | 2000 | 1500 |

2500 B.C.

c. 1500 B.C. The nomadic Aryans settle in the Indus Valley. They compose sacred hymns called the Vedas, still recited today.

A.D. 320–467 During India's Gupta Dynasty, the Hindu religion prospers. Hindus write down great poems, including a tale about a hero named Rama. Indian children (above) still act out this tale. The mask (left) represents Hanuman, the monkey god who helped Rama.

1000	500	B.C.	A.D.	500

c. 500 B.C. A new religion, Buddhism, arises from the teachings of Siddhartha Gautama.

A.D. 467

L E S S O N   1

The Indus Valley Civilization

THINKING FOCUS

What evidence have archaeologists found of a highly developed civilization in the Indus River Valley?

Key Terms

- subcontinent
- silt

➤ *The strange symbols on this water buffalo seal still puzzle decoders.*

> *The seal is a smooth black stone without polish. On it is engraved very deeply a bull . . . Above the bull there is an inscription in six characters, which are quite unknown to me . . .*
>
> *Archaeological Survey of India, 1872–1873*

Those are the words used by archaeologist Alexander Cunningham in 1873 to describe a curious, cracker-sized object much like the one shown on this page. He identified it as a seal, an object commonly used to imprint pictures, writing, or numbers. Cunningham had found the seal in Harappa, a mysterious, ruined city in what is now northern Pakistan.

The seal and the strange writing captured Cunningham's attention, but he could not solve the riddle of their origin. Though we now know more about the history of the seal, the script on its surface still remains a mystery.

The trail that led Cunningham to the seal began in the early 1800s with travelers' accounts of Harappa. Partly buried beneath mounds of earth, Harappa had long been deserted. Yet the ruins that remained above ground showed that this was a highly developed civilization. Who were the builders? No one knew.

The reports of Harappa eventually reached Cunningham, who was a leading British archaeologist working in India. He decided to visit the ruins. It was on his third trip that Cunningham came upon the puzzling seal.

In the years that followed Cunningham's find, other archaeologists explored Harappa and Mohenjo-Daro, a ruined city 400 miles southwest of Harappa. What they found was astonishing: traces of a civilization thousands of years older than anything ever before discovered in India. This civilization became known as the Indus Valley civilization. It thrived for approximately 1,000 years from about 2500 to 1500 B.C.

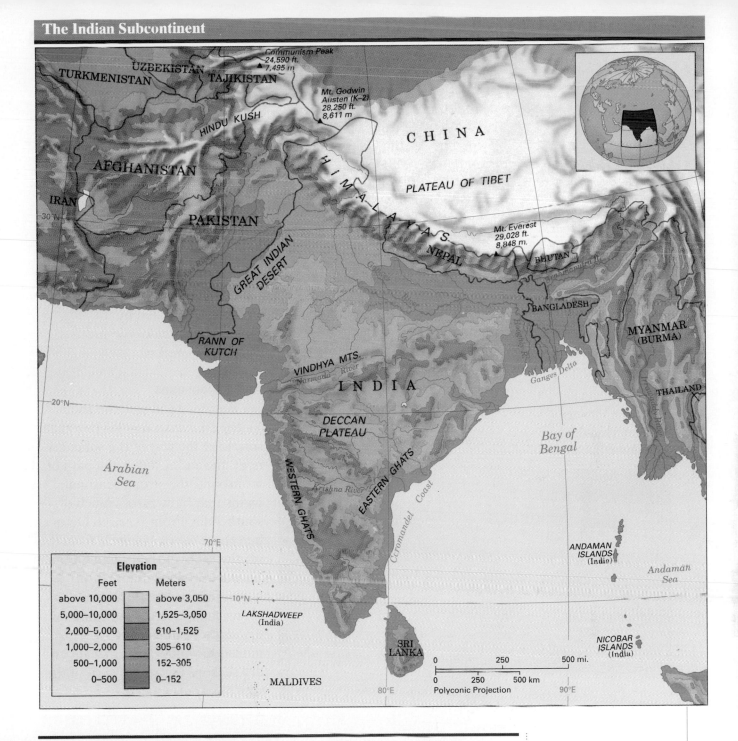

Elevation

Feet	Meters
above 10,000	above 3,050
5,000–10,000	1,525–3,050
2,000–5,000	610–1,525
1,000–2,000	305–610
500–1,000	152–305
0–500	0–152

Almost a Continent

The discovery of the cities Harappa and Mohenjo-Daro took archaeologists by surprise, but what did not surprise them was that a great civilization had developed in the Indus River Valley. The mountains, rivers, and fertile soil made this region an ideal place for people to settle. The rivers offered water for irrigation. They also provided people with water routes for building up trade.

Locate on the above map the rugged Himalayan and Hindu Kush mountain ranges that separate the Indian region from the rest of Asia. Geographers call this area a **subcontinent,** a large land mass that's somewhat separated yet still part of a continent.

▲ *The subcontinent features plains, plateaus, and the highest mountains in the world, the Himalayas. Look for Mt. Everest in this range. It's more than five miles high.*

223

Ancient India

The Indus Valley is no longer a well-watered plain. The Indus River passes through a barren, desertlike landscape. This area was not altered by a change in climate, but by cutting down trees and overgrazing.

The Himalayas are more than just a natural boundary. They are also the source of three major river systems. Starting amid snow-crowned peaks, the Ganges and Brahmaputra rivers flow southeast into the Bay of Bengal. The Indus River flows southwest into the Arabian Sea.

The Indus River System

As the map on this page shows, the Indus River stretches across the northwestern part of the sub-continent in an area that is now part of Pakistan. The river's source lies high atop Himalayan peaks, where melting snow feeds dozens of trickling mountain streams.

These streams join as they flow down rugged slopes, eventually forming small rivers.

Find on the map where these small rivers unite to form the great Indus River. Now locate the city of Mohenjo-Daro about 250 miles from the coast.

In ancient times, the Indus flooded frequently. When the river overflowed its banks, flood waters left a rich, fine-grained soil called **silt** upon the banks and neighboring lands. Enriched by the silt, crops in the area of the Indus River grew well.

Asian Monsoons

Besides good soil, the Indus Valley enjoyed a regular rainy season. Like the rest of the subcontinent, the valley lies in the path of monsoons, the strong seasonal winds that blow across much of south Asia. From April to October, these winds sweep in from the southwest over the Indian Ocean. They carry heavy rains. From November to March, the monsoons change direction, bringing dry air from the northeast. Thus, monsoon winds cause the wet and dry seasons that are typical of the subcontinent.

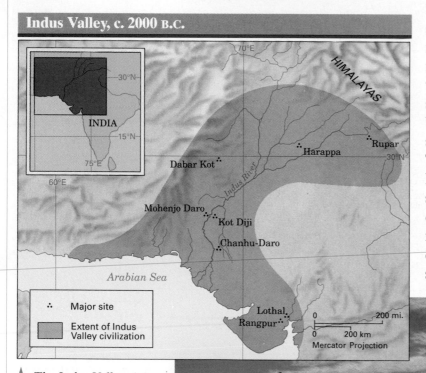

Indus Valley, c. 2000 B.C.

INDIA
30°N
15°N
75°E
60°E
70°E
HIMALAYAS
Rupar
Harappa
30°N
Dabar Kot
Indus River
Mohenjo Daro
Kot Diji
Chanhu-Daro
Arabian Sea

∴ Major site

▨ Extent of Indus Valley civilization

Lothal
Rangpur

0   200 mi.
0   200 km
Mercator Projection

▲ The Indus Valley civilization depended upon its network of rivers.

➤ Looking downstream of the Indus River in modern Pakistan. On the right are the Himalayas.

The Indus Valley was once a well-watered plain that may have provided homes for the animals shown on the carved seals. Although these animals are no longer found in the valley, it must have once been their home.

Blessed with fertile fields and water, the people of the Indus Valley raised wheat and barley year after year. This stable food supply encouraged others to settle in the area. Eventually, these people began to build cities. ■

■ *How did the geographical location of the Indus Valley make possible the growth of a civilization there?*

The Great River Civilization

Besides Mohenjo-Daro and Harappa, more than 70 other sites have been discovered in the Indus Valley. Even though no written records that modern historians can read have been found, archaeologists have learned much about this civilization.

Central Planning

The Indus sites are scattered across the river plain, and area three times larger than California. Archaeological digs reveal that most of these towns were neatly laid out according to similar plans. Workers constructed the buildings, streets, and sewer systems with skill and care. Even their bricks were equal in size and shape.

This matching suggests a strong central government for the entire area with information flowing freely between towns. To achieve such order, a central group must have planned the projects and overseen the work in the various towns.

Widespread Trade

Besides being in contact with their neighbors along the river, the people of the Indus Valley traded with communities many miles away. We have learned this from Mesopotamian writings that refer to trade between the Indus Valley and Sumer. In addition, stone beads, bone inlays, and seals from

◄ *This rhinoceros seal uncovered by archaeologists helps to confirm that this animal once lived in the Indus River Valley.*

the Indus Valley have been discovered in Mesopotamia. Traces of Indus products also were found near the Persian Gulf.

Cube-shaped stone weights for use by merchants give further evidence of trade. These finely crafted and apparently accurate weights were unearthed throughout the Indus Valley. Some were tiny enough to balance small amounts of gold, while others were so large they had to be hoisted with ropes.

Historians also believe that merchants had their own trademarks that were carved on stone seals. An example is pictured on this page. Merchants used these seals to stamp their identification on their belongings. In A Closer Look, on pages 226 and 227, you'll learn more about archaeological discoveries made at the Mohenjo-Daro site in the Indus Valley. ■

▲ *Can you imagine an ancient merchant using these weights to measure out grain and gold?*

■ *What products did the Indus Valley cities export, and how do we know?*

225

Ancient India

Mohenjo-Daro

This was once a busy city of 35,000 people, filled with footsteps, shouts, laughter, and the smells of food cooking. What was it like to live here? What skills and ideas did people have? The clues found at Mohenjo-Daro can help tell us.

What does it take to build a city with straight streets and well-designed sewers? It takes smart engineers to plan the streets and sewers so they are level and the water runs where it's supposed to. The sewers made Mohenjo-Daro cleaner and more healthful than most other ancient cities.

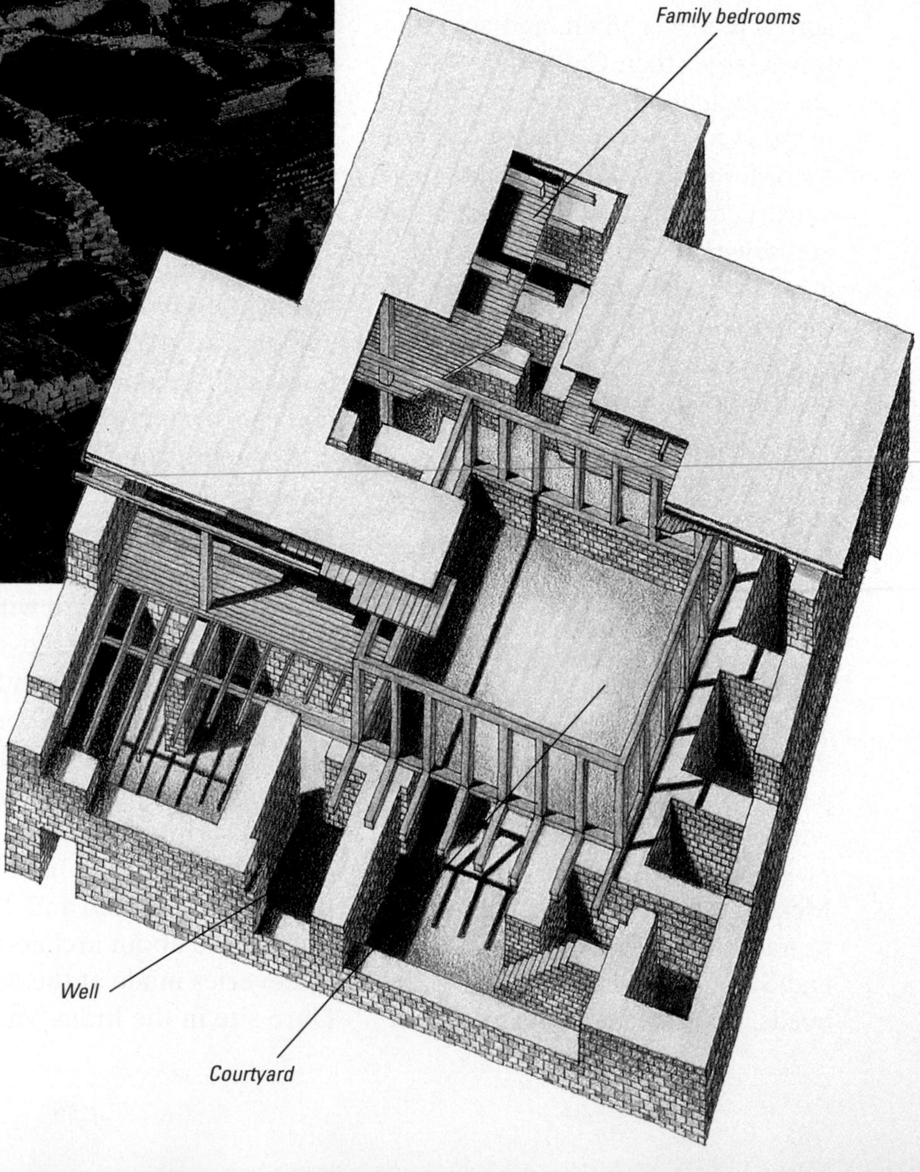

Family bedrooms

The layout of brick walls tells us that some houses were very large. Some historians think that the second floors of big houses may have been used for bedrooms since they would be cooler at night.

Well

Courtyard

Look at the clothing carved on this statue, which may represent a priest or a king. Based on carvings like this and scraps of cotton cloth archaeologists think that both women and men dressed in colorful robes.

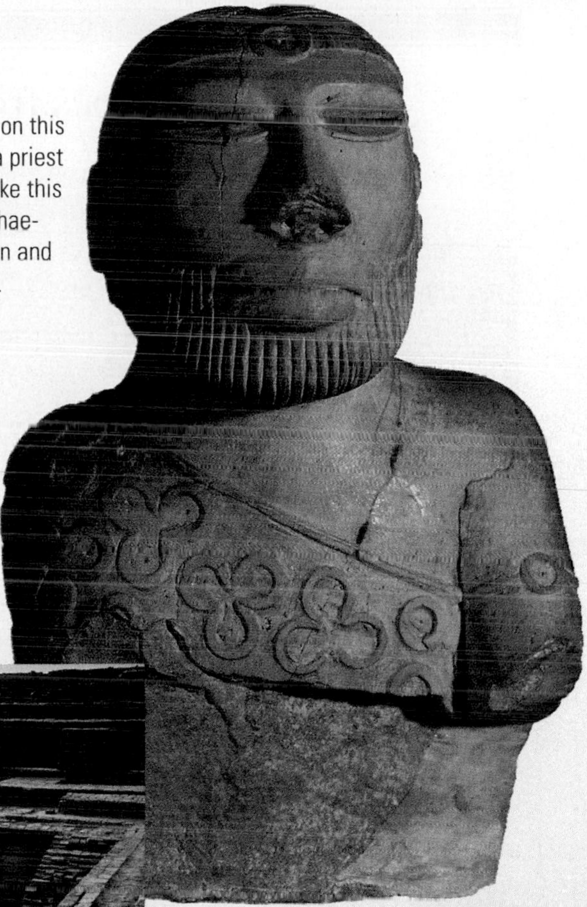

This pool with steps leading into it is known as the Great Bath. Why did the ancient citizens put this pool in the most important part of town? Since ritual bathing is still an important part of some present-day Indian religions, perhaps the Great Bath was a part of Mohenjo-Daro's religious life.

Thin, light, and strong, this pottery is of very high quality. The quality and the beautiful designs show us that a skilled potter made this piece.

What's for dinner? Archaeologists found tiny bits of food in huge grain storage rooms in the center of the city. These clues suggest that dinner in Mohenjo-Daro could have been warm, tasty wheat bread served with barley or rice.

227

Ancient India

Echoes from Abandoned Cities

The Indus Valley people perfected the two-wheeled cart.

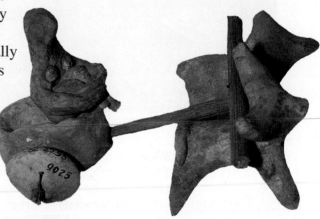

➤ *This miniature cart of terra cotta pulled by two bulls was discovered in the Mohenjo-Daro ruins.*

■ *What evidence of the Indus Valley civilization is found in modern India?*

After lasting for 1,000 years, the Indus Valley civilization finally declined. No one knows exactly why, but there are clues. Perhaps an earthquake caused great floods. Human skeletons were found huddled together in the digs at Mohenjo-Daro, as if they were trapped in such a disaster. Or, a decline in trade and wealth may have made life difficult in the cities. People may have gradually moved back to farming villages because they could no longer make a living in the cities.

In the search for answers, archaeologists have found new evidence that this civilization was one of the largest in the ancient world.

The ruins of hundreds of cities dot the river valleys of northeastern India. Other cities have been uncovered in Pakistan and one has been found in present-day Afghanistan.

After the decline of the Indus Valley cities, some parts of their culture survived. Among treasures found at Mohenjo-Daro was a statue of a woman wearing bracelets. In India and Pakistan today, many women wear similar jewelry.

The people of the Indus Valley were the first to raise chickens for food. Today, chicken appears on menus worldwide.

By 2000 B.C., the Indus people had begun to spin and weave cotton cloth. Today, the making of cotton cloth is a very important industry in Pakistan and India. ■

REVIEW

1. **FOCUS** What evidence have archaeologists found of a highly developed civilization in the Indus River Valley?
2. **CONNECT** Compare the rise of civilization in the Nile River Valley and the Indus River Valley.
3. **CULTURE** What do the large, well-constructed houses at Mohenjo-Daro tell us about the people who lived there 4,500 years ago?
4. **CRITICAL THINKING** Archaeologists discovered 10 cities at Mohenjo-Daro, built one on top of the other, each less carefully built than the one before. What conclusions can you draw from this?
5. **ACTIVITY** List five imaginary finds from an archaeological site. Exchange lists. Tell what these finds reveal about the early inhabitants.

LESSON 2

Arrival of the Aryans

L et's travel back in time about 3,500 years to a large plain in the Indus Valley. It is a day for chariot racing. Your uncle is there with his fastest horses. Imagine standing at the edge of the dusty plain with the other spectators waiting for the race to begin. You fiddle with the bangles on your arm turning them around and around. A bird repeats its high *trwee-trwee* call. And everywhere the god called Surya shines in the sky and fills the air with heat.

The men stand upright in their chariots and wait for the starting signal. One more half-second to shake the reins and they are off!

The wooden wheels of the chariots jerk into motion. There is a jumble of hooves, wheels, and waving arms as the racers try to take the lead. You squint your eyes and stand on tiptoe to see who has won the race. From the yelling, you know that it is the raja *(RAH jah)*. Maybe that is best. He is the ruler and it is good that he is kept happy.

What did the Aryans contribute to Indian culture?

Key Terms

- Aryan
- migration
- caste

From Where Did the Aryans Come?

The people racing their chariots were **Aryans**. Historians don't agree about where the Aryans came from. One theory is that Aryan culture grew out of the Indus Valley civilization that you read about in Lesson 1.

Other historians believe that the Aryans migrated to India over a long period of time and developed alongside the Indus Valley civilization. They believe that the Aryans and the Indus Valley people are two separate groups because their languages were so different.

The Indus Valley people spoke a language that scholars have not been able to read. The Aryans

spoke a language called ancient Sanskrit. Like Russian, Persian, and English, Sanskrit is part of the Indo-European family of languages.

Indo-European Migrations

According to the migration theory, the Aryans lived in the grasslands of eastern Europe north of the Black and Caspian seas long before they reached India. They were part of a larger group we now call the Indo-Europeans.

The Indo-Europeans were a seminomadic people who herded cattle, goats, and sheep. They generally traveled from place to place in tribes, groups made up of

229

Ancient India

The adz side (left) of this Aryan tool shaped wood; the ax chopped it.

■ *What advantages enabled the Aryans to successfully take over the Indus Valley?*

▼ *Aryans pushed their way through passes in the Hindu Kush mountain range, like this one near Kabul, Afghanistan.*

related families. Because the Indo-Europeans were on the move much of the time, they didn't build cities. But they did tame the horse and develop a sturdy wheel with spokes for their two-wheeled chariots. These speedy chariots allowed them to move freely over large areas and to wage war more effectively than warriors on foot.

About 2000 B.C., conditions in the Indo-European homeland changed. Historians aren't exactly sure what happened. Perhaps the Indo-Europeans ran out of good grazing pasture for their herds. Perhaps their population had simply grown so much that they needed more space. Or they may have suffered an outbreak of disease or an attack by invaders.

Whatever the reason, sometime around 2000 B.C., huge groups of Indo-Europeans left their homes and began moving to new regions. This movement of people to new surroundings is called **migration.** As the map on page 231 shows, some groups of Indo-Europeans moved west and south. Others, the Aryans, moved east toward the Indian subcontinent.

Through the Mountain Passes

By around 1500 B.C., the first Aryans found their way through the difficult, high passes in the Hindu Kush, the mountains along the northwestern edge of the Indian subcontinent. One route was through the Khyber Pass. These passes would serve as highways for other migrating and invading peoples for the next 3,000 years.

Aryan Hymns: The Vedas

Although we have little archaeological evidence of the early Aryans, we do have other sources of information. Aryan beliefs and daily life are described in the Vedas *(VAY duhs),* a collection of sacred hymns and poems. They were composed over hundreds of years starting around 1500 B.C.

The early Aryans had no written language, yet they passed down the Vedas for centuries. Aryan priests memorized the Vedas and taught younger priests. Imagine memorizing long school books, word for word, by having them read aloud to you. That gives you some idea of what the Aryan priests did. Passing knowledge from generation to generation by oral tradition wasn't an easy task. ■

The Aryans who rode into India were not the only people at that time who were on the move. Similar migrations of people took place east, south, and west of the Indo-European homelands in eastern Europe.

What is a migration? What causes people to leave their homes and move thousands of miles to places they may never have seen? What happens when migrating people meet the people already there?

A Trip Isn't Migration

A migration is a permanent move, not a short-term one. About 200 years ago, Indians such as the Pawnee were often on the move. They hunted the many buffalo that roamed the midwestern plains. Once or twice a year they went on trips to hunt buffalo. The Pawnee carried everything they needed with them, and set up temporary wood-and-skin homes called tepees. But the Pawnee were not migrating. They always returned to their permanent villages.

Why People Migrate

People migrate to leave where they are, as well as to arrive at a new place. Natural disasters such as floods or earthquakes may push people out of their homes. Or, invaders may force them out. The attraction of more food or better jobs may pull people to a new place. Historians call this the "push-pull" of migration.

Some Major Migrations

Major migrations have taken place throughout history. Thousands of years ago people settled North and South America by crossing the Bering Strait from Asia. Bantu migrations took place in Africa around A.D. 700, in 1200, and again in 1800. In the 1990s, many people from Latin America migrated to the United States.

Results of Migration

People who migrate are influenced by the culture of their new land. But they also cause changes in that culture. The map below shows how the Indo-Europeans fanned out in different directions on their migrations. With them, they took their flocks, their horses, chariots, clothes, and weapons. But they also took along something more lasting: their language.

As they settled in their new homelands, their Indo-European language was taken into the cultures already there. Language experts have discovered that many of the languages spoken in Europe and India today have the same root: the language spoken by Indo-Europeans. In this way, those early migrations made a lasting imprint on history.

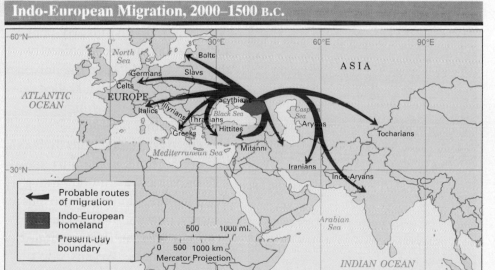

Indo-European Migration, 2000–1500 B.C.

Legend:
- Probable routes of migration
- Indo-European homeland
- Present-day boundary

0   500   1000 mi.
0   500 1000 km
Mercator Projection

What Do the Vedas Reveal?

How Do We Know?

HISTORY *Most information about the Aryans comes from the Vedas. All other evidence is scarce. When the Aryans first arrived in the Indus Valley, they were still seminomadic. They probably built their houses with the materials at hand—mud, wood, and reeds. Unlike brick, mud crumbles easily; wood and reeds quickly decay. Thus, little physical evidence of these early settlements remains.*

The Vedas are the main source of information about the Aryan people and their way of life. For this reason, historians call the period from about 1500 to 600 B.C. the Vedic Period.

The Aryans first settled in northwestern India in an area now known as the Punjab. From the Indus Valley people, they learned to grow grains, such as wheat and barley. They also continued to raise livestock. In fact, cows were so highly prized by the Aryans that these animals were used as a kind of money. According to the Vedas, Aryan priests were paid in cows for performing religious services.

Aryan Religion

The Vedas describe the universe as divided into three regions—earth, atmosphere, and sky. Aryans worshiped divine beings, or gods, who occupied these regions and had power over the forces of nature.

➤ *Indra, the mighty storm god, rides across the sky on his white elephant in this Indian painting from the 1600s. Indra has answered the call of the priests who are tending the sacred fire.*

One of the most powerful gods was Indra. Indra was the god of war and a thrower of thunderbolts. Each morning, Indra defeated a dragon of darkness. Indra's victory allowed the sun to rise and the dawn goddess to arrive. Indra was the guardian of cosmic order in the world. The power of Indra is shown in the *Rig Veda*, one of the Vedic books:

I ndra, who wields the thunderbolt in his hand, is the king of that which moves and that which rests, of the tame and of the horned. He rules the people as their king, encircling all this as a rim encircles spokes.

The Aryan Fire Sacrifice

The main ceremony in Aryan religion was the fire sacrifice. Sometimes animals were sacrificed into the fire, but it was more common to offer milk, clarified butter, vegetable cakes, or grains. A person making a sacrifice might want more sons, cattle, or earthly happiness from the gods.

Priests called to the gods during the ceremony by singing and chanting Vedic hymns. By performing the sacrifices correctly, the priests could keep the universe in harmony, the way a skilled mechanic tunes the running of a huge machine.

The Aryans saw both divisions and connections in the universe. The universe was divided into three regions of earth, atmosphere, and sky, and yet there were connections between these regions. For example, the Aryans saw a connection between the heat in a

fire sacrifice, the heat that caused a fruit to ripen, and the god who ruled the heat of the sun. One of the goals of worship then, was to honor and celebrate these connections.

Social Classes

When the Aryans first came to India, their social system had three classes—the ruler, or raja, and his warriors; the priests; and the commoners.

Eventually, a new four-class system emerged. These four classes have remained the same for centuries. The Vedas describe the four social classes, or *varnas*, and their responsibilities.

In this system, priests, or *brahmins*, were the most powerful class. Their responsibility was to feed the community with spiritual nourishment. The second class, made up of rulers and warriors, ruled and protected society. The merchants and common people were the third class. They gave supplies and food to the community.

The fourth class, the servants, gave their service to the three other classes.

The Aryans valued the class system because it worked to bring harmony and order to society. Just as religious sacrifices had an important role in keeping order in the universe, so the Vedas gave classes a very powerful role in keeping order in society.

Little by little as people learned new jobs, new groups formed within the classes. These subgroups were named **castes**. For example, there was an ivory-carvers caste and a spice-sellers caste. Both belonged to the third class, the merchants. Castes were ranked one above the other like steps on a ladder. You were born within a caste, and you stayed there all your lifetime. Your job, your family life, your marriage, and your daily activities, were all shaped by your caste. Even though castes and classes are different, people often use the word *caste* to refer to both groupings. ■

■ *What do the Vedas reveal about the Aryan society and religion?*

233

Ancient India

What Remains Today of Aryan Ways?

■ *What evidence of the Aryan tradition is found in modern India?*

▼ *A Vedic fire is still used at some weddings in India.*

As the centuries passed, the growing Aryan population continued to spread over the region. By 1000 B.C., these one-time nomads had reached as far east as the fertile banks of the Ganges River.

They still raised livestock, but gradually they began to settle down. They had learned how to work with iron to make stronger axes and plows. With these tools, they could cut down forests to create new farmlands. They grew a variety of crops, including rice.

Crafts and trades had also increased. The Aryans now had skilled weavers, dyers, jewelers, and potters. This new settled life brought about another change, too. Slowly, the Aryan people began to establish small kingdoms.

The Aryans first migrated to India more than 3,500 years ago. Remarkably, the effects of that migration are still seen in India today. Sanskrit, the language spoken by the Aryans, is the root of many Indian languages including Hindi. Hindi is the most widespread language in modern India.

Castes, too, are important in some ways in modern India. Many people still marry and choose jobs within their family's caste. Religion, however, is the most lasting heritage of the Aryans. The Vedas are studied and memorized today. The Upanishads, a part of the Vedas, hold special meaning for many people because they treat deep subjects such as a person's place in the universe. ■

REVIEW

1. **FOCUS** What did the Aryans contribute to Indian culture?
2. **CONNECT** Contrast the Aryans with the Indus Valley people. Be sure to include way of life, power structure, tools, and equipment.
3. **HISTORY** Who were the Indo-Europeans, and how is their influence felt in the world today?
4. **CRITICAL THINKING** Since the Vedas were composed by Aryans, the information is presented from an Aryan point of view. Why is this important?
5. **ACTIVITY** Draw a map of present-day India and Pakistan. Label the Aryans' route through the Khyber Pass. Also show how they later spread eastward to the Ganges River.

On the 49th day, Siddhartha discovered the truth he sought. He now had found a way to escape suffering. Understanding had flooded his mind like a great light. From that time on, he was called the Buddha, a title meaning "enlightened one." He had reached the height of understanding that the Buddhists call enlightenment.

The Peaceful Road

The Buddha then began to teach, speaking to five followers in a park near Sarnath. Within days, 60 more joined him. He sent them in all directions to spread the Buddha dharma *(DUR muh)*, the law or teachings. The Buddha traveled and taught, stopping whenever and wherever people gathered and listened. He lived his days in peace, teaching until his death at the age of 80. ■

▲ *The Buddha receives his enlightenment beneath the sacred tree. This sculpture stands about two feet high.*

■ *What events do Buddhists believe led to Siddhartha's enlightenment?*

Teachings of Buddhism

Amid the religious stirrings of the times, the Buddha found listentua. His teachings didn't meet the Sords of everyone who searched wotruth. But for some, his words sign wisdom. Why?

that first, his dharma freed people kingthe priests' control. He spiritu that everyone could find come t without the aid of the

The rituals. The Buddha held his son t to all, men and women, follow spoung, rulers and servants, king decioor.

ture. He st, the Buddha did not ac-dhartha firste system that placed According ne social group for their dered that e taught that all people or injury be that everyone should roads when S to try to live a better about in his cl

prince lived a as against religious ury. More than animals were put row during his eddha believed it

was wrong to take a life. Some people welcomed this message because there were far too many sacrifices. They were costly, too.

The Middle Way

Following his days of meditation beneath the sacred tree, the Buddha set forth his Four Noble Truths. These teachings give the Buddhist view on why people suffer and how suffering can be avoided. The chart below explains these beliefs.

▼ *In his Four Noble Truths, the Buddha explained why suffering occurs and how it ceases.*

The Four Noble Truths

1. People experience suffering and sorrow.

2. Suffering and sorrow are caused by people's greed, hatred, and ignorance.

3. We can be freed from suffering by overcoming its cause.

4. People can overcome their greed, hatred, and ignorance by practicing the Eightfold Path. This path gives eight steps for living a correct, or right life.

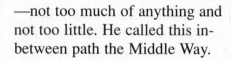

The Eightfold Path	
Step	**Description**
Right view	Believing in the Four Noble Truths and the Eightfold Path
Right resolve	Making a firm decision to live according to the Eightfold Path
Right speech	Speaking in a manner that doesn't harm others; not gossiping, lying or using angry words
Right conduct	Acting in a way that doesn't harm others; not killing, not stealing and also not acting selfishly
Right livelihood	Earning a living in a way that doesn't harm others
Right effort	Striving to get rid of any unwholesome action or attitude
Right mindfulness	Having constant awareness and attention in all activities
Right meditation	Developing tranquility and concentration of mind, which lead to insight into reality

➤ *When following the Eightfold Path, a Buddhist tries to live all eight steps at once, not one after the other.*

The Buddha's teaching centered on how people should think and act. He realized that greed for possessions and power was wrong. Yet he didn't want people to give up necessities, like food. The Buddha's answer was **moderation** —not too much of anything and not too little. He called this in-between path the Middle Way.

Karma and Rebirth

The thoughts, speech, and action a person performs during a lifetime are called karma *(KAHR muh)*. Buddhists teach that both an individual's wholesome karma (or good deeds) and the unwholesome karma (or bad deeds) travel into the next life. This karma causes **rebirth**. However, a person's personality does not make this journey. Buddhists do not believe in a soul or in any kind of creator God. What continues lifetime after lifetime is the karma that has been set in motion by all one's thoughts, words, and deeds—like the ripples caused by a stone thrown into a pond.

The Buddha taught that life is continual change. If human beings try to hold onto a personality, they will suffer. It is better to see oneself as part of the flow, part of the change, and interconnected with everything else. Once a person is successful in giving up all desires

➤ *In this sculpture the Buddha is preaching his first sermon at Deer Park in Sarnath, India.*

and in overcoming ignorance, that person will reach the goal of enlightenment. The Buddha taught that compassion and selfless love help one toward this goal.

Meditation, or focusing one's thinking, is an important part of Buddhism. Buddhists teach that meditation calms the mind and allows a person to let go of desires and possessions and be part of the universe. This discipline can be compared to setting a pail of muddy water in a still place until the mud sinks to the bottom and the water is clear.

The Three Jewels

The Buddhist tradition is made up of three parts called The Three Jewels. The first jewel is the Buddha himself. The second jewel is the dharma, the law the Buddha passed on to his followers.

The third jewel is Buddhism's religious community, called the *sangha*. In the sangha are monks and nuns. As time went on, devoted monks built centers of learning,

which are called monasteries. Here, they practiced the Buddha's way of life.

Gradually, Buddhism extended beyond the subcontinent. Missionaries first traveled to the island of Ceylon, southeast of India, now called Sri Lanka. By about A.D. 650, Buddhism extended to China, Korea, Japan, Tibet, Burma, and other areas of Southeast Asia. Today more than 325 million people throughout the world practice Buddhism. ■

▲ *A Buddhist monk studies today in a monastery in northern India.*

■ *What is the Eightfold Path, and where does it lead?*

A Great Buddhist Ruler

Buddhism found a faithful follower in the emperor, Asoka *(Ah SOH kah).* He was the first ruler to send missionaries beyond Indian borders. Thus, he started Buddhism on its worldwide path.

Asoka belonged to a line of conquering kings known as the Mauryas, who ruled from about 324 to 183 B.C. The Mauryas built the first great Indian empire. It was the largest empire on the subcontinent until the British claimed India in 1876. Note on the map the empire's boundaries during Asoka's rule.

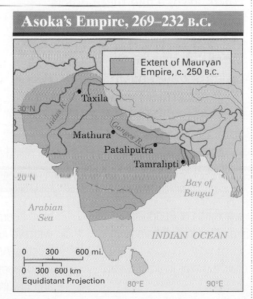

Asoka's Empire, 269–232 B.C.

Extent of Mauryan Empire, c. 250 B.C.

Taxila
Mathura
Pataliputra
Tamralipti

30°N
20°N

Indus R.
Ganges R.

Bay of Bengal

Arabian Sea

INDIAN OCEAN

0 300 600 mi.
0 300 600 km
Equidistant Projection

80°E   90°E

◀ *Within his Mauryan empire, Asoka built public wells and baths, free clinics for the sick, rest houses for travelers, and watering places for cattle.*

Asoka's Conversion

Not long after Asoka came to power in 269 B.C., he went to war. He set out to conquer Kalinga, an independent area in eastern India.

Asoka won that war. But the campaign was extremely cruel. The battles were horribly bloody. A short while after that experience, Asoka converted to Buddhism. During the rest of his rule, he spread the dharma by sending Buddhist missionaries to many places around the subcontinent. In addition, he sent missionaries to Ceylon, Burma, and the high Himalayan regions.

Asoka's Edicts

The Buddhist beliefs of the emperor were spelled out for the people in his public announcements, or edicts. Asoka had these edicts carved into rocks and pillars around the empire. Beautiful carvings often decorated the tops, or capitals, of the pillars.

Rock Edict I explains Asoka's support of ahimsa *(uh HIHM sah)*, which is the Buddhist belief in nonviolence. It forbids harming humans or animals.

> *No living creature shall be slaughtered here . . . Many hundreds of thousand living creatures were formerly slaughtered every day for curries in the kitchens of His Majesty. At present, when this edict on Dharma is inscribed, only three living creatures are killed daily, two peacocks and a deer . . . In the future, not even these three animals shall be slaughtered.*

The Kalinga Edict II in eastern India shows how Asoka felt toward his people:

> *All men are my children. Just as I seek the welfare and happiness of my own children in this world and the next, I seek the same things for all men.*

Breakup of the Mauryan Empire

After the emperor Asoka's death in 232 B.C., the rulers that followed him couldn't hold the Mauryan empire together. Gradually, it broke down into many little warring kingdoms.

Within 50 years, the last Mauryan ruler was killed by his own army commander. This violent deed contrasted sharply with Asoka's hopes for an Indian empire of nonviolence. ■

▲ *This lion capital sits atop an Asokan pillar. India's national emblem is patterned from it.*

■ *How did Asoka's Buddhist beliefs influence his rule?*

R E V I E W

1. **FOCUS** What are the main teachings of Buddhism?
2. **CONNECT** How did Buddhism differ from the Vedic religion?
3. **GEOGRAPHY** Trace a map of Asia. Color in areas where Buddhism had spread by A.D. 650.
4. **CRITICAL THINKING** Why might the merchant class

have been particularly attracted to Buddhism?

5. **WRITING ACTIVITY** In 50 words or less, write a column edict as Asoka might have done. In you edict, instruct people how to act toward other human beings and toward animals. Draw your pillar. Design a carving for its capital.

Recognizing the Buddha

Here's Why

Suppose you visited a museum. How would you be able to recognize a statue of Buddha?

You identify individuals through visuals features such as curly hair or brown eyes. In the same way, you can use identifying features to help you recognize symbols such as the Buddha.

Here's How

Some 600 to 700 years after the Buddha's death, his followers wanted a painting or statue of him to worship. However, no one who was alive then knew exactly what the Buddha had looked like.

You will remember that at Gautama's birth, a wise man predicted that the child would become a great man. This was because he had 32 identifying marks, or features, on his body. Some of them are shown on the diagram below. These identifying features, when they come together, create a symbol of the Buddha. The Buddha symbol represents both the great man and his teachings. Artists still use such features to represent the Buddha.

Not all these features are clearly visible on all images of the Buddha. But when you see three or four of these features together, you'll know that you are looking at the Buddha.

Try It

Look at the sculpture of the Buddha on page 237. Compare it to the diagram below. Which identifying features do you see? In what other ways are the two images alike?

Apply It

Choose a religious figure such as Moses or Jesus. Look in books for pictures of this person. What identifying features help you to recognize him?

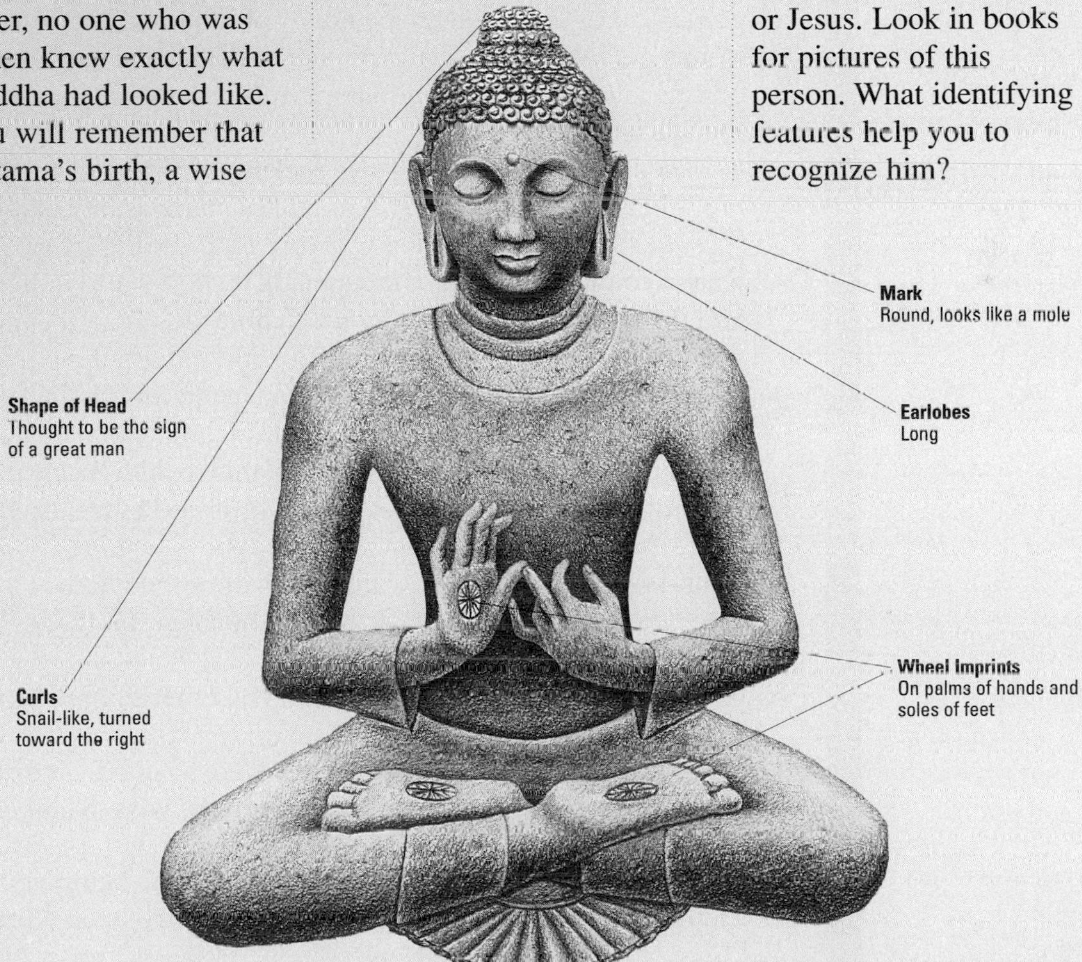

Mark
Round, looks like a mole

Earlobes
Long

Shape of Head
Thought to be the sign of a great man

Wheel Imprints
On palms of hands and soles of feet

Curls
Snail-like, turned toward the right

241

Ancient India

Popularity

A Jataka Tale

The Buddha told as many as 500 stories that taught about human behavior. Today these stories are known as Jataka *tales. This modern version of one of the stories appears in the book* Jataka Tales, *edited by Nancy DeRoin.*

As you learned in the last lesson, the Buddha taught that greed is wrong. Here is one of his teachings on a certain kind of greed.

Jataka (JAH duh kuh)
Dhananajaya
(duhn uhn JY uh)
Potthapada
(puht duh PAH duh)

Once upon a time when Dhananjaya was king of Benares, two parrots lived in the nearby forest. One was named Radha, the other Potthapada. Both were big and perfectly formed. Their feathers were beautiful to see.

A hunter, seeking the king's favor, trapped these two birds and gave them to the king as a present.

Pleased with the beautiful birds, the king put the pair in a golden cage. They were given honey and parched corn to eat from a golden dish and sugar water to drink. The king spent a lot of time talking to them, and the parrots became the favorites of the whole court.

Then one day a forester, also seeking the favor of the king, brought a big black monkey named Kalabahu as a present.

Quickly, all the attention was turned to the big monkey. He was so comical! His funny faces made the lords and ladies laugh, and the king himself was very much amused when the monkey played the clown. No one payed any attention to the parrots anymore, although they were still fed and cared for.

The older parrot, Radha, said nothing. But the younger bird, Potthapada, complained. "Brother, in this royal house we used to get much praise. Now we get none. Lords and ladies used to give us treats to eat. Now we get our daily food. The king used to visit us and talk to us daily. Now he passes our cage without looking. And," he wept, "that monkey has all the attention that belongs to us!"

Radha said to his brother parrot, "By what right does it belong to us?"

Potthapada replied, "Because we were so good, so true, so loyal. We never bit, we never squawked. We were well-behaved birds!"

"And why not?" Radha asked. "If you were being yourself, brother, you have no cause to complain. Perhaps you were just putting on an act to please the king."

Potthapada hung his head in shame.

Things continued as they were for a long while. But, at last, the monkey (who was only a foolish fellow) grew bored with his pleasant life. He even grew tired of all the good things he had to eat and drink. He became devilish and began to steal. When caught, he would put on a long face and everyone could not help but laugh.

Then, not knowing what to do next, the monkey began to amuse himself by frightening the king's children. When they came near, he would shake his ears and show his teeth. The children cried and ran away. Soon they would not enter the room for fear of the monkey. The king asked them one day why they were so afraid of Kalabahu, and the children told him how the monkey had been scaring them.

The king became angry and ordered his men to drive the monkey out of the palace and back into the forest. The parrots once again became the favorites. Potthapada sang for joy, but his brother, Radha, warned him to remember:

> Gain and loss, and praise and blame,
> Pleasure, pain, dishonor, fame,
> All come and go like wind and rain!

Further Reading

The Five Sons of King Pandu. Elizabeth Seeger. The author retells the story of the *Muhabharata*, a 2,500-year-old epic poem of India.

Jataka Tales. Nancy DeRoin, editor. This is a collection of 30 of the Buddha's stories, including *Popularity*.

Seasons of Splendour: Tales, Myths and Legends of India. Madhur Jaffrey. This book retells many of the myths about the Hindu gods.

The Golden Age

What are some of the main features of Hinduism?

Key Terms

- Hinduism
- guild
- epic

► *This miniature painting from the* Maha-bharata *shows Arjuna and Krishna in battle. You can usually find Krishna because his face is painted blue. Krishna means "the dark one."*

Drumbeats thunder across the plain. Cymbals clash while horns blare. Warriors and chariots stand ready, their horses stomping nervously. Then the trumpeting of elephants pierces the air.

Arjuna prepares for battle. He's a skilled archer and a mighty warrior. He has proved his bravery many times before. Looking across the battlefield, he searches the faces of the foe. In the enemy lines, he can see his uncles, his cousins, and friends. He wants to get his kingdom back, yet how can he kill them?

This civil war has set family members against each other. Arjuna cries, "I see no good in killing my kinsmen in battle. . . . I do not want to kill them even if I am killed."

Troubled, he turns to his charioteer, Krishna, for advice. Krishna is no ordinary man. Hindus believe that he is God in human form. Krishna puts a stop to Arjuna's confusion. Arjuna must fight. He was born into the warrior class. Fighting a just war is his duty.

"If you fail to wage this war of sacred duty, you will abandon your own duty and fame only to gain evil," says Krishna. "Rise to the fight, Arjuna!"

Beliefs of Hinduism

The dialog of Arjuna and Krishna is part of the literature of **Hinduism,** the major religion of India today. The followers of Hinduism are known as Hindus.

For centuries, Hindu parents have handed down stories of Krishna to their children. The story you just read comes from the *Bhagavad Gita,* a well-loved poem. It is part of a larger epic poem called the *Mahabharata,* a saga of two families fighting over the kingdom of India. In these stories, Krishna guides humans away from evil and teaches them self-lessness, love, peace, and ethics.

A Way of Life

The *Bhagavad Gita* was widely read during India's classical period that began around A.D. 300. The roots of Hinduism, however, go back farther than that. Hinduism had its beginnings before Buddhism. Its roots include the Vedic religion of the Aryan people (1500-600 B.C.).

Over the centuries, Hinduism has been shaped into a faith that touches every corner of its followers' lives. Hindus follow daily rituals for washing and prayer. There are strict rules for what a Hindu eats. Every Hindu home has a spot reserved for meditation. Through these actions, Hindus believe they are bringing holiness into their lives.

Caste and Duty

The four classes of the Vedic period, as well as various castes, continued into Hindu times. In ancient days, castes gave Hindus a sense of security. Each caste cared for its members.

Hinduism has always been linked to the class and caste system, but it is *dharma* which has kept the society running smoothly. Dharma can be translated as duty, justice, or social obligation. Arjuna was obeying his dharma when he fought for a just cause. Dharma also means being able to live in an unselfish way without thinking about the results of your actions. As explained in the *Bhagavad Gita,* "There is more joy in doing one's own duty imperfectly than in doing another man's duty well."

◀ *The God Shiva reveals his divine identity to the bowing goddess, Parvati. Brahma, Krishna, and other gods also bow while heavenly musicians play. This painting, created about 1770 in the Punjab Hills, illustrates a work by the famous Indian poet, Kalidasa, of the Gupta period.*

► *Lamps burn brightly when Hindus mark their New Year. The celebration, which comes in either October or November, honors the goddess of plenty.*

Karma and Rebirth

Hindus believe that everyone carries a moral backpack, filled with karma, the good and bad results of their actions. Karma is what decides whether the soul will be reborn in a better or worse form in the next life. Good deeds lead to a better next life. When there is no evil remaining, rebirth no longer takes place and a person becomes one with *Brahman*, or God.

Life's Stages

Only Hindu males of the three upper classes are allowed to read the Vedas. Once they undertake this sacred study, they're called "twice born." For these males, life is divided into four stages.

In the first stage, a young boy studies the Vedas with a guru, or spiritual teacher.

In the second stage of his life, a young man marries and raises a family. For the young woman he marries, this is supposed to be the most important stage of her life. A wife has important religious duties. She is not allowed to read the sacred Vedas, but some women are educated according to the standards of the time. In stage three, men and women can choose to live in a forest and meditate. During the fourth stage, a few men and women give up everything, including caste membership, to become a holy person.

What if you had been a boy of the warrior class in ancient India? How would you have entered stage one? Let's look back.

You're 11 years old. You've waited impatiently for this special day because you're about to be "twice born." You're about to go through the sacred ceremony that begins your religious studies.

Your head has been shaved except for a topknot. You wear new ceremonial clothes, too. Your parents, relatives, and friends cluster around the sacred fire, waiting and watching. With dignity, you stand before your guru.

Guru and Pupil

9:13 A.M., November 17, A.D. 406
Forest School near Kashi, India

Earlobes

The guru's earlobes held heavy gold earrings for 20 years. On the day his first grandson was born, the guru took the earrings off, gave up everything he owned, and became a teacher in the forest.

Topknot

The guru won't shave off this tuft of hair until he enters the next stage of life and becomes a wandering holy man.

Lines

The ash marks on their foreheads and shoulders show that the guru and pupil worship Shiva above all other Hindu gods.

Fingers

For the very first time, the pupil recites one whole book of the *Rig Veda*—1,080 verses. His fingers help him keep the rhythm of the lines.

Crossed Legs

His legs would usually be tired after sitting cross-legged for three hours. But today he feels only excitement about doing so well with the poem he's memorized.

Sacred Thread

Guru and pupil both wear this cotton cord. The guru will break the thread when he leaves his forest home to wander alone.

247

During the ceremony, your guru places a sacred cord over your shoulder. You will wear such a cord always, a sign that you've been "twice born." Now, for the first time, you announce in public the secret name given to you at birth. The guru then hands you an antelope skin, symbol of strength and bravery. You will sometimes sit on it when you meditate. This ceremony marks a new beginning for you, the start of your studies.

Shiva and Vishnu

Hindus worship the absolute reality, called Brahman, in different ways. Brahman is represented by the God Vishnu as an all-knowing, merciful master. Shiva is another representation of Brahman and is known as a Lord who lies behind both birth and death. Shiva is often shown seated in meditation or in his role as Lord of the Dance.

According to Hinduism, God can appear on earth in various forms called incarnations. Hindus believe that Vishnu has appeared on earth in nine of his 10 incarnations. These earthly forms included a fish, a tortoise, and a dwarf. One of Vishnu's most important incarnations was Prince Rama, who represented the ideal human. Another important incarnation was Krishna. ■

■ *In what ways is Hinduism a way of life?*

The Gupta Empire

Between A.D. 320 and 467, Hinduism reached new heights. The rulers during this time were the Guptas. Although they ruled less than 200 years, they brought a Golden Age to ancient India. Not only did Hinduism flower, but borders expanded and trade boomed.

By conquering neighboring areas, the Guptas created an Indian empire. Compare the Gupta boundaries on this map with the Mauryan empire on page 239.

Ships and Caravans

Gupta trade routes hummed with activity. Elephants and ox-drawn carts loaded with goods bumped along the overland trails. Carts' wooden wheels creaked through desert, forest, and jungle. Cargo ships also sailed the seas. Huge eyes sometimes decorated a ship's prow. They were put at the front of a ship to scare the imagined monsters of the deep.

Westward, Gupta trade routes led to Rome and the rest of the Mediterranean, as well as to Africa. Eastward, trade was carried on with China, Southeast Asia, and Indonesia. The Guptas offered luxury exports—gems; pearls; perfumes; pepper, ginger, cinnamon, and other spices; finely woven cotton cloth; red dye; and

► *The Gupta Empire brought splendor to the northern portion of the subcontinent.*

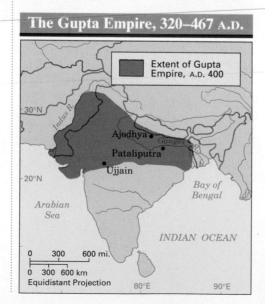

The Gupta Empire, 320–467 A.D.

Extent of Gupta Empire, A.D. 400

30°N
Indus R.
Ajodhya
Ganges
Pataliputra
Ujjain
20°N
Arabian Sea
Bay of Bengal
INDIAN OCEAN
0   300   600 mi.
0 300 600 km
Equidistant Projection
80°E   90°E

timber such as teak and ebony. Goods flowing into the Gupta empire included gold from Rome, silk from China, and horses from Saudi Arabia and Central Asia.

Town Trade and Guilds

Trade in towns bustled, too. Crowds jammed the cobblestone streets. Some shoppers walked while the wealthy were carried in curtained litters, or chairs. Peddlers balanced baskets on their heads, offering their fruits and flowers. Edging each side of the street were covered stalls. Here, men and women traders sat cross-legged all day, selling their wares.

Along with Gupta's increased trade came the growth of **guilds,** groups of craftspeople and merchants who did the same type of work. Each guild occupied its own section of town. For example, the weavers worked and lived together; so did the potters, the ivory carvers, and the carpenters. The guilds set prices and wages, checked the quality of work, and looked after the needs and interests of their members.

Guilds and castes aren't the same. Yet, they sometimes overlap. Guilds are organized according to crafts and trades, castes according to social levels. ■

■ *Where did trade routes lead during Gupta times, and what was traded?*

Achievements of Ancient India

Ancient India's scholars in the arts, sciences, and technology gave golden gifts to future generations. In Gupta days, both rulers and merchants helped to pay for these great achievements.

Famous Poetic Tales

Hindus learned much about their gods, myths, and religious duties from two glorious **epics**—long poems in fine language. An epic usually tells of heroic deeds. For years, these epics had made their way from generation to generation through oral tradition. But in Gupta times, they were written down in a regular form.

The first epic, known as the *Mahabharata,* tells of a great civil war between two branches of a ruling family. It's probably the world's longest poem. One section of this poetic work is the *Bhagavad Gita.* A much shorter epic, the *Ramayana,* tells the story of Rama, the princely incarnation of the God

Vishnu. This tale tells of Rama's rescue of his wife, who was stolen by a terrible demon.

Other Advances

Scholars excelled in science, too. In astronomy, Aryabhata determined that the world was a sphere, rotating around the sun. Some Europeans still hadn't accepted this fact 1,000 years later when Columbus sailed for the Indies in 1492. Aryabhata also figured out that the solar year had 365.358 days. Today's figures say 365.242. Aryabhata missed by about three hours.

The mathematicians of ancient India also made advances that were astounding.

▼ *This 11th century sculpture of the god Ganesha shows the continuing influence of the Gupta period.*

► *A kathakali dancer from South India puts finishing touches to his costume. He'll take part in a dance drama performed in the ancient tradition. The sacred epics are among the performances these dancers give.*

► *Gold came to ancient India from Rome. Metalworkers then crafted it into golden coins showing Gupta scenes.*

■ *Explain some of the achievements of the Gupta Period.*

They gave you the number system that you use in your math classes today. This system features nine digits, the zero, and the decimal.

Metalwork also stands high on the Guptas' list of accomplishments. Proof of the great skill of ironworkers is the one-piece pillar that stands 23 feet high at Mehrauli, near the city of Delhi. Modern ironworkers had been unable to duplicate this feat until the 1800s. Because of the iron's purity, the pillar shows few signs of rust even though it has been battered by more than 1,500 monsoon rains.

Gupta Days and Decline

An eyewitness account of Gupta's golden days comes to us from Faxian *(fah shee AHN)*, a Buddhist monk from China. He took notes in his diary while traveling through India in A.D. 399. He wrote that "the people are prosperous and happy." His diary tells, too, that there was little crime, and in certain areas, hospitals gave free care to the poor and helpless.

Fifty years after Faxian's travels, the Gupta empire began to decline. Invaders called White Huns swooped down from Central Asia. The attacks weakened the empire, causing it to break up into small kingdoms. By A.D. 467, India's Golden Age was almost over. ■

R E V I E W

1. **FOCUS** What are some of the main features of Hinduism?
2. **CONNECT** How did the Mauryan and Gupta empires differ in boundaries?
3. **ECONOMICS** Why do you think Gupta guilds were important?
4. **CRITICAL THINKING** In earlier times, Hindus were required to marry within their caste. How did this duty help to strengthen the caste system?
5. **ACTIVITY** Draw a "Moment in Time" picture of you and one of your teachers. Write short paragraphs that point out significant details about each of you.

Computing Travel Time

Here's Why

Suppose you want to figure out how long it took the Buddhist monk Faxian to walk from his home in Changan, China, to a shrine in Kara-shahr, China. If you know how to calculate the real distance between points on a map, you can compute his travel time.

Here's How

Look at the map of Faxian's travels. The scale shows that $5/8$ inch on the map stands for 600 miles on the earth.

To measure the distance between two points on a map along a straight route, use a ruler or a piece of paper. If the route you are measuring is not straight, use a piece of string.

To measure the distance between Changan and Kara-shahr, lay a small piece of string on the map so it follows Faxian's route. Put a mark on the string next to each city.

To find the number of miles, compare the distance marked on the string to the map scale. The distance between marks on the string is about $2^{1}/_{2}$ times the length of the scale, or about 1,500 miles. So, Faxian traveled 1,500 miles from Changan to Kara-shahr.

Historical records show that Faxian may have walked about 25 miles a day. Divide the total number of miles (1,500) by the number of miles he could walk in a day (25). The answer will tell you how long it took Faxian to complete the walk—60 days.

Try It

Measure the sea route between Tamluk, India, and Trincomalee, Ceylon (now Sri Lanka). What is the distance in miles? Traveling by water, Faxian could cover 21 miles per day. How long would the trip from Tamluk to Trincomalee take him?

Apply It

Look at the map of North America shown on page 512 of the Atlas. If you traveled at 55 miles per hour, how long would it take to go from Los Angeles, California, to Seattle, Washington?

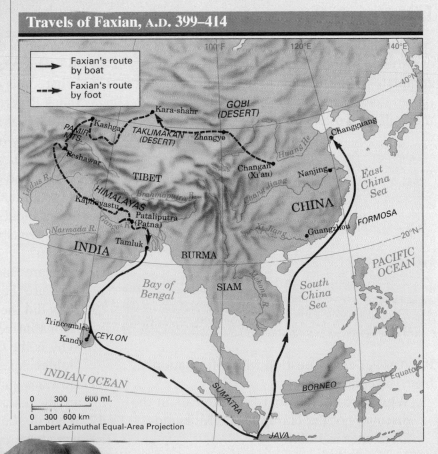

Travels of Faxian, A.D. 399–414

→ Faxian's route by boat

--→ Faxian's route by foot

Chapter Review

Reviewing Key Terms

Aryan (p. 229)
Buddhism (p. 236)
caste (p. 232)
epic (p. 249)
guild (p. 249)
Hinduism (p. 245)

migration (p. 230)
moderation (p. 238)
rebirth (p. 238)
silt (p. 224)
subcontinent (p.223)

A. In each statement below, a key term has been used incorrectly. Rewrite each sentence using the correct key term.

1 The busy trade and commerce of the Gupta period encouraged the growth of *castes*—groups of craftspeople and merchants.

2. History has seen many periods of *rebirth*, in which whole populations move from one area to another.

3. *Buddhists* who migrated to northern India introduced a new religion.

4. *Moderation* helped the Indus Valley farmers to grow their crops.

5. The *guild* system has been an important part of Hinduism.

B. Use a dictionary to find the origins of the following words. Then explain how the meaning of the word applies to India.

1. subcontinent
2. Buddhism
3. moderation
4. rebirth
5. Hinduism

Exploring Concepts

A. Reminders of India's ancient civilizations can still be found in today's world. Copy and complete the following chart on your own paper. List at least two examples of the past that still exist today.

Civilization	Modern Reminders
Indus Valley Civilization	
Aryans	
Mauryan Empire	spread of Buddhism India's national emblem
Gupta Empire	

B. Answer each question with information from the chapter.

1. Why were archaeologists excited about the discovery of the Harappa and Mohenjo-Daro sites in India?

2. What helped the people of the Indus Valley to be successful in their farming?

3. What kinds of evidence still exist of the Indus River civilization?

4. How was the Aryan society different from the society of the Indus Valley?

5. Why were the Vedas important to the Aryans and to archaeologists?

6. How did the migration of Aryans influence life in India?

7. What are two characteristics of the caste system?

8. How are Buddhism and Hinduism similar? How are they different?

9. How did the religious beliefs of Emperor Asoka influence his rule?

10. Why is the Gupta period often called a Golden Age?

11. How are guilds different from castes? How are they similar?

12. What do the *Mahabharata* and the *Ramayana* have in common?

Reviewing Skills

1. Look at the sculpture of the Buddha receiving his enlightenment on page 237. What identifying marks help you know that this is the Buddha?
2. Look at the map on this page. Imagine that you are an archaeologist in Karachi, Pakistan. Using the map scale, figure out how far it is to travel to Harappa. At 20 mph, how long would it take?
3. Look at the map on this page. Using the grid, estimate Mohenjo-Daro's location. Your answer should give the latitude first, then the longitude.
4. Imagine that you are writing an archaeological report on artifacts you have discovered. The report has two parts: first, a description of the artifacts; second, your ideas about their importance. How is the first part of your report different from the second part?

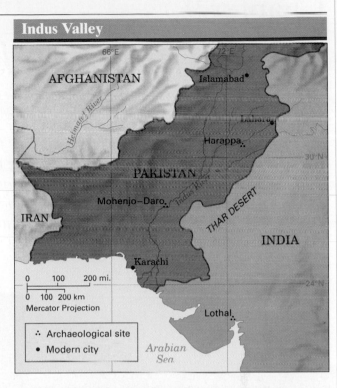

Indus Valley

AFGHANISTAN
Islamabad
Lahore
Harappa
PAKISTAN
Mohenjo-Daro
IRAN
THAR DESERT
INDIA
Karachi
Lothal
Arabian Sea

0   100   200 mi.
0   100 200 km
Mercator Projection

∴ Archaeological site
• Modern city

Using Critical Thinking

1. The success of crops and trade depended on the regular monsoons. What might have happened if the monsoon was early or late?
2. About 2,500 years ago, the Buddha stated that suffering and sorrow are caused by the greedy desire for power, pleasure, and possessions. Do you think this is true today? Explain your answer.
3. In the Buddha's time, priests, rulers, and warriors were in the upper class. How might they have felt about Buddhism? Why?
4. Under the Guptas, art and science prospered along with trade and commerce. Do you think there is a connection? Explain.

Preparing for Citizenship

1. **COLLECTING INFORMATION** Archaeologists find, record, and interpret traces of past life. Your community has a past. Discover any traces left from its past inhabitants. You could interview older residents; research photographs, maps, and books; or study the buildings and land. Share your research with the class.
2. **GROUP ACTIVITY** The Buddhist teachings focus on how people should think and act. In small groups, make a set of laws for your school. What do you think is good school behavior? Display your laws on a poster.
3. **COLLABORATIVE LEARNING** The Indus Valley and the United States both received migrating peoples. In small groups, give a presentation on a migrant culture in America. Have one person discover the reasons why the migration took place. Have another find photographs or articles from that time period. A third person can interview someone from the migrant culture, and a fourth could research the native culture to discover how it differs from ours. Everyone should then decide on how to present your findings to the class.

253

Chapter 9

Ancient China

For many centuries, China lay far away from other ancient civilizations. Towering mountains, vast deserts, and the Pacific Ocean made contact with the rest of the world difficult, though not impossible. In this varied land the Chinese developed a unique civilization—one of the oldest to live on into the present.

c. 750–500 B.C. Before the Chinese used wooden strips, they wrote on pottery, bones, and bronze. Some historians believe that Chinese writing is among the oldest in the world.

2500	2000	1500	1000

2200 B.C.

c. 1600 B.C. During the Shang dynasty, metalworkers learn to make bronze from copper and tin. Soon craftspersons create works of art like the giant cooking pot above.

Han artists crafted masterpieces in bronze, like this statue of a horse and rider.

202 B.C.–A.D. 220 During the Han Dynasty, the Chinese invent paper and a device for detecting earthquakes.

500	B.C.	A.D.	500	1000

221 B.C. Emperor Qin Shihuangdi unifies China.

214 B.C. Chinese laborers begin building the Great Wall, which eventually stretches for 1,500 miles across northern China.

A.D. 220

Meng-Jiang Nyu

Yin-lien C. Chin, Yetta S. Center, and Mildred Ross

The Great Wall of China, which spans 1,500 miles, was built to prevent invasions from the north. But the construction itself cost thousands of Chinese lives. This selection from Traditional Chinese Folktales *tells how the Great Wall project affected the lives of an ordinary Chinese man and woman.*

In Lesson 3 you will learn about the history of the Great Wall of China.

Meng-Jiang Nyu (muhng jyahng nyoo)
Wan Chi-liang (wan chy lyahng)

Meng-Jiang Nyu was eighteen on the day of her marriage to Wan Chi-liang. Everyone delighted in the lovely couple. She, dainty as a flower in her red wedding dress, glowed with happiness. And Chi-liang in his new, belted tunic was a handsome groom. The entire village was invited to witness the ceremony and partake of the feast that lasted for several days. The festivities over, the young bride and groom settled down to the routines of village life. They thought of themselves as truly fortunate, for they never felt hunger nor suffered from the cold. Deeply in love with his wife, Chi-liang found pleasure in fulfilling her every wish.

Their peaceful life was shattered one late summer day. Barely moments after they had come in from the fields, a stranger appeared at their door. He was dressed in an official's gown, and behind him stood two men in army uniform. With no word of explanation, he commanded his soldiers to seize Chi-liang and take him outside. Meng-Jiang Nyu, a look of bewilderment on her face, watched them push her husband toward the milling crowd assembled in the center of the village road.

The younger men from the neighboring cottages had all been rounded up, and they stood in a tight knot ringed by armed guards. Women, children, and older people had been ordered to remain at some distance.

Meng-Jiang Nyu's pounding heart made it difficult for her to breathe. As she approached the villagers, she heard a woman ask, "Could the emperor be conscripting men again? How well I remember when they took my father. I was just a young girl. I never saw him again."

Grandfather Hu, a village elder who was respected by all, offered his opinion. "The emperor has probably been convinced by his advisers to undertake another one of his foolish projects. No

conscripting forcing people to enlist in the army

256

good can come of this."

Children fidgeted and cried, while the restlessness of the by-standers increased as their anxiety mounted.

"Silence!" shouted the official. "I bring an order from the emperor." The murmuring ceased. "Wild horsemen are attacking from the north. These barbarians are looting and killing, burning whole villages to the ground. The emperor has issued a call for all able-bodied men to build a great wall, the highest and thickest wall ever built by men. The enemy will never be able to break through its impenetrable defense, and our people will be able to live in peace. It is the duty of every man to obey the emperor's summons. Anyone who refuses does so on pain of death."

"Forward!" he commanded. Lined up three abreast, the men were marched off. Soldiers carrying spears walked along the sides of the column. Escape was impossible.

Tearful parents, wives, and children were left behind to fend for themselves. An old farmer leaning on a cane shook his head sadly.

"Heaven alone knows if I shall ever see my son before my life is over," he said in a hoarse whisper.

Only a few months had passed since that terrifying day, but for Meng-Jiang Nyu it seemed like ages. Without her husband at her side, time dragged interminably. In her fervent prayers she asked that he be kept from hunger and thirst. The winter would bring its bitter winds that blow unceasingly from the mountains. How was Chi-liang going to survive in so hostile a climate without a warm jacket and cotton quilted shoes?

The last days of autumn were drawing to an end. It was the time of year when the dusk came early, but Meng-Jiang Nyu would not stop until darkness forced her to lay aside her sewing. Her needle flew ever faster as she layered fabric with cotton padding, fashioning a comfortable outer garment. She took particular care to design thick-soled shoes, sewing them with extra strong thread. Time was her enemy as she worked to finish the task she had set for herself.

Meng-Jiang Nyu swore a solemn oath. Chi-liang would not do without winter clothes. This she vowed. No matter how perilous the journey, she would take them to him herself. A woman traveling alone might encounter unexpected dangers, and she wondered if she would endure the long trek on foot. But she banished the troubling thoughts from her mind.

The evening before her departure, she prepared a small bag of rice and another of millet, only the barest necessities to sustain her along the way. On a large cloth square she placed Chi-liang's jacket and shoes. By tying the opposite corners of the square together, she made a bundle to carry over her arm.

Before daybreak she left her home. No one was yet awake,

impenetrable can't be entered or crossed

interminably without end; tiresomely long

and the narrow streets of the village were deserted. It was still quite dark. In the east, Meng-Jiang Nyu saw a rosy glow that announced the beginning of a new day. "A good omen," she mused.

Word had come back to the village that the section of the wall where Chi-liang was working lay at a great distance. If the snows came early, there was no telling how long it would take to get there. Meng-Jiang Nyu had learned that she must travel in a northwesterly direction, but beyond that she did not even know for certain where she would find her husband.

Never having traveled more than a few miles from her village, she could not imagine the vastness that lay beyond it. Nor could she conceive, in her wildest flight of fancy, the size and length of the wall that the emperor had planned. Neither could she picture a wall three thousand miles long that would climb over high mountains, descend into deep valleys, and cross forbidding deserts. But the grandeur of the emperor's ambitious undertaking meant nothing to her. She only knew she must plod ahead for as long as it would take her to join Chi-liang.

As the days wore on, Meng-Jiang Nyu found she had to rest more and more frequently. Often, as she passed through little villages, she begged for food. She had finished her rice and millet long ago. People who spoke to her and learned where she was bound praised her devotion but shook their heads in disbelief.

Once she heard a woman lamenting loudly to a friend, "Our sons are gone, our daughters widowed, and the pile of dead grows ever larger at the foot of the emperor's great wall." Meng-Jiang Nyu shuddered.

doggedly stubbornly

From sunrise to sunset she doggedly trudged on. When darkness fell, she looked for a place to lay her head. Many a night her bed was just a pile of scratchy straw.

The day Meng-Jiang Nyu reached the Yellow River, her strength was beginning to fail. At the point where she stood, the river was wide and the current of its silt-laden water, swift. For the peasants who lived along its banks it was life-sustaining, but for Meng-Jiang Nyu it was yet another obstacle that had to be overcome. Except for a lone shepherd grazing his flock of sheep, there was not a soul in sight.

"I have not come this far in vain," she thought. "I will not turn back!"

With determination born of despair, she walked into the water holding Chi-liang's clothes over her head to keep them dry. A few yards out from the shore her feet could no longer touch bottom, and she tried to swim. The effort to keep afloat was beyond her endurance. Finally she gave up the struggle and let the river claim her. The cold water dragged her toward the murky bottom— down, down into an inky blackness.

Meng-Jiang Nyu's distress did not go unnoticed. A river god

came to her rescue, plucking her from the deep and carrying her to the opposite shore.

When Meng-Jiang Nyu opened her eyes, a shadowy specter was hovering over her.

"My brave child, do not abandon hope," it soothed. "All the spirits along the way will help you to the end of your journey." The shadow drifted away and melted into the air. Meng-Jiang Nyu was alone. She had no recollection of how she had reached the other side of the river. Nor was she sure she had heard the encouraging promise of help.

Wearily, she picked up her bundle. Everything was wet through. Before moving on she would have to wait for the clothes to dry. She wrung out Chi-liang's jacket and spread it on the ground. When she reached for his shoes, a miracle occurred. Spellbound, she saw the shoes turn into two blackbirds. From then on, never ceasing their shrill chatter, the blackbirds led her day after day in a northerly direction. Whenever she tired, they alighted on the ground near her and waited until she had regained her strength. At night they roosted in a nearby tree while she slept. One morning, Meng-Jiang Nyu awoke, trembling with cold. Her fingers and toes were numb and she ached all over. Reaching to pick up her bundle, she was surprised to see Chi-liang's shoes standing neatly, side by side. The blackbirds, her guides and constant companions, were gone. They had fulfilled their mission, for they had led Meng-Jiang Nyu close to her destination.

Meng-Jiang Nyu dragged her swollen, painful feet along a dusty road. At first the road was flat; then it began to climb steeply. When she reached high ground, her eyes took in an incredible scene. The figures she saw moving about resembled a scurrying swarm of ants. She quickened her pace. Now she could see more clearly. Files of men, backs bent under the weight of heavy stones, were struggling to the top of the unfinished wall. Others were lugging buckets of mortar to fill the spaces between the rocks. Covered from head to foot by the dry, brown sand, they were indistinguishable, one from the other. How could she ever find Chi-liang among that multitude?

With unaccustomed boldness, she approached a small group of men who were attempting to warm their hands over a smoldering fire. Timidly she explained, "I am looking for my husband. He is called Chi-liang." She told them the name of their village and the day on which he was conscripted, but they only looked at her with pity.

specter a ghost; phantom

"I am sorry I cannot help you," said one of the men. "This wall has no beginning and no end. The wind batters us, the white snow blinds us, we have little food and no warm clothing. There is only toil without rest. Every day we see good comrades fall, and many more will die of exhaustion. Hundreds are already buried inside the wall. We admire your loyalty to your husband, but you should not endanger your own life trying to do the impossible. Better that you return home. You will never find him."

But Meng-Jiang Nyu could not be discouraged. Bravely she continued to search. Wherever she went she asked for Chi-liang. The relentless wind tore at her clothing, her face and hands became rough and red from exposure. She ate very little and slept hardly a wink. At last, fatigue conquered her, and Meng-Jiang Nyu fell asleep on the frozen ground. She did not know how much time had passed before she became aware of someone prodding her. "You must not lie here or you will freeze to death," a man warned.

Shaking uncontrollably, she managed to say, "I am looking for my husband. He bears the name Chi-liang." Once again, she recited the name of their village and the date on which he was taken.

"Yes, I knew your husband," the stranger responded. "I remember him well. We were assigned the task of making bricks and he was the best worker in the section. It pains me to tell you that we found him one morning covered by newly fallen snow, lifeless. With many others he lies buried within the wall."

Meng-Jiang Nyu could not hold back the flood of salty tears that stung her cold cheeks. She blamed herself for Chi-liang's death. She had come too late to save him.

"How can it be that so gentle a husband has perished so young? The Great Wall takes more lives than the plundering enemy."

A wife's devotion can sometimes move mountains. Wailing bitterly, Meng-Jiang Nyu cried out to heaven. The sun vanished behind threatening clouds. A violent tempest churned up the powdery sand, and rain fell in icy sheets. Bolts of lightning streaked through the sky. With a deafening clap of thunder, a section of the wall collapsed, bricks and stones spilling out together with human bones and skulls.

"Do not be alarmed, brave wife of Chi-liang. Heaven has witnessed your sorrow. You will seek out your husband's bones from among all the others." The words were sharp and clear, but there was not a soul in sight. Meng-Jiang Nyu stood transfixed amid the pile of rubble.

"But how will I know which among the many are his?"

"Have no fear. You will succeed, for when love is sincere and true, two people become as one. They share thoughts, hopes,

plundering stealing; taking by force

feelings. Their blood, their bones, their very tissues mingle. Do not despair, you will find a way."

"Alas," moaned Meng-Jiang Nyu. "In this jumble lying here, strewn this way and that, are the bones of Chi-liang. Oh mountains, hills, desert of yellow sands," she pleaded, "favor me, and give me a sign that I may recognize those that belong to him. I cannot choose for I cannot tell one from another." Unaware of what she was doing, she bit down on her thumb until she drew blood. She watched a drop fall upon a bone, slide off the surface, and reach the ground. Suddenly the words she had just heard took on meaning.

"If the bones are Chi-liang's, my blood will mingle with his and sink into them. If the bones belong to others, the blood will remain apart."

This time, with determination, she bit down harder and then shook her hand, spattering the blood about. What she hoped for did not happen. Again, and still again, she tried. Each time her blood slid quickly off the bones. "One last time," she told herself. Though the pain brought tears to her eyes, she bit down with all her might. The blood flowed freely and she flung it as far and as wide as she could. One quivering red dot landed on a bone lying apart from the others. At once the blood sank into its chalky whiteness. This bone must belong to Chi-liang. Of this she was certain. Feverishly she continued to search, and soon she recovered the rest. Chi-liang's bones would receive a proper burial, and his soul would not have to wander aimlessly in search of peace.

Laden with the heavy blow fate had dealt her, Meng-Jiang Nyu turned to the south and began her sad journey homeward.

Further Reading

China Homecoming. Jean Fritz. In this book Jean Fritz returns to the country where she spent her childhood.

Heaven's Reward: Fairy Tales from China. Catherine Edwards. These six fairy tales present Confucian and Taoist philosophies.

Homesick: My Own Story. Jean Fritz. The author describes her experiences as the child of American missionary parents in China.

Young Fu of the Upper Yangtze. Elizabeth Lewis. A teenage country boy travels to the city of Chongqing to become a coppersmith's apprentice in the 1930s.

LESSON 1

China's Early History

What advances were made by these ancient cultures—the Yangshao, the Lungshan, the Xia, the Shang, and the Zhou?

Key Terms

- ancestor
- oracle
- feudalism
- dialect

> *High peaks, fertile valleys, desert wastes— these are some of the varied land forms of China.*

*T*he towering heights of the Southern Mountains
Soar dizzily like a stack of cooking pots,
Precipitous and sheer.
Their sides are furrowed with ravines and valleys. . . .
While from their folds the mountain streams leap and tumble,
Spilling out upon the level plains.
There they flow a thousand miles along smooth beds,
Their banks lined with dikes
Blanketed with green orchids.

From "The Shanglin Park"

More than 2,000 years ago, the Chinese poet Sima Xiangru *(suh mah shahng roo)* wrote these lines about his native land. He described a rugged land of towering mountains, powerful rivers, and vast plains. Look at the physical map of China on the next page. What major land forms can you identify?

On the southwest, China is bounded by huge mountains. On the north and west lie more mountains and deserts. And on the east, the ocean stretches to the horizon. These land forms act as natural barriers. They set China apart from the rest of the world. They help to preserve one of the oldest continuous civilizations in the world, dating back almost 4,000 years.

China's Geography

The geography of China has helped to create numerous regions within this vast land. Regions developed separately from each other. Thus China became a patchwork of different customs, cultures, and languages. The task of unifying this varied land has never been an easy one.

To understand why, look at the map below. Mountain ranges ripple across the land, making travel and communication difficult. Find the Himalayas *(hihm uh LAY uhz)* in the southwestern part of China. These are the world's highest mountains. Many peaks rise more than 24,000 feet above sea level. Mount Everest, the highest mountain in the world, soars to 29,028 feet. Other great mountain ranges are the Kunlun Shan, the Tian Shan, and the Altai in the west and the Da Xing'an Ling in the north.

Deserts also create barriers within China. Across the north and northwest regions lie dry wastelands. The greatest of China's deserts is the massive Gobi. Find it on the map.

Though mountains and deserts have served to divide the Chinese, rivers have helped to link them. Trace China's major rivers on the map. The Huang He *(hwahng huh)* begins within the Plateau of Tibet and runs across the farmlands of

▼ *As the map shows, nature built a wall around China with mountains, plateaus, seas, and deserts.*

China

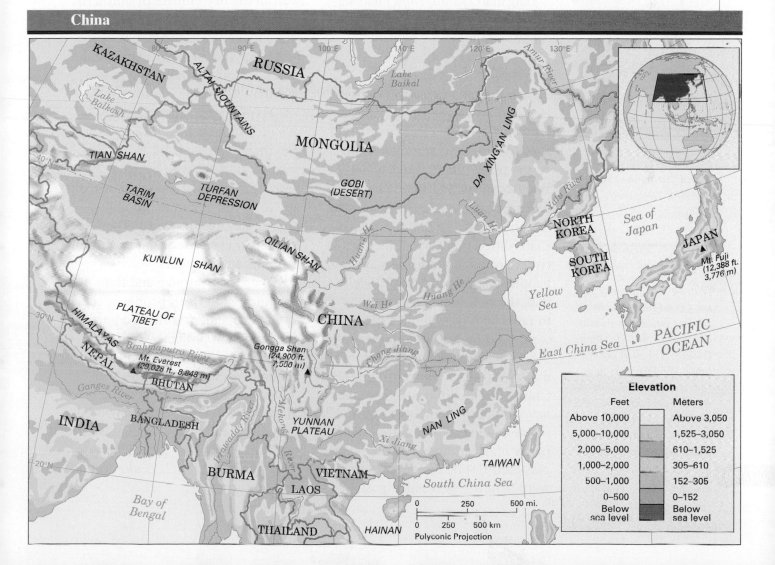

northeastern China. Rich in minerals, it gets its name—meaning "Yellow River"—from the rich yellow dirt that it leaves behind when it overflows its banks.

Along with the minerals that enrich the soil, these floods often bring disaster. The Huang He is nicknamed "China's Sorrow." It has destroyed property and claimed the lives of thousands who have been swept away in its swirling waters.

Another river, the Chang Jiang *(chahng jyahng)*—also known as the Yangzi *(YANG see)*—winds across the farmlands of central and southern China. Trace the Chang Jiang on the map. Farmers use the river's many tributaries to send their crops easily and cheaply to Pacific ports. ■

■ *How did geography isolate ancient China from the rest of the world?*

Prehistoric Cultures

Like the other great ancient civilizations—Mesopotamia, Egypt, and India—the earliest known Chinese civilization started along a river. By about 10,000 B.C., a group of Neolithic people called the Yangshao *(yahng show)* had settled near the Huang He in north central China.

Two Neolithic Cultures

On the map, trace the Huang He from its source in the Tibetan Highlands. Follow its course as it flows north, east, and then south. At the place where it meets the Wei *(way)*, the Huang He bends like an elbow and heads northeast. It's not surprising that the Yangshao settled there. First, the two rivers provided plenty of water for people, animals and crops. Second, the rich, sandy soil was easy to farm with the simple tools that were used by Neolithic farmers.

Archaeologists have uncovered many Yangshao villages in northern China. In one village, Banpo, they have found the remains of farmhouses, many of which were built partly underground. The houses had plastered floors, and their roofs were held up by wooden posts.

By about 3000 B.C., another Neolithic culture, the Longshan, had developed in northeast China. The Longshan people were farmers too. They raised cattle, sheep, pigs, and dogs. They grew wheat and millet, two grain crops that grow well in the dry climate of northern China. They also hunted, fished, and gathered wild foods. Over time, Longshan farmers also settled in the south of China. It rained more there, and they were able to grow rice.

The Longshan people were advanced for their time. For example, they harvested silk from silkworms and used it to weave fine fabrics. They used a potter's wheel, and they baked strong, durable pottery in kilns, or ovens. The Longshan even used simple written symbols and numbers.

In order to survive and farm the land along the river, people needed to work together on flood control and irrigation projects. Gradually, leaders arose in different places in China to organize these projects. According to Chinese legends, one of the leaders was a man named Yu, the "Great Engineer." Legend said he founded the first great Chinese dynasty, the Xia *(SHEE ah)* around 2000 B.C.

▲ *Prehistoric Chinese pottery demonstrates both skill and artistry. This painted ceramic cup was found during the excavation of a Yangshao village.*

Across Time & Space

Don't get confused if you see China's capital city of Beijing written as Peking *or* Peiping *on older maps. Beijing is spelled according to the Pinyin system for writing Chinese in our Roman alphabet. In 1958, the Chinese officially adopted Pinyin, replacing earlier systems.*

A Legendary Dynasty

Knowledge of the Xia dynasty comes mostly from legend. There are no written records. Legend tells us the Xia ruled for nearly 300 years. The last Xia ruler, Jie (CHEE uh), was an evil king

Cheng Tang (chahng tahng), or Tang the Successful, defeated Jie in 1766 B.C. Tang's victory marked the beginning of a new dynasty called the Shang (shahng). The Shang dynasty ruled China for over 700 years, from 1766 to 1122 B.C. ■

■ What were some achievements of China's Neolithic river cultures, the Yangshao and the Longshan?

The Shang Dynasty

Trace the boundaries of the Shang dynasty on the map below. Notice that Shang China included much of the Huang He plain.

During the Shang dynasty, most people were still peasants, or poor farmers. They lived in villages and spent their lives working in the fields and struggling to control the flooding rivers. They farmed small plots of land and lived in simple houses.

Walled Cities

Archaeologists have discovered that most Shang people lived in farming villages. Some, however, lived in large walled cities. For example, one Shang city was surrounded by an earth wall 30 feet high, 65 feet thick, and four and a half miles long. With simple hand tools, it would probably have taken 10,000 workers 18 years to build such a wall. To complete it, Shang rulers must have developed complex ways of organizing people. They must also have become skillful in engineering.

Within the walls lived rulers, priests, and warriors. Their huge temples and palaces were built on raised earth terraces. Skilled craftworkers lived outside the walls in neighborhoods made up of people who practiced the same craft. Farmers lived in nearby villages.

In the Shang capital of Anyang, archaeologists have found thousands of cowrie shells like those shown on this page. Cowrie shells served as an early form of money to buy small items like tools and weapons. They were used in the 1000s B.C., before the Bronze Age brought the use of metal coins.

The Bronze Age

Around 1600 B.C., Shang craftworkers in the city of Yanshi (yen shir) made an important discovery. They learned to mix tin and copper to produce a hard and beautiful metal called bronze. This new metal was quite valuable because bronze was much stronger than tin or copper. In Anyang, archaeologists have found bronze pots, plates, ceremonial vessels,

▲ Cowries are snails found in the coastal waters of the Pacific and Indian oceans. The shells shown here are life-sized.

▼ Find the Huang He on this map. Shang farmers learned to tame the wild water buffalo that roamed the river's flood plain.

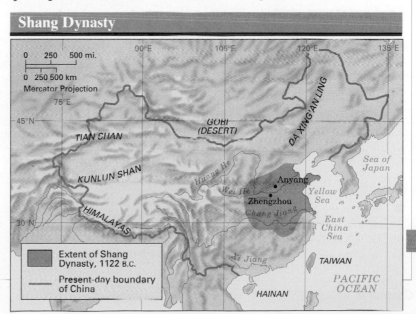

Shang Dynasty

0 250 500 mi.
0 250 500 km
Mercator Projection

90°E 105°E 120°E 135°E
75°E
45°N

TIAN SHAN
GOBI (DESERT)
DA XINGAN LING
KUNLUN SHAN
Huang He
Anyang
Wei He
Yellow Sea
Zhengzhou
Sea of Japan
Chang Jiang
HIMALAYAS
30°N
East China Sea
Xi Jiang
TAIWAN
PACIFIC OCEAN
HAINAN

Extent of Shang Dynasty, 1122 B.C.

Present-day boundary of China

Shang craftworkers created this 14-inch-high bronze vessel in the shape of a man within a tiger's open jaws. No one knows whether the tiger is protecting the man or eating him. What do you think?

Across Time & Space

Westerners wear black as the color of mourning when someone dies. The Chinese wear white. These seem the opposite until you realize that both cultures are really doing the same thing—avoiding colorful clothing.

■ *How did the Shang people live, and how did their religious beliefs affect their lives?*

spears, and even chariots. These Shang pieces are skillfully decorated with complex patterns and animal faces.

Religion

The early Chinese believed in many gods. They worshiped individual gods that they believed controlled the sun, moon, stars, rivers, and mountains. They also worshiped a supreme god, Shang Di *(shahng dee),* who took a personal interest in the world and its people. They believed their priests could communicate directly with Shang Di.

Ancestor Worship

As important to the Shang as their gods were their **ancestors—**relatives who had lived before them. The Chinese believed that the wise spirits of their ancestors controlled every part of their lives. Chinese fathers, as the heads of their households, made frequent offerings to their ancestors. Even the king would make offerings to his ancestors at special religious ceremonies.

Burials

Shang leaders believed that when they died, they joined their ancestors. They were buried in deep pits dug in the shape of a cross. Like the Egyptian pharaohs, Shang kings were buried with the things they might need in the next life. These included pottery jars, bronze weapons, jade ornaments, and even war chariots.

In one royal tomb at Anyang, archaeologists found the remains of nine guards and nine dogs that had been killed and placed around the prince's coffin. They also found the prince's chariot with its four horses and three armed warriors buried alongside.

Oracle Bones

To guide them in this world, Shang kings consulted their ancestors by means of oracle bones. An **oracle** is a prediction about the future. First, the priest would carve the king's question on an animal bone or a turtle shell. Then he would drill holes in one side of the bone and heat it. When the heated bone cracked, the priest looked at the pattern of cracks to find the oracle and answer the king's question.

Kings often asked questions about daily life—for example, whether the day's hunt would be successful. Like us, they also wanted predictions about the weather. The question on one oracle bone reads, "Will the weather be fine tomorrow?" The priest's forecast was, "This evening it will rain; tomorrow, it will be fine." Some of the bones have notes telling whether the oracle was correct. This priest was apparently a good weather forecaster. The bone notes, "In the night rain was granted; the next day it was fine."

Archaeologists have found more than 100,000 of these oracle bones. They contain the earliest known examples of Chinese writing. Readers today can recognize many of the more than 2,000 characters engraved on the 3,600-year-old bones. Read A Closer Look on page 267 to discover more about the development of Chinese writing. ■

Chinese Writing

The brush races across the paper as your Chinese friend draws the word you see below. Can you guess what it means? It's the word for horse! Chinese writing has a long history. Look how the word for horse developed step by step.

Turtle shells were sometimes used to write on in ancient China. The writing on this shell was done around 1200 B.C. Notice that the writing uses mostly straight lines, which are easy to draw.

c. 2000 B.C.
The earliest writers scratched small pictures like this onto bones and shells.

c. 600 B.C.
In this period, writing started to look less like a picture.

C. A.D. 300
When writers began to use brushes, their lines got longer. Where are the horse's feet?

Present
Today the Chinese are trying to simplify their writing by using characters like this one.

Jade brush rest

Signature seal

Take this stick of ink and grind it slowly back and forth on this ink stone. Add water until the ink is just the shade you want it, from the deepest black to the palest gray. Now you are ready to dip your brush and paint the word *horse*.

Is this writing or painting? Chinese people began to write with brushes over 2,000 years ago. For centuries writers in China have worked to make their words look as beautiful as possible. So, making a Chinese letter or poem is actually both writing and painting.

267

Ancient China

The Zhou Dynasty

In the Wei Valley, west of the bend in the Huang He, lived a group of people called the Zhou (*joh*). The Zhou were farmers. They also helped their Shang rulers by patrolling the country's borders, guarding them against raiders from the west.

One Zhou leader, King Wen, tried to overthrow the Shang. Eventually King Wen's son, Wu the Martial, became the leader of the Zhou. True to his name, Wu the Martial carried out his father's wishes and conquered the Shang. In 1050 B.C., Wu's forces attacked the Shang king. They burned the royal palace and set up their own dynasty. The Zhou dynasty would be the longest in China's history.

The Mandate of Heaven

The Zhou worshiped an impersonal power called *tian,* or heaven. Unlike the Shang, the Zhou did not believe their priests could communicate with *tian.* Instead, they believed *tian* was simply a power that demanded right behavior and good government. They believed that *tian* required this especially of the king, whom they called the "son of heaven." If a king ruled well, he earned heaven's support, called the "mandate of heaven." If he ruled poorly or was evil, he lost the mandate of heaven and was overthrown. The Zhou used this idea to justify their overthrow of the last Shang ruler.

Feudalism

Zhou kings spread their rule over China through a system called **feudalism** (*FYOOD uh lihz uhm*). Under a feudal system, nobles own the farmland, which is worked by peasants, or serfs. In feudal China, the Zhou put their relatives and even some Shang nobles in charge of the land. The serfs paid the nobles for the use of the land. In turn, the nobles paid the king a portion of what their peasants produced. The nobles also promised to send the king soldiers in times of war.

The king granted each noble complete control of his own land. The noble was like a king on his land. A noble's land consisted of a walled town and the farms around it. By about 700 B.C., there were 200 of these feudal states, each with its own government.

▲ *This bronze ceremonial vessel in the shape of a rhinoceros suggests the playful side of the artisan who designed it. The vessel dates from the late Shang or early Zhou period.*

➤ *To the ancient Chinese, the imaginary dragon was king of all animals. Dragons with five claws on each foot symbolized an emperor. Nonroyal dragons had four claws.*

As methods of farming improved, the nobles' stores of surplus grain grew. Since grain was valuable, the nobles became richer and more powerful. They grew greedy and waged wars against each other to gain even more land.

To run their powerful states and do business with neighbors, the nobles needed skilled and educated people. They needed engineers to plan and build flood control projects. They needed tax collectors to gather payments from their serfs. And because few people could read or write, they needed scholars to keep records and to advise them. In fact, men who could read and write wandered through China, offering their services to the nobles. For a fee, these wandering scholars also taught common people to read and write. The earliest surviving Chinese books were written during the Zhou period.

Wider Use of Writing

During the Zhou dynasty, as today, people in China's many regions spoke a variety of languages and dialects. **Dialects** are different forms of the same language. Thus, communication from region to region was often a problem.

To solve this problem, the Zhou built on the Shang practice of writing on oracle bones. They

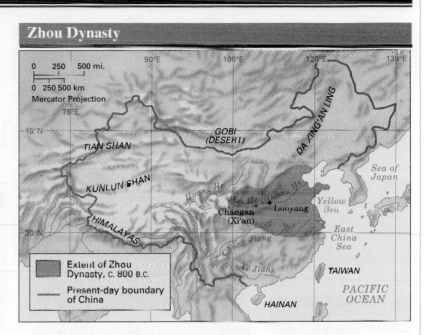

Zhou Dynasty

0   250   500 mi.
0 250 500 km
Mercator Projection

Extent of Zhou Dynasty, c. 800 B.C.

Present-day boundary of China

China under the Zhou dynasty was made up of feudal states ruled by powerful nobles.

expanded the use of writing by using bronze, wood, and bamboo for recording information. No matter how a word was pronounced in different parts of China, its written form could be understood everywhere.

In the time of the Zhou, the Chinese language had more than 3,000 written characters. At last, people from feudal states hundreds of miles apart, speaking different dialects, could communicate with each other.

Writing helped to bridge the barriers created by China's geography. Writing helped to unify the Chinese people. Finally, writing made possible the growth and spread of China's unique culture and civilization. ■

In what ways were the Zhou walled cities like small countries?

R E V I E W

1. **FOCUS** What advances were made by these ancient cultures—the Yangshao, the Longshan, the Xia, the Shang, and the Zhou?

2. **CONNECT** How did China's Neolithic cultures resemble those of Mesopotamia and Egypt?

3. **GEOGRAPHY** How did China's geography affect its early history? Consider both the regions within China, and China's relationship to the rest of the world.

4. **CRITICAL THINKING** How did the Shang and Zhou religions differ? How did each religion give a special role to the king?

5. **ACTIVITY** Imagine that you are a feudal noble. Make a chart comparing the advantages and disadvantages of your position. List the benefits on one side and the risks and responsibilities on the other side.

Ancient China

LESSON 2

The Age of Confucius

How did the teachings of Confucius compare with those of the Moists, the Legalists, and the Daoists?

Key Terms

- nobility
- Confucianism

➤ *The portrait of Confucius on this page was made from an ancient marble relief.*

T he gentleman first practices what he preaches and then preaches what he practices."

"Do not do to others what you would not want others to do to you."

China's greatest teacher, Confucius *(kuhn FYOO shuhs)*, taught such rules for living about 2,500 years ago. Some of his ideas may even sound familiar to you. Wise people throughout history have taught us the same lessons. Indeed, Confucius's advice on how to treat others has echoed down through the ages.

About 20 B.C., the great Jewish teacher Hillel said, "What is hateful to yourself, do not do to your neighbor." And in the Christian New Testament, the same message is written in the following way: "Treat others as you would like them to treat you."

At the root of Confucius's teachings lay a basic idea—that people could get along peacefully if only they followed the rules of good behavior. In a time of chaos and change, this great thinker longed for order and mutual respect among people. Little did he know that his simple lessons for living would instruct and inspire millions for centuries to come.

An Age of Change

Confucius lived during the last years of the Zhou dynasty. Gradually, the Zhou had lost more and more power. By the time of Confucius, they were rulers in name only. And as the rule of the Zhou weakened, China tumbled into chaos.

How did the Zhou fall from power? They needed help ruling China's vast lands, and so they sent military leaders to control faraway outposts. These leaders, or lords, ruled walled cities and maintained powerful armies. Soon, independent lords governed their own lands. Finally, in 771 B.C., powerful lords invaded the Zhou capital and drove out the rulers.

The Zhou moved their capital east to Luoyang *(loh YAHNG)*, far from enemy territory. Officially, the Zhou still ruled China. In fact, they had little power by this time. The true rulers were the heads of the strongest feudal states.

During this time of chaos, a number of great thinkers were seeking ways to put Chinese society back in order. They traveled, looking for work as government officials or as advisors. Each hoped to persuade rulers and commoners to accept his view of the world.

Like the Buddha in India, these great Chinese teachers questioned their society's rules and values. So many teachers wrote and debated that the Chinese later named this period "The Hundred Schools."

Among these great thinkers, one stands out. Even today, Chinese people still follow the wisdom of Confucius. ■

■ *Why did the Zhou kings lose their power, and who controlled China after them?*

Confucius the Teacher

Confucius lived from 551 to 479 B.C. He was born in the state of Lu in northeastern China. His family belonged to the **nobility,** people of high rank or social position. Still, they were very poor. Confucius became an orphan when he was young. He studied hard and became one of the best-educated Chinese of his time.

As Confucius got older, he looked for work as a political official. He was never able to get a government post. Even so, he became one of the most successful teachers the world has ever known. His ideas, known as **Confucianism,** continue to influence Chinese thought after almost 2,500 years.

What were the ideas of Confucius? What made those ideas so powerful? Confucianism is a code of behavior. A central idea of Confucianism is *ren*. Examine the Chinese characters in the margin to learn how the word *ren* is formed and what it means.

Five Basic Relationships

Confucius taught that there are five basic relationships. They are husband and wife, father and son, older and younger brother, friend and friend, and ruler and subject. The foundation for each relationship, he said, should be sincerity, loyalty, and mutual respect.

Three of Confucius's basic relationships are between family members. Indeed, the family has always been the most important unit in Chinese society. Children, Confucius believed, should respect their parents at all times. Parents today would surely agree with Confucius when he said: "In serving his parents, a child may gently disagree with them. If they refuse to listen to his argument, he should remain reverent and obedient."

Over the centuries, Chinese homes have reflected Confucius's ideas about the family. Traditionally, families shared their homes with several generations. Children would often have grandparents and perhaps aunts and uncles living with them. At age 15 or 16, a son might bring his new wife into the family home. A daughter would marry and move to her husband's home. Families tried to stay in one place because family members were buried in plots near

▲ *The brush strokes at the top represent the Chinese word for* man. *The two middle strokes represent the number* two. *When written together, these characters form* ren *—one person existing in harmony with another. It can also mean benevolence or humaneness. The relationship between two people is central to Confucianism.*

271

the farm home, and people did not want to move away from their ancestors' graves.

Rulers and Their Subjects

Confucius used the family as a model of how rulers should behave. A ruler, he believed, should act like a good father to his people. If a ruler were wise and good, people would follow that example and be wise and good themselves.

Thus, Confucius longed for traditional Chinese values, such as obedience and order. He was a traditional thinker in other ways too. He never questioned the right of the great lords to rule. Still, he broke with tradition, especially on how government should be run.

Ideas About Government

First, Confucius believed that government should be based on virtue, or goodness, not on laws and punishment. Confucius said,

"If the ruler himself is upright, all will go well, even though he does not give orders. But if he himself is not upright, even though he gives orders, they will not be obeyed."

Second, Confucius argued that government officials should earn their jobs through education and talent. They should not use family connections to get their jobs as so many did. Confucius said this:

> Riches and honor are what everyone desires, but if they can be gained only by doing evil, they must not be held. Don't worry about not being in office; worry about qualifying yourself for office. Don't worry that no one knows you, but seek to be worthy of being known.
>
> Confucius, *The Analects*

Truly, this teacher had wise advice for everyone—rulers and commoners alike.

► *Confucius talks with his disciples in this scroll painting from the Tang dynasty, A.D. 618–906.*

A Follower of Confucius

About 100 years after Confucius died, his disciple Mencius (*MEHN shee uhs*) began spreading the ideas of Confucianism. Mencius had his own ideas too. He felt that human nature is good. People should extend the love and respect they felt for family members to people outside their families.

Mencius also had strong beliefs about rulers. He thought that a bad king should be driven from the throne. Of the evil Xia and Shang kings, he said: "Losing the throne arose from . . . losing the people, and to lose the people means to lose their hearts. There is a way to get the kingdom: get the people and the kingdom is got." ∎

∎ *What were some basic teachings of Confucius?*

Opponents of Confucianism

Not all scholars supported the teachings of Confucius. For example, Moists (*MOH ihts*), people who followed the teachings of Mozi (*MOHD zuh*), believed in universal love, equal love for all people—not just rulers and family members. Universal love, they believed, would bring benefits such as peace.

Another group, the Legalists, held a different view. They thought that people were bad by nature. Only a strong government, with strict laws and harsh punishments, would keep evil under control.

The Daoists (*DOW ihsts*) were a third group. Their first great teacher was Laozi (*LAOW dzuh*), who may have been a legendary figure. Laozi said that the best leaders work quietly in the background, not taking credit for what they do. The Daoists wanted a small, simple society. Their aim was to find Dao, or "the Way" of the universe, by being in harmony with nature and inner feelings. The followers of Confucius, on the other hand, looked for Dao in the smooth workings of society and the correct relationships between people.

Imagine you are on a busy street corner in a Chinese marketplace around 250 B.C. You listen as three men engage in a heated debate. A thin man, a Moist, seated on a box, waves his arms excitedly as he speaks: "Confucius believed that men of learning should guide rulers, but why shouldn't men of learning *be* rulers?"

"That's an easy question," replies the large man they call a Legalist. "Rulers must make strict laws because people are evil. The ruler must be an all-powerful king. Now here's another question

◄ *This wooden carving shows a Daoist wise man. The 12-inch carving dates from the Southern Song dynasty, A.D. 1127–1279.*

273

Ancient China

Two Schools of Chinese Thought

	Confucianism	Legalism
Goal	Virtuous conduct, peaceful society	All power in the hands of the ruler
Government	Rule by good example	Rule by law, including rewards and punishments
Emphasis	The past	The present

for you," he goes on. "Confucius said rulers should govern by virtue, not by power. But when powerful states fight with one another, who wins?"

"The most powerful leader wins," admits the Moist. "But going to war is the biggest waste of time and money."

The third man, who is a Daoist, smiles at the others. "Arguing about these things is silly," he says. "And working in government is pointless. After all, the world is neither good nor evil. It certainly can't be changed by anything that people do."

The thin Moist answers, "You seem to be saying that there's nothing to be done at all. But we should love everyone as much as we love ourselves. What could be a better way of showing love than feeding the hungry and housing the poor? Whatever enriches the country and brings order to society is good."

The Legalist shifts his bulky weight to his other leg. "You have

■ *In what ways did each of these—Moists, Legalists, and Daoists—disagree with Confucius?*

a good point," he says. "If we keep trying to rule by looking back to the past, as Confucius did, we're just like the man of Song. Then the Legalist goes on to tell this story:

"Once there was a man of Song who plowed his field around a tree stump that stood in the center. One day, a hare, running at full speed, bumped into the stump, broke its neck, and died. So the farmer left his plow and kept watch at the stump. He always hoped to catch another hare, but he never did. Those who try to rule today the way the early kings ruled are doing the same thing as that foolish man of Song!"

The stories and arguments went on and on as the day drew to an end. Soon the merchants would be counting their money and packing up their wares. The horse-drawn carts would be plowing their way through the muddy streets. And finally the three arguing scholars would go home to their beds, each one dreaming his own vision of China's future. ■

R E V I E W

1. **FOCUS** How did the teachings of Confucius compare with those of the Moists, the Legalists, and the Daoists?

2. **CONNECT** What might Confucius say about evil kings such as the last ruler of the Xia dynasty?

3. **POLITICAL SYSTEMS** What were Confucius's ideas about how a government should be run?

4. **CRITICAL THINKING** What might Confucius say about the relationships between family members in U.S. society today?

5. **ACTIVITY** Form groups of four and discuss the ideas presented in the imaginary debate. Then let each member take one of the four roles. Act out a debate in which Confucius answers the arguments of the other three.

Evaluating Arguments

Here's Why

People often disagree about things. In any debate, you need to be able to understand the arguments on both sides of a question to figure out which one makes the most sense.

You have learned that philosophers of the Hundred Schools debated many subjects. Often the cause of their disagreements was a basic difference in how they saw the world. For example, Confucius believed that humans are good by nature; others disagreed. Who was right?

To respond to such questions, you must be able to evaluate ideas or arguments as they are presented. You must ask which ideas fit the point.

Here's How

Read the paragraph below. It was written by Han Fei Zi, a Legalist. To evaluate his argument, first identify its main point: Love spoils people, but punishment makes them obedient. Then identify his supporting arguments. Decide whether the arguments are consistent —do they agree with other ideas presented? Also ask whether the arguments are relevant—do they fit the point he is making? For example, if you take out the sentence "His friends may like him," does it change the argument? No, because the statement is irrelevant to the argument. Statements of this type weaken the debater's position.

Try It

What would you identify as the main point of the argument if it ended with the following sentence? "With a boy who is a good character, however, love of parents, conduct of neighbors, and wisdom of teachers have a positive and lasting effect." Which sentence in the paragraph would be inconsistent with this ending?

Apply It

Prepare a written argument for or against this idea: "Every citizen should vote." Be sure to use supporting arguments. Then trade papers with a classmate. Evaluate each other's work, looking for inconsistencies and irrelevant statements.

Irrelevant. This says nothing about how or what a person learns of morality.

Consistent. This summarizes the argument.

Take a boy who is a bad character. His parents may get angry with him; he does not change. His teachers may teach him moral conduct; he does not conform. His friends may like him. Parents' love and teachers' wisdom have no effect on him. Not a hair on his shins changes. But when the police come around looking for wicked characters, he becomes afraid, changes his principles, and reforms his conduct. The love of parents is not enough to teach a boy morality; the severe punishments of the law are needed. People become naturally spoiled by love but obedient to severity.

Inconsistent. Showing anger is not necessarily love; it may really be punishment.

Relevant. This emphasizes the major point of the argument.

LESSON 3

A Unified China

THINKING FOCUS

How did Qin Shihuangdi unify China, and what did he do to maintain his empire?

Key Terms

• province
• bureaucracy
• censorship

▼ This striking photo shows a small part of Qin Shihuangdi's amazing clay army.

Imagine facing an army of fearsome warriors from more than 2,000 years in the past. That's what journalist Audrey Topping saw in 1974 near the ancient Chinese city of Xian (*shee YAHN*). The troops were, in fact, life-sized pottery figures. Yet Topping still felt a sense of awe as she looked upon the legions of warriors.

Looking into the pit . . . was like looking back more than two thousand years at an ancient battlefield. . . . Some figures were almost completely unearthed and stood as if poised to attack; others were half buried, or smashed and scattered. . . . Proud heads, fallen

from broken bodies, looked up from their centuries-old grave, their fierce eyes fixed on us.

Audrey Topping, "Clay Soldiers: The Army of Emperor Ch'in"

Peasants had made the discovery while drilling a well. Topping was the first Western reporter to visit the site. The huge clay army consisted of more than 6,000 life-sized warriors, plus horses and chariots. Armed with swords, spears, and crossbows, the clay warriors appeared ready for battle. Nearby in his ancient grave lay the once-powerful ruler—Qin Shihuangdi (*chihn shee hwahng dee*). The statues had been crafted to guard the emperor in his afterlife.

The Qin Dynasty

In the last years of the Zhou dynasty, the feudal state of Qin became very powerful. In 256 B.C., Qin forces defeated the last Zhou ruler. They spread their control over more and more of China.

In 246 B.C., Zheng, who later was the emperor Qin Shihuangdi, became king of the state of Qin. Twenty-five years later, he led his mighty state to victory over its final rival. Now he ruled all of China. Note the extent of the Qin dynasty on the map below.

The new ruler wanted a new title. For 1,500 years, Shang and Zhou rulers had been called *wang*, meaning "king." But this wasn't good enough. Believing his family's rule over China would last 10,000 generations, the king added *shi*, meaning "first," to *huangdi*, meaning "emperor," and called himself Qin Shihuangdi. The Qin dynasty lasted only 15 years, but Chinese emperors were called *huangdi* until 1912.

No matter how fine his title, an emperor cannot rule without power. Qin Shihuangdi knew this well. He set out to run the empire as he had run the state of Qin. He worked to unify the many warring states. To do so, he divided the empire into 36 **provinces,** or territories. He divided each of the provinces into districts. Over each province were two officials, a governor and a defender. Thus, the emperor kept firm control over his entire empire.

Qin Shihuangdi also set up a system of rewards and punishments. He urged people to spy on neighbors and turn in lawbreakers. This system strengthened his control and gave him power to make great changes in his empire. ■

◄ *This life-sized clay soldier appears ready to defend his emperor Qin Shihuangdi from any foe.*

■ *What did Qin Shihuangdi hope to accomplish by appointing governors to rule the provinces?*

◄ *Compare the extent of the Qin dynasty with the Shang and Zhou dynasties shown on pages 265 and 269.*

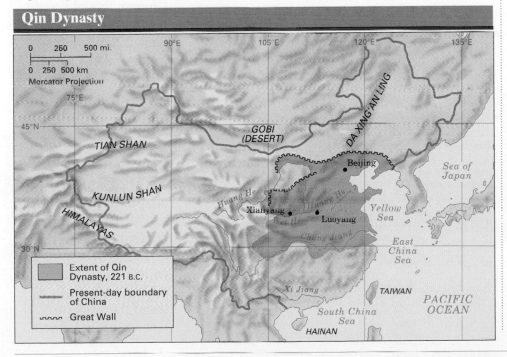

Qin Dynasty

0   250   500 mi.
0   250   500 km
Mercator Projection

75°E
45°N
TIAN SHAN
GOBI (DESERT)
DA XING AN LING
Beijing
Sea of Japan
KUNLUN SHAN
Huang He
Huang He
HIMALAYAS
Xianyang
Wei He
Luoyang
Yellow Sea
Chang Jiang
East China Sea
30°N
Xi Jiang
TAIWAN
PACIFIC OCEAN
South China Sea
HAINAN

Extent of Qin Dynasty, 221 B.C.
Present-day boundary of China
Great Wall

90°E   105°E   120°E   135°E

277

Ancient China

The Legacy of Qin

Could Qin Shihuangdi rule all China from his palace? Even with governors and defenders, he needed more help. The emperor set up a new system that would be used in China for centuries to come.

Qin Shihuangdi's New System

Before Qin Shihuangdi, officials passed their jobs on to their sons. Qin Shihuangdi changed all that. He set up a **bureaucracy** *(byoo RAHK ruh see),* a system in which each worker is appointed to a job and is trained for that job. Each worker gets a salary, follows strict rules, and answers to a superior. People at each level supervise those below them.

Heading the bureaucracy was the emperor Qin Shihuangdi. Eleven chamberlains managed the emperor's household. Three high officials, sometimes called the "Three Dukes," held the highest government and military posts. Find their titles on the chart below. The chart shows only the top levels of the Qin bureaucracy.

Beneath all the officials on the chart labored a host of minor officials.

New Standards

Qin Shihuangdi made other changes to help unify his empire. People in different parts of China had developed their own systems of measurement and money. Over time, different regions had even come to use different characters for writing.

The emperor set new standards for all of China. All measurements had to be the same, and only one kind of money was legal. He also decreed standard written characters. Now people all over China could communicate in writing. To this day, Chinese writing remains much the same as in Qin Shihuangdi's time.

Land Ownership

Qin Shihuangdi also changed the rules about ownership of land. He feared the nobles as a threat to his power, so he took land away from thousands of noble families. Thus Qin Shihuangdi ended the Chinese feudal system. Now any man, rich or poor, could own land, as long as he paid the land tax. And now Qin Shihuangdi's government, not the lords, controlled the peasants.

Book Burnings

The emperor's advisor, Li Si *(lee suh),* saw still another way for Qin Shihuangdi's government to strengthen its control. Like other Legalists, Li Si hated the works of Confucius and others

▼ The most powerful persons in a bureaucracy are usually those with the most people working beneath them. Use this chart to compare the positions of the "Three Dukes." Which one seems to have had the most power? You're right if you said the Counselor-in-chief. What officials were beneath him?

Qin Bureaucracy

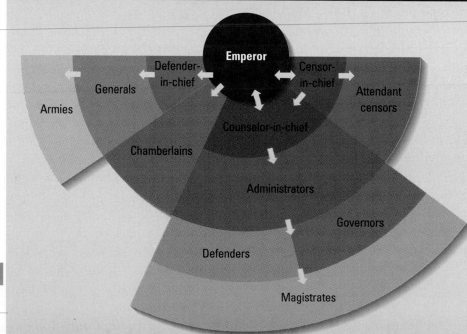

Emperor
Defender-in-chief
Censor-in-chief
Generals
Attendant censors
Armies
Counselor-in-chief
Chamberlains
Administrators
Governors
Defenders
Magistrates

who disagreed with Legalism. In 213 B.C., he ordered the burning of "useless" books. According to Li Si, all books were useless unless they were about medicine, agriculture, or prophecy.

The government attacked writers and readers as well as their books. "Anyone referring to the past to criticize the present . . . should be put to death," Li Si told the emperor.

Several hundred scholars who criticized the government were buried alive or punished in other ways.

Qin Shihuangdi's book burning was an early example of **censorship**—control of what people read, write, hear, or see. Look again at the bureaucracy chart on page 278. How does it show that censorship was important in Qin Shihuangdi's government?

UNDERSTANDING CENSORSHIP

*T*he idea for burning books came from Qin Shihuangdi's advisor, Li Si. "Your servant suggests that all books in the imperial archives, except records of the Qin dynasty, be burned." Li Si was telling the emperor to stop people from reading, writing, saying, or even hearing words that might challenge the government. Efforts such as these to prohibit free expression are called censorship.

A Matter of Policy

Your local bookstore can choose not to sell a certain book or magazine. That isn't censorship. Censorship is an official policy of stopping the spread of works and ideas that the government or some other group does not like.

A Long History

Censorship has been practiced throughout history. Around 500 B.C. leaders of the Greek city-state of Sparta banned poems and music that they felt made people behave badly. About 2,000 years later, King Henry VIII of England ordered his officials to read every piece of writing before it was printed.

In June 1989, Chinese college students staged a peaceful demonstration in Beijing. They demanded rights such as freedom of speech. But the Chinese government sent troops into the crowd, killing many people. Officials insisted there had been no killings—despite photographs and videotapes of the massacre. They did not allow Chinese television or newspapers to report what really happened.

An Ancient Debate

Throughout history, the debate over censorship has raged. On one side are those who believe that people should have free access to all ideas. On the other side are those who fear the consequences of freedom. They fear that knowledge might make people dissatisfied. It might lead to criticism of the government or even rebellion.

A Reason for Alertness

Citizens of a democracy cherish their freedom of expression. That freedom can be threatened, even in a democracy. We need to be alert when people tell us what Li Si told the emperor—that certain books or other kinds of expression are "dangerous" and ought to be censored.

This picture shows part of the Great Wall of China as it is today. Some emperors after Qin Shihuangdi extended and strengthened the Wall.

■ *What are three things that Qin Shihuangdi standardized, and how did each change affect China?*

for enemy forces. They signaled invasions with flags or fires, holding off the enemy until help came.

To complete this massive structure, Qin Shihuangdi used a forced-labor crew of 300,000 men. These workers connected several existing walls to form one single, massive wall. The Great Wall is nearly 30 feet high. At most points, it is wide enough to allow five horses to run atop it side by side. If it were in the United States, the Great Wall would stretch from Washington, D.C., to Denver, Colorado.

The Wall was not a complete success. First, it never really kept out invaders. They swarmed over and around it. Second, thousands of workers died on the long journey to the Wall. Thousands more died while building it. The folktale "Meng-Jiang Nyu," on pages 256 to 261, shows how some lives were changed by the Great Wall.

The Great Wall

Some of the scholars punished under Li Si were sent to work on the emperor's huge building project. That project would later be known as the Great Wall of China.

The Great Wall still stands. It snakes through the mountains of northern China for more than 1,500 miles. The wall was built to keep out enemy invaders. Guards on its watchtowers kept a lookout

A Unified Empire

In a sense, Qin Shihuangdi, a brilliant and sometimes cruel emperor, gained the immortality he wanted. In his lifetime, he unified states that had been fighting for centuries. And even today outsiders call the land "China" from *Qin* (or *Ch'in*), the name of its first emperor. ■

R E V I E W

1. **FOCUS** How did Qin Shihuangdi unify China, and what did he do to maintain his empire?
2. **CONNECT** Qin Shihuangdi unified China. Who were the rulers that unified Mesopotamia and Egypt? How did each ruler create a unified empire?
3. **GOVERNMENT** How was Qin Shihuangdi's rule different from the rule of the Shang and the Zhou?

4. **CRITICAL THINKING** What would you have liked about living under Qin Shihuangdi's rule? What would you have disliked? Explain.
5. **WRITING ACTIVITY** If you lived in Qin Shihuangdi's China, what occupation would you choose? Scholar? Bureaucrat? Peasant? Write a day's entry in your diary discussing your job, your problems, and your life in general.

LESSON 4

The Han Dynasty

> *O* n one occasion one of the dragons let fall a ball from its mouth though no perceptible shock could be felt. All the scholars at the capital were astonished at this strange effect occurring without any evidence of an earthquake to cause it. But several days later a messenger arrived bringing news of an earthquake in Longxi [Kansu, about 400 miles away to the northwest].
>
> Han court historian, A.D. 132

What is this mysterious instrument that tells of a faraway earthquake? The carved bronze dragons and the toads below them are fine works of art. But this amazing device is much more than art. Today we call it a **seismograph** (*SYZ muh graf*), a machine that detects earthquakes.

Here's how the Han dragon-and-toad seismograph worked. In the center of the huge jar stood a pendulum. With the slightest shaking from a far-off earthquake, the pendulum would fall into one of the slots, hitting a rod. The rod would slip into the dragon's mouth, hitting a ball. The ball would fall into the mouth of a toad. The loud crack of bronze against bronze signaled that an earthquake had happened. But it told even more. It told what part of the country had suffered the quake. The ball fell into the mouth of the toad that stood in that direction.

Key Terms

- seismograph
- middleman

◀ *This seismograph is a copy of the Han dynasty model. The drawing shows its inner workings.*

0   6 ft.

281

Ancient China

Han rulers needed to know when earthquakes happened. Frequent quakes destroyed farms, roads, and cities, causing food shortages. Starving peasants often revolted. Informed by the dragon-and-toad seismograph, the rulers could rush food supplies and soldiers to the earthquake area.

Indeed, this brilliant invention seems to symbolize the explosion of scientific advances that were made during the Han dynasty. The Han rulers were in power from 206 B.C. to A.D. 220. During this time, China seemed centuries ahead of the rest of the world in science, art, and culture.

Revival of Confucianism

During this period of creativity, Han scholars, like Zhou scholars before them, searched for new ideas. They looked for new ways to organize China's political life. Legalist teachings had helped Qin Shihuangdi to unite China's states under a single government. But as a Legalist, Qin Shihuangdi ruled harshly. He ignored moral principles such as kindness and respect. As a result, only a few people supported his rule. Finally, soldiers and peasants rebelled, overthrowing the Qin dynasty a few years after Qin Shihuangdi's death. One leader of the rebellion became the first emperor of the Han dynasty.

Legalism and Confucianism

The Han leaders saw that China's government could not be based on Legalism alone. Confucianism—the belief in moral behavior and rule by good example —became popular again.

The first Han emperor, Han Gaozu *(hahn kow dzuh)*, was uneducated. He appointed learned people to help him run the government. Some were Confucian scholars. Gaozu even lifted the Qin ban on books in 191 B.C. and permitted scholars to rewrite some old Confucian texts from memory.

Government officials no longer destroyed books on Confucianism.

➤ *Compare the Han empire in this map with the Shang dynasty shown on page 265.*

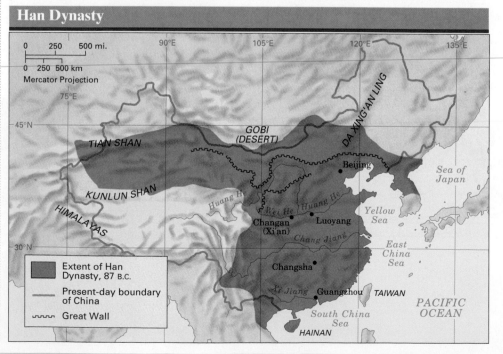

Han Dynasty

0 250 500 mi.
0 250 500 km
Mercator Projection

75°E
90°E
105°E
120°E
135°E
45°N
30°N

TIAN SHAN
KUNLUN SHAN
HIMALAYAS
GOBI (DESERT)
DA XING AN LING
Huang He
Wei He
Huang He
Changan (Xi'an)
Luoyang
Beijing
Changsha
Chang Jiang
Xi Jiang
Guangzhou
TAIWAN
HAINAN
Sea of Japan
Yellow Sea
East China Sea
South China Sea
PACIFIC OCEAN

Extent of Han Dynasty, 87 B.C.
Present-day boundary of China
Great Wall

Instead, they began to study them. Later, in 136 B.C., emperor Wudi (*woo dee*) made Confucianism part of the law of the empire. Students even read Confucian books in school.

Yet Confucianism alone was not enough to guide the government. In fact, the Han rulers combined Confucianism with Legalism. They kept the Legalist ideas of a strong ruler and a strict set of laws. But they added the Confucian view that the emperor was a "good father"to his people. He ruled by setting a good example, not by threats of punishment.

Confucianism and Legalism may seem like opposites. In some ways they are. But the Chinese understood how such opposites could work together through the idea of Yin and Yang.

Yin and Yang

During the late Zhou dynasty, some thinkers had explained life as a blend of two opposing forces—Yin and Yang. *Yin* means "the dark side of the hill." Yin has the qualities of darkness, calm, and weakness. Earth, winter, sorrow, and death are examples of Yin. *Yang* means "the bright side of the hill." Yang is active and strong. Examples include heaven, summer, joy, and life.

The Chinese knew that opposites depend on each other. There can be no light without darkness, or life without death. And opposites, they knew, often take turns, as day gives way to night. Thus, a combination of opposites such as Confucianism and Legalism seemed reasonable. ■

▲ *The Yin and Yang symbol is the center of this design, which is part of a carved door ornament.*

■ *How did the Han and Qin governments differ?*

Daily Life in the Empire

Written records tell us little about how the Han Chinese lived their daily lives. Han tombs, however, contain a wealth of information. For example, the Han people buried their dead in underground tombs decorated with paintings of scenes from daily life. They also buried small pottery models like those you see below. These models tell much about the furniture, houses, and villages of China 2,000 years ago.

Life in the Country

Then, as now, most of China's people were farmers. Han farmers lived in mud houses that stood on earthen platforms. Tile or thatched roofs topped these one-story or two-story houses. Rough hemp curtains covered the farmhouse windows. Barns and other buildings surrounded the houses. Often several farm families lived together

▼ *These clay figures, found in a Han tomb, show an ordinary farm scene. Like the ancient Egyptians, the Han believed such images might be useful in the afterlife.*

283

This funeral suit, made of a green stone called jade, covered the body of the princess Tou Wan, who lived before 100 B.C. Some people believed jade would prevent the body from decaying, and small pieces of jade were sometimes buried with the bodies. This princess went further. Her suit has 2,160 jade pieces.

■ *How were the lives of China's wealthy farmers different from the lives of poor farmers?*

in small villages. In this way, they could work the fields together.

A wealthy farmer could afford strong oxen to pull his carts and iron tips to strengthen the ends of his plows. He used simple machines to carry water to his fields.

His poorer neighbor worked with wooden hand tools. To water his fields, the poorer farmer hauled heavy buckets of water on his shoulders. He lugged the buckets on a yoke across his back, carrying two buckets at a time.

These Chinese farmers dressed in simple, rough clothes. They wore shirts and pants made of scratchy cloth. They wore sandals made of straw. In cold weather, they wore clothing that was padded, stuffed like a quilt to keep them warm.

Farmers cooked their simple meals in boxlike stoves. They steamed much of their food over boiling water, as Chinese people still do. Those living in the north ate wheat or a grain called millet. Those living in the south ate rice. Farmers enjoyed steamed dumplings, small portions of fish, and even smaller portions of meat. Many families planted garden plots and grew ginger, garlic, and onions. These crops added flavor to their meals and could even be sold at the market to bring them a few coins.

Life in the City

By the time of the Han dynasty, perhaps one in 10 Chinese people lived in a city. The cities were laid out neatly according to compass directions. They had earthen and stone walls so strong that some are still standing today. The cities were centers of government, education, and trade. There, in busy marketplaces, merchants traded everything from coarse cloth to fine silk, from the heaviest ox cart to the most elegant horse-drawn carriage.

Then, as now, rich and poor shared city life. According to one writer of the time, the poor lived in houses packed together as tightly as the teeth of a comb. And then, as now, some youngsters joined street gangs. These gangs roamed the city, terrorizing its people. Gang members also wore special clothes and armor.

Rich city people lived in huge houses built so that they opened onto courtyards. They decorated their houses with woolen rugs and fine draperies. They wore belted robes with long sleeves. In winter, the rich wrapped themselves in squirrel or fox furs. They slipped their feet into leather slippers lined with silk.

City life also included lively entertainment. Musicians played bells, drums, and wind and string instruments. Jugglers and acrobats delighted audiences with their tricks and stunts. ■

Achievements of the Han Dynasty

Early Han rulers ended many of the harsh Qin laws and heavy taxes. Thus, the Han gained their subjects' loyalty as Qin Shihuangdi never could. With peace and prosperity, the Han dynasty marked the beginning of an age of creativity at home and expansion abroad.

Expansion of the Empire

Emperor Wudi, who ruled from 141 to 87 B.C., sent out armies to expand the empire. His soldiers captured lands in southern China and started colonies in what are now North Korea and North Vietnam. Wudi's troops also crossed the Great Wall. They subdued the raiding tribes of the Gobi Desert and brought these northern people under Chinese rule.

In 139 B.C., Wudi sent out Zhang Qian (jahng chyee YAHN), a military officer and explorer. He journeyed west into what is now Afghanistan. When he returned to China 10 years later, he described the fabulous riches and wonders of the West. He brought back tales of new plants—alfalfa and grapes. He told of splendid, swift horses that "sweat blood when they perspire." His stories stirred the emperor's curiosity.

Zhang Qian added, "There are cities with mansions and houses, as in China." He gave the first hint that a civilized world lay beyond China.

Zhang Qian's explorations and Wudi's new interest in the West resulted in the growth of a major trade route— the Silk Road. Along the Silk Road, traders exchanged China's fine silk for Western goods such as glassware from Syria and gold from Rome.

Advances and Inventions

Since prehistoric times, only the Chinese knew how to make silk. Skilled Chinese silk makers unwound the long threads from the silkworm's cocoon. Then they wove the thread into strong, beautiful cloth. For hundreds of years, China guarded the secret of how to make silk. Rulers even threatened a horrible death to anyone who told an outsider the secret, or gave away a silk moth.

Chinese workers used foot-pedaled looms to weave complex patterns into the silk. Silk became even more precious to the world beyond China.

People of the West knew little about the land that produced silk. Han rulers kept their lands closed

In this painting from a vase of the Ming dynasty, A.D. 1368–1644, two women are spinning silk cloth. What else do you see in the painting?

Ancient China

➤ *This bronze leopard illustrates the fine work of Han artisans. Less than one and a half inches high, it is inlaid with silver and precious stones called garnets. Four of them were found in the princess Tou Wan's tomb, dating from about 100 B.C.*

▼ *In Afghanistan, the explorer Zhang Qian saw horses that were larger and finer than any the Chinese had known. In 101 B.C., the Chinese brought some of these horses home. This 26-inch pottery figure, made in the first century B.C., shows one of those early horses.*

to outsiders. They used **middlemen** —agents who go between the buyer and seller. These middlemen from neighboring lands—now known as India, Pakistan, and Afghanistan—carried on most of the Silk Road trade. Thus, China's other advances were almost as well hidden as the secret of making silk.

For example, you've read about the seismograph. Its inventor was

Zhang Heng. He and other Chinese astronomers learned how to predict eclipses and how to calculate the length of a year.

Han doctors understood many kinds of medicine. They studied the healing powers of herbs and plants. They invented the unique Chinese medical practice with needles called acupuncture.

Chinese engineers of the Han period were the first to use iron-tipped bamboo poles for deep drilling. They drilled salt water out of mines thousands of feet underground. They heated the water with piped-in natural gas until it evaporated, leaving salt.

The Han Chinese invented paper, too. Papermakers beat mulberry bark fibers into tiny particles. They mixed these and other fibers with water and poured the mixture out on a flat mold. There it dried, forming a sheet of paper.

Han artists also produced exceptional art and writing. Han artisans crafted bronze and gold belt hooks, glazed pottery dishes, and jade jewelry. Han writers wrote dozens of great books. Historian Sima Qian *(soo muhn chih ehn)* completed the first full history of China during Wudi's reign. He set a high standard for later historians.

Han writers also wrote brilliant works in the fields of mathematics, medicine, and poetry. They enriched the written language itself, increasing the number of characters from 3,000 to 9,000 by about A.D. 100. At that time, scholars completed the first Chinese dictionary.

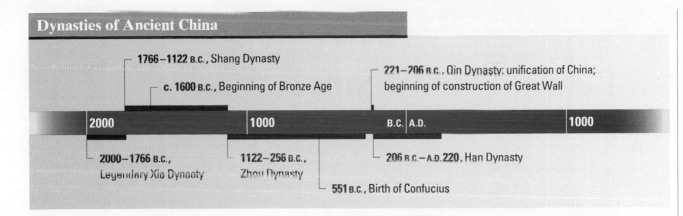

Dynasties of Ancient China

1766–1122 B.C., Shang Dynasty

c. 1600 B.C., Beginning of Bronze Age

221–206 B.C., Qin Dynasty: unification of China; beginning of construction of Great Wall

| 2000 | 1000 | B.C. | A.D. | 1000 |

2000–1766 B.C., Legendary Xia Dynasty

1122–256 B.C., Zhou Dynasty

206 B.C.–A.D. 220, Han Dynasty

551 B.C., Birth of Confucius

Ban Zhao

Late in the Han dynasty a woman sat in the emperor's court writing beautiful poems and essays that were enough to fill 16 books. Her name was Ban Zhao *(bahn jow)* and she worked in the court of Emperor He. Even hundreds of years after she lived, Chinese women still studied her advice on how to conduct themselves. In her society, good conduct meant obedience. "Yet only to teach men and not to teach women,—is that not ignoring the essential relation between them?" Ban Zhao wrote in *The Admonitions of the Instructress of Court Ladies.*

Ban Zhao came from a family that valued learning. She was a mathematician, an astronomer, and a poet. The emperor called her to his court to teach the empress and to finish writing the history of the Han dynasty.

Considering the many Han accomplishments and inventions, it is not surprising that the Chinese still refer to themselves as Han people. Yet the Han empire fell in A.D. 220, and another period of warfare between the states followed. Not until A.D. 589 would the empire again become united. ■

▲ *How long did each ancient Chinese dynasty last? What was one major achievement of each dynasty?*

■ *What were some of China's greatest achievements under the Han dynasty?*

◄ *Ban Zhao taught the empress and the ladies who served her as well as writing a history of the Han dynasty.*

R E V I E W

1. **FOCUS** What kind of government did Han rulers create, and how did it affect people's lives?
2. **CONNECT** Compare the burial practices of the Han with those of the Egyptians. How do their burial practices tell us about the daily lives of people in those cultures?
3. **HISTORY** Why did the Han rulers need the ideas of both Confucianism and Legalism?

4. **CRITICAL THINKING** What feelings about the outside world might have led the Chinese to use middlemen for trade?
5. **ACTIVITY** Draw or paint a picture showing one important aspect of Han life. For example, you might draw a scene from daily farm life, or one showing some people using a Chinese invention.

Learning How Silk Is Made

Here's Why

In many cases the most effective way to explain or describe something is to use a picture of it. One special kind of picture that can help make an explanation clearer to you is a process diagram.

You are probably familiar with some process diagrams already. Manufacturers often provide process diagrams with products that you must put together. For example, instructions for building a model airplane are likely to include a process diagram; so are instructions for assembling a bicycle. Manufacturers know that it is often easier for people to understand how something is done or made by seeing pictures of the process than by reading a description with no pictures.

Suppose you want to understand the steps involved in the making of silk. The drawings on this page and the facing page show you how diagrams can help explain the process of making silk.

Here's How

The fine fiber used to produce beautiful silk fabric is made by silkworms. Like other caterpillars, the silkworm wraps itself in a cocoon. There, the silkworm spends several weeks before it emerges as an adult moth, as shown in the photo on page 289.

The silkworm makes its cocoon by spinning a fine silken fiber around itself. To produce this fiber, the silkworm forces a gummy substance out from two openings beneath its mouth. This sticky material dries into a delicate strand of silk as soon as it is exposed to the air. The silkworm spins one continuous thread to make its cocoon.

Workers gather the cocoons and carefully unwind the silk threads. They must be extremely skillful to avoid breaking the threads.

The diagram below shows how the delicate strands of silk are unwound from several cocoons and twisted together to form a single, stronger silk thread. The thread can then be combined with other silk threads and woven into silk fabric.

Notice that labels identify each part of the process. Arrows show the direction of movement. In this case, the arrows show you that the crank moves clockwise, turning the reel toward you. Diagrams that describe longer processes often use numbers or letters to show the order of steps.

Try It

The diagram on page 289 shows another part of the silk-making process—preparing skeins of silk thread for

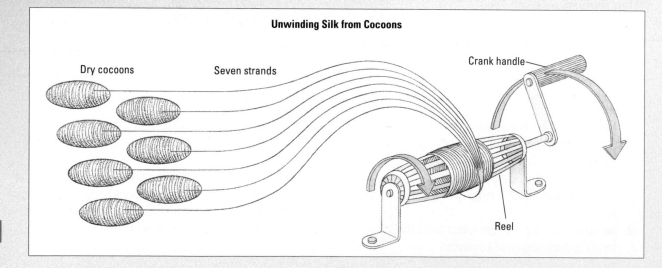

Unwinding Silk from Cocoons

Dry cocoons   Seven strands   Crank handle

Reel

dyeing. Twisting the silk into skeins keeps the threads from becoming tangled while they are being dyed. Study the diagram below. See how well you understand the process based on looking at the diagram by answering the following questions:

1. What parts of the diagram show movement?
2. Which way are the silk threads moving, up or down?
3. As the silk threads are pulled from the reels at the bottom onto the take-up reel, what do they pass through?
4. What makes the threads move?

5. Which way does the crank handle turn, clockwise or counterclockwise?
6. Does the take-up reel turn in the same direction as the crank handle, or does it turn in the opposite direction?
7. What is the final product of this process?

8. Does the diagram tell you what a skein is? Where can you go to find this information?

Apply It

Now that you know how to read a process diagram, try making one of your own. Think of some process you perform in your daily life. It can be something as simple as making a sandwich for lunch or as complex as operating a video game. Make sure that you clearly label all important parts of your diagram. Also be sure that you use arrows to show the proper direction of all movements. If necessary, number the steps in your diagram so that someone else can follow them.

When you complete your diagram, exchange diagrams with a classmate. Read each other's diagrams to see whether you can each describe the process the other is explaining.

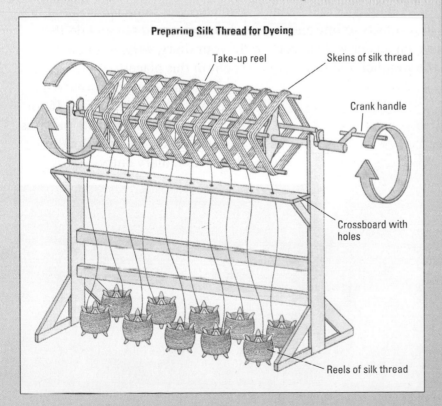

Preparing Silk Thread for Dyeing

Take-up reel

Skeins of silk thread

Crank handle

Crossboard with holes

Reels of silk thread

The Silk Road

For hundreds of years, people, animals, and goods streamed along the Silk Road. This famous route linked China with the Middle East and Europe. East met West in gorgeous fabrics, precious metals, food, and wine.

▲ *This pottery figure of a Middle Eastern wine merchant was made in China. It serves as evidence of trade between East and West.*

Get Ready

Take a notebook and a pen to your school or local library. You'll need reference books and magazines to help you imagine a journey on the Silk Road.

Find Out

First, decide whether you are a merchant, a caravan leader, or an adventurer. A merchant will be interested in products to buy and sell. A caravan leader will concentrate on the weather and terrain.

He will also see that the camels and horses have enough food and water and time to rest. An adventurer will focus on new experiences, unfamiliar sights, unusual sounds, and new people and customs.

Next, choose a place along the Silk Road (use the map to help you). The books and magazines will give you some ideas about what you would see and do there. In your diary, write about a day spent in this place.

You may draw pictures to go along with your diary entry. If you prefer, you may substitute pictures of your day on the Silk Road for the written diary entry.

Move Ahead

Separate into groups based on the place you wrote about or drew. Read your diary entry or show your pictures to a classmate who chose the same character you did. How does your information compare? How does it contrast?

Display your group's pictures on the bulletin board. What items are included in most of the pictures? Camels? Silk?

Find two classmates who chose to be the other two characters. Use your diaries to write a short skit. The characters can talk and interact as they visit a stopping-place along the Silk Road.

Explore Some More

Visit a shopping area and look at silk products. You'll find them in sporting goods stores as well as in clothing stores. Check labels to see what countries silk comes from now. Then look at other types of products, such as shoes, watches, or radios. Make a list of the countries that produce them. Which countries appear most often on your list? Find these countries on a world map or globe.

▲ *These Chinese pottery figures show a merchant and his camel loaded with trade goods.*

◄ *Traders on the Silk Road crossed the mountains of Afghanistan, shown at the left, and the vast Gobi, pictured below.*

The Silk Road

Map: THE SILK ROAD

EUROPE
Rome
Mediterranean Sea
Antioch
Baghdad
Alexandria
AFRICA
ARABIA
Arabian Sea
Samarkand
Bactria
PAMIRS
HINDU KUSH
Begram
Kashgar
TAKLA MAKAN DESERT
TIBET
HIMALAYAS
INDIA
Bay of Bengal
ASIA
GOBI DESERT
Jade Gate Pass
Great Wall of China
CHINA
South China Sea
INDIAN OCEAN

THE SILK ROAD
— The Silk Road
— Other land routes
— Sea routes

0   1000 mi.
0   1000 km

Chapter Review

Reviewing Key Terms

ancestor (p. 266)
bureaucracy (p. 278)
censorship (p. 279)
Confucianism (p. 271)
dialect (p. 269)
feudalism (p. 268)
middleman (p. 286)
nobility (p. 271)
oracle (p. 266)
province (p. 277)
seismograph (p. 281)

Be sure you understand the meanings of the key terms. Then answer each question by writing one or more sentences.

1. How might your dialect tell people where you have lived?
2. If an ancient Chinese farmer had used oracle bones, what might he have asked?
3. If you lived in a feudal society, would you rather be a serf or a noble? Why?
4. Why would a bureaucracy not work in a one-person business?
5. Why do people value a seismograph?
6. If you followed Confucianism, how would you behave toward your parents?
7. Why would a newspaper reporter dislike censorship?
8. What are some ways of finding out about your ancestors?
9. How is a middleman used if two people have something to sell to each other?
10. Why would an emperor decide to form 36 provinces?
11. Why would you expect a military commander to be a member of the nobility?

Exploring Concepts

A. Five dynasties of China appear on the timeline below. Copy the timeline. Fill in the items associated with each dynasty from this list: the Great Wall of China, the Mandate of Heaven, the dragon-and-toad seismograph, the Bronze Age, bureaucracy, Confucius the teacher, oracle bones, feudalism, the invention of acupuncture, the Silk Road. Choose two related items and discuss the relationship between them.

B. The Chinese people were responsible for many inventions and ideas. Complete the following statements by telling why each invention or idea came about.

1. Irrigation of fields began when . . .
2. A new metal called bronze resulted . . .
3. A picture language developed because . . .
4. Feudalism was the outgrowth of . . .
5. A bureaucracy was formed to . . .
6. The seismograph was necessary because . . .
7. Emperor Wudi governed through Legalism and Confucianism because . . .
8. The concept of using a middleman developed because the emperors . . .
9. Iron-tipped drilling poles were invented because of a need to . . .
10. Li Si advised Qin Shihuangdi to censor writer, scholars, and books because . . .

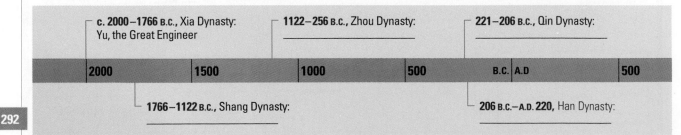

c. 2000–1766 B.C., Xia Dynasty: Yu, the Great Engineer

1122–256 B.C., Zhou Dynasty: _____

221–206 B.C., Qin Dynasty: _____

2000   1500   1000   500   B.C. | A.D   500

1766–1122 B.C., Shang Dynasty: _____

206 B.C.–A.D. 220, Han Dynasty: _____

Reviewing Skills

1. In the heated debate recorded on pages 273 and 274, the Moist asks the question "why shouldn't men of learning be rulers?" The Legalist's response contains some points that are irrelevant. Identify those points.
2. What point does the Moist make that is also irrelevant?
3. List four pieces of equipment shown in the paper-making process diagram on the right.
4. Using the diagram, write a brief description of the paper-making process.
5. Look at the map on page 265 of the Shang Dynasty in 1122 B.C. and the map on page 282 of the Han Dynasty in 87 B.C. What hypothesis can you make based on a comparison of the two maps?
6. The Yin-Yang stands for the blend of life's two opposing forces: the dark side and the bright side. What do you call something that stands for an idea?

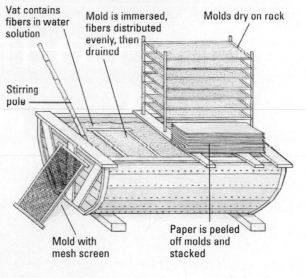

Paper-making Process

Vat contains fibers in water solution

Mold is immersed, fibers distributed evenly, then drained

Molds dry on rack

Stirring pole

Mold with mesh screen

Paper is peeled off molds and stacked

Using Critical Thinking

1. The thinkers of the Zhou dynasty explained life as a blend of two opposing forces—Yin, "the dark side of the hill," and Yang, "the bright side of the hill." How would you apply this idea to present-day events in the world or the nation? Which events are Yin, and which are Yang?
2. Ancestor worship and respect for the past were important ideas in ancient China. How do these ideas compare to present-day attitudes in America toward elderly people and toward the past?
3. During the Qin dynasty, an advisor named Li Si decreed that all books were useless unless they were about agriculture, medicine, or prophecy. What would you say to convince Li Si that other kinds of books are valuable too?

Preparing for Citizenship

1. **WRITING ACTIVITY** If you could ask Confucius which qualities he thinks a candidate for president of the United States should have, what do you think he might reply? Base your answer on information concerning his teachings and beliefs that you read in this chapter or in other sources.
2. **COLLABORATIVE ACTIVITY** Reread the description of the Qin bureaucracy on pages 278–280. Think about the needs and responsibilities you have in working together as a class. Then set up a bureaucratic form of government in your class for a specified time. In class discussions, decide how many levels you will have and what they will be. Team up with two other people and choose a level. Each person on the team is responsible for one of the following decisions:
   (1) what the jobs will be at your level,
   (2) how you will determine who will do each job, and
   (3) what written rules you will need.
   Share your decisions with the other teams. Implement all decisions. At the end of the time allowed, each team should decide how well this system of government worked.

The Foundation of Western Ideas

Just as these graceful columns support this Greek temple, the contributions of the Greeks and Israelites support our civilization today. The Greeks gave us basic ideas about government, arts, and thought. The Israelites contributed religious ideas that led to present-day Judaism and Christianity. The world we live in has its roots in all the peoples of the past. Yet our civilization— Western civilization—owes a special debt to the ancient Greeks and Israelites.

2500 B.C.

The Erechtheum, located on the Acropolis at Athens, Greece, built 421–405 B.C.

323 B.C.

Chapter 10
The Ancient Israelites

Time after time, conquerors invaded Jerusalem, a city in present-day Israel. Twice they destroyed its holy temple and drove its people away. But each time, the faith of the people drew them back. Jerusalem holds an important place in the history of three religions—Judaism, Christianity, and Islam. The shared traditions of the three religions helped shape Western civilization.

The story of the Israelites, told in the Jewish Bible, is also part of the Old Testament of the Christian Bible (below).

2000   1500   1000

1900 B.C.

c. 1000 B.C. David, shown playing a harp in the painting above, becomes king of the Israelites. Under his leadership, they make Jerusalem their capital.

The original Jewish temple in Jerusalem was built on the site where the gold-domed mosque now stands.

Prayer shawls like this one are still used by many Jews today.

587 B.C. The Babylonians destroy Jerusalem and force the Jews into exile.

c. 4 B.C. The Christian story begins with the birth of Jesus. The painting above, from the A.D. 1400s, shows Mary, Joseph, and the baby Jesus.

500

B.C. A.D.

500

A.D. 70 After a Jewish revolt, Romans destroy the temple in Jerusalem. Yet the Jewish religion endures.

A.D. 135

LESSON 1

Early Biblical History

Key Terms

- monotheism
- Judaism
- Exodus
- covenant

➤ *Biblical stories have inspired many artists. This version of Moses and the Israelites escaping from the Egyptians, painted in the A.D. 1400s, shows how Europeans interpreted biblical events.*

Chapter 10

Was it for want of graves in Egypt that you brought us to die in the wilderness?" That is the question the Israelites asked their leader, Moses, as thousands of Egyptian soldiers chased them toward the sea in about 1250 B.C.

The Israelites were the early ancestors of the Jewish people. According to the Torah, the sacred book of the Jewish religion, the Israelites were fleeing from slavery in Egypt. But they were trapped. They had no way to get across the Red Sea. The Torah tells the story of what happened next:

> *Then Moses held out his arms over the sea and the Lord drove back the sea with a strong east wind all that night, and turned the sea into dry ground. The waters were split, and the Israelites went into the sea on dry ground, the waters forming a wall for them on their right and on their left.*
>
> Exodus 14: 21–22

Egyptian soldiers followed Moses and the Israelites, but the Torah teaches that Moses held out his arms, and the waters crashed down on the Egyptians. The entire army drowned.

The Belief of the Israelites

The Israelites believed God made their escape from Egypt possible. In fact, the Israelites saw themselves as God's chosen people.

The God of the Israelites

The Israelites believed that there was only one true God. This idea was new to the ancient world. For example, the people of Mesopotamia had more than 3,000 gods. The Egyptians worshiped nature gods, the sun and spirits, and their own kings. In contrast, the God of the Israelites was all-powerful, all-knowing, and present everywhere. **Monotheism** is the belief that there is only one God. This idea has had a lasting impact on Western civilization.

Many of our present-day beliefs about how people should treat each other can be traced to people, events, and ideas you will study in this chapter. And like the ancient Israelites, many people today find meaning in history by viewing it as directed by one all-powerful God.

The History of Biblical Times

The story of how the Israelites developed as a people is found in the first five books of the Hebrew Bible. In **Judaism**, or the religion of the Jewish people, these books are called the Torah. The Torah contains the central religious teachings of Judaism and traces the history of the Israelites through the 1200s B.C. In the Christian Bible, these books are the first five books of the Old Testament.

Historians rely on the accounts in the Bible to understand the history of the Israelites and the development of their belief in one God. But it is important to remember that for Jews, these stories explain their faith in God. The Torah celebrates the power of God over nature and history.

Many people believe that the scriptures are a factual record of biblical times. Historians often combine the Bible with other kinds of evidence. They use the Bible, archaeological artifacts, and other written records to interpret the events and ideas of biblical times. ■

Before Judaism, mankind worshiped many gods, including Baal, shown in this goldplated bronze statuette from about 1300 B.C. However, the Israelites came to believe that there was only one true God.

The Origins of the Israelites

According to Genesis, the first book of the Torah, God created the heavens and earth. Genesis tells of how God commanded a shepherd named Abraham from the city of Ur in Mesopotamia to move to Canaan in about 1900 B.C. God told him, "Go forth from your native land and from your father's house to the land that I will show you. I will make of you a great nation." (Genesis 12:1–2)

■ *What is monotheism?*

Genesis tells how God brought this new nation into being, beginning with the descendants of Abraham. They were called Hebrews.

The Land of the Israelites

Canaan was a small area, but it held an important place in the ancient world because of its location. Find Canaan on the map below. Why do you think the location was so important to the neighboring nations?

Canaan was an important trading route, marketplace, and battlefield. It lay in the path of expansion for Egypt, one of the larger and more powerful nations of the ancient world. The land of

Canaan was quite varied. It included fertile plains, grassy slopes, rocky hills, and arid deserts.

Most people in Canaan were herders rather than farmers. These nomads lived in tents and traveled from place to place seeking pasture for their sheep, goats, or cattle.

Jacob, the grandson of Abraham, was one of these herders. The book of Genesis tells how Jacob spent a night wrestling with a man. This man appeared to be sent by God because he blessed Jacob after the long struggle. At daybreak the man told Jacob: "Your name shall no longer be Jacob, but Israel, for you have wrestled with God and men, and have prevailed." (Genesis 32:29)

▼ *Where was Canaan in relation to Babylonia and Egypt?*

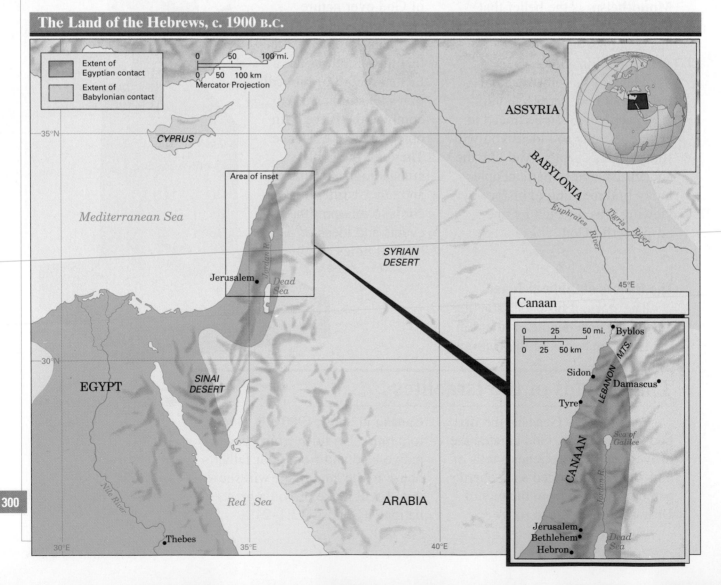

The Land of the Hebrews, c. 1900 B.C.

Extent of Egyptian contact

Extent of Babylonian contact

0   50   100 mi.
0 50 100 km
Mercator Projection

CYPRUS

ASSYRIA

BABYLONIA

35°N

Area of inset

Mediterranean Sea

Jordan R.

Jerusalem

Dead Sea

SYRIAN DESERT

Euphrates River

Tigris River

45°E

EGYPT

SINAI DESERT

30°N

Red Sea

ARABIA

Nile River

Thebes

30°E   35°E   40°E

Canaan

0   25   50 mi.
0 25 50 km

Byblos

Sidon

Tyre

LEBANON MTS.

Damascus

CANAAN

Jordan R.

Sea of Galilee

Jerusalem
Bethlehem
Hebron

Dead Sea

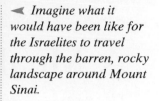

Across Time & Space

HISTORY *The Bible is an important source of historical information. In addition to explaining the faith of the Israelites, the Bible describes events of biblical times. It also provides a record of the thoughts, ideas, and laws of the people in the land.*

The name "Israel" means "the one who wrestles with God." Jacob's children, and the generations of believers in this God, came to be known as Israelites.

According to the Torah, some of the Israelites migrated into Egypt after suffering through several famines in Canaan. This was around 1700 B.C. For the next 430 years the Israelites were slaves in Egypt.

The Leadership of Moses

The Israelites bitterly resented their slavery in Egypt. Finally, in the early 1200s B.C., the Israelites found a strong leader in Moses. According to the Torah, God armed Moses with miraculous powers to persuade the Egyptian ruler to free the Israelites. Terrifying plagues, or outbreaks of disease and destruction, rained down on the Egyptians. Water turned into blood. Frogs, lice, and insects swarmed over Egyptian cities and fields. Hail, thunder, locusts, and darkness also covered the land. After each plague, the frightened pharaoh agreed to free the Israelites. But time and again he changed his mind.

The tenth plague was the most terrible. According to the Torah, God killed the first-born son in every family in Egypt. However, God passed over the houses of the Israelites and none of their children died. When the pharaoh saw that so many of his people were dead, he let the Israelites go. Moses led them across the sea.

The escape was the beginning of a difficult journey back to their homeland. This journey is called the **Exodus,** or departure. Great stretches of desert wilderness separated the Israelites from their homeland. As the map on page 303 shows, the Israelites took a roundabout route. The Torah states that the trek to reach their homeland lasted 40 years. The Exodus is celebrated in the Jewish festival of Passover. Refer to A Closer Look on page 302. What parts of the Seder ceremony relate to Exodus experiences? ■

▲ *According to the Torah, a plague of locusts descended on Egypt, ruining crops.*

■ *Trace the origins of the Israelites.*

301

The Ancient Israelites

A Meal That Tells a Story

The Seder is a meal Jews eat during the springtime holiday of Passover. Every item on the table symbolizes part of the Passover story.

A roasted egg stands for spring as well as ancient holiday offerings.

A special bowl and pitcher are often part of the opening ceremonies of the Seder. The pitcher holds water used for a ritual washing of the hands.

Flat matza bread reminds Jews how quickly their ancestors left Egypt: they had no time to let bread dough rise.

Four cups of wine remind the drinker of the four promises God made to the Israelites.

When the temple stood in Jerusalem, priests sacrificed a lamb at Passover. The roasted bone symbolizes that ancient rite.

Like salty tears of slavery, a green vegetable dipped in salt water symbolizes the captivity and renewal of the Jewish people.

The sharp taste of bitter herbs (horseradish) recalls the bitterness of slavery.

A mixture of apples, honey, nuts, wine, and spices, Charoset stands for the mortar binding the bricks that the enslaved Jews baked for the Egyptians.

An Agreement with God

The Torah teaches that during the Exodus Moses climbed to the top of Mount Sinai, where God spoke to him and gave him a message to pass on to his people. This message was about a **covenant,** or special agreement, that would bind the Israelites to God. According to the covenant, God promised to love and protect the Israelites. In return, the Israelites agreed to love God and follow God's laws: "And now, O Israel, what does the Lord your God demand of you? Only this: to revere the Lord your God, to walk only in His paths, to love Him, and to serve the Lord your God with all your heart and soul." (Deuteronomy 10:12)

The Torah explains that ten important laws were engraved on two stone tablets that Moses carried down from Mount Sinai. These written laws are known as the Decalogue or the Ten Commandments:

> I the Lord am your God who brought you out of the land of Egypt, the house of bondage: You shall have no other gods besides Me.
>
> You shall not make for yourself a sculptured image. . . .
>
> You shall not swear falsely by the name of the Lord your God . . .
>
> Remember the sabbath day and keep it holy. . . .
>
> Honor your father and your mother, that you may long endure on the land that the Lord your God is assigning to you.
>
> You shall not murder.
>
> You shall not commit adultery.
>
> You shall not steal.
>
> You shall not bear false witness against your neighbor.
>
> You shall not covet [desire] . . . anything that is your neighbor's.
>
> Exodus 20: 3–14

By accepting the covenant, the Israelites accepted God as their king. They accepted the commandments as laws of God's kingdom.

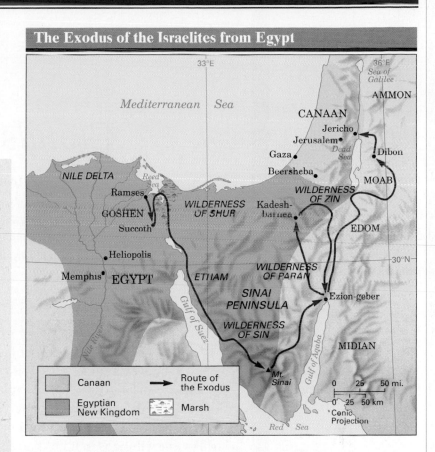

The Exodus of the Israelites from Egypt

In the centuries that followed, this religious idea of a covenant between a single God and a people would become the basis for both Judaism and Christianity. The Jewish and Christian belief that people serve God by acting responsibly toward each other can be traced directly to the special covenant made by the Israelites. In addition, the Ten Commandments form the basis of much of the Western world's ideas about law and justice. ■

▲ Today, scholars are not sure which mountain is Mt. Sinai. The map above shows the location of the mountain traditionally considered Mt. Sinai. Find it on the map.

■ Why did the Israelites agree to obey the Ten Commandments?

R E V I E W

1. **FOCUS** What role did the Israelites' relationship with God play in the formation of their nation?

2. **CONNECT** The Ten Commandments contained rules of conduct for the Israelites to follow. What teachings of Buddhism contained rules of conduct for Buddhists to follow?

3. **BELIEF SYSTEMS** Explain the covenant the Israelites made with God.

4. **CRITICAL THINKING** The Torah explains how the Israelites became a people and developed their belief in God. Why would this be important to historians?

5. **ACTIVITY** The land of ancient Israelites is now divided into several nations. Use the map on page 300 and the maps of the Time/Space Databank to find out what nations now occupy the land.

Clouds of Glory

Miriam Chaikin

Over the centuries, Jewish religious teachers pondered the meaning of the Bible. Sometimes their explanations of the Bible took the form of stories. These are called Midrash stories. The following excerpts are from the book, Clouds of Glory.

In Lesson 1 you read about Abraham. Now read a Midrash about him and his wife, Sarah.

vast large

rabbi Jewish religious teacher

motif a theme

prophet one of a group of people during biblical times who urged Israel to obey God

There is a vast body of Jewish literature that is little known even among Jews. It is called Midrash. The Hebrew word means "search and explain." Ancient rabbis, who originated the Midrash stories, believed that the Bible held the answer to all questions. "Turn it and turn it," they said of the Bible's pages. "For everything is in it." When something in the Bible puzzled them, they searched its pages for an answer.

The explanation they found is a Midrash—Midrashim in the plural.

The rabbis used Midrashim to teach the Bible and to enliven their sermons. They wove in folktale motifs and other story elements. They added to existing Midrashim, creating new ones. And the body of literature known as Midrash grew and grew.

A sample midrash concerns the story of Creation. The Bible tells that God made seas, heavens, lands, trees, plants, and animals. Someone wondered: "How did God make the heavens?"

The rabbis would have answered that this was not a human concern, that the secrets of heaven belong to God. All the same, they would have quoted the prophet Isaiah: "He stretched out the heavens as a curtain, and spread them out as a tent."

The answer is a Midrash. . . .

To qualify as a Midrash, a story must answer a question that the Bible raises, and it must be based on Bible teachings:

God created the universe and all life.
God created a wonderful world for people to enjoy.
God is goodness and wants us to be like him.

What is *goodness?* That question also generated many Midrashim:

Goodness is loving kindness.
Love your neighbor as yourself.
Do not do to others what you would not want them to do to you.

*Be thoughtful of the stranger, eyes for the blind, feet to the lame, care-
takers of the poor.*
Loving kindness should extend to animals as well.

---

*In this Midrash, Abraham is working in an idol shop in the city of Ur. The
Holy One mentioned at the beginning is God. Abraham and his wife Sarah turn
from idol worship and teach others what they know about the one God.*

*T*he Holy One had for so long refused to look at the
world. Now, hearing these words, he turned with
interest toward the world, sending his gaze
over Aram, over the city of Ur, and focusing on the idol shop. The
angels, following his gaze, looked with him and watched Abraham
rise from his stool to greet a customer.

"Peace be yours, Abraham," said the customer.

"And yours as well, my friend," Abraham said. "Is your planting over? Your cucumbers, are they in the ground?"

"They are," the farmer said. "I have done my part, but the goddess Asherah is not able to do hers."

"And why is that?" Abraham asked.

"The wind that came last night," the farmer said. "It knocked
her down. She lies in pieces, strewn across my field."

"It is a sad story," Abraham said.

It was an odd response and the farmer looked at him. "I did
not come for your sympathy, Abraham," he said. "I came for a new
goddess."

"To keep the crows away?" Abraham said.

The farmer again looked at him strangely. "To worship, so she
will grant me a good crop," he said.

Abraham went to the Asherahs lined up against the wall.
"Which of these would you like?"

The farmer pointed. "That one—"

"It was made this morning," Abraham said.

"This morning, last week, I don't care—" the farmer said, losing
patience.

"My friend," Abraham said. "You have been growing cucumbers for fifty years. Woe to you, if you think this day-old idol can
help you more than your own two hands."

The farmer became red in the face and left, and as he went out,
Plonit the widow came in shaking her head.

"What is this world coming to?" she said. "While I was at the
public baths, a thief entered my house and stole my god of protection. Give me a new one, Abraham."

"Good Plonit," Abraham said, "if the god couldn't protect itself from thieves, how can it protect you?"

Plonit was silent.

"Your god is made of clay," Abraham said. "It has a mouth but cannot speak, feet that cannot move, eyes that do not see. It is a dead thing. How can it help you?"

"There are gods," Plonit said. "A person must appeal to them, rely on them—"

"There is only one God," Abraham said. "One God who made heaven and earth and everything in between."

The words entered Plonit's heart. She stood looking at him. "Speak to me of your God," she said after a moment.

Abraham told her of his thoughts, the understanding that had come to him. When he was through speaking, the widow Plonit left without an idol. Watching her go, Abraham saw his parents returning up the lane. Sarah, he knew, had gone home to their tent at the edge of the city. Quickly, Abraham took a stick and went about the shop smashing idols. He left one standing, a large Baal, and put the stick in its hand.

When Terah and Emtelai entered, they were speechless. They stood looking at the floor, covered from end to end with broken idol parts—noses, limbs, chests, arms, heads.

"What is this?" Terah said.

Abraham nodded toward the standing Baal. "He did it," he said. "The idols began arguing about who was the most powerful. To show them who he was, he took a stick and smashed them to bits."

His parents glared at him.

"You fool in the world!" Terah said. "Idols can't argue. They can't hold sticks!"

"They can't do anything," Emtelai said.

"Father, Mother," Abraham said. "Do your ears hear what your mouth is saying?"

The silence that filled the room indicated that Terah and Emtelai had heard. Suddenly, they understood what Abraham and Sarah had been telling them about the one God.

The attention of heaven remained on Ur as Terah and Emtelai closed the idol shop, as the widow Plonit sealed up her home, and as all three went to help Abraham and Sarah in their tent at the edge of the city.

And what was this tent? A place known to travelers as the Tent of the Servants of God. It was a shelter where visitors arriving thirsty and dusty from the road could receive food and water. When the visitors were refreshed and said, "Thank you," a conversation opened up. And Abraham and Sarah began teaching about God.

"Do not thank us, thank God," they said. "The bread and water are his, he made them."

"How do you know this?"

seal to close

"The garment you wear, who made it?" they said. "A weaver, of course."

"How do you know this?" they said.

The travelers, understanding their meaning, said nothing.

"Open your eyes and you will see for yourself," they said. "Study the creatures, the fields and streams, the mountains and valleys, the woods and forests. They will help you see God. Ask the birds of the air, they will tell you. The plants of the earth, they will teach you."

The travelers, listening with interest, asked, "How do we thank him?"

"The food on your table comes from his earth. Thank him when you sit down to eat."

"Where is he, to hear us?"

"He is everywhere."

"No god can be everywhere."

"This God, the one God in heaven, can."

It was a hard thought. The travelers set it aside.

"What does he want of us?"

"He wants you to stop worshiping idols and to worship only him."

"The way we serve the idols, by animal sacrifice?"

"That is just a ceremony. He prefers another way."

"Which is?"

"Your actions. You worship him by being good."

"How does that serve him?"

"He wants to be in the world with us."

"If he can do all that you say, why can't he come down?"

"Our good deeds form an invisible ladder to heaven. On it, we rise up to meet him. On it, he comes down to meet us."

So it went, and so it went.

The amber rays of Glory sparkled merrily as the Holy One said to the angels, "These two are making me known on earth."

Further Reading

Angels, Prophets, Rabbis, and Kings from the Stories of the Jewish People. José Patterson. A collection of stories in the Bible, traditional Jewish legends from the earliest times, stories of the rabbis, and tales from the communities of medieval Europe.

Menorahs, Mezuzas, and Other Jewish Symbols. Miriam Chaikin. This book explains the history of many Jewish symbols and how they are used in holiday celebrations.

Miriam's Well: Stories About Women in the Bible. Alice Bach and J. Cheryl Exum. Thirteen stories give voices to some remarkable women.

L E S S O N   2

Kings, Prophets, and Priests

THINKING
FOCUS

How did Israel develop as an independent Jewish nation?

Key Terms

- prophet
- messiah

Day and night for 40 days, the giant Goliath shouted his challenge to the soldiers of Israel. According to the story told in the Bible, Goliath was the great warrior of the Philistines, a people who were fighting the Israelites for control of Canaan during the 1000s B.C. No one in the Israelite camp would accept Goliath's challenge to fight him. No one, that is, until a boy named David came into the camp.

David gathered five smooth stones, and put them in his leather bag. Then he went out to face the giant.

He said to Goliath, "You come against me with sword and spear and javelin; but I come against you in the name of the Lord of Hosts, the God of the armies of Israel. . . ." According to the Bible,

> **D**avid put his hand into the bag; he took out a stone and slung it. It struck the Philistine in the forehead; the stone sank into his forehead, and he fell face down on the ground. Thus David bested the Philistine with sling and stone; he struck him down and killed him.
>
> I Samuel 17:49–50

When the Philistines saw their warrior dead, they ran. The Israelites treated David as a hero. This young boy grew up to become a king of the Israelites.

➤ *In the time of David, slings and stones were common weapons. This stone carving illustrates the Bible story of David slaying Goliath.*

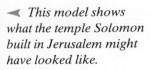

◄ This model shows what the temple Solomon built in Jerusalem might have looked like.

The Monarchy

The battle with the Philistines was one of many the Israelites fought with other peoples living in Canaan between the 1200s and the 1000s B.C. During this time, the Israelites formed a loose association of tribes in the central hill country of Canaan. However, the battles between the Israelites and other peoples for the control of Canaan convinced the Israelites that they needed a king to unite them and lead them.

Around 1020 B.C., the Israelites chose a man named Saul as their first king. Saul led the Israelites in the fight against the Philistines, but he was unable to defeat them. That job fell to David, who became the second king of the Israelites.

The Reign of David

David was 30 years old when he became king, and he governed Israel for 40 years. David brought together all the tribes of Israel. Under his leadership, the Israelites were finally able to defeat the Philistines. They also captured the city of Jerusalem and made it the capital of the Israelite nation. The Israelite empire grew to include land from the Sinai Peninsula as far east as Damascus.

David began a dynasty that lasted for more than 400 years. According to the Bible, the dynasty fulfilled a pledge God made to David: "I will establish a home for My people Israel and will plant them firm, so that they shall dwell secure and shall tremble no more." (II Samuel 7: 10–11)

When David died in 961 B.C., his son Solomon came to power. During Solomon's rule the kingdom was at peace. Solomon showed his skill as a diplomat by making treaties with the pharaoh of Egypt and other rulers. These treaties assured Israel's safety.

Solomon also found new trading partners so that the Israelites could increase the country's wealth. Finally, he began a royal building program, constructing a temple and many palaces and forts throughout the land.

A Temple for Jerusalem

Solomon's most famous building project was the main temple in Jerusalem. The temple became the center of religious life for the

Across Time & Space

Over the centuries, the land of the Israelites has gone by many names. Many different powers have ruled it. The present nation of Israel was formed in 1948. It covers most of the land that made up the kingdoms of Judah and Israel in the 900s B.C.

309

The Ancient Israelites

Israelites and a symbol of their faith. The Bible tells of the great beauty of the temple. Cedar beams specially brought from Lebanon held up the roof. Ivory covered the outer doors. Gold decorated the walls of the holiest rooms.

When Solomon died in 922 B.C., Israel was a much stronger nation. But its growth had put a burden of heavy taxes on the people. These taxes were needed to pay for the building projects. King Solomon also required the men of Israel to work on the buildings without pay.

Two Kingdoms

People began to resent the burden the king placed upon them. After Solomon's death, this resentment turned into revolt. The tribes in the northern part of Israel chose their own king and later moved their capital to Samaria.

The land of the Israelites was divided into two kingdoms. The northern kingdom continued to be known as Israel. The southern kingdom, with its capital city Jerusalem, was renamed Judah. (The word "Jew" comes from the name Judah.)

Because the temple was there, Jerusalem remained an important city. The two kingdoms were divided politically, but they remained united by their religion.

The two kingdoms existed side by side for about 200 years. Then both fell to foreign powers. The Assyrians conquered Israel in 721 B.C. and invaded Judah. In 586 B.C., Judah fell to the Babylonians. ■

■ *What caused Israel to be divided into two kingdoms?*

The Message of the Prophets

The Babylonians not only took control of Judah but destroyed the entire city of Jerusalem and the temple. About 15,000 Jews were taken away to Babylonia as prisoners.

At this point, the future of the Israelites looked very bleak. Had the God of the Israelites abandoned the chosen people? According to a remarkable group of men known as the prophets, the answer to this question was no.

The **prophets,** who interpreted the will of God, told the Jews that they had only themselves to blame. The Jews had failed to obey God's teachings—they had broken their covenant with God.

The prophets were not fortune tellers who predicted the future. They preached a message about how the people should act in the present and warned that God would punish greed, unfairness to others, and worship of other gods.

➤ *The French artist Jean Fouquet painted this version of the destruction of Jerusalem by the Babylonians. The painting dates from the A.D. 1400s.*

Jeremiah, one of the better-known prophets, preached during the time that the Babylonians conquered Judah. Jeremiah urged the Jews to change their ways, telling them that God declares:

> *If you do not oppress the stranger, the orphan, and the widow; if you do not shed the blood of the innocent in this place; if you do not follow other gods, to your own hurt—then only will I let you dwell in this place, in the land that I gave to your fathers for all time.*
>
> Jeremiah 7:6–7

According to the prophets, the people did not heed the warning. As a result, the Jews were exiled from the promised land when the Babylonians conquered them.

However, by accepting the prophets' explanation for the disaster, the Jews could keep their faith in God and survive exile. In this way, the prophets offered hope for the future. They preached that if the Jews obeyed the laws of God, they would someday be able to return to their homeland. The Jews came to believe that God alone controls all nations and directs the course of history. ■

■ *According to the prophets, why was Judah captured by Babylonia?*

A People Governed by Priests

The exile of the Jews in Babylon lasted about 50 years. Then in 540 B.C., the Persian ruler Cyrus the Great took control of Babylon.

Cryus allowed the Jews in Babylon to return to Judah. However, the Jews were not allowed to rule their homeland. Jerusalem and the surrounding territory remained a province of the Persian empire.

Without a king of their own, the leadership of the Jewish people fell to their priests. They saw to it that the great temple of Jerusalem was rebuilt. These priests, called *kohanim (ko HA neem)*, inherited their position from their fathers and could marry. They guided the people in celebrating religious holidays and in following Jewish law. The Jews used their religious beliefs to govern themselves.

The Formation of the Torah

In the 400s B.C., a priest and scribe named Ezra returned from exile in Babylon. He brought with him a collection of the many versions of holy writings that had been put together by Jewish scribes in Babylon. This document was the Torah, the sacred history and laws of the Israelite people. The Torah contains the five books of Genesis, Exodus, Leviticus, Numbers, and Deuteronomy, which then became what is today the first part of the Jewish Bible.

Some Jews believe that the entire Torah came from God in the exact words in which it is written today. Others believe that over the centuries people wrote down what they understood to be God's messages. Ezra then edited these documents into what is now the Torah. Jews believe that the Torah is God's will for humanity. *Torah* is a Hebrew word that can be translated as "instruction." The Torah defines Israel's relationship with God. It gives Israel's obligations to love and serve God and

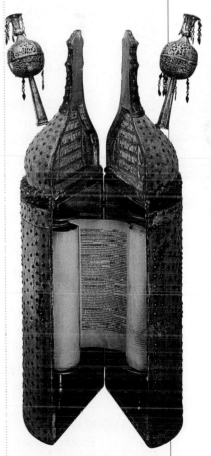

▲ *Ancient scribes copied the Torah onto scrolls.*

As a sign of devotion to God and of obedience to God's commandments, some Jewish men wear phylacteries during their weekday morning prayers. These are cases that contain Torah texts. They are strapped to the arm and the forehead.

tells of God's love and care for His children, such as in the following passage:

> "The beloved of the Lord shall dwell in safety by Him; Ever does He protect him, as he rests between His shoulders."
>
> Deuteronomy 33:12

The Torah brought back by Ezra became the accepted version of Judaism's holiest writings. With the backing of the Persian authorities, Erza demanded that the Jews obey the Torah and separate themselves from the people who did not. From the 400s B.C., Judaism was defined by obediance to the Torah.

The Torah was a written

UNDERSTANDING LAW

When Ezra, the priest and scribe, returned to Jerusalem from exile in Babylon in the 400s B.C., he carried with him a letter from the King of Persia. The letter told Ezra's duty: "For you are commissioned by the king and his seven advisers to regulate Judah and Jerusalem according to the law of your God, which is in your care." (Ezra 7: 14)

All societies establish laws to govern themselves. The authority may come from a supreme leader or from the people. In most societies, an important part of law is a sense of justice, or fairness.

What Is Law?

Every society or group of people needs to establish customs, rules, and patterns of accepted behavior. Law is the set of guidelines a group of people or society uses to govern itself.

However, law is more than just individual rules. Law is a code of conduct for a group of people. The law of the Torah established the religious and social rules by which the Jews governed themselves. The law code of a nation establishes the rules governing both the rights and obligations of its people.

Who Makes Laws?

In early societies, laws often came from the authority of the king or ruler. One of the early written codes was Hammurabi's code. This was a set of rules of behavior and punishments established by the Babylonian king Hammurabi in the 1700s B.C. The Jews believed that the law of the Torah came from the authority of God, whom the Jews accepted as their king.

In the United States today, federal, state, and local officials elected by the people have the power to make laws. The courts have the power to review laws and even change them to make sure they are just. The courts also decide the punishments for breaking laws.

What Is Justice?

Today, most people agree that laws should be just—they should be applied in a way that treats people fairly. The law of the Torah played an important role in establishing the ideal of justice. In the book of Leviticus, judges are told that they "must not make an unfair decision. Do not favor the poor or show deference to the rich. Judge your neighbor fairly." (Leviticus 19: 15)

document, but it also had a rich oral tradition. Religious teachers and the scribes who copied the scrolls of the Torah pondered its teachings. Through preaching and discussions this oral tradition grew. At a much later date, it too, became a written document.

The Hope for a Messiah

In the 400s B.C., the Jews had both the Torah and a rebuilt temple to help them guide their faith. However, they did not have their independence. Many Jews hoped that one day Israel would again be an independent nation, as it had been during the time of King David.

The Jews continued to govern themselves by the laws of the Torah for about 200 years, even though the Persians and then the Egyptians were their overlords. Then around 200 B.C., new rulers from Syria took over Israel. Many Jews yearned for a leader who would free them from foreign rule. The name they gave this hoped-for leader was **messiah** (*muh SY uh*), which means "anointed one." As

far back as the time of the prophets, the Jews had spoken of the Messiah. They believed the Messiah would bring universal peace and justice. The prophet Isaiah wrote about this universal peace: "Nation shall not lift up sword against nation, neither shall they learn war any more." (Isaiah 2:4) The idea that a messiah would someday come, free the people and bring world peace, became a part of Jewish belief. ■

▲ Jews examine a Torah scroll in Jerusalem, near the site of the original temple.

■ *How was the Torah of central importance to the Jews?*

The Revolt of the Maccabees

The Syrians who ruled Israel brought ideas with them from the Greek culture that had flourished for centuries in the countries across the Mediterranean Sea.

Some Jews admired Greek culture and learned to speak Greek. They gave themselves Greek names. Some even accepted Greek religious ideas.

Many other Jews, especially highly religious Jews, rejected Greek religious beliefs. Religious Jews did not object to Syrian rule, but they did not want Syrian rulers

to interfere in Jewish religious practices.

In 175 B.C., a new ruler, Antiochus (*ahn TEE uh kuhs*), came to power in Syria. Antiochus forced Jews to adopt Greek customs. He outlawed the study of the Torah. Officers of the Syrian king went throughout the land ordering Jewish priests to make offerings to the Greek gods.

However, a Jewish priest named Mattathias refused. He and his five sons fled into the hills of Judah to organize a revolt. Many

313

> *When the Jews dedicated the temple after defeating the Syrians, they only had enough oil to light their holy lamps for one day. Yet according to tradition, the lamps burned for eight days. Today, during the festival of Chanukah, Jews light the candles of the menorah to celebrate this event.*

■ *What was the result of the revolt of the Maccabees?*

Jews joined the fight, hoping for a chance to free their land from foreign rule and gain independence. Led by Mattathias's son Judah Maccabee, the rebels fought a two-year war against the Syrian soldiers.

The word *Maccabee* means "hammer." Like hammers, Judah Maccabee and his followers were hard-hitting fighters. They were known as the Maccabees. They used hit-and-run tactics against the Syrians. The Maccabees attacked in the dark and set fire to Syrian camps. They hid themselves behind rocks and jumped down on the Syrians as they came through narrow paths in the hills.

In 164 B.C., the Maccabees drove the Syrians out of the area around Jerusalem. The reign of the Torah was restored. The Jews had control of their temple once again.

The temple in Jerusalem was rededicated with a special service in December of 164 B.C. Since that time, Jews everywhere have celebrated the victory of Maccabean rebels on the eight-day festival known as Chanukah *(HAH nuh kuh).* ■

R E V I E W

1. FOCUS How did Israel develop as an independent Jewish nation?

2. CONNECT Why did King Nebuchadnezzar of Babylonia conquer Judah in 586 B.C. and force the Jews into exile?

3. BELIEF SYSTEMS The prophets said that the Jews had broken their covenant with God. Summarize the things the Jews needed to do to return to their homeland.

4. HISTORY How did the Maccabees defeat the Syrians?

5. CRITICAL THINKING The land of the Jews was conquered by several foreign powers. Why was Judaism able to survive and prosper?

6. WRITING ACTIVITY Imagine you were with the Jews when they were conquered by the Babylonians and forced into exile. Write a journal entry describing what it is like to be forced to live away from your homeland.

L E S S O N   3

Religious Developments

T here was a man who had two sons," the story goes. The younger son left his father's house for a distant country. There he wasted the money his father gave him, got a miserable job feeding pigs, almost starved, and finally wanted to go home. When his father saw him returning, he ran to meet him. He planned a big celebration. Meanwhile, the older son was jealous because no one had ever given him a party. He complained to his father who told him, "My child, you have always been with me, and all that is mine is yours. But we had to be merry and rejoice, for this brother of yours was dead and has begun to live, and was lost and has been found." (Luke 15:31,32)

THINKING FOCUS

How are Judaism and Christianity related?

Key Terms

- parable
- disciple
- Resurrection
- Christianity
- diaspora
- rabbi
- synagogue

◄ *The teacher called Jesus is shown spreading his message in this Italian painting from the A.D. 1400s. There are no paintings of Jesus from the time in which he lived.*

315

➤ *Many artists have represented what Jesus may have looked like. This mosaic, from A.D. 1148, is inside the apse of the cathedral in Cefalu in northern Sicily.*

Across Time & Space

The New Testament was written in Greek, between A.D. 50 and 100. The Gospels, or first four books of the New Testament, give the life and teachings of Jesus. Gospel means "good news" in Greek. The rest of the New Testament contains the history and teachings of the early Christian Church. The New Testament, together with the Jewish Bible, which Christians know as the Old Testament, form the Christian Bible.

This story comes from the New Testament of the Christian Bible. It is a **parable**, a story that teaches a moral and spiritual lesson. In the first century A.D., a Jewish teacher named Jesus told this parable of the Prodigal Son. (Prodigal means reckless and wasteful.) Jesus used the lessons in his many parables— like the two sons who learn about their father's great love—to teach about the Kingdom of God. What Jesus said about the forgiveness of sins and the equality of rich and poor in God's sight were welcome news to many listeners. In time, his ideas and the events of his life would grow into a new religion.

The Life of Jesus

The story of the life, deeds, and teachings of Jesus is told in the New Testament of the Bible. Followers of Jesus today study the New Testament as a record inspired by God of the events in Jesus' life. Historians use the New Testament to help them understand the origin and beliefs of a new religion.

According to the New Testament, an angel appeared to a woman named Mary in the city of Nazareth about 2,000 years ago. The angel told her that she would have a child. The angel told Mary to name the child Jesus.

Mary and her husband Joseph were Jews, and when Jesus was born they raised him as a Jew. Jesus learned the laws and customs of Judaism and studied the Torah.

There is not much about Jesus' childhood in the New Testament, but it does say that Mary found him discussing religion with the elders in the temple at Jerusalem at the age of 12. When asked why he was there, Jesus told his mother that he was doing the work of his Father. Jesus called God his Father.

The Teachings of Jesus

Some of Jesus' teachings were based on traditional Jewish law. For example, he put special emphasis on two great rules in the Torah, "Love the Lord your God" and "Love your neighbor as yourself."

One subject came up again and again in Jesus' preaching: the Kingdom of God. His listeners knew he was talking about God's power over all creation and God's final victory over evil in the world. Jesus' new message was that his life and actions were the sign that God's kingdom was already at hand.

Jesus taught a sermon that has since been named the Sermon on the Mount. In it, he described what the Kingdom of God is like. Jesus began the sermon with the following list of blessings, known as the Beatitudes:

According to the New Testament, Jesus healed the sick and performed miracles to demonstrate the power of God.

> **B**lessed are the poor in spirit, for theirs is the kingdom of heaven.
> Blessed are those who mourn, for they will be comforted.
> Blessed are the meek, for they will inherit the earth.
> Blessed are those who hunger and thirst for righteousness, for they will be filled.
> Blessed are the merciful, for they will be shown mercy.
> Blessed are the pure in heart, for they will see God.
> Blessed are the peacemakers, for they will be called sons of God.
> Blessed are those who are persecuted because of righteousness, for theirs is the kingdom of heaven.
>
> Matthew 5: 3–10

There are many stories in the Gospels, the first four books of the New Testament, that tell how Jesus performed wonders as signs of God's kingdom. One day, after Jesus spoke to a gathering of 5,000 hungry people, he fed them all with only five loaves of bread and two fish. Jesus took the loaves and the fish, blessed them, broke them, and told his disciples to give them to the crowd. After everyone ate, they collected what was left over—enough to fill 12 baskets.

Jesus said that he had come to save humanity. He preached that God's gift of salvation made it possible for people to give up sin and gain eternal life.

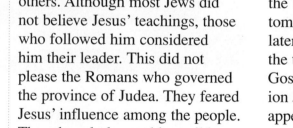

Jesus ate a final meal called the Last Supper with his disciples. The chalice, or cup, like the one used by Jesus in the Last Supper (below), is today used in some Christian services.

■ *What did Jesus teach about the kingdom of God?*

Roman Rule

During the lifetime of Jesus, Judah was governed by the Romans. Rome had conquered Judah in 63 B.C. and made it a Roman province, which it called Judea *(joo Dee uh)*. It was a time of unrest. Many different religious groups looked for solutions to the problems of their day. The Jews hoped that one day Judea would be independent. One radical religious group hoped to revolt and overthrow the Romans. Other Jewish religious leaders urged their followers instead to obey the laws of the Torah and to depend on God's help.

Jesus, too, formed a group of followers. His twelve closest followers, called **disciples**, traveled with him as he taught.

Jesus interpreted Judaism in a specific way, teaching some points and disagreeing with others. Although most Jews did not believe Jesus' teachings, those who followed him considered him their leader. This did not please the Romans who governed the province of Judea. They feared Jesus' influence among the people. They thought he could possibly lead the Jews in a revolt against Roman rule.

The Origins of Christianity

Finally, in about A.D. 33, Jesus' opponents acted. Jesus and his disciples came to Jerusalem to celebrate the Jewish festival of Passover. According to the New Testament, people gathered and cheered Jesus as he entered the city. Nevertheless, he was arrested just after he ate the traditional Passover meal. According to the New Testament, Jesus' opponents took him before the Roman governor, Pontius Pilate. They said Jesus claimed to be king of the Jews. They charged him with treason against Rome. Pilate ordered that Jesus be put to death. He was crucified—nailed to a cross and left to die—by Roman guards, according to Roman custom. Jesus said while on the cross, "Father, forgive them, for they know not what they do."

The New Testament says that the body of Jesus was placed in a tomb of solid rock. Three days later, however, a woman returned to the tomb and found it empty. The Gospels say that after his crucifixion Jesus rose from the dead and appeared to his disciples. This event is called the **Resurrection**. It convinced the disciples that Jesus was the Son of God. They spread the gospel, or "good news," about Jesus and his teachings.

In the New Testament, Jesus is given the title *Christ*. Christ is the Greek word for messiah. The religion based on the teachings of Jesus is called **Christianity**. The New Testament says that on a day called Pentecost, Jesus' disciples were filled with the Holy Spirit. On that day thousands of people began following the new religion. You will read about how Christianity spread in Chapter 15. ■

Origins of Religious Observances

Religion	Event	Observance
Judaism	Creation of the World Rededication of the Temple Exodus of Israelites from Egypt Revelation to Moses of the Ten Commandments	Rosh Hashanah Chanukah Passover Shavuot
Christianity	Birth of Jesus Crucifixion of Jesus Resurrection of Jesus Descent of the Holy Spirit	Christmas Good Friday Easter Pentecost

◄ *Present-day Jewish and Christian religious observances can be traced to events of biblical times.*

Judaism in the First Century

The death of Jesus was an important event in the history of Christianity, but it went largely unnoticed by the Roman rulers of Judea. To them, Jesus was one of thousands who were killed to keep the Jews from revolting.

The Revolt Against the Romans

In A.D. 66, a group of Jews called Zealots *(ZEHL uhts)* rebelled against Roman rule. Like the Maccabees two centuries earlier, they used hit-and-run tactics against the Romans. They drove out the Romans for a time, but the Romans fought back.

When the fighting spread to Jerusalem, Roman leaders took strong steps to bring the Jews under control. A general named Titus came to Jerusalem with 60,000 soldiers and the most modern weapons of the time. The Jewish troops that opposed him numbered only about 25,000.

Although the Jews were outnumbered, they put up a strong fight. When Titus and his army marched on Jerusalem, the Jews inside the city walls held out for five months. But finally, in August of A.D. 70, the city fell.

The Romans burned down the temple and destroyed the city. All that remained was the Western Wall of the temple area. Jews still go to the Western Wall to mourn the destruction of their temple and to mark their attachment to this ancient, holy site.

The Fall of Masada

Three more years passed before the Romans could conquer the other centers of Jewish resistance. The last fort to fall was Masada *(muh SAH duh)*. Perched atop a 1,400-foot-tall rock on the edge of the Judean desert, Masada could not be attacked easily.

The Romans discovered that they could not climb the steep sides of the rock. Instead, they spent seven months building a ramp of wood and earth up to the fort.

Throughout one night, Roman soldiers battered the wall of the fort again and again with their battering ram.

According to Jewish tradition, the wall came crashing down early in the morning. However, the crash was followed by an eerie silence.

What the soldiers saw inside was a horrifying sight: 960 men,

■ *Why did the Romans attack Masaada?*

women, and children lay dead inside the fort. As a final act of resistance, they had killed themselves.

The Great Revolt had ended. Jerusalem was in ruins, and the temple was destroyed. Many Jews were taken by the Romans to other parts of the empire to work as slaves. The word used for the scattering of Jewish settlements by force is **diaspora** *(dy AS pur ah).*

The Jews revolted once again in A.D. 132, but the power of the Roman Empire was too strong. After three years, the Romans crushed the Jewish resistance. After this last revolt, the Romans prohibited Jews from living in Jerusalem, though many Jews remained in the city. ■

The Jewish Legacy

The battles with the Romans left the Jews without their temple, their priests, and their homeland. Yet the Jewish people did not disappear from history as some other ancient peoples had. The Jews adapted to their new situation.

Wherever Jews settled, they kept their religion by relying on the Torah. The Torah was their reassurance that God was wherever they found themselves, for they could study the word of God anywhere.

They also had **rabbis** to teach them the Torah. Rabbi is the Hebrew word for master or teacher.

Beginning about the first century A.D., this title was given to teachers of the Torah. Over time, a rabbi came to mean someone who could decide questions of Jewish law.

As Jews settled in other lands, rabbis helped them continue to learn about and practice Jewish traditions. Rabbis were leaders of the community as well. They settled arguments and taught people how to treat each other fairly according to the laws of the Torah. Some of the rabbis' wisdom was collected and written down. For example,

Simon the Just said: "The world rests upon three things: on study of the Torah, on service of God, and on deeds of love. (*Ethics of the Fathers 1:2*)

In addition to relying on the Torah and the rabbis, the Jews built **synagogues**, the Jewish houses of worship. After the destruction of the temple in Jerusalem, the synagogue became the center of Jewish religious and community life. In their new homelands, Jews made the synagogue a place for social gatherings as well as religious worship.

Because the rabbis of this period were so important, the form of Judaism that began in the first century is called rabbinic Judaism.

Over many centuries rabbis had explained the meaning of the Torah. Around the year A.D. 200, rabbis took all of the oral tradition that had been passed from rabbi to student since the time of Moses and wrote the *Mishnah*. Then oral commentaries began on the Mishnah. The Mishnah plus its commentaries make up the *Talmud*. Rabbi Hillel, one of the most important rabbis, wrote in the Talmud:

> *What is hateful to yourself, do not do to anybody else. That is the whole of the Torah. All the rest is commentary."*
>
> Talmud, Shabbat 31a

The Torah and the Talmud have guided traditional Jewish belief and practice up to the present day.

Even though the Jewish people did not have a homeland after the Romans defeated them, their religion did not die out and they always believed that they would return to their homeland. By relying on the Torah and the teachings of the rabbis, the Jews developed ways of practicing their religion and ideas of social justice that are still ongoing today. ■

■ *How did the Jewish religion survive after the Roman attacks?*

▼ *Trace the early history of the Jewish people.*

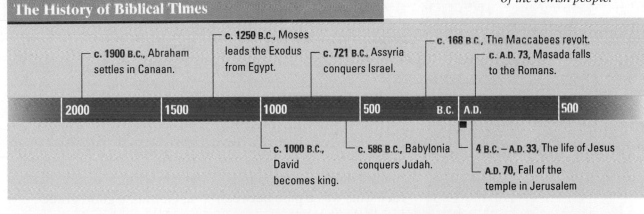

The History of Biblical Times

- c. 1900 B.C., Abraham settles in Canaan.
- c. 1250 B.C., Moses leads the Exodus from Egypt.
- c. 721 B.C., Assyria conquers Israel.
- c. 168 B.C., The Maccabees revolt.
- c. A.D. 73, Masada falls to the Romans.

2000 | 1500 | 1000 | 500 | B.C. | A.D. | 500

- c. 1000 B.C., David becomes king.
- c. 586 B.C., Babylonia conquers Judah.
- 4 B.C. – A.D. 33, The life of Jesus
- A.D. 70, Fall of the temple in Jerusalem

R E V I E W

1. **FOCUS** How are Judaism and Christianity related?
2. **CONNECT** How did Egyptian rule over the Israelites compare to Roman rule over the Jews?
3. **BELIEF SYSTEMS** The Jewish people did not disappear from history after the Romans put down the Jewish revolts. Summarize the ways the Jews kept their religion alive.

4. **CRITICAL THINKING** Why were Roman leaders more concerned with Jesus' power as a leader than with his religious teachings?
5. **ACTIVITY** Imagine you are a television reporter covering the Roman assault on Masada. Prepare a news report on this event. Be sure to answer the questions who, what, when, where, why, and how.

The Ancient Israelites

Using Analogies

Here's Why

Sometimes the best way of explaining something is to compare it to something else, more familiar. When you compare two things that have something in common but are otherwise quite different, you are using an analogy.

Jesus, like many other wise teachers before and since, often used analogies to make a point. His parables were more easily understood when he compared the unfamiliar with the familiar. By learning about analogies you will more quickly uncover their messages. You will also be able to use analogies yourself, to make your points more effectively.

Here's How

Jesus sometimes told people who came to hear him that if they wanted to become one of his followers they would have to sell all that they owned. On one occasion, he said:

> Truly I say to you, it will be hard for a rich man to enter the kingdom of heaven. Again I tell you, it is easier for a camel to go through the eye of a needle than for a rich man to enter the kingdom of God.
>
> Matthew 19:23-24

The "eye of a needle" to which Jesus referred was actually a land formation in Israel. This was a pass between two rocks that was so narrow that camels had to be unloaded before they could squeeze through. Jesus was not saying that rich men and camels were alike. But a rich man, like the camel, had to be willing to give up some things in order to enter heaven.

Try It

If you wanted to make a similar point now, how would you express it? What analogy could you use instead of a camel? How would you replace the "eye of the needle"?

Here is another analogy, this time from Hebrew scriptures:

> Like a loose tooth and an unsteady leg, Is a treacherous support in time of trouble.
>
> Proverbs 25:19

What is the analogy used here? What things are being compared? How would you make the same point if you were talking to one of your friends today?

Apply It

Write some analogies of your own, and be prepared to read them to the class. In each case use for your comparison something that your classmates will understand. Begin with these:

1. Getting a good grade when you've cheated on an exam is like _____ .
2. An unfaithful friend is like _____ .
3. A kind word on a sad day is like _____ .
4. Not doing the best you can is like _____ .
5. Missing the school bus is like _____ .

Using Constructive Criticism

Here's Why

Have your feelings ever been hurt because of something critical someone has said to you? Sometimes the criticism is well-intended, but it hurts because of the way it is said.

In school you and your classmates are often asked to present your work to the rest of the class. How can you comment on other people's work without hurting their feelings? Learning to give constructive criticism will help you.

Here's How

If you try hard enough, you can usually find something good to say about anyone's presentation. Suppose you are listening while another student presents a report. Listen carefully and try to comment on what the student has done well. If you can't think of anything to say, use the checklist in the box above to help you.

Sometimes, to be truthful, you need to point out something that is wrong with another person's work. Perhaps a good friend asks you to read a report before handing it in. How do you handle that?

One thing to remember is to always criticize the work, not the person.

1. Facts are accurate.
2. Speaker spoke clearly, without hesitation.
3. Speaker looked directly at the audience while speaking.
4. Ideas were creative and original.
5. The idea worked for me!

Another is to focus first on what is good about the work. (Study the list in the box again for suggestions.) If you start with something positive, then the negative things you have to say won't be so difficult to hear. In fact, your friend will probably thank you for your help.

Try It

Take your turn at presenting your analogies to the class and at reviewing the analogies of the others. When it is your turn to review others, use the suggestions in the box or use your own words to say something positive about each person.

Apply It

Keep a diary during a 24-hour period at home and at school. Write down every time you say something constructive about a person. What reactions did you get? Were your family and friends pleased? Did your constructive criticism help others?

Chapter Review

Reviewing Key Terms

Christianity (p. 318)
covenant (p.302)
diaspora (p. 320)
disciple (p. 318)
Exodus (p.301)
Judaism (p. 299)
messiah (p.313)

monotheism (p. 299)
parable (p. 316)
prophet (p. 310)
rabbi (p. 320)
Resurrection (p. 318)
synagogue (p. 321)

Some of the following statements are true. The rest are false. Write *True* or *False* for each statement. Then rewrite the false statements to make them true.

1. People who practice Judaism believe in monotheism.
2. The story of the Exodus tells how Abraham led his people from Canaan to Egypt.
3. In a covenant with God, the Jewish people promised not to worship other gods.
4. A prophet was an Israelite who revolted against his or her captors.
5. The Jews waited for a leader they called the messiah, or anointed one.
6. All those Jews who were taken by force and scattered make up the diaspora.
7. Rabbis were priests appointed by Moses.
8. The synagogue was the sacred place that was destroyed by the Romans in A.D. 70.
9. Christianity began with Jesus' disciples telling of his resurrection.
10. A parable teaches a moral and spiritual lesson.

Exploring Concepts

A. Copy the cause-and-effect chart on your own paper. For each effect, add the correct cause from the list below the chart.

Cause	Effect
The Israelites could not survive as separate groups fighting against stonger enemies.	The Israelites chose Saul to be their king.
	Priests became the leaders of the Jews.
	The Romans put down the Jewish rebellion.
	The Jews settled in areas outside of Israel.

Causes
 a. Under the Persian Empire, the Jews could not have their own king.
 b. The Roman forces greatly outnumbered the Jews and were too well armed.
 c. As separate groups fighting against strong enemies, the Israelites could not survive.
 d. The Jews were exiled from their homeland.

B. Answer each question below with the information you have gained from reading the chapter.

1. Explain how the Jews got their freedom from any two of their captors.
2. When and how did the Torah come into being? What was its importance from that point on?
3. Describe the accomplishments of three different leaders of the Jews before Roman times.
4. Describe how the concepts of law, justice, and love are related within Judaism.
5. Describe the importance of the Talmud to Jewish belief.

Reviewing Skills

1. Explain this analogy from a speech by Jesus called the "Sermon on the Mount":

> Enter by the narrow gate; for the gate is wide and the way is easy, that leads to destruction, and those who enter by it are many. For the gate is narrow and the way is hard, that leads to life, and those who find it are few.
>
> Matthew 7:13–14

2. Your best friend asks you to look at her science project on frogs. The presentation is good but very messy. What do you say?

3. Look at the map of Jerusalem on pages 492 and 493 of the Minipedia. Find the fortress and the road leading away from the fortress. What does that suggest to you about the enemies of Jerusalem? Were they more likely to be from Gaza, Jericho, or Bethlehem? Why do you think so?

4. Now look at the walls on the map. Where do you think the earliest city of Jerusalem was located? Compare the houses on either side of the Theater and its wall. What hypothesis might you make about the people who lived in each area?

5. Suppose you wanted to present a comparison of the Revolt of the Maccabees and the Revolt of A.D. 66. In your presentation, you would like to show the differences clearly. What would be the best way to do it?

Using Critical Thinking

1. In most major religions, there are groups of people who share the same basic beliefs but differ as to how scriptures and laws should be interpreted. Why do you think such groups arise?

2. Passover is a Jewish tradition not commonly observed by Christians today. Yet the events celebrated at Passover, as well as the celebration itself, are part of Christian tradition. Explain why both the story and the observance of Passover are important in Christian history.

Preparing for Citizenship

1. **WRITING ACTIVITY** When the word *exodus* is not capitalized, it refers to large numbers of people leaving an area. Examples of exoduses include the migrations of southern black people to northern cities, of Vietnamese "boat people" to the United States, and of eastern Europeans to the West in the 1980s. Learn all you can about an exodus. Then write a paragraph about it.

2. **WRITING ACTIVITY** Write an imaginary diary entry for a boy or girl who might have lived in Canaan, Israel, or Judah during the time period covered by the chapter. The entry should cover one day. It can be about an important event as seen through that boy or girl's eyes, or it can be about daily life. Give the entry a specific date.

3. **COLLABORATIVE LEARNING** Make a class bulletin board on the history and culture of the Jews from their beginnings around 1900 B.C. up to A.D. 400. To do this, form four to seven groups. Each group should then decide what to contribute to the bulletin board. For example, your group might work on the Hebrew calendar, language and writing, the Temple, King David, King Solomon, or dates and events. After each group has decided what to contribute, work as a whole class to plan the entire bulletin board. Then each group should complete its part of the bulletin board. For a look at Jerusalem see pages 492 and 493 in the Minipedia, and for important dates refer to the chapter.

Chapter 11

The Ancient Greeks

The blue waters of the Aegean Sea and the rugged mountains rising from its shores helped shape the civilization of the ancient Greeks. The mountains and the sea divided Greece into separate city-states. Shared customs and backgrounds drew these communities together. But at times bitter rivalries tore them apart.

c. 2000–1450 B.C. The Minoan civilization prospers on the island of Crete. The Minoans used golden axes like this one in religious ceremonies.

2500	2000	1500

2500 B.C.

c. 1450–1100 B.C. The Mycenaeans, the first mainland Greek civilization, conquer the Minoans and rule the Aegean region.

Spartan warriors march into battle on this vase, painted about 640 B.C.

Steep mountains limited travel on land, as this map from a later period shows. The Greeks turned to the sea instead.

c. 500 B.C. The city-state Athens, named after the Greek goddess Athena, develops the world's first democracy. Athena, shown above, was the goddess of warfare and wisdom.

1000	500	B.C.	A.D.

c. 700 B.C. Sparta becomes one of the most powerful city-states in Greece.

479 B.C.

The Early Greeks

> *B*ut come now, put it for me clearly, tell me the sea ways that you wandered, and the shores you touched; the cities, and the men therein, uncivilized, if such there were, and hostile, and those god-fearing who had kindly manners.
>
> Homer, the *Odyssey*, c. 700 B.C.

THINKING FOCUS

What were some of the forces that influenced the rise of civilization in ancient Greece?

Key Term

- city-state

An ancient king made this request of a great Greek hero named Odysseus *(oh DIHS yoos)*, according to the *Odyssey*, an early masterpiece of Greek literature. The *Odyssey* retells the legends of the travels and adventures of Odysseus 3,000 years ago.

For 10 years, Odysseus wandered among the islands and coastal regions of what is now Greece, according to the tale. He endured shipwrecks, escaped from strange creatures such as a one-eyed giant called a cyclops, and met a variety of strange and wonderful people. Finally, he found his way back to his home.

These tales are just part of the rich heritage of the Greeks, a people who have had a lasting impact on Western civilization. Many present-day concepts of government, art, literature, science, and ideas can be traced to the ancient Greeks.

➤ *The ancient Greeks sailed in warships like the one shown on this vase painting. Note the soldiers' shields displayed above the oars.*

The Land Around the Sea

According to the *Odyssey*, Odysseus wandered throughout the region known today as the Aegean *(ih JEE uhn)* Sea. He was seeking to return to his home in Ithaca after fighting in the Trojan War. Find the Aegean Sea and Ithaca on the map below. What do you notice about the geography of the region?

The Geography of Greece

The area in which the ancient Greeks lived was centered on the Aegean. Between the 2000s B.C. and 100 B.C., these people developed a civilization there that grew to control the ancient world. Although many people settled on the peninsula called the Peloponnesus *(pehl oh puh NEE suhs)*, others settled on the numerous islands sprinkled throughout the Aegean.

The rugged mountains and the bays and inlets of the seas divided Greece into many small, isolated regions. The people who settled in each region formed closely knit communities. Sometimes neighboring groups became bitter enemies. At various times in Greek

▲ *The blue water of the Aegean Sea along the coast of Samos is shown above. Find Samos on the map below.*

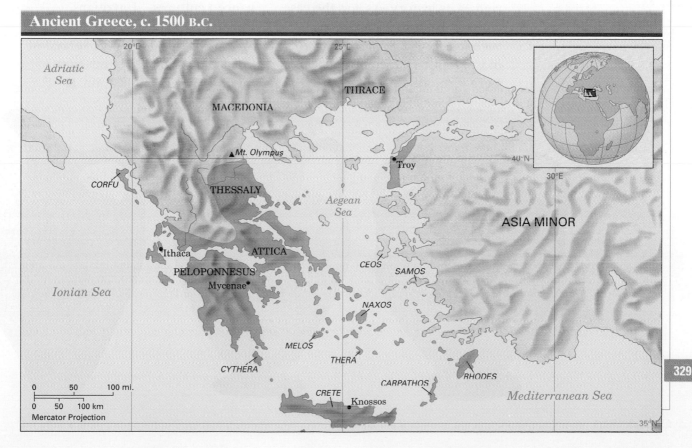

Ancient Greece, c. 1500 B.C.

Adriatic Sea
20°E
25°E
THRACE
MACEDONIA
▲ Mt. Olympus
40°N
30°E
Troy
CORFU
THESSALY
Aegean Sea
ASIA MINOR
Ithaca
ATTICA
CEOS
SAMOS
PELOPONNESUS
Mycenae
NAXOS
Ionian Sea
MELOS
THERA
CYTHERA
CARPATHOS
RHODES
0   50   100 mi.
0   50   100 km
Mercator Projection
CRETE
Knossos
Mediterranean Sea
35°N

Greece had a climate similar to that of southern California—mild winters and hot, sunny summers. As a result, farmers could raise crops all year round.

In spring and summer, Greek farmers tended vineyards and olive groves. In fall they harvested grapes and olives, and they also planted wheat and barley. They harvested these crops in the spring.

The hilly terrain was ideal for growing grapes and olives, so the Greeks could produce plenty of these crops. However, less than one-fourth of Greece's land was level enough for planting grains, so at times grains were scarce. To supplement their stores of wheat and barley, the Greeks sailed west to Sicily and east to the Black Sea region to trade for grains. They may also have sailed south to trade with the Egyptians.

Greece was ideally located for sea trade. The Greeks made extensive contacts with people from advanced cultures—Egyptians, Phoenicians, Persians, and others. These contacts led to the spread of ideas that spurred the development of Greek civilization. ■

▲ *The main crops grown in ancient Greece were grapes, grain, and olives (above). The vases below were used in the 500s B.C. to store crops. What crops were stored in each jar?*

■ *How did sea trade influence the growth of civilization in Greece?*

history, these fierce rivalries erupted into wars.

The sea connected the peoples who became known as the Greeks. In fact, no point on the mainland is more than 40 miles from the sea. As a result, the sea became the Greeks' link to other peoples, products, and ideas.

Farming in Ancient Greece

The geography of Greece helped to shape its economy as well as its history. As was the case with other ancient civilizations, such as those in Sumer and Egypt, most people in ancient Greece were farmers.

Early Civilizations

The roots of Greek civilization can be traced to two nearby cultures that flourished and declined between 3000 B.C. and 1100 B.C. Find Crete on the map on page 329. On this island the first major civilization of the region arose. According to legend, its leader was a conqueror and lawgiver named King Minos. The period from about 2000 B.C. to 1400 B.C. is called the Minoan Age.

Minoan Civilization

The Minoans developed a system of writing, and they created fine artwork, including carved statuettes, pottery, metal bowls, jewelry, and weavings. The Minoans also were great sailors. They carried on a rich trade with the people of Egypt, Phoenicia, and Mesopotamia.

The Minoans were master builders as well. At Crete's main city, Knossos *(NAHS uhs)*, and in other cities they built huge palaces. These palaces had a mazelike series of rooms surrounding a central courtyard.

Although they were built nearly 4,000 years ago, the palaces were quite advanced . The Minoans equipped them with underground plumbing and piped running water to luxurious bathing rooms. The walls of the palaces

▼ *An acrobat leaps over a charging bull in this Minoan bronze sculpture from about 1600 B.C. (shown full size). The sport, called bull dancing, was popular in ancient Crete.*

▼ *Trace the early history of the ancient Greeks.*

Origins of the Greeks

1400–1100 B.C., Mycenaean Age

In the **1200s B.C.,** the lion's gate guarded the entrance to the city of Mycenae.

700–500 B.C., Age of Expansion

2000	1500	1000	500	B.C.	A.D.

2000–1400 B.C., Minoan Age

Mycenaean gold cup, **c. 1500 B.C.,** illustrates how people caught bulls on the range.

1100–800 B.C., Dark Age

A scene from Homer's *Odyssey* appears on this vase, **c. 480 B.C.**

331

▲ *Much of the palace of Knossos was restored in the early 1900s. Colorful paintings like the one shown at right once decorated palace walls.*

How Do We Know?

HISTORY *In the early 1900s, British archaeologist Sir Arthur Evans excavated the ruins of an ancient palace in Knossos. Among the many artifacts Evans found was a set of clay tablets. The information on these tablets showed that the Minoan king at Knossos headed a strong central government, which controlled the whole island of Crete.*

■ *What did the Minoan and Mycenaean civilizations have in common?*

were decorated with colorful murals of daily life in ancient Crete.

Mycenaean Civilization

While the Minoan civilization was thriving on the island of Crete, people began settling on the Greek mainland as well. About 1900 B.C., they began building cities high on hilltops, overlooking the surrounding countryside and the sea. The largest of these cities was Mycenae *(my SEE nee).* Find Mycenae on the map on page 329.

Like the Minoans, the Mycenaeans *(my suh NEE uhnz)* built a large fleet of ships. They set out to capture rich trade routes and establish colonies. The Mycenaeans learned from the Minoans. They built palaces in the Minoan style and adopted the Minoan system of writing. Gradually, they became more powerful.

Then, in about 1450 B.C., the Mycenaeans conquered the Minoans. With the downfall of the Minoans, the Mycenaeans became the dominant civilization in the Aegean region. The period between 1400 B.C. and 1100 B.C. is called the Mycenaean Age.

The Dark Age

In the 1100s B.C., the Mycenaean culture began to decline. No one knows for sure why, but by about 1150 B.C. Mycenae fell to invaders. Soon afterwards, the Dorians, who were groups of related peoples from the northern part of Greece, moved into the area. Many Mycenaeans fled. Greece was entering a period of decline called the Dark Age.

During the Dark Age, which lasted from about 1100 B.C. to 800 B.C., trade came to a standstill. The written language disappeared. People lived in isolated villages.

However, the early history of Greece was not lost during this time. The oral tradition kept the history alive. Storytellers retold the legends and myths of their past. About 800 B.C., the Greeks began to write again, using an alphabet based on the system of the Phoenicians. During the 700s B.C., the poet Homer wrote down long poems, called epic poems, based on these oral tales. His epic poem the *Odyssey* was one of the most important literary achievements of the early Greeks. ■

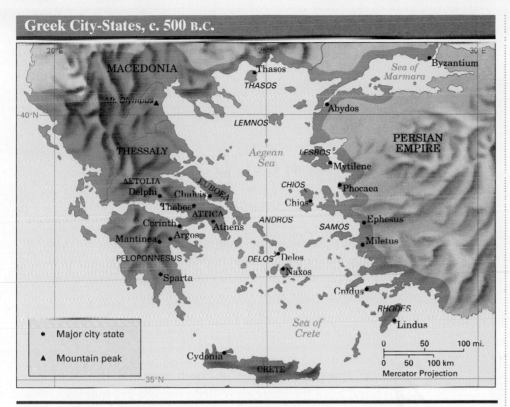

◀ *Which city-states were located on the Peloponnesus? Which ones were in Attica? Look at the map on page 51 to see the wider Mediterranean world in which trade and ideas flowed back and forth.*

The Rise of the City-States

Around 750 B.C., Greece's Dark Age came to an end. The population of Greece had increased during the Dark Age, and the isolated villages began to develop into cities. As the cities grew, trade increased. People in each city traded among themselves. They also traded with people living in neighboring cities. Leaders arose among the people in each city.

The isolated cities of the Dark Ages developed into **city-states**—independent, self-governing units. Each city-state included a city and the territory surrounding the city. As the city-states grew, however, they sometimes did not have enough farmland to support their people. They began to fight with one another over boundaries and other matters. Many Greek colonists left their city-states and founded new ones. Look at the map above. How far east did the city-states extend? How far north did they extend?

In the 600s and 500s B.C. the Greek city-states flourished. This period is called the Age of Expansion. In the next lessons, you will read about the great achievements of the city-states in government, art, literature, and science. ■

■ *What was the Age of Expansion?*

1. **FOCUS** What were some of the forces that influenced the rise of civilization in ancient Greece?

2. **CONNECT** In what ways were the Greek city-states described above similar to the cities of ancient Mesopotamia?

3. **CULTURE** How did the Greeks keep their history alive during the Dark Age?

4. **GEOGRAPHY** Why did Greece develop as a group of individual city-states rather than a unified state?

5. **CRITICAL THINKING** Why are epic poems such as the *Odyssey* important sources of information about the Greek civilization?

6. **WRITING ACTIVITY** Imagine that you had traveled with Odysseus. Write an account of what you saw.

The Cyclops's Cave

Bernard Evslin

Odysseus, known as Ulysses to the Romans, encountered many troubles on his way home after the Trojan War. In this excerpt from Greeks Bearing Gifts, *Ulysses and his crew land on the island of the Cyclopes, one-eyed giants. They enter a cave where they are trapped by one of the giants.*

A s Ulysses and his horrified men watched, the great hand bore the struggling little men to the giant's mouth. He ate them, still wriggling, the way a cat eats a grasshopper; he ate them clothes and all, growling over their raw bones.

The men had fallen to their knees and were whimpering like terrified children, but Ulysses stood there, sword in hand, his agile brain working more swiftly than it ever had before.

"Greetings," he called. "May I know to whom we are indebted for such hospitality?"

The giant belched and spat buttons. "I am Polyphemus," he growled. "This is my cave, my mountain, and everything that comes here is mine. I do hope you can all stay to dinner. There are just enough of you to make a meal. Ho, ho. . . ." And he laughed a great, choking phlegmy laugh, swiftly lunged, and caught another sailor, whom he lifted into the air and held before his face.

"Wait!" cried Ulysses.

"What for?"

"You won't enjoy him that way. He is from Attica, where the olives grow. He was raised on olives and has a very delicate oily flavor. But to appreciate it, you must taste the wine of the country."

"Wine? What is wine?"

"It is a drink. Made from pressed grapes. Have you never drunk it?"

"We drink nothing but ox blood and buttermilk here."

"Ah, you do not know what you have missed, gentle Polyphemus. Meat-eaters, in particular, love wine. Here, try it for yourself."

Ulysses unslung from his belt a full flask of unwatered wine. He gave it to the giant, who put it to his lips and gulped. He coughed violently, and stuck the sailor in a little niche high up in

---

The Odyssey *was based on an oral tradition about the Greek hero. Here is another version of one of Odysseus's adventures.*

Polyphemus (pahl uh FEE muhs)

phlegmy   full of mucus

the cave wall, then leaned his great slab of a face toward Ulysses and said:

"What did you say this drink was?"

"Wine. A gift of the gods to man, to make women look better and food taste better. And now it is my gift to you."

"It's good, very good." He put the bottle to his lips and swallowed again. "You are very polite. What's your name?"

"My name? Why I am—nobody."

"Nobody. . . . Well, Nobody, I like you. You're a good fellow. And do you know what I'm going to do? I'm going to save you till last. Yes, I'll eat all your friends first, and give you extra time, that's what I'm going to do."

Ulysses looked up into the great eye and saw that it was redder than ever. It was all a swimming redness. He had given the monster, who had never drunk spirits before, undiluted wine. Surely it must make him sleepy. But was a gallon enough for that great gullet? Enough to put him to sleep—or would he want to eat again first?

"Eat 'em all up, Nobody—save you till later. Sleep a little first. Shall I? Won't try to run away, will you? No—you can't, can't open the door—too heavy, ha, ha. . . . You take a nap too, Nobody. I'll wake you for breakfast. Breakfast. . . ."

The great body crashed full-length on the cave floor, making the very walls of the mountain shake. Polyphemus lay on his back, snoring like a powersaw. The sailors were still on the floor, almost dead from fear.

"Up!" cried Ulysses. "Stand up like men! Do what must be done! Or you will be devoured like chickens."

He got them to their feet and drew them about him as he explained his plan.

"Listen now, and listen well, for we have no time. I made him drunk, but we cannot tell how long it will last."

Ulysses thrust his sword into the fire; they saw it glow white-hot.

"There are ten of us," he said. "Two of us have been eaten, and one of our friends is still unconscious up there on his shelf of rock. You four get on one side of his head, and the rest on the other side. When I give the word, lay hold of the ear on your side, each of you. And hang on, no matter how he thrashes, for I am going to put out his eye. And if I am to be sure of my stroke you must hold his head still. One stroke is all I will be allowed."

Then Ulysses rolled a boulder next to the giant's head and climbed on it, so that he was looking down into the eye. It was lidless and misted with sleep—big as a furnace door and glowing softly like a banked fire. Ulysses looked at his men. They had done what he said, broken into two parties, one group at each ear. He lifted his white-hot sword.

"Now!" he cried.

Driving down with both hands, and all the strength of his back and shoulders, and all his rage and all his fear, Ulysses stabbed the glowing spike into the giant's eye.

His sword jerked out of his hand as the head flailed upward, men pelted to the ground as they lost their hold. A huge screeching curdling bellow split the air.

"This way!" shouted Ulysses.

He motioned to his men, and they crawled on their bellies toward the far end of the cave where the herd of goats were tethered. They slipped into the herd and lay among the goats as the giant stomped about the cave, slapping the walls with great blows of his hands, picking up boulders and cracking them together in agony, splitting them to flinders, clutching his eye, a scorched hole now from which the brown blood jelled. He moaned and gibbered and bellowed in frightful pain; his groping hand found the sailor in the wall, and he tore him to pieces between his fingers. Ulysses could not even hear the man scream because the giant was bellowing so.

Now Ulysses saw that the Cyclops's wild stampeding was giving place to a plan. For now he was stamping the floor in a regular pattern, trying to find and crush them beneath his feet. He stopped moaning and listened. The sudden silence dazed the men with fear. They held their breath and tried to muffle the sound of their beating hearts; all the giant heard was the breathing of the goats. Then Ulysses saw him go to the mouth of the cave, and swing the great slab aside, and stand there. He realized just in time that the goats would rush outside, which is what the giant wanted, for then he could search the whole cave.

Ulysses whispered, "Quickly, swing under the bellies of the rams. Hurry, hurry!"

Luckily, they were giant goats and thus able to carry the men who had swung themselves under their bellies and were clinging to the wiry wool. Ulysses himself chose the largest ram. They moved toward the mouth of the cave, and crowded through. The Cyclops's hands came down and brushed across the goats' backs feeling for the men, but the animals were huddled too closely together for him to reach between and search under their bellies, so he let them pass through.

Now, the Cyclops rushed to the corner where the goats had been tethered, and stamped, searched, and roared through the whole cave again, bellowing with fury when he did not find them. The herd grazed on the slope of the hill beneath the cave. There was a full moon; it was almost as bright as day.

"Stay where you are," Ulysses whispered.

He heard a crashing, peered out, and saw great shadowy figures converging on the cave. He knew that the other Cyclopes of the island must have heard the noise and come to see. He heard the giant bellow.

The others called to him: "Who has done it? Who has blinded you?"

"Nobody. Nobody did it. Nobody blinded me."

"Ah, you have done it yourself. What a tragic accident."

And they went back to their own caves.

"Now! said Ulysses. "Follow me!"

He swung himself out from under the belly of the ram, and raced down the hill. The others raced after him. They were halfway across the valley when they heard great footsteps rushing after them, and Polyphemus bellowing nearer and nearer.

"He's coming!" cried Ulysses. "Run for your lives!"

They ran as they had never run before, but the giant could cover fifty yards at a stride. It was only because he could not see and kept bumping into trees and rocks that they were able to reach the skiff and push out on the silver water before Polyphemus burst out of the grove of trees and rushed onto the beach. They bent to the oars, and the boat scudded toward the fleet.

Polyphemus heard the dip of the oars and the groaning of the oarlocks, and, aiming at the sound, hurled huge boulders after them. They fell around the ship, but did not hit. The skiff reached Ulysses' ship, and the sailors climbed aboard.

"Haul anchor, and away!" cried Ulysses. And then called to the Cyclops, "Poor fool! Poor blinded drunken gluttonous fool—if anyone else asks you, it is not Nobody, but Ulysses who has done this to you."

But he was to regret this final taunt. The gods honor courage, but punish pride.

Polyphemus, wild with rage, waded out chest-deep and hurled a last boulder, which hit mid-deck, almost sunk the ship, and killed most of the crew—among them seven of the nine men who had just escaped.

And Polyphemus prayed to Poseidon, "God of the Sea, I beg you, punish Ulysses for this. Visit him with storm and shipwreck and sorceries. Let him wander many years before he reaches home, and when he gets there let him find himself forgotten, unwanted, a stranger."

Poseidon heard this prayer, and made it all happen just that way.

skiff a flat-bottomed open boat

scudded skimmed swiftly

Poseidon (poh SYD n)

sorceries acts of evil supernatural power

Further Reading

Ancient Greece. Susan Purdy. Step-by-step directions show how to make models of ancient Greek columns, statues, and catapults.

The God Beneath the Sea. Leon Garfield and Edward Blishen. This book retells Greek myths about the gods and goddesses on Olympia.

LESSON 2

Athens: A City-State

THINKING FOCUS

How did democracy develop and work in Athens?

Key Terms

- democracy
- monarchy
- oligarchy
- tyrant
- barter

▼ *The ancient Greeks used these tokens to cast their votes.*

The trial promised to be one of the most important the citizens of Athens would hear all year. In 406 B.C., six navy generals were accused of abandoning hundreds of shipwrecked soldiers and leaving them to drown. Were the generals guilty of causing the deaths of these men? A jury of 2,000 Athenian citizens would decide the fate of the generals.

Early in the morning, the trial began. First the six generals took the stand. They testified that they had done all they could to save the men. The deaths were just an unfortunate turn of fate.

Next, witnesses testified, including a survivor who had floated to shore in a flour barrel. He claimed that the spirits of his drowned comrades urged him to testify against the generals.

Professional mourners, dressed in black, made their way through the crowd. They hoped to convince the jurors to convict the generals.

Xenophon (*ZEHN uh fuhn*), a Greek historian, told of a public crier who announced how the jury would decide:

> L et every one who finds the generals guilty of not rescuing the heroes of the late sea-fight deposit his vote in one urn. Let him who is of the contrary opinion deposit his vote in the other urn. Further, in the event of the aforesaid generals being found guilty, let death be the penalty.
>
> Xenophon, *Hellenica*, Book I
> c. 400 B.C.

The jurors' tokens were counted. The generals were found guilty and sentenced to death.

The Evolution of Democracy

Trials such as the one of the navy generals were an important part of the government developed by the citizens of Athens. Between the 700s and 400s B.C., the Athenians developed a new form of government that put the power to make decisions into the hands of the people. This form of government is called a **democracy,** which means government by the people.

The Origins of Democracy

The idea of democracy was developed over several centuries. Before the Dark Age, the people in the Greek city-states were ruled by kings. A system of government in which a king rules over a group of people is called a **monarchy.** In ancient Greece, the king of a city state was also usually the head of the most powerful family. When the king died, he usually passed on his power to govern to his eldest son.

During the Dark Age, Greek kings began to rely on wealthy landowners, or nobles, to help them defend their land from invaders. Not surprisingly, the nobles began to demand some of the king's powers. By the end of the Dark Age, a small group of nobles shared power equally with the king in many city-states. This system of government, in which a few people hold power over a larger group, is called an **oligarchy.**

The leaders of the oligarchies improved the government of the city-states, but during the 500s B.C., some city-states had problems of a different kind.

◄ *The earliest governments of Greece were monarchies. This mask shows the face of a king who ruled about 1500 B.C.*

Some grew to be so large that their farmers could not provide enough food. Food shortages caused unrest and discontent. During this period, poorer farmers suffered greatly. Many lost their land to the wealthy and were forced to sell themselves into slavery. The discontent with the leaders of the oligarchies led to the rise of new leaders called tyrants.

The Rule of Tyrants

Greeks called a leader who seized power by force and ruled the city-state single-handedly a **tyrant**. Many people supported tyrants because these leaders promised to reform the laws and to aid the poor. The tyrants of Athens, for example, promoted building projects and religious festivals, and allowed

UNDERSTANDING DEMOCRACY

When the tyrant Hippias was driven out of Athens in 510 B.C., the people of Athens established a form of government that was new to the ancient world. This government—a democracy— has had a lasting impact on Western civilization.

A democracy is a form of government that places the power in the hands of the citizens. Some democracies are governed directly by the citizens, and some are governed by elected representatives.

Rule of the People

The word *democracy* comes from two Greek words, *demos*, meaning people, and *kratos*, meaning "rule." Thus democracy means "rule of the people."

Unlike an oligarchy, in which only a few rule, all citizens take part in the government of a democracy.

However, democracies can take different forms.

Forms of Democracy

In ancient Greece, the citizens met regularly in an assembly to vote on important issues. This type of democracy is known as direct democracy because all the citizens take part directly. For smaller communities, such as the early Greek city-states, direct democracy worked because it was possible to bring together all citizens to make decisions.

Many democracies today are representative democracies. In a representative democracy, the citizens elect representatives to make decisions for them.

The United States, Zimbabwe, and Venezuela, are examples of representative democracies. This form of democracy is more practical for nations who cannot

get all of their people together at one time to make decisions.

Even in ancient Greece, the people gave some decision-making power to representatives. One feature of Athenian democracy was a council of 500 citizens. They were chosen each year to propose new laws for the assembly of all citizens to consider.

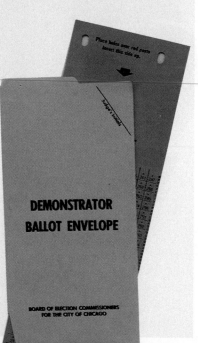

DEMONSTRATOR
BALLOT ENVELOPE

BOARD OF ELECTION COMMISSIONERS
FOR THE CITY OF CHICAGO

other people besides the nobles to have a say in government.

The tyrants played an important role in the development of democracy. They taught citizens that by uniting behind a leader, they could gain the power to make changes. However, some tyrants were harsh and greedy. The people of a city-state sometimes threw out one tyrant and replaced him with another.

The Democracy of Athens

About 510 B.C., the citizens of Athens became upset with the harsh rule of a tyrant named Hippias. With the help of soldiers from the city-state of Sparta, Hippias was driven out of Athens. But he was not replaced by a new tyrant. Instead, the citizens of Athens chose to share the decision-making power among themselves. This was the beginning of the world's first democracy.

Several institutions assured citizens of Athens a voice in their government. A council of 500 citizens, chosen at random every year, proposed new laws. An assembly of all the citizens of Athens met about every nine days to vote on the laws. In the law courts, citizens served as jurors. They interpreted the laws and decided guilt or innocence in cases such as that of the navy generals.

All of these institutions had existed before 500 B.C. However, now they were open to more people and they were administered more fairly. For example, the government of Athens paid council members and jurors for their ser-

A tyrant is put to death in this vase painting.

vices. Thus, poorer citizens, as well as rich ones, could afford to take time off from their work to take part in the government of their city-state.

Not all citizens of Athens liked this new form of government. Some wealthy citizens believed the democracy gave too much power to poor citizens. Nevertheless, most Athenians appreciated their form of government.

The development of democracy has greatly influenced Western civilization. It also was an important step for the Athenians.

> ### Across Time & Space
>
> *Today the word* tyrant *means "dictator" or "a ruler who governs in a harsh or cruel way." However, in ancient Greece the word did not have those negative meanings. Although the Greek tyrants took power by force, often they ruled well and fairly.*

Athenians voted to banish people from a city. They wrote the name of the person they wanted to banish on pieces of clay pottery.

341

The Ancient Greeks

The Greek historian Herodotus (*hih RAHD uh tuhs*) wrote that when the Athenians were ruled by tyrants, they "were not a whit more valiant than any of their neighbors." But when they established their democracy,

> They became decidedly the first of all. These things show that, while undergoing oppression, they let themselves be beaten, since then they worked for a master; but so soon as they got their freedom, each man was eager to do the best he could for himself.
>
> Herodotus, *The Persian Wars*, c. 430 B.C.

Athens was not the only city-state with a democratic government. Several other ancient Greek city-states developed democracies. However the democracy that developed in Athens was the most successful. ■

■ *Trace the development of democracy from the monarchy.*

Citizenship in Athens

The democracy of Athens opened participation in government to all citizens. However, citizenship was a privilege reserved for relatively few people. Only men over the age of 18 could become citizens. And except under special circumstances, a man became a citizen only if his father had been a citizen. After 451 B.C., the rules regarding citizenship became stricter. A man became a citizen only if both his father and his mother's father were citizens.

Of the 300,000 inhabitants of Athens, only about 45,000 of them were citizens. Their wives and children, who were not citizens, accounted for about 145,000 inhabitants. Note that women, whether they were married or unmarried, had no political rights and they could not own land.

About 35,000 residents of Athens were metics, or foreigners. They came from other Greek city-states or from other parts of the Mediterranean region. Many were traders, shopkeepers, craftsmen, or moneylenders. Metics could not vote or hold public office, but they were protected by Athenian law.

Slaves made up the rest of Athens's population. Many had been captured during foreign wars. Slaves could not vote, and they could not choose their jobs. They were not even allowed to have a family without the permission of their master. They had to do the jobs their owners assigned them. Many worked as farmhands. Others did household chores. Some learned crafts such as metalwork or pottery. These slaves were paid for their work. A few of them earned enough money to buy their freedom from their owners. ■

➤ *What group of people made up the largest part of Athenian society?*

■ *Find evidence in the lesson to disprove this statement: In Athens everyone took part in the government.*

Population of Athens

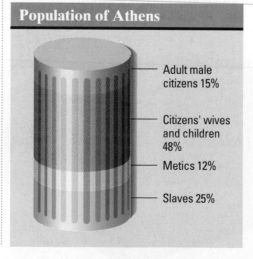

Adult male citizens 15%

Citizens' wives and children 48%

Metics 12%

Slaves 25%

The Economy of Athens

Farming was the main economic activity in Athenian society. Most citizens owned just enough land to support their families. However, some wealthy Athenians owned large estates on which slaves did most of the work. On other estates, tenant farmers worked the land. These farmers leased plots from the owner and paid rent by giving the owner part of their crops.

Trade and Coinage

Until the 500s B.C., Athenians did most of their trading through **barter.** Using this system people exchanged one type of product, such as grain, directly for another, such as olives. As Athens became an international trading center around 600 B.C., barter became an inconvenient way to trade.

Trade in Athens became easier around 570 B.C., when the government began to make silver coins. People were willing to exchange their goods for coins. In contrast to the barter system, the system of trade using coins allowed the purchase of any product.

Redistributing Wealth

The use of coins spurred the Athenian economy, and Athens became a very wealthy city. The active trade drew many foreigners, who came to Athens to make their fortunes.

However, wealthy people in Athens usually did not hold on to their wealth for many generations. Foreigners who became wealthy usually went back to their own city-states. Wealthy citizens were expected to contribute large amounts of money to government projects. For example, they might have been asked to give money to outfit one of the navy's ships or sponsor a religious festival.

The cost of the Athenian government was high. As a result, few families managed to stay rich for more than three generations. By then the family had used up its wealth on projects that benefited all Athenians. This system kept money flowing to citizens throughout the city-state. It also gave work to merchants and craftsmen. ■

▼ *Greeks traded with these coins during the 500s and 400s B.C.*

■ *Why did wealthy families in Athens have difficulty staying rich?*

REVIEW

1. **FOCUS** How did democracy develop and work in Athens?

2. **CONNECT** How was the democracy of Athens different from the governments led by the pharaohs of Egypt and the kings of Mesopotamia?

3. **ECONOMICS** What were the advantages for Athens' of coined money?

4. **CRITICAL THINKING** How was the democracy in Athens similar to the democracy in the United States today? How was it different?

5. **WRITING ACTIVITY** Write a journal entry on what it would be like to be a noncitizen in Athens. You can choose to write from the point of view of a slave, metic, woman, or child.

Comparing Graphs

Here's Why

Graphs can help you organize information. They can help you see patterns and make comparisons. Certain kinds of graphs are best used to present particular kinds of information.

The graphs on this page are based on estimates of the population in ancient Greece. They show information in different ways. One is a line graph; the other is a pie graph.

By comparing the two graphs, you can get more information than you can from a single graph. Also, by understanding what each graph does best, you will learn which type of graph to choose to present your own information.

Here's How

A line graph shows change over time. The line graph at the lower left shows that 30,000 male citizens lived in Athens in 500 B.C. The upward slope of the line to the right of 500 B.C. shows that the male population increased to about 45,000 during the 50 years between 500 B.C. and 450 B.C. The downward slope of the line from about 450 B.C. to about 325 B.C. shows a decrease in the male population during that time.

A pie graph shows how something is divided into parts. For example, if you created a pie graph of your class, you might show how the class is divided into boys and girls.

The pie graph at the lower right shows the five groups that made up the estimated 300,000 people living in Athens in 451 B.C. Each section of the pie shows how the number of people in that group relates to the total population. For example, 75,000 slaves equals 25 percent of the total pie.

Try It

Suppose that by 200 B.C. the population of Athens had fallen to 100,000. Suppose that of that 100,000, there were about 20,000 male citizens, 20,000 wives of citizens, 35,000 children of citizens, 15,000 metics, and 10,000 slaves.

Use this information to make two graphs—Male Citizens of Athens, 500–200 B.C., and Population of Athens, 200 B.C.

Apply It

Find out your school's total enrollment each year for the past 10 years and the number of students who participated in various sports. For each set of data, decide whether a line graph or a pie graph is more appropriate. Then create the graphs.

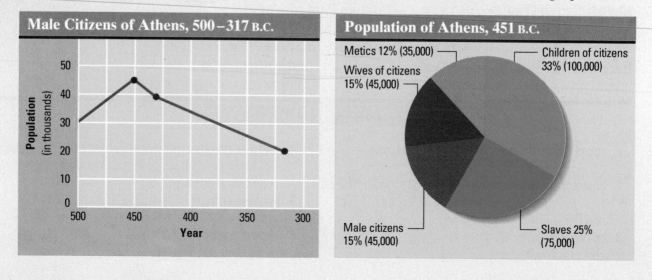

Male Citizens of Athens, 500–317 B.C.

Population of Athens, 451 B.C.

Metics 12% (35,000)
Wives of citizens 15% (45,000)
Children of citizens 33% (100,000)
Male citizens 15% (45,000)
Slaves 25% (75,000)

LESSON 3

Ancient Greek Culture

A crowd of 45,000 gathered on the grassy slopes of the stadium at Olympia one summer afternoon in 776 B.C. Below them, the runners prepared for the foot-race. The race began, and the crowd rose and cheered as one runner burst ahead of the others. He was Coroebus, a cook from the nearby city of Elis. When he crossed the finish line, Coroebus became the first recorded winner at the Olympic games.

Sports events were important in ancient Greece, just as they are in the United States today. Every four years, beginning in 776 B.C., the Greeks held an athletic competition called the Olympics, which was open to all Greek men. At first this competition consisted of one event, a foot-race of about 200 yards. Later the Olympics were expanded to include longer races, wrestling, boxing, discus throwing, horse races, and chariot races. The modern-day Olympics are modeled after these Greek games.

The Greeks considered the Olympics so important that nothing, not even war, was allowed to interfere with them. However, the function of these competitions was not simply to entertain. The main purpose of the Olympics and other public events and festivals was to honor the gods.

THINKING FOCUS

What religious beliefs and customs did all Greeks share?

Key Terms

- sanctuary
- tragedy
- comedy

◄ *An Olympic athlete throwing the discus is shown in this Roman copy of a Greek sculpture from about 450 B.C.*

345

The Family of Greek Gods

The Olympic Games honored Zeus, the father of the Greek gods. The games were named after the city of Olympia. The Greeks believed that Zeus sat on a golden throne atop Mount Olympus and ruled all other gods and all of the Greeks. In fact, they thought of Zeus as master of the entire world.

All Greeks, no matter what city-state they lived in, worshiped Zeus and his family of gods. The Greeks thought these gods controlled both the world of nature and the human world.

The myths and legends of the Greeks celebrated their gods. These traditional stories explained the roles of the gods in creating the world and causing natural events.

The stories also told of the great power of their gods. For example, Zeus was portrayed as powerful, stern, and commanding. In Homer's poem the *Iliad*, Zeus boasts about how he could control the world with a cord of gold dropped from the sky.

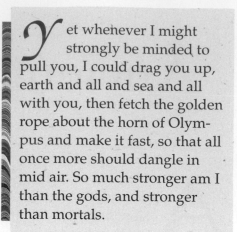

Yet whenever I might strongly be minded to pull you, I could drag you up, earth and all and sea and all with you, then fetch the golden rope about the horn of Olympus and make it fast, so that all once more should dangle in mid air. So much stronger am I than the gods, and stronger than mortals.

The Roles of the Gods

The gods of Greek myths formed a family, and each member had a specific role with particular duties and powers. Zeus, as head of the family, set standards of justice and made sure that humans and gods followed them. He also controlled the weather and punished wrongdoing with bolts of thunder and raging storms.

Poseidon, Zeus's brother, was the god of the sea. Hera, Zeus's wife, was the goddess of marriage. Zeus's son Ares was the god of war. Another of his sons, Dionysus *(dy uh NY suhs)*, was the god of wine. His son Apollo was the god of light, who drove the sun across the sky each day in his golden carriage. Apollo also was the god of health, herding, and prophecy.

Worshiping the Gods

The Greeks prayed to specific gods for things they wanted. For example, a sick person might pray to Apollo for a speedy recovery. The Greeks thanked the gods by making animal sacrifices when their prayers were granted. They also made sacrifices to the gods before competing in sports, going

The image painted on an Athenian cup about 550 B.C. shows the birth of Athena. According to Greek myth, Athena sprang full grown from the head of Zeus, which was split open by an ax.

off to war, or setting sail on a long voyage.

The Greeks also built sacred places called **sanctuaries** to honor their gods. People from the entire Aegean world traveled to these sanctuaries to worship their many gods. ■

■ *Describe some of the Greek gods and their powers.*

Sanctuaries to the Gods

The sanctuaries were built in areas of great natural beauty. Each sacred site had its own unique traditions that had been established over hundreds of years. Find the four sanctuaries on the map on page 348.

Olympia

Olympia, where the Olympic games were held, was a sanctuary to Zeus. A winding river ran through the site, and a thickly wooded area made it a place of peace and serenity. Olympia was a perfect site for sports competition, because the land in the broad river valley was flat. On this level plain, the Greeks easily laid out large courses on which the foot races, horse races, and chariot races could be run during the Olympics. The Greeks believed that Zeus and the other gods took special delight in watching great athletes display their skill and strength in open competition.

Delphi

The Greeks honored Apollo at Delphi *(DEHL fy)*. Each city-state sent gifts to the sanctuary. Because the site was considered sacred, no thief would think of robbing it. Therefore, many people left their gold and silver in the shrines at Delphi for safekeeping.

Located halfway up a mountain overlooking a lush river valley, Delphi was a most impressive site. The sanctuary was most fa-mous for its oracle to the god Apollo. Like the ancient Chinese, the Greeks believed oracles were predictions. The Greeks believed gods and goddesses revealed hidden knowledge through these oracles. The Greeks also called the shrines where these messages were revealed oracles.

At these oracles, priests or priestesses interpreted the messages of the gods. The messages were often hard to understand. For example, the Athenian generals appealed to the Delphic oracle for advice during the Persian Wars in the late 400s B.C. The generals wanted to know how they could turn back the Persian invaders. The message they received from the oracle was that "wooden walls" would save Athens. After much debate, the generals decided that wooden walls meant new wooden ships. The generals built a new fleet of ships, and the fleet played

▼ *To please the gods, Greeks sacrificed animals in the temples of the sanctuaries. This mosaic shows a sheep being led to a sacrificial altar.*

347

The Ancient Greeks

a crucial role in defeating Persia. Therefore, the Greeks believed the oracle was right.

The oracle at Delphi was considered the most powerful of the Greek oracles. People from all over the Aegean world came to Delphi seeking advice.

Delos and Eleusis

According to Greek myth, the island of Delos *(DEE lohs)* was Apollo's birthplace. Like Delphi, the Delos sanctuary had an oracle to Apollo. Every five years the Greeks held a sports competition there to honor Apollo.

Eleusis *(ih LOO suhs)*, on the coast of mainland Greece near Athens, was the site of a sanctuary to Demeter *(dih MEET ur)*, the goddess of grain. Athenians made pilgrimages each year to Eleusis during the planting and harvest seasons. They also made sacrifices to Demeter and offered prayers for an abundant harvest. These religious rituals highlighted the importance of agriculture in ancient Greece.

Religious Festivals

The Greeks also honored their gods and goddesses by holding religious festivals. Many of these festivals, such as the Olympic games, centered on sports. Other ceremonies featured religious rituals and animal sacrifices.

One group of festivals has had a lasting influence on Western civilization. These were the drama festivals honoring Dionysus, the god of wine. ■

■ *How did the Greek people use sanctuaries?*

➤ *The ruins at Delphi of the Temple of the Treasury of the Athenians are shown at the right. Find the treasuries at Delphi on the map below.*

Major Sanctuaries of Ancient Greece

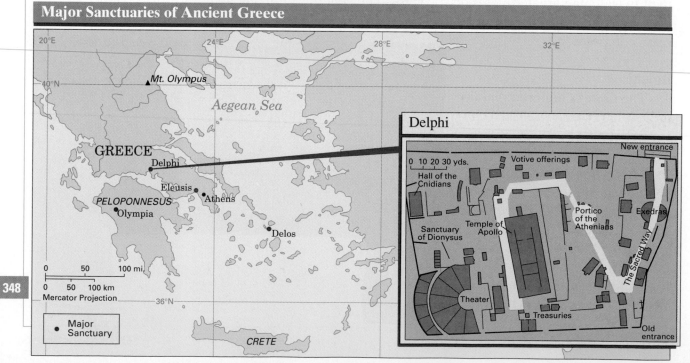

348

A Greek Actor

10:00 A.M., March 24, 441 B.C.
Theater of Dionysus, Athens

Mouth Hole
The opening allows the actor's fine voice to project the words of Sophocles' play *Antigone* all the way to the last row. Our actor is just about to step back out onto the stage.

Mask
Newly made of linen and smelling of fresh paint, the mask is much better than the ones at last year's festival. The citizen who is paying for this year's plays has spent a lot more money on costumes.

Padding
A band around the actor's head holds his mask in place. He hopes to exchange the band for the wreath of ivy leaves given to the festival's best actor.

Goose Bumps
He's not only chilled by the cold morning air. He's also nervous about remembering his lines, which are very important.

Sash
His belt is smaller than the one he wore at the festival last year because he has been fasting to improve his voice.

Long Sleeves
Earlier in the play, these sleeves hid the actor's manly arms when he acted the part of a young woman. Today he will play eight different parts in three brand-new tragedies by Sophocles.

Cape
Purple, the color of kings, tells the audience that the actor is playing the role of King Creon. Our actor is happy because Creon is a very important part with many good lines.

Greek Drama

Twice a year, writers throughout Greece composed plays that were presented at festivals in Athens to honor Dionysus. The plays produced on the Athenian stages are one of the lasting contributions of the Greeks.

Most of the plays told stories about Greek gods or heroes. They combined religion and history with entertainment. Most popular were the **tragedies,** sad stories in which the hero was brought to ruin by a flaw in his character.

Look at the Moment in Time on page 349. The actor is preparing to appear in the tragedy *Antigone (an TIHG uh nee)* by Sophocles. The actor will be playing a king who ordered the death of the woman his son loved. The son, stricken with grief, then killed himself as well. Here are the sad lines the king will speak as he gazes at his son's body.

> Sirs, ye behold the slayer and the slain.
> Such is the end my schemes unblessed have won,
> By a boy's blow
> Undone, undone!
> For you have died, have willed to go,
> And I was all to blame, not you, my son, my son.
>
> Sophocles, *Antigone*, 441 B.C.

During a festival for Dionysus, plays were presented from dawn until dark for four days. Three days were devoted to tragic plays. **Comedies**—funny plays—were presented for only one day during the festival. Like comedies today, the Greek comedies made fun of a wide range of topics, from politics to everyday life.

All businesses in Athens closed during the festivals to Dionysus. Thousands of people headed to the open-air amphitheater to watch the plays. The city even released prisoners from jail so that they could go to the festival.

A jury of Athenian citizens judged the plays and awarded ivy crowns to the writers of the winning plays. Many of the prize-winning plays are still performed today. ■

▲ *By wearing different masks, actors in Athenian plays could play more than one part.*

■ *How was the festival of Dionysus different from the festivals to other gods?*

REVIEW

1. **FOCUS** What religious beliefs and customs did all Greeks share?
2. **CONNECT** Compare the Greek gods to the Egyptian gods and the Mesopotamian gods.
3. **CULTURE** What is a tragedy?
4. **CRITICAL THINKING** Why were plays and sports competitions considered important religious events by the ancient Greeks?
5. **WRITING ACTIVITY** Make up a story about the Greek god Zeus and one of his children mentioned in the chapter. You might use your story to explain an event in Greek history, an aspect of Greek culture, or a natural phenomenon such as a thunderstorm, earthquake, or flood.

LESSON 4

A Tale of Two City-States

In 490 B.C., Persia's fleet of 600 ships loomed off the Greek shores not far from Athens. According to legend, the general of the Athenian troops sent his fastest runner, Phidippides *(fy DIHP uh deez)*, to ask for help from Sparta. Phidippides ran for two days and two nights to reach Sparta, about 140 miles away. He gave the message to the Spartans. They agreed to send troops—but not for nine days, when their religious festival would be completed.

Phidippides ran back to Athens with the Spartans' reply. The Athenian general decided he could not wait that long. He ordered his troops to advance and meet the Persians before the invaders could move inland toward Athens. The two armies clashed at a town called Marathon. The lightly armed Persian soldiers were no match for the well-disciplined Greek forces. The Greeks reported that about 6,400 Persian soldiers were killed, while the Athenians lost only 192 men.

According to legend, the Athenian general ordered Phidippides to run back to Athens and spread the good news. The distance between Marathon and Athens was about 25 miles, a short distance for a professional runner such as Phidippides. But he was still exhausted from his long run to Sparta. Nevertheless, he set out for Athens, running as fast as he could. When he reached Athens, he managed to gasp, "Rejoice! We won." Then he fell to the ground and died.

THINKING FOCUS

How were the cultures of Athens and Sparta similar? How were they different?

Key Terms

- ephor
- helot

Sparta and Athens

At the time of the battle of Marathon, Sparta and Athens were the two largest city-states in Greece. Size, however, was about all the two cities had in common. Events that took place over the preceding centuries had pointed Sparta and Athens in different directions.

Although Athens lost wealth and territory, it was not destroyed. Sparta was invaded and conquered by the Dorians around 1100 B.C. During the next few hundred years, the Dorians took over the region surrounding the city-state of Sparta. They enslaved the former inhabitants of

351

The Ancient Greeks

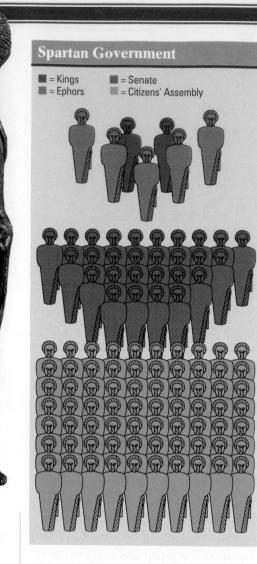

Spartan Government

■ = Kings   ■ = Senate
■ = Ephors   ■ = Citizens' Assembly

The Government of Sparta

Like the government of Athens, Sparta's government began as a monarchy. However, Sparta had two kings who ruled together. This custom probably began because the original Dorian invaders of Sparta included two tribes, each with its own leader. Later, the two kings became part of a 30-man senate. The kings continued to have powers that the senate did not have. The members of the senate were elected by the citizens, who included all male landholders over age 30. However, a person could not become a senator until he was 60 years old.

All Spartan citizens belonged to an assembly similar to the one held in Athens. However, Spartan citizens could not propose laws. They could only vote for or against laws proposed by the senate or by the **ephors** (EHF awrz), five government leaders elected by the assembly. Even if the assembly voted down a law, the senate and ephors often ignored this vote.

Although the Spartans had an assembly and held elections for government offices, power was really in the hands of a few families. These families dominated the senate and could control the ephors. A democratic government never developed in Sparta. This city-state remained an oligarchy.

The Economy of Sparta

Sparta's emphasis on maintaining a strong army shaped the economy. By law, the only occupation a Spartan man could hold was that of a soldier. The people living in the communities around Sparta provided trade and craft items for

▲ *This bronze sculpture from about 500 B.C. (shown full size) represents a Spartan warrior. How did the Spartans govern themselves?*

Sparta. Although people in towns near Sparta remained free, they were forced to serve in the Spartan army.

The slave population of Sparta was much larger than the population of Spartan citizens. When Sparta was at the height of its power, its population consisted of 10,000 citizens and 250,000 slaves. The Spartans feared the possibility of uprisings by their slaves. Because of this, they built a strong army. In fact, Spartan men spent almost their entire adult lives in military service. The Spartans bragged that they needed no walls to protect their city; their soldiers were the only walls they needed.

the city-state. During much of Sparta's history, the government forbade Spartans to have luxury goods. Thus, Spartans led very simple lives. Today we refer to a simple lifestyle without luxuries as "spartan."

Each Spartan citizen received a plot of land from the government. **Helots** (*HEHL uhts*)–state slaves assigned to a particular plot—farmed the land. They received some of the crops as wages and turned over the rest to the owner. The owner gave a portion of his crops to the government, which provided him with daily meals. If, for some reason, a Spartan could not pay for these meals, he lost his rights as a citizen. ■

■ *Why did the economy of Sparta center on a strong army?*

Education in Sparta and Athens

The differences between the two city-states were also reflected in the ways children were treated. Look at the chart on page 354. How did growing up differ in Sparta and Athens?

The Spartan government had a huge influence on the daily lives of its citizens. In fact, when a Spartan baby was born, a government inspector came to look it over. If the baby did not seem healthy, the inspector took the baby to a distant cave on a mountainside and left it there to die. The Spartans wanted only babies who they thought would grow into strong adults.

Training Spartan Children

All Spartan children lived at home until they were seven years old. Then the boys had to leave their families to live in barracks with other boys their own age. From that moment on, the government took over their education and controlled their lives.

Although the boys were taught to read and write, their training emphasized physical skills, including running, jumping, boxing, and wrestling. Conditions in the Spartan schools were harsh, and discipline was strict. The boys slept on the floor. Even when the weather was cold, they wore only light clothes. The Spartans thought that such hardships made the boys stronger. Anyone who disobeyed orders received severe punishment. Even obedient children were whipped from time to time. According to the Spartans, such beatings were good training for soldiers.

Beginning at age 18, young men devoted all their time to the army. By age 30, a Spartan man

▼ *Many Spartan girls excelled at sports. This bronze sculpture from about 520 B.C. shows a girl running.*

Growing Up in Sparta and Athens

Citizens	Ages 0–7	Ages 7–18	Ages 18–?
Spartan	A government inspector decides whether the new-born baby is healthy; if not, the baby is taken to a cave and left to die. Children remain in the home, learning traditional discipline.	Boys leave their homes and live in barracks with other boys as they begin their education. Physical education and military training are stressed. Girls receive training in physical education. Girls often marry at age 15.	Men enter the army and continue military training. At age 30, men complete their military training and gain full citizenship. Women take care of the home and raise children.
Athenian	Baby boys are more prized than girls. Some girls are left at the gates of the city, where people passing by might find them and raise them. Children in wealthy families may begin their education with a private tutor.	Wealthy Athenian boys attend school, receiving training in reading, writing, arithmetic, fine arts, and athletics. Girls remain at home, learning crafts and poetry from their mothers. Girls often marry at age 15.	Men enter the army for two years. Then they enter the army reserve force. Men manage farms or estates and participate in the government. Women take care of the home and raise children.

▲ *Compare and contrast the lives of girls and boys in Sparta and Athens.*

completed his military training and gained full citizenship. However, even if he married, he continued to eat his meals in the mess hall with other soldiers. He also continued to devote much of his time to taking part in military exercises.

Although the training Spartan girls received was not as extensive as that of boys, the girls did get a strong physical education. They practiced running, wrestling, and discus throwing. The Spartans believed that girls had to be strong in order to bear healthy children.

Although the Spartans emphasized military training, they also enjoyed several forms of entertainment. At religious festivals they participated in chorus contests, with boys and girls singing traditional songs. Dance contests were also popular.

Training Athenian Children

The Athenians valued cultural education as well as physical education. However, only boys in wealthy families received formal education. Upon reaching seven years of age, wealthy Athenian boys began school. Unlike Spartan boys, however, Athenian boys did not have to live in barracks with other boys. They lived at home with their families.

Athenian schoolboys learned reading, writing, arithmetic, poetry, music, and dance. They also devoted much time to athletics. When they reached 18 years of age, they joined the army for two years of military training. Upon graduation, these young men received a shield and spear and joined a reserve force. The reserve force was called to duty in times of war.

Unlike the Spartan government, which trained girls in athletics, the Athenian government basically ignored the training of women. Girls learned crafts and poetry from their mothers.

Because of the rich culture of Athens, an Athenian's education continued throughout his or her adult life. Athenians often discussed the myths about the gods and the poetry of Homer. They looked forward to seeing new plays at the yearly festival to Dionysus. In addition, during the late 300s B.C., Athens developed academies where wealthy adults could continue their schooling.

Comparing Cultures

The differing values of Sparta and Athens produced different cultures. Ancient Greek thinkers admired the Spartans because their military background made for a stable society. Although Athens is admired today for its democracy and its personal freedoms, many ancient Greeks thought Athenian freedom made its citizens restless and unpredictable. ■

◄ *Athenians continued their education as adults by discussing myths. This vase painting from the 500s B.C. illustrates the myth of the twin gods Kastor and Pollux.*

■ *How did education differ in Sparta and in Athens?*

Allies Against Persia

Although Sparta and Athens were quite different, their leaders occasionally put their differences aside and joined together to fight a common enemy. The greatest foreign challenge to the Greek city-states came from the Persian empire in the 490s B.C.

During the 500s B.C., Persia built a vast empire in what is today called the Middle East. Stretching from Egypt in the west to the Indus River in the east, the Persian empire brought the entire region under one ruler. The Persians began to extend their control into the city-states along the eastern edge of the Aegean Sea.

In 499 B.C., Athens sent soldiers to help these city-states fight off the Persians. After five years of fighting, Persia crushed the revolt. However, Persia's king Darius wanted to punish Athens for aiding the rebellion.

In 490, the Persians sailed toward Athens, landing at the Bay of Marathon. As you have read, the Athenian forces defeated the invaders. The Persians fled, leaving thousands of dead soldiers on the battlefield. However, the Persians did not give up their desire to pun-ish Athens. They hoped to extend their power into Greece.

Fighting Xerxes' Army

Ten years later, in 480 B.C., the Persian army returned under Darius' son Xerxes *(ZURK sees)*. Historians estimate that as many as 200,000 soldiers set sail from Persia. When the Greek city-states learned of this huge army about to attack them, some banded together under the military leadership of the Spartans.

The first battle between the combined Greek forces and the Persians took place at Thermopylae *(thur MAHP uh lee)*, a mountain pass on the Greek mainland. The Greeks sent about 7,000 soldiers to guard the pass. For two days, the Greek soldiers held off the Persians. On the second night, however, a Greek traitor led a group of Persians over a secret mountain path so that they could attack the Greek forces from the rear. Most of the Greek army retreated to avoid being surrounded. However, 300 Spartan soldiers remained at the pass, fighting to the death. Although the Greeks lost the battle at Thermopylae, the

355

1 In the Battle of Salamis, the Greek ships (in red) were clustered at the island of Salamis. The Persians divided their fleet (in yellow), sending some ships around the island to cut off the Greeks. However, those ships did not arrive in time to fight in the battle.

2 As the Greek ships left the island, the remaining Persian ships sailed into the narrow passage between the island and the Greek mainland.

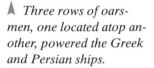

Three rows of oars-men, one located atop another, powered the Greek and Persian ships.

■ *How did the Greeks finally win the Persian Wars?*

brave stand of the Spartans allowed the rest of the Greek army to withdraw.

After the battle of Thermopylae, the Persian army overran mainland Greece and burned many parts of Athens. However, most Athenians had escaped by ship to the island of Salamis. Thus, "wooden walls" did indeed save the Athenians as the oracle at Delphi had predicted.

The Final Battles

The next major battle in the Persian Wars took place off the coast of Salamis about a month after the battle of Thermopylae. Look at the illustrations above. How did the Greeks trick the Persians and defeat them?

The Greeks sank about half the Persian fleet. Xerxes led his remaining troops back to Persia. The following summer, in 479 B.C., the Persians tried one more time to invade Greece. At the battle of Plataea *(pluh TEE uh)*, Greek forces led by the Spartans overwhelmed the Persians. By banding together, the Greek city-states defeated the immense Persian army. This victory showed the amazing things Athens and Sparta could achieve when they united. In the next chapter, you will read about the terrible destruction that resulted when they fought. ■

▲ *Both the Persians and the Greeks sailed in ships called triremes. The ships had strong bronze bows that were used as battering rams.*

3
The Greeks tricked the Persians into believing the Greek ships were retreating. The Persian fleet bunched together as it prepared to attack.

4
The Greeks reversed their course and attacked first. They surrounded the Persian ships and rammed them. About 200 Persian ships were sunk. The Greeks lost only 40 ships.

REVIEW

1. **FOCUS** How were the cultures of Athens and Sparta similar? How were they different?

2. **CONNECT** How was the economy of Sparta different from the economy of Athens?

3. **SOCIAL SYSTEMS** Why did some ancient Greek thinkers admire Sparta more than Athens?

4. **CRITICAL THINKING** If you had a choice, would you rather be an Athenian or a Spartan? Why?

5. **WRITING ACTIVITY** Write a newspaper account describing the battle between the Greek and Persian fleets off the coast of Salamis.

The Ancient Greeks

Chapter Review

Reviewing Key Terms

barter (p. 343)
city-state (p. 333)
comedy (p. 350)
democracy (p. 339)
ephor (p. 352)
helot (p. 353)

monarchy (p. 339)
oligarchy (p. 339)
sanctuary (p. 347)
tragedy (p. 350)
tyrant (p. 340)

A. On your own paper, use each word below in a sentence that shows what the word means. Write your sentence as if it were the beginning of a story.
1. monarchy
2. tyrant
3. barter
4. sanctuary
5. city-state

B. Answer the following questions about the key terms.
1. Which three key terms are words for people? If you could be one of these people, which would you be? Why?
2. Which two words describe a play? If you could see one of these plays, which would you see? Why?
3. Which three words name forms of government? If you could live under one of these governments, which would you choose? Why?
4. Which word names a method of trading? If you use this method, what problems might occur?

Exploring Concepts

A. Copy the timeline below. After each date, write the importance of the date in the history of ancient Greece. The first entry is done for you. Choose two entries and write a paragraph for each one that explains the historical event more fully. Use information from the chapter.

B. Answer each question with information from the chapter.
1. How did living within 40 miles of the sea affect the unity of the Greeks?
2. How did geography help Greek civilization advance?
3. Describe the first Aegean civilization.
4. How did the first Aegean civilization influence the Mycenaeans?
5. Describe the four different forms of government used in ancient Greece.
6. Using facts in the chapter, tell how the ancient Olympics differed from today's.
7. How did the Greeks individually worship their gods?
8. How did the governments of Athens and Sparta develop differently?
9. How were Spartan boys trained for the military?
10. How did the Spartans help lead the Greeks to victory over the Persians?

2000 B.C., Minoan Age begins in Crete.

1100 B.C., ____

776 B.C., ____

570 B.C., ____

| 2000 | 1750 | 1500 | 1250 | 1000 | 750 | 500 |

1400 B.C., ____

600 B.C., ____

479 B.C., ____

Reviewing Skills

1. The table at the right gives information about the discus throw event in the Olympics. What kind of graph would be the best one to use to show this information? Explain why this is the best graph to use.

2. On your own paper, create a graph using the information from the table at the right. Make the kind of graph you chose as your answer to question 1.

3. Decide which kind of graph would best show the following information about Spartan life. Then create the graph on your own paper.

Age	Living Quarters /Activity
0–7	Home/early training
7–18	Barracks/physical training
18–20	Barracks/army training

4. Look at the detailed map of Delphi on page 348. Based on the information on this map, what could you say about the people who lived there?

Olympic Discus Records

Year	Distance (in nearest feet)
1896	96
1912	148
1932	162
1956	185
1972	211
1988	226

5. It is 400 B.C. You are a metalworker who makes coins. You have decided that you want to record the coinmaking process for future generations. How would you choose to show it? Name the type of drawing you might make.

Using Critical Thinking

1. One reason Spartan men spent most of their adult lives in the military service was that Spartans were concerned about uprisings by their slaves. Do you think the history of ancient Greece might have been different if Sparta had had fewer slaves? Explain why you think as you do.

2. Because a young girl in Athens was not educated, she could not take part in the political life of her community. Do you think this strengthens or weakens a society? Explain your answer, thinking about what life in your community would be like if only boys went to school.

3. The Olympic Games were an important part of Greek life. Do sports play an important role in your school or community? Do you think good athletes should concentrate on athletics instead of school subjects? Why or why not?

Preparing for Citizenship

1. **COLLECTING INFORMATION** Look in a dictionary for words with Greek origins. Write the definitions of five words you find.

2. **WRITING ACTIVITY** Long ago, myths were used to explain natural events. Sometimes mythic characters acted out qualities that a society admired or disliked. Find a Greek myth to read. Does any character act out a quality that we admire or dislike? Explain.

3. **COLLABORATIVE LEARNING** In small groups, plan brief Athenian-style trials to present to the class. One group member is accused of a crime. A witness supports the innocence of the accused. A second witness denies the innocence of the accused. A public crier announces the decision facing the jurors. The class (the jury) decides each case.

359

Chapter 12
Classical Greece

"Our city is an education to Greece," boasted Pericles, the leader of Athens, in 430 B.C. This was Greece's Golden Age, when Athens blossomed as a center of democratic government and achievements in the arts and sciences. Although Athens and the other Greek city-states eventually fell to foreign invaders, their accomplishments have been passed down through the ages.

550	500	450

447–405 B.C. The Athenians build beautiful temples on a rocky hill called the Acropolis. The Parthenon (above) is a marble temple dedicated to the goddess Athena.

500 B.C.

During the 400s B.C., Greek playwrights staged tragedies and comedies at the Dionysus Theater (left). Actors could play many parts with a quick change of masks, like those shown in the mosaic below.

338 B.C. The northern kingdom of Macedonia defeats the Greeks. Led by Alexander the Great, its powerful army spreads Greek culture as far as Egypt and India. Macedonian soldiers wore helmets like the one at right.

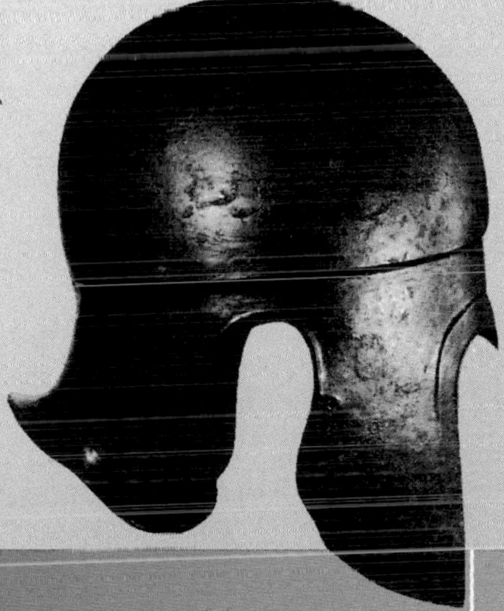

400

350

300

404 B.C. Sparta conquers Athens, bringing an end to the Peloponnesian War.

323 B.C.

LESSON 1

The Golden Age of Athens

THINKING FOCUS

Why were the years of Pericles' leadership called the Golden Age of Athens?

Key Term

- agora

➤ *Pericles led Athens during much of its Golden Age. This bust portrays him as a general with his helmet on.*

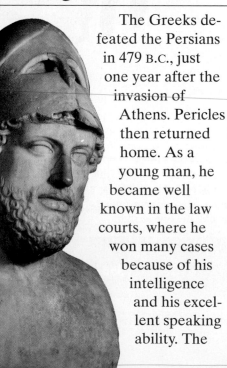

The messengers sent to Athens in 480 B.C. urgently sounded an alert: The Persians are going to invade. Everyone leave the city immediately!

A 15-year-old boy named Pericles *(PEHR ih kleez)* heard the warning, and he fled from Athens with the other citizens. They escaped to an island off the southern coast of Greece. Soon, terrifying news reached them: the Persians had burned their great city. Athens had been destroyed.

Was it at that moment that young Pericles vowed to build up Athens again and make it the greatest city of its time? No one can know for sure. But Pericles did return to Athens, and he became its most outstanding leader. From 460 to 429 B.C., Pericles led Athens through an age so glorious that it became known as the Golden Age of Athens.

The Age of Pericles

The Greeks defeated the Persians in 479 B.C., just one year after the invasion of Athens. Pericles then returned home. As a young man, he became well known in the law courts, where he won many cases because of his intelligence and his excellent speaking ability. The Greek historian Plutarch wrote the following about Pericles' ability: "Like Zeus, he was said to speak with thundering and lightning, and to wield a dreadful thunderbolt in his tongue."

Because he was a persuasive speaker, Pericles was able to convince the citizens that his ideas were important. As a result, in 460 B.C. they elected him as one of the 10 generals, the main elected officers in the Athenian democracy. The term for generals lasted just one year, but Pericles was elected over and over again.

Pericles set three major goals for Athens. His military goal was to protect Athens. His artistic goal was to make Athens beautiful. His political goal was to strengthen democracy.

Protection

Pericles' first goal was to protect Athens from its enemies. He was determined to prevent another disaster such as the burning of the city by the Persians just 20 years earlier.

The Athenians had already built a strong stone wall around Athens after the war with Persia. But enemies could still surround the city and block Athens from Piraeus, its harbor five miles away. If that happened, the city would be cut off from necessary food supplies that came into the city by ship. So the Athenians extended the wall to the sea. The new barricaded corridor became known as the Long Walls.

To protect their city further, the Athenians also built up a very powerful navy. In the years to come, Athens's navy would be the key to its defense.

Beautification

Pericles' second goal was to make Athens the most beautiful city in the world. To do that, the Athenians built new public buildings and temples. Plutarch wrote that the buildings "gave most pleasure and ornament to the city of Athens, and the greatest admiration and even astonishment to all strangers."

The most magnificent of these buildings were built on the Acropolis (uh KRAHP ah lihs). The Acropolis was a flat-topped, fortified hill in the middle of Athens. It stood about 200 feet above the rest

▲ *During the Golden Age of Athens, the Athenians beautified their city greatly. One of the most beautiful buildings from that age was the Temple of Nike, the goddess of victory.*

of the city and covered a little more than 10 acres. Temples had adorned the Acropolis for many years. But the Persian troops had destroyed all of them when they invaded the city.

The most beautiful new temple, called the Parthenon, was dedicated to Athena, the city's patron goddess. The Parthenon was 60 feet high, built from marble, and surrounded by 46 tall, graceful columns. Inside the Parthenon stood a 40-foot-tall gold and ivory statue of the goddess Athena. The Parthenon was a tribute to the outstanding artistry of the Athenians during the Golden Age. Many historians consider it to be the most beautiful building in ancient Greece.

As many as 20,000 citizens were paid by the government during the Golden Age. Everyone in the government received a salary. As a result, even poor male citizens could afford to hold office and have their voices heard.

Athens's Golden Age

During the Golden Age, Pericles called Athens the "school of Greece," because it was a center for art, literature, and ideas. In the same speech in which he praised the Athenian democracy, Pericles stated some of the basic beliefs of the Athenians:

> Our love of what is beautiful does not lead to extravagance; our love of things of the mind does not make us soft. We regard wealth as something to be properly used, rather than as something to boast about. As for poverty, no one need be ashamed to admit it: the real shame is in not taking practical measure to escape from it. Here each individual is interested not only in his own affairs but in the affairs of the state as well.

Note how these beliefs differ from those of Athens's rival, Sparta. ■

▲ *The Parthenon can still be seen today. It has been badly damaged by pollution and by an explosion that occurred in 1687 when Turkish troops were storing gunpowder in the Parthenon.*

How Do We Know?

HISTORY *Pericles gave his speech to the citizens of Athens in 430 B.C., after the first year of fighting in a war with Sparta. The speech was recorded by Thucydides, one of the first great historians. Thucydides spent 27 years writing a history of the war with Sparta.*

■ *What were Pericles' three major goals for Athens?*

Democracy

Pericles wanted to make Athenian democracy even stronger by spreading power more evenly between rich and poor. He said to the citizens of Athens:

> It is true that we are called a democracy, for the administration is in the hands of the many and not of the few. When it is a question of settling private disputes, everyone is equal before the law; when it is a question of putting one person before another in positions of public responsibility, what counts is not membership of a particular class, but the actual ability which the man possesses.

Life in a Citizen Family

The citizens of Athens generally enjoyed a pleasant life during the Golden Age. Here is an account of how a rich family in Athens might have spent a typical day. As the first few rays of sunlight shimmered into the center courtyard of a citizen's house, the family would begin to prepare for their day. A typical household included a mother, father, two or three children, and one or two slaves or hired servants.

Men at the Marketplace

Everyone in the family ate a light breakfast of pieces of bread soaked in wine mixed with water. Afterward, the father headed down the narrow, crooked streets toward the **agora,** or marketplace. The agora was a large, open square located near the Acropolis. Beautiful public buildings and temples lined two sides of the square. On the other sides of the square, men debated the issues of the day. In the huge open center, vendors sold items ranging from food and pottery to goats and sheep. Athenian merchants hawked their wares or argued with customers over prices.

Each man walking in the agora was dressed in the usual Greek fashion—a woolen tunic that fell either to his knees or ankles. Only the richest men could afford cotton or linen tunics.

Men also might go to the Assembly or serve as jurors at the law courts. At the Assembly, citizens debated current political issues. Some of these debates were so important that citizens walked into the city from 10 to 20 miles away to hear them. At the law courts, jurors listened to speeches for and against an accused person. Then the jury members cast votes of guilty or innocent. Juries in Athens consisted of between 201 and 2,501 citizens.

In the afternoons, Athenian men went to

▼ *Athenian men spent much of their day at the gymnasium. Here they took part in sports such as boxing, discus and javelin throwing, and wrestling. The gymnasium was also a popular place for conversation.*

Athenian women did many of the household tasks. This vase shows women collecting water. Athenian homes did not have indoor plumbing, and so women had to carry water from wells to their homes.

Athenian women spent most of their time in the house. There they might work in the looming room upstairs, making clothing, and the kitchen downstairs, making bread.

one of the outdoor gymnasiums and exercised. In the evenings, the men socialized together as well.

Women and Children at Home

While men were in the agora, women were at home. Women were not allowed to vote or hold office. Instead, a woman spent much of her time in a double room called the looming room. There she made the family clothes. First she spun sheep's wool into threads on a spinning wheel. Then she dyed the threads red, yellow, black, blue, or green. Finally, she wove the threads into fabrics.

Next to the looming room was a small kitchen. There women ground grain for bread and baked the bread in small clay ovens. Preparing bread was an important task, because bread was a staple of the family's diet.

Women did all of the other cooking over a small portable hearth. During a festival, however, a family often hired a cook to roast an animal.

Women also cared for their young children. Once sons reached the age of seven, they attended school during the day. Daughters stayed home and learned how to do household tasks.

Most girls married around the age of 15. Generally their fathers chose the girls' future husbands. Sometimes a father might arrange a marriage years before the marriage was to occur. Such an arrangement made sure that the girl would marry into a good family.

The houses where women spent much of their time generally looked alike. They were made out of mud bricks that had been dried in the sun. Roofs were made from baked tiles. A door from the street

opened onto a courtyard that had an altar to Zeus at its center. The rooms surrounding the courtyard were dark because they had no windows. These rooms stayed cool in the summer and warm in the winter.

Many rich citizens could have lived in more luxury. However, they believed that their wealth should be used for the good of the whole community. The famous Greek speaker Demosthenes *(dih MAHS thuh neez)* noted that the Athenians made public buildings that "their successors can never surpass; but in private life, they practiced so great a moderation" that an observer would not be able to tell the homes of the rich from the homes of the poor.

Evenings in the Home

As the sun started to set, the men returned home for dinner. A husband and his wife ate together only if he had not invited guests. Often, however, a husband would bring home several friends. The men ate in a separate room called the men's dining room. This room was bare except for some couches against the walls where the men reclined as they ate.

Wives joined their husbands publicly for only two events. They might attend a play together or a religious parade or festival. ■

■ *How did citizens of Athens spend their days?*

Life for Noncitizens

One reason wealthy citizens enjoyed a pleasant lifestyle was that noncitizens did much of the work. Two groups of noncitizens, metics and slaves, lived in Athens.

Metics and Slaves

In order to live and work in Athens, metics were required to register with the government and to pay a monthly tax. They could not own property in Athens. Metics were allowed to attend the theater and religious festivals, and they had the right to use the law courts.

Citizens looked down on metics as inferior or second-class people. However, many metics became wealthy in Athens and returned to their own city-states, where they enjoyed both wealth and all the benefits of citizenship.

In contrast to metics, slaves had no legal rights. Most Athenian citizens owned at least one slave. Wealthy landowners often kept several slaves to farm their land, including one slave to oversee the others. Even an ordinary farmer kept one slave so the farmer could be free on certain days to go into Athens and attend the Assembly.

Slaves often did the same jobs as other Athenians, sometimes

◄ *Athenians and their slaves dressed similarly. This vase shows a slave handing a pot to her mistress. Notice the similarity of their dress.*

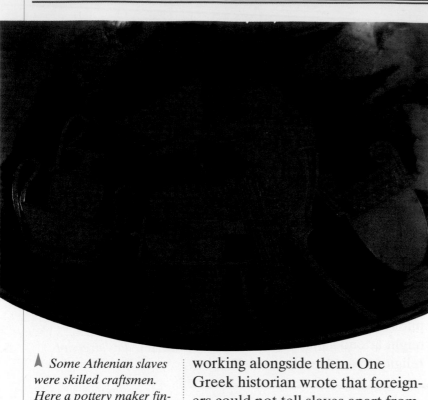

Some Athenian slaves were skilled craftsmen. Here a pottery maker finishes a pot while his completed work lies around him.

in charge of his bank. Pasion made so much money that his owner not only set him free, but also gave Pasion the bank. Over the years, Pasion multiplied his wealth and used his money to acquire a shield factory. He probably had many slaves of his own working there. A generous man, Pasion donated large sums of money for government projects in Athens. Before his death in 370 B.C., the grateful Athenians made him a citizen.

The Mining Slaves

In sharp contrast to Pasion's pleasant life were the terrible lives of the slaves who worked in the silver mines. As many as 40,000 slaves at a time worked in the mines. These slaves, who were owned by the state, had perhaps the worst lives in all of Athens. Forced to work 10-hour shifts while chained to rocks, the slaves had to crawl in tunnels that were only three feet high. They worked all day in near-darkness, chipping at stone with small picks. Many mining slaves died from overwork or disease.

Except for the miners, slaves in Athens were generally treated well, especially compared to other Greek city-states. All ancient societies had slaves. And Athens—as advanced as it was in politics and the arts—was no exception. ■

working alongside them. One Greek historian wrote that foreigners could not tell slaves apart from citizens because "they [citizens] are no better dressed and no better in appearance."

The better-off slaves held jobs that required great skill, such as goldsmithing or pottery making. Their owners often paid these slaves for their services. Slaves who saved enough of their earnings could buy their freedom. Once freed, however, slaves did not become citizens. They could only move into the ranks of metics.

One talented slave named Pasion did become a citizen as a result of his skill. Because Pasion was very smart, his master put him

■ *How was a metic's life different from a slave's?*

R E V I E W

1. **FOCUS** Why were the years of Pericles' leadership called the Golden Age of Athens?
2. **CONNECT** How was life in Athens during the Golden Age different from life in Greece during the earlier Dark Age?
3. **CITIZENSHIP** What were the roles of men and women in a citizen family?

4. **CRITICAL THINKING** Do you think life for citizens would have been different if Athens had not allowed slavery? Explain your answer.
5. **WRITING ACTIVITY** Divide a paper into two columns marked Citizens and Noncitizens. Compare and contrast the lives of these two groups in Athens during the Golden Age.

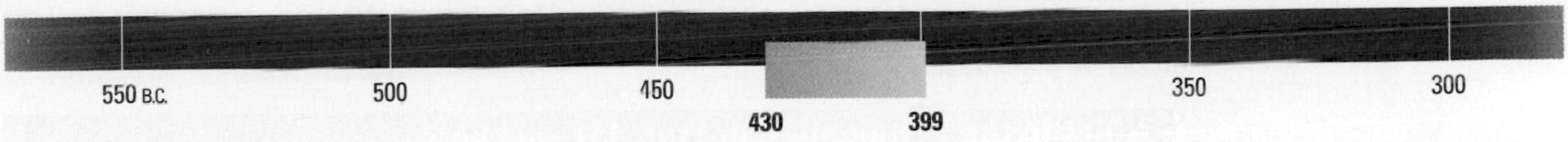

LESSON 2

The Peloponnesian War

Words indeed fail one when one tries to give a general picture of this disease; and as for the sufferings of individuals, they seemed almost beyond the capacity of human nature to endure.

Thucydides, *The Peloponnesian War*

The Greek historian Thucydides *(thoo SIHD ih deez)* wrote that description of the **plague,** a disease that swept through Athens in 430 B.C. Most victims of the plague died within a week, but they suffered terrible pain before dying.

The great disaster of the plague, as described by Thucydides, was made worse by the fact that Athens was overcrowded at this time. In addition, the Spartans had invaded Attica. To protect the Athenians who lived in the countryside surrounding the city, Pericles had called everyone into the city for protection.

Yet inside the city walls, the Athenians found despair and disease. Both the plague and the war were to change Athens, and Greece, forever.

THINKING
FOCUS

Why did the Golden Age come to an end?

Key Terms

- plague
- alliance
- philosopher

Athens and Sparta

A year before the plague struck, Sparta and her allies in the Peloponnesian League declared war against Athens. The rivalry between Athens and Sparta had existed for years. And during the Golden Age, Sparta's fear of Athens had grown more intense as a result of Athens's increasing power. After the Persian Wars, Athens had formed an **alliance,** or agreement, between city-states. This alliance, called the Delian League, was formed to protect Greece from further Persian invasions. But during the Golden Age, Athens had taken over the league, changing it from an alliance to an empire. Athens forced many

Greek city-states to remain in the league, even when these cities wanted to withdraw. The Athenians used the money they collected from this league to rebuild Athens after the Persian Wars.

In addition, Athens had begun to attack cities outside Greece. During its Golden Age, the population of Athens had increased tremendously. To ensure that everyone would have enough food, Pericles insisted that Athens control

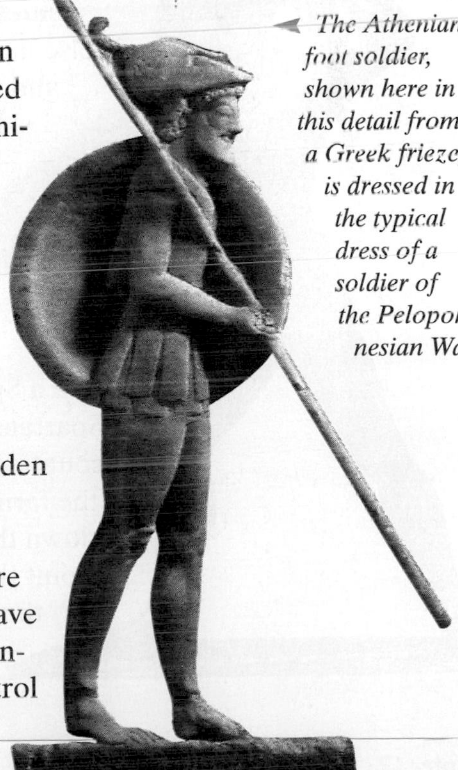

The Athenian foot soldier, shown here in this detail from a Greek frieze, is dressed in the typical dress of a soldier of the Peloponnesian War.

► Note the territories
allied with Athens and
Sparta at the start of the
Peloponnesian War.

Allies in the Peloponnesian War, 431–404 B.C.

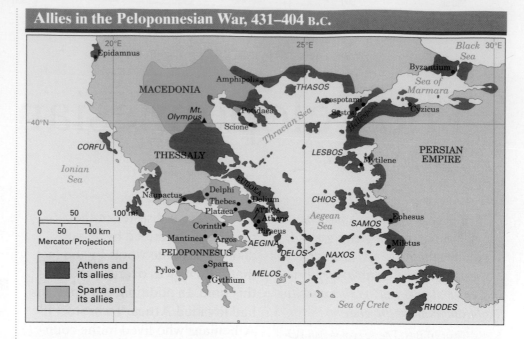

▼ Spartan foot soldiers
attacked Athens every
year during the war.

the trade routes through which grain and other food reached Athens. As a result, the mighty Athenian navy attacked and captured cities along both shores of the Aegean Sea.

Sparta felt threatened by Athens's rise in power. In 431 B.C., Sparta and her allies finally gave Athens an ultimatum: free all of the cities under your control or else face war. Athens refused, and the Peloponnesian War began.

War Begins

The walls of Athens protected the city from a Spartan invasion. The Spartans invaded Athens's countryside instead, burning the farmhouses and cutting down the grain. It was at this point that Pericles called all the outlying citizens into the city. Pericles wanted to

avoid fighting the powerful Spartan army on land. He also wanted to protect all Athenians. His plan might have worked if the plague had not hit Athens in 430 B.C.

The plague spread quickly and easily through the overcrowded streets of Athens. Within months, one of every four people in Athens had died. One of the victims was Pericles himself, who died of the plague in 429 B.C. The death of Pericles and the worsening of the war marked the beginning of the end of the Golden Age of Athens.

Athens During the War

During the war, Athens suffered through a long, hard period that contrasted greatly with the splendor of the Golden Age. Deaths from the plague affected almost every family. Food was scarce because the Spartans kept invading Athens's countryside each year and burning its crops. The labor force was weakened because many slaves were able to escape when Sparta invaded the land near Athens.

Meanwhile, the war against Sparta and her allies went on relentlessly. For many years, neither side seemed to be winning. Sparta had the more powerful army, and Athens had the more powerful navy. Therefore, the war was often at a deadlock.

A turning point in the war came in 413 B.C., when the Athenian troops suffered a serious defeat at Sicily. Many of the small cities of the Delian League that had been ruled by Athens decided to take advantage of the weakened condition of the Athenians. To free themselves from Athens's control, these cities joined forces with Sparta.

The fighting continued in Greece for another 10 years. Athens's final defeat became nearly certain when Persia agreed to give Sparta funds to build a bigger and better fleet. Although Persia was still an enemy of all of Greece, the Persians gave Sparta funds because they hoped that the Greek city-states would destroy each other.

End of the War

Meanwhile, in one last effort to defend themselves, the Athenians melted down the gold and silver ornaments in the temples to pay for building new ships. However, in 405 B.C., the Athenians made a mistake so crucial that it led to their final defeat.

The battlefront had moved to the coastal cities of the Hellespont. In the summer of 405 B.C., the Athenians sailed their fleet to a port called Aegospotami (*EE guh SPAHT uh mee*). For five days, the Spartans did not begin a battle. Believing that the harbor was safe, the Athenians went ashore to obtain badly needed food and supplies. While they were gone, the Spartan forces captured almost the entire Athenian fleet—without a single fight.

When news of the defeat at Aegospotami reached Athens, the citizens reacted with despair. In his description of that dreadful time, the Greek historian Xenophon wrote,

> On that night no man slept. There was mourning and sorrow for those that were lost, but the lamentation [expression of grief] was merged in even greater sorrow for themselves, as they pictured the evils they were about to suffer.
>
> Xenophon, *Hellenica*, c. 400 B.C.

The Athenians refused to surrender immediately. Instead, they barricaded themselves inside the city walls for several months. In the meantime, the Spartans cut off their grain supply by both land and sea. Starvation at last set in and forced the Athenians to surrender in 404 B.C. ■

Across Time & Space

Outbreaks of the plague have devastated many other societies. In A.D. 262, about 5,000 people a day died in Rome. From 1334 to 1351, plague swept through China, India, Persia, Russia, Italy, France, England, Germany, and Norway. Between 1894 and 1914, more than 10 million people in India died of the plague.

◄ Athens suffered greatly as a result of the Peloponnesian War. This funeral sculpture honors a dead soldier. Thousands of Greeks died as a result of the wars.

■ What caused the Peloponnesian War, and what were its consequences?

End of the Golden Age

The Peloponnesian War had raged for 27 years. Xenophon recorded the bleak terms of the Athenian surrender.

> That the Long Walls . . . should be destroyed; that the Athenian fleet, with the exception of twelve vessels, should be surrendered; that the exiles should be restored; and lastly, that the Athenians should acknowledge the [leadership] of Sparta in peace and war.
>
> Xenophon, *Hellenica*

Many Spartans wanted to burn Athens to the ground and sell its citizens into slavery. However, Spartan leaders decided to spare Athens. They recognized that Athens had saved all of Greece from the Persians at the battles of Marathon and Salamis.

Decline of the Democracy

At first, the Spartans destroyed the Athenian democracy and set up government by a few harsh rulers. By 430 B.C., the Athenians had forced out the rulers. The Spartan king allowed them to restore their democracy. However, their feelings for democracy no longer were as strong as they had been during the Golden Age.

A great number of citizens—especially the younger citizens— refused to take any role in public affairs after the war. Other citizens became suspicious of anyone who seemed the least bit antidemocratic. One of the great tragedies of this stormy time was the death of one of Greece's greatest teachers, Socrates.

The Trial of Socrates

Socrates was a **philosopher,** a person who searches for the truth and the meaning of life. He asked the following questions: What is justice? What is wisdom? What is goodness?

Socrates became a well-known teacher in Athens. His primary method of teaching was to ask questions that made his pupils examine their own beliefs. However, his method upset many Athenian leaders. They thought that by teaching the young to question every aspect of life, Socrates was challenging the authority of the government.

In the period of suspicion following the war, Socrates was arrested. He was charged with neglecting the worship of the gods and "corrupting the youth."

Socrates stood trial in 399 B.C. In those times, most men on trial tried to gain the sympathy of the jury by bringing their weeping wives and children to court or by dressing in poor or dirty clothes. Socrates refused

to use any such tactic. Instead, he stood with dignity before a jury of 700 Athenian citizens and pleaded his own case. However, the jury convicted Socrates by a narrow margin. His penalty was death by drinking hemlock, the juice from a poisonous plant.

During the month between the famous trial and his death, Socrates could have escaped several times. Seventy years old by that time, Socrates explained to his friends that he had obeyed the law throughout his long life and would not break it then. Later, a student of Socrates' named Plato (*PLAY toh*), wrote the following about his teacher's last moments:

H*e raised the cup to his lips and very cheerfully and quietly drained it. Up to that time most of us had been able to restrain our tears fairly well, but when we watched him drinking and saw that he had drunk the poison, we could do so no longer, but in spite of myself my tears rolled down in floods, so that I wrapped my face in my cloak and wept for myself.*

Plato honored his teacher when he said, "It was not for him [Socrates] that I wept, but for my own misfortune in being deprived of such a friend." ■

▲ *Socrates' death is illustrated in this French painting from the 1700s by Jacques Louis David. What attitude toward his death does Socrates seem to have in this painting?*

■ *Why did the teachings of Socrates upset Athenian leaders?*

R E V I E W

1. **FOCUS** Why did the Golden Age come to an end?
2. **CONNECT** Was Athens justified in forming the Delian League? Why?
3. **HISTORY** How might the plague have affected the outcome of the Peloponnesian War?
4. **CRITICAL THINKING** How did democracy in Athens differ before and after the Golden Age?
5. **ACTIVITY** Socrates taught his pupils to question every aspect of life. Athenian leaders thought his questioning threatened the democracy. Who do you think was right? Prepare and give a speech defending either Socrates or the Athenian leaders.

373

Classical Greece

LESSON 3

Alexander the Great and His Influence

How did Alexander the Great spread Greek culture throughout the ancient world?

Key Terms

• conquest
• Hellenistic

King Philip of Macedonia and many of his subjects looked on one day in 342 B.C. as men attempted to tame a horse. The huge horse kept rearing up, kicking its legs wildly and throwing its head back and forth. The king wanted to buy the horse, but he decided it was too mean and wild. Then his 14-year-old son Alexander spoke up. "What a horse they are losing, and all because they don't know how to handle him, or dare not try!" According to the historian Plutarch:

Philip kept quiet at first, but when he heard Alexander repeat these words several times and saw that he was upset, he asked him, "Are you finding fault with your elders because you think you know more than they do, or can manage a horse better?" "At least I could manage this one better," explained Alexander.

Alexander bet his father that he could ride the horse. Alexander approached the horse and stroked it to calm it down. Then Alexander mounted it and galloped around the field. Plutarch wrote:

Thereupon the rest of the company broke into loud applause, while his father, we are told, actually wept for joy. And when Alexander had dismounted he kissed him and said, "My boy, you must find a kingdom big enough for your ambitions. Macedonia is too small for you."

► *Alexander rode his horse Bucephalus on most of his military campaigns. Bucephalus fell in battle on the Hydaspes River in 326 B.C.*

Alexander would indeed follow his father's advice. Riding this horse, he would venture far beyond Macedonia to create the largest kingdom the ancient western world had yet known.

The Rise of Macedonia

From 399 B.C. to 338 B.C., individual Greek city-states fought each other for power. However, no city-state could establish the kind of power Athens had enjoyed during the Golden Age.

The Rise of Macedonia

Macedonia was a large state just north of Greece. It had little power because it was far less organized than the smaller Greek city-states. However, when King Philip, Alexander's father, took the throne in 359 B.C., he turned Macedonia into a military power.

Most ancient armies were made up of soldiers who served for a limited time and then returned home. Philip, however, established a professional army of full-time, well-paid, highly skilled soldiers.

A military genius, Philip developed new battle formations and a large number of weapons for his army. These new weapons included catapults, machines that could hurl burning spears or 50-pound rocks over walls, and battering rams on wheels that could smash through locked doors and closed gates.

Greece Falls to Macedonia

Philip used his powerful army to build an empire. Soon after coming to rule in 359 B.C., he defeated large tribes to the north and west of Macedonia. Then he turned south to Greece. The Greek armies were no match for the Macedonian military and fell at the Battle of Chaeronea *(KEHR uh NEE uh)*. In 338 B.C., Philip became ruler of Greece.

Philip might have ended Greece's independence after his victory. Yet he did not. After he had defeated the Greeks, Philip ordered that Athens not be destroyed because he admired its culture. Philip had gained respect for Greek ways during his youth when he spent three years in Thebes as a hostage.

When Philip defeated the Greeks, he reorganized their armies and combined them with Macedonia's troops. Philip then set out to conquer the great Persian empire with his powerful army. However, shortly before his first expedition to Persia, Philip was murdered. Philip's son Alexander would have to fulfill Philip's dreams of empire. ■

▲ *This gilded sheeting for a bow-and-arrow case is believed to have been Philip's. It gives an idea of the wealth and power of Philip and his son.*

■ *How did Macedonia become a powerful state?*

Alexander's Conquests

Alexander was only 20 when his father was murdered in 336 B.C. But he firmly took charge of his father's kingdom. He put down the revolts that sprang up. Then he turned his ambitions toward winning new lands.

With his troops, Alexander began a 20,000-mile journey of **conquest,** or victory by force over other peoples. Look at the map in A Closer Look on pages 376 and 377. How far south did Alexander extend his empire? How far east? ■

■ *How did Alexander build an empire?*

Alexander's Conquests

*Alexander the Great was a brilliant general.
By outwitting his enemies, he defeated armies
much larger than his own. Alexander was only
16 when he joined his father's army. For the
rest of his life, he marched from battle to battle.*

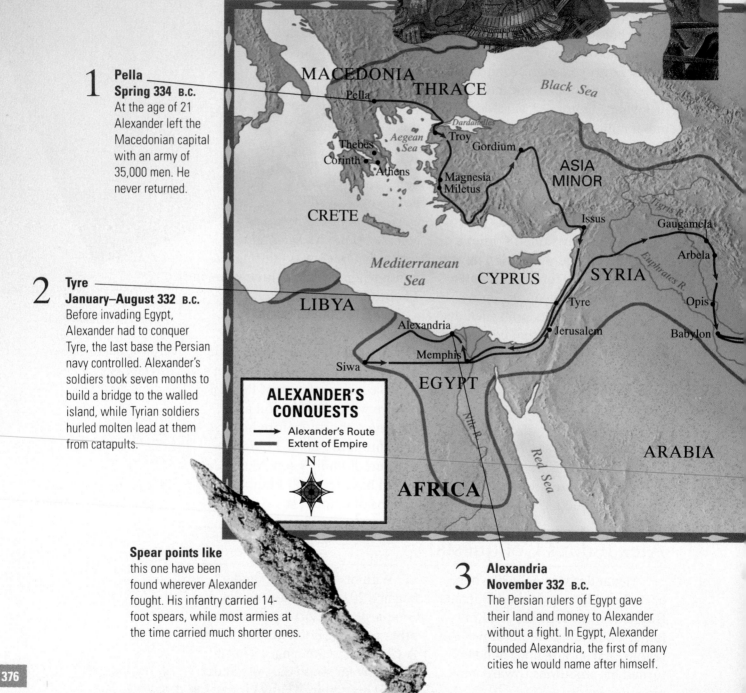

**1 Pella
Spring 334 B.C.**
At the age of 21
Alexander left the
Macedonian capital
with an army of
35,000 men. He
never returned.

**2 Tyre
January–August 332 B.C.**
Before invading Egypt,
Alexander had to conquer
Tyre, the last base the Persian
navy controlled. Alexander's
soldiers took seven months to
build a bridge to the walled
island, while Tyrian soldiers
hurled molten lead at them
from catapults.

ALEXANDER'S CONQUESTS
→ Alexander's Route
━ Extent of Empire

N

Spear points like
this one have been
found wherever Alexander
fought. His infantry carried 14-
foot spears, while most armies at
the time carried much shorter ones.

**3 Alexandria
November 332 B.C.**
The Persian rulers of Egypt gave
their land and money to Alexander
without a fight. In Egypt, Alexander
founded Alexandria, the first of many
cities he would name after himself.

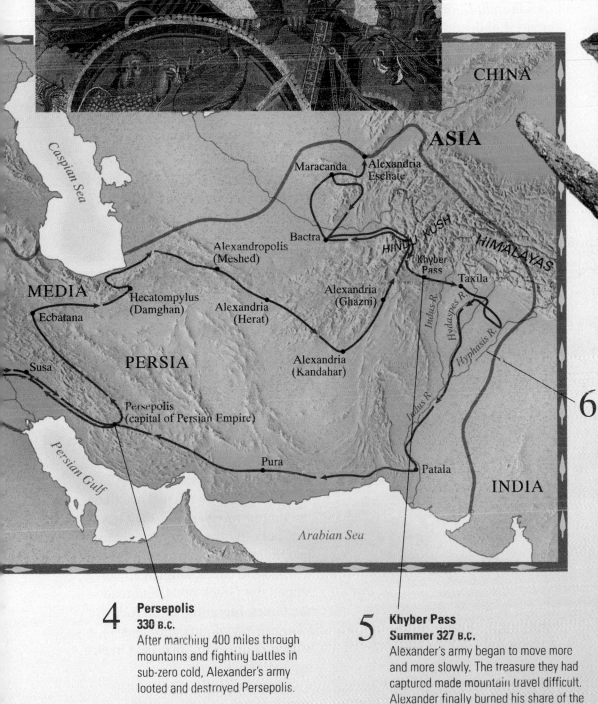

King Darius III of Persia stood between Alexander and the rest of Asia. Their armies fought at the Gulf of Issus in 333 B.C. and at Guagamela two years later. Each time Darius had more soldiers. But Alexander's clever planning won the battles, forcing Darius to flee for his life.

Roman mural from the first century A.D. shows Alexander (left) and Darius (right)

CHINA

ASIA

Maracanda

Alexandria Eschate

Caspian Sea

Bactra

HINDU KUSH

HIMALAYAS

Alexandropolis (Meshed)

Khyber Pass

Taxila

MEDIA

Hecatompylus (Damghan)

Alexandria (Ghazni)

Alexandria (Herat)

Indus R.

Hydaspes R.

Hyphasis R.

Ecbatana

Alexandria (Kandahar)

Susa

PERSIA

Indus R.

Persepolis (capital of Persian Empire)

6 Hyphasis River Summer 326 B.C.
After months of heat and rain, the army reached the Hyphasis River and refused to go any farther. To punish the army, Alexander led them on a harsh homeward route through the desert. Three years later, at the age of 33, Alexander became ill and died in Babylon.

Persian Gulf

Pura

Patala

INDIA

Arabian Sea

4 Persepolis 330 B.C.
After marching 400 miles through mountains and fighting battles in sub-zero cold, Alexander's army looted and destroyed Persepolis.

5 Khyber Pass Summer 327 B.C.
Alexander's army began to move more and more slowly. The treasure they had captured made mountain travel difficult. Alexander finally burned his share of the loot and ordered his men to do the same.

377

Classical Greece

The Spread of Greek Culture

Today Alexandria is the chief port of Egypt. It also is the second largest city in Egypt, after Cairo, the nation's capital.

▼ *The legend of Alexander lived on. This Persian painting from the 1500s shows Alexander as a horseman dressed in Persian clothing.*

Like his father, Alexander had both a military genius and an appreciation for Greek culture. Alexander had learned to appreciate the accomplishments of Greek culture as a child. In fact, his father, Philip, had hired Aristotle *(AR ih staht l),* one of Greece's greatest philosophers, to teach Alexander about literature, philosophy, and science. Years later, Alexander would tell people that from his father, he had received life, but from Aristotle he had learned how to lead a good life.

Historians have given Alexander the title of "Alexander the Great." His greatness is remembered not only because he created a vast empire, but also because the influence of Greek culture remained long after Alexander's empire fell apart. The legend of Alexander remained even longer. Alexander's life and conquests continued to be a popular topic for stories and paintings for more than a thousand years in India, Persia, and Egypt.

New Greek Colonies

As Alexander conquered lands, he established colonies and built cities modeled after Greek cities in the conquered lands. Alexander realized that he could not maintain control over these conquered lands with force alone. W0hen he and his armies moved on, Alexander left behind Greeks to rule these lands.

In addition, he adopted some features of the conquered cultures. For instance, Alexander began to wear Persian clothing and brought Persian soldiers into his army as he moved into central Asia. It was Alexander's hope that by doing these things the Persians would not see Greek rule as alien. Thus they would not rebel against the Greeks. Not only did they not rebel, many people in these countries actually learned the Greek language, worshiped the Greek gods, and read the Greek literature. Even today, there are people in central Asia who proudly claim that the Greeks are their ancestors.

Eventually, the Greek influence became so widespread that the period from Alexander's rule

to 146 B.C. became known as the Hellenistic Age. **Hellenistic** means "Greek-like." The art and culture of the Hellenistic period was a mixture of Greek and Eastern art and culture. During the Hellenistic Age, Greece became the teacher of the western world in the areas of science, art, literature, and philosophy.

Most of the lands that Alexander had conquered, such as Egypt and Persia, did not give up their own cultures altogether. Instead, these countries adopted two systems of life. One system was Greek for the people who lived in the cities. The other system was a native system for the people who lived in the country and therefore were not in close contact with the Greeks.

The Museum at Alexandria

During the Hellenistic Age, the center of Greek culture shifted from Athens to the new city of Alexandria—named after Alexander the Great. Located in Egypt, Alexandria was founded by Alexander in 332 B.C.

A magnificent museum, which was the intellectual center of the world during the Hellenistic Age,

▲ *The Alexander legend also continued in India. This Indian painting from the 1500s supposedly illustrates an event from Alexander's life. According to the legend, Alexander had asked to be lowered into the sea in a glass barrel. Alexander hoped to study marine life while under water.*

was built at Alexandria. At the museum, mathematicians, poets, philosophers, and astronomers gathered to explore the mysteries of numbers, words, ideas, and the heavens.

To help the scholars do their research, the museum opened a library. This library, which grew into the largest library in the ancient world, had a collection of both Greek and non-Greek scrolls. Scholars at the library translated these non-Greek scrolls into

Classical Greece

Greek. In fact, some scientists believe that the oldest manuscript of the Old Testament—still in existence today—was first translated into Greek at the great museum in Alexandria.

Besides having a huge impact on the ancient world, the museum at Alexandria influenced future generations. It remained an important intellectual center for about seven centuries, until it was destroyed in the A.D. 200s. Thus, Alexander's conquests continued to affect the world for years after his death. ■

■ *What is Hellenistic culture?*

UNDERSTANDING CONQUEST

Alexander the Great's many conquests built the greatest empire that the world had known up to that time. What is conquest? Why do leaders and nations set out on conquests? What are the results of conquest?

Victory Is Not Conquest

A conquest begins when one power overcomes another power in a war. However, conquest is more than just the defeat of one army by another. During a conquest, the conquerors remain in the lands that they have won and control the defeated people by establishing a new system of government. In addition, the conquerors use the resources of the defeated country as they see fit.

Leaders Make Conquests

Leaders and nations generally make conquests to increase their power and wealth. For example, 100 years after Alexander's death, Rome, a powerful city-state in Italy, began making conquests. The Romans hoped to increase their power by controlling trade in the lands around the Mediterranean.

Sometimes a rival nation may have great wealth but may at the same time lack the power to defend itself. The potential conqueror then attempts to conquer the rival nation to gain that wealth. For example, in the early 1500s, Spain began making conquests in the Americas. Spain wanted to acquire silver and gold from mines in America and to build Spain into a world power.

Conquest Brings Change

The results of conquest are similar in some ways to the results of migration. Defeated peoples adopt elements of their conquerors' cultures, and conquerors borrow from the cultures of the defeated. For example, in Latin America today, the majority of the people speak Spanish. However, the people of Spanish descent in Latin America eat many foods that were adopted from the native population, including corn and beans.

In much the same way, Alexander's armies spread Greek language and culture throughout the vast empire. But Greeks eventually began to build enormous monuments and palaces that looked more Persian than Greek. The merging of Greek and eastern cultures through conquest was to change both cultures forever.

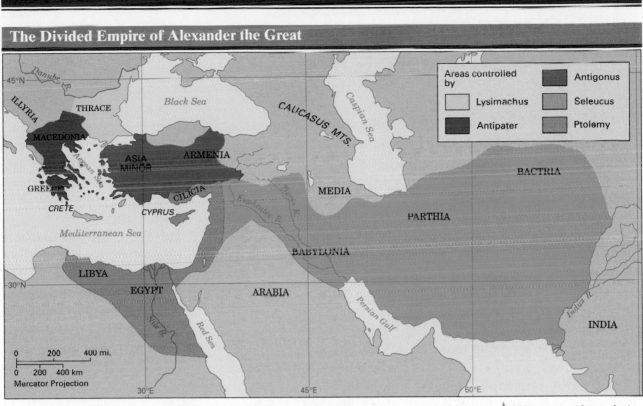

The Divided Empire of Alexander the Great

Areas controlled by
- Lysimachus
- Antipater
- Antigonus
- Seleucus
- Ptolemy

ILLYRIA · THRACE · MACEDONIA · GREECE · CRETE · Aegean Sea · Danube R. · Black Sea · CAUCASUS MTS. · Caspian Sea · ASIA MINOR · ARMENIA · CILICIA · CYPRUS · Mediterranean Sea · Euphrates R. · Tigris R. · MEDIA · BACTRIA · PARTHIA · BABYLONIA · LIBYA · EGYPT · Nile R. · Red Sea · ARABIA · Persian Gulf · Indus R. · INDIA

0 200 400 mi.
0 200 400 km
Mercator Projection

45°N · 30°N · 30°E · 45°E · 60°E

How was Alexander's empire divided after his death?

After Alexander

In 323 B.C., Alexander suddenly died of a fever. He was 33 years old. During the 13 years of his rule, he had created the largest empire in the western world.

After Alexander's death in 323 B.C., Greek culture still united the empire. But politically the empire broke apart because no single leader had enough power to take Alexander's place.

When Alexander the Great died, his generals split his empire among themselves. The giant empire was cut up into as many as 34 kingdoms. In bloody fighting, five generals took control of different parts of the empire, as shown on the map above. Which three generals controlled the largest areas? Eventually, the regions led by Antigonus (an TIHG uh nuhs), Seleucus (sih LOO kuhs), and Ptolemy (TAHL uh mee) became stronger than the rest. Yet even these had only a fraction of the power and size of the former empire of Alexander the Great. ∎

Why did Alexander's empire decline after his death?

R E V I E W

1. **FOCUS** How did Alexander the Great spread Greek culture throughout the ancient world?
2. **CONNECT** What methods did Alexander use to rule his empire? How did these methods differ from the methods the Athenians used to rule the Delian League?
3. **GEOGRAPHY** What were the major regions included in Alexander's vast empire?
4. **CRITICAL THINKING** What qualities do you think made Alexander a great leader?
5. **WRITING ACTIVITY** Imagine you are a soldier traveling with Alexander on his great march of conquests. Write a letter home telling about some of your adventures.

381

Presenting Information

Here's Why

Writing a report is a good way to add to your knowledge and to share information with others. Suppose you were asked to write a report about the outcome of the Peloponnesian War. Would you know what to do? Where would you begin?

Here's How

Here are six basic steps for writing a good report.

1. **Explore your topic.** Make a list of five things you want to know about your topic. Consider narrowing your topic to one of the five questions.

2. **Do research.** You can find a lot of information about the Peloponnesian War in this chapter, but you should use other sources (encyclopedias, books, and magazines) also.

3. **Take notes.** As you read, record information on note cards like those below. Write each different idea on a separate note card. When you finish taking notes, group the cards according to the main ideas.

4. **Write an outline.** Look at the outline below. Notice how the important ideas from the note cards become the main points shown by Roman numerals in the outline. After you identify the main parts, go back and fill in the details. Notice how the details from the note cards become the subheads listed on the outline.

5. **Write a first draft.** Use the items with Roman numerals in your outline as paragraph topic sentences in your report. Use the subheads as supporting details. Write in complete sentences and paragraphs.

6. **Revise, proofread, and copy.** After completing your first draft, read it over to see how you can improve it and to correct any mistakes you may find. Then prepare the final copy.

Try It

Follow the first four steps of writing a report. Use the following topic: Some people say Sparta won the Peloponnesian War; others say Athens lost it.

Apply It

Use the first three steps of writing a report to learn more about a hobby. Then make an outline.

The Peloponnesian War

I. Sparta invades athenian countryside
  A. Farmhouses burned
  B. Crops destroyed
  C. Athenian citizens forced into the walled city
II. Plague hits Athens
  A. Spreads in overcrowded city
    1. One in four die
    2. Pericles dies

A
Spartan Invasion
Spartans burn athenian farmhouses

B
Spartan Invasion
Spartans destroy crops of athenians

C
Spartan Invasion
citizens of athens forced into walled city of athens

LESSON 4

Contributions of the Greeks

High on a hill, a Greek temple overlooks the riverfront. Along the banks of the river, the reflection of graceful Greek columns and simple Greek shapes shimmer in the water. Could this scene, pictured below, be a photograph of a well-preserved section of Greece?

Actually, it's a photograph of present-day Philadelphia. The Philadelphia Museum of Art, the temple on the hill, was modeled after the temples built by the Greeks 2,500 years ago. It was even painted with the bright colors favored by the ancient Greeks. Likewise, the buildings along the banks of the river were built in the classic Greek style. Even the name Philadelphia comes from the Greek word for "brotherly love."

The influence of the ancient Greeks can be seen throughout the United States. Many of our houses, churches, government buildings, and schools have been built in the style that can be traced to the ancient Greeks. And the influence is not only found in architecture. It's also in artwork, literature, history, philosophy, science, and mathematics.

THINKING FOCUS

How does the culture of ancient Greece still influence our lives today?

Key Term

• lyric poetry

◄ *The riverfront of Philadelphia shows the strong influence of Greek architecture today.*

383

Classical Greece

The theater at Epidaurus, shown at right, was built over 2,300 years ago. Even today, because the theater was so well designed, anyone sitting in one of the theater's 14,000 seats can hear the faintest whisper.

Because Greek theaters were so large, actors wore masks so everyone in the audience could see them. Note the two masks sitting next to two of the actors in the mosaic below.

Greek Arts

You have probably seen many buildings that look Greek. Greek styles have influenced architecture in many countries during the past 2,000 years. Look at the Minipedia on pages 490 and 491 to see the features of Greek architecture.

The most noticeable feature of Greek architecture is the use of columns to support the roof. The three types of Greek columns are illustrated in the Minipedia article on page 490.

Literature

Many of the forms of literature that have been popular throughout history can be traced to the Greeks. Although the Greeks did not invent these literary forms, they did perfect them. One popular Greek literary form was epic poetry, long poems celebrating heroic deeds. You have read about the epic poems of Homer, the *Odyssey* and the *Iliad*. The Greeks also wrote a shorter form of poetry called **lyric poetry.** Lyric poetry deals with personal feelings rather than great events. One of the greatest Greek lyric poets was Sappho *(SAF oh)*. She wrote poems celebrating friendship and love in the 600s B.C.

Perhaps the greatest contribution of Greek literature was Greek theater. Greek tragic plays are still admired today because they deal

with timeless issues about how people behave.

The Greeks also introduced styles of comedy that we still see today. For example, in the 400s B.C., Greeks enjoyed biting comedies that made fun of politics, public figures, and social issues. One of the most popular Greek writers of such comedy was Aristophanes *(ar ih STAHF uh neez)*, who often made fun of important people in his plays.

Art and Sculpture

Painters and sculptors throughout history have learned from the Greeks. Look at the sculpture pictured here. Notice the natural and lifelike form. The body looks almost real. The Greeks showed the human body in a way that is both beautiful and without flaws. As with Greek architecture, other cultures greatly admired and copied Greek art and then passed it on to future generations.

History

The Greeks were the first people to examine the past critically and write down their findings. In the 400s B.C., two Greeks wrote accounts of wars that changed the way history was written.

The historian Herodotus *(hih RAHD uh tuhs)* is called the "father of history." His history of the Persian Wars was one of the first factual accounts of a past event. The word *history* actually comes from the Greek word that Herodotus uses in his first line, *historia*, meaning researches or inquiries. In the opening sentence of his book, he wrote:

These are the researches of Herodotus of Halicarnassus, which he publishes with a view to preserving from oblivion [from being forgotten] the remembrance of what men have done. Thus, the great and wonderful deeds of the Greeks and foreign peoples will not lose the acclaim that is due them. At the same time, the reasons for their hostility will be put on record.

The other great historian of the 400s B.C., Thucydides, took history a step further when he wrote an account of the Peloponnesian War. In his history, Herodotus had traced many events to the will of the gods. Thucydides, on the other hand, tried to understand events from people's actions. He also used sources and documents and interviewed eyewitnesses. His method of sifting through evidence set a new standard for future historians. ■

■ What are three forms of literature that the Greeks are famous for?

◄ *This statue, believed to be Zeus preparing to throw a thunderbolt, illustrates the ancient Greek style of sculpture. Note how real the figure looks.*

► *The Socratic method of questioning students rather than lecturing to them is used today in most law schools in the United States. Note also the auditorium style of the room, similar to the seating at a Greek theater.*

Greek Ideas

Just as Thucydides looked beyond the will of the gods to explain history, Greek philosophers and scientists looked beyond the gods for answers to other questions about the world. The Greeks thought people themselves could answer these questions.

Philosophy

The search for answers, however, was not always successful. For example, Greeks at the time of Homer had believed that Poseidon, the god of the waters, caused earthquakes. In the 500s B.C., the first Greek philosopher, Thales, challenged that belief. Thales claimed that the world rested on water. Therefore, he concluded, earthquakes resulted from wind making waves in the water. Thales' explanation was wrong, but he had taken a first step in searching for explanations rather than blaming the gods.

Later philosophers, such as Socrates, Plato, and Aristotle, continued this search for explanations. These philosophers developed ways of seeking knowledge that are still used today. In particular, many American universities use Socrates' method of repeatedly questioning students rather than lecturing to them.

Science

The Greeks also asked basic questions about the natural world. These questions led them to make early discoveries in such diverse areas as astronomy, medicine, and mathematics.

The Greek astronomer Aristarchus *(ar ih STAHR kuhs)* was one of these early discoverers. He expressed a theory in the 200s B.C. that the earth revolved around the sun. Until Aristarchus was proven correct a thousand years later, many Europeans continued to believe that the sun revolved around the earth.

A mathematician named Pythagoras *(pih THAG ur uhs)*

Oath. Medical doctors still take that oath today. Part of it reads,

> I will follow that method of treatment which, according to my ability and judgment, I consider for the benefit of my patients, and abstain from whatever is [harmful].

◄ *The Greeks became famous for their medicine. This relief shows an ancient doctor treating a patient.*

made important discoveries in a field of mathematics called geometry. Today, students still learn about some of Pythagoras's discoveries. Another great Greek mathematician, Euclid, is sometimes called the father of geometry. He wrote a book explaining geometry that was used as a textbook until about 1900.

In medicine, Hippocrates (*hih PAHK ruh teez*) was one of the first doctors who looked for natural causes for diseases. Previously, people had believed that acts of the gods caused diseases. In the 400s B.C., Hippocrates also wrote a pledge about the duty of doctors, called the Hippocratic

The Legacy of Greece

In addition to their great achievements in the arts and sciences, the Greeks' ideas about democracy and government have been passed down through the centuries. In fact, the Greek civilization is sometimes called the starting point of Western civilization. ■

▼ *The drawing illustrates a famous theorem of Pythagoras. Adding together the squares of the lengths of two sides of a right triangle you get the square of the length of the third side. Try writing an equation that describes the triangle below.*

■ *How did Greek philosophers and scientists react to and try to understand the natural world?*

REVIEW

1. **FOCUS** How does the culture of ancient Greece still influence our lives today?
2. **CONNECT** Think about the philosophers and scientists from the other cultures you have learned about. Choose one, such as Confucius or Asoka. How did their works differ from the works of Greek philosophers and scientists?
3. **CULTURE** Why is the Greek civilization considered the starting point of Western civilization?
4. **CRITICAL THINKING** Many American government buildings are designed in the Greek style. In addition to the beauty of the Greek style, what do you think are the reasons why government officials choose to use the Greek style?
5. **ACTIVITY** How does ancient Greece influence your daily life? For one week, keep track of the things you see and do that have been influenced by the Greeks. Make a chart listing the items you discover under headings such as math and science, art, literature, and government.

The Internet and Ancient Civilizations

Years ago, people who wanted to learn more about early civilizations had to travel to ancient sites or to the library to find information. Today, the Internet has opened a new way to do research for millions of people. The Internet is a network of computers that connects people, businesses, and institutions all over the world. You can learn about almost any topic by searching the Internet.

Get Ready

The Internet can help you learn more about ancient civilizations, such as the one in Greece. You'll need a computer with Internet access, which allows you to connect to the World Wide Web. Be sure the computer has a Web browser, which is the software that enables you to "travel" to Web sites. A Web site is a collection of "pages" with information on specific topics. A Web site is located by its address, or URL (Uniform Resource Locator).

To best use the Internet for research, you must decide what you want to know. The more specific you can be in your research topic, the more likely you are to find helpful information.

▶ Internet Service Providers give computers access to the Internet. Usually you connect to your Internet Service Provider through a modem.

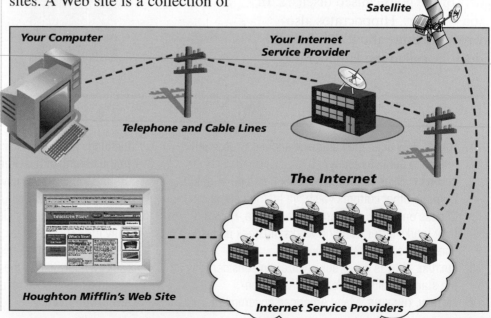

Your Computer

Your Internet Service Provider

Satellite

Telephone and Cable Lines

The Internet

Houghton Mifflin's Web Site

Internet Service Providers

388

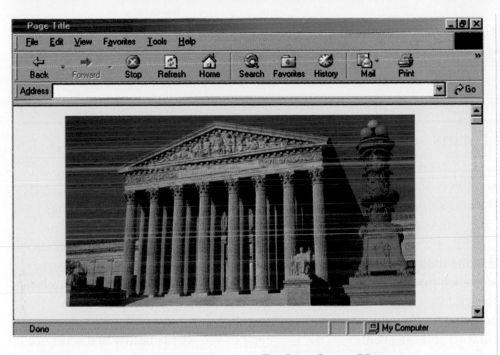

◄ This Web site provides information on Greek architecture's continuing influence.

Find Out

Suppose you wish to learn more about Greek architecture. You can practice using the Internet to research this topic by visiting the Web site **Education Place** at www.eduplace.com/kids/.

When you get to the site, you will find "Brain Power." Click on "Using the Web," choose Grades 6-8, and you will find a step-by-step process for doing research on the Web.

Move Ahead

When you do research on the Internet, you must record your findings, just as you would if you found information in a book or in a visit. Take notes on the information you read on a Web site. Be sure to record the name and address (URL) of the Web site as your source of information. Also note the day on which you recorded your notes because information on the Internet can change often.

Explore Some More

Web sites often have links to other sources of information. These links connect to other places on the Internet, such as other Web sites or pages within the same Web site.

By searching the Internet, you can find many more Web sites with information on Greek architecture. You can use a search engine to help you find these sites. (A search engine lets you find Web pages that contain specific information.) Type in the key words, "Greek architecture."

Be sure to record the site name and the date of your research when you record the information you find. Remember, not all Web sites have accurate, unbiased information. You need to check the source of the Web site.

▲ The top of a Greek column is called its capital.

389

Classical Greece

Chapter Review

Reviewing Key Terms

agora (p. 365)
alliance (p. 369)
conquest (p. 380)
Hellenistic (p. 379)

lyric poetry (p. 384)
philosopher (p. 372)
plague (p. 369)

A. Be sure you understand the meanings of the key terms. Then answer each question by writing one or more sentences.

1. How were the daily activities in the agora in ancient Greece similar to and different from those in the downtown part of a large city today?
2. What benefits and problems did belonging to an alliance present to a city-state?
3. What was the effect of plague on Athens?
4. Why is Alexander the Great sometimes called Alexander the Conqueror?
5. Find the origin of the word lyric in the dictionary. What does the origin of the word tell you about the meaning of the term lyric poetry?

B. Use each of the words below in a sentence that gives a specific fact about ancient Greece.

1. agora
2. plague
3. philosopher
4. Hellenistic

Exploring Concepts

A. The timeline below covers the span of time roughly from the birth of Pericles to the death of Alexander. Copy the timeline on your own paper. For each event, fill in the date on your timeline. For each date, fill in the event. Then color the span of Pericles' lifetime in one color and the span of Alexander's lifetime in another.

B. Answer each question with information from the chapter.

1. In what years did the Golden Age of Athens begin and end? What important event took place in each of those two years?
2. How did the lives of men and women differ during the Golden Age?
3. What rights and privileges did metics have that slaves did not have?
4. What other extremely important event took place about the same time Athens suffered an outbreak of plague?
5. Why didn't the Spartans destroy Athens after the Athenian defeat?
6. Why did the part of the world around the eastern Mediterranean Sea become Hellenized under Alexander?
7. Why was Alexander's life remarkable?
8. Compare the outcome of the Peloponnesian Wars with that of Alexander's conquests. Think of the span of time in each.
9. Describe the contributions of ancient Greece to each of the following:
   a. architecture
   b. the study of history
   c. drama and literature

479 B.C., Greeks defeat Persians.

431 B.C., ____

____ B.C., Philip becomes king of Macedonia.

332 B.C., ____

| 500 | 475 | 450 | 425 | 400 | 375 | 350 | 325 | 300 |

460 B.C., ____

404 B.C., ____

336 B.C., ____

Reviewing Skills

1. Reread the section The Trial of Socrates on pages 372 and 373, and make a list of five questions you might want to explore in research if you were writing a report about Socrates.
2. Make a list of resources you would use to find information to answer your questions about Socrates.
3. Place the following six steps for writing a report in the proper order:
   Do research.
   Write an outline.
   Explore your topic.
   Take notes.
   Write a first draft.
   Revise, proofread, and copy.
4. Choose two sports with which you are familiar. Compare and contrast them by finding at least two similarities and two differences.
5. You know that Greek culture spread far and wide during the time of Alexander the Great, but you want to know just how far. What kind of resource would best help you determine the distance from one end of Alexander's empire to the other? Describe how you would use that resource to find out how far Alexander spread Greek culture.

Using Critical Thinking

1. During its Golden Age, Athens forced many other city-states to remain in the Delian League. Athens's navy attacked and captured cities along the Aegean Sea. The Parthenon was paid for with money taken from Athens's allies. Write one argument that supports Athens's policies and one argument against those policies.
2. In ancient Athens there were three social classes: slaves, metics, and citizens. Only male citizens had political power. Women were not allowed to participate in government. And yet the Athenian form of government was called a "democracy"—a political system in which the people rule. In what way was Athens a democracy? Would you be satisfied with that kind of a democracy today? Write a paragraph in which you explain why or why not.

Preparing for Citizenship

1. **ARTS ACTIVITY** Design a building in the ancient Greek style of architecture. For ideas, use pictures and information about Greek architecture from the chapter and the Explore feature. Also use information in the Minipedia article on Architecture on pages 490–491. Carefully draw three different views of your building. Show the building's proportions and the design of its columns. Indicate how large the building would be. Either give measurements on your drawing or draw objects such as trees for comparison.
2. **COLLABORATIVE LEARNING** In groups of four, discuss the question of why there could or could not be an Alexander the Great today. Assignments should be made as follows. One person in each group should learn in detail what Alexander did. Another should learn about "balance of power," especially as that term is used today. Each should report to the group what they have learned. Based on that information, the third group member should write an explanation of what it would mean to be an Alexander the Great today. The group then should come up with a written statement of its position, with reasons for taking that position. This statement should be revised until all group members agree to it. The fourth group member then will speak for the group in a class debate with the other groups' spokespeople.

Classical Greece

Rome: A World Power

A row of soldiers, strong and proud, stands as a symbol of Rome at the peak of its power. Rome began as a humble village in what is now Italy. The Romans used their military strength to build a vast empire. They developed ideas of government and law to unite this empire. Over a 1,000-year period, Rome grew to rule the Mediterranean world.

753 B.C.

Marble relief of a cavalry parade from the base of the column of Emperor Antoninus Pius in Rome. A.D. 161

A.D. 476

Chapter 13

The Rise of Rome

At a time when Greece was home to powerful city-states, Rome was just a village of straw-roofed huts. But the Romans learned quickly from their contacts with other civilizations. Within 600 years, Rome had conquered Greece and much of the rest of the Mediterranean world.

The Romans adopted many ideas from the Greeks. This Roman wall painting of a funeral dance from the 500s B.C. reflects the influence of Greek art.

1000	750	500

753 B.C.

c. 575 B.C. The Etruscans of northern Italy conquer Rome and spread their culture among the Romans. The helmet (above) is from the tomb of an Etruscan warrior.

The wolf symbolizes the legend of Rome's founding.

146 B.C. With its victory over Greece, Rome now rules the Mediterranean world. The center of Roman government is the Forum, a great open-air market and meeting place (above).

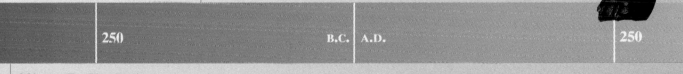

| 250 | | B.C. | A.D. | | 250 |

264 B.C. The First Punic War marks the beginning of Rome's overseas expansion.

49 B.C.

LESSON 1

The Birth of Rome

THINKING FOCUS

How was Rome founded, and how did it grow?

Key Terms

- omen
- Senate

Down the river floated a tiny reed basket carrying two babies, left to die. The basket came ashore at the foot of a hill. There a wolf found the crying orphans and cared for them. Later, a shepherd came upon the children and took them home to raise as his own. They were twin boys, and he named them Romulus and Remus.

Years later, the two brothers decided to build a city. This would be a city where others who were homeless, as they once were, could come to live. But the brothers argued over where to build the city.

One night Romulus and Remus agreed to watch for an **omen,** a sign from the gods, to settle their argument. At dawn, Remus saw six vultures flying overhead. However, as the sun rose higher in the sky, Romulus saw 12 vultures.

The brothers quarreled over the meaning of the omens, and in a rage, Romulus killed Remus. He then began to build his city on the spot he had chosen—the hill where the tiny basket containing the two babies had come to rest years before. He named his new city after himself—Rome.

➤ *According to legend, Romulus and Remus floated down the Tiber River. At the right is the Tiber as it looks today.*

Seven Kings

Much of the early history of Rome comes to us in the form of legends, like the story of Romulus and Remus. Though they are not historically accurate, legends are useful. They tell us what qualities people admired and the values they wished to pass on to future generations.

Rome's Early Kings

According to legend, Rome was founded in 753 B.C., and Romulus was the first of seven kings. He was believed to be a great warrior-king and is credited with starting Rome's first army and its first government.

Rome's second king was Numa Pompilius. He brought peace to Rome and, according to legend, founded the Roman religion.

The early kings were advised by a **Senate** (from the Latin word for "old men"), a council of elders from Rome's leading families. A citizens' assembly voted on decisions made by the king and the Senate.

At the time of the early kings, government and religion were closely linked. The king was also the chief priest. He chose other priests from members of the Senate. In addition, the king and his priests performed religious duties and interpreted omens.

The Etruscans

During the rule of the early Roman kings, Rome's powerful neighbors to the north, the Etruscans, were expanding their territory, Etruria. The Etruscans traded in the western Mediterranean and had established many wealthy

city-states in northern Italy. About 575 B.C., the Etruscans moved into Rome. Etruscan kings ruled Rome for the next 66 years.

The Etruscans had an older, more advanced civilization. Rome made rapid progress under their influence. The Etruscans introduced their alphabet and taught the Romans new building techniques, including the use of the arch.

Under the Etruscan kings, Rome grew from a village of straw-roofed huts into a walled city with paved streets. During this time, the Romans began a tradition of great building that eventually far

▲ This Etruscan fresco, or wall painting, shows the advanced art of the Etruscans.

▼ Prehistoric villagers of central Italy lived in simple huts like this one.

surpassed that of their teachers. The Romans built the Circus Maximus, an arena that seated thousands, and the Temple of Jupiter in honor of their highest god. They also built the Cloaca Maxima *(kloh AY kuh MAX suh muh)*, a sewer that is still in use today. The sewer drained a marshy valley that became the Forum.

Rome flourished under the Etruscans, until Tarquin the Proud, the seventh and last Roman king, came to power. He was a cruel ruler who ignored the Senate and terrorized the people. In 509 B.C., the people rebelled against him and finally sent him into exile. Never again would Romans be ruled by a king. ■

Midpoint of the Mediterranean

At the time of the early kings, Rome was just one of many city-states in Italy, a peninsula centrally located in the Mediterranean Sea. Rome lay near the center of that peninsula on a broad plain known as Latium. Archaeologists have found evidence of settlements dating to the 1100s B.C. throughout the region.

The Latium Plain

The area once known as Latium has a typical Mediterranean climate. Summers are hot and dry, and winters are wet and

▲ *The inkwell above is inscribed with the Etruscan alphabet.*

■ *How did the Etruscans influence the Romans?*

➤ *In 509 B.C., Rome shared the Italian peninsula with the Etruscans to the north and Greek settlers to the south.*

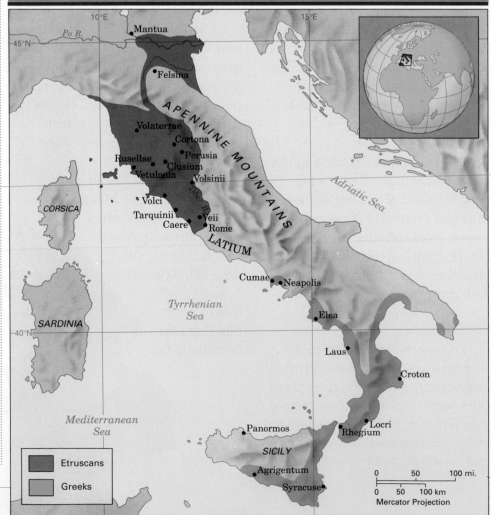

Settlement of Italy, c. 509 B.C.

Map showing the Italian peninsula with locations including Mantua, Felsina, Volaterrae, Cortona, Perusia, Rusellae, Clusium, Vetulonia, Volsinii, Volci, Tarquinii, Veii, Caere, Rome, LATIUM, Cumae, Neapolis, Elea, Laus, Croton, Panormos, Locri, Rhegium, SICILY, Agrigentum, Syracuse. Surrounded by the Adriatic Sea, Tyrrhenian Sea, and Mediterranean Sea. Corsica and Sardinia islands to the west. Apennine Mountains and Po R. labeled.

Legend: Etruscans, Greeks

0   50   100 mi.
0   50   100 km
Mercator Projection

mild. The people of Latium were called Latins, and they spoke the same language, Latin. Like other Mediterranean peoples, the early Latins were herders and farmers who harvested wheat, grapes, and olives.

To the north of Rome lay the Etruscan city-states, and to the south lay Greek colonies. The Etruscans and the Greeks carried on much trade in the Mediterranean. Look at the map on page 398. Which power controlled the greater portion of the Italian peninsula?

The Advantages of Latium

Rome's location offered many advantages. As the Roman historian Livy described it, "Not without good reason did gods and men choose this spot as the site of a city."

Livy, who lived from 59 B.C. to A.D. 17, noted that Rome was built on several hills, which made the city a difficult place for enemies to attack. He also pointed out the advantages of being on the Tiber River, "by means of which the produce of inland countries may be brought down and inland supplies obtained." The Tiber flows into the Mediterranean Sea 15 miles away, which means Rome is "near enough [to the sea] for all useful purposes, but not so near as to be exposed to danger from foreign

fleets." Livy wrote that Rome was "in the very center of Italy, in a word, a position singularly adapted by nature for the growth of a city."

From its location in the center of the Italian peninsula and

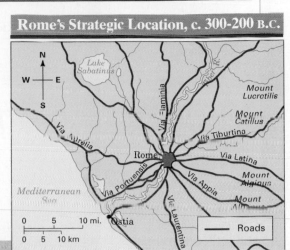

Rome's Strategic Location, c. 300–200 B.C.

▲ A network of roads connected the city of Rome to the countryside.

◄ Rich farmland near Rome was one advantage of the city's location. Farming is still important here.

the center of the Mediterranean, Rome was within easy reach of Greece to the east, Spain to the west, and the northern coast of Africa to the south. In the centuries that followed, Rome expanded to all of these areas. Eventually, the Romans would rename the Mediterranean *Mare Nostrum*— "our sea." ■

■ What part did geography play in the development of Rome?

REVIEW

1. **FOCUS** How was Rome founded, and how did it grow?
2. **CONNECT** Compare the early government of Rome with the early government of Greece.
3. **CULTURE** What contributions did the Etruscans make to Roman society?
4. **CRITICAL THINKING** What does the legend of Romulus

and Remus tell you about early Roman life? What kind of people do you think the early Romans were?

5. **WRITING ACTIVITY** Write a news story that describes how Romulus and Remus tried to found the city of Rome. Be sure to tell who, what, when, where, and how.

The War over Latium

Alfred J. Church

After Troy was destroyed by the Greeks, the hero Aeneas and the other Trojan survivors left to find a new home in Italy. In this story from The Aeneid for Boys and Girls, *the goddess Juno, who hates Aeneas, is determined to keep the Trojans from settling in the Latium Plain. She decides to seek help from the underworld.*

The Roman poet Virgil wrote the Aeneid (ih NEE uhd), *an epic poem about the beginnings of Rome. Here is a retelling of parts of the Aeneid.*

Aeneas (ih NEE uhs)

treachery betrayal

Juno went down into the lower parts of the earth, and called to her Alecto, who was one of the Furies, who loved anger and war and treachery, and all evil and hateful things. Even her own sisters, the Furies, could not bear to look on her, so dreadful was she to behold. Juno said to her: "Daughter of Night, I have suffered a great wrong and disgrace, and I want you to help me. A man whom I hate, Aeneas by name, desires to have a kingdom in Italy; keep him from it. He wishes to have Lavinia, the daughter of King Latinus, to wife: see that he does not. You can set brother against brother; you can bring strife into kingdoms and into homes. Break this peace that the Latins and the Trojans are making. Bring about some occasion of war."

Alecto first went to the palace of Latinus. There she found the queen, Amata by name, in great anger and trouble. She was much displeased by the doings of the king, her husband. She did not wish to have Aeneas for her son-in-law, and she loved the prince Turnus with all her heart. Then the Fury thought to herself: "The queen hates Aeneas already; I will turn her hatred into madness." So she took a snake out of her hair and thrust it into the bosom of the queen. The evil beast crept about her so that the poison got into her heart; then it changed itself into a collar, as of twisted gold, round her neck, and poisoned her very breath.

At the first, before the evil altogether overpowered her, she spoke gently to her husband, weeping as a mother might weep when she is afraid that she may lose her daughter. She said: "Are you not afraid, my husband, to give Lavinia to this exile from Troy? Have you no pity for her or me or yourself? Well I know that so soon as the north wind begins to blow, he will fly from this land and carry her away with him. Do you not care for the promise that you made to Turnus—yes, made with an oath—that he should have Lavinia for his wife? You say that she must marry a stranger. Is he not a stranger? Are not all who are not subjects of your kingdom strangers? This, and this only, is what the gods command. Further, if you look into the matter, you will see that he is a stranger also in race, for he is of the family of Inachus, and is by race a Greek."

Inachus (IHN uh kuhs)

But when she saw that her husband was not moved at all by her words, the madness altogether overcame her. She rushed out of the palace, and through the streets of the city, taking her daughter with her. And, as she went, she called to the other women to follow her, so that a whole multitude went after her. Like so many wild creatures, they ran through the woods, the queen leading them, holding a burning torch in her hand, and singing the marriage song of her daughter and Turnus.

The next thing that the Fury did was that she went to the city where Turnus lived. He was asleep, and the Fury went in and stood by his bedside. She had taken the shape of an old woman, the priestess of the Temple of Juno, and she said: "Turnus, are you content that you should lose that which is your right, and that your kingdom should be taken from you? King Latinus takes from you the wife that he had promised, and is about to hand over his kingdom to a stranger from over the sea. Juno bade me come and tell you this. Arm your people; drive these strangers out of the land, and burn their ships with fire. And if the king will not keep his promise, let him learn for himself that Turnus is not one who will suffer wrong."

So the old woman spoke, and Turnus answered—for so it seemed to him in his dream—"Old woman, I know that the ships of the strangers have come to the Tiber. But these are idle tales that you tell me. I know that Queen Juno cares for me; therefore, I am not afraid. But you, mother, are old, and wander somewhat in your wits, and trouble yourself for nothing, and are afraid when there is nothing to fear. Keep, I pray you, to your own business; serve the temples of the gods, but leave war and the things of war to men, for such matters belong to them."

And then it seemed to Turnus in his dream that the old woman grew very angry, yea, that she changed into the shape of a Fury, and that a thousand snakes hissed round her. And when he tried to speak again, the words would not come, and when he would have risen from his bed, she thrust him back, and caught two snakes from her hair and lashed him with them, crying: "I am old, forsooth! and I wander from my wits! and I am afraid when I have nothing to fear! Nay, but I am the greatest of the Furies, and war and death are in my hands." And it seemed to him, still in his dream, that she threw a lighted torch at him, and that it fixed itself in his heart. Then he woke with a great start. He did not know whether the things which he had seen and heard in his sleep were

forsooth indeed

true or not, but his heart was full of anger. He called for his arms, and commanded all the young men to make themselves ready for war. "I will drive these Trojans," he cried, "out of Italy, and if Latinus and his people stand by them, then they shall go also."

And now there was one thing left for the Fury to do, and this was to make a cause of quarrel. King Latinus had a man to keep his cattle, and this man's daughter, Silvia by name, had a tame stag which her brothers had found when it was a fawn, and had brought to her. The girl was very fond of the creature, and would put garlands of flowers about its neck, and comb its hair, and give it a bath. All day long the stag would wander about the woods, and at night it came back to the house. Now it so happened that Ascanius, with other Trojan lads, was hunting that day, and his dogs caught the scent of the stag and followed it. And Ascanius, riding after them, saw the beast, and shot an arrow at it, and hit it, for the Fury took care that the arrow should not miss its aim. Then the stag, being wounded to death, ran back to the herdsman's house, and filled it with most lamentable cries. Silvia heard it, and was greatly grieved to see her dear pet in such a case, and cried out for help. And here again the Fury—for she was hiding in the woods—did all she could to increase the trouble. From all sides the country folk came together, each picking up for a weapon anything that came to hand. One had a brand that had been half burned in the fire, and another a great stick with knots in it. The herdsman himself carried an ax in his hand. On the other hand, the Trojans ran together to help Ascanius, and soon there was a regular battle. Some were slain both on the one side and on the other.

Now the scene is set for war. Driven to anger by the Fury, Turnus gathers an army of Latin soldiers to try to force the Trojans to leave. One of the greatest Latin soldiers is Camilla.

Now the story of Camilla is this. She was the daughter of a certain king, Metabus by name, who was driven out of his kingdom by his subjects on account of his cruelty. He fled for his life, taking with him his little daughter, whom he carried in his arms. He came in his flight to a certain river, and the river was swollen with rain, so that it ran high and strong. The man could not swim with the child in his arms, and his enemies were close behind, so he took the spear that he carried on his back, and bound the child to it, with strips of bark, and made ready to throw it. As he balanced it in his hand, he prayed to Diana, saying: "O Goddess! I give thee this child to be thy servant forever, if thou wilt save her now." Then he cast the spear across the river with all his might, and, Diana giving strength to his arm, it fell on the other side. Then he himself leaped into the water, and, swimming across, so escaped from his enemies. After this he never lived in house or town, but with the shepherds on the hills, and the child he fed with mare's milk and the like things. As soon as she could walk he gave her a little javelin to carry, and when she was a little stronger, a bow and arrows. She wore no gold or jewels, nor had she long skirts like a girl. From a child she could sling a stone in a wonderful way, hitting the cranes and the wild swans as they flew high in the air. Tall and strong and beautiful was she when she grew up, and many Tuscan mothers desired to have her for a daughter-in-law, but she had no thought of marriage, only of hunting and fighting.

The goddess Diana, as she sat in heaven, said to Opis, who was chief of the nymphs who waited on her: "Opis, Camilla goes to fight in this war. Would that she had not thought of it! There is not a girl in Italy that I love more, and have loved her ever since she was a child. But her fate is on her, and she must die. Now I give you this charge. Go down to the Latin land, where they are beginning just now this evil war; take with you your bow and your arrows, and see that any man who harms her shall himself be slain. And when she is dead no man shall spoil her of her arms; but I will carry back her body to her native land."

And now Aeneas and the Trojans came towards the city, the horsemen being in front. One of these, a Tuscan, was the first to kill his man. He charged against a Latin chief, and drove him from his horse, making him fly through the air, as a stone flies from an engine. When the Latins saw him, they turned and fled. And the Trojans and Tuscans followed them. But when they came near the city, then those that stood upon the walls, the old men and the boys and the women, threw sticks and stones at them, and the soldiers took courage and faced about. Then the Trojans, in their turn, fled, and the Latins pursued them. So it happened twice. But when they met for the third time, then neither would the one side nor the other give way. Both of them stood firm, and there was a great slaughter. Many died valiantly, but none was equal to Camilla. Sometimes she would fight with a battle-ax and sometimes with her bows and arrows. Never did she strike a man with her battle-ax but she laid him low upon the earth; never did she aim an arrow at a man, but she killed him. One of these was the hunter Ornytus, who was the tallest of the Tuscans. He had a wolf's head with great white teeth for a helmet, and in his hand he carried a hunting spear. But strong as he was, Camilla overcame him, and as he lay dying on the ground she mocked him: "Did you think, O Tuscan, that you were hunting wild beasts today? Lo! a woman's arms have brought all your boasts to nothing." So she raged through the field, slaying Trojans and Tuscans

nymphs in Greek and Roman mythology, one of the female spirits representing nature

Ornytus
(AWR nih tuhs)

alike. One of the Ligurians, the son of Aunus, thought to escape in this way. He said to her: "Let us fight on foot; you have so swift a horse that no one can fight with you on equal terms." Camilla answered: "Be it so; we will fight on foot." And she leaped from her horse, and gave it to one of her companions to hold. But the other turned his horse to flee, foolish man, not knowing that Camilla could run faster than any horse in the world. But so it was, she outran the horse, and stood in front of it, catching the reins in her hand, and so killed him.

Then Tarchon the Tuscan shouted out to his horsemen: "What is this, you cowards? Shall a woman drive you before her? You are ready for the dance and feast, and you lag behind in battle. Follow me." And he rode at Venulus, prince of Tibur, and caught him in his arms, dragging him from his horse. So an eagle catches up a snake in his claws and carries him off, and the snake winds himself round the bird, and hisses. Thus did Tarchon carry off his enemy, looking for a place where to strike him, for he was covered with armor, and the man tried to keep the sword from his throat. When the Trojans and the Tuscans saw this, they took courage again.

All this time a certain Arruns, a great archer, was watching Camilla, looking for a chance to kill her. There was a certain priest who was riding in the midst of the battle very splendidly adorned. There were clasps of gold on his armor and the armor of his horse. He wore a purple robe which had come from Tyre; he had a Lycian bow, adorned with gold; his helmet also shone with gold; and his scarf had a ring of gold, and his tunic was rich with the finest needlework. Never was there such a sight to see.

And Camilla, having a woman's love of beautiful things, followed him, caring for nothing, and thinking of nothing, but how she might take these splendid spoils. Now Arruns lay in ambush, and when he saw Camilla, how she followed the priest, and thought of nothing else, he said to himself, "Now is the time." And he prayed to Apollo: "Lord of the bow, help me now, if ever I and my people have done honor to you. I ask no glory for myself. Only let me slay this fury, though I go back to my country without honor." Part of this prayer the god heard and answered, but part was scattered by the winds. For he drew his bow to the full, and let fly the arrow. And when the people heard the twang of the bow, for they could not see the man, they all turned. But

spoils   goods or property taken from a victim

404

Camilla took no heed; she had no thought of the arrow till it struck her under the left breast. She reeled upon her horse, and her companions closed round her and caught her as she fell. Once she laid her hand on the arrow and would have drawn it out, but it had gone too deep. Then her eyes swam in death, and the color that was as the color of a rose faded from her cheek. Only as she died, she said, for her thoughts were still with the battle, so keen a fighter was she: "Acca, my sister, tell Turnus to come forth from his ambush, and join in the battle, if he would keep the Trojans from the walls of the city." So she died.

Now Arruns, at the first, lay in hiding, for he was afraid, so great a deed had he done. After a while, he came out from his place, and began to boast. Then Opis drew her bow with all her strength, till the ends came almost together. With her right hand she held the bow-string, and with her left the arrowhead. So she let the shaft fly. Arruns heard the twang, and even while he heard it, he fell dead upon the plain. And now the companions of Camilla flew, as did also the Latins and the allies. The dust of the battle came nearer and nearer to the walls, and a great cry went up to the heaven. Great was the fear and the confusion. Some were trodden down by their own people, so that they died even in sight of their own homes. And the keepers of the gates shut them close, so that their own friends were left outside.

And now Acca had carried to Turnus, as he lay in ambush, the news of how her sister was dead, and how the battle went against his people. Immediately he rose up from his place, and made all haste to the city. And it chanced that at the very same time Aeneas had come through the valley and passed over the ridge. The two saw each other; but the night was now falling, so that they could not meet in battle.

Further Reading

City. David Macaulay. Detailed illustrations of a Roman city explain the Roman approach to construction and planning.

They Marched with Spartacus. Eric Houghton. During the time of the rebellion of Spartacus, a young slave confronts his Roman captors.

The White Wall. Eric Houghton. In this story a young boy joins Hannibal's army after his village is destroyed by a warlike tribe.

The Rise of the Republic

What internal and external struggles occurred during the rise of the Roman Republic?

Key Terms

- republic
- consul
- patrician
- plebeian
- debt bondage

> *There was great panic in the city, and through mutual fear, all was suspense. The people left in the city dreaded [feared] the violence of the senators; the senators dreaded the people remaining in the city, uncertain whether they should prefer to stay or to depart; but how long would the multitude [crowd] which had seceded [left] remain quiet? What were to be the consequences then, if, in the meantime, any foreign war should break out?*

Livy wrote that description, telling of the crisis in Rome in 494 B.C. The common people of Rome had seceded, or moved out of the city. They were very angry over their treatment by the rich and powerful leaders of Rome. The leaders knew that their city was in serious danger unless the common people returned. So they agreed to give the people more rights. This crisis between the Roman leaders and the people marked the beginning of a 200-year struggle by the common people of Rome to gain equal rights.

Patricians and Plebeians

With the overthrow of the last Etruscan king in 509 B.C., Roman leaders adopted a very new form of government—a republic. In a **republic,** citizens elect leaders to run their government. The leaders the citizens elected to replace the king were called consuls. These **consuls** were leaders elected by a citizen assembly and advised by a Senate. Although the citizens elected their representatives, the early Roman Republic was not a democracy because not every citizen had the same economic power.

Citizens were divided into two classes, patricians and plebeians. **Patricians** *(puh TRISH uhns)* were members of the small number of wealthy Roman families. **Plebeians** *(plih BEE uhns)* were the bulk of the population—artisans, shopkeepers, and peasants. Class was determined by birth.

As citizens, both patricians and plebeians had the right to vote. However, only patricians could hold political, military, or religious offices. All power was in the hands of the patricians.

Though most plebeians were poor, some were quite wealthy. They believed that they should have the same social and political rights as the patricians.

The poor plebeians, too, believed that the system was unfair. When a poor plebeian had to borrow money from the rich to survive, he and his family were forced into debt bondage. A man in **debt bondage** became a servant of the man to whom he owed the money. He was treated almost like a slave, and, without wages, he could never get the money he needed to regain his freedom. Yet the patrician government did nothing to end this cruel practice.

Roman citizens were divided into patricians and plebeians. But Roman society as a whole was also divided into two groups: citizen and slave. Adult male citizens had certain rights,

Patrician women, like the one at left, often had slaves to assist them with their elaborate hairdos.

such as the right to vote and to own property. Women citizens, however, had limited rights. They could not vote or take part in the government but were protected by Roman laws. Slaves, war captives, were owned by citizens and had no rights. ■

Many plebeians were farmers, like the one in this Etruscan bronze figure of the 300s B.C.

■ *What were the differences between patricians and plebeians in the early Republic?*

Struggle for Rights

Although the plebeians had fewer rights than the patricians, they still had to serve in the army and pay taxes to the very forces that were oppressing them. By 494 B.C., the plebeians had suffered

long enough. They withdrew from Rome and formed their own assembly, which was known as the Council of Plebeians. They also elected their own officials, who were called tribunes.

When Rome was ruled by kings, the Roman people were subjects of the king. A subject is someone who is completely under a king's power and who owes loyalty to him. The people had no rights except those the king gave them.

When Rome became a republic, the people became citizens. The word *citizen* comes from the Latin word *civitas*, meaning "membership in a city." The Roman idea of citizenship, like the Greek idea, was based on the relations between the state and its citizens. That is, the Roman republic began when the people insisted on their right to become full citizens of the state.

Citizens are expected to be loyal. In return, they are granted such benefits as the right to vote and the protection of the state.

You might compare citizenship to being a member of a club. If you are a member of a club, you have the right to take part in its activities. Others may include the right to vote for club officials. But you may also have duties, such as paying dues or serving on club committees.

For citizens, the state or nation is the club. Rights may include the right to vote and to hold public office, as in Greece. Duties may be paying taxes and serving in the military, as in Rome.

Not all residents of ancient Rome and Greece were citizens, however. Some residents were slaves or foreigners. A person had to be born a citizen, though not all citizens had equal rights. While the Greeks granted rights fairly evenly among male citizens, the Roman plebeians fought over 200 years to gain the same rights held by the patricians. In ancient Greece or Rome, women citizens were not allowed to vote or hold office. But as Rome expanded its territory, it granted citizenship to many of its conquered peoples, something Greece did not do.

Citizenship Today

Today, in many countries, such as Great Britain and the United States, everyone born in the country is automatically granted citizenship. Other people must apply to become citizens. This process is called naturalization.

One of the most important benefits of citizenship is the right to vote. However, there are countries today where elections are not held and citizens cannot vote. Citizens of these countries have no say in how they are governed.

U.S. Citizenship

Like the ancient Romans and Greeks, U.S. citizens have the right to vote and take part in government. Duties include paying taxes and serving in the military when required. U.S. citizens have additional rights guaranteed by the Constitution's Bill of Rights, such as freedom of speech, freedom of religion, and freedom of the press.

Citizenship in ancient Rome was more limited. Although a large number of Roman citizens enjoyed many rights, some Romans, such as slaves and women, had very few rights at all.

During the 300s B.C., the plebeians gained more and more of the rights already held by the patricians. The priesthood was opened to plebeians. Debt bondage was outlawed. Eventually, plebeians even won the right to become members of the Senate.

Though the plebeians had made many gains, the plebeians and patricians still had separate political bodies. The laws passed

◄ *The ruins of the Forum shown at the far left were photographed from the Palatine hill. Below is a reconstruction of the Forum, looking towards Capitoline Hill. You can find more information about architecture like this in the Minipedia*

As you have read, the patricians were desperate. They knew that Rome could not survive without plebeians. Who would do the work? Who would protect the Republic from enemy attacks?

The patricians had no choice but to let the plebeians keep their assembly and their tribunes. Tribunes were to protect plebeian rights. The plebeians could vote against any unjust law passed by the Senate.

Next, the plebeians demanded a reform of the laws. Rome's laws had never been written down. The plebeians believed that patrician judges took advantage of this fact to rule unfairly against plebeians.

The Twelve Tables

Finally in 450 B.C., the laws were engraved on 12 bronze tablets called the Twelve Tables. The tablets were then displayed in the Forum, so all citizens could appeal to them, though few could actually read them.

by the patrician Senate applied to everyone. However, the laws passed by the plebeian assembly applied only to plebeians.

Equality for Plebeians

The plebeians demanded that the laws passed by their assembly apply to all citizens, plebeian and patrician alike. Once again, the plebeians forced the issue by withdrawing from Rome. This time, the patricians gave in and, in 287 B.C., agreed to meet the demands of the plebeians. After more than 200 years of struggle, plebeians and patricians were finally equal under Roman law. ■

■ *What were the major steps in the plebeians' struggle for greater rights?*

Roman Government

The U.S. Constitution owes one of its very basic concepts to the Romans. Neither the President, nor the Congress, nor the courts can dominate the government. Each branch of government has ways to check the actions of the others, and the actions of each branch balance the others. This idea of checks and balances was first developed in the government of the Roman Republic.

■ *How was the government of the Roman Republic organized?*

As the plebeians gained power, the Republic became more democratic. Since 509 B.C., the Roman government had been headed by two consuls. By 367 B.C., one of the consuls had to be a plebeian. The consuls had the same powers as the early kings, but with two important limitations. To avoid one-person rule, consuls were elected to serve only one year, and each consul could veto the other's actions. Our word *veto* is from the Latin word meaning "I forbid."

The consuls carried on the daily business of the government and commanded the army. They were also advised by the Senate of about 300 citizens. The Senate controlled the Roman treasury and foreign policy. Most of the senators were members of wealthy families. Though the consuls changed each year, senators held their positions for life. The Senate was the most powerful group in the government of Rome.

Laws proposed by the Senate could be approved or disapproved by citizen assemblies. Candidates for consul were also elected by these assemblies. The government of the Republic spread its power among many groups.■

➤ *The chart of Roman government structure shows how the power of each level was balanced by the power of the other levels.*

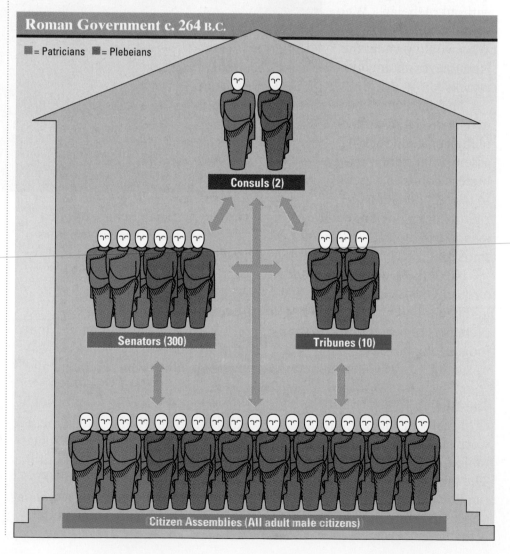

Roman Government c. 264 B.C.

■ = Patricians   ■ = Plebeians

Consuls (2)

Senators (300)

Tribunes (10)

Citizen Assemblies (All adult male citizens)

Early Expansion

While the patricians and plebeians struggled for power within the city's walls, other battles raged on the outside. Year after year, the Roman army marched off to wage war against its neighbors and to expand the area under Roman control. The army was not always victorious, however. In fact, in 390 B.C., Rome itself was attacked and destroyed by the Gauls, a warlike people from the north.

Nevertheless, Rome rebuilt and continued to grow. By 338 B.C., Rome had conquered Latium and Etruria. By 275 B.C., Rome ruled the whole Italian peninsula.

Rome was so successful, in part, because instead of punishing the people it conquered, Rome made them allies. As allies, they had to fight for Rome in any future wars. In return, Rome promised them protection and a share in the profits from future victories. In some cases, Rome even granted citizenship to conquered peoples.

By 270 B.C., Rome had more citizens and well-trained soldiers than any other Mediterranean power. During the next century, Rome used those resources to conquer the Mediterranean world. ■

◄ *Roman legionaries like this one were stationed in the various provinces of Rome, but never in Rome itself.*

■ *What made the Romans successful conquerors?*

REVIEW

1. **FOCUS** What internal and external struggles occurred during the rise of the Roman Republic?
2. **CONNECT** Compare the Roman government of the Republic with that of the Athenians in the 400s B.C.
3. **HISTORY** How did the Roman Republic expand its territory beyond Italy?
4. **LEGAL SYSTEMS** What was important about the Twelve Tables, and how did they help the plebeians?
5. **CRITICAL THINKING** How was the government of the Roman Republic like that of the United States today? How was it different?
6. **ACTIVITY** Make a chart that compares the rights of the plebeians and the patricians. You might compare their political rights, their social rights, and their economic rights.

270   49

Overseas Expansion

Let's leave Rome for a moment and travel across the Mediterranean to the coast of North Africa. The time is 238 B.C. The place is the Phoenician city of Carthage. The great Carthaginian *(kahr thuh JIHN ee uhn)* general, Hamilcar, is preparing to leave for Phoenician outposts in Spain where he hopes to raise a new army. Carthage has just been defeated in a long and bitter war with Rome for the island of Sicily, and the general is angry and humiliated at the loss.

Hamilcar is making sacrifices to the gods, so that they will bring him good luck in Spain. His young son, Hannibal, looks on. Livy describes the scene:

Hannibal, then about nine years old, was childishly teasing his father to take him too. His father, still angry at the loss [to the Romans] led him to the altar and made him swear to be the enemy of Rome as soon as he was able.

Hamilcar took the young boy to Spain with him and taught him to be a soldier. Twenty years later, Hannibal fulfilled his oath to his father. He became a brilliant general, one of the greatest foes Rome ever faced.

The Punic Wars

In the 200s B.C., Rome was conquering Italy. Another power, Carthage, existed on the opposite side of the Mediterranean. It was a prosperous Phoenician city with trading posts all around the Mediterranean. Carthage and Rome became fierce rivals and fought three long and bloody wars over which power would control the Mediterranean.

The First Punic War

Find Rome and Carthage on the map on the next page. What large island lies between them at the tip of the Italian peninsula? By the 200s B.C., Carthage had settlements on Sicily. Rome feared it would gain complete control of the island. In 264 B.C., the two powers went

▼ *Notice the plank at the front of the Roman boat. What advantage did it give the Romans in sea battles?*

to war over Sicily. This struggle marked the beginning of the First Punic *(PYOO nihk)* War. *Punici* was the Roman word for the people of Carthage.

The fighting raged on land and sea. Rome had a stronger army and soon controlled Sicily's inland. But Carthage controlled the coast with its stronger navy.

In fact, at the beginning of the war, Rome had few ships and little experience at sea. Yet the Romans found a clever answer to their problem. They invented a device called a "crow," a kind of gangplank with clawlike hooks. The crow was held upright until the Romans pulled their ship up next to an enemy ship. Then they swiftly lowered the crow so the hooks caught in the enemy ship's deck. The crow thus served as a bridge, allowing Roman soldiers to board the enemy ship easily.

The First Punic War lasted 23 years. Rome was in a better position than Carthage to withstand the heavy losses because of its huge army and loyal allies.

By 241 B.C., the Carthaginian army, led by General Hamilcar, was forced to admit defeat. Sicily became the first territory outside of the Italian peninsula to come under Rome's control. Rome had begun its expansion into the Mediterranean world.

The Second Punic War

Despite its defeat at the hands of the Romans, Carthage remained

▼ *Use the map below to help you follow the Punic Wars between Carthage and Rome.*

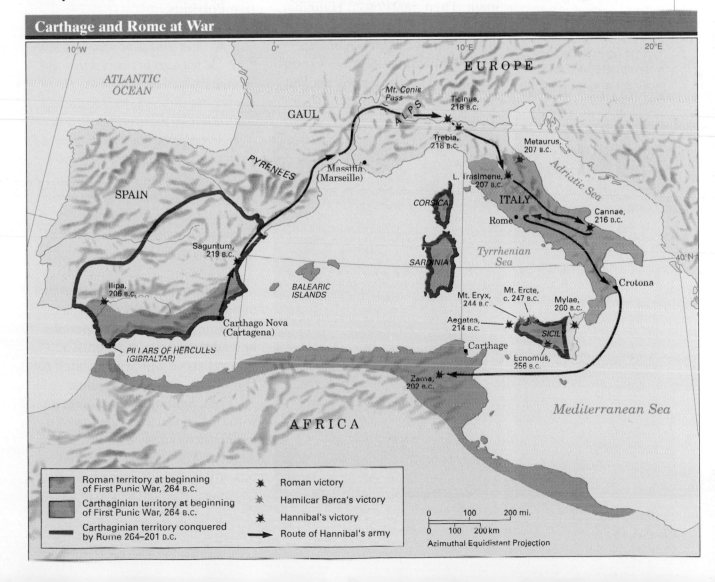

Carthage and Rome at War

Legend:
- Roman territory at beginning of First Punic War, 264 B.C.
- Carthaginian territory at beginning of First Punic War, 264 B.C.
- Carthaginian territory conquered by Rome 264–201 B.C.
- ✷ Roman victory
- ✷ Hamilcar Barca's victory
- ✷ Hannibal's victory
- → Route of Hannibal's army

0 100 200 mi.
0 100 200 km
Azimuthal Equidistant Projection

► *This coin from Spain shows one of Hannibal's elephants, the symbol of his daring expedition across the Alps.*

Across Time & Space

Carthage was rebuilt after the Third Punic War. However, it was finally destroyed by Arab invaders in A.D. 698. All that remains of the once great city are a few ruins near the present city of Tunis, Tunisia. Find Tunisia on the map of Eurasia in the Atlas.

▼ *This French tapestry, woven in the late 1600s, pictures the meeting of Hannibal and Scipio.*

an important power. It immediately began to rebuild its empire, starting in Spain, where it already had numerous trading posts.

Under the leadership of General Hamilcar, Carthage succeeded in expanding its holdings in Spain. In 229 B.C., however, Hamilcar was killed in battle. His successor was assassinated, and in 221 B.C., the army elected Hannibal commander. Hamilcar's son was only 26 years old, but it was time for him to fulfill the oath he had made as a child.

Rome watched anxiously as Carthage expanded its empire in Spain. Then, in 219 B.C., Hannibal attacked Saguntum, one of Rome's allies in Spain. After Saguntum had fallen, Rome declared war on Carthage. Thus began the Second Punic War, which ended in 201 B.C.

The Romans sent troops to Saguntum, but Hannibal had other plans. True to his oath, he decided to invade Italy.

He gathered an army of 60,000 soldiers, 6,000 horses, and 37 elephants. They marched across the Pyrenees Mountains in Spain and through southern Gaul, crossed the Rhone River with trumpeting elephants on rafts, and reached the Alps five months later, in winter. Only one-half of the army was left, and they still had to cross the craggy, wind-whipped Alps to reach Italy.

Try to imagine the scene as it was described by the Greek historian Polybius:

A fter nine days' climb Hannibal's army reached the snowcovered summit of the pass over the Alps—all the time being attacked by the mountain tribes. However, when the enemy now attacked the column, the elephants were of great use to the Carthaginians. The enemy was so terrified of the animals' strange appearance that they dared not come anywhere near them.

Hannibal crushed the Romans in battle after battle. Only the determination of Rome's people helped them to survive until a general arose who was a match for Hannibal—Scipio Africanus.

First, Scipio made a secret pact with one of Carthage's allies, Numidia, the country now known as Algeria. Then, while Hannibal was still in Italy, Scipio attacked Carthage. But just as Carthage

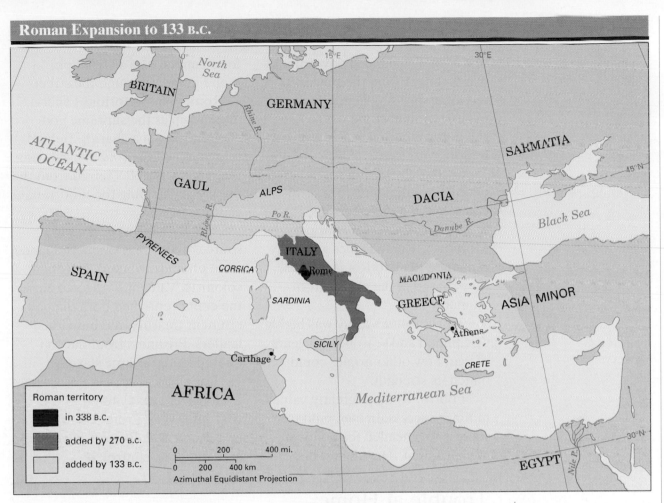

Roman territory

- in 338 B.C.
- added by 270 B.C.
- added by 133 B.C.

0   200   400 mi.
0 200 400 km
Azimuthal Equidistant Projection

was about to admit defeat, Hannibal returned from Italy. Scipio fought Hannibal at Zama, a town near Carthage. With the help of the Numidians, Scipio won. He was given the name "Africanus" in honor of this victory in northern Africa.

This defeat marked the end of Carthage's empire. Carthage was forced to give up its territories and its ships, and to pay Rome vast sums of money.

In 149 B.C., Carthage rebelled against Rome, thus beginning the Third Punic War. Rome once again defeated Carthage. And as punishment, Rome sold all of the surviving Carthaginians into slavery and leveled the city. ■

▲ *Notice how Rome increased its influence in the Mediterranean area between 338 and 133 B.C.*

■ *What were the Punic Wars?*

Conquest of the Eastern Mediterranean

With the defeat of Carthage, Rome became the most important power in the western Mediterranean. Next, Rome turned eastward, conquering Greece and Macedonia, the country to the north of Greece, by 146 B.C.

By 50 B.C., Rome controlled the entire area around the Mediterranean. Find these Roman provinces on the map above:

Greece, Spain, Gaul, Asia Minor, and North Africa.

How was it possible for Rome to conquer so much so quickly? Historians give several reasons. First, the Romans took great pride in their Republic and fiercely defended it. The Greek historian Polybius, who lived among the Romans in the 100s B.C., wrote that the power of the Roman people

415

The Rise of Rome

under their balanced government was stronger than the power of any one opposing leader. Not even Hannibal could overcome the determination of the Roman people.

Second, by treating conquered peoples as allies and, in several cases, making them citizens, Rome was able to raise a large army. Moreover, Rome's allies generally remained loyal to Rome because they shared in the profits from Roman wars.

Third, Rome's army was highly disciplined and seasoned by years of war. Few other armies could match its strength.

Fourth, Romans greatly valued military success. In fact, military success was needed for political advancement. The highest honor for a general was a "triumph," a grand parade through the streets of Rome. The victorious general, dressed up as the supreme god Jupiter, rode in a chariot. Behind him marched the soldiers, carrying the many valuables seized from the enemy and leading the unfortunate captives of war.

Finally, wars were a great source of wealth. Conquered lands were often distributed to Roman colonists. Valuables seized from the enemy enriched both the government treasury and individual leaders. Prisoners from the conquered lands became slaves.

For all these reasons, Roman leaders were ready to go to war year after year. From 338 to 50 B.C., Rome steadily extended the area under its control. ■

■ *How could Rome conquer so much of the Mediterranean so quickly?*

Trouble at Home

By 50 B.C., Rome ruled the Mediterranean world, but it had serious problems at home. Before the Punic Wars, Italy was a land of small family farms and farmer-soldiers. Wars were fought nearby between planting and harvest. In 458 B.C., Cincinnatus, a citizen farmer, laid down his plow to lead the Roman army. At the request of his fellow citizens, he was made dictator. According to legend, within 16 days he had defeated the neighboring tribe, resigned his dictatorship, and gone back to his farm.

However, as Rome expanded, wars were fought farther away, and farmers were gone for longer periods of time. Many of them were killed in battle.

The Second Punic War had destroyed Roman farms. Returning from war, farmers often did not have the money needed to buy oxen, tools, and seed to begin farming again. Wealthy Romans bought the land and created plantations run by slave labor.

Many landless farmers moved to the city, but there were not enough jobs for the newcomers. People without skills had the hardest time finding work. As the numbers of poor and unemployed people grew, the Roman leaders feared that violent mobs would demand a solution to their troubles. Some Roman leaders wanted to help the poor, but their efforts were blocked by wealthy senators. In fact, two tribunes who tried to help the poor were killed for their efforts.

▼ *The message on this slave tag promised a reward for the return of the runaway slave.*

Rome's large population of slaves caused other problems. Most slaves, who had been free in their homelands, were treated brutally by their Roman masters. Desperate for freedom, the slaves rebelled. In 73 B.C., the slave Spartacus gathered an army of more than 100,000. They fought the Roman army for two years. In 71 B.C., the Romans killed Spartacus and crucified 6,000 slaves. ■

■ *What problems did Rome have at home?*

Fall of the Roman Republic

By 50 B.C., Rome ruled an area about the size of the United States. Rapid expansion brought about change in the Republic. The small farm society had changed, the gap between rich and poor had grown, and the slave population had greatly increased. And wealth from the wars had made Roman leaders greedy.

Dishonest leaders had huge incomes and ignored the poor. The poor, in turn, felt no loyalty to a government that was keeping them poor. Conflicts broke out between rich and poor.

Also, by 50 B.C., the army was made up of professional soldiers, mostly poor citizens who couldn't find work elsewhere. They were fighting for money, not for Rome. And money depended on victory in battle. Thus, these soldiers were loyal only to the generals, who hired them and paid them with land and money. Power-hungry generals fought one another for control of the government.

One of those generals was Julius Caesar. Caesar came from an old patrician family, and he was very ambitious. In 59 B.C., Caesar

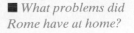
Across Time & Space

One of Julius Caesar's accomplishments was the development of a new calendar. By 46 B.C., the Roman calendar was three months behind the sun. Caesar added the three months and then changed the way the calendar was arranged. For his efforts, the Senate named the month of July in his honor, a name still in use today.

◀ *Andrea Mantegna painted* Triumph of Caesar *in the late 1400s. Notice the banner with the letters SPQR. These are the initials for the Latin words "The Senate and the people of Rome."*

417

The Rise of Rome

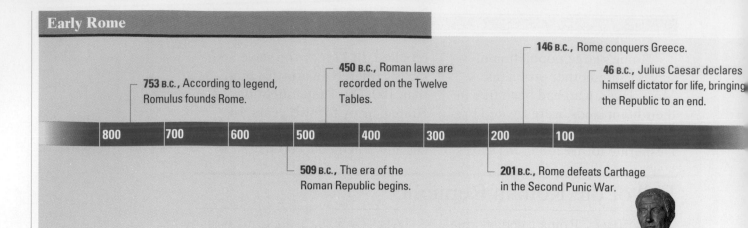

753 B.C., According to legend, Romulus founds Rome.

450 B.C., Roman laws are recorded on the Twelve Tables.

146 B.C., Rome conquers Greece.

46 B.C., Julius Caesar declares himself dictator for life, bringing the Republic to an end.

509 B.C., The era of the Roman Republic begins.

201 B.C., Rome defeats Carthage in the Second Punic War.

Trace the events of early Roman history on the timeline above.

➤ *Julius Caesar's great popularity among his troops enabled him to become dictator.*

■ *Who was Julius Caesar?*

was elected consul, but he knew he must win military glory to fulfill his ambitions. He took command of Roman troops and left to tame the Gauls. Nine years later he had succeeded.

Caesar's successes in Gaul worried his rivals in Rome. They feared that Ceasar was becoming too powerful. They called him a public enemy and persuaded the Senate to declare Caesar a threat to Rome.

The Senate ordered Caesar to return to Rome without his troops. But Caesar feared that if he did, his life would be in great danger. Instead, he decided to lead his troops to Rome.

On January 11, 49 B.C., Caesar and his army crossed the Rubicon River, which divided Gaul and Italy. Since it was treason for a general to leave his assigned province and bring his army to Rome, this was a serious action. Caesar

knew he must win or die.

Civil war broke out and lasted for three years. Eventually, Caesar defeated his rival, Pompey, and in 46 B.C. declared himself dictator. A **dictator** is a ruler who has absolute power.

Earlier Roman dictators had been chosen by the city officials only for emergencies. The citizen farmer, Lucius Cincinnatus, you recall, resigned 16 days after saving the city. When Caesar made himself dictator for life, he ended the Republican system. ■

R E V I E W

1. **FOCUS** How was Rome able to control the Mediterranean world?

2. **CONNECT** Compare Hannibal as a leader with Pericles of Athens. How successful was each in battle? Why is Hannibal considered a great general?

3. **ECONOMICS** In what ways did wars make Rome strong economically? How did wars weaken Rome?

4. **HISTORY** Why didn't Rome's allies in Italy defect to join Hannibal?

5. **CRITICAL THINKING** Caesar crossed the Rubicon River during his return to Rome. Today, we use the expression "crossing the Rubicon" as a figure of speech. What does it mean? Have you ever crossed a Rubicon?

6. **ACTIVITY** One of the "weapons" used by Hannibal's army was the elephant. Use your imagination to draw a war elephant. You might show it wearing armor and carrying soldiers.

Evaluating Sources

Here's Why

To learn about the past, we rely on the eyewitness accounts of events and records left behind. As you know, sources produced at the time of the event are *primary sources*. Sources produced after the event and that use primary sources for information are *secondary sources*.

You learned in Lesson 3 about some of Hannibal's remarkable deeds in the Punic Wars. Suppose you wanted to learn more about Hannibal. You might look for primary or secondary sources about him and then evaluate them.

Here's How

In order to evaluate a primary or secondary source, you can apply the questions used by historians. See the box at the bottom of this page.

First find out whether the source is primary or secondary. Try answering the first question. The passage on the right was written sometime between 27 and 25 B.C. The Punic Wars took place between 264 and 149 B.C. Obviously, this passage is a secondary source, because it was not produced at the same time as the event it tells about.

Look at the second question. Since this is a secondary source, it is not an eyewitness account.

Next find out who the writer was. The writer of this source, Titus Livius, or Livy, was a well-known Roman historian.

Next determine the type of source you are reading. The passage on this page is from a history book, Livy's history of Rome.

Finally, it is important to know why the source was written. A campaign poster about a person will have a different slant than will a historical account of the same person. The passage on this page was written by Livy to give an idea of how forceful a leader Hannibal was.

> . . . It was under Hannibal that the soldiers displayed greatest confidence and daring. He was fearless in undertaking dangerous enterprises, he was prudent in discharging them. Toil could not weary his body or subdue his spirit. Heat and cold he endured alike.

Try It

Apply the five questions for evaluating sources to all of Lesson 3 in this chapter. Use what you know about primary and secondary sources, and about the parts of a book. Then tell whether Lesson 3 is a primary source or a secondary source.

Apply It

Newspapers and books of today will be sources that people of the future will use to learn about our times. Find two articles about the U.S. President. Apply the five questions for evaluating sources. Then decide how reliable each source is.

1. When was the source produced? (Was it at the time of the event—primary source; or some time after the event —secondary source?)
2. Where was the source produced? (Was it an eyewitness account or a secondhand account?)
3. Who was the writer? (How might the writer's background affect the account?)
4. What kind of source is it? (Is it a letter, speech, or book?)
5. Why was the source produced? (To describe, to prove a point, or to comment?)

LESSON 4

Greece and Rome

How strong was Greece's influence on Rome?

Key Term

• aqueduct

➤ *Romans admired and imitated many Greek sculptures like the famous Nike of Samothrace, c. 200-190 B.C. This statue is often called* Winged Victory.

"Although we con-quered Greece, she conquered us: She brought Art to rustic Rome," wrote Horace, the great Roman poet, in about 35 B.C. Many Roman citizens agreed with him. The Romans may have triumphed militarily over Greece in 146 B.C. However, the resulting close contact with Greek culture dramatically changed many parts of Roman life. Greek ideas, art, and customs all were to become an important part of the Roman heritage.

Greek Influence on Rome

The Greek roots of Roman culture run deep. As early as the 600s B.C., Greece had established powerful colonies in southern Italy and Sicily. Greek culture spread quickly as Greek merchants traded Greek goods, such as fine pottery and metalwork, with neighboring peoples. By the 200s B.C., the Greek epic poem the *Odyssey* had been translated into Latin.

Greek influence grew even more when the two cultures came into greater contact after Rome's conquest of Greece. Victorious Roman troops brought Greek stat-ues and paintings back to Rome, where they were admired and cop-ied. Greek scholars were brought to Rome as slaves to teach wealthy Roman children.

In fact, Greek culture influ-enced Roman culture so much that the result is called Greco-Roman culture. With the growth of the Roman Republic, Greco-Roman culture spread throughout the Mediterranean world.

The Romans borrowed heavily from the Greeks. They worshiped Greek gods and gave them Roman names. The Greek god Zeus became the Roman god Jupiter; Aphrodite, goddess of love, became Venus; Ares, the god of war, became Mars.

Roman writers often turned to the Greeks for inspiration. The Roman poet Virgil used a Greek myth to begin his epic poem, the *Aeneid (ih NEE uhd)*.

In architecture, the Romans adopted basic Greek forms. Many Roman temples, for example, have columns surrounding the structure, just as most Greek temples do.

Education

School took place at home early in Roman history, when most Romans lived in the countryside. Girls were taught by their mothers, and boys learned from their fathers and served in the army. Roman parents taught their children the values of citizenship and service.

As Romans had more contact with the Greek world, they started studying Greek literature and philosophy. The Roman historian, Sallust, praised a woman he admired as "well educated in Greek and Latin literature." Roman children learned Greek early in grammar school. These schools were started by freed Greek slaves. If you came from a rich Roman family, you might be taught at home by a professional Greek philosopher. Julius Caesar, and other young Roman men, were sent to Greece to finish their education. ■

■ *What is Greco-Roman culture?*

Roman Genius

The Greeks were inventive, bringing out new ideas and new art forms. The Romans were practical, using and adapting whatever ideas and forms suited their needs. The early Romans were bent on expansion, and they mastered the skills necessary for building and governing an empire. Among these skills were military organization, legal administration, and special engineering ability.

Military Organization

The Roman army was one of the greatest military forces the world has ever seen. Before the Romans, most armies triumphed over their enemies simply by outnumbering them. The Roman army, however, won its victories mainly because of its determination and discipline.

Although the early Republic relied on citizen-farmers, after about 100 B.C., Rome began to build a full-time army. Roman soldiers enlisted for periods of up to

▼ *The Romans took care to protect themselves from attack. How many lines of defense are in the sketch of Roman siegeworks below?*

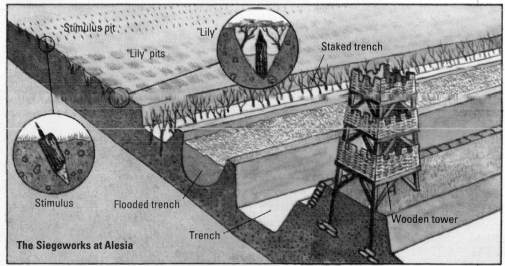

Stimulus pit

"Lily" pits

"Lily"

Staked trench

Stimulus

Flooded trench

Trench

Wooden tower

The Siegeworks at Alesia

20 years. They became hardened by years of fighting.

The Roman army was well organized with a strict chain of command. The army was divided into legions of 6,000 men each. Each legion was a self-contained unit with all the workers necessary to supply the army during long campaigns. Arrow makers, nurses, and engineers traveled with the soldiers. Thus the army could wage long battles without returning to Rome for supplies.

The Roman army was also unusually good at adapting to changing conditions. Specially trained troops of skilled archers, spear throwers, or horse riders could be called into battle.

In contrast, most Greek city-states (except for Sparta) had small armies of citizens, not professional soldiers. These armies served only when needed.

▲ *The Appian Way, which leads through the countryside to the city of Rome, is still used today.*

Engineering Skill

To unify and control their huge Republic, the Romans built more than 50,000 miles of roads—many of them paved with stone. With the paved roads, both messengers and troops could race to remote Roman provinces in case of enemy attack. The network of roads was also a great help to trade and communication.

Roman roads were built so well that some are still in use. In the city of Rome, honking cars and buses filled with commuters and sightseers clatter over the Appian Way, one of the very first Roman roads, built in 312 B.C.

In contrast, the mountainous countryside of Greece made road-building difficult. Since no part of their country was very far from the sea, the Greeks turned to it instead. Sea lanes became Greek highways.

Romans also used their engineering skills to perfect the arch they had inherited from the Etruscans. In addition, they invented a new building material—concrete. Concrete is long-lasting, but compared to stone, lightweight. With arches and concrete, the Romans were able to build huge public works—bridges, aqueducts, and stadiums.

Among the engineering skills developed by Roman builders was surveying. In A Moment in Time on page 423, you see a Roman surveyor at work.

► *In this cross section of a Roman road, you can see that the Romans built their roads to last.*

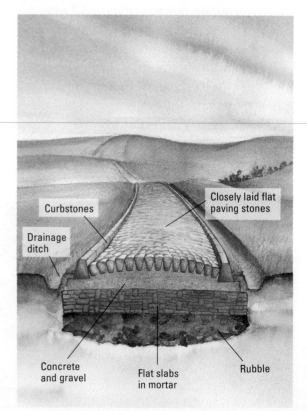

Curbstones

Closely laid flat paving stones

Drainage ditch

Concrete and gravel

Flat slabs in mortar

Rubble

A Roman Engineer

8:42 A.M., August 26, 109 B.C.
On what will be the Via Aemilia Scauri outside Pisa

Crossbars
Now that the top of his surveying instrument is level, he can look ahead to where his assistant is standing. He shouts directions to the assistant, who marks the ground where the road should go.

Ear
Our engineer can hear the shouts of slaves and prisoners digging half a mile away. The diggers are already working on the stretch of road he planned just days ago.

Clasp
This gift was sent by his wife in Rome. Because of the excellent roads, it reached him in only three days.

Robe
He's wearing his finest today despite the heat. The official in charge will come by soon to inspect. Our engineer wants to look his best.

Measuring Cord
Besides the mathematics he needs to make accurate measurements, our engineer has studied music, astronomy, and medicine. The best engineers know all the arts and sciences.

Metal Point
He likes the moments each day when he moves his equipment ahead and plants it in a new place. The army is anxious to have this road finished, and movement means progress.

> ➤ *This aqueduct in Nimes, France, was built in 16 B.C.*

■ *At what skills did the Romans excel?*

Romans used arches and concrete to build huge bridgelike structures. These **aqueducts** were built to carry water from mountain springs to the public fountains and baths in nearby cities. One of the longest of these supplied water to the Roman city of Carthage. It ran for more than 50 miles from its source in the mountains to the city.

Legal Administration

Roman laws were first written as the Twelve Tables in 450 B.C. Over time, the Romans developed a legal system with courts, judges, and lawyers. Judges based their decisions on common sense, fairness, and individual rights.

The Athenian system of justice was more direct. There were no judges or lawyers. Instead, the accused and accuser argued their own cases before the assembly, which acted as a jury.

As the Romans extended citizenship to a conquered people, they spread their legal system throughout the Mediterranean world. Roman law is the origin of modern-day legal systems in many parts of the world.

The Romans owed much to Greek culture. Yet in practical matters, such as military organization, engineering, and legal administration, the Romans made their own mark on the world. ■

<hr>

REVIEW

1. **FOCUS** How strong was Greece's influence on Rome?
2. **CONNECT** Name two ways Greek culture influenced Roman culture.
3. **CULTURE** How did Greek education influence Rome?
4. **HISTORY** Why is the Roman army considered one of the greatest military forces the world has ever seen?
5. **CRITICAL THINKING** How did Roman engineers use the environment to meet the needs of the Republic?

6. **CRITICAL THINKING** Reread the quotation from the Roman poet Horace at the beginning of the lesson. Do you think the Greeks "conquered" the Romans? Explain your answer.
7. **WRITING ACTIVITY** Write a one-minute speech describing the ways Roman genius has benefited the world. Give concrete examples.

Comparing Greece and Rome

Here's Why

It is hard to remember everything you read. Identifying the main ideas can help. The conclusion of a section of text is often also its main idea.

A conclusion is a reasoned judgment based on evidence. The lesson that compared Rome and Greece presented a great deal of evidence about both of these powers.

Here's How

Use the summary below of Military Organization from Lesson 4 to draw a conclusion about the strength of Roman army legions compared to Greek armies. Follow these steps:

1. **Study the evidence.** As you read, look for facts. Facts in the paragraph on military organization include these important points:
   a. Roman soldiers were professionals.
   b. Greek soldiers were citizen-soldiers.

2. **Draw a conclusion.** Use the facts from step 1 along with anything else you know about the subject. Here, it is reasonable to conclude that the Roman legions were stronger than the Greek armies, because professional soldiers are probably better than part-time soldiers.

3. **Think about the evidence again.** Does it support the conclusion? Be ready to change your conclusion if necessary. The evidence is this: Roman troops spent 20 years as professional soldiers. The legions were well supplied and organized, and they had specially trained troops to adapt to changing battle conditions. The conclusion is supported.

Try It

Read the summary of Engineering Skill below. What facts are given about Roman and Greek achievements? What conclusion can you draw?

Apply It

Find an article in a local newspaper or magazine. Use the three-step strategy to draw a conclusion from it.

Military Organization

The Roman army was a powerful military force. Unlike other armies, it defeated enemies with its determination and discipline. Whereas most Greek city-states relied on small armies of citizen-soldiers, Roman soldiers were professionals who remained in the army for 20 years. The Roman legions traveled with workers to supply them with arms and medical help, so they seldom needed to return to Rome. Moreover, they adapted to changing battle conditions by using specially trained troops, something less organized armies could not do.

Engineering Skill

The Romans owed much to Greek culture but made many important practical achievements of their own. Engineering skill enabled the Romans to build long-lasting roads throughout the empire. Greeks, by contrast, used the sea for most transportation, because Greek mountains made road building difficult. The Roman invention of concrete helped not only with road building but also with huge public works—bridges, aqueducts, and stadiums. The most impressive of these projects are the Appian Way and the 50-mile aqueduct to Carthage.

Chapter Review

Reviewing Key Terms

aqueduct (p. 424)
consul (p. 406)
debt bondage (p. 407)
dictator (p. 418)
omen (p. 396)

patrician (p. 406)
plebeian (p. 406)
republic (p. 406)
Senate (p. 397)

A. Some of the following statements are true. The rest are false. Write *True* or *False* for each statement. Then rewrite the false statements to make them true.

1. Ancient Romans often waited for omens from Senators before making decisions.
2. Young patricians made up the Senate.
3. In the Roman republic, a series of kings passed down leadership.
4. People had more to say about who became consuls than who became kings.
5. If a plebeian borrowed money from a patrician, he was forced into debt bondage and treated almost as a slave.
6. Julius Caesar became dictator of Rome because the Romans knew he would seek wise advice from his advisors.
7. Romans in the cities were able to get fresh water from an aqueduct.

B. Write a sentence to answer each question. Use at least one key term in each sentence.

1. Which terms listed above are related to government even today? Explain.
2. Which ones are related to social class? Explain.
3. Which one describes something outlawed by the Romans? Explain.

Exploring Concepts

A. In this chapter, you learned about the history of the city of Rome. Write a four-paragraph summary of the chapter based on the following information.

I. The birth of Rome
  A. Seven kings
  B. Midpoint of the Mediterranean
II. The rise of the republic
  A. Patricians and plebeians
  B. Struggle for rights
  C. Roman government
  D. Early expansion
III. Overseas expansion
  A. The Punic wars
  B. Control of eastern Mediterranean
  C. Trouble at home
  D. Fall of the Roman republic
IV. Greece and Rome

B. Support each statement with facts and details from the chapter.

1. The Etruscans were more advanced than the early Romans in some areas.
2. With effort and time, the plebeians gained legal rights that made them equal to the patricians.
3. The Roman government set an example for modern balance of power.
4. Romans treated people in areas they conquered in a special way.
5. The First Punic War lasted 23 years because both sides had strengths in certain areas.
6. Scipio Africanus was given his last name as an honor.
7. Spartacus was an important leader.
8. Crossing the Rubicon River was extremely risky for Julius Caesar.
9. Roman culture borrowed heavily from Greek culture.

Reviewing Skills

1. Read the quotation from Livy's history of Rome on this page. This account describes the suffering of one man, a plebeian soldier. Use it to list ways that the Roman system was unfair to plebeians. How does this primary source help us to sympathize with a man who lived over 2,000 years ago?

2. Reread Midpoint of the Mediterranean on pages 398 and 399. Draw conclusions about these questions: Would Rome have been as successful if it were located on the coast of Spain? Of France? Of Sardinia? What evidence supports your ideas?

3. On the map of Eurasia on pages 508 and 509 of the Atlas, find the cities of Rome, Italy, and Athens, Greece. Using the scale, calculate the distance of the most direct route between the two cities.

4. Suppose you want to review events from the founding of Rome through its control of the Mediterranean region. What is a helpful study aid?

An old man entered the forum. His clothing was covered with filth, and his pale and emaciated condition was shocking. . . . When he was asked the cause of his wretched condition he declared to all that while he had been fighting in the Sabine War all his property had been burned, the crops in his fields devastated, his flocks driven off; and when a special emergency tax was exacted. . . he was driven into debt. As this debt had accumulated with excessive interest rates, it had first deprived him of his farm   then of the rest of his belongings...he had been dragged by his creditor not just into slavery, but into a place of punishment and torture.

Using Critical Thinking

1. Romans disagreed about whether foreign cultures weakened early Roman culture. Today, Americans disagree about the same issue in America. What do you think the effects of other cultures are on American culture? Explain.

2. Rome's location on the Tiber, on hills near the sea, gave the city advantages in ancient times. Is Rome's location still a good one today? Explain. Think about how transportation affects the way countries get along with each other.

3. In early Rome, farming was the main way of life. On page 416, you read about Lucius Cincinnatus. Look for more information about him in the library and write a short report. Discuss how his values affected what he did for his country. What do you think his decision would be if he were in that situation today?

Preparing for Citizenship

1. **WRITING ACTIVITY** Imagine that you live at the time of Romulus and Remus. You know they disagree about where to build their city. You be the peacemaker; write them a letter in which you suggest how they could solve their dispute.

2. **COLLABORATIVE LEARNING** Just as legends of ancient civilizations reveal their spirit, so do legends of modern peoples. (Paul Bunyan is an example of a modern legend.) For a class project, create a book of modern legends. Form groups of three, with each person in a group choosing a legend. Decide which of the three legends is most interesting. One person in the group will illustrate the story, one will write about the culture from which it came, and one will print it. Choose a member to meet with the other groups to decide how to put together the book.

Chapter 14
The Roman Empire

With the end of the Roman Republic, a new era began. During the next 200 years, the Romans conquered new lands and built a vast empire. Rome itself prospered. The years from 27 B.C. to A.D. 180 are remembered as the Pax Romana, *a time of peace and prosperity.*

This couple, a baker and his wife, lived in the Roman city of Pompeii during the *Pax Romana.*

100	50	B.C.	A.D.	50

49 B.C.

27 B.C. Augustus (above left) becomes Rome's first emperor. He reforms the government and begins the era of the Roman Empire.

Roman soldiers pushed the borders of the empire north to what is now Britain, west to the Atlantic Ocean, south into Africa, and east into Asia. This map from a later period shows much of the world that was once under Roman control.

A.D. 80 The 50,000-seat Colosseum opens in Rome (far right). To celebrate the event, coins like this were given away.

100	150	200	250

A.D. 180 The *Pax Romana* ends with the death of emperor Marcus Aurelius.

A.D. 235

LESSON 1

The Early Empire

THINKING
FOCUS

How did the Romans build a peaceful and prosperous empire?

Key Terms

• assassinate
• province

➤ *No sculpture of Julius Caesar made in his own lifetime still exists. This later one is thought to be the best likeness of Caesar. With it is a broken crown of laurel. In the ancient world, laurel crowns were often used to honor heroes.*

eware the ides of March," the fortune-teller whispered in Julius Caesar's ear. "I have seen many warnings of danger in your future." But Caesar, confident of his power in early 44 B.C., simply went on about his business. He was even bold enough to dismiss his bodyguards. However, March 15, referred to in the Roman calendar as the "ides" of March, turned out to be the day of Caesar's undoing.

As Caesar strode into the senate that day, a group of men gathered around him as if to pay their respects. One of them took hold of Caesar's robe and said, "Friends, what are you waiting for?" That was the signal to attack. Several men drew daggers from their robes and began stabbing Caesar. He tried to defend himself, but then he recognized one of the men. It was Brutus, a man Caesar thought was his friend. *"Et tu, Brute?"*

("You too, Brutus?") Caesar asked. Realizing that even his friend had turned against him, he stopped resisting. Caesar fell to the floor and died. He had been stabbed 23 times.

Brutus jumped up, waving his bloody knife. He announced that he and his men had saved the Roman Republic by killing Caesar. However, the death of Caesar did not restore the Republic. Instead, it sparked 13 years of civil war as various groups struggled to control Rome.

Establishing Peace and Order

Caesar had seized control of the government of the Roman world in 49 B.C., making himself dictator for life. As dictator, Caesar seemed to have little respect for the constitution. According to the constitution, a Roman leader was supposed to share power with the senators. But many senators thought Caesar acted as if he were above the law. They thought he treated them as servants. They saw his behavior as haughty and insulting. Many began to think of him as both a personal enemy and an enemy of the Roman Republic.

Senators and other Roman citizens whispered among themselves that Caesar intended to make himself king. If he did so, he could establish a dynasty. His family line would rule the Roman world even after his death, and the Senate would then have no role in choosing the next leader. Outraged, more than 60 senators met secretly. They planned how they would **assassinate** Caesar—murder him for political reasons. One leader of the group was Brutus, the so-called friend of Caesar.

When Brutus and his men killed Caesar on the ides of March, they thought they had saved the Republic. But by the end of that day, the assassins had to hide from angry mobs of Roman citizens. Many were outraged by Caesar's murder. Caesar was well liked because he made many reforms that improved people's lives. For example, he reorganized the government and lowered taxes. He founded new colonies and gave people land to farm. He hired people to build temples and public buildings. He made citizens of many people in the colonies.

A power struggle followed Caesar's death. Caesar's adopted son Octavian *(ahk TAY vee uhn)* was the leader of one group that was fighting to control Rome. He defeated his rivals in 31 B.C. and led Rome into a new era.

The Empire of Augustus

Octavian brought peace to the Roman Empire and became a popular leader. In 27 B.C., the Senate voted to give him the title Augustus *(aw GUHS tuhs),* meaning "respected one." He ruled the empire until A.D. 14.

Augustus learned from his father's mistakes. He continued many of the reforms that had been started by Caesar. He knew that the people wanted a republic, so he showed respect for the Senate and asked for its cooperation in running the empire.

But Augustus held the real power. He controlled almost all of the military troops. He appointed the most important officials of the government—those who governed the provinces. He carefully avoided using the title of king. Instead, he called himself "first citizen" to show that he was one of the people.

Augustus ruled an empire. He is considered to be the

▼ *This detail from a tomb relief, carved in the A.D. 100s, shows work in progress on a building project in Rome. Notice that the machine moving the building materials looks something like a modern crane.*

The Roman Empire

► *In modern Morocco, these ruins, once part of the Roman city of Volubilis, are reminders of how vast the Roman Empire was.*

first Roman emperor. The people welcomed him because they craved a strong leader. They desperately wanted peace and order after the time of turmoil that followed Caesar's death.

Order in the City

Augustus once boasted, "I found Rome built of sun-dried bricks. I leave her covered in marble." During the 41 years of his rule, Augustus built or restored 82 temples. Most of them were dressed in the smooth marble from the quarries that were just opening north of Rome.

Augustus also worked to improve life in the city of Rome. With a population of nearly one million people, Rome had no city services. Some of the worst problems were hunger and poverty. Violence and disorder increased, and Rome had a major crime problem. In addition, fires regularly swept through the city. Augustus created a police force and a fire brigade. He set up a department to supply food to the city's citizens.

Growth in the Provinces

The Roman Empire beyond Italy was divided into about 40 **provinces,** or territories. Each province had a governor, who was appointed by the emperor or named by the Senate. The governors' work included keeping order and collecting taxes.

Augustus and the emperors who followed him expanded the empire by conquering new territories. Look at the map on page 433 to see how the Roman Empire grew in the 200 years after Augustus came to power. At its peak in A.D. 117, the Roman Empire had a population of about 60 million. This was more than one-fifth of the total population of the world at that time.

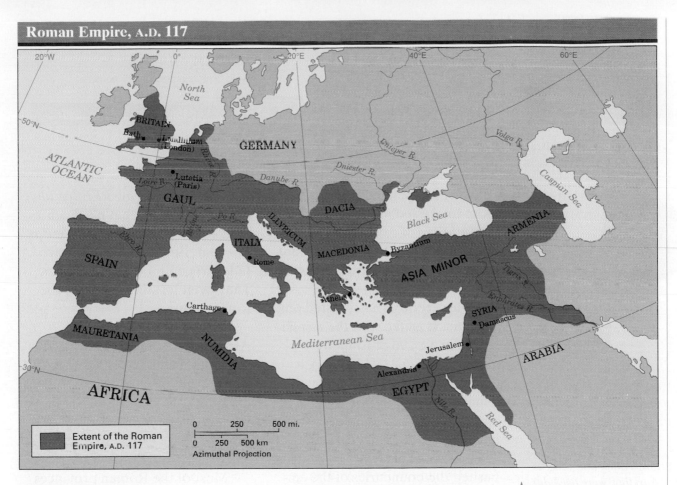

Extent of the Roman Empire, A.D. 117

0   250   500 mi.
0   250   500 km
Azimuthal Projection

The *Pax Romana*

Augustus's reign marked the beginning of a remarkable period in Rome's history. For more than 200 years, the vast Roman Empire was united and, for the most part, peaceful. This period from 27 B.C. to A.D. 180 is called the *Pax Romana (paks roh MAH nuh)*, or "Peace of Rome." ■

Ruling the Empire

Remember the problems that arose after Caesar's death over who would be the next emperor. Augustus hoped to avoid the same problems. He wanted his stepson Tiberius *(ty BIHR ee uhs)* to be the next emperor. To make sure it would happen, Augustus began to share his power with Tiberius. When Augustus died in A.D. 14, Tiberius stepped into his step-father's position. In that way, Augustus established a new way of choosing emperors. Each emperor chose his successor from his family or adopted someone he thought would make a good emperor.

During the 200 years after Augustus's death, four family lines, or dynasties, ruled the Roman Empire. Some emperors in each dynasty ruled wisely. Others were cruel or foolish. Each of the four dynasties ended with the violent overthrow of an unpopular or unfit emperor.

The Dynasties

Augustus's family line ended in disgrace in A.D. 68 with Emperor Nero *(NEE roh)*. Nero came to power when he was just a boy of 17. He did not gain the respect of the senators or the army. Many

▲ *Notice that Roman rule extended as far north as Britain. Where were the western and eastern borders? How far south did the empire extend?*

■ *What did Augustus do for the city of Rome and for the provinces?*

433

The Roman Empire

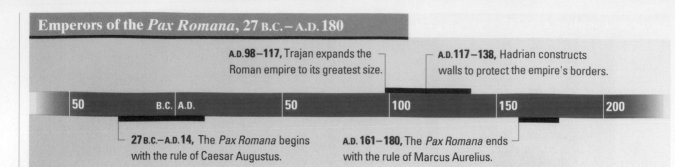

A.D. 98–117, Trajan expands the Roman empire to its greatest size.

A.D. 117–138, Hadrian constructs walls to protect the empire's borders.

| 50 | B.C. | A.D. | 50 | 100 | 150 | 200 |

27 B.C.–A.D. 14, The *Pax Romana* begins with the rule of Caesar Augustus.

A.D. 161–180, The *Pax Romana* ends with the rule of Marcus Aurelius.

Examine the timeline to see which emperor had the longest reign. The Roman coins, which picture Trajan and Marcus Aurelius, were used during their reigns.

■ *How did the reigns of the "good emperors" contrast with the reigns of Nero and Domitian?*

Romans complained that he was more interested in entertaining himself than in governing the empire. Opposition to his rule mounted. A bloody civil war broke out, and Nero committed suicide.

The second dynasty lasted only 26 years. It ended with the assassination in A.D. 96 of Emperor Domitian *(duh MIHSH uhn)*, a cruel and ruthless leader. The third dynasty became known as the dynasty of the "good emperors." It included five talented emperors. Trajan *(TRAY juhn)*, for example, pushed the boundaries of the empire beyond the Danube and into Armenia and Mesopotamia. He also gave low-cost loans to farmers and helped support poor children and orphans.

Hadrian *(HAY dree uhn)* was the first emperor to protect the borders with walls. Under Hadrian, small settlements around forts and castles became towns and cities.

Marcus Aurelius *(aw REE lee uhs)* protected borders, but his death marked the gradual end of the *Pax Romana*. Emperors who followed failed to control the vast empire. They even lost the respect of the Roman army.

Finally, Emperor Severus Alexander was assassinated by his own soliders in A.D. 235. His death was the end of the dynasties and the start of 50 years of civil war within the empire.

Rebellion in the Provinces

Most of the Roman provinces lived in peace during the *Pax Romana*. However, a few areas resisted Roman rule. The Roman army had to put down rebellions in Gaul and Britain. The greatest resistance, however, came from the Jews in Judea. The Jews rebelled in A.D. 66 and again in A.D. 132. Each time, the Roman army crushed the Jewish resistance. ■

Unifying the Empire

Despite resistance to Roman rule in some provinces, the empire remained unified during the *Pax Romana*. However, maintaining unity was a large task. Over the centuries, the Romans conquered vast areas and diverse peoples. These people spoke different languages, had different customs, and worshiped different gods. The Roman emperors, though, managed to hold the empire together. They

did so in several ways. They encouraged the conquered people to build cities. They made some of the people Roman citizens. And they involved them in the government.

Policies for the Provinces

These new cities that the people in the provinces built followed the model of Rome. The city center surrounded a main square

Across Time & Space

In Britain, Emperor Hadrian ordered his soldiers to build a stone wall 73 miles long to keep invaders out of the empire. Parts of Hadrian's Wall are still standing today.

434

called the forum, like the one in Rome. The new cities also had temples for Roman gods, an amphitheater for games, and public baths. These and other public buildings were patterned after the ones in the city of Rome. The ideas of the Romans, their customs, and their Latin language gradually spread from the cities into the surrounding areas.

As a second way of unifying the empire, Rome gradually granted citizenship to people in the provinces. In A.D. 212, Emperor Caracalla granted citizenship to the entire free population of the empire. As citizens, the people gained some important new rights. For example, citizens were protected by Roman law. They could do business and own property in Rome. They could also pass their property and citizenship on to their children.

As a third means of unifying the empire, Rome allowed officials in the provinces to govern their own cities. They collected taxes and kept order on Rome's behalf.

Rome allowed some of these officials from the provinces to participate in the central government in Rome. By A.D. 200, more than half of the 600 senators came from the provinces. Some of these senators even became emperors. Emperor Trajan, for example, came from Spain. Septimius Severus, who ruled from A.D. 193 to 211, came from North Africa.

These policies of Rome made the people who lived in the provinces feel that they were a part of the empire. Therefore, most of them did not have any reason to rebel.

Rome at Its Peak

One of Rome's greatest poets described the purpose of the empire in this way:

> *R*emember, Roman, that it is for you to rule the nations. This shall be your task: to impose the ways of peace, to spare the vanquished and to tame the proud by war.
>
> Virgil, *Aeneid*, c. 19 B.C.

For 200 years, Rome did just that. The *Pax Romana* is remembered as the period during which Rome reached the peak of its political and cultural achievement. ■

▲ *The city of Bath, England, is a health resort noted for its warm springs. This photo shows the public baths that were built there under the Romans.*

■ *What policies did the Roman emperors follow in order to unify the empire?*

R E V I E W

1. **FOCUS** How did the Romans build a peaceful and prosperous empire?

2. **CONNECT** Caesar's assassins thought the assassination had saved the Republic. Why do you think they might have expected the Roman people to approve?

3. **GOVERNMENT** Why did the Roman people welcome Augustus's rule?

4. **HISTORY** In what ways was the *Pax Romana* a remarkable period in Rome's history?

5. **CRITICAL THINKING** The Roman people did not want a king or dictator. Do you think Augustus and the emperors that followed him were different from kings or dictators? Explain your answer.

6. **ACTIVITY** Imagine that you live in the Roman province of Gaul, and you have heard rumors of a rebellion against Rome. Discuss the rumors with a partner, taking opposite sides about whether you ought to join the rebels.

LESSON 2

Social Rank in the Empire

I t's a beautiful day in A.D. 150. The people of ancient Rome are heading eagerly to the Colosseum. They are going to watch an afternoon of games in which professional fighters called gladiators will fight lions, bears, other wild beasts—and each other. "Such a throng flocked to all these shows," wrote Suetonius, "that many strangers had to lodge in tents pitched . . . along the roads, and the press was often such that many were crushed to death."

Now the people are pushing and shoving as they scramble toward the entrances to the giant outdoor stadium. Like sports fans today, the Romans pass through the gates and head for their seats.

Where they sit, however, depends on their social status. The emperor and his guests are seated nearest the field on a magnificent platform. In the first rows are senators and other wealthy Romans. They wear flowing white robes called togas. The togas are trimmed with purple borders—the mark of the **elite,** the upper class.

Sitting in the rows above the elite are ordinary citizens, also dressed in togas. Their togas are plain white. Only the elite are allowed to wear the purple border.

Crowded near the top of the stadium, above the ordinary citizens, are poor people and slaves in drab, grey clothes. They have no seats and must stand for hours waiting for the games to begin.

➤ *Gladiators like these, pictured in a detail from a Roman mosaic, often faced each other in the Colosseum and in other arenas.*

Three Social Classes

Roman social status determined what people could wear, where they could sit—even what their job could be. Roman society was divided into three major classes—the elite, the "more humble," and the slaves. Birth and wealth determined social class.

The Elite Class

The best seats at the Colosseum were saved for the elite. This group included senators and other government officials and wealthy citizens. The elite made up less than 2 per cent of the people, but they were the most powerful. They even had special legal rights. If they were guilty of a crime, they could not be punished as severely as ordinary citizens or slaves.

Only a few jobs were acceptable for a man of the elite class. The emperor appointed members of the elite class to serve as government officials. Also acceptable for the elite were jobs in law and ownership of farms. Jobs in business were not acceptable. If a man of the elite class wanted to make money in business, he would hire someone of the "more humble" class to do it for him.

The "More Humble" Class

The people seated above the elite in the Colosseum were the ordinary citizens, who belonged to the "more humble" class. The more humble class included most of the free men and women in the empire. Farmers, laborers, shopkeepers, soldiers, and other working people were in the more humble class. Some of the more humble were fairly wealthy. Others just scraped by.

The Slaves

Crammed together with the poorest people at the top of the Colosseum were the slaves—

The Colosseum was completed in A.D. 80. It had four stories and covered over seven and one-half acres. Its 80 entrances allowed 50,000 spectators to find seats in 10 minutes. The emperor's family came in through a special gate. Wild animals were kept in cages under the floor.

Slaves

Ordinary citizens

Elite

437

The Roman Empire

human property that could be bought and sold. Slaves could not own property. By some estimates, slaves made up as much as a third of the people of Roman Italy during the empire.

Rome also had a large population of "freedmen." They were ex-slaves who were freed by their masters. As government workers for Emperor Augustus, freedmen gained great influence in Rome.

Besides working in households and on farms, trained slaves worked in mining, shipping, road building, and construction. Slaves also might hold office jobs in the provinces. Conditions for slaves varied widely. Slaves on the farms worked long hours in the fields. Sometimes they were chained together.

Slaves in cities usually worked as servants in the homes of wealthy masters. They had an easier life than the slaves on farms. Some city slaves even gained important positions as heads of household staffs. But all slaves were at the mercy of their masters, who could beat or torture them.

Some Romans complained about the mistreatment of slaves. However, this system was the foundation of the Roman economy. No one in the ancient world thought seriously about the end of slavery. ■

■ *How did life differ for people in the three Roman social classes?*

The Importance of Social Level

Social level was important to all Romans. Let's visit the home of an elite Roman to see the role it played at a dinner party.

A Roman Dinner Party

As the guests arrive, they are led to the special dining room. Painted on the walls are sayings like this: "Let the slave wash and dry the feet of the guests, and let him be mindful to spread a linen cloth on the cushions of the couches."

Couches rather than chairs surround the tables because Romans prefer to lean back as they eat. Eating in a reclining position is considered a mark of elegance. Only children and slaves sit upright as they eat. On holidays, the slaves in this house are allowed to recline like their masters.

Elite Romans follow a complex formula for seating people according to their social status. The most honored guests may even be served better food than the other guests. Pliny the Younger once complained about the favoritism shown by a host: ". . . very elegant dishes were served up to himself and a few more of the company; while those placed before the rest were cheap and paltry."

▼ *This painting found at Pompeii shows some elite Romans being entertained at a dinner party.*

The host at this dinner party has invited a man who belongs to the "more humble" class. The invitation is a reward for services performed. Unfortunately, the other guests treat this man as an inferior. They joke about his clothes, his table manners, and his vocabulary.

Slaves serve the dinner. The Roman writer Seneca described such slaves: "The unfortunate slaves are not allowed to move their lips, let alone talk. . . . A cough, a sneeze, a hiccup is rewarded by a flogging, with no exceptions."

Changes in Social Level

As this dinner party shows, social divisions were clearly defined in ancient Rome. However, people were occasionally able to improve their social position. The key was gaining wealth, and for most, becoming wealthy was impossible. According to Juvenal, the Romans decided the importance of a man in this way:

T he first question to be asked will be about his wealth, the last about his character. How many slaves does he maintain? How much land does he possess? How many courses does he have served at table and how much does he provide for his guests?

Romans could improve their social position if they became wealthy. If they lost wealth, however, they could lose their social status. Raising one's social level was not easy. The great majority of people in the "more humble" class worked on farms, and they were usually lucky just to get by each year. They had little chance of becoming rich. Soldiers had a better chance. Some earned promotions and wealth during long military careers. When they retired, they were rich and respected enough to join the elite class.

Even slaves had a chance to better themselves by buying their freedom. Wealthy Romans sometimes helped their former slaves start a business in exchange for a share in the profits. Rural slaves had harder lives and fewer opportunities. They had little chance of gaining freedom or improving their lot in life. ■

▼ *Wealthy Roman families used beautiful dishes like this plate and pitcher.*

■ *How could Romans improve their social position?*

1. **FOCUS** What role did social rank play in Roman life?
2. **CONNECT** Compare the Roman social class system with the caste system of ancient India.
3. **SOCIAL SCIENCE** How did the ancient Romans feel about slavery? How would you compare their attitude with ours today?
4. **CRITICAL THINKING** Compare the Roman system for seating people in the Colosseum with the way people

are seated at sporting events today. Who gets the best seats, and why?

5. **ACTIVITY** According to the U.S. Declaration of Independence, all people are created equal. Plan a debate about equality. Have one side, the Romans, argue that people are unequal and should be treated as such. Have the other side, the Americans, explain what the Declaration means by equality.

LESSON 3

Daily Life in Ancient Rome

THINKING
FOCUS

How was daily life different for rich and poor Romans?

Key Terms

- rhetoric
- ritual

> **B**efore it is light I wake up, and, sitting on the edge of my bed, I put on my shoes and leg-wraps because it is cold. . . . Taking off my nightshirt I put on my tunic and belt; I put oil on my hair, comb it, wrap a scarf around my neck and put on my white cloak. Followed by my school attendant and my nurse I go to say good morning to daddy and mummy and I kiss them both. I find my writing things and exercise book and give them to a slave. I set off to school followed by my school attendant. . . .
>
> I go into the schoolroom and say "Good morning master." He kisses me and returns my greeting. The slave gives me my wax tablets, my writing things and ruler. . . . When I finish learning my lesson I ask the master to let me go home to lunch. . . . Reaching home I change, take some white bread, olives, cheese, dried figs, and nuts and drink some cold water. After lunch I go back to school where the master is beginning to read. He says, "Let's begin work."
>
> At the end of the afternoon I'm off to the Baths with some towels with my slave. I run up to meet the people going to the Baths and we all say to each other "Have a good bathe and a good supper."
>
> A Roman schoolboy, quoted by F. R. Cowell,
> *Everyday Life in Ancient Rome*

A boy from a wealthy Roman family wrote the above description of a typical day in about A.D. 300.

Accounts like this are one source of information about daily life in ancient Rome.

Rich and Poor

The boy who wrote this account belonged to an elite family in Rome. Only the rich could send their children to school and have slaves wait on them. His home may have looked like the Roman house shown in A Closer Look on page 442. What parts of the house were open to let in light, air, and rain? Where would you spend the most time if you lived in this house?

A rich family in one of these homes might own 500 slaves. Some very wealthy Roman families

might own 4,000 slaves. An emperor might command a personal slave population of 20,000. Household slaves did just about every job imaginable. They cooked, served meals, cleaned, and took care of the children. Each slave might have only one job—folding the master's clothes or fixing the mistress's hair, for example.

In contrast, the vast majority of those who lived in the city had tiny apartments in five-story apartment buildings called *insulae* (*IHN suh ly*). In some cases, an entire family would crowd into a single room.

For every wealthy home in Rome, there were 26 blocks of *insulae*. Most *insulae* were dark and dirty and had no heat or running water. The poor got water from public fountains outside.

The Roman writer Juvenal described the poorer neighborhoods of Rome in the A.D. 100s:

> Most of the city [is] propped up with planks to stop it collapsing. Your landlord stands in front of cracks that have been there for years and says, "Sleep well!" although he knows that the house itself may not last the night. I wish I lived where there were no fires, no midnight panics.

In these crowded conditions, fires and crime were serious problems. Lack of sanitation also contributed to the spread of disease. The problem was so severe that about one-fourth of the babies born in Rome did not live through their first year. Half of all Roman children did not live to be 10 years old. ■

▲ *The Roman father and son in this marble relief are shown at different stages of the son's life. In the last scene, the boy may be answering the age-old question, "What did you learn in school today?"*

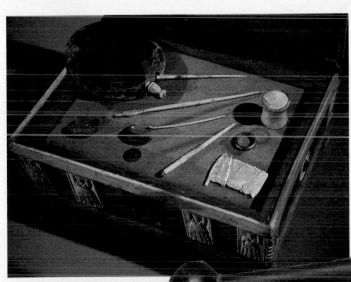

◄ *This make-up box and the hairpin shown with it once belonged to a wealthy Roman woman.*

■ *How did the housing of the rich Romans compare with the housing of the poor?*

441

The Roman Empire

A Roman House

Imagine living in a home that was also your parents' work place. Relatives, friends, servants, and clients would always be coming and going. There might be a vegetable garden and a couple of stores under your roof, too.

If you put out this dog-shaped oil lamp, your bedroom would be totally dark—even during the day! That's because bedrooms rarely had windows.

Would you walk on your artwork? The Romans did. Romans decorated their floors with mosaics like this one.

The father of the family sits here, where he can see all the action.

Back yard

Garden

Kitchen

Statue of great-grandfather

Reading room

Stores

Door, open all day

Bedroom

Can you eat lying down? Romans held dinner parties in a room called the *triclinium*, which means "three-couch place." The room had three couches, and dinner guests ate while lying on their sides.

Like a living room today, the *atrium* was the place where Roman families entertained their guests. But the Roman living room had a hole in its roof. Rainwater poured into a pool where it was stored for drinking and washing.

Only the rich could afford glass pitchers and bowls like these.

Family Life in the Empire

By the time Rome had become the center of an empire, family life was changing. In the days of the Republic, the father was the undisputed head of the family. He could even sell his children as slaves. He could arrange marriages for his daughters when they were only 12 to 15 years old. He would do this for the political and economic benefits it would bring to the family. The young bride and groom had little to say about it.

By the A.D. 100s, however, family discipline had become less harsh, and the father's power had been reduced. A father no longer had the right to sell his children or to force marriages. In addition, women had more freedom. Unlike women in other ancient cultures such as Greece, Roman women were independent under the law. They could have their own property and slaves.

Families that could afford the cost of private education sent their children and even household slaves to school beginning at about age seven. These children studied basic reading, writing, and arithmetic. The schools were small, and one teacher was responsible for all subjects. Teachers followed the rule of the Greek playwright Menander: "A man who has not been flogged [beaten] is not trained."

Girls usually did not have any formal education after age 15. Usually at 15, the sons of wealthy parents continued their education by taking classes in Latin and Greek literature and **rhetoric**—the art of effective writing and speaking. Students needed to learn rhetoric in order to enter law or politics. Romans believed that skill in rhetoric was the mark of a gentleman.

The Roman schools rarely had classes in science, engineering, or complex mathematics. The few professional people—engineers, doctors, or lawyers, for example—learned through apprenticeships, not through formal education. ■

▲ *Some people in Pompeii were eating their midday meal when Vesuvius erupted. (See How Do We Know? on page 444.) Several foods, preserved intact under the ashes, can be seen today in the Pompeii Museum, including this loaf of bread.*

◄ *This young Roman student looks thoughtful. Is she thinking about the day's lesson?*

■ *What were family life and schooling like for young people growing up in the Roman Empire?*

Benefits of Life in Rome

The city of Rome was a crowded, busy, thriving place—the center for the best and worst of the Mediterranean world. Disease, crime, and fires raged there. But life in Rome also had its benefits. The emperors made a point of trying to keep the city people happy.

HISTORY *In A.D. 79, Mount Vesuvius, a volcano in southern Italy, erupted. Afterward, nearly 13 feet of ash and stone covered the nearby town of Pompeii. During the past two centuries, archaeologists have rediscovered the town. Studying what remains of Pompeii has given archaeologists a clear picture of daily life in the Roman Empire.*

▼ *The Roman public baths were complex structures. (1) A furnace heated (2) a tank of water. (3) Pipes carried the hot water to the pools. The Romans began their bath in a hot-water pool, continued it in (4) a warm-water pool, and ended it in (5) a cool-water pool.*

Public Services

The government gave free wheat to male citizens on a regular basis. This gift of food was important to the poor people of Rome, who often went hungry. On special occasions, the emperor also gave money to the citizens of Rome. The wheat and money came from taxes that farmers and other people in the provinces paid.

Another benefit of living in Rome was the plentiful water supply. The system of aqueducts carried 200 million gallons of water to Rome daily. With so much water available, the city built public baths where residents, rich and poor, could bathe and swim for a small fee. These baths became important gathering places.

Entertainment

The emperors spent enormous sums of money to entertain the people. In fact, 159 days each year had been declared holidays by the A.D. 50s. Later emperors found it necessary to limit the number of holidays each year. Still, nearly one-third of the days of each year remained holidays throughout the A.D. 100s.

On these holidays the emperors provided elaborate circuses and games to keep the people content. The Circus Maximus was a gigantic Roman arena that could hold nearly 200,000 spectators. There, spectacular daredevil chariot races took place. "All Rome today is in the circus," wrote Juvenal. "Such sights are for the young, whom it befits to shout and make bold wagers with a smart damsel by their side."

Chariot racing was also popular at the Colosseum, but so were some of the more bloody sports. Wild beasts were hunted and killed by the hundreds. Gladiators fought each other to the death. During the years A.D. 106 to 114, 23,000 gladiators fought to entertain the citizens. The Romans were so fond of bloody events that during the intermissions, Roman officials executed condemned criminals for the entertainment of the audience.

However, the benefits of life in Rome such as free food and spectacular entertainment did not appeal to all Romans. Some claimed that the citizens took too much interest in those things and not enough interest in their government. Even members of the elite class, who benefited the most, saw problems. The Roman historian

Tacitus said that the empire made slaves of free men. The Roman writer Juvenal also complained that the public "longs for just two things—bread and circuses." ■

Circuses were a major form of entertainment in the Roman Empire. This "Mosaic of the Circus Games" was found in Roman Gaul. It dates from about A.D. 175.

■ *How did the emperors provide "bread and circuses" for the people of Rome?*

Religious Practices

Many Romans believed that they had been able to build their empire and find peace because they had kept their gods happy. Like many other ancient peoples, the Romans had gods for every act and event in their lives.

The Many Gods of the Romans

The great gods of the Roman state were Jupiter, Juno, and Minerva. Jupiter was the supreme god. He controlled the thunder and lightning and was the special guardian of Rome. Juno was his wife. She was the queen of the gods and the protector of women. Minerva was the goddess of wisdom and guardian of craftworkers. The Romans joined together on specific days to worship these gods. In this way they showed their unity and their loyalty to the state.

At home, the Romans worshiped household gods, such as Vesta, Lares *(LAIR eez),* and Penates *(puh NAY teez).* Vesta guarded the fireside, where people

cooked and kept warm. Lares guarded the land, and Penates watched over the stored food. Family members made daily offerings to these gods and asked for protection in exchange.

Many of these Roman gods had been borrowed from the Greeks at an earlier time. For example, Jupiter was the Greek god Zeus, and Juno was the Greek goddess Hera. Diana, the Roman goddess of the hunt, was the Greek goddess Artemis. Mars, the Roman god of war, was the Greek god Ares.

In A.D. 126, the Romans erected a magnificent temple called the Pantheon *(PAN thee uhn)* to honor all the Roman gods and goddesses. They built it in the shape of a drum, with a dome rising 14 stories above the ground. They covered the dome with gleaming brass so that people could see it

▼ *Found in the ruins of Pompeii, this household shrine contains small statues that include one of Lares, the guardian of houses.*

shining all over the city. The Pantheon is still standing today.

During the empire, the Romans also began to worship their emperors. The emperor was not a god like Jupiter, but he was so powerful that people believed he was divine.

► *This statue of Jupiter, the supreme god of the Romans, was found with a statue of his wife Juno. It is made of terra cotta, a hard ceramic clay.*

Religious Ceremonies

The Roman religion was based on **rituals,** or ceremonies, rather than a written creed or right behavior. If a priest carried out the rituals properly, the Romans thought that the gods would be happy and would reward them with protection and wealth.

In one of the most important rituals, priests sacrificed animals to please the gods. The priests also made sacrifices in order to find signs, or omens, in the organs of the sacrificed animals. These signs, the people believed, would tell the will of the gods and would help them make decisions. How were the beliefs of the Romans similar to certain ideas of the ancient Greeks and Chinese?

■ *What was the Roman state religion like, and why were some people dissatisfied with it?*

Other Religions

The state religion did not teach about how people ought to act, so some Romans started looking for other religions. Gods and religious beliefs from Greece, Asia, Persia, and Egypt began to gain popularity during the first two centuries A.D. People in many parts of the empire, including women and the "more humble" class, were becoming Christians. Like the Jews, the Christians believed in just one God. They honored their God above the gods of the empire or the orders of the emperor.

For the most part, the Romans were tolerant of other religions within the empire. However, when the fortunes of the empire began to decline, emperors tried to force people to follow the state religion. A struggle lay ahead over what religious beliefs should guide the Roman people. ■

R E V I E W

1. **FOCUS** How was daily life different for rich and poor Romans?
2. **CONNECT** How does the class system help to explain why the only Romans who studied rhetoric were wealthy men?
3. **BELIEF SYSTEMS** How did their religion make the Romans feel they had some control over the unknown?

4. **CRITICAL THINKING** Why did the emperors of Rome go to so much effort and expense to entertain the poor people? What might have happened if they had ignored the poor?
5. **ACTIVITY** Make a chart listing the pros and cons of having as many holidays as the Romans had. Consider both Roman society and our own.

L E S S O N   4

The Roman Economy

In 1957, a 16-year-old boy who was skin-diving near the Italian island of Sardinia made an important discovery. He saw a group of large jars on the floor of the sea, about 65 feet below the surface. These jars turned out to be amphorae from a Roman ship that had sunk more than 2,000 years ago.

A team of underwater archaeologists was called in to investigate. To search the floor of the sea, they used techniques similar to those used in excavations on land. They took underwater photographs of the area. They placed a grid of tape over the area so that they could make records about where they found evidence. Then they brought the amphorae up to the surface.

From what the archaeologists found, they determined that the ship had probably set sail from a port in Italy. It had run aground near the little island of Sparghi off the coast of Sardinia.

The Sparghi ship, as it is now called, was part of the vast fleet of ships that carried goods between ports on the Mediterranean Sea beginning in the 200s B.C. By the time of the Roman Empire, the Romans sent ships to the far corners of the ancient world as they knew it. The olive oil and wine found on the Sparghi ship were probably on their way from Italian farms to people in Spain or Gaul.

THINKING FOCUS

What were some important products of the Roman economy, and why were they important?

Key Term

- market

◀ *This marble relief shows a Roman ship from about A.D. 200. The sails were probably of cloth, reinforced with leather at the corners. The relief, which was found in Carthage, was probably made in the country that is present-day Tunisia.*

447

The Roman Empire

An Agricultural Economy

Agriculture was the backbone of the Roman economy. In Italy itself, farmers grew grain and planted olive groves and vineyards. Olive oil and wine were shipped to cities throughout the empire. As the empire expanded, olive oil and wine were also produced in Gaul, Spain, and North Africa as well as Italy.

But on the whole, Roman farming methods were not very advanced. As a result, crops were small, and many people were needed to work the land. Four out of five people in the Roman Empire worked on farms. Compare that with about one in forty-five people who farm in America today. What does the comparison

UNDERSTANDING EMPIRE

Rome began as a village, a dot on the map of Italy. Yet by A.D. 117, Rome controlled the Mediterranean world. The Roman Empire spread out in all directions from its capital of Rome.

A Nation Is Not an Empire

Remember that an empire is made up of a nation and the nations it has conquered, under one ruler. The Roman Empire under Augustus is an example. An empire usually covers a large territory, but size alone doesn't make an empire. Both Canada and the United States are large, yet neither is an empire.

Building an Empire

A nation may conquer new territories for a number of reasons. For one, it may be seeking natural resources. The Romans needed grain to feed their people. When Egypt became part of the Roman Empire, it had to give Rome grain as payment of taxes.

A nation might expand, too, as it seeks borders it can defend. Mountain ranges and bodies of water make good natural borders. The Roman Empire at some points extended north to the Danube River.

Often the native people in the new territories, or colonies, have cultures and languages different from those of the ruling power. These colonies may even be located thousands of miles away. Portugal, for example, set up colonies in Africa and Brazil during the 1500s.

The conquered peoples in an empire often resent foreign rule and rebel against it. Beginning some 300 years ago, the British built the largest empire ever known. The eastern United States was once part of it. Most colonial Americans shared British culture, but they rebelled against British rule in 1776.

Results of Empire Building

As it works to unify its empire, the ruling power spreads its culture—sometimes by force. In that way it leaves its mark on its colonies, sometimes long after the empire breaks up.

The Roman Empire is a good example. Its language, Latin, spread throughout the empire. French, Spanish, and Italian are called "Romance languages" because of their roots in Latin.

tell you about Roman agriculture? Another reason for the poor performance of Roman agriculture was taxation. The emperors required farmers to give most of their surplus grain to the government in taxes. Farmers could not make money by selling surplus grain at a profit, and so they had little to spend.

The Market for Roman Industry

One result was a limited demand for manufactured items. Modern industry employs so many people and produces so many items because there is a large **market,** or demand, for its products. In ancient Rome, most people could afford only simple clothes and inexpensive pottery. Only the wealthy could afford decorated pottery and fine jewelry. As a result, the market for such items was small.

Most manufacturing plants in ancient Rome were small. An example is the pottery shop in Arretium *(uh REE shuhm)*, one of the empire's best-known manufacturing operations. It employed only about 50 slaves. In contrast, a modern manufacturing plant might employ thousands of workers.

For all its accomplishments, the Roman Empire never developed a complex economy. It did not create large banks and other financial institutions. Instead, the Roman economy was mainly concerned with the basic task of feeding the empire's soldiers and city dwellers. This same basic task made Rome the hub of an extensive network of trade routes. ■

▲ *This branch was part of an olive tree, a plant that had great importance to the ancient Romans. Even today, Italy leads the world in production of olives.*

■ *Why was Roman farming so poor?*

▼ *This olive crusher was a useful tool for a Roman farmer. The wheels and basin are made of lava from Vesuvius. The crosspiece is wooden. The wheels rotate against an iron pin inside the basin, separating the pulp from the seeds.*

Trade in the Empire

Here's how the Greek writer Aelius Aristides *(air ih STY deez)* described Roman shipping in the A.D. 100s:

So many merchant ships arrive in Rome with cargoes from everywhere, at all times of the year, and after each harvest, that the city seems like the world's warehouse. The arrival and departure of ships never stops—it's amazing that the sea, not to mention the harbor, is big enough for these merchant ships.

Ships hauled goods, such as wine, grain, and exotic animals, to and from ports in every part of the Roman Empire. On land, carts pulled by oxen or mules and even caravans of camels carried such items as lumber, clothing, and household goods over the empire's extensive system of roads. A side benefit was that trade brought news of other cultures and foreign places.

Feeding the Empire

The most important item that the Romans traded for was grain. Wheat and barley were used in making the bread

449

Just as ancient Rome could not produce enough grain for its people, many modern nations must seek grain from other sources. The United States supplies grain to such countries as the Soviet Union, China, Argentina, and Australia.

▼ *The Romans traded for wheat, barley, and other foods they needed for survival. They also imported luxury items like marble, gold, and ostrich eggs.*

and other foods that formed most of the Roman diet. Grain was needed for the people of the cities as well as the army legions throughout the empire. Providing enough was a constant challenge.

Rome itself had become a city with about one million people by the A.D. 100s. The farmland around Rome could not grow enough grain to feed everyone. Therefore, the city depended heavily on products imported from North Africa, Egypt, and Sicily. Look at the map on page 451 to see the main regions that sent grain to the city.

An added problem was that as many as 300,000 people in the city of Rome were so poor that they could not buy grain. The government had to give it to them. Free handouts became important to the peace of the city. An emperor might face riots if he did not provide enough grain for the people.

Another 300,000 men in the army stationed in the empire's provinces also had to be fed. Food was generally supplied by the provinces where the men were stationed. Sometimes, though, the provinces could not produce enough for themselves and the army too. Then the government had to send more grain from other parts of the empire.

Manufacturing and Mining

The largest industry in the empire was mining. Marble and other materials for the empire's great building projects were mined in Greece and northern Italy. Gold and silver came from mines in Spain. Lead and tin came from Britain. The metals were needed to manufacture weapons and other items, including coins for trade within the empire. Metals were also exchanged for luxury goods from foreign lands.

Italian communities manufactured pottery, glassware, weapons, tools, and textiles for use in Rome and for trade throughout the empire. In contrast to farm products, however, trade in manufactured goods was limited.

Luxury Trade

The trade in luxury goods made up the smallest part of the Roman economy. Not many people had enough money for luxuries.

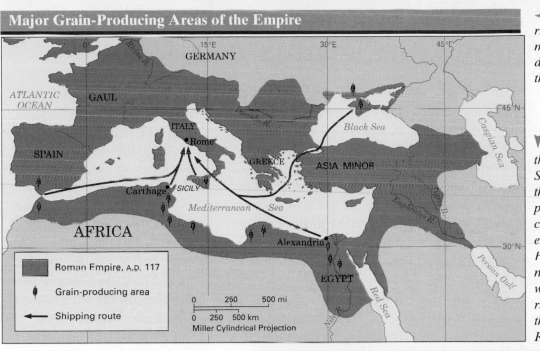

Major Grain-Producing Areas of the Empire

Roman Empire, A.D. 117

Grain-producing area

Shipping route

0   250   500 mi
0   250   500 km
Miller Cylindrical Projection

◄ *What seas and rivers watered the major grain-producing regions of the empire?*

▼ *Roman trade in the Mediterranean Sea increased as the empire expanded and decreased as the empire declined. How does the number of shipwrecks reflect the rise, the peak, and the decline of the Roman Empire?*

However, traders traveled far beyond the borders of the empire to bring back unusual items for wealthy Romans.

Traders went south into the Sahara and brought back ostrich eggs and ivory, which were strange and wonderful to the Romans. They went north and brought back blond slaves from the land that is now Germany. These blond slaves were so intriguing to the dark-haired Romans that some rich Romans even began wearing blond wigs. The traders also went into the Far East, bringing back silks from China, and spices and gems from India.

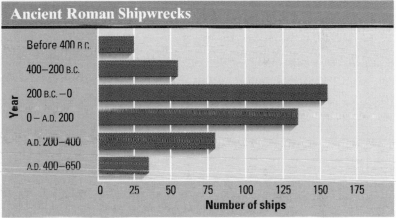

Ancient Roman Shipwrecks

Year / Number of ships

Such items, of course, were always far less important than grain. Remember that both trade and agriculture had the same primary purpose. They provided food for the vast numbers of people in the Roman Empire. ■

■ *Why did the Romans need to import grain?*

R E V I E W

1. **FOCUS** What were some important products of the Roman economy, and why were they important?

2. **CONNECT** How was Rome's economy similar to that of other ancient civilizations?

3. **ECONOMICS** People are productive when they expect to be rewarded for their efforts. Relate this idea to the poor productivity of Roman farmers.

4. **CRITICAL THINKING** The Roman culture was not an innovative culture—one that tried new ways of doing things. Is our culture innovative? Explain.

5. **WRITING ACTIVITY** Imagine that you are a farmer in a province of the Roman Empire. You have just found out that you have to give one-third of your wheat crop in taxes. Your grain is needed to feed the poor people of Rome. Write a newspaper editorial explaining your opinion of the tax.

Reading Cartograms

Here's Why

Maps can show statistical information, such as population, rainfall, or yearly income, in many ways. For example, cartographers may choose to use a standard map base and then add thematic information. Or they might use a cartogram.

Cartograms are chart maps that present statistical information. On a cartogram, the sizes of geographic areas are changed, or distorted, in order to help show the statistical information. Thus, cartograms allow you to see

facts at a glance and to make comparisons quickly.

Approximately 60 million people lived in the Roman Empire at its height. Suppose you want to know about population distribution in that part of the world today. A cartogram can help you.

Here's How

Look at the maps on these pages. Read the titles; then find out how each map shows information.

The map on the left is a thematic map. It shows the extent of the Roman Empire

at its height, around A.D. 117. As the key indicates, color is used to show which areas were part of the Empire.

The map also includes modern political boundaries to show you which modern nations contain land that was once part of the Roman Empire. The scale tells you how distance on the map relates to distance on the earth.

Now look at the cartogram on page 453. Each shape represents a country. Notice that the cartogram has no scale of miles. The sentence in the lower left

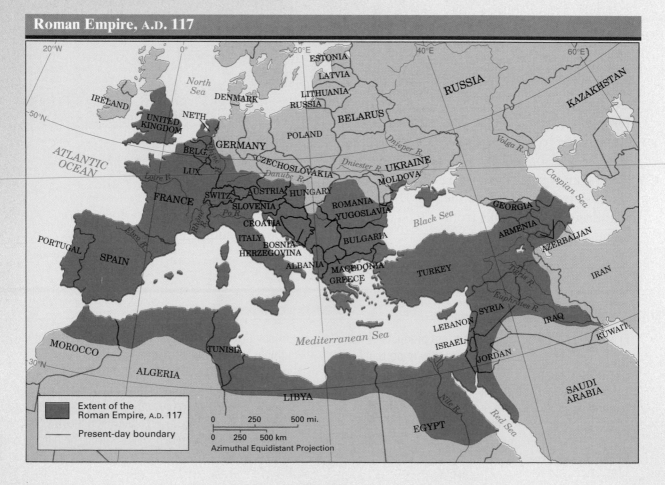

Roman Empire, A.D. 117

Extent of the Roman Empire, A.D. 117

Present-day boundary

0   250   500 mi.
0   250   500 km
Azimuthal Equidistant Projection

corner tells you that the size of each country is related to the size of its population. The cartogram distorts the actual size and shape of countries to show how populations compare. For example, the map on the left shows that France and Spain are about the same size. On the cartogram, however, France is larger than Spain because France's population is greater.

The key in the lower left corner of the cartogram explains how the colors show population statistics. By using the key, you can find out more about how the populations of Spain and France compare.

Try It

Compare the cartogram on this page with the World Population cartogram on page 517. How do they differ? Which one would you use to compare the populations of Turkey and Saudi Arabia? Find the United States on the World Population cartogram on page 517. How does the population of the United States compare to the population of Canada?

Apply It

Find out how many students are in each classroom at your school. Then make a cartogram of the classrooms. Remember that the placement of the rooms on the cartogram shows where the classrooms are located, but the size of the rooms should show how many students are in them. Or try drawing a cartogram of the United States where the size of each state reflects the size of its population, like the one below.

The Roman World in 2000: Population

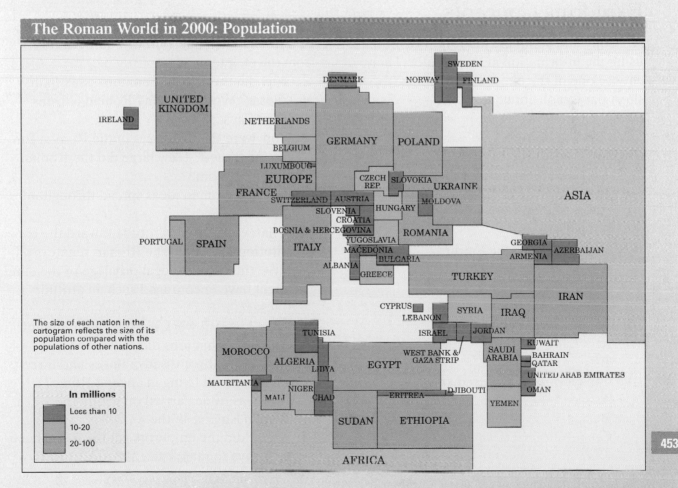

The size of each nation in the cartogram reflects the size of its population compared with the populations of other nations.

In millions
- Less than 10
- 10–20
- 20–100

The Roman Empire

Chapter Review

Reviewing Key Terms

assassinate (p. 431)   province (p. 432)
elite (p. 436)   rhetoric (p. 443)
market (p. 449)   ritual (p. 446)

A. Answer the questions below about the key terms. Use the information in the chapter.
1. Where would you need a governor to collect taxes? Tell why.
2. Which word names something a product needs? What does the word mean in the chapter?
3. Who were the most powerful people in Ancient Rome? What kinds of work did these people do?

B. Each phrase below could be the title of an article about the Roman Empire. For each phrase, write a sentence that could be the first sentence of the article. Use at least one key term in each sentence you write.
1. The Betrayal of Julius Caesar
2. Trade in the Roman Empire
3. Special Treatment for a Few
4. Beyond Italy—A Vast Empire
5. A Good Education in Ancient Rome
6. Keeping the Roman Gods Happy
7. The Ancient Art of Speaking Well
8. Religious Practices of the Romans
9. The rising demand for wheat in Rome

Exploring Concepts

A. Copy and complete the following outline using the information in the chapter. Then choose one of the major heads and write a short paragraph about it.

The Roman Empire
I. Emperors of the *Pax Romana*
   A. Caesar Augustus
   B. Trajan
   C. Marcus Aurelius
   D. Hadrian
II. Social classes in the Empire
   A.
   B.
   C.
III. Homes of the rich and poor
   A.
   B.
IV. Transportation over trade routes
   A.
   B.
   C.

B. Answer each question with information from the chapter.
1. Why did the Roman senators assassinate Caesar? Why had many Roman citizens liked Caesar?
2. How were the provinces of the Roman Empire governed? How large did the Roman Empire become?
3. How did Roman ideas spread throughout the empire?
4. What was Caesar's attitude toward the constitution? How did the Roman senators observe this? Which legal privilege of the elite might have encouraged such an attitude in Caesar?
5. What kinds of work did the "more humble" class do? What jobs did slaves do?
6. What were three disadvantages and three advantages of living in ancient Rome?
7. How was trade carried on within the Roman Empire in the A.D. 100s?
8. Where did the emperors get the free wheat they gave to male citizens?

Reviewing Skills

1. Look at the map and cartograms on pages 452 and 453. On the standard map on the left, Libya is larger than Italy. Why is Italy larger than Libya on the cartogram?

2. Turn to the World Population cartogram on page 517. In this cartogram, why is India shown larger than Russia? Why is Australia shown as one of the smallest nations? What does the cartogram's color coding tell you about the population in Bangladesh?

3. Prepare an opening or closing statement for a debate on the following: "The system of rule by emperors improved people's lives during the time period called the *Pax Romana*." Evaluate your work. Make sure your written statement is clear and forceful.

4. Suppose you are a close friend of Nero. He asks you to tell him how highly the people think of him. How could you answer him truthfully without making the emperor angry?

Using Critical Thinking

1. Look at the map on page 499 of the Minipedia. Find the Roman Empire, the Han Dynasty, and the Gupta Empire. Which empire spans the greatest distance? Would you expect communication within the empire you chose to be easier or more difficult than in the other two empires? Explain your answer.

2. One Roman writer said that Romans wanted only "bread and circuses." What did this writer mean? Do you think people in the United States today want only "bread and circuses"? Use examples to explain your answer.

3. In ancient Rome, birth and wealth determined everyone's social class. Social class determined what people's legal rights were, where they sat in the Colosseum, what clothes they wore, and what kinds of jobs they held. Think about the social system in the United States today. How do you think it compares to the social system of ancient Rome?

Preparing for Citizenship

1. **COLLECTING INFORMATION** By the terms of the Roman constitution, a leader was expected to share power with the senate. Think about Caesar's attitude toward the senate. Then study the United States Constitution. Write down two powers the president shares with Congress. Do you think that sharing power in government is a good idea? Why or why not?

2. **WRITING ACTIVITY** A 13-year struggle for power followed Caesar's assassination. Look up *presidential succession* in an encyclopedia. Find out what would happen if both the president and vice president were unable to complete their terms of office. Imagine that someone is proposing to change the existing laws about presidential succession. Write a letter to your senator or Congressional representative. Tell why you are for or against the proposed change.

3. **COLLABORATIVE LEARNING** The ancient Romans respected both Caesar and Augustus because of what they did to improve people's lives. Divide the class into two groups, one researching improvements under Augustus and the other researching improvements under Caesar. Then form small groups, each with representatives of both rulers. Plan how you will present the contributions of both rulers to the class. After the class presentations, discuss some improvements that modern leaders have brought into people's lives.

Chapter 15

Christianity and the Fall of Rome

By the A.D. 200s, Rome's great era of peace and prosperity was just a memory. Military leaders fought each other for power. Invaders from beyond the borders defeated the mighty Roman army. The economy crumbled. As Rome declined, another power rose—the Christian Church.

A.D. 200–300 Barbarian invasions weaken the empire. This relief from a stone coffin shows a bitter battle between the Romans and invaders from the north.

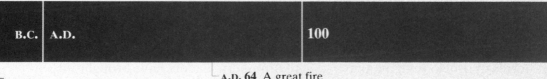

| B.C. | A.D. | | 100 | | 200 |

A.D. 36

A.D. 64 A great fire sweeps through Rome. Emperor Nero blames Christians for the fire and orders them killed.

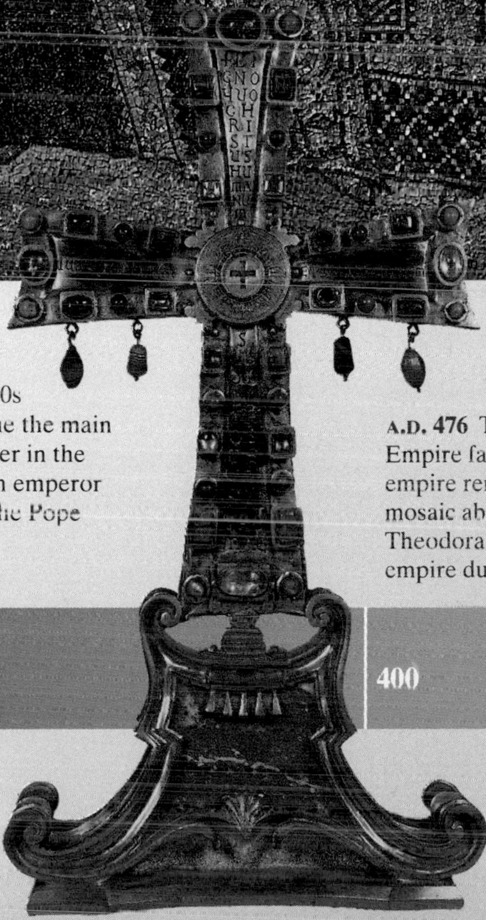

During the A.D. 300s Christianity became the main religion and a power in the empire. An eastern emperor gave this cross to the Pope around A.D. 570.

A.D. 476 The Western Roman Empire falls, but the eastern empire remains strong. The mosaic above shows Empress Theodora, a ruler of the eastern empire during the A.D. 500s.

300

400

500

A.D. 330 Emperor Constantine builds the capital of Constantinople for the eastern empire.

A.D. 476

LESSON 1

The Early Christians

Key Terms

- persecute
- conversion
- sect
- Gentile

The New Testament of the Christian Bible tells of a man named Saul who came from Tarsus, a city in the Eastern Mediterranean region of the Roman Empire. Saul opposed those Jews who followed the teachings of Jesus. One day, in about A.D. 36, he was on the road to Damascus, a city in ancient Syria.

The New Testament goes on to describe what Christians believe happened next:

Now as he journeyed he approached Damascus, and suddenly a light from heaven flashed about him. And he fell to

the ground and heard a voice saying to him, "Saul, Saul, why do you persecute me?" And he said, "Who are you, Lord?" And he said, "I am Jesus, whom you are persecuting; but rise and enter the city, and you will be told what you are to do."

Acts 9: 3–6

(To **persecute** is to treat cruelly.)

According to the New Testament, Saul was blinded by the light from heaven. He did not regain his sight until a follower of Jesus touched him. Saul's life changed forever. He became one of the most devoted followers of the faith that would become Christianity.

► *In the A.D. 1400s, the French artist Jean Fouquet painted this version of Saul's conversion to Christianity.*

The New Faith

Saul's **conversion**, or change from one belief to another, came a few years after Jesus' life which you read about in Chapter 10. At the time of Saul's conversion, the followers of Jesus were considered a **sect**, or group, among Jews.

Religions in the Roman Empire

Judaism was one of many religions practiced in the Roman Empire. The Romans themselves followed a number of religions. Romans were even willing to accept the gods of other people alongside their own. They also allowed a great deal of freedom to different religious groups, as long as the groups respected the gods of the Roman state.

Nevertheless, the beliefs of the Jews and the Christians clashed with those of the Romans. The Jews believed in one God, and they were unwilling to worship the many Roman gods. The Jews also lived by the laws of God, as set forth in the Torah, and the teaching of their prophets. The Romans believed in serving their gods by following certain rituals, such as sacrificing animals. They believed that keeping their gods happy would keep the empire strong.

Even so, Judaism was a legal religion in the Roman Empire and Jews were allowed to practice their religion. Jews and Romans disagreed mainly on political grounds. However, Jews and Christians disagreed on religious grounds. As a result, Christianity slowly became a separate religion. Both religions have had a lasting impact on Western civilization.

New Testament

At first, few people in the Roman Empire took much notice of the Christians. This is why there are few written accounts of the early Christians, other than the New Testament.

The New Testament was written between A.D. 50 and 100 to teach and inspire the Christians and to separate them from the religions they had followed in the past. As a result, the New Testament tells the story of Christianity from the point of view of Christians only.

Besides giving an account of the life and ministry of Jesus, the New Testament tells of the birth and early development of Christianity, including the story of Saul and his conversion. It ends with a collection of letters to some of the new churches in the Mediterranean world. ■

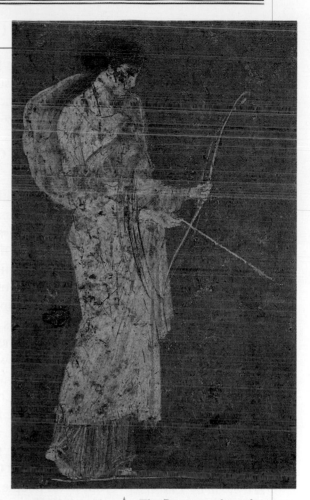

▲ *The Romans adopted gods and goddesses from other religions. This wall painting from around A.D. 60 shows the Roman goddess Diana, who is based on the Greek goddess Artemis.*

■ *How did the Jewish and Christian religious beliefs differ from those of the Romans?*

◄ *The fish was one of the earliest Christian symbols. The Greek word for fish contains the first initials of the words,* Jesus Christ, Son of God, Savior.

Jews and Christians

Most of the first disciples and followers of Jesus were Jews. The biggest difference between them and their fellow Jews was that these Christians believed that Jesus was the Son of God and the Messiah.

Jews and Gentiles

Nevertheless, the Jewish roots of Christianity ran deep. In addition to sharing many beliefs, Jews and Christians lived in the same communities. Jews had been gathering together in communities within the cities of the Roman Empire since the diaspora, the scattering of Jewish settlements throughout the Mediterranean.

The early Christians concentrated on trying to convert other Jews. However, a serious debate came up within the early Christian church: Should Christians reach out to all people, or just to other Jews? Both the Jews and the Christians saw the world as divided into two groups—Jews and **Gentiles**, or non-Jews. At first, the Christians were deeply against preaching to the Gentiles. They felt Jesus had come to rescue the Jews, not to save the Gentiles. In their view, the Gentiles would first have to become Jews before they could accept the teachings of Jesus.

Preaching to Gentiles

According to the New Testament, the turning point came in about A.D. 45. That was when Peter, one of Jesus' disciples, was instructed in a vision from God to go to a city where many Gentiles lived. There he went to the home of a Roman soldier and visited with a group of Gentiles. After Peter preached to them, the soldier and the people who were with him became Christians.

Christians who were in favor of converting the Gentiles used this event to persuade other members of the church. As it turned out, it wasn't Peter who went on to preach the gospel to the Gentiles. It was Saul. He came to be known by the Roman name of Paul and traveled throughout the Roman Empire spreading the teachings of Christianity. ■

➤ *This wall painting is from the first century A.D. This Roman woman may have been a Jew, a Christian, or a worshiper of the Roman gods.*

■ *Why did the Christians resist preaching to the Gentiles at first?*

▼ *The Psalms, shown on this fragment from a Greek manuscript, are scriptures that are studied by both Christians and Jews.*

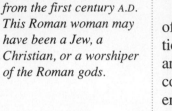

The Work of Paul

Paul played an important role in early Christianity. Because he had been a devout Jew, he could speak to fellow Jews. He was also a Roman citizen. Not only could he claim all the benefits of citizenship, but he could be seen by the Romans as one of their own. Finally, he was a passionate supporter of the new faith.

From about A.D. 47 until his death in about A.D. 64, Paul made three long journeys during which he spread Christian teachings. As the map on this page shows, Paul's second journey began in Asia Minor and took him through much of the eastern Mediterranean region. How far west did Paul travel during this second journey?

Several factors helped spread the message of Christianity throughout the Roman Empire. As you know, the Romans were expert road builders and Paul traveled on good roads. The roads were mostly free from robbers. Small inns with food and lodging dotted the countryside. Secondly, the Roman world spoke Greek, so Paul had no difficulty being understood wherever he preached. Finally, the cities were full of travelers from all over the empire. These different people were open to new ideas.

According to Paul's letters in the New Testament, his journeys were not easy. He tells of being shipwrecked three times. Crowds sometimes threw stones at him or beat him. Paul described his travels this way, "I have labored and toiled and have often gone without sleep; I have known hunger and thirst and have often gone without food; I have been cold and naked. Besides everything else I face daily the pressure of my concern for all the churches."

On Paul's journeys, he started new groups of Christians. He

▼ *On his second journey, Paul visited many important cities in Asia Minor and Greece.*

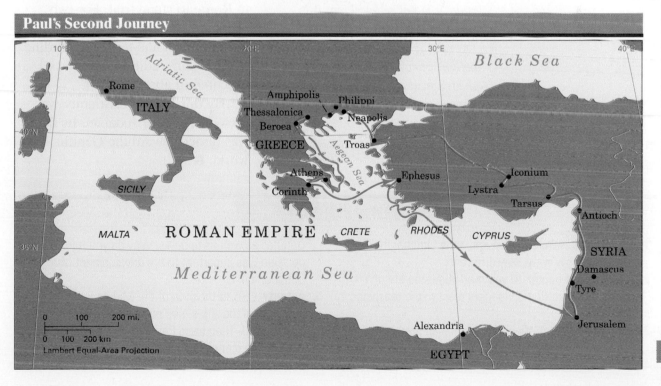

Paul's Second Journey

Christianity and the Fall of Rome

The ruins of Corinth, one of the cities Paul visited on his second journey, are pictured at the right. Find Corinth on the map on page 461.

preached to them, wrote to them, encouraged them, and corrected them. Churches sprang up in places like Ephesus, Philippi, and Corinth. (Find them on the map on page 461.) In a letter to the church in Corinth, Paul wrote:

> *L*ove is patient, love is kind. *It does not envy, it does not boast, it is not proud. It is not rude, it is not self-seeking, it is not easily angered, it keeps no record of wrongs. Love does not delight in evil but rejoices with the truth. It always protects, always trusts, always hopes, always perseveres.*
>
> I Corinthians 13:4–7

■ *How did Paul help spread Christianity?*

What attracted the Gentiles to Paul's message? Paul taught that through accepting Jesus as the Christ, the love of God and eternal life was open to all, including the Gentiles.

By encouraging Romans to join the new faith, Paul was becoming a troublemaker in the eyes of the Roman authorities. He was eventually arrested in Jerusalem and went to Rome to stand trial. For two years, he remained there, continuing to preach and teach. According to Christian tradition, Paul was executed in about A.D. 64.

By this time, Christianity was no longer part of Judaism. Its face was turned toward the Gentile world. ■

REVIEW

1. **FOCUS** How were Judaism and early Christianity alike, and how were they different?

2. **CONNECT** In Chapter 10 you read about the life of Jesus. How did Roman leaders react to the teachings of Jesus?

3. **GEOGRAPHY** What effect did the Roman road system have on Paul's travels?

4. **CRITICAL THINKING** The Christians decided to preach to

Gentiles as well as to Jews. Why do you think that decision was important to the development of Christianity?

5. **ACTIVITY** Look at the map of the Middle East today on page 510 of the Atlas, and compare it with the map on page 461. Then trace Paul's second journey through the modern world. List the countries he passed through.

LESSON 2

Rome and the Christians

In A.D. 64, a great fire swept through Rome. It burned for six days, and it destroyed much of the city. Here is how the Roman historian Tacitus described the scene:

> First, the fire swept violently over the level spaces. Then it climbed the hills—but returned to ravage the lower ground again. When people looked back, menacing flames sprang up before them or outflanked them. When they escaped to a neighboring quarter, the fire followed. . . . Some who had lost everything—even their food for the day—could have escaped, but preferred to die.
>
> Tacitus, *Annals*, c. A.D. 120

Look at the map at the right. What parts of Rome suffered the greatest damage in the fire? What important buildings were destroyed?

At the time of the fire, Nero was the emperor. He was a young man who was known for his ruthless hunger for power, not for his leadership. In fact, Nero's poor leadership made many Romans turn against him.

Some people even accused him of setting the fire, although no proof of his guilt exists. Nero was crafty, though. He knew that he

needed to blame someone for starting the fire. He chose the Christians. They were already unpopular with most people in Rome because they refused to worship the Roman gods.

Emperor Nero gave orders that the Christians be killed for starting the fire. Tacitus described the cruel way in which they were put to death:

> Mockery of every sort was added to their deaths. Covered with the skins of beasts, they were torn by dogs and perished, or were nailed to crosses, or were doomed to the flames and burnt.

THINKING
FOCUS

How did Christianity grow between A.D. 64 and A.D. 400?

Key Terms

- martyr
- excommunication
- pagan

▼ *The great fire destroyed central Rome.*

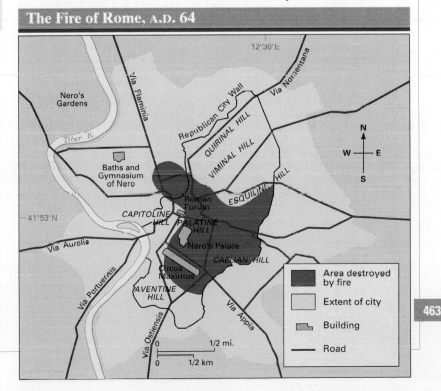

The Fire of Rome, A.D. 64

12°30'E

Nero's Gardens

Via Flaminia

Via Nomentana

Republican City Wall

QUIRINAL HILL

VIMINAL HILL

Tiber R.

Baths and Gymnasium of Nero

41°53'N

Roman Forum

ESQUILINE HILL

CAPITOLINE HILL

PALATINE HILL

Via Aurelia

Nero's Palace

CAELIAN HILL

Via Portuensis

Circus Maximus

AVENTINE HILL

Via Appia

Via Ostiensis

Area destroyed by fire

Extent of city

Building

Road

0   1/2 mi.

0   1/2 km

463

Rome's Early Response

How Do We Know?

HISTORY *A major source for information on Rome up to* A.D. *100 is the historian Tacitus. In fact, some consider Tacitus to be Rome's greatest historian. He wrote the* Annals, *a year-by-year history of the empire from* A.D. *14 to 68. In this book, he told the story of the fire of Rome.*

▼ *This painting illustrates two New Testament events from Paul's travels. On the left, Paul defends himself in front of a Roman governor. On the right, he is lowered from the walls of Damascus to escape.*

Tacitus, like many Romans, did not really believe that the Christians had set Rome on fire. Yet he shared the view of many Romans that Christians should be convicted, "not so much of the crime of firing the city, as of hatred against mankind."

The Christians did not act like other Romans, and this made some Romans suspicious. Christians kept to themselves—almost like a secret club. Since they did not worship Roman gods or the emperor, Christians no longer went to public festivals.

Some Christian ideas, too, seemed shocking. Wealth and private property, for example, were measures of a person's success in Roman society. Yet the Christians taught that worldly riches should be given up and that property should be shared with the poor.

The early Christian churches often gave food to the poor—especially widows and orphans. Around A.D. 250, the church in Rome was feeding 1,500 people.

Christians, like the Jews, had to decide matters of conscience in daily life. A Christian sculptor could carve monuments, but would not carve a lion, a whale, or a bull, if it represented a Roman god. Many Christians chose not to serve in the army because it went against Jesus' teaching to love one's enemies. Was it right to buy meat in the market that had been offered first as a sacrifice to the gods? Christians had to make these choices.

Religious Practices

The first Christian churches were in private homes. The leader of the Christians in each city was called a bishop. All religious services were held in Greek.

Two ceremonies were very important in the Christian churches: baptism and the Lord's Supper. Bringing a new member into the Church was celebrated by baptism, a blessing with water. Baptism means different things to different Christian churches today. One meaning is that a person, after being baptised, turns away from sin and starts living a Christian life.

The early Christians met together on Sunday nights for what they called the Lord's Supper. Rumors spread that Christians were cannibals because they spoke of eating the body of Christ. In fact, they were celebrating the presence and spirit of Christ among them. At this service they remembered Jesus' sacrifice and

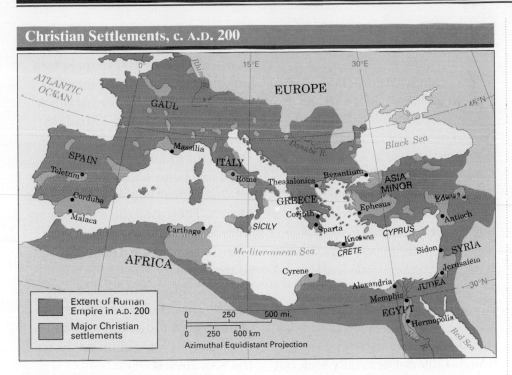

Christian Settlements, c. A.D. 200

Extent of Roman Empire in A.D. 200

Major Christian settlements

0   250   500 mi.

0   250   500 km

Azimuthal Equidistant Projection

◄ *By the year A.D. 200, Christianity had spread throughout the empire. In these areas, Christians gathered to practice their religion.*

his instructions that they should love and serve one another.

Roman Law and Early Christians

For the most part, before A.D. 64, the Roman government ignored the early Christians. Emperor Nero's treatment of the Christians was unusually harsh, and not typical.

The Romans generally did not try to change the differing religious beliefs of the people in the empire. And Christian leaders such as Paul taught Christians to obey Roman laws. "Let every person be subject to the governing authorities," Paul wrote in his letter to the Romans. "Pay all of them their dues, taxes to whom taxes are due, revenue to whom revenue is due, respect to whom respect is due, honor to whom honor is due."

Christianity, however, was not one of the legal religions in the empire. By A.D. 100, Roman law stated that anyone who admitted to being a Christian must be killed. This policy was seldom enforced.

In general, the Roman emperor let officials in the provinces decide how Christians should be treated. But these officials were often unsure of what to do. In fact, written records indicate that many Roman officials had little experience in dealing with Christians. The governor of Asia Minor, Pliny the Younger, wrote to Emperor Trajan, in about A.D. 110:

S o far, this is how I have dealt with people who were brought to me for being Christians. I ask them if they are Christians: if they admit it, I ask them twice more, and warn them what the punishment is: if they persist I order them to be executed.

But the Christians were not a real danger to Pliny. "If we give these Christians a chance to repent, a large number of people could be brought back on to the right path," he said.

Trajan agreed with Pliny's actions. His response indicates

Christianity and the Fall of Rome

that the Romans did not actively seek to persecute Christians.

> *I*t is not possible to lay down strict rules to deal with every case, but certainly the Christians must not be hunted down. But if they are brought to you and found guilty, then they must be punished, with this exception: if anyone denies he is a Christian, and makes this fact quite clear by praying to the Roman gods, he must be pardoned, whatever his previous record.
>
> Pliny, *Epistles*, c. A.D. 112

As the above exchange shows, Romans did not generally seek out Christians for punishment. In fact, Christian settlements existed in North Africa for 100 years before the first Christian was executed.

Still, Christians were at times treated cruelly. Some Christians were even put into an arena to fight lions as entertainment for Romans. Later Christian writers attached great importance to these events. They used the events to reinforce the suffering endured by Christians who remained faithful to their beliefs.

However, historians do not believe that many Christians were actually sent to the lions. Overall, most Christians lived in peace until the A.D. 200s. ■

■ *What was the attitude of Romans towards the early Christians?*

The Roman Catacombs

You enter a small chapel outside the city of Rome and walk down a stone staircase. You are in the catacombs, underground cemeteries built and used by the early Christians.

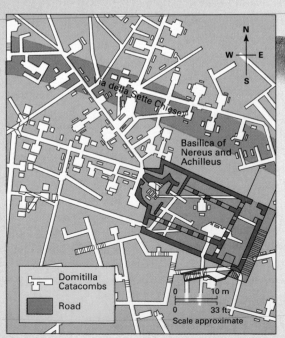

Side view of a Roman catacomb

Via della Sette Chiese

Basilica of Nereus and Achilleus

This map shows one series of Roman catacombs called the Domitilla Catacombs. Catacomb cemeteries of Christians were located outside the walls of Rome, because burials were forbidden inside the city.

Domitilla Catacombs

Road

0   10 m
0   33 ft
Scale approximate

466

The Attack on Christianity

By the early 200s, the Roman Empire was facing serious problems. Many Romans believed their troubles were a sign that the gods were angry. So in A.D. 250, Emperor Decius ordered all citizens to worship the Roman gods and make public sacrifices.

Decius believed that these offerings would please the gods and ease the troubles in the empire. The Christians, however, refused to follow his orders. Decius then ordered his soldiers to execute all Christians who refused.

Some Christians chose death These **martyrs,** people who chose to die rather than give up their religious beliefs, became important symbols for the church. Their courage inspired other Christians and created new converts. Below, A Closer Look shows the Christian burial chambers built beneath the city of Rome. How did the Christians honor martyrs in the catacombs?

Emperor Decius died in A.D. 251, and the persecution ended for a time. The Christians, though, were now marked as unpatriotic because they had refused to follow Decius's orders. In A.D. 257 and 258, Emperor Valerian carried out another wave of persecution, seizing the property of wealthy

Jesus' Last Supper is just one of the many paintings found on catacomb walls. Martyrs' tombs were often decorated with paintings. Early Christians held religious ceremonies near these special tombs. Imagine holding a ceremony in a place like the catacombs!

To find their way in the pitch-black catacombs, people carried oil-burning lamps like this one. These lamps were small enough to fit in the palm of your hand.

Thousands of people were buried in the catacombs. The dead were wrapped in linen and brought down into these damp tunnels. Then they were placed in tombs carved in the walls and sealed inside. Tombs of Christian martyrs became shrines, and people wanted to be buried near them.

Christianity and the Fall of Rome

Christians. The most violent and systematic persecution of Christians started around A.D. 300 during the reign of the emperor Diocletian *(dy uh KLEE shuhn)*.

Roman mobs destroyed many churches, broke Christian crosses, and burned sacred books. Christians were fired from Roman jobs, forced out of the army, attacked, and killed.

The wave of persecution that had begun under Diocletian continued until A.D. 311. The next year, however, a new emperor came to power and the official Roman position toward Christianity began to change. ■

■ *Why and how did Decius, Diocletian, and other emperors persecute the early Christians?*

The Rise of Christianity

▲ *This painting from the catacombs shows St. Agnes, a Christian martyr killed during the persecution by Emperor Diocletian.*

In A.D. 312, Rome witnessed a struggle for power. One army leader fighting to become emperor was named Constantine.

According to Christian historians, before Constantine went into battle, he saw a vision of a cross with the sun behind it. Although Constantine was not a Christian, the vision convinced him that his men would win if they fought under the sign of Christ. He ordered his soldiers to paint a Christian symbol called a chi-rho *(ky roh)* on their shields.

Constantine's men won the battle, and that year Constantine became emperor. At the beginning of his rule, perhaps as little as 10 per cent of the empire's population was Christian. But with his support, Christianity became the main religion in the Roman Empire.

Constantine was not baptized a Christian until shortly before his death in A.D. 337. Nevertheless, he promoted Christianity throughout his reign. In A.D. 313, he issued an order that allowed Romans the freedom to follow any religion they wanted to. This act ended the official persecution of Christians. He also contributed vast sums of money to repair churches that had been damaged earlier. He even gave church leaders money to build new churches.

Church and State

Constantine took an active interest in the operations of the Christian church. He held meetings with church leaders to settle disputes among Christian leaders.

In earlier times Christians had believed that religion and government should be separate. Now, Constantine's decisions on behalf of the church had the power of the Roman Empire behind them. He even persecuted church members who opposed his views. Just as earlier emperors persecuted Christians for fear of displeasing Roman gods, Constantine now persecuted Romans for fear of displeasing the Christian God. Constantine was the first emperor to pass laws limiting the Jews' rights as Roman citizens.

Membership in the Christian Church now included many educated people who held jobs in government. The government passed laws that favored Christianity. It contributed money to help the churches feed the widows and the sick. Churches did not have to pay taxes. Church leaders who used to meet in secret were allowed to meet publicly.

Constantine's interest in Christianity helped to strengthen the religion. People who were attracted to Christianity because of its message of salvation could join the church without fear. At the same time, the relationship between Constantine and the church brought up an issue that is still the subject of debate today—how much the church should be separated from the state.

The Power Shift

By the end of the A.D. 300s, church leaders felt powerful enough to give orders to emperors—or even to punish them. For example, in A.D. 390, Christian leaders punished Emperor Theodosius for ordering the massacre of a rebellious village. Bishop Ambrose of Milan threatened Theodosius with **excommunication,** or being banned from the church until he repented his actions.

The fact that a Roman emperor would consider excommunication as punishment shows how powerful the church had become.

Just as Roman leaders had persecuted Christians when they were in power, now some fanatical Christians persecuted **pagans,** people who were not Christians or Jews. These Christians burned pagan temples. Then, in A.D. 391, Theodosius outlawed all pagan religions.

By the end of the A.D. 300s, the new faith had become a well-organized community with churches, priests, and bishops throughout the empire. In fact, Christianity was gaining power and members as the Roman Empire was declining. ■

▼ *The chi-rho combines the Greek letters* chi(X) *and* rho(P), *the first two letters of* Christos, *the Greek word for Christ.*

■ *How did Constantine help Christianity become the main religion in the empire?*

R E V I E W

1. **FOCUS** How did Christianity grow between A.D. 64 and A.D. 400?

2. **CONNECT** In Chapter 10 you studied how the Romans treated the Jews. How was Roman treatment of Jews similar to Roman treatment of Christians? How was it different?

3. **BELIEF SYSTEMS** How did the persecution of the Christians hurt the growth of Christianity? How did it help?

4. **CRITICAL THINKING** How are early Christian ideas about charity seen in Christian churches today?

5. **WRITING ACTIVITY** Imagine you could explore the catacombs described in A Closer Look on pages 466 and 467. Write a journal entry about the experience. Describe what you would see and how you would feel exploring the underground.

Christianity and the Fall of Rome

Comparing Art Forms

Here's Why

A work of art not only shows its subject. It also tells about the beliefs and culture of the artist's times. Choice of tools and materials, and the artist's personal style will also affect the work. While many works of art may present the same subject, each will reflect its artist's vision.

Below are two works of art that probably depict Jesus of Nazareth. No one knows what he really looked like. Artists show Jesus as they understand him. Comparing different artists' visions of a subject provides a broader view of the subject through different times and cultures.

Here's How

The sculpture shows a shepherd carrying a lamb on his shoulders. Many scholars believe the statue by an unknown Roman artist depicts Jesus. What qualities of Jesus do you think the artist was attempting to convey?

Note that the sculptor shows Jesus with short, curly hair and wearing a Roman tunic. Why, do you suppose, did the artist depict Jesus in Roman dress and hairstyle?

On the right is a 12th-century mosaic from the Cathedral of Torcello, an island in a lagoon north of Venice, Italy. Mosaics are formed by placing small bits of colored glass or stone in mortar. This mosaic shows Jesus as a mature man with a beard and a serious face.

Note the halo and the rich use of gold. Christians believe that Jesus, as the son of God, was both human and divine. Which aspect of Jesus do you think the mosaic artist was emphasizing?

Try It

The painting of Jesus healing on page 317 is by Sebastiano Ricci, who lived from 1659 to 1734. How is the background in the painting different from the sculpture or the mosaic? What does this painting tell about how the artist and the people of his time viewed Jesus?

Apply It

Draw a picture of the President of the United States. Compare it to pictures drawn by your classmates. How do differences in the pictures reflect each person's views?

L E S S O N   3

The Decline of Rome

I n A.D. 192, the signs for the future of Rome were not good. The Roman historian Dio Cassius wrote that, "many eagles of ill omen soared about the Capitol and moreover uttered screams that boded nothing peaceful, and an owl hooted there." Then a fire swept through some of Rome's government buildings, destroying many of the empire's records. Dio Cassius warned,

> T his, in particular, made it clear that the evil would not be confined to the City, but would extend over the entire civilized world under its sway.
>
> Dio Cassius, *History*, c. A.D. 192

Dio Cassius, who was a senator at the time, believed bad times were ahead for the empire. Indeed, the Roman Empire was beginning a century of decline.

T H I N K I N G
F O C U S

Why did the Roman Empire begin to decline?

Key Term

* edict

The End of the *Pax Romana*

The *Pax Romana* had been a 200-year period of peace and great achievements for Rome. But by the time Emperor Marcus Aurelius died in A.D. 180, Rome had political problems. Commodus, a son of Marcus Aurelius, proved to be an unpopular and wicked ruler. He was killed in A.D. 193. This was the beginning of a period when military leaders fought for power and the empire began to decline.

Commodus was followed by Emperor Septimius Severus, a strong ruler who held the empire together by his tough military leadership. When he died in A.D. 211, the dynasty of Severus continued to rule Rome. Yet conditions in the empire got worse. The last emperor of this dynasty, Severus Alexander, was finally killed by his own men in A.D. 235.

Even worse times were ahead. In the next 50 years, 25 different emperors ruled Rome. Some ruled only a few months. All but one were killed.

Political upset was only one of the many problems troubling the empire. The

◄ *Commodus was only 19 when he became emperor.*

471

238, Four emperors die in one year.

244, Emperor Gordian III is murdered.

250, Emperor Decius orders first large-scale persecution of Christians.

268, Emperor Gallienus is assassinated.

| | 240 | | 250 | | 260 | | 270 | | 280 |

238, Emperor Maximinus is declared a public enemy.

249, Emperor Philip is killed in battle with foreign invaders.

257, Emperor Valerian orders second wave of persecution.

| | 150 | | 200 | | 250 | | 300 | | 350 |

193–235, Severan Dynasty

235–284, Period of Unrest

284–305, Reign of Diocletian

312–337, Reign of Constantine

■ *What problems did the Empire face after the Pax Romana?*

▼ *Diocletian divided the empire. He ruled the Eastern empire and Maximian, the Western empire. They are shown below.*

economy was a disaster. Prices were out of control. In Egypt, 30 liters of wheat had cost 12 to 20 drachmas, an ancient coin, in the early A.D. 200s. By the 280s, the same amount of wheat cost 120,000 drachmas.

At the same time, the empire was under attack from outside forces. Tribes from northern Europe overran the borders.

To pay for the empire's defense, the government raised taxes. Many people left their farms and jobs because they could no longer pay the high taxes that Rome demanded.

Warfare left much of the empire in ruins. There wasn't enough food to go around. Trade was disrupted. Poverty and unemployment increased. Some Romans believed the empire stretched across too many lands to be well managed. With unrest inside and threats from outside, the empire badly needed strong leadership. ■

The Reign of Diocletian

Finally, in A.D. 284, the army declared Diocletian emperor. Diocletian then ordered the persecution of Christians in the hope of making the gods look with favor upon the empire once again. However, he also used more direct means to restore order.

The "New Empire"

Diocletian introduced a number of major reforms. That is why his reign is called the "New Empire."

In order to improve the economy, Diocletian issued the Edict on Prices. This **edict,** or command, told farmers and merchants how much they could charge for various items. If a seller tried to charge higher prices, the penalty was death. But the edict failed to control the economy, and prices continued to rise.

To fight off foreign threats, Diocletian increased the size of the army from about 300,000 to 450,000 soldiers. He also increased both the size and complexity of the government.

To run his huge empire more efficiently, he divided it into regions. Each one had its own government and army. Although this new government was more efficient, it was also more costly. To pay for it, Diocletian created a new tax system and raised taxes.

In order to keep this new system running, the government had to make sure that its citizens worked hard and paid their taxes. Strict laws were passed to keep people on the job. Farmers could not leave their farms, and workers could not change or leave their jobs. Children had to work at the same job as their parents. Sons of soldiers had to enter the army.

Diocletian's actions reestablished order, but they also brought about a harsher style of rule. The emperors who ruled during the *Pax Romana* had come from the Senate and were called "first citizen." Beginning with Diocletian, emperors came from the army and were called dominus, or "master."

A Divided Empire

Diocletian also tried to put an end to the civil wars which had troubled the empire following the death of emperors from A.D. 235 to 284. He shared his power with another emperor and divided the empire in two. Both the eastern and western portions had their own emperor. Each emperor gave part of his territory to an emperor-in-waiting. After each emperor's reign, power would transfer peacefully to the next emperor.

However, when Diocletian retired in A.D. 305, his system did not work. Civil war broke out again, and military leaders fought for power for the next seven years. Finally, in A.D. 312, Constantine became emperor of the western part of the empire. Twelve years later, Constantine took control of the entire empire. ■

Across Time & Space

HISTORY *The city of Constantinople is known today as Istanbul. The name Istanbul comes from a phrase used by Arab settlers in the 1200s that means "in the city." Istanbul is now the largest city of the Turkish Republic.*

■ *Why was Diocletian's reign called the "New Empire"?*

▼ *Today, Constantinople is called Istanbul.*

The Reign of Constantine

Under the reign of Constantine, Christianity became the main religion in the empire. However, Constantine's importance as a leader went far beyond church affairs. He also completed the reorganization of the government that had been started by Diocletian. And he built a new capital for the empire.

A New Capital for the Empire

He chose for his capital the ancient Greek city of Byzantium, which he renamed Constantinople after himself. Constantinople had several advantages as a capital city.

Notice on the map on page 474 that it was centrally located between Greece and Asia Minor, connecting Europe and Asia. It could easily be reached both by land and sea, making it ideal for trade. And the empire's richest provinces were in the eastern empire.

The location was also ideal for defense. The new capital was on a narrow peninsula, so the Roman army could

473

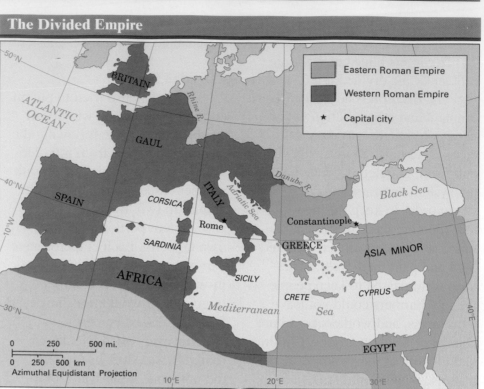

The Divided Empire

Eastern Roman Empire

Western Roman Empire

★ Capital city

Azimuthal Equidistant Projection

0   250   500 mi.
0 250 500 km

▼ *Constantine, shown below on a coin from A.D. 320, established the capital for the Eastern empire. Find the capitals of the Eastern and Western Roman Empire on the map.*

easily ward off enemy attacks. The capital was also closer to the empire's eastern frontier, so troops could reach it more quickly.

Constantine rebuilt the city, making it a magnificent capital. To decorate the new buildings, he brought statues and artwork from pagan temples in other cities. Constantinople was dedicated in A.D. 330, and it became the "new Rome."

A Split in the Empire

When Emperor Constantine died in A.D. 337, his two sons and two nephews fought for control of the Roman empire. One of his

■ *What were the major accomplishments of Constantine?*

nephews, Julian, became emperor in A.D. 361 and tried to restore the pagan religion. However, his effort failed, and by A.D. 400, Christianity became the official religion of the empire. During this period, the church continued to gain strength and support, but the once all-powerful empire was in decline.

By A.D. 400, the empire had permanently split into two parts. The Eastern Roman Empire, with Constantinople as its capital, was to last for another 1,000 years. The Western Roman Empire, with Rome as its capital, was nearing its end. ■

REVIEW

1. **FOCUS** Why did the Roman Empire begin to decline?
2. **CONNECT** Compare and contrast the growth of Christianity and the decline of the Roman Empire during the first 400 years A.D.
3. **POLITICAL SYSTEMS** What were three governmental reforms made by Emperor Diocletian?
4. **CRITICAL THINKING** Before Diocletian, emperors were

known as "first citizen." Afterwards, emperors were known as *dominus*, or "master." Why was that change important for the people living in the empire?

5. **ACTIVITY** Make a timeline showing the important events in the history of the Roman Empire from A.D. 284 to A.D. 400.

474

LESSON 4

The Fall of Rome

Alaric is at the gates, and Rome trembles. He encircles the city; there is panic; he bursts in; but not before giving his instructions, that all those seeking asylum in the holy-places and especially in the churches of the apostles St. Peter and St. Paul must be left untouched and unharmed. The invading army was also to refrain from bloodshed, while gorging itself on as many valuables as it could find.

Orosius, *Histories*, c. A.D. 417

That is how the early Christian historian Orosius described the invasion of Rome. In A.D. 410, the once-proud capital of the Roman Empire was captured by a tribe of invaders from the north called the Visigoths, led by a leader named Alaric. Mighty Rome, itself once the conqueror of a vast empire, had finally met its downfall.

THINKING
FOCUS

Why did the Roman Empire fall?

Key Terms

- barbarian
- monastery

◄ *Today, the Forum, the grand public square of ancient Rome, lies in ruins.*

Barbarian Invasions

Rome did not fall as the result of a single invasion. The pressures that brought it down had been weakening it for centuries. Since the time of the *Pax Romana*, the empire had been fighting off attacks from outsiders. Romans called the invaders **barbarians,** which meant people from beyond the Roman frontier.

Over a period of about 300 years, many barbarian tribes made their way south into the Roman Empire. Look at the map below. Where did Franks, Vandals, and Goths begin their journeys into the empire?

These barbarian tribes were trying to escape the attacks of other tribes migrating into their own territories from Asia. In addition, they were attracted by the wealthy cities and fertile farmlands of the empire.

The Romans looked down on the barbarians as uncivilized. The Roman historian Tacitus drew this unfavorable picture:

> *When they are not fighting, they spend little time in hunting, much more in doing nothing. They devote themselves to sleeping and eating. Even the bravest and most warlike are quite idle.*
>
> Tacitus, *Germania*, A.D. 98

However, Romans looked down on barbarians partly because they were different from Romans. They did not share Roman ideas about government and culture. Yet the barbarian tribes had their own

▼ *What was the first barbarian tribe to enter the empire?*

Barbarian Invasions

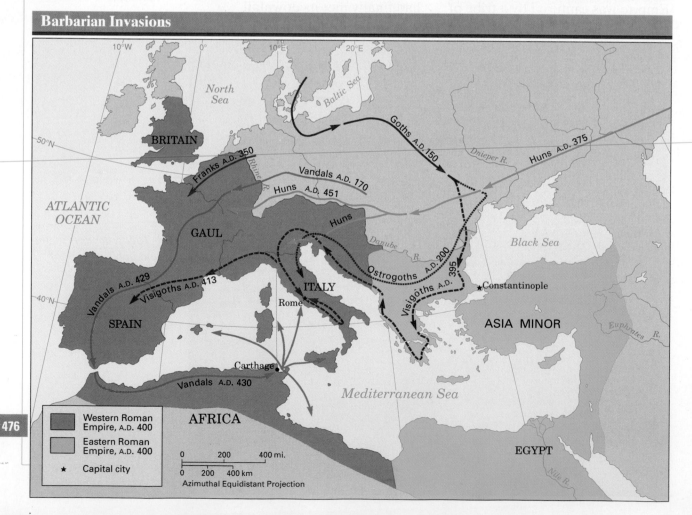

Western Roman Empire, A.D. 400
Eastern Roman Empire, A.D. 400
★ Capital city

0   200   400 mi.
0 200 400 km
Azimuthal Equidistant Projection

government systems, including elected assemblies, and their own cultural values.

Battles with the Barbarians

In the A.D. 200s, the Romans' internal troubles allowed barbarian invasions to reach the heart of the empire. Diocletian and the emperors who followed him fought the invaders to make the frontiers of the empire secure.

As the invasions continued, the empire needed more soldiers to defend itself. Look at the chart on the right. How did the army grow from A.D. 117 to A.D. 425?

To relieve the pressure of barbarian attacks, some Roman emperors tried to "buy off" the invaders. These emperors gave the tribes land to live on, and they hired barbarians to serve in the army. By the A.D. 200s, the frontier of the empire was no longer a clear-cut boundary between the barbarians and the Roman world. The barbarians were gradually becoming part of the empire.

In the late A.D. 300s, pressure from the barbarians was growing. In A.D. 378, the Visigoths, who had settled in the eastern part of the

empire, revolted against the Romans. They killed the leader of the eastern part of the empire, Emperor Valens, and defeated his army. Then, encouraged by their victory, the Visigoths marched into Rome in A.D. 410.

The Fall of the Empire

The success of the invasions showed the weakness of the Roman army. Gradually, the emperors were losing control of their territories. In the early A.D. 400s, the barbarians overran and looted Britain, Gaul, Spain, and North Africa.

In fact, barbarian chiefs took control of much of the western part of the empire during the A.D. 400s.

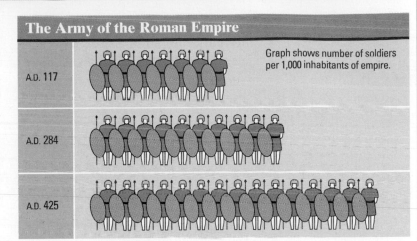

The Army of the Roman Empire

Graph shows number of soldiers per 1,000 inhabitants of empire.

A.D. 117	
A.D. 284	
A.D. 425	

▲ *How many soldiers did Rome have for every 1,000 people in A.D. 425?*

◄ *Hadrian's wall in Britain, built in the A.D. 120s, marked the northern boundary of the empire. From the A.D. 200s on, barbarians repeatedly overran that border.*

■ *Who were the barbarians?*

Historians use the year A.D. 476 to mark the fall of Rome. In that year, the Germanic chief Odoacer (*oh doh AY suhr*) forced the last emperor out of the western part of the empire. Unlike Rome, Constantinople withstood barbarian attacks. The eastern part of the Roman Empire remained intact for another thousand years. ■

Growth of the Church

As the Roman empire grew weaker under the pressure of barbarian attacks, Christianity grew stronger. During the A.D. 300s and 400s, even barbarian tribes such as the Goths, Vandals, and Franks had converted to Christianity.

UNDERSTANDING BARBARIANS

The Roman historian Tacitus said of the barbarians, "they love idleness yet hate peace." As his description shows, Romans thought barbarians were uncivilized and warlike people.

Barbarian is a term that shows a point of view. It expresses the attitudes of one group of people toward another. It indicates the fears groups have about people they do not understand.

The Roman Point of View

The word *barbarian* comes from a Greek word. It means a person from another country. The Romans used the word to refer to the people beyond the frontier. However, a barbarian was not just a foreigner. A barbarian was someone the Romans believed was less refined or had lower social and cultural standards.

A Lack of Respect

Although many barbarians entered the empire peacefully, they were still outsiders. They had different beliefs and values. Throughout history, groups have tended to look down on others who were different from themselves.

For example, the European settlers who came to America in the 1700s and 1800s called American Indians "savages and barbarians." The settlers did not respect the American Indians and felt justified in driving these people from their lands.

An Outside Threat

Groups also tend to feel threatened by people who are different from themselves. The Romans felt threatened because they didn't understand the culture of the barbarians. As the barbarians continued to move into the empire, the barbarians became a more direct threat. They invaded Roman cities and drove out Roman leaders.

As a result, the Romans looked upon barbarians as fierce, brutal, and cruel invaders. That viewpoint has shaped the way barbarians are remembered today.

One of the barbarian tribes is remembered in an even more negative way. Today, *vandal* means someone who destroys things without reason. At the time of the fall of Rome, the Vandals were one of the many barbarian tribes that destroyed cities of the Roman Empire.

478

Nevertheless, some Romans blamed the empire's many problems on the widespread growth of Christianity.

Pagan Romans were upset and angered to see the empire decline under Christian leadership. They blamed the decline on the fact that the Romans had abandoned their pagan gods. In past centuries, the pagans argued, Romans had made sacrifices to the pagan gods, and the empire had gotten stronger. Now Romans were no longer allowed to make these pagan sacrifices. The Christian God, they said, did absolutely nothing to protect the empire.

This charge against Christianity was so serious that a church leader named St. Augustine felt he needed to respond. In the early A.D. 400s, he spent 13 years writing a book called *The City of God*. This book, consisting of 22 volumes, explained what Christians

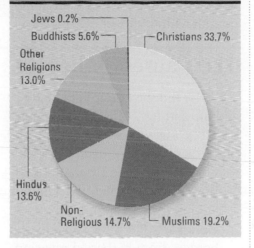

Religious Populations Today

- Jews 0.2%
- Buddhists 5.6%
- Other Religions 13.0%
- Christians 33.7%
- Hindus 13.6%
- Non-Religious 14.7%
- Muslims 19.2%

◄ *How much of the world's population today practices a religion?*

believed to be the role of God in human history.

In *The City of God*, St. Augustine argued that the decline of Rome taught an important lesson. Cities such as Rome, like all worldly things, break down, he wrote. But the city of God, which for St. Augustine represented the Christian faith and its believers, would last forever.

▼ *Even after the fall of the Western Roman Empire, Christianity played an important role in the Eastern Roman Empire. This mosaic from the A.D. 500s shows Justinian, emperor of the Eastern empire, presenting a gold plate to church leaders.*

Why did St. Augustine write The City of God?

When the Roman Empire finally fell in the west, the church did not fall with it. In fact, Christianity continued to grow and increase its influence in the centuries that followed. ■

The Causes of the Fall

Why did the empire gradually decline and fall? Historians do not have one answer. Still, these factors played an important part:

- **Geography** The Roman Empire was shaped like a donut around the Mediterranean. Defending the weak western borders from barbarian invasion took a large number of soldiers and resources away from Rome.
- **Economic decline** In the last century of the empire, both the army and the government kept growing. In addition, Romans continued to import luxury items from distant lands. The Roman economy was not strong enough to support such activities.
- **Growth of government** The large government kept demanding more of the people. Government officials were often dishonest and used their power to get rich. Civil wars wasted Rome's valuable resources of people and money as leaders fought over who would be emperor.
- **Decline in the work force** A high death rate among Romans and a decrease in the number of slaves meant that the empire had fewer workers and fewer soldiers.
- **Lack of technology** Fewer workers now had to produce more goods to meet the demands of defending the empire. Rome had very little machinery that would make human labor more productive. The upper class Romans did not direct their interest and attention to developing ways to save labor.
- **Military defeat** The Roman army was no longer strong enough to defeat the barbarians.

As the power of Rome declined, the power of the Christian church and barbarian tribes increased. This painting from the A.D. 1500s by the Italian artist Raphael shows Pope Leo persuading the barbarian leader Attila to withdraw from Rome in A.D. 452.

As you learn about why Rome fell, you can see the challenge of studying history. You cannot understand the past just by collecting facts and dates. History is also explaining the facts and dates.

Historians have studied for centuries the causes that led to the fall of Rome. Yet they have come to many different conclusions about which causes were the most important. The more you learn, the more skilled you will be at understanding the puzzles of history. ■

■ What are the major causes that led to the fall of Rome?

The Roman Legacy

After the great Roman Empire fell to the German barbarians, Europe entered 500 years of decline. This period is known to historians as the Early Middle Ages.

European cities that had just begun to blossom declined as increased warfare disrupted trade. The education system broke down. In many communities the priests were the only people who knew how to read and write.

Day-to-day survival became the main concern for most people. Under these conditions, the learning of the Greeks and Romans could easily have been lost to the world. Fortunately, several factors kept that from happening.

In Europe, the church began to develop religious communities known as monasteries. These **monasteries** were centers of learning containing schools and libraries. They preserved Rome's heritage in book form.

Centers of learning were also found in the Eastern Roman Empire, which did not fall with Rome. In Constantinople, the capital, scholars copied the many important works of the Greeks and Romans for study.

Through the efforts of scholars at these centers of learning and others like them, the ideas of Greco-Roman civilization were saved for future generations. The achievements of the ancient Greeks and Romans have made lasting impressions on Western civilization. ■

◄ *The Eastern Roman Empire continued to flourish after the fall of Rome. This mosaic from the A.D. 500s shows Theodora, the wife of Emperor Justinian. She is considered the most powerful woman in the history of the Eastern empire.*

■ What were the Early Middle Ages?

R E V I E W

1. **FOCUS** Why did the Roman Empire fall?
2. **CONNECT** How was the fall of Greece to the Macedonians similar to the fall of Rome to the barbarians? How was it different?
3. **HISTORY** Who were the barbarians that invaded the Roman Empire? What drew them to the empire?
4. **CITIZENSHIP** How can studying the reasons for the fall of Rome help you understand events of today?
5. **CRITICAL THINKING** Not all historians agree on the reasons for the fall of Rome. What do you think were the most important reasons? Why?
6. **WRITING ACTIVITY** You have read Tacitus's description of the barbarians. Now imagine that you are a Visigoth and write a short description of your encounters with the people of the Roman Empire.

481

Christianity and the Fall of Rome

Public Policy: Spend Less? Raise Taxes?

U ncontrolled prices are widespread in the sales taking place in the markets and in the daily life of the cities. . . we have decided that maximum prices of articles for sale must be established. . . Thus, when the pressure of high prices appears anywhere . . . [greed] will be checked by the limits. . . of the law.

Emperor Diocletian, *Edict on Prices*, A.D. 301

W hen . . . he brought about enormously high prices, he attempted to legislate the prices of [goods]. Then much blood was spilled. . . nothing appeared on the market because of fear, and prices soared much higher. In the end, after many people had lost their lives, it became absolutely necessary to repeal the law.

Lactantius, Christian writer living in Rome, A.D. 245-325

▼ *Diocletian and his co-emperor Maximian ruled the empire together.*

Background

When Diocletian became emperor of Rome in A.D. 284, he faced an empire in crisis. Enemies along the empire's borders were constantly waging war against Rome. The once-powerful Roman army was no longer strong enough to fight off their attacks. Warfare left the cities and countryside in ruins.

In addition, the empire had grown so large that the government in Rome wasn't able to rule it efficiently. Lawsuits in distant provinces were often left unsettled because there were no government officials to hear them.

Closer to home, arguments and civil wars broke out each time an emperor died or retired: Who would follow him to the throne? Prices were also rising rapidly, making it harder for people to survive.

Finally, the treasury—the money used to pay for the government and army—was running out. The empire was falling apart. What could Diocletian do to save it?

Diocletian began by making a number of decisions. First he reorganized the government. He appointed a co-emperor and two junior emperors. Each of these men ruled a portion of the empire. In this way a local problem could be quickly brought to the attention of one of the rulers. This same system would help ensure a peaceful transfer of power at the end of an emperor's reign.

The four regions of the empire were further divided into more than a hundred provinces—double the number that had existed before. Each province was run by a governor and hundreds of government officials.

To safeguard the borders, Diocletian increased the size of the army. In addition to the troops stationed along the empire's frontiers, he created specially trained troops stationed in cities nearby. These troops stood ready to move quickly to any point along the border in case of enemy attack.

To fight rising prices, Diocletian issued his Edict on Prices, setting the top price to be charged or paid for any item. He also introduced a new system of coins.

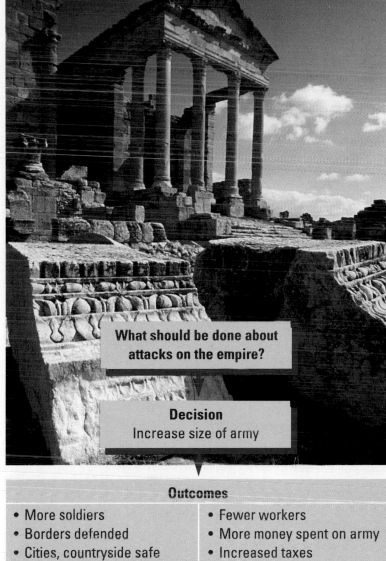

What should be done about attacks on the empire?

Decision
Increase size of army

Outcomes

• More soldiers	• Fewer workers
• Borders defended	• More money spent on army
• Cities, countryside safe	• Increased taxes
• Empire strong, unified	• Unhappy taxpayers

The Cost of Decisions

What did Diocletian hope to achieve with these changes? He wanted to bring peace and make the empire secure. He also wanted to make government more effective and efficient and to keep the economy stable.

Though many Romans agreed that these were worthy goals, some of the decisions Diocletian made based on these goals were not so popular. All of these changes cost money, and that meant higher taxes. Now there were four royal courts to pay for, not just one. There were nearly three times the number of government workers as before, and all of these workers had to be paid. As the army increased in size, more money had to be spent on soldiers' salaries, training, and supplies.

▲ What were the goals behind Diocletian's decision to increase the size of the army? Did the outcome of that decision support his goals?

Christianity and the Fall of Rome

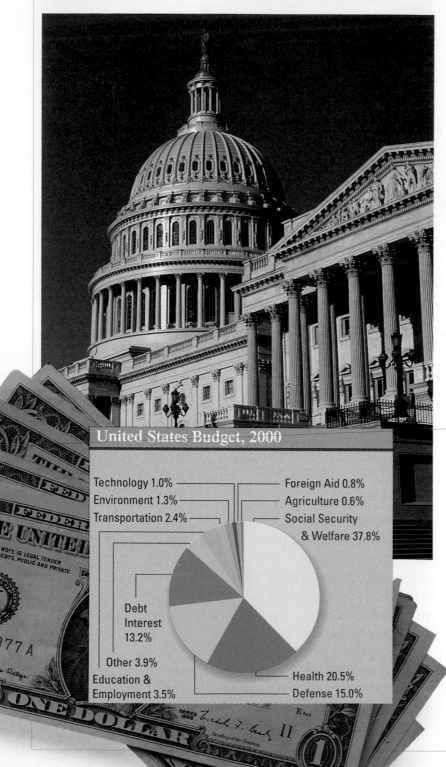

The U.S. Congress meets in the Capitol building in Washington, D.C. The pie chart represents the total amount of money that the federal government has to work with and how it can be spent in the year 2000.

United States Budget, 2000

Technology 1.0%
Environment 1.3%
Transportation 2.4%
Foreign Aid 0.8%
Agriculture 0.6%
Social Security & Welfare 37.8%
Debt Interest 13.2%
Other 3.9%
Education & Employment 3.5%
Health 20.5%
Defense 15.0%

Enforcing new laws, like the Edict on Prices, meant more money for officials, lawyers, and courts.

Many Romans suffered under the huge tax burden. Lactantius complained that, "The number of those receiving [pay from the state] was so much larger than the number of those paying [taxes] that . . . the resources of the tenant farmers were exhausted [and] fields were abandoned."

As emperor, Diocletian had no need to ask for support from the public or even from the Senate. He could simply raise taxes to pay for his reforms.

Like Diocletian, our representatives at the local, state, and national levels must pass laws and provide services that people need. They must also find ways to pay for them. In our democratic system, however, government leaders must consider the goals and values of the people they represent as well as their own.

Decision Point

1. What were the goals and values that led to each of Diocletian's decisions? What were some of the outcomes of each decision? Did the outcomes support the goals?

2. Look in a newspaper or magazine for information about a federal government program whose goals you support. How much will the program cost?

3. Look at the pie chart on this page. Where does your program fit?

4. Suppose you are a U.S. representative. What arguments would you present to persuade other representatives to spend money on your program?

5. Whenever Congress adds a new government program, it must pay for it by raising taxes, reducing spending on some other programs, or borrowing the money. What are the advantages and disadvantages of each of these alternatives?

Chapter Review

Reviewing Key Terms

barbarian (p. 476)
conversion (p. 459)
edict (p. 472)
excommunication (p. 469)
Gentile (p. 460)

martyr (p. 467)
monastery (p. 481)
pagan (p. 469)
persecute (p. 458)
sect (p. 459)

A. Write a sentence to answer each question. Each sentence you write should include the key term in parentheses following the question.

1. Why did Saul of Tarsus, a hunter of Christians, suddenly begin risking his life to spread the Christian message? (conversion)
2. In what way did the Bishop of Milan's threat to Emperor Theodosius in A.D. 390 show how powerful the church had become? (excommunication)

3. Who took control of much of the western part of the Roman Empire during the A.D. 400s? (barbarian)
4. How did Diocletian set the prices that farmers and merchants could charge for goods? (edict)
5. Where did most learning take place during the Early Middle Ages? (monastery)

B. For each pair of words, write one sentence that includes both words and that gives information from the chapter.

1. conversion, Gentiles
2. persecute, pagan
3. sect, martyr

Exploring Concepts

A. On your own paper, copy and complete the following summary of events.

> The first ___?___ years A.D. saw the rise of the ___?___ religion and the ___?___ of the Roman Empire. The Romans ___?___ Christians on and off for the first 300 years A.D. Rome blamed many of its problems on Christians' refusal to worship Roman ___?___. Two problems facing the empire were ___?___ and ___?___. To solve these problems, Emperor ___?___ started policies that greatly limited individual freedom. Soon after ___?___ became emperor in A.D. 312, ___?___ became the main religion of the empire. After Constantine's death, the empire split into two parts, the ___?___ and the ___?___ Roman Empires. In A.D. 410, the ___?___ invaded the city of Rome. The Roman Empire ended when Odoacer, a ___?___, forced out the last emperor of the ___?___ in A.D. 476.

B. Support each statement with facts and details from the chapter.

1. Some Christian values seemed to conflict with Roman values.
2. The Greek language helped Christianity spread.
3. By A.D. 280, the economy of Rome was a disaster.
4. By A.D. 280, Rome's government had become very unstable.
5. Many individual freedoms vanished under the emperor Diocletian.
6. Although not himself a Christian until late in his life, Constantine promoted Christianity throughout the Roman Empire.
7. The Roman Empire had encountered barbarians long before Rome was invaded in A.D. 410.
8. Although the rise of Christianity and the fall of the Roman Empire took place in the same time span, Christianity itself did not cause the empire to fall.

485

Reviewing Skills

1. Look at the bust of Socrates on page 372 and at the painting of the death of Socrates on page 373. Describe your impressions of Socrates from each of these. What was the main idea or feeling that each artist was trying to convey?

2. a. Make a timeline showing the dates of these important events in Roman history from 0 to 476 A.D.

0—200	*Pax Romana*
303	Diocletian persecutes Christians
410	City of Rome falls to Visigoths
313	Emperor Constantine gives religious freedom
100	Roman courts execute Christians
64	Rome burns during Nero's reign
250	Emperor Decius orders Roman gods worshiped
395	Roman Empire splits
476	Roman Empire falls

   b. Find the dates of the following events in the chapter. Show these dates on a telescoping timeline based on the timeline you made in *a*.

   Saul converts to Christianity
   Christians begin preaching to Gentiles
   Paul executed
   New Testament books collected

   c. Find the dates of the following events in the chapter. Show these dates on a telescoping timeline based on the timeline you made in *a*.

   Emperor Constantine gives religious freedom
   Constantine becomes a Christian
   Julian tries to restore pre-Christian religions

3. Suppose you are a historian. You are interested in adding to our factual knowledge of the early Christian church. What kinds of written sources might contain the information you are looking for?

Using Critical Thinking

1. The fall of the Roman Empire had many causes. Think of an example of a problem today that has many causes. Pollution is one example. In a paragraph, describe the problem and some of its causes. Then explain the danger of finding only one cause and acting on that information.

2. The emperors Decius and Diocletian adopted some very harsh policies. Write a paragraph explaining what those policies were intended to accomplish. Then suggest some solutions to the problems of the Roman Empire during the A.D. 200s. Why might your solutions have worked?

Preparing for Citizenship

1. **COLLECTING INFORMATION** During the first 400 years A.D., the Roman Empire suffered an economic collapse. Clip newspaper articles about economic problems around the world today. Look for words in headlines such as economy, shortages, prices, and supply. List causes of economic problems and their effects on the people of a country. Use the library to find more information.

2. **COLLABORATIVE LEARNING** Constantinople, once Byzantium, is now Istanbul, Turkey. In groups of three, find an interesting way to present the city's three historical periods. Your group might produce an illustrated timeline, an oral report, or written descriptions. Each group member should research one historical period. The group should work together on the final presentation.

Time/Space
Databank

Alphabet

Alphabet is the series of letters used in writing a language. The name means exactly what the term ABC´s means as a name for the 26 letters of our alphabet. The word comes from *alpha* and *beta,* the first two letters of the Greek alphabet.

Most books, magazines, and newspapers are printed in the 26-letter alphabet called *Roman.* But the Romans did not invent it. They put finishing touches on a system that had been growing for thousands of years.

The earliest writing

In early times, people could communicate with one another only by speaking or by making gestures. They had no way to keep records of important events, unless they memorized the story of a great battle or important happening. They had no way to send messages over long distances unless they passed them from one person to the next by word of mouth, or had one person

memorize the message and then deliver it.

The first stage in writing came when people learned to draw pictures to express their ideas. In *ideography,* each picture conveyed an idea. Ideography enabled even people who did not speak the same language to communicate with each other. Then people learned *logography,* expressing ideas indirectly by using signs to stand for the words of the idea. Instead of drawing pictures of five sheep to show a herd of five animals, a person could draw one sign for the numeral "five" and one for "sheep." Gradually people learned to use a *syllabic* system, in which a sign that stood for one word could be used not only for that word but also for any phonetic combination that sounded like that word. This is what we call *rebus writing.* If we used rebus writing in English, we could draw a sign for the word "bee" followed by a sign for the word "leaf" to stand for the word "belief." Finally, people developed alphabets in which indi-

Development of the English alphabet The English alphabet developed from a number of early writing systems, beginning with the sign writing of Ancient Egypt. The Romans had given most capital letters their modern form by A.D. 114. But the letters *J, U,* and *W* were not added to the alphabet until the Middle Ages.

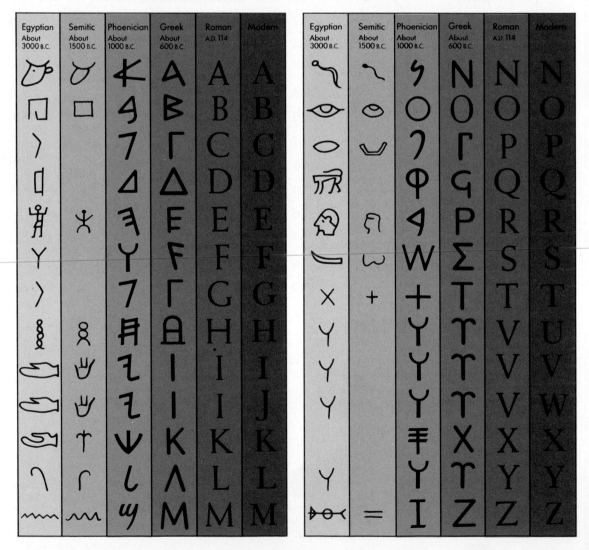

Egyptian About 3000 B.C.	Semitic About 1500 B.C.	Phoenician About 1000 B.C.	Greek About 600 B.C.	Roman A.D. 114	Modern
			A	A	A
			B	B	B
			Γ	C	C
			Δ	D	D
			E	E	E
			F	F	F
			Γ	G	G
			H	H	H
			I	I	I
			I	I	J
			K	K	K
			Λ	L	L
			M	M	M

Egyptian About 3000 B.C.	Semitic About 1500 B.C.	Phoenician About 1000 B.C.	Greek About 600 B.C.	Roman A.D. 114	Modern
			N	N	N
			O	O	O
			Γ	P	P
			Φ	Q	Q
			P	R	R
			Σ	S	S
			T	T	T
			Υ	V	U
			Υ	V	V
			X	X	W
			Υ	Y	X
			Υ	Y	Y
			I	Z	Z

Some important alphabets   The alphabets of five important languages are shown below. Hindi is India's most widely spoken language. People throughout the Middle East and northern Africa use Arabic, which is read from right to left. Gaelic, along with English, is the official language of Ireland.

Greek   Α Β Γ Δ Ε Ζ Η Θ Ι Κ Λ Μ Ν Ξ Ο Π Ρ Σ Τ Υ Φ Χ Ψ Ω

Russian   АБВГДЕЁЖЗИЙКЛМНОПРСТУФХЦЧШЩЪЫЬЭЮЯ

Hindi   अ आ इ ई उ ऊ ऋ ए ऐ ओ औ क ख ग घ ङ च छ ज झ ञ ट ठ ड ढ ण त थ द ध न प फ ब भ म य र ल व श ष स ह

Arabic   ا ب ت ث ج ح خ د ذ ر ز س ش ص ض ط ظ ع غ ف ق ك ل م ن ه و ي

Gaelic   ᚪ ᚠ ᚲ ᚦ ᚢ ᚨ ᚷ ᚺ ᛁ ᛚ ᛗ ᚾ ᚮ ᛈ ᚱ ᛏ ᚢ

vidual signs stood for particular sounds. Today, most written languages in the world use alphabetic writing systems.

The earliest alphabets

The Egyptians used a system of several hundred signs that stood for full words or for syllables. They could write the word *nefer,* or *good,* with a single sign for the whole word, or with three signs, for the sounds *n, f,* and *r.* These signs specified the consonants in syllables, but not the vowels. Egyptian writing, which developed around 3000 B.C., was formally a picture writing, and structurally a word and syllabic writing.

The Semites, who lived in Syria and Palestine, knew something of the Egyptian writing system. They worked out an alphabetic writing about 1500 B.C. They used signs to show the consonants of syllables, just as the Egyptians did. The Semites seem to have adapted some of the pictures from Egyptian hieroglyphics, but they used these symbols for sounds in their own language. The oldest known Semitic alphabets have been found in Syria and at a Semitic outpost in the Sinai Peninsula.

The Phoenicians, who lived along the coast of the Mediterranean Sea, developed a system of 22 signs about 1000 B.C. Their alphabet was structurally related to Semitic and Egyptian, with signs for consonant sounds, not vowel sounds. Early Phoenician writing consists partly of pictographic forms, which they may have borrowed from older pictographic systems, and partly of geometric or diagrammatic signs that they invented. Historians find it difficult to trace the formal relations between Semitic and Phoenician signs, because Phoenician has both pictographic and diagrammatic signs, and because so little is known of the ancient systems used in Syria and Palestine.

The Cypriots, the people of the island of Cyprus, developed an alphabet of their own. Starting with an unknown word-syllable system, they worked out an alphabet of 56 signs, each standing for an initial consonant and a different vowel. The next step was to create separate signs for vowels and consonants.

The Greeks came in contact with Phoenician traders, and learned from them the idea of writing individual sounds of the language. Sometime during the period before 800 B.C., they borrowed Phoenician symbols and modified them to form the Greek alphabet. The Phoeni-

cian alphabet included more consonants than the Greeks needed for their language, so they used the extra signs for vowel sounds. In this way, the Greeks improved on both Phoenician and Cypriot ideas, because they could combine individual letters for both consonants and vowels to spell any word they wanted.

The Greeks took over the Phoenician names for their signs, and in most cases the signs themselves. The first letter of the Phoenician alphabet, ✕, and its name, *aleph,* meaning *ox,* became ◁, or *alpha* in Greek. The second letter, ⅁ , or *beth,* meaning *house,* became Β, or *beta* in Greek. The Greeks later modified the shapes of these letters, adding and dropping some letters, to form the 24-letter Greek alphabet of today.

The Roman alphabet

The Etruscans moved to central Italy from somewhere in the eastern Mediterranean region sometime after 1000 B.C. They carried the Greek alphabet with them. The Romans learned the alphabet from the Etruscans, and gave it much the same form we use today. The early Roman alphabet had about 20 letters, and gradually gained 3 more.

Capital letters were the only forms used for hundreds of years. Many people consider the Roman alphabet to have been perfected by A.D. 114. That year, sculptors carved the inscriptions on a memorial column built to honor the emperor Trajan. The style of lettering they used is considered one of the most beautiful in the world.

Carving letters in stone is not an easy job, and Roman stonecutters rounded or squared, simplified, and polished their letters. They developed the beautiful thick-and-thin strokes we use today. They also added *serifs* (little finishing strokes) at the tops and bottoms of many letters. The practical reason for serifs was that the carvers found it difficult to end wide strokes without ugly blunt lines. And if a chisel slipped while squaring off an end, they could not erase the mistake. But serifs also added a touch of strength and grace to Roman lettering, and are still used today.

Small letters gradually developed from capitals. Scribes who copied books often used *uncials* (rounded letters) that were easier to form than some capitals. True lower-case letters developed later, when scribes saved space in books by using the smaller letters.

Excerpted from the Alphabet article in *World Book.*
Copyright © 1998 by World Book, Inc.

Architecture

Architectural terms

Ambulatory is a continuous aisle in a circular building. In a church, the ambulatory serves as a semicircular aisle that encloses the apse.

Apse is a semicircular area. In most churches, the apse is at one end of the building and contains the main altar.

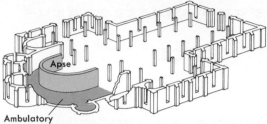

Arcade refers to a series of arches supported by columns or piers. A passageway formed by the arches is also called an arcade.

Arch is a curved structure used to support the weight of the material above it. A stone at the top of an arch, called the *keystone,* holds the other parts in place.

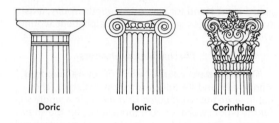

Architrave makes up the lowest part of an entablature. It rests on the capital of a column. For a drawing of an architrave, see Entablature on the opposite page.

Buttress is a support built against an outside wall of a building. A *flying buttress* is an arched support that extends from a column or pier to the wall.

Buttress   Flying Buttress

Cantilever is a horizontal projection, such as a balcony or a beam, which is supported only at one end.

Cantilevers

Capital, in an order, forms the upper part of a column. It separates the shaft from the entablature.

Doric   Ionic   Corinthian

Colonnade means a row of columns, each set an equal distance apart.

Column is a vertical support. In an order, it consists of a shaft and a capital and often rests on a base.

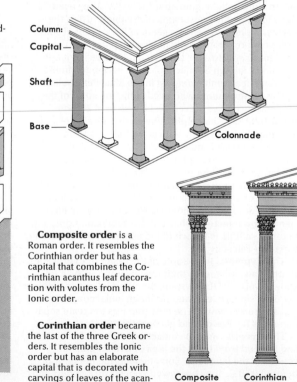

Column:
Capital
Shaft
Base
Colonnade

Composite order is a Roman order. It resembles the Corinthian order but has a capital that combines the Corinthian acanthus leaf decoration with volutes from the Ionic order.

Corinthian order became the last of the three Greek orders. It resembles the Ionic order but has an elaborate capital that is decorated with carvings of leaves of the acanthus plant.

Composite Order   Corinthian Order

Cornice forms the upper part of an entablature and extends beyond the frieze.

Doric order was the first and simplest of the three Greek orders. The Doric is the only order that normally has no base.

Entablature refers to the upper horizontal part of an order between a capital and the roof. It consists of three major parts—the architrave, frieze, and cornice.

Facade is the front of a building. Most facades contain an entrance.

Frieze forms the middle part of an entablature and is often decorated with a horizontal band of relief sculpture.

Ionic order was the second of the three Greek orders. It has a capital decorated with carved spiral scrolls called *volutes*.

Module is a measurement, such as the diameter of a column, which architects use to establish the proportions of an entire structure.

Nave is the chief area within a church. It extends from the main entrance to the transept.

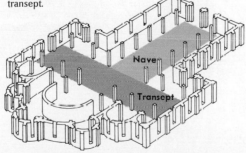

Order, in classical architecture, consisted of a column and an entablature. Orders served as the basic elements of Greek and Roman architecture and influenced many later styles.

Pediment is a triangular segment between the horizontal entablature and the sloping roof at the front of a classical-style building.

Pendentive is a curved support shaped like an inverted triangle. Pendentives hold up a dome.

Pier refers to a large pillar used to support a roof.

Post and lintel is a method of construction in which vertical beams (posts) support a horizontal beam (lintel).

Shaft is the main part of a column below the capital. Many shafts have shallow vertical grooves called *fluting*.

Transept forms the arms in a T- or cross-shaped church.

Tuscan order, a Roman order, resembles the Doric order, but the shaft has no fluting.

Vault is an arched brick or stone ceiling or roof. A *barrel vault,* the simplest form of vault, is a single continuous arch. A *groined vault* is formed by joining two barrel vaults at right angles. A *ribbed vault* has diagonal arches that project from the surface.

Barrel Vault   **Groined Vault**   **Ribbed Vault**

Jerusalem in the First Century

No one knows exactly what Jerusalem looked like during the first century. This exclusive *World Book* illustration is based on research by a scholar dealing with how the city may have appeared at that time. The index at the right identifies the points of interest numbered on the illustration. The Temple (13), which was the largest building in the city, stood on a hill in eastern Jerusalem. West and north of the Temple lay a small area of shops, stores, and houses. The First Wall (24) almost encircled southern Jerusalem. A shorter, jagged wall cut across this area and separated sections called the Lower City and the Upper City. The crowded Lower City, east of the jagged wall, was the commercial and industrial center of Jerusalem and the chief residential area of its poor. Most of Jerusalem's wealthy people lived in the Upper City, west of the jagged wall. There, King Herod's Palace (35) and many large homes had spacious courtyards with gardens and pools.

1. Road to Galilee
2. Wood Market and Stores
3. North Gate
4. Second Wall
5. Hill of Calvary (Golgotha)
6. Stores
7. Barracks
8. Market Halls
9. Fortress of Antonia
10. Jannaeus Monument
11. Sheep Pool and Market

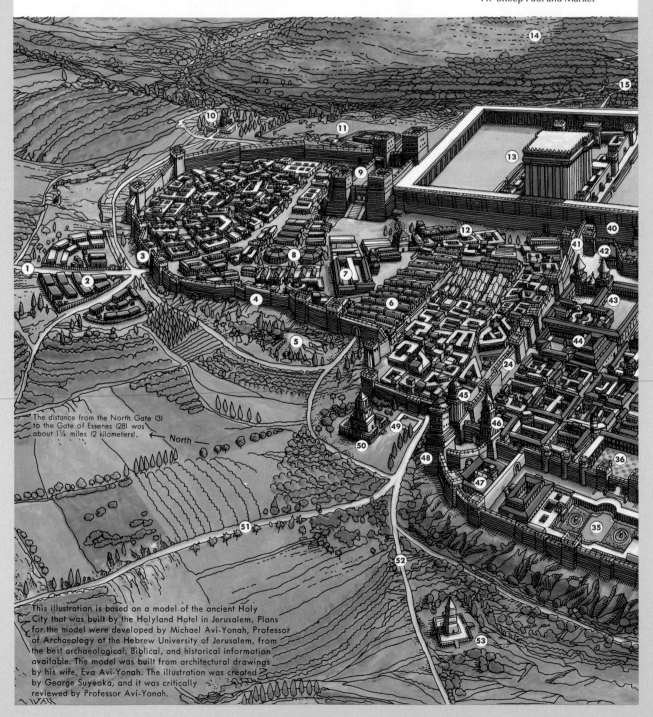

The distance from the North Gate (3) to the Gate of Essenes (28) was about 1¼ miles (2 kilometers).

← North

This illustration is based on a model of the ancient Holy City that was built by the Holyland Hotel in Jerusalem. Plans for the model were developed by Michael Avi-Yonah, Professor of Archaeology at the Hebrew University of Jerusalem, from the best archaeological, Biblical, and historical information available. The model was built from architectural drawings by his wife, Eva Avi-Yonah. The illustration was created by George Suyeoka, and it was critically reviewed by Professor Avi-Yonah.

Jerusalem

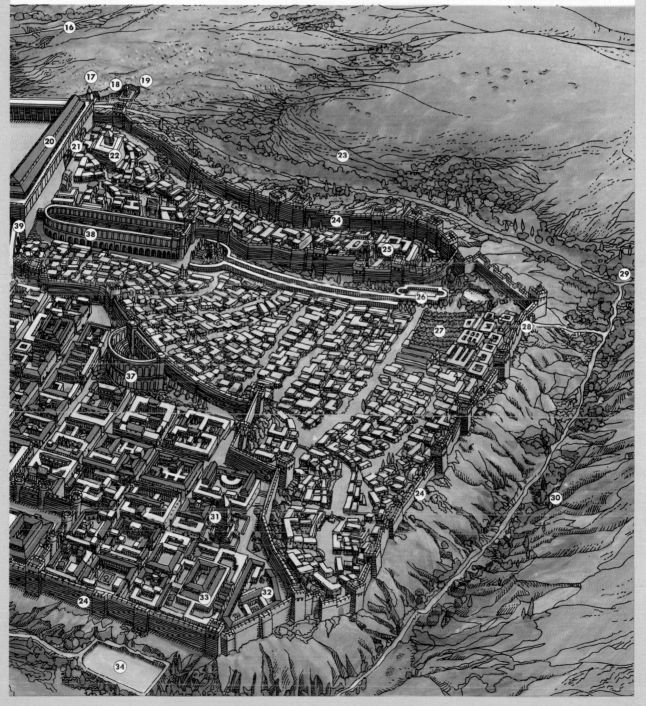

Seven Wonders of the Ancient World

Ancient Greeks and Romans made up many lists of notable objects. These illustrations show the objects that have been most commonly listed as the Seven Wonders of the Ancient World. The map, *below right,* shows the location of the Seven Wonders of the Ancient World in red.

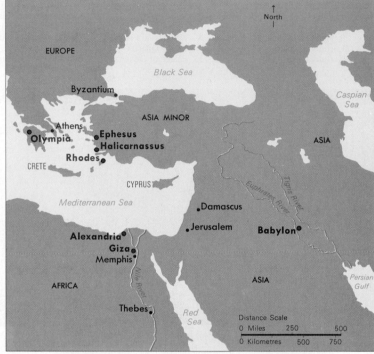

WORLD BOOK map

The Temple of Artemis at Ephesus was one of the largest temples built by the Greeks. It was famous for its decoration and extensive use of marble.

The statue of Zeus at Olympia, Greece, was probably the most famous statue made by the Greeks. People who came to watch the Olympic Games admired this gold and ivory figure.

The pyramids of Egypt at Giza are the best preserved of the Seven Wonders of the Ancient World. They still attract many visitors to Giza, just outside the present-day city of Cairo.

Seven Wonders of the Ancient World

The Mausoleum at Halicarnassus was a great marble tomb. It was built for Mausolus, a local ruler, by some of the most famous Greek sculptors and architects.

The Lighthouse of Alexandria, Egypt, was the world's first important lighthouse. It guided ships into the city's harbor for about 1,500 years before being toppled by an earthquake.

WORLD BOOK illustrations by Birney Lettick

The Hanging Gardens of Babylon probably were built by King Nebuchadnezzar II after he married a mountain princess. He apparently hoped the gardens would make her feel at home.

The Colossus of Rhodes was built in honor of the sun god Helios. It was constructed after the people of Rhodes survived a yearlong siege by a large force of Macedonians.

World
Independent countries of the world*

Name	Area In sq. mi.	In km²	Rank in area	Population†	Rank in population	Capital	Map key	
Afghanistan	251,773	652,090	40	23,731,000	41	Kabul	D	11
Albania	11,100	28,748	140	3,548,000	125	Tiranë	C	11
Algeria	919,595	2,381,741	11	29,806,000	35	Algiers	D	10
Andorra	175	453	178	75,000	181	Andorra la Vella	C	10‡
Angola	481,354	1,246,700	22	12,212,000	62	Luanda	F	10
Antigua and Barbuda	171	442	179	67,000	183	St. John's	E	6
Argentina	1,073,519	2,780,400	8	35,805,000	31	Buenos Aires	G	6
Armenia	11,506	29,800	138	3,726,000	119	Yerevan	D	13
Australia	2,978,147	7,713,364	6	18,758,000	52	Canberra	G	16
Austria	32,378	83,859	113	8,076,000	86	Vienna	C	10
Azerbaijan	33,436	86,600	112	7,801,000	88	Baku	D	13
Bahamas	5,358	13,878	154	287,000	166	Nassau	D	6
Bahrain	268	694	173	604,000	157	Manama	D	12
Bangladesh	55,598	143,998	92	128,558,000	8	Dhaka	D	14
Barbados	166	430	180	266,000	169	Bridgetown	E	7
Belarus	80,155	207,600	83	10,048,000	78	Minsk	C	11
Belgium	11,783	30,519	136	10,273,000	75	Brussels	C	10
Belize	8,763	22,696	147	232,000	170	Belmopan	E	5
Benin	43,484	112,622	99	5,900,000	99	Porto-Novo	E	10
Bhutan	18,147	47,000	128	1,756,000	141	Thimphu	D	14
Bolivia	424,165	1,098,581	27	7,944,000	87	La Paz; Sucre	F	6
Bosnia-Herzegovina	19,741	51,129	124	3,947,000	117	Sarajevo	C	10
Botswana	224,607	581,730	45	1,620,000	144	Gaborone	G	11
Brazil	3,286,488	8,511,965	5	169,430,000	5	Brasília	F	7
Brunei	2,226	5,765	161	300,000	165	Bandar Seri Begawan	E	15
Bulgaria	42,823	110,912	102	8,654,000	84	Sofia	C	11
Burkina Faso	105,792	274,000	72	11,119,000	70	Ouagadougou	E	9
Burma (Myanmar)	261,228	676,578	39	49,447,000	24	Rangoon	D	14
Burundi	10,747	27,834	142	6,937,000	93	Bujumbura	F	11
Cambodia	69,898	181,035	87	11,052,000	71	Phnom Penh	E	15
Cameroon	183,569	475,442	52	14,389,000	60	Yaoundé	E	10
Canada	3,849,674	9,970,610	2	29,450,000	36	Ottawa	C	4
Cape Verde	1,557	4,033	163	424,000	161	Praia	E	8
Central African Republic	240,535	622,984	42	3,555,000	124	Bangui	E	10
Chad	495,755	1,284,000	20	6,904,000	94	N'Djamena	E	10
Chile	292,135	756,626	37	14,878,000	59	Santiago	G	6
China	3,705,822	9,598,036	3	1,265,413,000	1	Beijing	D	14
Colombia	439,737	1,138,914	25	36,694,000	30	Bogotá	E	6
Comoros	863	2,235	166	724,000	155	Moroni	F	12
Congo (Brazzaville)	132,047	342,000	63	2,809,000	130	Brazzaville	F	10
Congo (Kinshasa)	905,355	2,344,858	12	48,042,000	25	Kinshasa	F	11
Costa Rica	19,730	51,100	125	3,641,000	122	San José	E	5
Croatia	34,022	88,117	111	4,457,000	114	Zagreb	C	10
Cuba	42,804	110,861	103	11,244,000	69	Havana	D	5
Cyprus	3,572	9,251	160	762,000	154	Nicosia	D	11
Czech Republic	30,450	78,864	115	10,327,000	74	Prague	C	10
Denmark	16,639	43,094	130	5,197,000	105	Copenhagen	C	10
Djibouti	8,958	23,200	146	616,000	156	Djibouti	E	12
Dominica	290	751	169	71,000	182	Roseau	E	6
Dominican Republic	18,816	48,734	127	8,217,000	85	Santo Domingo	E	6
Ecuador	109,484	283,561	71	12,151,000	63	Quito	F	6
Egypt	386,662	1,001,449	29	66,547,000	16	Cairo	D	11
El Salvador	8,124	21,041	149	6,150,000	96	San Salvador	E	5
Equatorial Guinea	10,831	28,051	141	430,000	160	Malabo	E	10
Eritrea	45,406	117,600	98	3,816,000	118	Asmara	E	12
Estonia	17,413	45,100	129	1,509,000	145	Tallinn	C	11
Ethiopia	426,373	1,104,300	26	60,053,000	19	Addis Ababa	E	11
Fiji	7,056	18,274	151	820,000	153	Suva	F	1
Finland	130,559	338,145	64	5,162,000	106	Helsinki	B	11
France	212,935	551,500	47	58,609,000	21	Paris	C	10
Gabon	103,347	267,668	74	1,161,000	148	Libreville	F	10
Gambia	4,361	11,295	156	1,217,000	147	Banjul	E	9
Georgia	26,911	69,700	119	5,500,000	101	Tbilisi	D	12
Germany	137,796	356,890	62	81,664,000	12	Berlin	C	10
Ghana	92,098	238,533	78	19,016,000	51	Accra	E	9
Greece	50,962	131,990	94	10,523,000	73	Athens	D	11
Grenada	133	344	182	93,000	178	St. George's	E	6
Guatemala	42,042	108,889	104	11,542,000	68	Guatemala City	E	5
Guinea	94,926	245,857	75	7,308,000	91	Conakry	E	9
Guinea-Bissau	13,948	36,125	133	1,142,000	150	Bissau	E	9
Guyana	83,000	214,969	81	864,000	152	Georgetown	E	7
Haiti	10,714	27,750	143	7,633,000	89	Port-au-Prince	E	6
Honduras	43,277	112,088	100	6,133,000	97	Tegucigalpa	E	5
Hungary	35,920	93,032	108	10,009,000	79	Budapest	C	10
Iceland	39,769	103,000	105	277,000	167	Reykjavik	B	9
India	1,269,346	3,287,590	7	986,026,000	2	New Delhi	D	13
Indonesia	735,358	1,904,569	15	206,491,000	4	Jakarta	F	16
Iran	630,577	1,633,188	17	71,569,000	15	Teheran	D	12
Iraq	169,235	438,317	57	22,345,000	46	Baghdad	D	12
Ireland	27,137	70,284	118	3,590,000	123	Dublin	C	9
Israel	8,130	21,056	148	5,883,000	100	Jerusalem	D	11
Italy	116,320	301,268	69	57,221,000	22	Rome	C	10
Ivory Coast (Côte d'Ivoire)	124,504	322,463	68	15,684,000	58	Abidjan	E	9
Jamaica	4,243	10,990	158	2,504,000	134	Kingston	E	6
Japan	145,870	377,801	61	125,922,000	9	Tokyo	D	16
Jordan	35,475	91,880	110	4,480,000	112	Amman	D	11
Kazakstan	1,049,156	2,717,300	9	17,457,000	54	Almaty	C	13
Kenya	224,081	580,367	46	30,738,000	33	Nairobi	E	11
Kiribati	280	726	171	84,000	179	Tarawa	F	1
Korea, North	46,540	120,538	96	25,121,000	39	Pyongyang	C	16
Korea, South	38,330	99,274	107	46,262,000	26	Seoul	D	16
Kuwait	6,880	17,818	152	1,702,000	142	Kuwait	D	12
Kyrgyzstan	76,641	198,500	84	4,960,000	107	Bishkek	C	15
Laos	91,429	236,800	80	5,296,000	104	Vientiane	E	15
Latvia	24,942	64,600	122	2,504,000	134	Riga	C	11
Lebanon	4,015	10,400	159	3,173,000	128	Beirut	D	11
Lesotho	11,720	30,355	137	2,216,000	137	Maseru	G	11
Liberia	43,000	111,369	101	3,339,000	126	Monrovia	E	9

Independent countries of the world*

Name	Area In sq. mi.	In km²	Rank in area	Population[†]	Rank in population	Capital	Map key	
Libya	679,362	1,759,540	16	5,965,000	98	Tripoli	D	10
Liechtenstein	62	160	187	31,000	187	Vaduz	C	10†
Lithuania	25,174	65,200	121	3,696,000	120	Vilnius	C	11
Luxembourg	998	2,586	165	418,000	162	Luxembourg	C	10
Macedonia	9,928	25,713	145	2,213,000	138	Skopje	C	10
Madagascar	226,658	587,041	44	14,125,000	61	Antananarivo	F	12
Malawi	45,747	118,484	97	11,724,000	67	Lilongwe	I	11
Malaysia	127,320	329,758	66	21,398,000	48	Kuala Lumpur	F	15
Maldives	115	298	184	269,000	168	Male	E	13
Mali	478,841	1,240,192	23	11,806,000	66	Bamako	E	9
Malta	122	316	183	373,000	164	Valletta	D	10
Marshall Islands	70	181	186	59,000	184	Majuro	E	18
Mauritania	395,956	1,025,520	28	2,450,000	135	Nouakchott	D	9
Mauritius	788	2,040	167	1,154,000	149	Port Louis	G	12
Mexico	756,066	1,958,201	14	98,766,000	11	Mexico City	D	4
Micronesia, Federated States of	271	702	172	135,000	175	Palikir	E	17
Moldova	13,012	33,700	135	4,479,000	113	Chisinau	C	11
Monaco	0.58	1.49	191	33,000	186	Monaco	C	10†
Mongolia	604,829	1,566,500	18	2,556,000	132	Ulan Bator	C	15
Morocco	172,414	446,550	56	28,548,000	37	Rabat	D	9
Mozambique	309,496	801,590	34	17,703,000	53	Maputo	F	11
Namibia	318,261	824,292	33	1,663,000	143	Windhoek	G	11
Nauru	8	21	190	12,000	190	—	F	18
Nepal	56,827	147,181	91	23,603,000	42	Kathmandu	D	14
Netherlands	16,003	41,447	131	15,760,000	57	Amsterdam	C	10
New Zealand	104,454	270,534	73	3,683,000	121	Wellington	G	18
Nicaragua	50,193	130,000	95	4,854,000	108	Managua	E	5
Niger	489,191	1,267,000	21	10,093,000	77	Niamey	E	10
Nigeria	356,669	923,768	30	121,513,000	10	Abuja	E	10
Norway	149,405	386,958	60	4,391,000	115	Oslo	B	10
Oman	82,030	212,457	82	2,425,000	136	Muscat	E	12
Pakistan	307,374	796,095	35	152,766,000	6	Islamabad	D	13
Palau	177	459	176	18,000	189	Koror	E	16
Panama	30,193	78,200	116	2,763,000	131	Panama City	E	5
Papua New Guinea	178,704	462,840	53	4,596,000	110	Port Moresby	F	17
Paraguay	157,048	406,752	58	5,337,000	103	Asunción	G	7
Peru	496,225	1,285,216	19	25,124,000	38	Lima	F	6
Philippines	115,831	300,000	70	71,654,000	14	Manila	E	16
Poland	124,808	323,250	67	40,858,000	28	Warsaw	C	10
Portugal	35,672	92,389	109	9,814,000	80	Lisbon	D	9
Qatar	4,247	11,000	157	582,000	158	Doha	D	12
Romania	92,043	238,391	79	22,698,000	45	Bucharest	C	11
Russia	6,592,850	17,075,400	1	146,120,000	7	Moscow	C	13
Rwanda	10,169	26,338	144	7,261,000	92	Kigali	F	11
St. Kitts and Nevis	101	261	185	41,000	185	Basseterre	E	6†
St. Lucia	240	622	174	148,000	173	Castries	E	6
St. Vincent and the Grenadines	150	388	181	115,000	176	Kingstown	E	6
San Marino	24	61	188	26,000	188	San Marino	C	10†
São Tomé and Príncipe	372	964	168	141,000	174	São Tomé	E	10
Saudi Arabia	830,000	2,149,690	13	19,801,000	49	Riyadh	D	12
Senegal	75,955	196,722	85	8,993,000	82	Dakar	E	9
Seychelles	176	455	177	75,000	181	Victoria	F	12
Sierra Leone	27,699	71,740	117	4,833,000	109	Freetown	E	9
Singapore	239	618	175	2,919,000	129	Singapore	E	15
Slovakia	18,924	49,013	126	5,422,000	102	Bratislava	C	11
Slovenia	7,821	20,256	150	1,945,000	140	Ljubljana	C	11
Solomon Islands	11,157	28,896	139	416,000	163	Honiara	F	18
Somalia	246,201	637,657	41	11,811,000	65	Mogadishu	E	12
South Africa	471,445	1,221,037	24	44,223,000	27	Cape Town; Pretoria; Bloemfontein	G	11
Spain	195,365	505,992	50	39,752,000	29	Madrid	C	9
Sri Lanka	25,328	65,600	120	19,034,000	50	Colombo	E	14
Sudan	967,500	2,505,813	10	30,392,000	34	Khartoum	E	11
Suriname	63,037	163,265	90	437,000	159	Paramaribo	E	7
Swaziland	6,704	17,364	153	928,000	151	Mbabane	G	11
Sweden	173,732	449,964	54	8,894,000	83	Stockholm	B	10
Switzerland	15,940	41,284	132	7,374,000	90	Bern	C	10
Syria	71,498	185,180	86	16,180,000	55	Damascus	D	11
Taiwan	13,892	35,980	134	22,106,000	47	Taipei	D	16
Tajikistan	55,251	143,100	93	6,603,000	95	Dushanbe	D	14
Tanzania	341,217	883,749	32	32,211,000	32	Dar es Salaam	F	11
Thailand	198,115	513,115	49	60,626,000	18	Bangkok	F	15
Togo	21,925	56,785	123	4,527,000	111	Lomé	E	9
Tonga	288	747	170	104,000	177	Nukualofa	F	1
Trinidad and Tobago	1,981	5,130	162	1,349,000	146	Port-of-Spain	E	6
Tunisia	63,170	163,610	89	9,363,000	81	Tunis	D	10
Turkey	299,158	774,815	36	65,331,000	17	Ankara	D	11
Turkmenistan	188,456	488,100	51	4,361,000	116	Ashgabat	D	13
Tuvalu	10	26	189	10,000	191	Funafuti	F	1
Uganda	93,065	241,038	77	23,204,000	43	Kampala	E	11
Ukraine	233,090	603,700	43	51,134,000	23	Kiev	C	11
United Arab Emirates	32,278	83,600	114	2,022,000	139	Abu Dhabi	D	12
United Kingdom	94,248	244,101	76	59,056,000	20	London	C	9
United States	3,615,292	9,363,563	4	270,002,000	3	Washington, D.C.	C	4
Uruguay	68,500	177,414	88	3,239,000	127	Montevideo	G	7
Uzbekistan	172,742	447,400	55	24,320,000	40	Tashkent	D	14
Vanuatu	4,706	12,189	155	182,000	171	Port-Vila	F	18
Vatican City	0.17	0.44	192	1,000	192	—	C	10†
Venezuela	352,145	912,050	31	23,195,000	44	Caracas	E	6
Vietnam	128,066	331,689	65	79,247,000	13	Hanoi	E	15
Western Samoa	1,093	2,831	164	180,000	172	Apia	F	1
Yemen	203,850	527,968	48	15,957,000	56	Sana	E	12
Yugoslavia	39,449	102,173	106	10,755,000	72	Belgrade	C	10
Zambia	290,587	752,618	38	10,204,000	76	Lusaka	F	11
Zimbabwe	150,872	390,757	59	11,989,000	64	Harare	G	11

*Each country listed has a separate article in *World Book.*
†Populations are 1998 estimates based on the latest figures from official government and United Nations sources.
‡Not on map; key shows general location.

World, History of the

Major developments in early centers of civilization

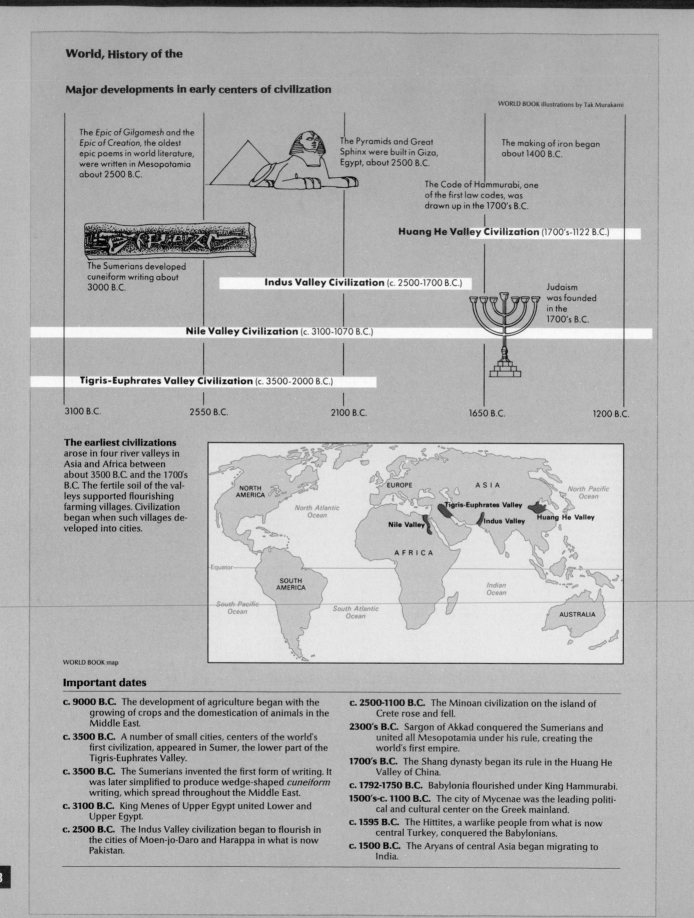

The *Epic of Gilgamesh* and the *Epic of Creation*, the oldest epic poems in world literature, were written in Mesopotamia about 2500 B.C.

The Pyramids and Great Sphinx were built in Giza, Egypt, about 2500 B.C.

The making of iron began about 1400 B.C.

The Code of Hammurabi, one of the first law codes, was drawn up in the 1700's B.C.

Huang He Valley Civilization (1700's-1122 B.C.)

The Sumerians developed cuneiform writing about 3000 B.C.

Indus Valley Civilization (c. 2500-1700 B.C.)

Judaism was founded in the 1700's B.C.

Nile Valley Civilization (c. 3100-1070 B.C.)

Tigris-Euphrates Valley Civilization (c. 3500-2000 B.C.)

3100 B.C.   2550 B.C.   2100 B.C.   1650 B.C.   1200 B.C.

The earliest civilizations arose in four river valleys in Asia and Africa between about 3500 B.C. and the 1700's B.C. The fertile soil of the valleys supported flourishing farming villages. Civilization began when such villages developed into cities.

WORLD BOOK map

Important dates

c. 9000 B.C. The development of agriculture began with the growing of crops and the domestication of animals in the Middle East.

c. 3500 B.C. A number of small cities, centers of the world's first civilization, appeared in Sumer, the lower part of the Tigris-Euphrates Valley.

c. 3500 B.C. The Sumerians invented the first form of writing. It was later simplified to produce wedge-shaped *cuneiform* writing, which spread throughout the Middle East.

c. 3100 B.C. King Menes of Upper Egypt united Lower and Upper Egypt.

c. 2500 B.C. The Indus Valley civilization began to flourish in the cities of Moen-jo-Daro and Harappa in what is now Pakistan.

c. 2500-1100 B.C. The Minoan civilization on the island of Crete rose and fell.

2300's B.C. Sargon of Akkad conquered the Sumerians and united all Mesopotamia under his rule, creating the world's first empire.

1700's B.C. The Shang dynasty began its rule in the Huang He Valley of China.

c. 1792-1750 B.C. Babylonia flourished under King Hammurabi.

1500's-c. 1100 B.C. The city of Mycenae was the leading political and cultural center on the Greek mainland.

c. 1595 B.C. The Hittites, a warlike people from what is now central Turkey, conquered the Babylonians.

c. 1500 B.C. The Aryans of central Asia began migrating to India.

Major developments from about 1200 B.C. to A.D. 500

WORLD BOOK illustrations by Tak Murakami

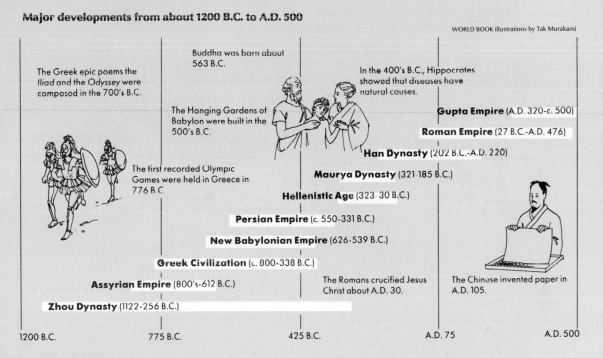

The Greek epic poems the *Iliad* and the *Odyssey* were composed in the 700's B.C.

Buddha was born about 563 B.C.

In the 400's B.C., Hippocrates showed that diseases have natural causes.

Gupta Empire (A.D. 320-c. 500)

The Hanging Gardens of Babylon were built in the 500's B.C.

Roman Empire (27 B.C.-A.D. 476)

Han Dynasty (202 B.C.-A.D. 220)

Maurya Dynasty (321-185 B.C.)

The first recorded Olympic Games were held in Greece in 776 B.C.

Hellenistic Age (323-30 B.C.)

Persian Empire (c. 550-331 B.C.)

New Babylonian Empire (626-539 B.C.)

Greek Civilization (c. 800-338 B.C.)

The Romans crucified Jesus Christ about A.D. 30.

The Chinese invented paper in A.D. 105.

Assyrian Empire (800's-612 B.C.)

Zhou Dynasty (1122-256 B.C.)

| 1200 B.C. | 775 B.C. | 425 B.C. | A.D. 75 | A.D. 500 |

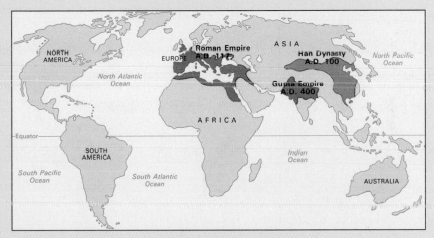

Powerful empires emerged as civilization advanced and spread between 1200 B.C. and A.D. 500. The Roman Empire covered much of Europe and the Middle East, and the north coast of Africa. The Han dynasty of China and the Gupta dynasty of India also ruled huge empires.

NORTH AMERICA · North Atlantic Ocean · EUROPE · Roman Empire A.D. 117 · ASIA · Han Dynasty A.D. 100 · North Pacific Ocean · Gupta Empire A.D. 400 · AFRICA · Equator · SOUTH AMERICA · South Pacific Ocean · South Atlantic Ocean · Indian Ocean · AUSTRALIA

WORLD BOOK map

Important dates

1020 B.C. The Hebrews founded a kingdom in what is now Palestine.

800's B.C. The Etruscans settled in west-central Italy.

750-338 B.C. Athens, Corinth, Sparta, and Thebes were the chief city-states of Greece.

c. 550 B.C. Cyrus the Great established the Persian Empire.

509 B.C. The people of Rome revolted against their Etruscan rulers and established a republic.

338 B.C. Philip II of Macedonia conquered the Greeks.

331 B.C. Alexander the Great won the Battle of Arbela, assuring his conquest of the Persian Empire.

221-206 B.C. The Qin dynasty established China's first strong central government.

202 B.C. The Han dynasty began its 400-year rule of China.

146 B.C. The Romans conquered Greece.

55-54 B.C. Julius Caesar led the Roman invasion of Britain.

27 B.C. Augustus became the first Roman emperor.

c. A.D. 250 The Maya Indians developed an advanced civilization in Central America and Mexico.

313 Constantine issued the Edict of Milan, which granted freedom of worship to Christians of the Roman Empire.

320 India began its golden age under the Gupta dynasty.

395 The Roman Empire split into the East Roman, or Byzantine, Empire and the West Roman Empire.

476 The Germanic chieftain Odoacer overthrew Romulus Augustulus, the last emperor of the West Roman Empire.

World, History of the

Major developments from A.D. 500 to about 1500

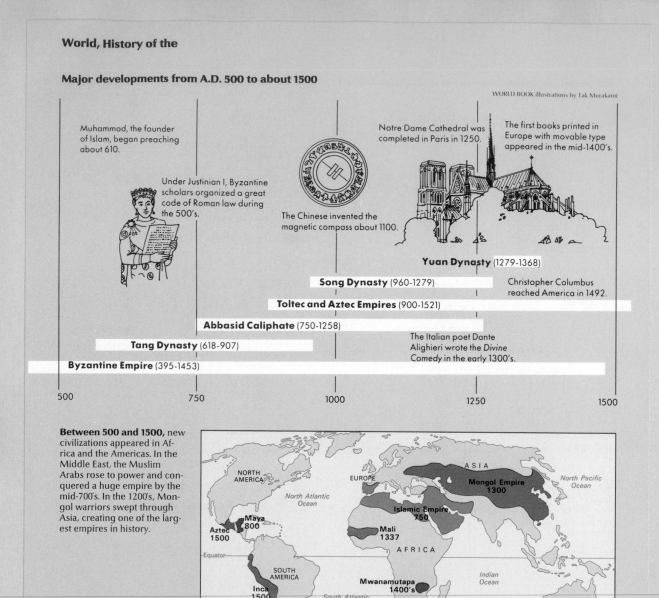

Muhammad, the founder of Islam, began preaching about 610.

Under Justinian I, Byzantine scholars organized a great code of Roman law during the 500's.

The Chinese invented the magnetic compass about 1100.

Notre Dame Cathedral was completed in Paris in 1250.

The first books printed in Europe with movable type appeared in the mid-1400's.

Yuan Dynasty (1279-1368)

Song Dynasty (960-1279)

Christopher Columbus reached America in 1492.

Toltec and Aztec Empires (900-1521)

Abbasid Caliphate (750-1258)

Tang Dynasty (618-907)

The Italian poet Dante Alighieri wrote the *Divine Comedy* in the early 1300's.

Byzantine Empire (395-1453)

500   750   1000   1250   1500

Between 500 and 1500, new civilizations appeared in Africa and the Americas. In the Middle East, the Muslim Arabs rose to power and conquered a huge empire by the mid-700's. In the 1200's, Mongol warriors swept through Asia, creating one of the largest empires in history.

ASIA
NORTH AMERICA
EUROPE
North Pacific Ocean
Mongol Empire 1300
North Atlantic Ocean
Islamic Empire 750
Maya 800
Aztec 1500
Mali 1337
Equator
AFRICA
SOUTH AMERICA
Mwanamutapa 1400's
Indian Ocean
Inca 1500
South Pacific Ocean
South Atlantic Ocean
AUSTRALIA

WORLD BOOK map

Important dates

300's-mid-1000's The Ghana Empire, the first great black empire in western Africa, existed as a trading state.

527-565 The Byzantine Empire reached its greatest extent under Emperor Justinian I.

622 Muhammad, prophet of Islam, fled from Mecca to Medina. His flight, called the Hegira, marks the beginning of the Islamic calendar.

732 Charles Martel and the Franks defeated invading Muslims in fighting in west-central France. The victory prevented the Muslims from overrunning Europe.

750 The Abbasids became the caliphs of the Islamic world.

800 Pope Leo III crowned Charlemagne, ruler of the Franks, emperor of the Romans.

988 Vladimir I converted the Russians to Christianity.

1054 Rivalries between the church in Rome and the church in Constantinople resulted in their separation as the Roman Catholic Church and Eastern Orthodox Churches, respectively.

1192 Yoritomo became the first shogun to rule Japan. Shogun rule lasted until 1867.

1215 English barons forced King John to grant a charter of liberties called Magna Carta.

1279 The Mongols gained control of all China.

1300's The Renaissance began in Italy.

1368 The Ming dynasty started its nearly 300-year rule of China.

1453 The Ottoman Turks captured Constantinople (Istanbul) and overthrew the Byzantine Empire.

Major developments

WORLD BOOK illustrations by Tak Murakami

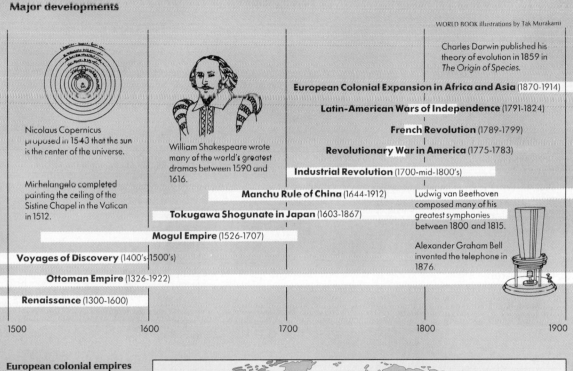

Charles Darwin published his theory of evolution in 1859 in *The Origin of Species.*

European Colonial Expansion in Africa and Asia (1870-1914)

Latin-American Wars of Independence (1791-1824)

French Revolution (1789-1799)

Revolutionary War in America (1775-1783)

Industrial Revolution (1700-mid-1800's)

Nicolaus Copernicus proposed in 1543 that the sun is the center of the universe.

William Shakespeare wrote many of the world's greatest dramas between 1590 and 1616.

Michelangelo completed painting the ceiling of the Sistine Chapel in the Vatican in 1512.

Manchu Rule of China (1644-1912)

Ludwig van Beethoven composed many of his greatest symphonies between 1800 and 1815.

Tokugawa Shogunate in Japan (1603-1867)

Mogul Empire (1526-1707)

Alexander Graham Bell invented the telephone in 1876.

Voyages of Discovery (1400's-1500's)

Ottoman Empire (1326-1922)

Renaissance (1300-1600)

| 1500 | 1600 | 1700 | 1800 | 1900 |

European colonial empires had spread over much of the world by the late 1800's. The largest empires of the period belonged to Great Britain, France, and Germany.

- Belgium
- France
- Germany
- Great Britain
- Italy
- Netherlands
- Portugal
- Spain

WORLD BOOK map

Important dates

1500's The Reformation led to the birth of Protestantism.

1519-1521 Ferdinand Magellan commanded the first globe-circling voyage, completed in 1522 after his death.

1521 The Spanish conquistador Hernando Cortés defeated the Aztec Indians of Mexico.

1526 Babar, a Muslim prince, invaded India and founded the Mogul Empire.

1588 The Royal Navy of England defeated the Spanish Armada, establishing England as a great naval power.

1644-1912 The Manchus ruled China as the Qing dynasty.

1776 The 13 American Colonies adopted the Declaration of Independence, establishing the United States of America.

1789 The French Revolution began.

1815 Napoleon Bonaparte was defeated in the Battle of Waterloo, ending his attempt to rule Europe.

1853-1854 Commodore Matthew Perry visited Japan and opened two ports to U.S. trade, ending Japan's isolation.

1858 Great Britain took over the rule of India from the East India Company after the Sepoy Rebellion.

1865 Union forces defeated the Confederates in the American Civil War after four years of fighting.

1869 The Suez Canal opened.

1871 Germany became united under the Prussian king, who ruled the new empire as Kaiser Wilhelm I.

1898 The United States took control of Guam, Puerto Rico, and the Philippines following the Spanish-American War.

WORLD: *Political*

ABBREVIATIONS

BOS. AND HERZ.
　　Bosnia and Herzegovina
CEN. AFR. REP.
　　Central African Republic
DEN. Denmark
FR. France
F.Y.R. MACE.
　　Former Yugoslav
　　Republic of Macedonia
GR. Greece
IT. Italy
N. North, Northern
NETH. Netherlands
N.Z. New Zealand
PORT. Portugal
S. South
SP. Spain
U.A.E. United Arab
　　Emirates
U.K. United Kingdom
U.S. United States
W. Western

——— National boundary

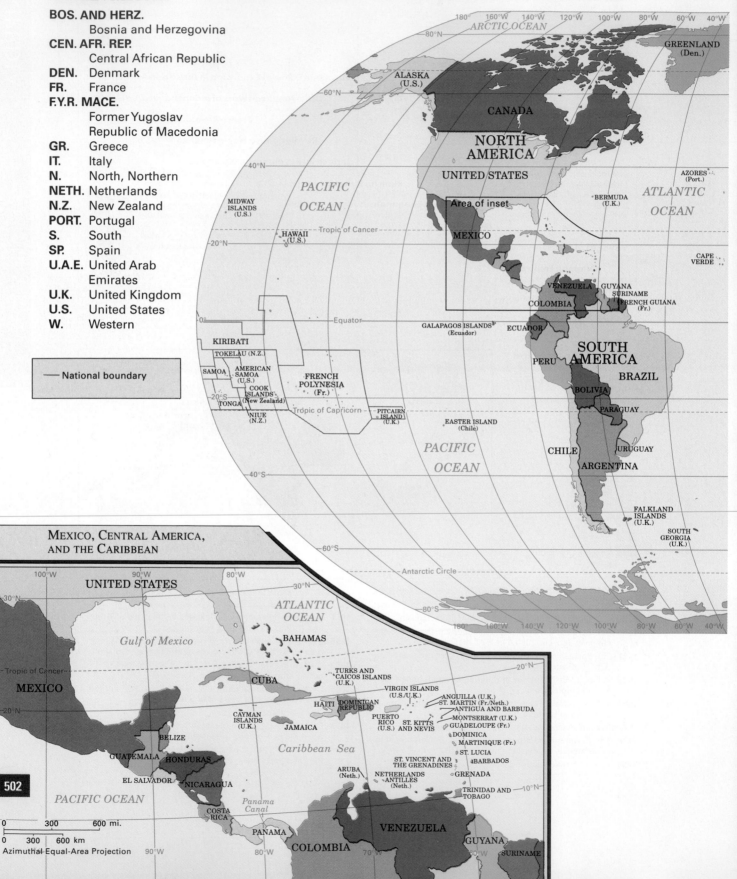

MEXICO, CENTRAL AMERICA, AND THE CARIBBEAN

Azimuthal Equal-Area Projection

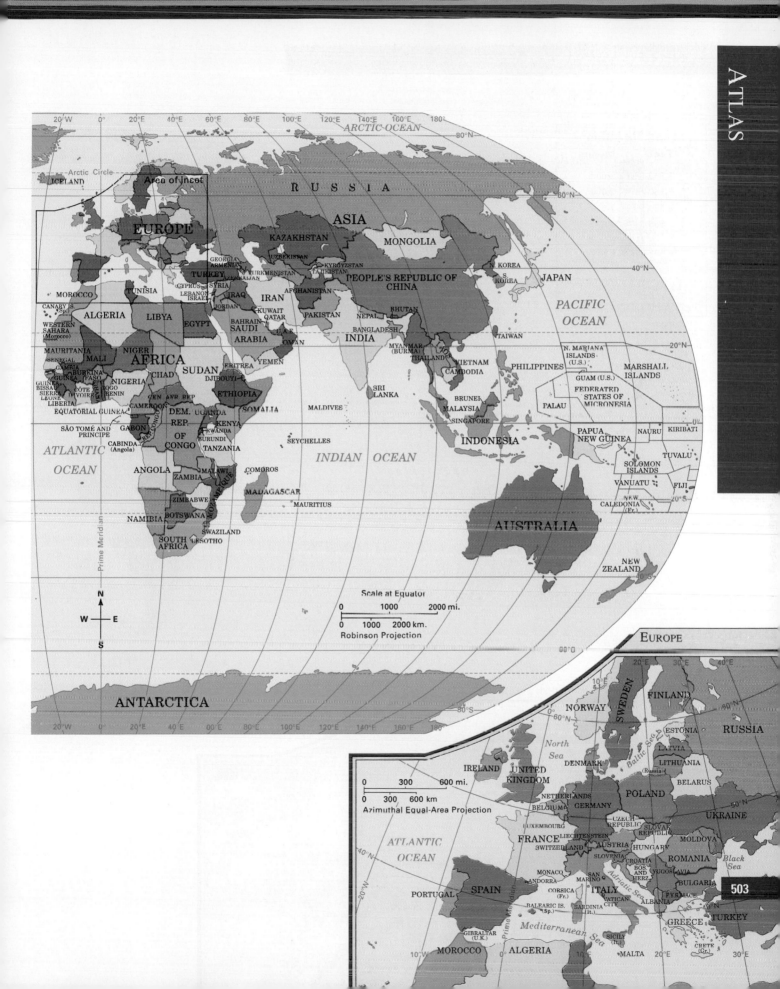

ARCTIC OCEAN

80°N

ICELAND

Arctic Circle

Area of Inset

RUSSIA

60°N

EUROPE

ASIA

KAZAKHSTAN

MONGOLIA

GEORGIA
ARMENIA
UZBEKISTAN
TURKMENISTAN
KYRGYZSTAN
TAJIKISTAN

40°N

TURKEY
AZERBAIJAN
CYPRUS SYRIA
LEBANON
ISRAEL
JORDAN
IRAQ

N. KOREA
S. KOREA

JAPAN

PEOPLE'S REPUBLIC OF
CHINA

MOROCCO

TUNISIA

IRAN

AFGHANISTAN

CANARY IS.
(Sp.)

ALGERIA

LIBYA

EGYPT

PAKISTAN

NEPAL BHUTAN

PACIFIC
OCEAN

BAHRAIN
QATAR

BANGLADESH

20°N

WESTERN
SAHARA
(Morocco)

SAUDI
ARABIA

U.A.E.

INDIA

TAIWAN

MAURITANIA

MALI

NIGER

OMAN

MYANMAR
(BURMA)
THAILAND

N. MARIANA
ISLANDS
(U.S.)

SENEGAL
GAMBIA
GUINEA
BISSAU
GUINEA
SIERRA
LEONE
LIBERIA
CÔTE
D'IVOIRE

AFRICA

BURKINA
FASO

NIGERIA

CHAD

YEMEN

SUDAN

DJIBOUTI

ERITREA

VIETNAM
CAMBODIA

PHILIPPINES

GUAM (U.S.)

MARSHALL
ISLANDS

FEDERATED
STATES OF
MICRONESIA

TOGO
BENIN

CEN. AFR. REP.

ETHIOPIA

SRI
LANKA

MALDIVES

PALAU

0°

EQUATORIAL GUINEA

CAMEROON

SÃO TOMÉ AND
PRINCIPE

GABON

DEM.
REP.
OF
CONGO

UGANDA
RWANDA
BURUNDI

SOMALIA

KENYA

BRUNEI

MALAYSIA

SINGAPORE

PAPUA
NEW GUINEA

NAURU KIRIBATI

ATLANTIC

OCEAN

CABINDA
(Angola)

CONGO

TANZANIA

SEYCHELLES

INDONESIA

INDIAN OCEAN

TUVALU

ANGOLA

MALAWI

ZAMBIA

COMOROS

SOLOMON
ISLANDS

ZIMBABWE

MOZAMBIQUE

MADAGASCAR

MAURITIUS

VANUATU

FIJI

20°S

NAMIBIA

BOTSWANA

NEW
CALEDONIA
(Fr.)

SOUTH
AFRICA

SWAZILAND

LESOTHO

AUSTRALIA

N

W   E

S

Scale at Equator

0   1000   2000 mi.

0   1000   2000 km.

Robinson Projection

NEW
ZEALAND

80°S

ANTARCTICA

20°W   0°   20°E   40°E   60°E   80°E   100°E   120°E   140°E   160°E   180°

SWEDEN

FINLAND

NORWAY

ESTONIA

RUSSIA

60°N

North
Sea

Baltic Sea
(Russia)

LATVIA

LITHUANIA

IRELAND

UNITED
KINGDOM

DENMARK

BELARUS

0   300   600 mi.

NETHERLANDS

POLAND

0   300   600 km

Azimuthal Equal-Area Projection

BELGIUM

GERMANY

50°N

UKRAINE

LUXEMBOURG

CZECH
REPUBLIC

SLOVAK
REPUBLIC

FRANCE

LIECHTENSTEIN

AUSTRIA

HUNGARY

MOLDOVA

SWITZERLAND

SLOVENIA

CROATIA

ROMANIA

ATLANTIC

OCEAN

MONACO

BOS.
AND
HERZ.

YUGOSLAVIA

Black
Sea

40°N

SAN
MARINO

BULGARIA

ANDORRA

ITALY

F.Y.R. MACE.

PORTUGAL

SPAIN

CORSICA
(Fr.)

VATICAN
CITY

ALBANIA

503

BALEARIC IS.
(Sp.)

SARDINIA
(It.)

GREECE

TURKEY

GIBRALTAR
(U.K.)

Mediterranean Sea

SICILY
(It.)

CRETE
(Gr.)

MOROCCO

ALGERIA

MALTA   20°E   30°E

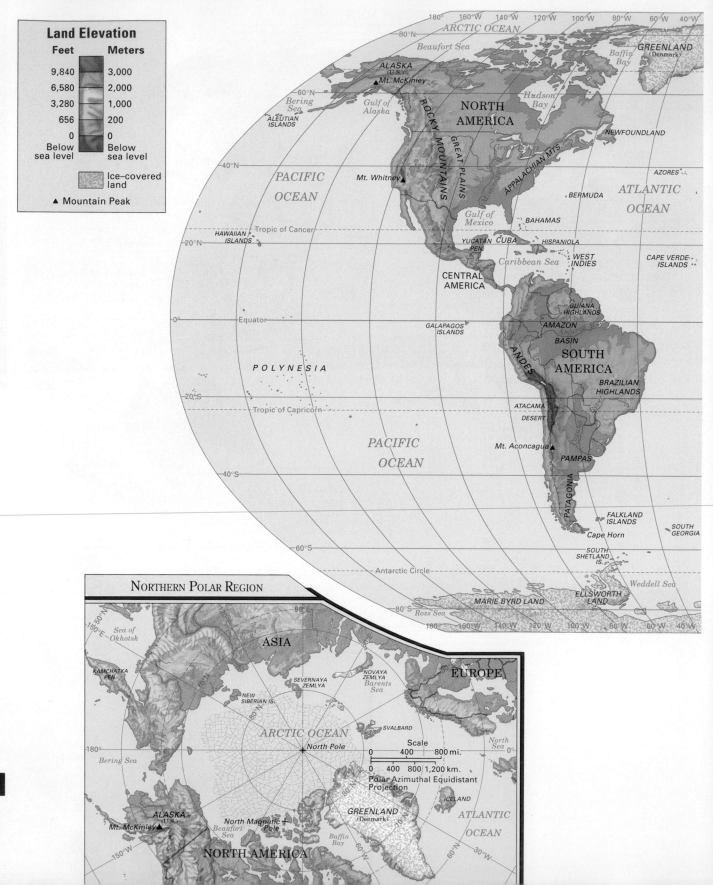

Land Elevation

Feet	Meters
9,840	3,000
6,580	2,000
3,280	1,000
656	200
0	0
Below sea level	Below sea level

Ice–covered land

▲ Mountain Peak

ARCTIC OCEAN
Beaufort Sea
GREENLAND (Denmark)
Baffin Bay
ALASKA (U.S.)
▲ Mt. McKinley
Bering Sea
Gulf of Alaska
NORTH AMERICA
Hudson Bay
NEWFOUNDLAND
ROCKY MOUNTAINS
GREAT PLAINS
APPALACHIAN MTS.
AZORES
ATLANTIC OCEAN
ALEUTIAN ISLANDS
PACIFIC OCEAN
Mt. Whitney ▲
BERMUDA
Gulf of Mexico
BAHAMAS
Tropic of Cancer
HAWAIIAN ISLANDS
YUCATAN PEN.
CUBA
HISPANIOLA
WEST INDIES
CAPE VERDE ISLANDS
Caribbean Sea
CENTRAL AMERICA
GUIANA HIGHLANDS
Equator
GALAPAGOS ISLANDS
AMAZON BASIN
SOUTH AMERICA
P O L Y N E S I A
ANDES
BRAZILIAN HIGHLANDS
Tropic of Capricorn
ATACAMA DESERT
PACIFIC OCEAN
Mt. Aconcagua ▲
PAMPAS
PATAGONIA
FALKLAND ISLANDS
SOUTH GEORGIA
Cape Horn
SOUTH SHETLAND IS.
Antarctic Circle
Weddell Sea
MARIE BYRD LAND
ELLSWORTH LAND
Ross Sea

NORTHERN POLAR REGION

Sea of Okhotsk
ASIA
KAMCHATKA PEN.
SEVERNAYA ZEMLYA
NOVAYA ZEMLYA
Barents Sea
EUROPE
NEW SIBERIAN IS.
SVALBARD
North Sea
ARCTIC OCEAN
North Pole
Scale
0   400   800 mi.
0   400   800 1,200 km.
Polar Azimuthal Equidistant Projection
Bering Sea
ALASKA (U.S.)
▲ Mt. McKinley
North Magnetic Pole
Beaufort Sea
GREENLAND (Denmark)
ICELAND
ATLANTIC OCEAN
Baffin Bay
NORTH AMERICA

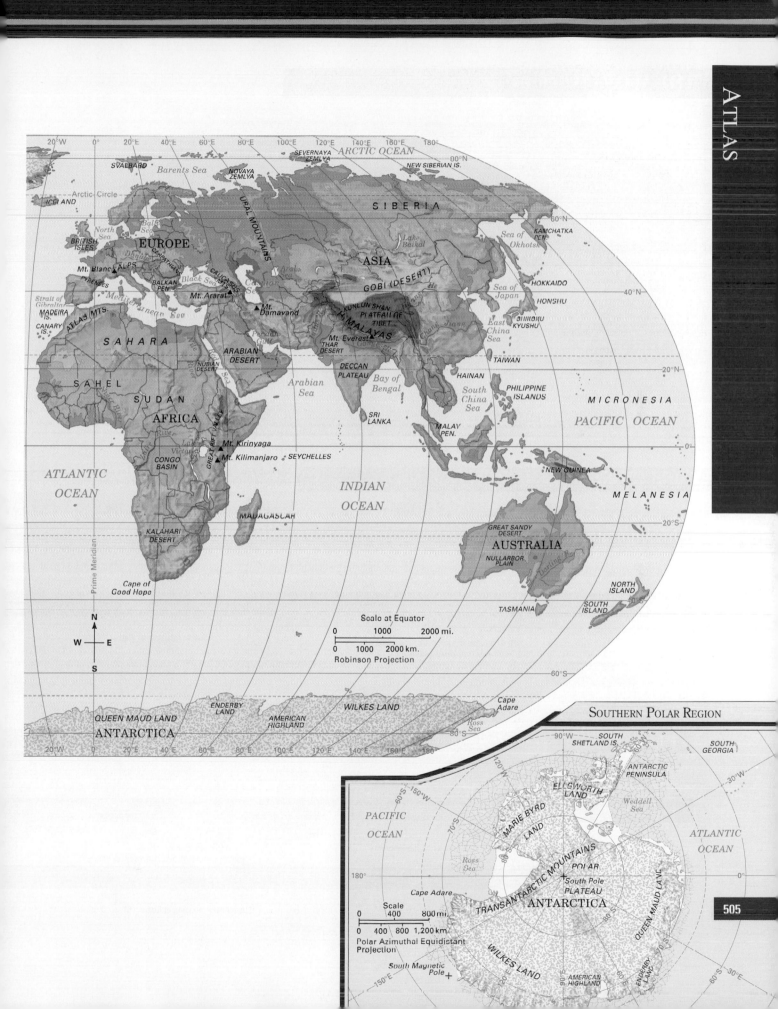

20°W 0° 20°E 40°E 60°E 80°E 100°E 120°E 140°E 160°E 180°

SVALBARD
Barents Sea
SEVERNAYA ZEMLYA
ARCTIC OCEAN
NEW SIBERIAN IS.
NOVAYA ZEMLYA
80°N
Arctic Circle
ICELAND
SIBERIA
60°N
North Sea
Baltic Sea
KAMCHATKA PEN.
BRITISH ISLES
EUROPE
Sea of Okhotsk
ASIA
Lake Baikal
Mt. Blanc ALPS
Carpathians
URAL MOUNTAINS
Aral Sea
HOKKAIDO
40°N
PYRENEES
BALKAN PEN.
Black Sea
CAUCASUS
Caspian Sea
GOBI (DESERT)
He
Sea of Japan
HONSHU
Strait of Gibraltar
Mt. Ararat
Mt. Damavand
KUNLUN SHAN
PLATEAU OF TIBET
SHIKOKU KYUSHU
East China Sea
Mediterranean Sea
MADEIRA IS.
ATLAS MTS.
Persian Gulf
HIMALAYAS
Mt. Everest
Chang Jiang
CANARY IS.
SAHARA
Nile
NUBIAN DESERT
ARABIAN DESERT
THAR DESERT
Ganges
TAIWAN
20°N
SAHEL
DECCAN PLATEAU
HAINAN
SUDAN
Arabian Sea
Bay of Bengal
PHILIPPINE ISLANDS
South China Sea
MICRONESIA
AFRICA
Niger River
SRI LANKA
MALAY PEN.
PACIFIC OCEAN
Mt. Kirinyaga
SEYCHELLES
0°
ATLANTIC OCEAN
Lake Victoria
GREAT RIFT VALLEY
Mt. Kilimanjaro
NEW GUINEA
CONGO BASIN
INDIAN OCEAN
MELANESIA
Zambezi River
MADAGASCAR
GREAT SANDY DESERT
20°S
KALAHARI DESERT
Prime Meridian
AUSTRALIA
NULLARBOR PLAIN
Darling
NORTH ISLAND
Cape of Good Hope
TASMANIA
SOUTH ISLAND

N
W   E
S

Scale at Equator
0   1000   2000 mi.
0   1000   2000 km.
Robinson Projection
60°S

QUEEN MAUD LAND
ENDERBY LAND
AMERICAN HIGHLAND
WILKES LAND
Cape Adare
Ross Sea
ANTARCTICA
80°S
20°W 0° 20°E 40°E 60°E 80°E 100°E 120°E 140°E 160°E 180°

Southern Polar Region

90°W
SOUTH SHETLAND IS.
60°W
SOUTH GEORGIA
PACIFIC OCEAN
ANTARCTIC PENINSULA
ELLSWORTH LAND
30°W
120°W
MARIE BYRD LAND
Weddell Sea
60°S
150°W
70°S
ATLANTIC OCEAN
Ross Sea
80°S
TRANSANTARCTIC MOUNTAINS
South Pole
POLAR PLATEAU
ANTARCTICA
0°
180°
Cape Adare
QUEEN MAUD LAND
Scale
0   400   800 mi.
0   400   800   1,200 km.
Polar Azimuthal Equidistant Projection
WILKES LAND
70°S
AMERICAN HIGHLAND
ENDERBY LAND
60°S
30°E
150°E
South Magnetic Pole
90°E

505

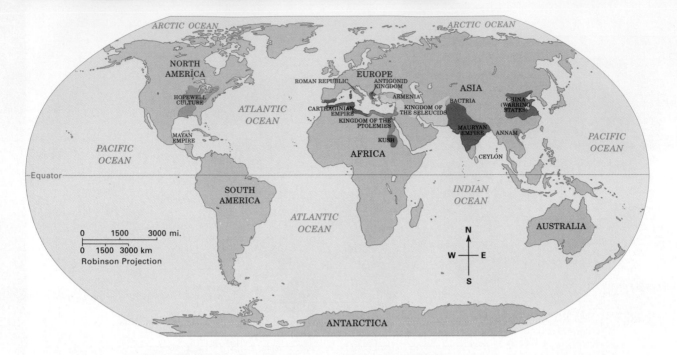

ARCTIC OCEAN · ARCTIC OCEAN

NORTH AMERICA

EUROPE
ROMAN REPUBLIC · ANTIGONID KINGDOM
ARMENIA
ASIA
BACTRIA
CHINA (WARRING STATES)

HOPEWELL CULTURE

ATLANTIC OCEAN

CARTHAGINIAN EMPIRE
KINGDOM OF THE SELEUCIDS
KINGDOM OF THE PTOLEMIES
MAURYAN EMPIRE
ANNAM

MAYAN EMPIRE

PACIFIC OCEAN

KUSH

AFRICA

CEYLON

PACIFIC OCEAN

Equator

SOUTH AMERICA

ATLANTIC OCEAN

INDIAN OCEAN

AUSTRALIA

0 1500 3000 mi.
0 1500 3000 km
Robinson Projection

N
W · E
S

ANTARCTICA

World Civilizations: 1500 B.C. – A.D. 500

The map above shows the world at 250 B.C. The timeline indicates major civilizations during, before, and after this time period.

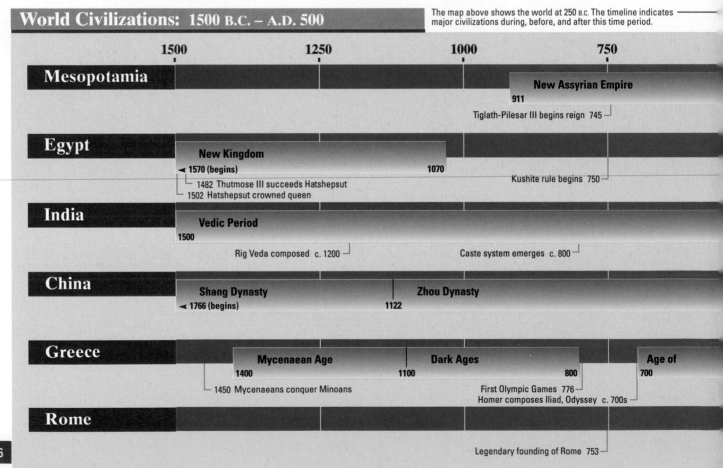

	1500	1250	1000	750
Mesopotamia				**New Assyrian Empire** 911 · Tiglath-Pilesar III begins reign 745
Egypt	**New Kingdom** 1570 (begins) · 1482 Thutmose III succeeds Hatshepsut · 1502 Hatshepsut crowned queen		1070 · Kushite rule begins 750	
India	**Vedic Period** 1500 · Rig Veda composed c. 1200		Caste system emerges c. 800	
China	**Shang Dynasty** 1766 (begins)	**Zhou Dynasty** 1122		
Greece	**Mycenaean Age** 1400 · 1450 Mycenaeans conquer Minoans	**Dark Ages** 1100	800 · First Olympic Games 776 · Homer composes Iliad, Odyssey c. 700s	**Age of** 700
Rome			Legendary founding of Rome 753	

THE WORLD: *A.D. 117*

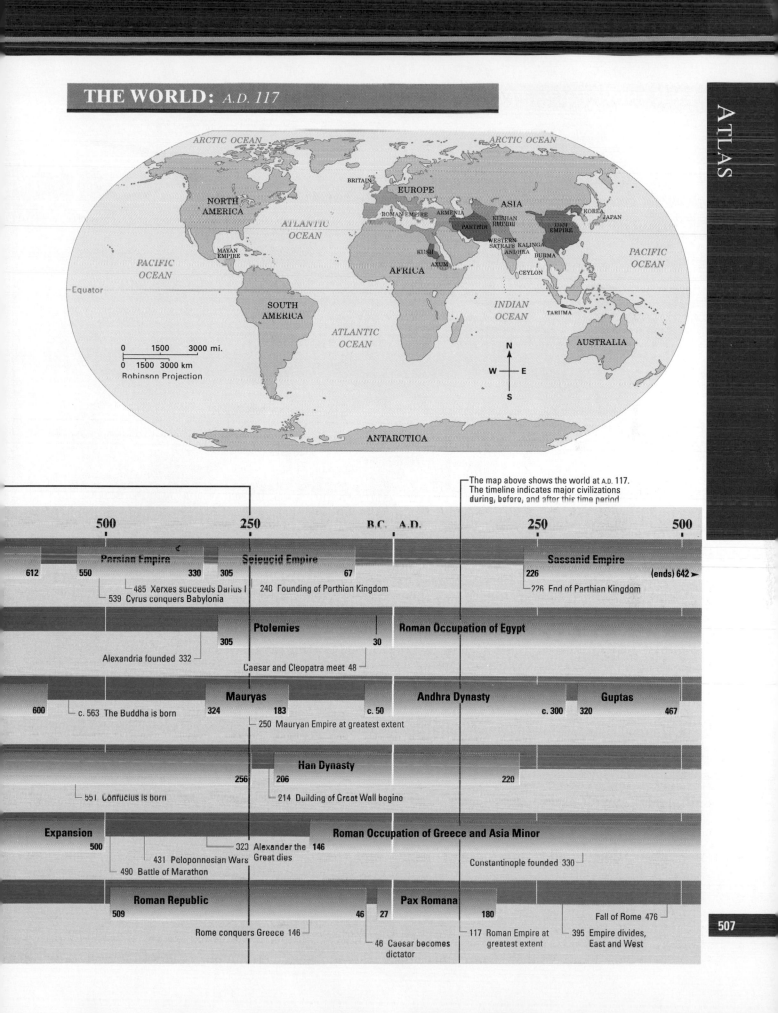

The map above shows the world at A.D. 117. The timeline indicates major civilizations during, before, and after this time period.

500	250	B.C.	A.D.	250	500

Persian Empire   **Seleucid Empire**   **Sassanid Empire**

612   550   330   305   67   226   (ends) 642 ►

485 Xerxes succeeds Darius I   240 Founding of Parthian Kingdom   226 End of Parthian Kingdom
539 Cyrus conquers Babylonia

Ptolemies   **Roman Occupation of Egypt**

305   30

Alexandria founded 332
Caesar and Cleopatra meet 48

Mauryas   **Andhra Dynasty**   **Guptas**

600   324   183   c. 50   c. 300   320   467

c. 563 The Buddha is born
250 Mauryan Empire at greatest extent

Han Dynasty

256   206   220

551 Confucius is born
214 Building of Great Wall begins

Expansion   **Roman Occupation of Greece and Asia Minor**

500   323   Alexander the   146
431 Peloponnesian Wars   Great dies
490 Battle of Marathon   Constantinople founded 330

Roman Republic   **Pax Romana**

509   46   27   180   Fall of Rome 476

Rome conquers Greece 146   117 Roman Empire at   395 Empire divides,
46 Caesar becomes   greatest extent   East and West
dictator

507

90°W   75°W   60°W   45°W   30°W   15°W   0°   15°E   30°E   45°E   60°E   75°E

SVALBARD (Norway)

FRANZ JOSEF LAND

NORTH AMERICA

Barents Sea

Norwegian Sea

NOVAYA ZEMLYA

75°N
45°W

Arctic Circle
30°W

Reykjavik ICELAND

Murmansk

R U S S I A

White Sea

Trondheim
NORWAY

SWEDEN

FINLAND

Helsinki

Oslo Stockholm

Lake Ladoga

St. Petersburg

Ob River

ATLANTIC OCEAN

60°N

Edinburgh

North Sea

Copenhagen
DENMARK

Tallinn
ESTONIA

Riga LATVIA

LITHUANIA

Moscow

Volga River

Samara

Novosibirsk

URAL MOUNTAINS

Irtysh River

Dublin
IRELAND

UNITED KINGDOM

Amsterdam
The Hague NETH.

Gdansk

(Russia)

Vilnius

Minsk
BELARUS

Astana

London BELG.
Brussels

Berlin
GERMANY

POLAND

Warsaw

Kiev
UKRAINE

Kharkiv

Volgograd

KIRGHIZ STEPPE

Lake Balkhash

Bonn
LUX.
Prague
CZECH REP.

Vistula R.

Dnieper River

MOLDOVA

KAZAKHSTAN

15°W

Paris
FRANCE

Rhine River
Loire R.

LIECH.
Bern SWITZ.
ALPS
AUST.

Vienna
SLOVAK REP.
Bratislava
HUNG.

Budapest
ROMANIA

CARPATHIANS
Chisinau

Dniester R.

Don River

Sea of Azov

Aral Sea

Almaty

45°N

Sea of Biscay

MONACO
SAN MARINO

Venice
CRO.
Zagreb

YUGO.
Belgrade

SLV.
BOS.

Sarajevo

Danube R.

Bucharest

BULGARIA

Sofia

Black Sea

GEORGIA
Tbilisi

CAUCASUS MTS.

Caspian Sea

UZBEKISTAN

Tashkent

Bishkek

KYRGYZSTAN

PAMIRS

ANDORRA
CORSICA (Fr.)

APENNINES

Rome
ITALY

Skopje
Tirane
ALB.

MAC.

Istanbul

Ankara

ARMENIA
Yerevan

AZERBAIJAN

Baku

TURKMENISTAN

Dushanbe

TAJIKISTAN

HINDU KUSH

KUNLUN

PORTUGAL
Lisbon

Barcelona
Madrid

SPAIN

PYRENEES

SARDINIA (Italy)

Tyrrhenian Sea

GREECE

Athens

ASIA MINOR

TURKEY

KURDISTAN

ELBURZ MTS.

Ashgabat

ZAGROS

Kabul

AFGHANISTAN

Islamabad

HIMALAYAS

BALEARIC ISLANDS (Sp.)

SICILY (Italy)

MALTA

Ionian Sea

Aegean Sea

Nicosia
CYPRUS

SYRIA

Euphrates R.

Tehran

PLATEAU OF IRAN

NEPAL

Mediterranean Sea

LEBANON
Beirut
Damascus

Baghdad

IRAN

Indus River

New Delhi

Kathmandu

30°N

Jerusalem
ISRAEL Amman
JORDAN

IRAQ

PAKISTAN

THAR DESERT

Ganges R.

INDIA

Kuwait
KUWAIT

MOUNTAINS

Persian Gulf

OMAN

Karachi

Tropic of Cancer

BAHRAIN

Riyadh

QATAR

Abu Dhabi
U.A.E.

Muscat

DECCAN PLATEAU

Red Sea

SAUDI ARABIA

Mecca

RUB AL KHALI (DESERT)

OMAN

Mumbai (Bombay)

Arabian Sea

WESTERN GHATS

EASTERN GHATS

15°N

AFRICA

Sanaa
YEMEN

Aden

SOCOTRA (Yemen)

Gulf of Aden

Channai (Madras)

LACCADIVE ISLANDS (India)

SRI LANKA

Colombo

Prime Meridian

0°

Equator

Male

MALDIVES

INDIAN OCEAN

15°S

0°   15°E   30°E   45°E   60°E   75°E

⊛ National capital

• Major city

— National boundary

N
W E
S

0   400   800 mi.

0   400   800 km.

Robinson Projection

ARCTIC OCEAN

75°N

NORTH
AMERICA

SIBERIA

60°N

Bering Sea

Iona   *River*

STANOVOI RANGE

Sea of
Okhotsk

SAKHALIN

Irkutsk

Lake
Baikal

Amur   *River*

DA HINGGAN LING

KURIL ISLANDS

180°

45°N

ALTAI MTS.

Ulaanbaatar

MONGOLIA

Harbin

Vladivostok

Sapporo

GOBI (DESERT)

Beijing

N. KOREA
Pyongyang

Sea of
Japan

JAPAN

SHAN

Huang He

Seoul
S. KOREA

Tokyo

Osaka

PLATEAU
OF
TIBET

PEOPLE'S REPUBLIC
OF CHINA

Yellow
Sea

30°N

Brahmaputra

Jinsha

Shanghai

Thimphu
BHUTAN

East
China
Sea

PACIFIC

BANGLADESH
Dhaka

Taipei
TAIWAN

OCEAN

Calcutta

MYANMAR
(BURMA)

LAOS

Guangzhou

MACAO
(Port.)

HONG
KONG

Mekong

Hanoi

15°N

Vientiane

HAINAN

Gulf
of
Tonkin

Philippine

Bay of
Bengal

Yangon
(Rangoon)

THAILAND

Da Nang

Sea

ANDAMAN
ISLANDS
(India)

Bangkok

CAMBODIA

VIETNAM

Manila

PHILIPPINES

NICOBAR
ISLANDS
(India)

Phnom
Penh

Ho Chi Minh City
(Saigon)

South China
Sea

Bandar Seri
Begawan

BRUNEI

MALAYSIA

Kuala Lumpur

MALAYSIA

Singapore
SINGAPORE

BORNEO

0°

SUMATRA

CELEBES

INDONESIA

NEW GUINEA

Java Sea

Jakarta

JAVA

Arafura Sea

15°S

Timor
Sea

AUSTRALIA

90°E   105°E   120°E   135°E   150°E   165°E

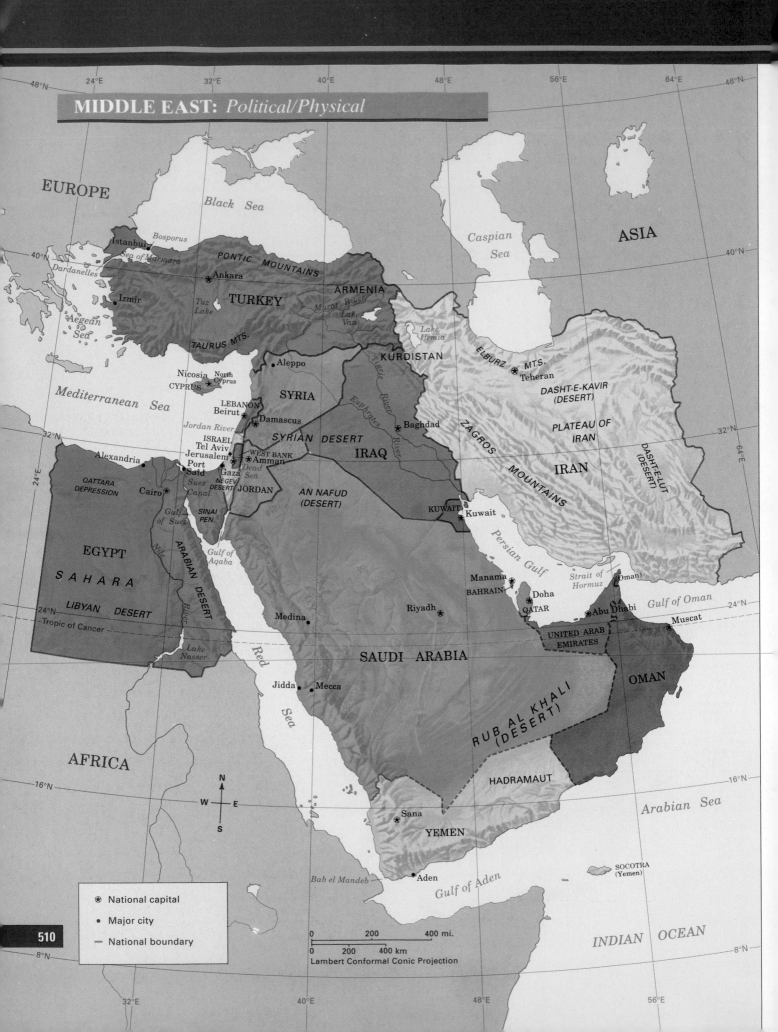

EUROPE

ASIA

Black Sea

Caspian Sea

Istanbul
Bosporus
Sea of Marmara
Dardanelles
PONTIC MOUNTAINS
⊛ Ankara
ARMENIA
Murat River
Izmir
Tuz Lake
TURKEY
Lake Van
Aegean Sea
TAURUS MTS.
ELBURZ MTS.
⊛ Teheran
KURDISTAN
Lake Urmia
DASHT-E-KAVIR (DESERT)
• Aleppo
Nicosia North
CYPRUS Cyprus ⊛
SYRIA
Tigris River
PLATEAU OF IRAN
Mediterranean Sea
LEBANON
Beirut ⊛
Damascus
Euphrates River
⊛ Baghdad
ZAGROS MOUNTAINS
DASHT-E-LUT (DESERT)
Jordan River
SYRIAN DESERT
ISRAEL
Tel Aviv
Jerusalem
WEST BANK
⊛ Amman
IRAQ
IRAN
Alexandria •
Port Said
Gaza
Dead Sea
QATTARA DEPRESSION
Cairo ⊛
Suez Canal
NEGEV DESERT
JORDAN
AN NAFUD (DESERT)
KUWAIT
⊛ Kuwait
Gulf of Suez
SINAI PEN.
ARABIAN DESERT
EGYPT
SAHARA
Nile River
Gulf of Aqaba
Manama ⊛
BAHRAIN
Doha
QATAR
Persian Gulf
Strait of Hormuz
⊛ (Oman)
Gulf of Oman
LIBYAN DESERT
Riyadh •
⊛ Abu Dhabi
Muscat ⊛
Tropic of Cancer
Lake Nasser
Medina •
UNITED ARAB EMIRATES
SAUDI ARABIA
OMAN
Red Sea
Jidda • • Mecca
AFRICA
RUB AL KHALI (DESERT)
HADRAMAUT
Arabian Sea
Sana ⊛
YEMEN
SOCOTRA (Yemen)
Bab el Mandeb
• Aden
Gulf of Aden

INDIAN OCEAN

Legend
⊛ National capital
• Major city
— National boundary

0   200   400 mi.
0   200   400 km
Lambert Conformal Conic Projection

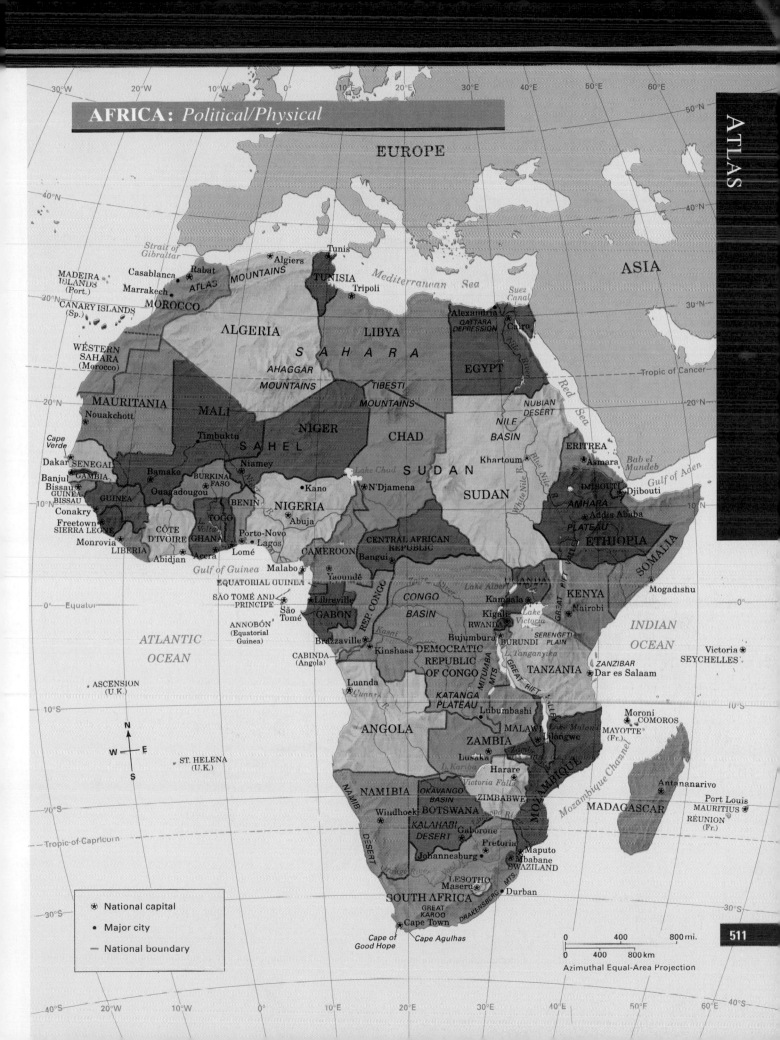

AFRICA: *Political/Physical*

EUROPE

ASIA

Mediterranean Sea

Strait of Gibraltar

Suez Canal

MADEIRA ISLANDS (Port.)

Casablanca • Rabat ✳
Marrakech •
ATLAS MOUNTAINS

CANARY ISLANDS (Sp.)

MOROCCO

Tunis ✳
TUNISIA
Tripoli ✳

Algiers ✳

Alexandria •
QATTARA DEPRESSION
Cairo ✳

WESTERN SAHARA (Morocco)

ALGERIA

LIBYA

EGYPT

S A H A R A

AHAGGAR MOUNTAINS

Tropic of Cancer

Red Sea

MAURITANIA

TIBESTI MOUNTAINS

Nouakchott ✳

MALI

NIGER

CHAD

NUBIAN DESERT

NILE BASIN

ERITREA
Asmara ✳
Bab el Mandeb

Gulf of Aden

Cape Verde

Timbuktu •
SAHEL

Khartoum ✳

Dakar ✳ SENEGAL
Banjul ✳ GAMBIA
Bissau ✳ GUINEA-BISSAU
GUINEA
Conakry ✳
Freetown ✳ SIERRA LEONE
Monrovia ✳ LIBERIA

Niamey ✳
Bamako ✳ BURKINA FASO
Ouagadougou ✳
BENIN

N'Djamena ✳

SUDAN

DJIBOUTI ✳ Djibouti

AMHARA
Addis Ababa ✳
PLATEAU

ETHIOPIA

SOMALIA

Kano •

SUDAN

NIGERIA
Abuja ✳
CÔTE D'IVOIRE
L. Volta
GHANA
TOGO
Porto-Novo ✳
Lomé ✳ Lagos •
Abidjan • Accra ✳

CAMEROON
Bangui ✳

CENTRAL AFRICAN REPUBLIC

Gulf of Guinea
Malabo ✳
EQUATORIAL GUINEA
Yaoundé ✳

Lake Albert
UGANDA
Kampala ✳
KENYA
Nairobi •

Mogadishu ✳

SÃO TOMÉ AND PRINCIPE
São Tomé ✳
Libreville ✳
REP. CONGO
GABON

CONGO BASIN

Kigali ✳
RWANDA
Lake Victoria
Bujumbura ✳ BURUNDI
SERENGETI PLAIN

INDIAN OCEAN

Victoria ✳
SEYCHELLES

Equator

ATLANTIC OCEAN

ANNOBÓN (Equatorial Guinea)

Brazzaville ✳
Kinshasa ✳
CABINDA (Angola)

Kasai R.

DEMOCRATIC REPUBLIC OF CONGO

L. Tanganyika
MITUMBA MTS.

TANZANIA
Dar es Salaam •
ZANZIBAR

ASCENSION (U.K.)

Luanda ✳
Cuanza R.

KATANGA PLATEAU

GREAT RIFT VALLEY

Lubumbashi •

Moroni ✳
COMOROS
MAYOTTE (Fr.)

ST. HELENA (U.K.)

ANGOLA

MALAWI
Lilongwe ✳
Lake Malawi

ZAMBIA
Lusaka ✳
L. Kariba
Harare ✳
Zambezi R.
Victoria Falls

Mozambique Channel

Antananarivo ✳

NAMIBIA
OKAVANGO BASIN
Windhoek ✳
BOTSWANA
ZIMBABWE

MOZAMBIQUE

MADAGASCAR

Port Louis ✳
MAURITIUS
RÉUNION (Fr.)

NAMIB DESERT

KALAHARI DESERT
Gaborone ✳
Pretoria ✳

Limpopo R.

Maputo ✳
Mbabane ✳ SWAZILAND

Tropic of Capricorn

Johannesburg •
Orange River
Vaal R.

LESOTHO
Maseru ✳
Durban •

SOUTH AFRICA
GREAT KAROO
DRAKENSBERG MTS.

Cape Town ✳
Cape of Good Hope   Cape Agulhas

N W E S

Legend:

- ✳ National capital
- • Major city
- — National boundary

0   400   800 mi.
0   400   800 km

Azimuthal Equal-Area Projection

511

NORTH AMERICA: *Political/Physical*

EUROPE

ASIA

ARCTIC OCEAN

Bering Sea

Bering Strait

BROOKS RANGE

Beaufort Sea

QUEEN ELIZABETH ISLANDS

ELLESMERE ISLAND

GREENLAND (Denmark)

Yukon River

ALASKA RANGE

Fairbanks

BANKS ISLAND

Baffin Bay

Anchorage

Gulf of Alaska

VICTORIA ISLAND

BAFFIN ISLAND

KODIAK ISLAND

ALEXANDER ARCHIPELAGO

Mackenzie River

Great Bear Lake

Labrador Sea

QUEEN CHARLOTTE ISLANDS

COAST MOUNTAINS

Great Slave Lake

UNGAVA PENINSULA

LAURENTIAN SHIELD

LABRADOR

VANCOUVER ISLAND

Edmonton

CANADA

Lake Winnipeg

NEWFOUNDLAND

Vancouver

Puget Sound

Calgary

PRINCE EDWARD ISLAND

CAPE BRETON ISLAND

Seattle

ROCKY MOUNTAINS

Winnipeg

L. Superior

Quebec

Portland

Montreal

Ottawa

Bay of Fundy

BLACK HILLS

Minneapolis

Lake Huron

Toronto

Boston

Cape Cod

SIERRA NEVADA

COAST RANGES

Great Salt Lake

Salt Lake City

Milwaukee

Chicago

Lake Michigan

L. Ontario

Lake Erie

New York

ATLANTIC OCEAN

San Francisco

Snake R.

Omaha

Detroit

Cleveland

Philadelphia

Denver

Indianapolis

APPALACHIAN MTS.

Baltimore

Washington

Colorado River

Kansas City

St. Louis

Ohio River

Louisville

Los Angeles

MOJAVE DESERT

GRAND CANYON

UNITED STATES

Nashville

Charlotte

Cape Hatteras

BERMUDA (U.K.)

San Diego

Phoenix

Red River

Atlanta

Birmingham

Fort Worth

Mississippi River

Jacksonville

Ciudad Juárez

Rio Grande

Austin

Houston

New Orleans

Cape Canaveral

Tropic of Cancer

Chihuahua

San Antonio

BAJA CALIFORNIA

Gulf of California

Miami

Nassau

BAHAMAS

PACIFIC OCEAN

Cabo San Lucas

Monterrey

SIERRA MADRE ORIENTAL

Gulf of Mexico

Havana

CUBA

San Juan

VIRGIN ISLANDS (U.S., U.K.)

MEXICO

Guadalajara

SIERRA MADRE OCCIDENTAL

PLATEAU OF MEXICO

Santiago de Cuba

DOMINICAN REPUBLIC

PUERTO RICO (U.S.)

ANGUILLA (U.K.)

ANTIGUA AND BARBUDA

ST. KITTS AND NEVIS

GUADELOUPE (Fr.)

Mexico City

Veracruz

YUCATÁN PENINSULA

CAYMAN ISLANDS (U.K.)

Port-au-Prince

HAITI

Santo Domingo

Roseau

DOMINICA

MARTINIQUE (Fr.)

Castries ST. LUCIA

Puebla

JAMAICA

Kingston

Bridgetown

BARBADOS

Acapulco

ISTHMUS OF TEHUANTEPEC

Belmopan

BELIZE

Kingstown

ST. VINCENT AND THE GRENADINES

Port-of-Spain

GUATEMALA

HONDURAS

Caribbean Sea

NETHERLANDS ANTILLES (Neth.)

St. George's

GRENADA

TRINIDAD AND TOBAGO

Guatemala City

San Salvador

EL SALVADOR

Tegucigalpa

NICARAGUA

MOSQUITO COAST

ARUBA (Neth.)

Managua

Lago de Nicaragua

San José

COSTA RICA

ISTHMUS OF PANAMA

Panama City

PANAMA

SOUTH AMERICA

Equator

⊛ National capital

● Major city

— National boundary

N W E S

0   400   800 mi.

0   400   800 km

Azimuthal Equal-Area Projection

512

SOUTH AMERICA: *Political/Physical*

CENTRAL
AMERICA

Caribbean Sea

ATLANTIC
OCEAN

Barranquilla
Cartagena
Maracaibo
Caracas

*Gulf of
Panama*

LLANOS
VENEZUELA
Orinoco River

Georgetown
Paramaribo

GUYANA
Cayenne

Medellín
Bogotá
COLOMBIA

GUIANA HIGHLANDS
SURINAME
FRENCH
GUIANA
(Fr.)

MALPELO
(Colombia)

Rio Negro

Quito
ECUADOR

AMAZON

Belém

0° Equator

GALÁPAGOS
ISLANDS
(Ecuador)

Guayaquil
*Gulf of
Guayaquil*

Iquitos

Manaus
Amazon River

BASIN

Solimões River

Madeira River

Tapajós River

Xingu River

Tocantins River

Fortaleza

Trujillo

PERU

BRAZIL

São Francisco River

Recife

A
N
D
E
S

Lima
Cuzco

Lake Titicaca

PACIFIC
OCEAN

Arequipa
La Paz
Sucre

ALTIPLANO
BOLIVIA

PLATEAU OF
MATO GROSSO

Brasília

BRAZILIAN

Salvador

HIGHLANDS

Belo Horizonte

Paraguay River

GRAN CHACO

PARAGUAY

Paraná River

São Paulo
Rio de Janeiro
Santos

Antofagasta

ATACAMA DESERT

Tropic of Capricorn

SAN FÉLIX
ISLAND
(Chile)
SAN AMBRÓSIO
ISLAND
(Chile)

Asunción

Salado River

Paraná River

Pôrto Alegre

A
N
D
E
S

Córdoba

CHILE

JUAN FERNÁNDEZ
ISLANDS
(Chile)

Rosario
URUGUAY

ATLANTIC

Valparaíso
Santiago

Buenos Aires
Montevideo

OCEAN

ARGENTINA
PAMPAS

Río de la Plata

Concepción

Colorado River
Bahía Blanca

Valdivia

Gulf of San Matías

N
W   E
S

PATAGONIA

Comodoro Rivadavia
Gulf of San Jorge

⊛	National capital
•	Major city
—	National boundary

*Strait of
Magellan*
FALKLAND
ISLANDS
(U.K.)

513

TIERRA
DEL FUEGO

0   400   800 mi.
0   400   800 km
Azimuthal Equal-Area Projection

Cape Horn

SOUTH GEORGIA
(U.K.)

Drake Passage

PACIFIC RIM: *Political/Physical*

ARCTIC OCEAN

Arctic Circle

RUSSIA

60°N

KAMCHATKA

Bering Sea

ALASKA (U.S.)

•Anchorage

60°N

ASIA

SAKHALIN

PACIFIC OCEAN

CANADA

NORTH AMERICA

MONGOLIA

KURIL IS. (Russia)

•Vladivostok

•Vancouver

•Seattle

•Ottawa

Beijing,✳

NORTH KOREA

Pyongyang✳
Seoul✳

JAPAN

UNITED STATES

•San
Francisco

Washington✳

PEOPLE'S
REPUBLIC
OF CHINA

SOUTH
KOREA

•Tokyo

•Los Angeles

Shanghai•

30°N

East
China
Sea

RYUKYU
IS.(Japan)

VOLCANO IS.
(Japan)

MIDWAY ISLANDS
(U.S.)

Tropic of Cancer

30°N

MEXICO

BAHAMAS

Hanoi•

✳Taipei

WAKE ISLAND
(U.S.)

•Honolulu

CUBA

LAOS

•HONG
KONG

TAIWAN

NORTHERN
MARIANA
ISLANDS
(U.S.)

HAWAII
(U.S.)

Mexico City•✳

BELIZE

HAITI

VIETNAM

Philippine
Sea

MARSHALL
ISLANDS

GUATEMALA
EL SALVADOR

HONDURAS

THAILAND

•Manila

MICRONESIA

GUAM (U.S.)

NICARAGUA

CAMBODIA

PHILIPPINES

✳Kolonia

•Majuro

COSTA RICA

PANAMA

Kuala
Lumpur

South
China
Sea

BRUNEI

FEDERATED STATES
OF MICRONESIA

PALAU

✳Tarawa

Bogotá✳

COLOMBIA

✳MALAYSIA

Yaren✳

Equator

GALAPAGOS IS.
(Ecuador)

ECUADOR

✳Quito

SINGAPORE

NAURU

KIRIBATI

Guayaquil•

INDONESIA

NEW
GUINEA

PAPUA
NEW GUINEA

SOLOMON
ISLANDS

TUVALU

Funafuti✳

POLYNESIA

PERU

Jakarta•

✳Port
Moresby

✳Honiara

TOKELAU
(N.Z.)

Lima✳

INDIAN
OCEAN

Timor
Sea

Arafura
Sea

Gulf of
Carpentaria

VANUATU

WALLIS AND
FUTUNA IS. (Fr.)

SAMOA

AMERICAN
SAMOA
(U.S.)

COOK
ISLANDS
(N.Z.)

FRENCH
POLYNESIA
(Fr.)

SOUTH
AMERICA

GREAT
SANDY
DESERT

Great
Barrier
Reef

✳Port
Vila

Apia✳

NIUE
(N.Z.)

Coral Sea

Suva✳

TONGA

MACDONNELL
RANGE

AUSTRALIA

FIJI

✳Nuku'alofa

Tropic of Capricorn

EASTER I.
(Chile)

CHILE

NEW CALEDONIA
(Fr.)

PITCAIRN I.
(U.K.)

Valparaíso✳

30°S

DARLING
RANGE

Great
Australian
Bight

•Sydney
✳Canberra

NORFOLK I.
(Aust.)

KERMADEC
ISLANDS
(N.Z.)

PACIFIC
OCEAN

Santiago

30°S

TASMANIA

NEW
ZEALAND

•Auckland

✳Wellington

Tasman
Sea

CHATHAM IS.
(N.Z.)

Scale at Equator

0   1000   2000 mi.

0   1000 2000 km

Miller Cylindrical Projection

60°S

60°S

Antarctic Circle

✳ National capital

• Major city

— National boundary

ANTARCTICA

120°E   150°E   180°   150°W   120°W   90°W

514

WORLD: *Religions*

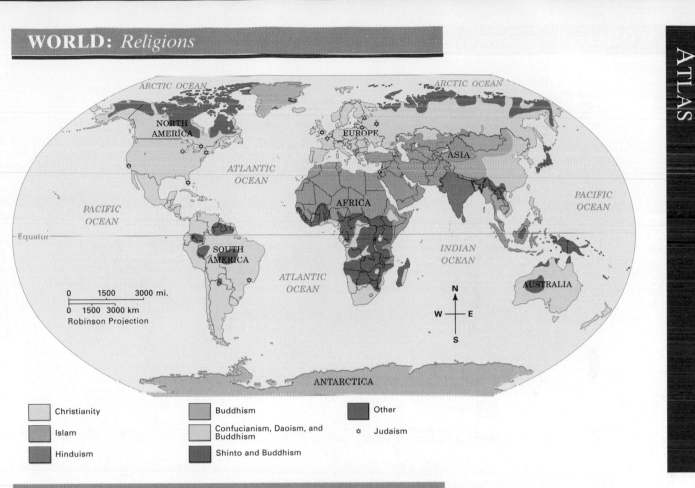

Legend:
- Christianity
- Islam
- Hinduism
- Buddhism
- Confucianism, Daoism, and Buddhism
- Shinto and Buddhism
- Other
- ✡ Judaism

WORLD: *Languages*

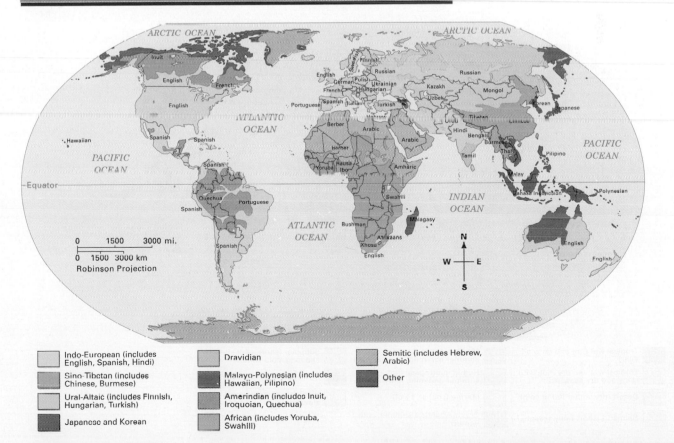

Legend:
- Indo-European (includes English, Spanish, Hindi)
- Sino-Tibetan (includes Chinese, Burmese)
- Ural-Altaic (includes Finnish, Hungarian, Turkish)
- Japanese and Korean
- Dravidian
- Malayo-Polynesian (includes Hawaiian, Pilipino)
- Amerindian (includes Inuit, Iroquoian, Quechua)
- African (includes Yoruba, Swahili)
- Semitic (includes Hebrew, Arabic)
- Other

WORLD: *Vegetation*

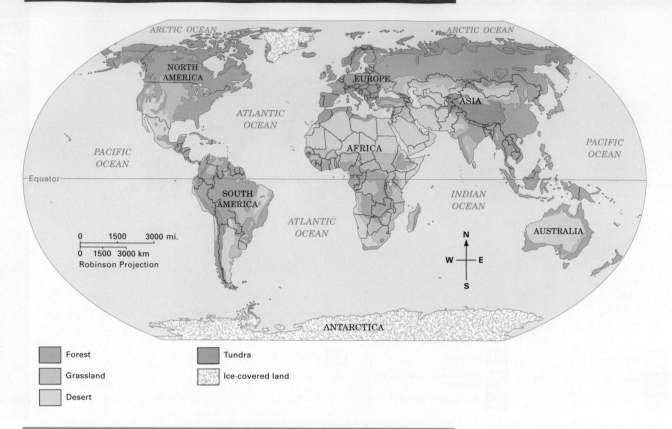

- Forest
- Grassland
- Desert
- Tundra
- Ice-covered land

0 1500 3000 mi.
0 1500 3000 km
Robinson Projection

WORLD: *Climate*

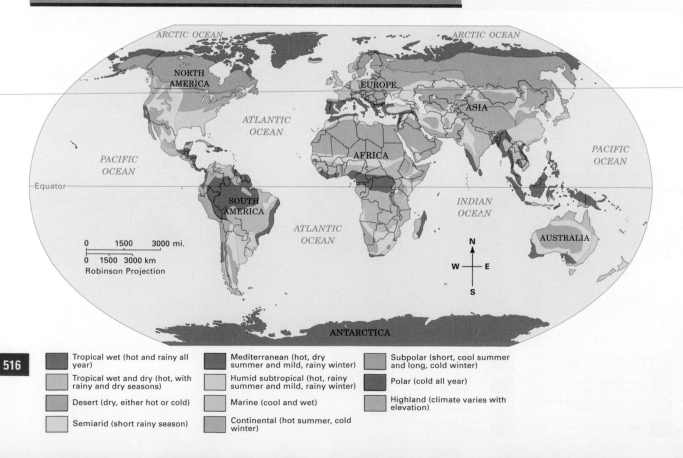

0 1500 3000 mi.
0 1500 3000 km
Robinson Projection

- Tropical wet (hot and rainy all year)
- Tropical wet and dry (hot, with rainy and dry seasons)
- Desert (dry, either hot or cold)
- Semiarid (short rainy season)
- Mediterranean (hot, dry summer and mild, rainy winter)
- Humid subtropical (hot, rainy summer and mild, rainy winter)
- Marine (cool and wet)
- Continental (hot summer, cold winter)
- Subpolar (short, cool summer and long, cold winter)
- Polar (cold all year)
- Highland (climate varies with elevation)

WORLD: *Population*

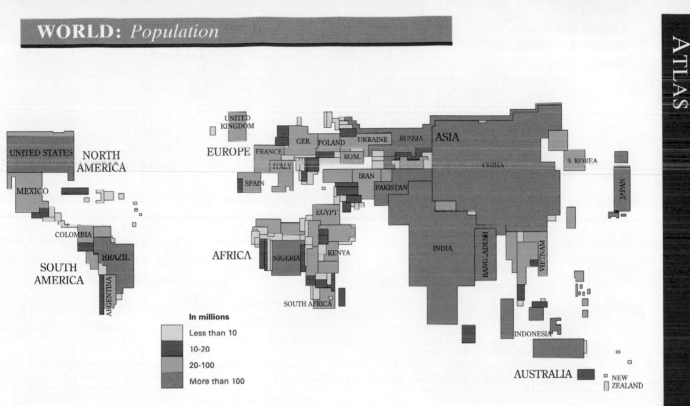

In millions

- Less than 10
- 10-20
- 20-100
- More than 100

Each country's size in the cartogram represents the size of its population compared with those of other countries in the world. Based on information in *Statistical Abstract of the United States 1995*.

WORLD: *Land Use, Land and Ocean Resources*

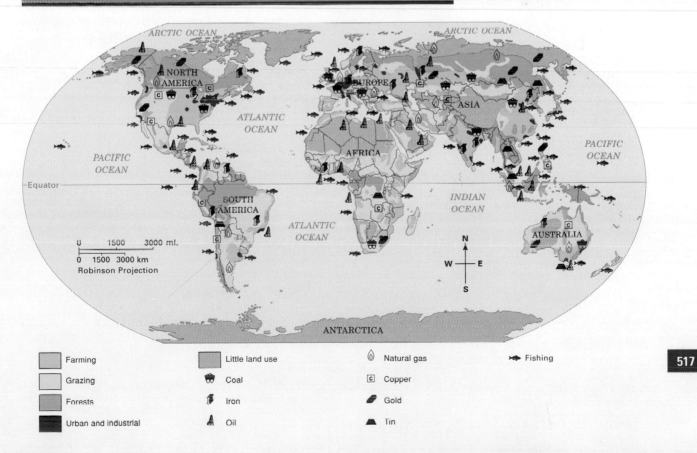

Farming		Little land use		Natural gas	Fishing
Grazing		Coal		Copper	
Forests		Iron		Gold	
Urban and industrial		Oil		Tin	

U   1500   3000 ml.

0   1500 3000 km
Robinson Projection

GLOSSARY OF GEOGRAPHIC TERMS

isthmus
a narrow strip of land connecting two large bodies of land

strait
a narrow strip of water connecting two large bodies of water

bay
part of an ocean or lake extending into the land

sea level
the level of the surface of the ocean

harbor
a sheltered area of water, a safe docking place for ships

flood plain
flat land near the edges of rivers formed by mud and silt deposited by floods

(river) mouth
the place where a river flows into a lake or ocean

volcano
an opening in the earth, usually raised, through which lava and gasses from the earth's interior escape

delta
a triangular area formed by deposits at the mouth of a river

swamp
an area of land that is partially covered by water

oasis
a spot of fertile land in a desert, fed by water from wells or underground springs

tributary
a stream or river that flows into a larger river

savanna
a region containing scattered trees and vegetation

desert
a dry area of land where few plants grow

butte
a raised, flat area of land with steep cliffs, smaller than a mesa

glacier
a large ice mass that moves slowly down a mountain or over land

plain
a broad, level area of land

mountain pass
a gap between mountains

valley
low land between hills or mountains

cataract
a large, powerful waterfall

mesa
a wide, flat-topped mountain with steep sides, found mostly in dry areas

cliff
the steep, almost vertical, edge of a hill, mountain, or plain

canyon
a narrow, deep valley with steep sides

plateau
a broad, flat area of land higher than the surrounding land

519

This Gazetteer will help you locate many of the places discussed in this book. Latitude and longitude given for large areas of land and water refers to the centermost point of the area; latitude and longitude of rivers refers to the river mouth. The page number tells you where to find each place on a map.

PLACE	LAT.	LONG.	PAGE
A			
Aegean Sea (in southern Europe)	39°N	25°E	**329**
Aegospotami (ancient town of Thrace)	40°N	26°E	**370**
Ain Mallaha (ancient settlement near Jordan R.)	32°N	35°E	**121**
Alexandria (city in Egypt founded by Alexander the Great)	31°N	30°E	**451**
Alps (mountain range in Europe crossed by Hannibal and his army)	46°N	9°E	**413**
Altai Mts. (mountain range in W. China)	49°N	87°E	**27**
Anyang (ancient capital of Shang dynasty)	36°N	114°E	**265**
Arabian Sea (in Asia; meets Indian Ocean)	16°N	65°E	**81**
Argos (ancient Greek city-state)	38°N	23°E	**333**
Assur (ancient city of Assyria)	35°N	43°E	**176**
Athens (ancient city-state; capital of modern Greece)	38°N	24°E	**370**
Attica (ancient region of central Greece)	38°N	24°E	**370**
B			
Babylon (ancient city-kingdom and capital of Babylonia)	33°N	45°N	**176**
Barcelona (ancient Carthaginian port; city in modern Spain)	41°N	2°E	**509**
Bath (ancient Roman city in England)	51°N	2°W	**433**
Beijing (capital of China)	40°N	116°E	**27**
Bengal, Bay of (part of Indian Ocean)	18°N	87°E	**223**
Bering Strait (water passage connecting Arctic Ocean and Bering Sea)	65°N	170°W	**512**
Bethlehem (ancient town of Judea; birthplace of Jesus)	32°N	35°E	**300**
Black Sea (between Europe and Asia)	43°N	32°E	**476**
Brahmaputra R. (in Tibet, India, and Bangladesh)	24°N	91°E	**223**

PLACE	LAT.	LONG.	PAGE
Byblos (ancient Phoenician city; modern Jubayl, Lebanon)	34°N	36°E	**300**
Byzantium (ancient city; site of modern Istanbul)	41°N	29°E	**81**
C			
Cairo (capital of Egypt)	30°N	31°E	**511**
Canaan (ancient Palestine)	33°N	36°E	**300**
Canary Islands (Spanish territory off W. coast of Africa)	29°N	17°W	**46**
Cartagena (ancient Carthago Nova; port on Mediterranean coast of Spain)	38°N	1°W	**413**
Carthage (ancient Phoenician city and state in N. Africa)	37°N	10°E	**413**
Carthago Nova (ancient Carthaginian port in Spain; modern Cartagena)	38°N	1°W	**39**
Caspian Sea (salt lake between Europe and Asia)	40°N	52°E	**433**
Çatal Hüyük (neolithic town in modern Turkey)	38°N	33°E	**121**
Chang Jiang (river in China; also known as Yangtze R.)	36°N	115°E	**27**
Changan (ancient capital of Emperor Shihuangdi of Qin dynasty; modern Xi'an)	34°N	110°E	**282**
Constantinople (ancient city of Turkey; modern Istanbul)	41°N	29°E	**474**
Corinth (ancient Greek commercial city)	38°N	23°E	**333**
Crete (island of Greece in Mediterranean Sea)	35°N	25°E	**465**
D			
Da Hinggan Ling (mountain range in E. China)	47°N	120°E	**27**
Damascus (capital of Syria)	34°N	36°E	**200**
Danube R. (second longest river in Europe)	45°N	30°E	**433**
Delos (island in Aegean Sea; legendary birthplace of Apollo)	37°N	25°E	**333**

PLACE	LAT.	LONG.	PAGE
Delphi (ancient site of oracle in Greece)	38°N	22°E	**348**

E

PLACE	LAT.	LONG.	PAGE
Ecbatana (ancient city of Iran; legendary site of tomb of Mordecai and Esther)	35°N	48°E	**81**
Eleusis (ancient Greek city)	38°N	24°E	**340**
Ephesus (ancient city near Athens)	38°N	27°E	**370**
Euphrates R. (in southwest Asia; along with Tigris R., site of several ancient civilizations)	36°N	40°E	**151**
Everest, Mt. (part of Himalaya range; highest mountain in the world: 29,028 ft.)	28°N	87°E	**223**

G

PLACE	LAT.	LONG.	PAGE
Gades (Phoenician trading colony in Spain; modern Cádiz)	37°N	6°W	**39**
Ganges R. (in India)	23°N	91°E	**223**
Gaul (ancient Roman province; modern France)	47°N	1°E	**433**
Gobi (desert mostly in Mongolia)	43°N	103°E	**27**
Guangzhou (city in China)	23°N	113°E	**27**
Gytta (Phoenician colony on W. Africa coast)	32°N	9°W	**46**

H

PLACE	LAT.	LONG.	PAGE
Hadar (site of discovery of australopithecine remains in Africa)	10°N	40°E	**93**
Harappa (site of ancient Indus Valley civilization in Pakistan)	31°N	73°E	**224**
Hebron (ancient town of Jordan; modern Al Khalil)	32°N	35°E	**300**
Hellespont (narrow strait between Turkey and Egypt; modern Dardanelles)	40°N	26°E	**370**
Himalayas (mountain system in S. Asia)	30°N	85°E	**223**
Hindu Kush (mountain range in Central Asia)	35°N	69°E	**223**
Hit (town in Iraq; ancient Is)	34°N	43°E	**151**
Huang He (river in China; also known as Yellow R.)	37°N	117°E	**27**

I

PLACE	LAT.	LONG.	PAGE
Iconium (ancient city in Turkey visited by Paul)	37°N	32°E	**461**
Indus R. (in Pakistan)	24°N	68°E	**223**
Istanbul (capital of Turkey; ancient Constantinople)	41°N	29°E	**508**
Ithuca (Greek island)	38°N	21°E	**329**

J

PLACE	LAT.	LONG.	PAGE
Jericho (ancient city in Jordan; modern Arīhā)	32°N	35°E	**303**
Jerusalem (ancient city; capital of modern Israel)	32°N	35°E	**200**
Jordan R. (forms boundary between Israel and Jordan)	32°N	36°E	**300**
Judea (ancient Roman province in Palestine)	31°N	34°E	**465**

K

PLACE	LAT.	LONG.	PAGE
Kabul (capital of Afghanistan)	35°N	69°E	**41**
Kapilavastu (town of ancient India; birthplace of the Buddha)	27°N	83°E	**251**
Kish (ancient city of Sumer)	33°N	45°E	**151**
Knossos (royal city of ancient Crete)	35°N	25°E	**465**
Kunlun Shan (mountain range in China)	35°N	83°E	**27**

L

PLACE	LAT.	LONG.	PAGE
Lagash (Sumerian city in Babylonia)	32°N	47°E	**151**
Leptis (ancient city of N. Africa)	34°N	14°E	**51**
London (capital of the United Kingdom)	52°N	0°W	**508**
Luoyang (city of E. China)	35°N	113°E	**211**

M

PLACE	LAT.	LONG.	PAGE
Macedonia (ancient kingdom N.W. of Aegean Sea)	41°N	22°E	**370**
Madeira Islands (territory of Portugal off W. coast of Africa)	33°N	16°W	**46**
Mediterranean Sea (between Europe and Africa)	36°N	13°E	**433**

PLACE	LAT.	LONG.	PAGE
Memphis (ancient city in Lower Egypt; capital of most rulers of Old Kingdom)	30°N	31°E	**187**
Meroë (ancient city on E. bank of Nile; capital of Nubia)	17°N	34°E	**211**
Mesopotamia (region in S.W. Asia; site of Babylonia and Assyria)	33°N	44°E	**151**
Miletus (ancient trade center in Turkey; conquered by Alexander the Great)	38°N	27°E	**370**
Mohenjo-Daro (Indus Valley civilization site in Pakistan)	27°N	68°E	**224**
Mycenae (ancient city of Greece; legendary capital of King Agammemnon)	38°N	23°E	**329**

N

PLACE	LAT.	LONG.	PAGE
Napata (ancient capital of Nubia in Egypt)	19°N	32°E	**211**
Neander Valley (site of Neanderthal burial mounds in W. Germany)	50°N	8°E	**93**
Nile R. (in Africa; longest in the world: 4,187 m.)	30°N	31°E	**200**
Nineveh (ancient capital of Assyria; in modern Iraq)	37°N	43°E	**121**
Nubia (ancient empire in E. Africa)	21°N	33°E	**187**

O

PLACE	LAT.	LONG.	PAGE
Olduvai Gorge (site of early human fossil beds in Africa)	2°S	35°E	**93**
Olympus, Mt. (range and peak in Thessaly, Greece)	40°N	22°E	**370**

P

PLACE	LAT.	LONG.	PAGE
Paris (capital of France; ancient Lutetia)	49°N	2°E	**508**
Patala (ancient trading city on Indus R. delta)	25°N	68°E	**48**
Pataliputra (ancient city of India; capital of empire of Asoka)	26°N	85°E	**81**
Peloponnesus (peninsula of Greece)	37°N	22°E	**370**
Persian Gulf (part of Arabian Sea)	28°N	51°E	**176**
Piraeus (ancient seaport of Athens)	38°N	24°E	**370**
Plataea (ancient city in central Greece)	36°N	23°E	**370**

PLACE	LAT.	LONG.	PAGE
Potidaea (ancient city of Macedonia)	40°N	23°E	**370**
Pyrenees (mountain range between France and Spain)	43°N	0°E	**413**

R

PLACE	LAT.	LONG.	PAGE
Red Sea (between Arabian Peninsula and N.E. Africa)	23°N	37°E	**200**
Rhône R. (in Switzerland and France)	43°N	5°E	**415**
Rome (capital of Italy; center of ancient empire)	42°N	13°E	**398**

S

PLACE	LAT.	LONG.	PAGE
Saguntum (city settled by Greeks in Spain; later allied with Rome; modern Sagunto)	40°N	0°W	**413**
Sahara (region of deserts and oases in N. Africa)	24°N	2°W	**511**
Samos (island in Aegean; commercial center of ancient Greece)	38°N	27°E	**329**
Sardinia (island country in Mediterranean Sea)	40°N	9°E	**474**
Segovia (ancient Roman city in Spain)	41°N	4°W	**39**
Sicily (island of Italy in Mediterranean Sea)	38°N	14°E	**398**
Sinai Peninsula (between Gulf of Suez and Gulf of 'Aqaba)	29°N	33°E	**303**
Sinai, Mt. (in S. Sinai Peninsula)	28°N	34°E	**303**
Sparta (ancient city-state of Greece)	37°N	22°E	**333**
Sudan (region of N. Central Africa; includes desert, plains, and grassy steppes)	14°N	28°E	**511**

T

PLACE	LAT.	LONG.	PAGE
Taung village (site of fossil skull found in S. Africa)	27°S	25°E	**93**
Thebes (ancient city of Egypt)	38°N	23°E	**187**
Tian Shan (mountain range in China, Kazakhstan, and Kyrgyzstan)	42°N	79°E	**27**
Tiber R. (in central Italy)	42°N	12°E	**398**

BIOGRAPHICAL DICTIONARY

This dictionary lists many of the important people introduced in this book. The page number refers to the main discussion of that person in the book. For more complete references see the Index.

Pronunciation Key

This chart presents the system of phonetic respellings used to indicate pronunciation in the Biographical Dictionary and in the chapters of this book.

Spellings	Symbol	Spellings	Symbol	Spellings	Symbol
pat	a	kick, cat, pique	k	thin, this	th
pay	ay	lid, needle	l	cut	uh
care	air	mum	m	urge, term, firm, word, heard	ur
father	ah	no, sudden	n		
bib	b	thing	ng	valve	v
church	ch	pot, horrid	ah	with	w
deed, milled	d	toe	oh	yes	y
pet	eh	caught, paw, for	aw	zebra, xylem	z
bee	ee	noise	oy	vision, pleasure, garage	zh
life, phase, rough	f	took	u		
gag	g	boot	oo	about, item, edible, gallop, circus	uh
hat	h	out	ow		
which	hw	pop	p	butter	ur
pit	ih	roar	r		
pie, by	eye, y	sauce	s	Capital letters indicate stressed syllables.	
pier	ihr	ship, dish	sh		
judge	j	tight, stopped	t		

A

Abraham c. 1900 B.C., first leader of Israelite nation (p. 299).

Adad-Nirari (*uh DAD nih RAH ree*) c. 911 B.C., king of Assyria (p. 176).

Aeneas (*ih NEE uhs*) c. 1200s B.C., Trojan hero in war against Greece; according to legend escaped to Italy where son, Romulus, founded Rome (p. 421).

Alaric c. 370–410, Visigoth king who conquered Rome in 410 (p. 475).

Alexander the Great 356–323 B.C., Macedonian king, 336–323 B.C., who conquered Greece, Persia, and Egypt (p. 378).

Ambrose of Milan, Bishop c. 340–397, bishop of Milan, 374–397 (p. 469).

Antigonus (*an TIHG uh nuhs*) 382–301 B.C., general of Alexander the Great who controlled Macedonia after Alexander's death (p. 381).

Antiochus (*ahn TEE uh kuhs*) ?–163 B.C., Syrian ruler, 175–163 B.C., whose order for Jews to worship Greek gods led to the Maccabean revolt (p. 313).

Archytas (*ahr KY tuhs*) 300s B.C., Greek who built wooden flying machine (p. 12).

Aristarchus (*ar ih STAHR kuhs*) 200s B.C., Greek astronomer who theorized that the earth revolved around the sun (p. 386).

Aristides (*air ih STY deez*) A.D. 100s, Greek writer (p. 449).

Aristophanes (*ar ih STAHF uh neez*) 400s B.C., Greek playwright (p. 385).

Aristotle (*AR ih staht l*) 384–322 B.C., Greek philosopher and teacher of Alexander the Great (p. 378).

Aryabhata c. 400s, Indian astronomer (p. 249).

Asoka (*ah SHOH kah*) 200s B.C., Buddhist ruler of Mauryan empire 269–232 B.C. (p. 239).

Attila the Hun c. 406–453, king of the Huns, a tribe of barbarians, and conqueror of Roman cities (p. 4).

Augustine, Saint 354–430, church leader, philosopher, and author of *The City of God* (p. 479).

Augustus (*aw GUHS tuhs*) 63 B.C.–A.D. 14, title meaning "respected one," given to Octavian, first Roman emperor, 27 B.C.–A.D. 14 (p. 431).

Aurelius *See* **Marcus Aurelius**

B

Ban Zhao (*bahn jow*) c. 45–115 A.D., Chinese scholar (p. 237)

Brutus c. 85–42 B.C., one of the Roman senators which assassinated Julius Caesar in 44 B.C. (p. 430).

Buddha, The c. 565–c. 483 B.C., Indian philosopher, teacher, and founder of Buddhism (p. 236). *See also* **Gautama, Siddhartha**

C

Caesar, Julius 100–44 B.C., Roman general who ended the Republic and ruled as dictator 46–44 B.C.; assassinated (p. 418).

C

Caesar, Julius 100–44 B.C., Roman general who ended the Republic and ruled as dictator 46–44 B.C.; assassinated (p. 418).

Caracalla 188–217, Roman emperor, 211–217; unified empire by granting citizenship to free population of empire (p. 435).

Carnarvon, Lord 1900s, wealthy English supporter of archaeological dig for King Tutankhamen's tomb (p. 71).

Carter, Howard 1873–1939, English archaeologist who discovered Egyptian king Tutankhamen's tomb in 1922 (p. 71).

Cato the Elder 234–149 B.C., Roman senator opposed to adopting Greek culture (p. 421).

Champollion, Jean 1790–1832, French scholar who decoded Egyptian hieroglyphics of the Rosetta Stone in 1822 (p. 196).

Chang Tang *(chahng tanhg)* 1700 B.C., Chinese ruler whose defeat of Chieh in 1766 B.C. began the Shang dynasty (p. 265).

Cheng *See* **Qin Shihuangdi**

Chieh *(CHEE uh)* c. 1700s B.C., last Xia king; defeated by Chang Tang in 1766 B.C. (p. 265).

Christ *See* **Jesus**

Cincinnatus, Lucius c. 519–439 B.C., citizen farmer made dictator in 458 B.C. to lead Roman army (p. 416).

Commodus 161–193, Roman emperor, 180–193; assassinated (p. 471).

Confucius *(kuhn FYOO shuhs)* 551–479 B.C., Chinese philosopher and teacher at end of Zhou dynasty (p. 270).

Constantine c. 280–337, Roman emperor, 306–337, who installed Christianity as main religion in Roman Empire and moved capital to Constantinople (p. 473).

Corebus c. 700s B.C., first recorded winner of Olympic games, 776 B.C. (p. 345).

Cunningham, Alexander 1800s, British archaeologist who led excavation of ancient ruins in Harappa, India (p. 222).

Cryus the Great c. 600–529 B.C., Persian ruler, 550–529 B.C., and conqueror of Babylon 540 B.C. (p. 180).

D

Darius c. 558–c. 486 B.C., Persian king, 521–486 B.C., who led war against Greek city-states in 490s B.C. (p. 355).

Dar, Raymond 1900s, first archaeologist to recognize humanlike features of australopithecine fossils (p. 92).

David, Jacques Louis 1748–1825, French painter (p. 373).

David c. 1010–c. 970 B.C., Israelite king who led defeat of Philistines and growth of Israelite empire (p. 309).

da Vinci, Leonardo *See* **Leonardo da Vinci**

Decius 201–251, Roman emperor, 249–251, who persecuted Christians (p. 467).

Demosthenes *(dih MAHS thuh neez)* c. 385–322 B.C., Greek speaker (p. 367).

Diocletian *(dy uh KLEE shuhn)* 245–313, Roman emperor, 284–305, and reformer of empire (p. 472).

Domitian *(duh MIHSH uhn)* 51–96, ruler of second Roman dynasty, 81–96 (p. 433).

Duncan, Donald 1900s, American inventor and producer of the yo-yo (p. 31).

E

Eratosthenes *(ehr uh TAHS thuh neez)* 200s B.C., Greek mathematician who used a gnomon to figure earth's circumference (p. 50).

Euclid c. 300 B.C., Greek mathematician and father of geometry (p. 387).

Evans, Arthur 1851–1941, English archaeologist who unearthed ancient palace ruins in Knossos (p. 332).

Ezana A.D. 300s, African king of Axum and conqueror of Meroë A.D. 350 (p. 214).

Erza 400s B.C., Jewish priest and scribe who brought Torah from Babylon (p. 312).

F

Faxian *(fah shee AHN)* A.D. 400s, Chinese Buddhist monk who wrote about travels to India (p. 250).

G

Gautama *(GAW tah mah)*, **Siddhartha** *(sihd DAHR tah)* *See* **Buddha**

Gilgamesh c. 2700 B.C., Sumerian king of Uruk and hero of epic *Gilgamesh* (p. 157).

Goliath 1000s B.C., legendary Philistine warrior defeated by David (p. 308).

Goode, Paul 1900s, American cartographer; creator of interrupted homolosine projection map (p. 45).

H

Hadrian 76–138, Roman emperor, 117–138; first to mark empire's borders with walls (p. 434).

Hamilcar c. 270–228 B.C., Carthaginian general during First Punic War (p. 413).

Hammurabi *(hah moo RAH bee)* d. 1750 B.C., Babylonian ruler, 1700s B.C.; created important code of written laws (p. 173).

Han Gaozu (*hahn kow dzuh*) c. 200 B.C., first emperor of Han dynasty, which began revival of Confucianism in China (p. 282).

Hannibal c. 247–183 B.C., Carthaginian general during Second Punic War (p. 414).

Hanno 400s B.C., Carthaginian commander who led voyage to west coast of Africa c. 480 B.C. (p. 46).

Hatshepsut (*hat SHEHP soot*) ruler of Egypt, 1503–1482 B.C. during the 18th dynasty; also daughter and wife of Egyptian rulers (p. 199).

Henry VIII 1491–1547, king of England 1509–1547 (p. 279).

Herodotus (*hih RAHD uh tuhs*) 400s B.C., Greek historian (p. 385).

Hillel 30 B.C.–A.D. 9, Jewish teacher (p. 270, p. 321).

Hippalus 1st century, Greek who discovered shorter trade route to India, c. A.D. 37 (p. 48).

Hipparchus (*hih PAHR kuhs*) 300s B.C., mapmaker who used latitude-longitude grid (p. 38).

Hippias 500s B.C., tyrant ruler of Athens, driven out c. 510 B.C. (p. 341).

Hippocrates c. 460–c. 377 B.C., Greek doctor and writer of Hippocratic Oath, a pledge of duty (p. 387).

Homer c. 700 B.C., Greek epic poet and author of *Iliad* and *Odyssey* (p. 332).

Horace 65–8 B.C., Roman poet (p. 420).

I

Imhotep 2600s B.C., adviser to ancient Egyptian king Zoser and designer of King Zoser's Step Pyramid (p. 191).

Ipuky (*ee POO kee*) c. 1380 B.C., Egyptian artist during New Kingdom period (p. 204).

J

Jacob c. 1800s–1700s B.C., Hebrew leader, given the name Israel, whose descendants became known as the Israelites (p. 301).

Jeremiah c. 600 B.C., Major Jewish prophet at the time of Babylonian conquest of Judah in 587 B.C. (p. 311).

Jesus c. A.D. 1–c. 33, Hebrew teacher and founder of Christianity (p. 316).

Johanson, Donald 1900s, leader of archaeological team that discovered Lucy, fossil skeleton of early human ancestors (p. 90).

Julian 331–363, Roman emperor, 361–363, and son of Constantine, who attempted to reinstate pagan religion (p. 474).

Justinian 483–565, Byzantine emperor, 527–565 (p. 479).

Juvenal c. 60–c. 140, Roman writer and social commentator (p. 441).

K

Kashta (*KAHSH tuh*) 700s B.C., Kushite ruler and conqueror of Upper Egypt 705 B.C. (p. 212).

L

Laozi (*LAOW dzuh*) 604–531 B.C., Founder of Taoism, a Chinese philosophy based on harmony with nature (p. 273).

Leakey, Louis 1903–1972, English archaeologist who found *Homo habilis* fossils in eastern Africa (p. 92).

Leakey, Mary b. 1913, English archaeologist who found *Homo habilis* fossils in eastern Africa (p. 92).

Leonardo da Vinci 1452–1519, Italian inventor and artist (p. 13).

Li Si (*lee suh*) 200s B.C., Legalist adviser to Chinese emperor Qin; court censor (p. 278).

Livy 59 B.C.–A.D. 17, Roman historian (p. 399).

Lugal-zaggesi (*LOO guhl zuh GEE see*) 2300s B.C., Sumerian king of Uruk defeated by Sargon of Akkad c. 2350 B.C. (p. 168).

M

Maccabee, Judah d. 160 B.C., leader of Jews who defeated Syrians in 164 B.C. (p. 314).

Marcus Aurelius (*aw REE lee uhs*) 121–180, last emperor of *Pax Romana*, 161–180 (p. 434).

Mattathias 100s B.C., Jewish priest whose revolt against Syrians in 175 B.C. sparked the revolt of the Maccabees (p. 313).

Maximian A.D. 200s, ruler of western empire, after Diocletian divided empire into eastern and western regions (p. 472).

Menander 300s B.C., Greek playwright (p. 443).

Mencius (*MEHN shee uhs*) 4th century B.C., Chinese disciple of Confucius (p. 273).

Menes (*MEE neez*) c. 3100 B.C., legendary king of Upper and Lower Egypt who began first Egyptian dynasty (p. 189).

Mercator, Gerhardus 1512–1594, German cartographer who published Mercator projection map in 1569 (p. 44).

Minos c. 2000 B.C., legendary king of Crete during its cultural height (p. 331).

Moses c. 1200 B.C., Hebrew who led Israelites out of Egyptian captivity (p. 301).

Mozi (*MOHD zuh*) c. 200s B.C., Chinese founder of Moism, a philosophy that stressed universal love (p. 273).

N

Nabonius *(na buh NY duhs)* 500s B.C., Babylonian king, 556–539 B.C., at time of Persia's defeat of Babylonia (p. 180).

Narmer c. 2900s B.C., Egyptian king who may have been King Menes of Egyptian legend (p. 190). *See also* **Menes**

Nebuchadnezzar c. 630–562 B.C., king of Babylon, 605–562 B.C., and conqueror of the Phonecians, Philistines, and Hebrews (p. 178).

Nero 37–68, Roman emperor, 54–68, and last ruler of Augustan dynasty (p. 433).

O

Octavian *See* **Augustus**

Orosius 300s–400s, Christian historian during the fall of the Roman Empire (p. 475).

P

Pasion d. 370 B.C., Greek slave who gained citizenship because of his craftsman's skills (p. 368).

Paul c. 5–64, former persecutor of Christians who became leader of early Christian movement (p. 461).

Pericles *(PEHR ih kleez)* d. 429 B.C., Athenian military and political leader during Golden Age, 460–429 B.C. (p. 362).

Peter 1st century, disciple of Jesus who declared in A.D. 48 that Christianity should be preached to Jews and Gentiles (p. 460).

Peters, Arno 1900s, West German cartographer whose projection map shows continents of correct size but distorted shape (p. 45)

Phidippides *(fy DIHP uh deez)* c. 400s B.C., legendary Athenian runner at Marathon (p. 351).

Philip 382–336 B.C., king of Macedonia, 359–336 B.C., and conqueror of Greece (p. 375).

Piankhy *(pee AHNG kee)* 700s B.C., Kushite conqueror of Lower Egypt (p. 212).

Picasso, Pablo 1881–1973, Spanish artist (p. 110).

Pilate, Pontius 1st century, Roman governor who ordered Jesus' execution in A.D. 33 (p. 318).

Plato *(PLAY toh)* c. 427–347 B.C., Greek philosopher and student of Socrates (p. 373).

Pliny the Elder 23–79, Roman scholar (p. 17)

Pliny the Younger 62–113, Roman writer and governor of Asia Minor (p. 56).

Plutarch c. 46–c. 120, Greek historian who recorded history of Alexander the Great (p. 374).

Polybius c. 205–c. 125 B.C., Greek historian (p. 414).

Pompey 106–46 B.C., Roman general, defeated by Caesar in 46 B.C. (p. 418)

Pompilius, Numa c. 700s B.C., second Roman king and supposed founder of Roman religion (p. 397).

Priscus c. 5th century, Roman historian (p. 4).

Ptolemy, Claudius 100s B.C. Greek geographer, astronomer, and author of *Guide to Geography* (p. 49).

Ptolemy *(TAHL uh mee)* c. 367–283 B.C., general of Alexander the Great who ruled Egypt after Alexander's death (p. 381).

Pythagoras *(pih THAG ur uhs)* 500s B.C., Greek mathematician, called father of geometry (p. 386).

Q

Qin Shihuangdi *(chin shee hwahng dee)* 200s B.C., emperor of Qin dynasty and unifier of China (p. 277). *See also* **Cheng**

R

Rehoboam c. 900s B.C., Israelite ruler at time of Israel's division; became king of Judah (p. 310).

Ricci, Sebastiano 1659–1734, Italian painter (p. 470).

Robinson, Arthur 1900s, American cartographer whose projection map is base for many world maps (p. 45).

S

Sargon of Akkad 2300s–2200s B.C., Mesopotamian ruler, c. 2334–c. 2279 B.C., and creator of world's first empire (p. 169)

Scipio Africanus *(SIHP ee oh af ruh KAHN uhs)* c. 237–183 B.C., Roman general who defeated Hannibal (p. 414).

Seleucus *(sih LOO kuhs)* c. 358–280 B.C., general of Alexander the Great and ruler of Syria after Alexander's death (p. 381).

Seneca 4 B.C.–A.D. 65, Roman writer and philosopher (p. 7).

Septimius Severus 146–211, Roman military leader and emperor, 193–211 (p. 471).

Severus Alexander 100s–200s, Roman emperor and last ruler of Severus dynasty; assassinated 235 (p. 471).

Shamshi-Adad 1800s–1700s B.C., Assyrian ruler and conqueror, c. 1813–1781 B.C. (p. 170).

Simon the Just c. 300s B.C., Jewish rabbi (p. 321).

Sima Jian *(soo muh chih yehn)* 100s B.C., Chinese historian during Han period (p. 286).

Sima Xiangru *(suh mah shahng roo)* 1st century B.C., Chinese poet (p. 262).

Snow, John 1800s English physician who used a map to trace cholera epidemic (p. 42).

Socrates c. 470–399 B.C., Greek philosopher; tried and executed for corrupting Athenian youths (p. 372).

Pronunciation Key

This chart presents the pronunciation key used in this Glossary. For a key to the phonetic respellings used to indicate pronunciation in the text of the chapters, see page 524.

Spellings	Symbol	Spellings	Symbol	Spellings	Symbol
pat	ă	kick, cat, pique	k	thin	th
pay	ā	lid, needle	l	this	*th*
care	âr	mum	m	cut	ŭ
father	ä	no, sudden	n	urge, term, firm, word, heard	ûr
bib	b	thing	ng		
church	ch	pot, horrid	ŏ	valve	v
deed, milled	d	toe	ō	with	w
pet	ĕ	caught, paw, for	ô	yes	y
bee	ē	noise	oi	zebra, xylem	z
life, phase, rough	f	took	o͝o	vision, pleasure, garage	zh
gag	g	boot	o͞o		
hat	h	out	ou	about, item, edible, gallop, circus	ə
which	hw	pop	p		
pit	ĭ	roar	r	butter	ər
pie, by	ī	sauce	s		
pier	îr	ship, dish	sh	Primary stress ´	
judge	j	tight, stopped	t	Secondary stress ˊ	

A

access (ăk´sĕs´) a means of entering; the right to enter or use (p. 211).

administrator (ăd-mĭn´ĭ-strā´tər) a manager; one who directs a government or organization (p. 154).

afterlife (ăf´tər-līf´) according to some beliefs, the life that follows death (p. 192).

agora (ăg´ə-rə) a marketplace in ancient Greece, commonly used as a meeting place (p. 365).

agriculture (ăg´rĭ-kŭl´chər) the science, art, and business of raising animals and plants to supply food for humans; farming (p. 125).

alliance (ə-lī´əns) a formal union between nations joined in a common cause (p. 369).

ancestor (ăn´sĕs´tər) a relative who lived in the past; a person from whom one is descended, especially more distant than a grandparent (p. 266).

aqueduct (ăk´wĭ-dŭkt´) a bridgelike structure built to carry water from a distant source (p. 424).

archaeology (är´kē-ŏl´ə-jē) the systematic recovery and study of tools, graves, buildings, pottery, and other remains of past human life and culture (p. 64).

artifact (är´tə-făkt´) an object made by humans that is of archaeological or historical interest (p. 57).

artisan (är´tĭ-zən) a worker who is skilled in making a particular product by hand (p. 155).

Aryan (âr´ē-ən) one of a group of seminomadic people that came from eastern Europe and spoke an Indo-European language (p. 229).

assassinate (ə-săs´ə-nāt´) to murder someone, especially for political reasons(p. 431).

astronomer (ə-strŏn´ə-mər) a scientist who observes and studies the universe beyond the earth, including the moon, planets, and stars and their motions (p. 179).

B

band (bănd) a group of people; a small, loosely organized group of hunter-gatherers, consisting of 20 to 30 individuals (p. 107).

barbarian (bär-bâr´ē-ən) in ancient Rome, a person from beyond the Roman frontier; a person considered by another group to be uncivilized (p. 476).

barter (bär´tər) a system of trading in which people exchange goods or services directly, without the use of money (p. 343).

Buddhism (bo͞o´dĭz´əm) a religion founded in India by Siddhartha Gautama; Buddhism stresses moderation and nonviolence (p. 236).

bureaucracy (byo͝o-rŏk´rə-sē) a type of organization structured like a pyramid, with one person at the top and many at the bottom; workers at each level supervise those below them (p. 278).

C

cartographer (kär-tŏg´rə-fər) a mapmaker (p. 39).

caste (kăst) a division within India's class system (p. 232).

cataract (kăt´ə-răkt´) steep rapids in a river; a very large waterfall (p. 187).

censorship (sĕn′sər-shĭp′) control of what people read or write or hear or see; efforts to prohibit free expression of ideas (p. 279).

Christianity (krĭs′chē-ăn′ĭ-tē) the Christian religion, founded on the teachings of Jesus (p. 318).

city-state (sĭt′ē-stāt′) a self-governing unit made up of a city and its surrounding villages and farmland (pp. 152 and 333).

civilization (sĭv′ə-lĭ-zā′shən) a complex society with a stable food supply, specialization of labor, a government, and a highly developed culture (p. 140).

climate (klī′mət) the average weather conditions in an area over a long period of time, especially temperature, precipitation, and wind (p. 28).

code (kōd) an organized set of laws or rules (p. 172).

comedy (kŏm′ĭ-dē) a humorous play that has a happy ending (p. 350).

Confucianism (kən-fyōō′shən-ĭz′əm) the ideas of Confucius, emphasizing such values as family, tradition, and mutual respect (p. 271).

conquest (kŏn′kwĕst′) the defeat of a nation or group, usually by force (p. 375).

consul (kōn′səl) either of the two main elected officials of the ancient Roman Republic (p. 406).

conversion (kən-vûr′zhən) a change in which one adopts a new religion (p. 459).

covenant (kŭv′ə-nənt) a binding agreement made by two or more people or groups; an agreement between a group of people and their god (p. 302).

culture (kŭl′chər) the attitudes, beliefs, customs, traditions, art, and achievements of a society that are passed from one generation to another (p. 14).

cuneiform (kyōō′nē-ə-fôrm′) wedge-shaped characters made with a reed stylus and used in writing several ancient languages (p. 160).

D

debt bondage (dĕt bŏn′dĭj) in ancient Rome, a condition in which a poor person became an unpaid servant to a wealthy person to whom he owed money (p. 407).

deforestation (dē-fôr′ĭ-stā′shən) the process of clearing away trees or forests (p. 17).

delta (dĕl′tə) a triangle-shaped deposit of soil near the mouth of a river (p. 187).

democracy (dĭ-mŏk′rə-sē) a system of government in which the people rule, either directly or through elected representatives (p. 339).

dialect (dī′ə-lĕkt′) a different form of the same language; the differences usually involve pronunciation, grammar, or vocabulary (p. 269).

diaspora (dī-ăs′pər-ə) the scattering of Jewish settlements outside of Israel (p. 320).

dictator (dĭk′tā′tər) a ruler who has absolute power (p. 418).

diffusion (dĭ-fyōō′zhən) the spread of ideas, values, and inventions from one culture to another (p. 30).

disciple (dĭ-sī′pəl) someone who follows the teachings of a master or leader and helps to spread those teachings (p. 318).

domesticate (də-mĕs′tĭ-kāt′) to train or adapt an animal or plant to live in a human environment, making it more useful to humans (p. 123).

dynasty (dī′nə-stē) a series of rulers from the same family (p. 190).

E

edict (ē′dĭkt) a formal command; a proclamation or announcement given out by an authority and having the force of law (p. 472).

elite (ĭ-lēt′) in ancient Rome, the upper class (p. 436).

embalm (ĕm-bäm′) to prevent the decay of a dead body by treating it with preservatives (p. 192).

empire (ĕm′pīr′) a nation and the other nations it has conquered; a political unit often made up of several nations under one leadership (p. 169).

environment (ĕn-vī′rən-mənt) all the living and nonliving things in a person's surroundings (p. 122).

ephor (ĕf′ôr′) one of five elected officals who supervised the kings of ancient Sparta (p. 352).

epic (ĕp′ĭk) a long poem in dignified language that tells the story of a hero (pp. 156 and 249).

excavation (ĕk′skə-vā′shən) in archaeology, the systematic digging of an area of ground to recover the archaeological record (p. 65).

excommunication (ĕks′kə-myōō′nĭ-kā′shən) official exclusion from a group; specifically, a formal punishment by church officials that takes away a person's membership in a church (p. 469).

exile (ĕg′zīl) enforced absence from one's own country (p. 178).

Exodus (ĕk′sə-dəs) the departure of the Israelites from Egypt (p. 301).

F

famine (făm′ĭn) a widespread shortage of food that threatens death from starvation (p. 137).

feudalism (fyōōd′l-ĭz′əm) an economic system in which nobles own the farmland and peasants work it; for example, the system in ancient China (p. 268).

fossil (fŏs′əl) the remains or imprint of a plant or animal from a past geological age (p. 57).

G

Gentile (jĕn′tīl′) one not of the Jewish faith (p. 460).

glacier (glā′shər) a huge, slow-moving mass of ice (p. 94).

guild (gĭld) an association of merchants or artisans who do the same type of work (p. 249).

H

Hellenistic (hĕl´ə-nĭs´tĭk) Greek-like; relating to Greek history and culture from the time of Alexander's rule to 146 B.C. (p. 379).

helot (hĕl´ət) a state slave in ancient Sparta (p. 353).

hieroglyphics (hī´ər-ə-glĭf´ĭks) the ancient Egyptian writing system in which pictorial symbols stand for words or sounds (p. 196).

Hinduism (hĭn´doo-ĭz´əm) the major religion and way of life in modern India (p. 245).

history (hĭs´tə-rē) a record of what happened in the past; the study of the past, including explanations of the events (p. 9).

hunter-gatherer (hŭn´tər-găth´ər-ər) a person who gets food by hunting wild animals and gathering wild plants, roots, nuts, and berries (p. 106).

I

inset (ĭn´sĕt´) a small map that appears within another map and shows some of the same area in greater detail (p. 40).

irrigation (ĭr´ĭ-gā´shən) the act of supplying dry lands with water by means of canals, ditches, pipes, and streams (p. 136).

J

Judaism (joo´dē-ĭz´əm) the monotheistic religion of the Jewish people (p. 299).

K

kitchen midden (kĭch´ən mĭd´n) a rubbish heap, including artifacts and bones, left in a settlement by people of the past (p. 73).

L

legend (lĕj´ənd) a story handed down from earlier times; also on maps, an explanation of the symbols (p. 39).

lyric poetry (lĭr´ĭk pō´ĭ-trē) poems that express personal emotions, often having musical sound patterns (p. 384).

M

market (mär´kĭt) a demand for goods; the opportunity to buy or sell (p. 449).

martyr (mär´tər) a person who chooses to die rather than give up religious beliefs (p. 467).

megalith (mĕg´ə-lĭth´) a very large stone used in various prehistoric buildings or monuments (p. 82).

messiah (mə-sī´ə) the hoped-for king who would free the Jewish people (p. 313).

middleman (mĭd´l-măn´) a trader who goes between two parties, buying from one and selling to another; a go-between (p. 286).

migration (mī-grā´shən) the permanent movement of people from one region and resettlement in another (p. 230).

moderation (mŏd´ə-rā´shən) the condition of not being excessive; not extreme (p. 238).

monarchy (mŏn´ər-kē) a system of government in which a monarch—a king, queen, or emperor—is the sole and absolute ruler (p. 339).

monastery (mŏn´ə-stĕr´ē) a dwelling place for persons living under religious vows (p. 481).

monotheism (mŏn´ə-thē-ĭz´əm) the belief that there is only one god (p. 299).

monsoon (mŏn-soon´) a wind system affecting the climate of India and southern Asia; reverses direction seasonally, producing a wet season and a dry season (p. 47).

mummy (mŭm´ē) a dead body embalmed in the manner of the ancient Egyptians (p. 192).

myth (mĭth) a traditional story about the origin and history of a people and their gods, ancestors, and heroes (p. 12).

N

nobility (nō-bĭl´ĭ-tē) a class of people having high birth or rank; aristocracy (p. 271).

nomad (nō´măd´) one of a group of people who move with their flocks and herds as the seasons change to find water and pasture (p. 157).

O

obelisk (ŏb´ə-lĭsk) a tall, four-sided stone pillar that tapers to a point like a pyramid (p. 200).

oligarchy (ŏl´ĭ-gär´kē) a system of government in which a few people rule (p. 339).

omen (ō´mən) a thing or event that is believed to foretell good or evil (p. 396).

oracle (ôr´ə-kəl) a prediction about the future; also, the person who makes such a prediction, believed to come from a god or an ancestor (p. 266).

oral tradition (ôr´əl trə-dĭsh´ən) the legends, myths, and beliefs that a culture passes from generation to generation by word of mouth (p. 57).

P

pagan (pā´gən) to the early Christians, a person who is not a Christian or Jew (p. 469).

papyrus (pə-pī´rəs) a long, thin reed; also, the paper-like writing material made by Egyptians from the reed's pith (p. 189).

parable (păr´ə-bəl) a story that teaches a moral or religious lesson (p. 315).

patrician (pə-trĭsh´ən) a member of the small class of wealthy families in ancient Rome (p. 406).

persecute (pûr´sĭ-kyo͞ot) to punish; to treat harshly or cruelly (p. 458).

pharaoh (fâr´ō) a ruler of ancient Egypt (p. 199).

philosopher (fĭ-lŏs´ə-fər) a person who seeks wisdom through intellectual means and moral discipline (p. 372).

pictograph (pĭk´tə-grăf´) a picture that stands for a word or idea; picture writing (p. 160).

plague (plāg) a highly contagious, widespread disease that is often fatal (p. 369).

plain (plān) a broad area of flat, open land (p. 151).

plateau (plă-tō´) an elevated area of flat land (p. 150).

plebeian (plĭ-bē´ən) in ancient Rome, a member of the large class of ordinary citizens (p. 406).

polytheism (pŏl´ē-thē-ĭz´əm) belief in more than one god (p. 158).

prehistory (prē-hĭs´tə-rē) the history of humans before the development of writing (p. 57).

primary source (prī´měr´ē sôrs) information about events recorded at the time of those events (p. 60).

projection (prə-jĕk´shən) a system for mapping the spherical earth on a flat surface (p. 44).

prophet (prŏf´ĭt) a person who expresses and explains the will of God (p. 310).

province (prŏv´ĭns) a territory governed as a unit within a country or empire (p. 277); in the ancient Roman Empire, any of the lands outside Italy conquered and ruled by the Romans (p. 432).

R

rabbi (răb´ī) teacher; the leader of a Jewish congregation (p. 321).

radiocarbon dating (rā´dē-ō-kär´bən dāt´ĭng) a method for determining the age of once-living things, based on the fact that their radioactive carbon content decays at a regular rate (p. 68).

rain forest (rān fôr´ĭst) a dense evergreen forest in a tropical area with an annual rainfall of at least 100 to 140 inches (p. 16).

region (rē´jən) an area with similar features that set it apart from surrounding areas (p. 31).

rebirth (rē-bûrth´) the belief in a new birth and life set in motion by a person's karma (p. 238).

republic (rĭ-pŭb´lĭk) a nation in which political power lies with the citizens, who elect leaders and representatives; the head of state in a republic is not a monarch (p. 406).

Resurrection (rĕz´ə-rĕk´shən) the rising of Jesus on the third day after his death (p. 318).

rhetoric (rĕt´ər-ĭk) the art of effective writing and public speaking (p. 443).

ritual (rĭch´o͞o-əl) a ceremony or rite; the prescribed form for a religious or solemn ceremony (p. 446).

S

sanctuary (săngk´cho͞o-ĕr´ē) a place of worship such as a church, temple, or mosque (p. 347).

sarcophagus (sär-kŏf´ə-gəs) a stone coffin; any coffin (p. 71).

scale (skāl) the proportion that exists between information on a graph and the amount or measure it represents; also in maps, the relationship between the actual size of an area and its size as shown on the map (p. 35).

scribe (skrīb) a professional writer or record keeper; a person whose job is to copy documents and manuscripts (p. 161).

secondary source (sĕk´ən-dĕr´ē sôrs) information about events recorded after those events by people who have studied the primary sources (p. 60).

sect (sĕkt) a group of people who form a distinct unit within a larger group, as for example, within a religious group (p. 459).

seismograph (sīz´mə-grăf´) an instrument for detecting and determining the direction, strength, and length of earthquakes and other ground movements (p. 281).

self-sufficient (sĕlf´sə-fĭsh´ənt) able to provide for oneself without the help of others (p. 130).

Senate (sĕn´ĭt) in ancient Rome, the supreme council of state of the Republic and later of the empire (p. 397).

shrine (shrīn) a place where people worship, usually containing a sacred object or statue (p. 129).

silt (sĭlt) a fine-grained soil, often deposited on riverbanks during floods (p. 224).

subcontinent (sŭb´kŏn´tə-nənt) a large landmass, such as India, that is part of a continent but is separated from it in some way (p. 223).

surplus (sûr´pləs) an extra amount; more than is needed (p. 121).

synagogue (sĭn´ə-gŏg´) a building or meeting place for Jewish worship and instruction (p. 321).

T

technology (tĕk-nŏl´ə-jē) the tools, machines, and methods used to make products, save time, or in some way improve people's lives (p. 99).

thematic map (thĭ-măt´ĭk măp) a map that gives information on a particular theme or subject (p. 43).

topography (tə-pŏg´rə-fē) the physical features of a region, such as mountains, plains, and rivers (p. 27).

tragedy (trăj´ĭ-dē) a serious drama in which the hero is brought to defeat by a character flaw (p. 350).

tribute (trĭb´yo͞ot) a gift or payment to show respect or admiration (p. 211).

tyrant (tī´rənt) a ruler who has total power, not limited by a constitution or by other officials; especially, one in ancient Greece (p. 340).

Italic numbers refer to pages on which illustrations appear.

Text *(continued from page iv)*

4 Excerpt by B.K. Workman from *They Saw It Happen in Classical Times*, ed. Dindorf. Copyright © 1964 by Basil Blackwell. Used by permission. 7 From *Through Roman Eyes* by Roger Nichols and Kenneth McLeish, London: Cambridge University Press, 1976. 8 From *Cradle of Civilization* by Samuel Kramer, New York: Time Inc., 1967. 9 From *The Rig Veda: An Anthology* translated by Wendy Doniger O'Flaherty, New York: Penguin, 1981. 16 "Enchanting Forest: South America Isn't the Only Place Where Nature Is Losing Ground" by Tom Masland from *Chicago Tribune*, May 31, 1989. Copyright © 1989 by Chicago Tribune Company. Used with permission. All rights reserved. 17 From *In the Rainforest* by Catherine Caufield, Chicago: University of Chicago Press, 1984. 26 Excerpt from *Riding the Iron Rooster* by Paul Theroux. Copyright © 1988 by Cape Cod Scriveners Company. 59 From *The Discoverers* by Daniel J. Boorstin, New York: Random House, 1983. 71 From *The Discovery of the Tomb of Tut Ankh Amen* by Howard Carter, New York: Dover, 1977. 73 From *Illustrated London News*, 12/9/22. 76–79 "The Henge" from *Sarum* by Edward Rutherford. Copyright © 1987 by Edward Rutherford. Reprinted by permission of Crown Publishers, Inc. 90 Excerpt from *Lucy, The Beginnings of Humankind* by Donald Johanson. Copyright © 1981 by Donald C. Johanson and Maitland A. Edey. Reprinted by permission of Simon & Schuster Children's Publishing. 102–105 Excerpt from *Attar of the Ice Valley* by Leonard Wibberley. Copyright © 1968 by Leonard Wibberley. Reprinted by permission of Farrar, Straus and Giroux, Inc. 135 From *Ur of the Chaldees* by Sir Leonard Woolley, Ithaca: Cornell University Press, 1982. 157 From *The Epic of Gilgamesh* edited by N. K. Sanders, New York: Penguin, 1960. 164–167 "The Luring of Enkidu" from *Gilgamesh* by Bernarda Bryson. Copyright © 1967 by Bernarda Bryson. Reprinted by permission of Bernarda Bryson Shahn. 206–209 "Isis and Osiris" from *The First Book of Tales of Ancient Egypt* by Charles Mozley, New York: Franklin Watts, 1960. 233 From *The Rig Veda: An Anthology* translated by Wendy Doniger O'Flaherty, New York: Penguin, 1981. 240 From *The Edicts of Asoka* translated by N. A. Nikam and Richard McKeon, Chicago: University of Chicago Press, 1959. 242–243 "Popularity" from *Jataka Tales* by Nancy DeRoin. Text copyright © 1975 by Nancy DeRoin. Art copyright © 1975 by Ellen Lanyon. Reprinted by permission of Houghton Mifflin Company. 256–261 "Meng-Jiang Nyu" from *Traditional Chinese Folktales* edited by Yin-lien C. Chin, Yetta S. Center and Mildred Ross. Copyright © 1989 by M.E. Sharpe, Inc. Reprinted by permission of M.E. Sharpe, Inc. 262 From *Anthology of Chinese Literature* compiled and edited by Cyril Birch, New York: Grove Press, Inc., 1965. 276 From *Horizon* magazine, January, 1977. 281 From *The Genius of China* by Robert Temple, New York: Simon and Schuster, 1987. 304–307 Excerpt from "Clouds of Glory" from *Clouds of Glory* by Miriam Chaikin. Text copyright © 1998 by Miriam Chaikin. Reprinted by permission of Clarion Books, a Houghton Mifflin Company and McIntosh and Otis, Inc. 328 From *The Odyssey* translated by Robert Fitzgerald, New York: Anchor Books, 1963. 334–337 "The Cyclops's Cave" from *Greeks Bearing Gifts. The Epics of Achilles and Ulysses* by Bernard Evslin. Text copyright © 1971 by Bernard Evslin. Reprinted with permission of Simon & Schuster Books for Young Readers, a division of Simon & Schuster Children's Publishing. 338 From *Greek Historians* edited by Truesdell S. Brown, Lexington: Heath, 1973. 346 From *The Iliad* of Homer translated by Richard Lattimore, Chicago: University of Chicago Press, 1951. 350 From *The Antigone of Sophocles* translated by Hugh Macnaghten, Cambridge: The University Press, 1926. 364 From *The Ancient Greeks* by Chester G. Starr, New York: Oxford University Press, 1971. 374 From *The Age of Alexander* translated by Ian Scott-Kilvert, New York: Penguin, 1973. 400–406 From *The Aeneid for Boys and Girls* by Alfred J. Church. Text copyright © 1908 by The Macmillan Co. Illustration by Eugene Karlin copyright © 1962 by Macmillan Publishing Company. Adapted with permission of Simon & Schuster Books for Young Readers, a division of Simon & Schuster Children's Publishing. 440 Excerpt from *Everyday Life in Ancient Rome* by F.R. Cowell. Copyright © 1961 by F.R. Cowell. Reprinted by permission of B.T. Batsford Ltd. 449 From *The Roman World* by Mike Corbishley, New York: Warwick Press, 1986. 463 From *Nero* by Michael Grant, New York: American Heritage Press, 1970. 465, 466, 475 From *Through Roman Eyes* by Roger Nichols and Kenneth McLeish, London: Cambridge University Press, 1976. 476 From *The Book of the Ancient Romans* by Dorothy Mills, New York: Putnam, 1937. 524 Pronunciation key copyright © 1985 by Houghton Mifflin Company. Adapted and reprinted by permission from *The American Heritage Dictionary*, Second College Edition. iv The material in the Minipedia is reprinted from *The World Book Encyclopedia* with the expressed permission of the publisher. Copyright ©1998 by World Book, Inc.

Illustrations

Literature border design by Peggy Skycraft.

Ligature 160, 196, 472. **Precision Graphics** 9, 15, 19, 68, 94, 96, 114, 116, 117, 124, 128, 140, 142, 144, 160, 163, 172, 174, 183, 188, 201, 216, 233, 237, 238, 252, 274, 278, 287, 292, 319, 321, 324, 331, 324, 331, 342, 344, 352, 354, 358, 359, 410, 418, 434, 451, 477, 556. **Brian Battles** 241, 247. **Alex Bloch** 356, 357. **John T. Burgoyne** 171, 349. **Ebet Dudley** 366. **Randall Fleck** 35, 124, 133 (t, b), 422. **Simon Galkin** 18, 67, 155, 230. **Henry Iken** 195, 365, 442, 444. **Phil Jones** 288, 289, 293. **Al Lorenz** 226, 437, 466, 467. **Charley Liu** 267, 271. **Rebecca Merilees** 189. **Dennis O'Brien** 112, 123, 138, 175, 215, 281, 412, 421. **Judy Reed** 35, 190. **Richard Waldrep** 6, 100, 423. **Gary Torissi** 518–519. **Kyuzo Tsugami** 129. **Other: 43** © London Transport Museum (t). **107** Adapted from "A Paleolithic Camp at Nice" by Henry de Lumey. Copyright © May 1969 by *Scientific American*, Inc. All rights reserved. (b). **111** Based on *The Cave of Lascaux: The Final Photographs* by Mario Ruspoli, Bordas, S.A., Paris 1986. (b). **128** Adapted from *The Hammond Past Worlds Atlas: The Times Atlas of Archeology*, Times Books, ed. 1988. (b). **153** From *History of Mankind: Cultural Development*, Vol I. © Unesco 1963. Reproduced by permission of Unesco. (b). **160** Adapted from *Sign, Symbol, Script* by Keith N. Scoville. Board of Regents of the University of Wisconsin System (Department of Hebrew and Semitic Studies, University of Wisconsin- Madison), 1984. (b). **180** By D.J. Wiseman from *Nebuchadrezzar and Babylon.* The British Academy, 1985. **536** From the "Trireme Sails Again"by John F. Coates. Copyright © April 1989 by *Scientific American*, Inc. All rights reserved.

Maps

© GeoSystems Global Corporation 502–517. **Mapping Specialists** G1– G15, 10, 11, 17, 23, 27, 28, 30, 33, 38, 39, 42, 43, 46, 48, 51, 53, 63, 81, 93, 95, 121, 126, 134, 141, 145, 151, 169, 176, 187, 200, 202, 211, 223, 224, 231, 239, 248, 251, 253, 263, 265, 269, 277, 282, 300, 303, 329, 333, 348, 370, 381, 398, 399, 413, 415, 433, 451, 452, 453, 461, 463, 465, 466, 474, 476. **Precision Graphics** 38, 44, 45. **XNR Productions** 291, 376–377. **Other: 42** Adapted from *Some Aspects of Medical Geography*, copyright © 1964 by the University of London. **43** Data reference from page 15 of 1997 World Bank Atlas, copyright © 1997. International Bank for Reconstruction and Development/The World Bank. **126** African information adapted from C. Ehret, *An African Classical Age*, University Press of Virginia, 1998. **466** From page 25 of *Katakomben und Basiliken* by Umberto M. Fasola, copyright 1981 by SCALA. Reprinted by permission of SCALA Instituto Fotografico Editoriale S.p.A.

Photographs

AR—Art Resource, New York; **BM**—British Museum, London; **MH**—Michael Holford; **RJB**—Ralph J. Brunke; **TIB**—The Image Bank

Cover: Egyptian galley, c. 1500 B.C., courtesy of The Museum of Science and Industry, Chicago; photo by Peter Busy. **Back Cover:** The Granger Collection. **ii:** Robert Harding Picture Library (t); BM, MH (b). **ii-iii:** BM, MH. **iii:** SCALA / AR. **v:** Giraudon / AR. **vi:** RJB (t); Wan-go H.C. Weng (b). **vii:** SCALA / AR (t); MH (b). **viii:** RJB (t); AR (b). **ix:** Giraudon / AR (t); BM, MH (c); The University Museum, University of Pennsylvania (b). **x:** SCALA / AR. **xi–1:** Louvre, AR. **2:** The Metropolitan Museum of Art. **2–3:** © Fong Siu Nang / TIB. **3:** AR. **4:** The Granger Collection. **5:** BM, MH (t); SEF, Turin, AR (b). **7:** Fairchild Tropical Gardens, Miami, RJB. **8:** AR (tr); Wan-go H. C. Weng (tl); National Museum, Naples (c). **13:** BM, MH (cl); RJB (c, br); Laurie Platt Winfrey, Inc. (tr). **14:** © Alain Evard / Photo Researchers, Inc. (tl); © Maria Taglienti / TIB (bl); © J. Brignolo / TIB (br). **16:** © George Holton / Photo Researchers, Inc. (l); © Gregory Dimijian / Photo Researchers, Inc. (r). **17:** RJB (t); © D.G. Barker / Tom Stack & Associates (b). **21:** RJB (t); © D.G. Barker / Tom Stack & Associates (c); © Peter Frey / TIB (b). **24:** BM, MH. **24–25:** The Granger Collection. **25:** Archaeological Museum, Palestrina, Italy / AR. **26:** © Rene Burri / Magnum Photos. **29:** SuperStock. **31:** RJB (t); © Grant V. Faint / TIB (b). **32:** © Eddie Hironaka / TIB. **34:** Pearson Graphics Corporation (l); © Peter LeGrand / Tony Stone Images (r). **36–37:** © Hans Wolf / TIB. **36:** RJB (tr); map from The World Book Encyclopedia © 1998 World Book, Inc. By permission of the publisher (l). **37:** RJB (br); map from The World Book Encyclopedia © 1998 World Book, Inc. By permission of the publisher (tr). **40:** © Ned Haines / Photo

ACKNOWLEDGMENTS

Researchers, Inc. **43:** London Transport Museum. **47:** RJB. **49:** BM, MH. **50:** SCALA / AR. **51:** RJB. **54:** BM, MH (l); AR (r). **55:** Robert Harding Picture Library (l); © Earthwatch (r). **56:** SCALA / AR. **57:** SCALA, AR (t); Bibliotheque Nationale, Paris (c); RJB (b). **58:** © Annie Griffiths Belt. **59:** RJB. **60:** © Wide World Photos. **61:** Clem Fiori, The Art Museum, Princeton University. **62:** Werner Forman Archive. **64:** SuperStock (t); Silkeborg Museum, Denmark (b). **66:** SCALA / AR(t, c); BM, MH (b). **67:** AR. **68:** RJB (t); Museum of the American Indian, New York (c); © Jim Cartier / Photo Researchers, Inc. (b). **69:** AR. **70:** BM. **72:** SCALA / AR (tl, bl, cr); RJB (tr); The Metropolitan Museum of Art (tc). **74:** RJB (tr); Center of American Archaeology (c, l). **75:** Dept. of Anthropology, Northwestern University, RJB (tl, tc, tr, cr); Center of American Archaeology (cl). **80:** Etruscan Museum, Vatican / AR. **82:** Comstock, Inc. **83:** RJB. **86–87:** BM, MH. **88:** © Timothy Beddow (t); AR (b). **88–89:** © Jean Clottes / Sygma. **89:** © Hurault, Museum of National Antiquities, Paris (b). **90:** David L. Brill, © National Geographic Society. **91:** David L. Brill, © National Geographic Society (t); © Jim Cartier / Photo Researchers, Inc. (b). **92:** Center for American Archaeology. **93:** David L. Brill, © National Geographic Society. **94:** © Emil Huensch / Photo Researchers, Inc. **97:** © Marvin E. Newman /TIB. **98:** © S. Achernar / TIB (l); BM, MH (r). **99:** BM, MH. **106:** RJB. **107:** RJB. **108:** RJB. **109:** Harper Horticulture Slide Library (c); © David L. Brill (b). **110:** National Antiquities Museum, Chateau de St. Germain, France. **111:** © Rene Burri / Magnum Photos. **112–13:** © Douglas Mazonowicz. **114:** BM, MH (tl, trc); Lee Boltin (tlc); Archaeological Museum, Madrid / AR (tr); © David L. Brill (cl); © G. Shilonsky SOVFOTO (cr); Musée de St. Germain (b). **115:** RJB. **118:** © Jonathan T. Wright / Bruce Coleman, Inc. (l); © David Hansen, Ervin Oekle, Steve Simmons, University of Minnesota, St. Paul, MN (r). **119:** SCALA / AR (t); © Michael Jennes, Robert Harding Picture Library (c); Field Museum of Natural History, Chicago, RJB (b). **121:** Centre de Recherche Français de Jerusalem. **122:** RJB. **122–23:** © Micha Bar Am / Magnum Photos. **123:** Field Museum of Natural History, RJB. **125:** RJB (c); © Don Smetzer / Tony Stone Images (b). **127:** The Oriental Institute, University of Chicago **130:** © James Melaart. **131:** SuperStock (t); American Museum of Natural History (b). **132:** RJB. **135:** BM, MH. **136:** BM, MH (t); © Michael Dannell, Robert Harding Picture Library (b). **137:** Lee Boltin. **138:** © Dr. Georg Gerster / Comstock. **139:** Lee Boltin. **140:** Iraq Museum, Baghdad / AR. **141:** AR. **142:** RJB. **143:** SuperStock (t); © Mathaux Photography / TIB (c); © Eric Meola/TIB (b). **146–47:** Egizio Museum, Turin. **148:** © Ian Griffiths / Robert Harding Picture Library. **149:** AR (tl, bl); BM, MH (cr). **151:** © Jonathan T. Wright / Bruce Coleman, Inc. **152:** Baghdad Museum / AR. **153:** New York Public Library. **154:** Deutsches Museum, Munich / AR (t); Trustees of the BM (b). **156:** Giraudon / AR. **157:** Robert Harding Picture Library. **158:** National Museum, Baghdad / AR (l, c,r). **159:** National Museum, Baghdad/AR. **160:** BM / Bridgeman Art Library / AR. **162:** SCALA / AR (cl). **162-63:** RJB. **163:** SCALA / AR. **168:** © Steve McCurry / Magnum Photos. **170:** The Granger Collection. **172:** © Steve McCurry / Magnum Photos (tl); BM, MH (tc, b); The Granger Collection (tr). **173:** BM, MH (l); © Steve McCurry Magnum Photos (r). **177:** BM, MH. **179:** © Steve McCurry / Magnum Photos (t); SuperStock (b). **181:** RJB. **184:** AR (l); SCALA, AR (r). **185:** © Gerard Chaplong / TIB (l); SuperStock (r); AR (b). **186:** © Allan Seiden / TIB. **187:** BM, MH. **188:** Borromco / AR. **190:** Egyptian Museum, Cairo, Giraudon / AR. **191:** © Louis Goldman / Photo Researchers, Inc. **192:** BM, MH (t); Giraudon / AR (b). **193:** BM, MH (t); The Metropolitan Museum of Art (b). **194:** The Metropolitan Museum of Art (tl); The Egyptian Museum , Cairo, Werner Forman Archive (tr); Egizio Museum, Turin / AR (cr); Archives Photographiques, Paris (bl); RJB (br). **195:** Egizio Museum, Vatican / AR. **196:** BM, MH. **197:** Louvre / AR. **198:** BM, MH. **199:** The Metropolitan Museum of Art. **201:** BM, MH. **203:** © Rene Burri / Magnum Photos. **204–05:** The Metropolitan Museum of Art. **208:** BM, MH. **210:** © Michael S. Yamashita. **212:** BM, MH. **213:** Werner Forman Archive (t); RJB (b). **214:** Museum of Egyptian Antiquities, Giraudon / AR. **218–19:** Robert Harding Picture Library. **220:** © J.H.C. Wilson / Robert Harding Picture Library (l); AR (r). **220–21:** © J.H.C. Wilson / Robert Harding Picture Library. **221:** RJB. **222:** © Jehangir Gazdar / Woodfin Camp & Associates. **224:** © Paolo Koch / Photo Researchers, Inc. **225:** AR (t); © Jehangir Gazdar / Woodfin Camp & Associates (cl, cr, b). **226:** © Paolo Koch / Photo Researchers, Inc. **227:** Karachi Museum, Pakistan / AR (t); © Dilip Mehta / Woodfin Camp & Associates (c); RJB (bl); Government of India, Dept. of Archaeology (br). **228:** © Woodfin Camp & Associates (t); Karachi Museum, Pakistan / AR (b). **230:** © John Elk III / Bruce Coleman, Inc. **232:** AR. **233:** © Edward S. Ross. **234:** © Marilyn Silverstone / Magnum Photos. **235:** BM / MH. **236:** South Asia Outreach Project, University of Chicago, RJB. **237:** AR. **238:** Press Information Bureau, Government of India. **239:** © Robert Frerck. **240:** Asoka School of Oriental and African Studies. **244:** BM, MH. **245:** Lee Boltin. **246:** SuperStock. **249:** © Pramod Chandra. **250:** © J. Schmitt / TIB (tr); New Delhi Museum, India / AR (tl, c, b).**251:** RJB. **254:** AR (l); © Wan-go H. C. Went (r). **255:** © Comstock (l); AR (r). **259:** © Michael Stuckey / Comstock. **262:** © George Bosio / Gamma-Liaison (t); © Manfred Gotschalk /Tom Stack & Associates (b). **264:** Giraudon / AR. **265:** RJB. **266:** BM, MH. **267:** Wan-go H. C. Weng (tr); Charles Liu, Westmont, Illinois, RJB (tl, bl, br). **268:** Laurie Platt Winfrey, Inc. (t); Minneapolis Institute of Arts (b). **270:** © Wan-go H. C. Weng. **272:** © Wan-go H. C. Weng. **273:** The Cleveland Museum of Art. **276:** © Gavin Hellier / Robert Harding Picture Library. **277:** © Seth Joel / Wheeler Pictures. **280:** © Dallas and John Heaton / Stock Boston. **281:** BM, MH. **283:** BM, MH (t); Wan-go H.C. Weng (b). **284:** Robert Harding Picture Library. **285:** RJB (t); Giraudon / AR (b). **286:** Robert Harding Picture Library. **287:** BM. **289:** © Harry Rogers / Photo Researchers, Inc. **290:** Laurie Platt Winfrey, Inc. (t); RJB (bl); © Guido Alberto Rossi / TIB (br). **291:** Giraudon / AR (t); © George Hunter / SuperStock (bl); Robert Harding Picture Library (br). **294–95:** © K-14 Group / TIB. **296:** Convent of San Paolo (l); Seabury Library, Northwestern University, RJB (r). **296–97:** © Ira Block / TIB. **297:** Tallit of Rabbi Arnold Rachlis, Evanston, IL, RJB (t); Uffizi, Florence / AR (b). **298:** AR. **299:** Oriental Institute, University of Chicago. **301:** © Marcello Bertinetti / Photo Researchers, Inc. (t); RJB (c, b). **302:** Spertus Museum of Judaica, Chicago, RJB. **308:** RJB; (l); Giraudon / AR (r). **309:** Photographic Archive of the Jewish Theological Seminary of America, New York. **310:** Bibliotheque Nationale, Paris. **311:** AR. **312:** International Cultured Pearls of the Orient, Inc., Chicago, RJB. **313:** © Paul Fusco / Magnum Photos. **314:** © Sid Bernstein / Photo Researchers, Inc. (l); © Gary Faber / TIB (r). **315:** AR. **316:** AR. **317:** AR. **318:** RJB (t); Giraudon / AR (b). **320:** © Nathan Berm / Stock Boston / PNI. **322:** RJB. **323:** RJB. **326:** The Museum of Fine Arts, Boston. **326–27:** New York Public Library. **327:** SCALA / AR (t); AR (r). **328:** SCALA / AR. **329:** © Michael Kuh / Photo Researchers, Inc. **330:** RJB (ti, tc, cl); Louvre (bl); BM / AR (bc); Herakleion Museum / Art Resource (br). **331:** BM, MH (t, br); © Farrell Grehan / Photo Researchers, Inc. (c); National Museum, Athens / AR (bl). **332:** © Lisle Dennis / T1B (l); © Linda Borcover (r). **338:** American School of Classical Studies, Newsweek Books. **339:** SCALA / AR. **340:** RJB. **341:** Martin von Wagner Museum University of Wuerzburg, photo K. Oehrlin (t); American School of Classical Studies (b). **343:** Lee Boltin (t, b); Ronald Sheridan (c). **345:** SCALA / AR. **346:** BM, MH. **347:** Herakleion Museum, Athens / AR. **348:** © Gianni Tortoli / Photo Researchers, Inc. **350:** Newsweek Books. **352:** Wadsworth Atheneum, J. Pierpont Morgan Collection. **353:** BM, MH. **355:** AR. **356:** © P. Sclarandis. **357:** © P. Sclarandis. **359:** © A. Hubrich / TIB. **360–61:** © Benn Mitchell / TIB. **361:** © Eliot Porter (t); AR (c); Greek Ministry of Culture and Sciences (b). **362:** BM, MH. **363:** © Eliot Porter. **364:** © SuperStock. **366:** The Bridgeman Art Library. **367:** National Museum. **368:** Robert Harding Picture Library. **369:** AR. **370:** Bildarchiv Foto Marburg, Germany / AR. **371:** National Museum, Athens / AR. **372:** SCALA / AR. **373:** The Metropolitan Museum of Art. **374:** BM, MH. **375:** AR. **376:** SCALA / AR (t); German State Archaeological Institute (b). 377. SCALA / AR (l); German State Archaeological Institute (r). **378:** Bibliotheque Nationale, Paris. **379:** The Metropolitan Museum of Art. **380:** Greek Ministry of Culture and Sciences / AR. **382:** RJB. **383:** © D. Winston / H. Armstorong Roberts, Inc. **384:** SCALA / AR (t); AR (b). **385:** National Museum, Athens / AR. **386:** © Steve Dunwell / TIB. **387:** BM, MH. **388:** Lee Snider / Corbis (t-inset). **389:** Lee Snider / Corbis (t); Araldo de Luca/Corbis (b). **392–93:** SCALA / AR. **394:** AR. **394–95:** AR. **395:** © Erich Hartmann / Magnum Photos (l); AR (r). **396:** RJB (l); © SuperStock (r). **397:** SCALA / AR. **398:** The Metropolitan Museum of Art. **399:** © Burt Glinn / Magnum Photos. **407:** © Capitoline Museum, Rome, Newsweek Books (t); SCALA / AR (b). **408:** © George Haling Productions / Photo Researchers, Inc. **409:** BM, MH (t); AR (b). **411:** BM, MH. **414:** American Numismatic Society (t); SCALA / AR (b). **416:** BM, MH. **417:** The Royal Collection. **418:** Capitoline Museum, Rome. **419:** American Numismatic Society. **420:** AR. **422:** © Eliot Erwitt / Magnum Photos. **424:** MH. **425:** RJB. **428:** Vatican Museum / AR (l); AR (r). **428–29:** AR. **429:** © Weinberg / Clark / TIB (r); © J. Powell, Rome (l). **430:** RJB (l); SCALA / AR (r). 431: SCALA / AR. 432: © Robert Harding Picture Library. **434:** American Numismatic Society (l); BM, MH (r). **435:** Blaine Harrington / The Stock Market. **436:** The Granger Collection. **438:** SCALA / AR. **439:** BM, MH. **441:** Louvre, Newsweek Books (t); © Erich Lessing / Magnum Photos (bl); SCALA / AR (br). **442:** SCALA / AR (tl); BM, MH (tr, b). **443:** AR (t); SCALA / AR (b). **445:** Musée Gallo Leon / Laurie Platt Winfrey, Inc. (t); Ronald Sheridan (b). **446:** SCALA / AR. **447:** BM, MH. **448:** The Art History Museum, Vienna, Newsweek Books. **449:** Garfield Park Conservatory, Chicago, RJB (t); SCALA, AR (b). **450:** BM, MH (jewelry); RJB (tl, bl, br). **456:** AR. **456–57:** AR. **457:** AR. **458:** Musée Conde, Chantilly, France, Giraudon / AR. **459:** AR (t); The Granger Collection (b). **460:** The University Museum, University of Pennsylvania (b); SCALA / Art Resource, NY (t). **462:** © Emil Muensch / Photo Researchers, Inc. **464:** AR. **465:** RJB (l); AR (r).**466:** RJB. **467:** AR (l); SCALA / AR (r). **468:** SCALA / AR. **469:** RJB. **470:** AR. **471:** Pius Clementine Museum, Vatican City / AR. **472:** BM, MH. **473:** © Louis Goldman / Photo Researchers, Inc. **474:** Ronald Sheridan. **475:** MH. **477:** © Brian Brake / Photo Researchers, Inc. **478:** Art History Museum, Vienna, Newsweek Books. **479:** SCALA / AR. **480:** Stanza of Heliodorus, Vatican Palace. **481:** SCALA / AR. **482:** Vatican Library / AR (l). **482-83:** © Ronald Sheridan / AR (b). **483:** © J. P. Kelly / TIB (t). **484:** © J. Ramey / TIB (t); RJB (b). **487:** Robert Harding Picture Library.

Picture Research by Carousel Research, Inc., and Meyers Photo-Art.